12/92

DATE DUE

AP 6'01			
NO 1'05			

DEMCO 38-296

Uniform Child Custody Jurisdiction Act:

A State-by-State Guide

THE PURPOSES OF THESE LAWS ARE TO:

■ Avoid jurisdictional competition and conflict with courts of other states in matters of child custody, which have in the past resulted in the shifting of children from state to state with harmful effects on their well-being.

■ Promote cooperation with the courts of other states to the end that a custody decree is rendered in that state which can best decide the case in the interest of the child.

■ Assure that litigation concerning the custody of a child take place ordinarily in the state with which the child and his family have the closest connection and where significant evidence concerning his care, protection, training, and personal relationships is most readily available.

■ Discourage continuing controversies over child custody, in the interest of greater stability of home environment and of secure family relationships for the child.

■ Deter abductions and other unilateral removals of children undertaken to obtain custody awards.

■ Avoid relitigation of custody decisions of other states insofar as feasible.

■ Facilitate the enforcement of custody decrees of other states.

■ Promote and expand the exchange of information and other forms of mutual assistance between the courts of other states concerned with the same child.

■ Make uniform the law of those states which enact it.

ISBN 0-922802-05-X

Published by:

Kessinger Publishing Company
P.O. Box 8933
Boise, ID 83707

ISBN 0-922802-05-X

Printed in U.S.A.

Disclaimer

This publication is designed to provide accurate and authoritative information in regard to the subject matter covered. It is sold with the understanding that the publisher and author are not engaged in rendering legal, accounting or other professional service. If legal advice or other expert assistance is required, the services of a competent professional person should be sought.—From a Declaration of Principles jointly adopted by a Committee of the American Bar Association and a Committee of Publishers and Associations.

The author has used his best efforts in collecting and preparing material for inclusion in this book, but does not warrant that the information herein is complete or accurate, and does not assume, and hereby disclaims, any liability to any person for any loss or damage caused by errors or omissions in this book whether such errors or omissions result from negligence, accident or any other cause.

This publication contains certain selected statutes only and is not intended to be complete or all inclusive in the subject matter presented. Although every effort has been made to ensure the accuracy of this information, it is not intended as a substitute for the law or for opinions and decisions of the courts.

The publisher and author will not be held responsible for typographical errors, misprints, and misinformation which may be found herein.

This publication is intended purely for educational purposes. Because the United States currently functions under an evolutionary legal system, the reader bears the burden of assuring that the principles of law stated in this work are current and binding at the time of any intended use or application. Caution: The law in this country is subject to change arbitrarily and without prior notice.

TABLE OF CONTENTS

ALABAMA

UNIFORM CHILD CUSTODY JURISDICTION ACT

§ 30-3-20. Short title.

This article may be cited as the Uniform Child Custody Jurisdiction Act.

§ 30-3-21. Purposes of article; construction of provisions.

(a) The general purposes of this article are to:

(1) Avoid jurisdictional competition and conflict with courts of other states in matters of child custody, which have in the past resulted in the shifting of children from state to state with harmful effects on their well-being;

(2) Promote cooperation with the courts of other states to the end that a custody decree is rendered in that state which can best decide the case in the interest of the child;

(3) Assure that litigation concerning the custody of a child take place ordinarily in the state with which the child and his family have the closest connection and where significant evidence concerning his care, protection, training, and personal relationships is most readily available, and that courts of this state decline the exercise of jurisdiction when the child and his family have a closer connection with another state;

(4) Discourage continuing controversies over child custody, in the interest of greater stability of home environment and of secure family relationships for the child;

(5) Deter abductions and other unilateral removals of children undertaken to obtain custody awards;

(6) Avoid relitigation of custody decisions of other states in this state insofar as feasible;

(7) Facilitate the enforcement of custody decrees of other states;

(8) Promote and expand the exchange of information and other forms of mutual assistance between the courts of this state and those of other states concerned with the same child; and

(9) Make uniform the law of those states which enact it.

(b) This article shall be construed to promote the general purposes stated in this section.

§ 30-3-22. Definitions.

As used in this article;

(1) CONTESTANT. A person, including a parent, who claims a right to custody or visitation rights with respect to a child;

(2) CUSTODY DETERMINATION. A court decision and court orders and instructions providing for the custody of a child, including visitation rights; it does not include a decision relating to child support or any other monetary obligation of any person;

(3) CUSTODY PROCEEDING. Includes proceedings in which a custody determination is one of several issues, such as an action for divorce or separation, and includes child neglect and dependency proceedings;

(4) DECREE OR CUSTODY DECREE. A custody determination contained in a judicial decree or order made in a custody proceeding, and includes an initial decree and a modification decree;

(5) HOME STATE. The state in which the child, immediately preceding the time involved, lived with his parents, a parent, or a person acting as parent, for at least six consecutive months, and in the case of a child less than six months old the state in which the child lived from birth with any of the persons mentioned. Periods of temporary absence of any of the named persons are counted as part of the six-month or other period;

(6) INITIAL DECREE. The first custody decree concerning a particular child;

(7) MODIFICATION DECREE. A custody decree which modifies or replaces a prior decree, whether made by the court which rendered the prior decree or by another court;

(8) PHYSICAL CUSTODY. Actual possession and control of a child;

(9) PERSON ACTING AS PARENT. A person, other than a parent, who has physical custody of a child and who has either been awarded custody by a court or claims a right to custody; and

(10) STATE. Any state, territory, or possession of the United States, the Commonwealth of Puerto Rico, and the District of Columbia.

§ 30-3-23. Jurisdiction to make child custody determination; effect of physical presence of child.

(a) A court of this state which is competent to decide child custody matters has jurisdiction to make a child custody determination by initial or modification decree if:

(1) This state:

a. Is the home state of the child at the time of commencement of the proceeding; or

b. Had been the child's home state within six months before commencement of the proceeding and the child is absent from this state because of his removal or retention by a person claiming his custody or for other reasons, and a parent or person acting as parent continues to live in this state; or

    (2) It is in the best interest of the child that a court of this state assume jurisdiction because:

        a. The child and his parents, or the child and at least one contestant, have a significant connection with this state; and

        b. There is available in this state substantial evidence concerning the child's present or future care, protection, training, and personal relationships; or

    (3) The child is physically present in this state and:

        a. The child has been abandoned; or

        b. It is necessary in an emergency to protect the child because he has been subjected to or threatened with mistreatment or abuse or is otherwise neglected or dependent; or

    (4) a. It appears that no other state would have jurisdiction under prerequisites substantially in accordance with subdivision (1), (2), or (3), or another state has declined to exercise jurisdiction on the grounds that this state is the more appropriate forum to determine the custody of the child; and

        b. It is in the best interest of the child that a court of this state assume jurisdiction.

  (b) Except under subdivisions (3) and (4) of subsection (a), physical presence in this state of the child, or of the child and one of the contestants, is not alone sufficient to confer jurisdiction on a court of this state to make a child custody determination.

  (c) Physical presence of the child, while desirable, is not a prerequisite for jurisdiction to determine his custody.

§ 30-3-24. Notice and opportunity to be heard.

  Before making a decree under this article, reasonable notice and opportunity to be heard shall be given to the contestants, any parent whose parental rights have not been previously terminated, and any person who has physical custody of the child. If any of these persons is outside this state, notice and opportunity to be heard shall be given pursuant to section 30-3-25.

§ 30-3-25. Notice to persons outside this state; proof of service; submission to jurisdiction.

  (a) Notice required for the exercise of jurisdiction over a person outside this state shall be given in a manner reasonably calculated to give actual notice, and may be:

    (1) By personal delivery outside this state in the manner prescribed for service of process within this state;

    (2) In the manner prescribed by the law of the place in which the service is made for service of process in that place in an action in any of its courts of general jurisdiction;

    (3) By any form of mail addressed to the person to be served and requesting a receipt; or

    (4) As directed by the court, including publication, if other means of notification are ineffective.

  (b) Notice under this section shall be served, mailed, or delivered, or last published, at least 20 days before any hearing in this state.

  (c) Proof of service outside this state may be made by affidavit of the individual who made the service or in the manner prescribed by the law of this state, the order pursuant to which the service or in the manner prescribed by the law of this state, the order pursuant to which the service is made, or the law of the place in which the service is made. If service is made by mail, proof may be a receipt signed by the addressee or other evidence of delivery to the addressee.

  (d) Notice is not required if a person submits to the jurisdiction of the court.

§ 30-3-26. Simultaneous proceedings in other states.

  (a) A court of this state shall not exercise its jurisdiction under this article if at the time of filing the petition a proceeding concerning the custody of the child was pending in a court of another state exercising jurisdiction substantially in conformity with this article, unless the proceeding is stayed by the court of the other state because this state is a more appropriate forum or for other reasons.

  (b) Before hearing the petition in a custody proceeding the court shall examine the pleadings and other information supplied by the parties under section 30-3-29 and shall consult the child custody registry established under section 30-3-36 concerning the dependency of proceedings with respect to the child in other states. If the court has reason to believe that proceedings may be pending in another state it shall direct an inquiry to the state court administrator or other appropriate official of the other state.

  (c) If the court is informed during the course of the proceeding that a proceeding concerning the custody of the child was pending in another state before the court assumed jurisdiction, it shall stay the proceeding and communicate with the court in which the other proceeding is pending, to the end that the issue may be litigated in the more appropriate forum and that information be exchanged in accordance with sections 30-3-39 through 30-3-42. If a court of this state has made a custody decree before being informed of a pending proceeding in a court of another state it shall immediately inform that court of the fact. If the court is informed that a proceeding was commenced in another state after it assumed jurisdiction it shall likewise inform the other court, to the end that the issues may be litigated in the more appropriate forum.

§ 30-3-27. Inconvenient forum; communication between courts; payment of expenses.

  (a) A court which has jurisdiction under this article to make an initial or modification decree may decline to exercise its jurisdiction any time before making a decree if it finds that it is an inconvenient forum to make a custody determination under the circumstances of the case and that a court of another state is a more appropriate forum.

(b) A finding of inconvenient forum may be made upon the court's own motion or upon motion of a party or a guardian ad litem or other representative of the child.

(c) In determining if it is an inconvenient forum, the court shall consider if it is in the interest of the child that another state assume jurisdiction. For this purpose it may take into account the following factors, among others:

(1) If another state is or recently was the child's home state;

(2) If another state has a closer connection with the child and his family or with the child and one or more of the contestants;

(3) If substantial evidence concerning the child's present or future care, protection, training, and personal relationships is more readily available in another state;

(4) If the parties have agreed on another forum which is no less appropriate; and

(5) If the exercise of jurisdiction by a court of this state would contravene any of the purposes stated in section 30-3-21.

(d) Before determining whether to decline or retain jurisdiction the court may communicate with a court of another state and exchange information pertinent to the assumption of jurisdiction by either court with a view to assuring that jurisdiction will be exercised by the more appropriate court and that a forum will be available to the parties.

(e) If the court finds that it is an inconvenient forum and that a court of another state is a more appropriate forum, it may dismiss the proceedings, or it may stay the proceedings upon condition that a custody proceeding be promptly commenced in another named state or upon any other conditions which may be just and proper, including the condition that a moving party stipulate his consent and submission to the jurisdiction of the other forum.

(f) The court may decline to exercise its jurisdiction under this article if a custody determination is incidental to an action for divorce or another proceeding, while retaining jurisdiction over the divorce or other proceeding.

(g) If it appears to the court that it is clearly an inappropriate forum it may require the party who commenced the proceedings to pay, in addition to the costs of the proceedings in this state, necessary travel and other expenses, including attorney's fees, incurred by other parties or their witnesses. Payment is to be made to the clerk of the court for remittance to the proper party.

(h) Upon dismissal or stay of proceedings under this section the court shall inform the court found to be the more appropriate forum of this fact or, if the court which would have jurisdiction in the other state is not certainly known, shall transmit the information to the court administrator or other appropriate official for forwarding to the appropriate court.

(i) Any communication received from another state informing this state of a finding of inconvenient forum because a court of this state is the more appropriate forum shall be filed in the custody registry of the appropriate court. Upon assuming jurisdiction the court of this state shall inform the original court of this fact.

§ 30-3-28. Jurisdiction declined by reason of conduct; expenses.

(a) If the petitioner for an initial decree has wrongfully taken the child from another state or has engaged in similar reprehensible conduct the court may decline to exercise jurisdiction if this is just and proper under the circumstances.

(b) Unless required in the interest of the child, the court shall not exercise its jurisdiction to modify a custody decree of another state if the petitioner, without consent of the person entitled to custody, has improperly removed the child from the physical custody of the person entitled to custody or has improperly retained the child after a visit or other temporary relinquishment of physical custody. If the petitioner has violated any other provision of a custody decree of another state the court may decline to exercise its jurisdiction if this is just and proper under the circumstances.

(c) In appropriate cases a court dismissing a petition under this section may charge the petitioner with necessary travel and other expenses, including attorneys' fees, incurred by other parties or their witnesses.

§ 30-3-29. Information under oath to be submitted to court; continuing duty to inform.

(a) Every party in a custody proceeding, in his first pleading or in an affidavit attached to that pleading, shall give information under oath as to the child's present address, the places where the child has lived within the last five years, and the names and present addresses of the persons with whom the child has lived during that period. In this pleading or affidavit every party shall further declare under oath whether:

(1) He has participated (as a party, witness, or in any other capacity) in any other litigation concerning the custody of the same child in this or any other state;

(2) He has information of any custody proceeding concerning the child pending in a court of this or any other state; and

(3) He knows of any person not a party to the proceedings who has physical custody of the child or claims to have custody or visitation rights with respect to the child.

(b) If the declaration as to any of the above items is in the affirmative the declarant shall give additional information under oath as required by the court. The court may examine the parties under oath as to details of the information furnished and as to other matters pertinent to the court's jurisdiction and the disposition of the case.

(c) Each party has a continuing duty to inform the court of any custody proceeding concerning the child in this or any other state of which he obtained information during this proceeding.

§ 30-3-30. Additional parties.

If the court learns from information furnished by the parties pursuant to section 30-3-29 or from other sources that a person not a party to the custody proceeding has physical custody of the child or claims to have custody or visitation rights with respect to the child, it shall order that person to be joined as a party and to be duly notified of the pendency of the proceeding and of his joinder as a party. If the person joined as a party is outside this state he shall be served with process or otherwise notified in accordance with section 30-3-25.

§ 30-3-31. Appearance of parties and child; notice; expenses.

(a) The court may order any party to the proceeding who is in this state to appear personally before the court. If that party has physical custody of the child the court may order that he appear personally with the child.

(b) If a party to the proceeding whose presence is desired by the court is outside this state with or without the child the court may order that the notice given under section 30-3-25 include a statement directing that party to appear personally with or without the child and declaring that failure to appear may result in a decision adverse to that party.

(c) If a party to the proceeding who is outside this state is directed to appear under subsection (b) or desires to appear personally before the court with or without the child, the court may require another party to pay to the clerk of the court travel and other necessary expenses of the party so appearing and of the child if this is just and proper under the circumstances.

§ 30-3-32. Binding force and res judicata effect of custody decree.

A custody decree rendered by a court of this state which had jurisdiction under section 30-3-23 binds all parties who have been served in this state or notified in accordance with section 30-3-25 or who have submitted to the jurisdiction of the court, and who have been given an opportunity to be heard. As to these parties the custody decree is conclusive as to all issues of law and fact decided and as to the custody determination made unless and until that determination is modified pursuant to law, including the provisions of this article.

§ 30-3-33. Recognition and enforcement of out-of-state custody decrees.

The courts of this state shall recognize and enforce an initial or modification decree of a court of another state which had assumed jurisdiction under statutory provisions substantially in accordance with this article or which was made under factual circumstances meeting the jurisdictional standards of this article, so long as this decree has not been modified in accordance with jurisdictional standards substantially similar to those of this article.

§ 30-3-34. Modification of custody decree of another state.

(a) If a court of another state has made a custody decree, a court of this state shall not modify that decree unless:

(1) It appears to the court of this state that the court which rendered the decree does not now have jurisdiction under jurisdictional prerequisites substantially in accordance with this article or has declined to assume jurisdiction to modify the decree; and

(2) The court of this state has jurisdiction.

(b) If a court of this state is authorized under subsection (a) and section 30-3-28 to modify a custody decree of another state it shall give due consideration to the transcript of the record and other documents of all previous proceedings submitted to it in accordance with section 30-3-42.

§ 30-3-35. Filing and enforcement of custody decree of another state; expenses.

(a) A certified copy of a custody decree of another state may be filed in the office of the clerk of any court of this state having jurisdiction over domestic relations matters. The clerk shall treat the decree in the same manner as the custody decree of any such court of this state. A custody decree so filed has the same effect and shall be enforced in like manner as a custody decree rendered by a court of this state.

(b) A person violating a custody decree of another state which makes it necessary to enforce the decree in this state may be required to pay necessary travel and other expenses, including attorneys' fees, incurred by the party entitled to the custody or his witnesses.

§ 30-3-36. Registry of out-of-state custody decrees and proceedings.

The clerk of each court having jurisdiction over domestic relations matters shall maintain a registry in which he shall enter the following:

(1) Certified copies of custody decrees of other states received for filing;

(2) Communications as to the pendency of custody proceedings in other states;

(3) Communications concerning a finding of inconvenient forum by a court of another state; and

(4) Other communications or documents concerning custody proceedings in another state which may affect the jurisdiction of a court of this state or the disposition to be made by it in a custody proceeding.

§ 30-3-37. Certified copies of custody decree.

The clerk of any court of this state having jurisdiction over domestic relations matters, at the request of the court of another state or at the request of any person who is affected by or has a legitimate interest in a custody decree, shall certify and forward a copy of the decree to that court or person.

§ 30-3-38. Taking testimony in another state.

In addition to other procedural devices available to a party, any party to the proceeding or a guardian ad litem or other representative of the child may adduce testimony of witnesses, including parties and the child, by deposition or otherwise, in another state. The court on its own motion may direct that the testimony of a person be taken in another state and may prescribe the manner in which and the terms upon which the testimony shall be taken.

§ 30-3-39. Hearings and studies in another state; orders to appear.

(a) A court of this state may request the appropriate court of another state to hold a hearing to adduce evidence, to order a party to produce or give evidence under other procedure of that state, or to have social studies made with respect to the custody of a child involved in proceedings pending in the court of this state and to forward to the court of this state certified copies of the transcript to the record of the hearing, the evidence otherwise adduced, or any social studies prepared in compliance with the request. The cost of the services may be assessed against the parties or, if necessary, ordered paid by the state.

(b) A court of this state may request the appropriate court of another state to order a party to custody proceedings pending in the court of this state to appear in the proceedings, and if that party has physical custody of the child, to appear with the child. The request may state that travel and other necessary expenses of the party and of the child whose appearance is desired will be assessed against another party or will otherwise be paid.

§ 30-3-40. Assistance to courts of other states.

(a) Upon request of the court of another state the courts of this state which are competent to hear custody matters may order a person in this state to appear at a hearing to adduce evidence or to produce or give evidence under other procedures available in this state. A certified copy of the transcript of the record of the hearing or the evidence otherwise adduced shall be forwarded by the clerk of the court to the requesting court.

(b) A person within this state may voluntarily give his testimony or statement in this state for use in a custody proceeding outside this state.

(c) Upon request of the court of another state, a competent court of this state may order a person in this state to appear alone or with the child in a custody proceeding in another state. The court may condition compliance with the request upon assurance by the other state that travel and other necessary expenses will be advanced or reimbursed.

§ 30-3-41. Preservation of documents for use in other states.

In any custody proceeding in this state the court shall preserve the pleadings, orders and decrees, any record that has been made of its hearings, social studies, and other pertinent documents until the child reaches 18 years of age. Upon appropriate request of the court of another state the court shall forward to the other court certified copies of any or all of such documents.

§ 30-3-42. Request for court records of another state.

If a custody decree has been rendered in another state concerning a child involved in a custody proceeding pending in a court of this state, the court of this state upon taking jurisdiction of the case shall request of the court of the other state a certified copy of the transcript of any court record and other documents mentioned in section 30-3-41.

§ 30-3-43. International application.

The general policies of this article extend to the international area. The provisions of this article relating to the recognition and enforcement of custody decrees of other states apply to custody decrees and decrees involving legal institutions similar in nature to custody institutions rendered by appropriate authorities of other nations if reasonable notice and opportunity to be heard were given to all affected persons.

§ 30-3-44. Priority.

Upon the request of a party to a custody proceeding which raises a question of existence or exercise of jurisdiction under this article the case shall be given calendar priority and handled expeditiously.

ALASKA

UNIFORM CHILD CUSTODY JURISDICTION ACT

Sec. 25.30.010. Purpose.
The general purposes of this chapter are to

(1) avoid jurisdictional competition and conflict with courts of other states in matters of child custody which have in the past resulted in the shifting of children from state to state with harmful effects on their well-being;

(2) promote cooperation with the courts of other states to the end that a custody decree is rendered in the state which can best decide the case in the interest of the child;

(3) assure that litigation concerning the custody of a child takes place ordinarily in the state with which the child and the child's family have the closest connection and where significant evidence concerning the child's care, protection, training, and personal relationships is most readily available, and that courts of this state decline the exercise of jurisdiction when the child and the child's family have a closer connection with another state;

(4) discourage continuing controversies over child custody in the interest of greater stability of home environment and of secure family relationships for the child;

(5) deter abductions and other unilateral removals of children undertaken to obtain custody awards;

(6) avoid re-litigation of custody decisions of other states in this state insofar as feasible;

(7) facilitate the enforcement of custody decrees of other states;

(8) promote and expand the exchange of information and other forms of mutual assistance between the courts of this state and those of other states concerned with the same child; and

(9) make uniform the law of those states which enact it.

Sec. 25.30.020. Jurisdiction.
(a) The superior court has jurisdiction to make a child custody determination by initial or modification decree if the conditions set out in any of the following paragraphs are met:

(1) this state

(A) is the home state of the child at the time of commencement of the proceeding, or

(B) had been the child's home state within six months before commencement of the proceeding and the child is absent from this state because of removal or retention by a person claiming custody or for other reasons, and a parent or person acting as parent continues to live in this state; or

(2) the child is physically present in this state and is a child in need of aid as defined in AS 47.10.290; or

(3) it

(A) appears that no other state would have jurisdiction under prerequisites substantially in accordance with (1) or (2) of this subsection, or another state has declined to exercise jurisdiction on the ground that this state is the more appropriate forum to determine the custody of the child, and

(B) is in the best interest of the child that this court assume jurisdiction.

(b) Except under (a)(2) and (3) of this section, physical presence in this state of the child, or of the child and one of the contestants, is not alone sufficient to confer jurisdiction on a court of this state to make a child custody determination.

(c) Physical presence of the child, while desirable, is not a prerequisite for jurisdiction to determine the child's custody.

Sec. 25.30.030. Notice and opportunity to be heard.
Before making a decree under this chapter, reasonable notice and opportunity to be heard, taking into account education and language differences which are known or reasonably ascertainable, shall be given to the contestants, any parent whose parental rights have not been previously terminated, and any person who has physical custody of the child. If any of these persons is outside this state, notice and opportunity to be heard shall be given under AS 25.30.040.

Sec. 25.30.040. Notice to persons outside this state; submission to jurisdiction.
(a) Notice required for the exercise of jurisdiction over a person outside this state shall be given in accordance with the provisions of Rule 4, Alaska Rules of Civil Procedure.

(b) Notice under this section shall be served, mailed, delivered, or published at least 20 days before any hearing in this state.

(c) Proof of service outside this state shall be made according to the provisions of Rule 4, Alaska Rules of Civil Procedure.

(d) Notice is not required if a person submits to the jurisdiction of the court.

Sec. 25.30.050. Simultaneous proceedings in other states.
(a) The superior court may not exercise its jurisdiction under this chapter if at the time of filing the petition a proceeding

concerning the custody of the child was pending in a court of another state exercising jurisdiction substantially in conformity with this chapter, unless the proceeding is stayed by the court of the other state because this state is a more appropriate forum or for other reasons.

(b) Before hearing the petition in a custody proceeding the court shall examine the pleadings and other information supplied by the parties under AS 25.30.080 and shall consult the child custody records maintained under AS 25.30.150 concerning the pendency of proceedings with respect to the state court administrator or other appropriate official of the other state.

(c) If the court is informed during the course of the proceeding that a proceeding concerning the custody of the child was pending in another state before the court assumed jurisdiction, it shall stay the proceeding and communicate with the court in which the other proceeding is pending so that the issue may be litigated in the more appropriate forum and information may be exchanged in accordance with AS 25.30.180 - 25.30.210. If a court of this state has made a custody decree before being informed that a proceeding was commenced in another state after it assumed jurisdiction, it shall likewise inform the other court to the end that the issues may be litigated in the more appropriate forum.

Sec. 25.30.060. Inconvenient forum.

(a) The superior court may decline to exercise its jurisdiction any time before issuing a decree if it finds that it is an inconvenient forum to make a custody determination under the circumstances of the case and that a court of another state is a more appropriate forum.

(b) A finding of inconvenient forum may be made upon the court's own motion or upon motion of a party or a guardian ad litem or other representative of the child.

(c) In determining if it is an inconvenient forum, the court shall consider if it is in the interest of the child that another state assume jurisdiction. For this purpose it may take into account the following factors, among others:

(1) if another state is or recently was the child's home state;

(2) if another state has a closer connection with the child and the child's family or with the child and one or more of the contestants;

(3) if better evidence concerning the child's present or future care, protection, training, and personal relationships is available in another state, or if equally substantial evidence is more readily available in another state;

(4) if the parties have agreed on another forum which is no less appropriate; and

(5) if the exercise of jurisdiction by a court of this state would contravene any of the purposes stated in AS 25.30.010.

(d) Before determining whether to decline or retain jurisdiction the court may communicate with a court of another state and exchange information pertinent to the assumption of jurisdiction by either court with a view to assuring that jurisdiction will be exercised by the more appropriate court and that a forum will be available to the parties.

(e) If the court finds that it is an inconvenient forum and that a court of another state is a more appropriate forum, it may dismiss the proceedings, or it may stay the proceedings upon condition that a custody proceeding be promptly commenced in another named state or upon any other conditions which may be just and proper, including the condition that a moving party stipulate consent and submission to the jurisdiction of the other forum.

(f) The court may decline to exercise its jurisdiction under this chapter if a custody determination is incidental to an action for divorce or dissolution of marriage or another proceeding while retaining jurisdiction over the divorce or other proceeding.

(g) If it appears to the court that it is clearly an inappropriate forum, it may require the party who commenced the proceedings to pay, in addition to the costs of the proceedings in this state, necessary travel and other expenses, including attorney fees, incurred by other parties or their witnesses. Payment is to be made to the clerk of the court for remittance to the proper party.

(h) Upon dismissal or stay of proceedings under this section the court shall inform the court found to be the more appropriate forum of this fact, or, if the court which would have jurisdiction in the other state is not certainly known, shall transmit the information to the court administrator or other appropriate official of the other state for forwarding to the appropriate court.

(i) Any communication received from another state informing this state of a finding of inconvenient forum because a court of this state is the more appropriate forum shall be filed in the custody records of the court in the appropriate judicial district. Upon assuming jurisdiction, the superior court of this state shall inform the original court of this fact.

Sec. 25.30.070. Jurisdiction declined by reason of conduct.

(a) If the petitioner for an initial decree has wrongfully taken the child from another state or has engaged in similar reprehensible conduct, the court may not exercise its jurisdiction unless it is necessary in an emergency to protect the child for reasons set out in AS 25.30.020(a)(2).

(b) If the petitioner for a modification decree has, without the consent of the person entitled to custody, improperly removed the child from the physical custody of the person entitled to custody or has improperly retained the child after a visit or other temporary relinquishment of physical custody, the court may not exercise its jurisdiction to modify a custody decree of another state unless it is necessary in an emergency to protect the child for reasons set out in AS 25.30.020(a)(2). If the petitioner has violated any other provision of a custody decree of another state, the court may decline to exercise its jurisdiction if this is just and proper under the circumstances.

(c) In appropriate cases a court dismissing a petition under this section may charge the petitioner with necessary travel and other expenses, including attorney fees, incurred by other parties or their witnesses.

Sec. 25.30.080. Information under oath to be submitted to the court.

(a) Every party in a custody proceeding in the party's first pleading or in an affidavit attached to that pleading shall give information under oath as to the child's present address, the places where the child has lived within the last five years, and the names and present addresses of the persons with whom the child has lived during that period. In this pleading or affidavit every party shall further declare under oath whether that party

(1) has participated, as a party, witness, or in any other capacity, in any other litigation concerning the custody of the same child in this or any other state;

(2) has information of any custody proceeding concerning the child pending in a court of this or any other state; and

(3) knows of any person not a party to the proceedings who has physical custody of the child or claims to have custody or visitation rights with respect to the child.

(b) If the declaration as to any of the matters specified in (a)(1) - (3) of this section is in the affirmative, the declarant shall give additional information under oath as required by the court. The court may examine the parties under oath as to details of the information furnished and as to other matters pertinent to the court's jurisdiction and the disposition of the case. All information obtained by the court shall be made available to counsel for the parties.

(c) Each party has a continuing duty to inform the court of any other custody proceeding concerning the child in this or any other state of which the party obtained information during this proceeding.

Sec. 25.30.090. Additional parties.

If the court learns from information furnished by the parties under AS 25.30.080 or from other sources that a person not a party to the custody proceeding has physical custody of the child or claims to have custody or visitation rights with respect to the child, it shall order that person to be joined as a party and to be properly notified of the pendency of the proceeding and of joinder as a party. If the person joined as a party is outside this state, the person shall be served with process or otherwise notified in accordance with AS 25.30.040.

Sec. 25.30.100. Appearance of parties and the child.

(a) The court may order any party to the proceeding who is in this state to appear personally before the court. If that party has physical custody of the child, the court may order that the party appear personally with the child.

(b) If a party to the proceeding whose presence is desired by the court is outside this state with or without the child, the court may order that the notice given under AS 25.30.040 include a statement directing that party to appear personally with or without the child and declaring that failure to appear may result in a decision adverse to that party.

(c) If a party to the proceeding who is outside this state is directed to appear under (b) of this section or desires to appear personally before the court with or without the child, the court may require another party to pay to the clerk of the court travel and other necessary expenses of the party so appearing and of the child if this is just and proper under the circumstances.

Sec. 25.30.110. Binding force and res judicata effect of custody decree.

A custody decree rendered by the superior court of this state having jurisdiction under AS 25.30.020 binds all parties who have been served in this state or notified in accordance with AS 25.30.040 or who have submitted to the jurisdiction of the court, and who have been given an opportunity to be heard. As to these parties the custody decree is conclusive as to all issues of law and fact decided and as to the custody determination made until that determination is modified in accordance with law, including the provisions of this chapter.

Sec. 25.30.120. Recognition of out-of-state custody decrees.

The superior court of this state shall recognize and enforce an initial or modification decree of a court of another state which had assumed jurisdiction under statutory provisions substantially in accordance with this chapter or which was made under factual circumstances meeting the jurisdictional standards of this chapter.

Sec. 25.30.130. Modification of custody decree of another state.

(a) If a court of another state has made a custody decree, a superior court of this state may not modify that decree unless

(1) it appears to the court of this state that the court which rendered the decree does not now have jurisdiction under jurisdictional prerequisites substantially in accordance with this chapter or has declined to assume jurisdiction to modify the decree, and

(2) the court of this state has jurisdiction.

(b) If a court of this state is authorized under (a) of this section and AS 25.30.070 to modify a custody decree of another state, it shall consider the transcript of the record and other documents of all previous proceedings submitted to it in accordance with AS 25.30.210.

Sec. 25.30.140. Filing and enforcement of custody decree of another state.

(a) A certified copy of a custody decree of another state may be filed in the office of the clerk of the trial courts of any judicial district of this state. A custody decree so filed has the same effect and shall be enforced in the same manner as a custody decree rendered by a court of this state.

(b) A person violating a custody decree of another state, which makes it necessary to enforce the decree in this state, may be required to pay necessary travel and other expenses, including attorney fees, incurred by the party entitled to the custody or the party's witness.

Sec. 25.30.150. Maintenance of out-of-state custody decrees and proceedings.

The clerk of the trial courts for each judicial district shall maintain the following;

(1) certified copies of custody decrees of other states received for filing;

(2) communications as to the pendency of custody proceedings in other states;

(3) communications concerning a finding of inconvenient forum by a court of another state; and

(4) other communications or documents concerning custody proceedings in another state which may affect the jurisdiction of a court of this state or the disposition to be made by it in a custody proceeding.

Sec. 25.30.160. Certified copies of custody decree.

The clerk of the trial courts for each judicial district of this state, at the request of the court of another state or at the request of any person who is affected by or has a legitimate interest in a custody decree, shall certify and forward a copy of the decree to that court or person, upon payment of a prescribed fee.

Sec. 25.30.170. Taking testimony in another state.

In addition to other procedural devices available to a party, any party to the proceeding or a guardian ad litem or other representative of the child may adduce testimony of witnesses, including parties and the child, by deposition or otherwise, in another state. The court on its own motion may direct that the testimony of a person be taken in another state and may prescribe the manner in which and the terms upon which the testimony shall be taken.

Sec. 25.30.180. Hearings and studies in another state; orders to appear.

(a) The superior court of this state may request the appropriate court of another state to hold a hearing to adduce evidence, to order a party to produce or give evidence under other procedures of that state, or to have social studies made with respect to the custody of a child involved in proceedings pending in the court of this state, and may request the other court to forward to the superior court of this state certified copies of the transcript of the record of the hearing, the evidence otherwise adduced, or any social studies prepared in compliance with the request. The cost of the services may be assessed against the parties or, if a party against whom the costs are assessed is determined by the court to be indigent, paid by the court.

(b) The superior court of this state may request the appropriate court of another state to order a party to custody proceedings pending in the superior court of this state to appear in the proceedings, and if that party has physical custody of the child, to appear with the child. The request may state that travel and other necessary expenses of the party and of the child whose appearance is desired will be assessed against another party or, if that party is determined by a court of this state to be indigent, that the costs will be paid by the court.

Sec. 25.30.190. Assistance to courts of other states.

(a) Upon request of the court of another state the superior court of this state may order a person in this state to appear at a hearing to adduce evidence or to produce or give evidence under other procedures available in this state or may order social studies to be made for use in a custody proceeding in another state. A certified copy of the transcript of the record of the hearing or the evidence otherwise adduced and any social studies prepared shall be forwarded by the clerk of the court to the requesting court upon receipt of payment from the requesting court.

(b) A person in this state may voluntarily give testimony or a statement in this state for use in a custody proceeding outside this state.

(c) Upon request of the court of another state, the superior court of this state may order a person in this state to appear alone or with the child in a custody proceeding in another state. The court may condition compliance with the request upon assurance by the other state that travel and other necessary expenses will be advanced or reimbursed.

Sec. 25.30.200. Preservation of documents for use in other states.

In any custody proceeding in this state, the court shall preserve the pleadings, orders and decrees, any record that has been made of its hearings, social studies, and other pertinent documents or a microphotographic film print or copy of any of the above papers until the child has reached majority or is emancipated under applicable law. Upon appropriate request of and payment from the court of another state, the court shall forward to the other court certified copies of any or all of those documents.

Sec. 25.30.210. Request for court records of another state.

If a custody decree has been rendered in another state concerning a child involved in a custody proceeding pending in a court of this state, the superior court of this state upon taking jurisdiction of the case shall request of the court of the other state a certified copy of the transcript of any court record and other documents mentioned in AS 25.30.200 and send payment for them.

Sec. 25.30.220. International application.
The general policies of this chapter extend to the international area. The provisions of this chapter relating to the recognition and enforcement of custody decrees of other states apply to custody decrees and decrees involving legal institutions similar in nature to custody rendered by appropriate authorities of other nations if reasonable notice and opportunity to be heard were given to all affected persons.

Sec. 25.30.230. Priority.
Upon the request of a party to a custody proceeding which raises a question of existence or exercise of jurisdiction under this chapter, the case shall be given calendar priority to the extent allowed by law and court rules, and shall be handled expeditiously.

Sec. 25.30.900. Definitions.
As used in this chapter,

(1) "contestant" means a person, including a parent, who claims a right to custody or visitation rights with respect to a child;

(2) "custody determination" means a court decision and court orders providing for the custody of a child, including visitation rights; it does not include a decision relating to child support or any other monetary obligation of any person;

(3) "custody proceeding" includes proceedings in which a custody determination is one of several issues, such as an action for divorce, dissolution of marriage, or legal separation, and includes child-in-need-of-aid proceedings;

(4) "decree" or "custody decree" means a custody determination contained in a judicial decree or order made in a custody proceeding, and includes an initial decree and a modification decree;

(5) "home state" means the state in which the child, immediately preceding the time involved, lived with the child's parents, a parent, or a person acting as parent, for at least six consecutive months, and, in the case of a child less than six months old, the state in which the child lived form birth with any of the persons mentioned; periods of temporary absence of any of the named persons are counted as part of the six-month or other period;

(6) "initial decree" means the first custody decree concerning a particular child;

(7) "modification decree" means a custody decree which modifies or replaces a prior decree, whether made by the court which rendered the prior decree or by another court;

(8) "physical custody" means actual possession and control of a child;

(9) "person acting as parent" means a person, other than a parent, who has physical custody of a child and who has either been awarded custody by a court or claims a right to custody;

(10) "state" means any state, territory, or possession of the United States, the Commonwealth of Puerto Rico, and the District of Columbia.

ARIZONA

UNIFORM CHILD CUSTODY JURISDICTION ACT

§ 8-401. Purposes of act; construction of provisions.
A. The general purposes of this chapter are to:

1. Avoid jurisdictional competition and conflict with courts of other states in matters of child custody which have in the past resulted in the shifting of children from state to state with harmful effects on their well-being.

2. Promote cooperation with the courts of other states to the end that a custody decree is rendered in that state which can best decide the case in the interest of the child.

3. Assure that litigation concerning the custody of a child take place ordinarily in the state with which the child and his family have the closest connection and where significant evidence concerning his care, protection, training and personal relationships is most readily available, and that courts of this state decline the exercise of jurisdiction when the child and his family have a closer connection with another state.

4. Discourage continuing controversies over child custody in the interest of greater stability of home environment and of secure family relationships for the child.

5. Deter abductions and other unilateral removals of children undertaken to obtain custody awards.

6. Avoid relitigation of custody decisions of other states in this state insofar as feasible.

7. Facilitate the enforcement of custody decrees of other states.

8. Promote and expand the exchange of information and other forms of mutual assistance between the courts of this state and those of other states concerned with the same child.

9. Make uniform the law of those states which enact the uniform child custody jurisdiction act.

B. This chapter shall be construed to promote the general purposes stated in this section.

§ 8-402. Definitions.

In this chapter, unless the context otherwise requires:

1. "Contestant" means a person, including a parent, who claims a right to custody or visitation rights with respect to a child.

2. "Custody determination" means a court decision and court orders and instructions providing for the custody of a child, including visitation rights. It does not include a decision relating to child support or any other monetary obligation of any person.

3. "Custody proceeding" means proceedings in which a custody determination is one of several issues, such as an action for divorce, dissolution of marriage or separation, and includes child neglect and dependency proceedings.

4. "Decree" or "custody decree" means a custody determination contained in a judicial decree or order made in a custody proceeding and includes an initial decree and a modification decree.

5. "Home state" means the state in which the child immediately preceding the time involved lived with his parents, a parent or a person acting as parent for at least six consecutive months, and in the case of a child less than six months old the state in which the child lived from birth with any of the persons mentioned. Periods of temporary absence of any of the named persons are counted as part of the six month or other period.

6. "Initial decree" means the first custody decree concerning a particular child.

7. "Modification decree" means a custody decree which modifies or replaces a prior decree, whether made by the court which rendered the prior decree or by another court.

8. "Person acting as parent" means a person, other than a parent, who has physical custody of a child and who has either been awarded custody by a court or claims a right to custody.

9. "Physical custody" means actual possession and control of a child.

10. "State" means any state, territory or possession of the United States, the Commonwealth of Puerto Rico and the District of Columbia.

§ 8-403. Jurisdiction.

A. The superior court of the state of Arizona is vested with jurisdiction to make a child custody determination by initial or modification decree if any of the following apply:

1. This state is the domicile or the home state of child at the time of commencement of the proceeding or had been the child's domicile or home state within six months before commencement of the proceeding and the child is absent from this state because of his removal or retention by a person claiming his custody or for other reasons, and a parent or person acting as parent continues to live in this state.

2. It is in the best interest of the child that a court of this state assume jurisdiction because the child and his parents, or the child and at least one contestant, have a significant connection with this state, and there is available in this state substantial evidence concerning the child's present or future care, protection, training and personal relationships.

3. The child is physically present in this state and the child has been abandoned or it is necessary in an emergency to protect the child because he has been subjected to or threatened with mistreatment or abuse or is otherwise neglected or dependent.

4. It appears that no other state would have jurisdiction under prerequisites substantially in accordance with paragraphs 1, 2 or 3 or another state has declined to exercise jurisdiction on the ground that this state is the more appropriate forum to determine the custody of the child, and it is in the best interest of the child that this court assume jurisdiction.

B. Except pursuant to subsection A, paragraphs 3 and 4, physical presence in this state of the child, or of the child and one of the contestants, is not alone sufficient to confer jurisdiction on a court of this state to make a child custody determination.

C. Physical presence of the child, while desirable, is not a prerequisite for jurisdiction to determine his custody.

§ 8-404. Notice and opportunity to be heard.

Before making a decree under this chapter, reasonable notice and opportunity to be heard shall be given to the contestants, any parent whose parental rights have not been previously terminated and any person who has physical custody of the child. If any of these persons is outside this state, notice and opportunity to be heard shall be given pursuant to § 8-405.

§ 8-405. Notice to persons outside this state; submission to jurisdiction.

A. Notice required for the exercise of jurisdiction over a person outside this state shall be given in a manner reasonably calculated to give actual notice and shall be any of the following:

1. By personal delivery outside this state in the manner prescribed for service of process within this state.

2. In the manner prescribed by the law of the place in which the service is made for service of process in that place in an action in any of its courts of general jurisdiction.

3. By any form of mail addressed to the person to be served and requesting a receipt.

4. As directed by the court, including publication, if other means of notification are ineffective.

B. Notice under this section shall be served, mailed, delivered or last published at least twenty days before any hearing in this state.

C. Proof of service outside this state may be made by affidavit of the individual who made the service, or in the manner prescribed by the law of this state, the order pursuant to which the service is made, or the law of the place in which the service is made. If service is made by mail, proof may be a receipt signed by the addressee or other evidence of delivery to the addressee.

D. Notice is not required if a person submits to the jurisdiction of the court.

§ 8-406. Simultaneous proceedings in other states.

A. A court of this state shall not exercise its jurisdiction under this chapter if at the time of filing the petition a proceeding concerning the custody of the child was pending in a court of another state exercising jurisdiction substantially in conformity with this chapter, unless the proceeding is stayed by the court of the other state because this state is a more appropriate forum or for other reasons.

B. Before hearing the petition in a custody proceeding the court shall examine the pleadings and other information supplied by the parties under § 8-409 and shall consult the child custody registry established under § 8-416 concerning the pendency of proceedings with respect to the child in other states. If the court has reason to believe that proceedings may be pending in another state it shall direct an inquiry to the state court administrator or other appropriate official of the other state.

C. If the court is informed during the course of the proceeding that a proceeding concerning the custody of the child was pending in another state before the court assumed jurisdiction it shall stay the proceeding and communicate with the court in which the other proceeding is pending to the end that the issue may be litigated in the more appropriate forum and that information be exchanged only in accordance with §§ 8-419 through 8-422. If a court of this state has made a custody decree before being informed of a pending proceeding in a court of another state it shall immediately inform that court of the fact. If the court is informed that a proceeding was commenced in another state after it assumed jurisdiction it shall likewise inform the other court to the end that the issues may be litigated in the more appropriate forum.

§ 8-407. Inconvenient forum.

A. A court which has jurisdiction under this chapter to make an initial or modification decree may decline to exercise its jurisdiction any time before making a decree it if finds that it is an inconvenient forum to make a custody determination under the circumstances of the case and that a court of another state is a more appropriate forum.

B. A finding of inconvenient forum may be made upon the court's own motion or upon motion of a party or a guardian ad litem or other representative of the child.

C. In determining if it is an inconvenient forum, the court shall consider if it is in the interest of the child that another state assume jurisdiction. For this purpose it may take into account the following factors, among other:

1. If another state is or recently was the child's home state.

2. If another state has a closer connection with the child and his family or with the child and one or more of the contestants.

3. If substantial evidence concerning the child's present or future care, protection, training and personal relationships is more readily available in another state.

4. If the parties have agreed on another forum which is no less appropriate.

5. If the exercise of jurisdiction by a court of this state would contravene any of the purposes stated in § 8-401.

D. Before determining whether to decline or retain jurisdiction the court may communicate with a court of another state and exchange information pertinent to the assumption of jurisdiction by either court with a view to assuring that jurisdiction will be exercised by the more appropriate court and that a forum will be available to the parties.

E. If the court finds that it is an inconvenient forum and that a court of another state is a more appropriate forum, it may dismiss the proceedings or it may stay the proceedings upon condition that a custody proceeding be promptly commenced in another named state or upon any other conditions which may be just and proper, including the condition that a moving party stipulate his consent and submission to the jurisdiction of the other forum.

F. The court may decline to exercise its jurisdiction under this chapter if a custody determination is incidental to an action for divorce, dissolution of marriage or another proceeding while retaining jurisdiction over the divorce, dissolution of marriage or other proceeding.

G. If it appears to the court that it is clearly an inappropriate forum it may require the party who commenced the proceedings to pay, in addition to the costs of the proceedings in this state, necessary travel and other expenses including attorneys' fees incurred by other parties or their witnesses. Payment is to be made to the clerk of the court for remittance to the proper party.

H. Upon dismissal or stay of proceedings under this section the court shall inform the court found to be the more appropriate forum of this fact, or if the court which would have jurisdiction in the other state is not certainly known shall transmit the information to the court administrator or other appropriate official for forwarding to the appropriate court.

I. Any communication received from another state informing this state of a finding of inconvenient forum because a court of this state is the more appropriate forum shall be filed in the custody registry of the appropriate court. Upon assuming jurisdiction the court of this state shall inform the original court of this fact.

§ 8-408. Jurisdiction declined by reason of conduct.

A. If the petitioner for an initial decree has wrongfully taken the child from another state or has engaged in similar reprehensible conduct, the court may decline to exercise jurisdiction if this is just and proper under the circumstances.

B. Unless required in the interest of the child, the court shall not exercise its jurisdiction to modify a custody decree of another state if the petitioner, without consent of the person entitled to custody, has improperly removed the child from the physical custody of the person entitled to custody or has improperly retained the child after a visit or other temporary relinquishment of physical custody. If the petitioner has violated any other provision of a custody decree of another state the court may decline to exercise its jurisdiction if this is just and proper under the circumstances.

C. In appropriate cases a court dismissing a petition under this section may charge the petitioner with necessary travel and other expenses, including attorneys' fees, incurred by other parties or their witnesses.

§ 8-409. Information under oath to be submitted to the court.

A. Every party in a custody proceeding in his first pleading or in an affidavit attached to that pleading shall give information under oath as to the child's present address, the places where the child has lived within the last five years and the names and present addresses of the persons with whom the child has lived during that period. In this pleading or affidavit every party shall further declare under oath whether:

1. He has participated, as a party, witness or in any other capacity, in any other litigation concerning the custody of the same child in this or any other state.

2. He has information of any custody proceeding concerning the child pending in a court of this or any other state.

3. He knows of any person not a party to the proceedings who has physical custody of the child or claims to have custody or visitation rights with respect to the child.

B. If the declaration as to any of the items in subsection A of this section is in the affirmative the declarant shall give additional information under oath as required by the court. The court may examine the parties under oath as to details of the information furnished and as to other matters pertinent to the court's jurisdiction and the disposition of the case.

C. Each party has a continuing duty to inform the court of any custody proceeding concerning the child in this or any other state of which he obtained information during this proceeding.

D. Notwithstanding this section or any other statute, if the person seeking custody of a child resides in a domestic violence shelter as defined in § 36-3001 or is a victim of domestic violence as defined in § 36-3001, the address of the person seeking custody or the domestic violence shelter shall not be disclosed, but a means of communicating with the resident, such as a post office box or address of his attorney, must be disclosed.

§ 8-410. Additional parties.

If the court learns from information furnished by the parties pursuant to § 8-409 or from other sources that a person not a party to the custody proceeding has physical custody of the child or claims to have custody or visitation rights with respect to the child, it shall order that person to be joined as a party and to be duly notified of the pendency of the proceeding and of his joinder as a party. If the person joined as a party is outside this state he shall be served with process or otherwise notified in accordance with §8-405.

§ 8-411. Appearance of parties and the child.

A. The court may order any party to the proceeding who is in this state to appear personally before the court. If that party has physical custody of the child the court may order that he appear personally with the child.

B. If a party to the proceeding whose presence is desired by the court is outside this state with or without the child the court may order that the notice given under § 8-405 include a statement directing that party to appear personally with or without the child and declaring that failure to appear may result in a decision adverse to that party.

C. If a party to the proceeding who is outside this state is directed to appear under subsection B of this section or desires to appear personally before the court with or without the child, the court may require the other party or parties to pay to the clerk of the court travel and other necessary expenses of the party so appearing and of the child if this is just and proper under the circumstances.

§ 8-412. Binding force and res judicata effect of custody decree.

A custody decree rendered by a court of this state which had jurisdiction under § 8-403 binds all parties who have been served in this state or notified in accordance with § 8-405 or who have submitted to the jurisdiction of the court and who have been given an opportunity to be heard. As to these parties the custody is conclusive as to all issues of law and fact decided and as to the custody determination made unless and until that determination is modified pursuant to law, including the provisions of this chapter.

§ 8-413. Recognition of out-of-state custody decrees.

The courts of this state shall recognize and enforce an initial or modification decree of a court of another state which had assumed jurisdiction under statutory provisions substantially in accordance with this chapter or which was made under factual circumstances meeting the jurisdictional standards of the chapter, so long as this decree has not been modified in accordance with jurisdictional standards substantially similar to those of this chapter.

§ 8-414. Modification of custody decree of another state.

A. If a court of another state has made a custody decree, a court of this state shall not modify that decree unless it appears to the court of this state that the court which rendered the decree does not now have jurisdiction under jurisdictional prerequisites substantially in accordance with this chapter or has declined to assume jurisdiction to modify the decree, and the court of this state has jurisdiction.

B. If a court of this state is authorized under subsection A of this section and § 8-408 to modify a custody decree of another state it shall give due consideration to the transcript of the record and other documents of all previous proceedings submitted to it in accordance with § 8-422.

§ 8-415. Filing and enforcement of custody decree of another state.

A. A certified copy of a custody decree of another state may be filed in the office of the clerk of any superior court of this state. The clerk shall treat the decree in the same manner as a custody decree of the superior court of this state. A custody decree so filed has the same effect and shall be enforced in like manner as a custody decree rendered by a court of this state.

B. A person violating a custody decree of another state which makes it necessary to enforce the decree in this state may be required to pay necessary travel and other expenses, including attorneys' fees, incurred by the party entitled to the custody or his witnesses.

§ 8-416. Registry of out-of-state custody decrees and proceedings.

The clerk of each superior court shall maintain a registry in which he shall enter the following:

1. Certified copies of custody decrees of other states received for filing.
2. Communications as to the pendency of custody proceedings in other states.
3. Communications concerning a finding of inconvenient forum by a court of another state.
4. Other communications or documents concerning custody proceedings in another state which may affect the jurisdiction of a court of this state or the disposition to be made by it in a custody proceedings.

8-417. Certified copies of custody decree.

The clerk of the superior court of this state, at the request of the court of another state or at the request of any person who is affected by or has a legitimate interest in a custody decree, shall certify and forward a copy of the decree to that court or person.

§ 8-418. Taking testimony in another state.

In addition to other procedural devices available to a party, any party to the proceeding or a guardian ad litem or other representative of the child may adduce testimony of witnesses, including parties and the child, by deposition or otherwise, in another state. The court on its own motion may direct that the testimony of a person be taken in another state and may prescribe the manner in which and the terms upon which the testimony shall be taken.

§ 8-419. Hearings and studies in another state; orders to appear.

A. A court of this state may request the appropriate court of another state to hold a hearing to adduce evidence, to order a party to produce or give evidence under other procedures of that state or to have social studies made with respect to the custody of a child involved in proceedings pending in the court of this state and to forward to the court of this state certified copies of the transcript of the record of the hearing, the evidence otherwise adduced or any social studies prepared in compliance with the request. The cost of the services may be assessed against the parties or, if necessary, ordered paid by the county.

B. A court of this state may request the appropriate court of another state to order a party to custody proceedings pending in the court of this state to appear in the proceedings and, if that party has physical custody of the child, to appear with the child. The request may state that travel and other necessary expenses of the party and of the child whose appearance is desired will be assessed against the other party or parties or will otherwise be paid.

§ 8-420. Assistance to courts of other states.

A. Upon request of the court of another state the superior court may order a person in this state to appear at a hearing to adduce evidence or to produce or give evidence under other procedures available in this state. A certified copy of the transcript of the record of the hearing or the evidence otherwise adduced shall be forwarded by the clerk of the court to the requesting court.

B. A person within this state may voluntarily give his testimony or statement in this state for use in a custody proceeding outside this state.

C. Upon request of the court of another state the superior court of this state may order a person in this state to appear along or with the child in a custody proceeding in another state. The court may condition compliance with the request upon assurance by the other state that state travel and other necessary expenses will be advanced or reimbursed.

§ 8-421. Preservation of documents for use in other states.

In any custody proceeding in this state the court shall preserve the pleadings, orders and decrees, any record that has been made of its hearings, social studies and other pertinent documents until the child reaches eighteen years of age. Upon appropriate request of the court of another state the court shall forward to the other court certified copies of any or all of such documents.

§ 8-422. Request for court records of another state.
If a custody decree has been rendered in another state concerning a child involved in a custody proceeding pending in a court of this state, the court of this state upon taking jurisdiction of the case shall request of the court of the other state a certified copy of the transcript of any court record and other documents mentioned in § 8-421.

§ 8-423. International application.
The general policies of this chapter may extend to the international area. The superior court of this state may consider the provisions of this chapter relating to the recognition and enforcement of custody decrees of other states to apply to custody decrees and decrees involving legal institutions similar in nature to custody institutions rendered by appropriate authorities of other nations if reasonable notice and opportunity to be heard were given to all affected persons.

§ 8-424. Severability.
If any provision of this chapter or the application of this chapter to any person or circumstance is held invalid, its invalidity does not affect other provisions or applications of the chapter which can be given effect without the invalid provision or application, and to this end the provisions of this chapter are severable.

ARKANSAS

UNIFORM CHILD CUSTODY JURISDICTION ACT

§ 9-13-201. Purposes of subchapter - Construction of provisions.
(a) The general purposes of this subchapter are to:

(1) Avoid jurisdictional competition and conflict with courts of other states in matters of child custody which have in the past resulted in the shifting of children from state to state with harmful effects on their well-being;

(2) Promote cooperation with the courts of other states to the end that a custody decree is rendered in that state which can best decide the case in the interest of the child;

(3) Assure that litigation concerning the custody of a child take place ordinarily in the state with which the child and his family have the closest connection and where significant evidence concerning his care, protection, training, and personal relationships are most readily available, and that courts of this state decline the exercise of jurisdiction when the child and his family have a closer connection with another state;

(4) Discourage continuing controversies over child custody in the interest of greater stability of home environment and of secure family relationships for the child;

(5) Deter abductions and other unilateral removals of children undertaken to obtain custody awards;

(6) Avoid relitigation of custody decisions of other states in this state insofar as feasible;

(7) Facilitate the enforcement of custody decrees of other states;

(8) Promote and expand the exchange of information and other forms of mutual assistance between the courts of this state and those of other states concerned with the same child; and

(9) Make uniform the law of those states which enact it.

(b) This subchapter shall be construed to promote the general purposes stated in this section.

§ 9-13-202. Definitions.
As used in this subchapter:

(1) "Contestant" means a person, including a parent, who claims a right to custody or visitation rights with respect to a child;

(2) "Custody determination" means a court decision and court orders and instructions providing for the custody of a child, including visitation rights. It does not include a decision relating to child support or any other monetary obligation of any person;

(3) "Custody proceeding" includes proceedings in which a custody determination is one of several issues, such as an action for divorce or separation, and includes child neglect and dependency proceedings;

(4) "Decree" or "custody decree" means a custody determination contained in a judicial decree or order made in a custody proceeding, and includes an initial decree and a modification decree;

(5) "Home state" means the state in which the child immediately preceding the time involved lived with his parents, a parent,

or a person acting as parent, for at least six (6) consecutive months, and in the case of a child less than (6) months old, the state in which the child lived from birth with any of the persons mentioned. Periods of temporary absence of any of the named persons are counted as part of the six-month or other period;

(6) "Initial decree" means the first custody decree concerning a particular child;

(7) "Modification decree" means a custody decree which modifies or replaces a prior decree, whether made by the court which rendered the prior decree or by another court;

(8) "Physical custody" means actual possession and control of a child;

(9) "Person acting as parent" means a person, other than a parent, who has physical custody of a child and who has neither been awarded custody by a court or claims a right to custody; and

(10) "State" means any state, territory, or possession of the United States, the Commonwealth of Puerto Rico, and the District of Columbia.

§ 9-13-203. Jurisdiction.

(a) A court of this state which is competent to decide child custody matters has jurisdiction to make a child custody determination by initial or modification decree if:

(1) This state (i) is the home state of the child at the time of commencement of the proceeding, or (ii) had been the child's home state within six (6) months before commencement of the proceeding and the child is absent from this state because of his removal or retention by a person claiming his custody or for other reasons, and a parent or person acting as parent continues to live in this state; or

(2) It is in the best interest of the child that a court of this state assume jurisdiction because (i) the child and his parents, or the child and at least one (1) contestant, have a significant connection with this state and (ii) there is available in this state substantial evidence concerning the child's present or future care, protection, training, and personal relationships; or

(3) The child is physically present in this state and (i) the child has been abandoned or (ii) it is necessary in an emergency to protect the child because he has been subjected to or threatened with mistreatment or abuse or is otherwise neglected or dependent; or

(4)(i) It appears that no other state would have jurisdiction under prerequisites substantially in accordance with subdivisions (a)(1), (2), or (3), or another state has declined to exercise jurisdiction on the ground that this state is the more appropriate forum to determine the custody of the child, and (ii) it is in the best interest of the child that this court assume jurisdiction.

(b) Except under subdivisions (a)(3) and (4), physical presence in this state of the child, or of the child and one (1) of the contestants, is not along sufficient to confer jurisdiction on a court of this state to make a child custody determination.

(c) Physical presence of the child, while desirable, is not a prerequisite for jurisdiction to determine his custody.

§ 9-13-204. Notice and opportunity to be heard - Inquiry about missing children.

(a) Before making a decree under this subchapter, reasonable notice and opportunity to be heard shall be given to the contestants, any parent whose parental rights have not been previously terminated, and any person who has physical custody of the child. If any of these persons is outside this state, notice and opportunity to be heard shall be given pursuant to § 9-13-205.

(b) In all proceedings for custody, when it appears from the pleadings or testimony that either parent resides at an unknown location, either parent is allegedly deceased, or personal service has not been perfected over either parent, the court shall, prior to the entry of a decree or modification concerning custody, inquire of the Missing Children Information Center within the Arkansas Crime Information Center to determine if such child or children have been reported missing. The inquiry shall be directed to the center through a local law enforcement agency having on-line access to the Arkansas Crime Information Center.

§ 9-13-205. Notice to persons outside this state.

(a) Notice required for the exercise of jurisdiction over a person outside this state shall be given in a manner reasonably calculated to give actual notice and may be:

(1) By personal delivery outside this state in the manner prescribed for service of process within this state;

(2) In the manner prescribed by the law of the place in which the service is made for service of process in that place in an action in any of its courts of general jurisdiction;

(3) By any form of mail addressed to the person to be served and requesting a receipt; or

(4) As directed by the court, including publication, if other means of notification are ineffective.

(b) Notice under this section shall be served, or delivered, at least ten (10) days before any hearing in this state. Where notice is published, publication shall be thirty (30) days prior to the hearing.

(c) Proof of service outside this state may be made by affidavit of the individual who made the service, or in the manner prescribed by the law of this state, by the order pursuant to which the service is made, or by the law of the place in which the service is made. If service is made by mail, proof may be a receipt signed by the addressee or other evidence of delivery to the addressee.

§ 9-13-206. Simultaneous proceedings in other states.

(a) A court of this state shall not exercise its jurisdiction under this subchapter if at the time of filing the petition a proceeding concerning the custody of the child was pending in a court of another state exercising jurisdiction substantially in conformity with this subchapter, unless the proceeding is stayed by the court of the other state because this state is a more appropriate forum or for other reasons.

(b) Before hearing the petition in a custody proceeding the court shall examine the pleadings and other information supplied by the parties under § 9-13-209, and shall consult the child custody registry established under § 9-13-216 concerning the pendency of proceedings with respect to the child in other states. If the court has reason to believe that proceedings may be pending in another state it shall direct an inquiry to the state court administrator or other appropriate official of the other state.

(c) If the court is informed during the course of the proceeding that a proceeding concerning the custody of the child is pending in another state before the court assumed jurisdiction, it shall stay the proceeding and communicate with the court in which the other proceeding is pending, to the end that the issue may be litigated in the more appropriate forum and that information be exchanged in accordance with §§ 9-13-219 - 9-13-222. If a court of this state has made a custody decree before being informed of a pending proceeding in a court of another state, it shall immediately inform that court of the fact. If the court is informed that a proceeding was commenced in another state after it assumed jurisdiction, it shall likewise inform the other court to the end that the issues may be litigated in the more appropriate forum.

§ 9-13-207. Inconvenient forum.

(a) A court which has jurisdiction under this subchapter to make an initial or modification decree may decline to exercise its jurisdiction any time before making a decree if it finds that it is an inconvenient forum to make a custody determination under the circumstances of the case and that a court of another state is a more appropriate forum.

(b) A finding of inconvenient forum may be made upon the court's own motion or upon motion of a party or a guardian ad litem or other representative of the child.

(c) In determining if it is an inconvenient forum, the court shall consider if it is in the interest of the child that another state assume jurisdiction. For this purpose, it may take into account the following factors, among others:

(1) If another state is or recently was the child's home state;

(2) If another state has a closer connection with the child and his family or with the child and one (1) or more of the contestants;

(3) If substantial evidence concerning the child's present or future care, protection, training, and personal relationships is more readily available in another state;

(4) If the parties have agreed on another forum which is no less appropriate; and

(5) If the exercise of jurisdiction by a court of this state would contravene any of the purposes stated in § 9-13-201.

(d) Before determining whether to decline or retain jurisdiction, the court may communicate with a court of another state and exchange information pertinent to the assumption of jurisdiction by either court, with a view to assuring that jurisdiction will be exercised by the more appropriate court and that a forum will be available to the parties.

(e) If the court finds that it is an inconvenient forum and that a court of another state is a more appropriate forum, it may dismiss the proceedings, or it may stay the proceedings upon condition that a custody proceeding be promptly commenced in another named state, or upon any other conditions which may be just and proper, including the condition that a moving party stipulate his consent and submission to the jurisdiction of the other forum.

(f) The court may decline to exercise its jurisdiction under this subchapter if a custody determination is incidental to an action for divorce or another proceeding while retaining jurisdiction over the divorce or other proceeding.

(g) If it appears to the court that it is clearly an inappropriate forum, it may require the party who commenced the proceedings to pay, in addition to the costs of the proceedings in this state, necessary travel and other expenses, including attorneys' fees, incurred by other parties or their witnesses. Payment is to be made to the clerk of the court for remittance to the proper party.

(h) Upon dismissal or stay of proceedings under this section, the court shall inform the court found to be the more appropriate forum of this fact or, if the court which would have jurisdiction in the other state is not certainly known, shall transmit the information to the court administrator or other appropriate official for forwarding to the appropriate court.

(i) Any communication received from another state informing this state of a finding of inconvenient forum because a court of this state is the more appropriate forum shall be filed in the custody registry of the appropriate court. Upon assuming jurisdiction, the court of this state shall inform the original court of this fact.

§ 9-13-208. Jurisdiction declined by reason of conduct.

(a) If the petitioner for an initial decree has wrongfully taken the child from another state or has engaged in similar reprehensible conduct, the court may decline to exercise jurisdiction if this is just and proper under the circumstances.

(b) Unless required in the interest of the child, the court shall not exercise its jurisdiction to modify a custody decree of another state if the petitioner, without consent of the person entitled to custody, has improperly removed the child from the physical custody of the person entitled to custody or has improperly retained the child after a visit or other temporary relinquishment of physical custody. If the petitioner has violated any other provision of a custody decree of another state, the court may decline to exercise its jurisdiction if this is just and proper under the circumstances.

(c) In appropriate cases, a court dismissing a petition under this section may charge the petitioner with necessary travel and other expenses, including attorneys' fees, incurred by other parties or their witnesses.

§ 9-13-209. Information under oath to be submitted to the court.

(a) Every party in a custody proceeding in his first pleading or in an affidavit attached to that pleading shall give information under oath as to the child's present address, the places where the child has lived within the last five (5) years, and the names and present addresses of the persons with whom the child has lived during that period. In this pleading or affidavit, every party shall further declare under oath whether:

(1) He has participated as a party, witness, or in any other capacity, in any other litigation concerning the custody of the same child in this or any other state;

(2) He has information of any custody proceeding concerning the child pending in a court of this or any other state; and

(3) He knows of any person not a party to the proceedings who has physical custody of the child or claims to have custody or visitation rights with respect to the child.

(b) If the declaration as to any of the above items is in the affirmative, the declarant shall give additional information under oath as required by the court. The court may examine the parties under oath as to details of the information furnished and as to other matters pertinent to the court's jurisdiction and the disposition of the case.

(c) Each party has a continuing duty to inform the court of any custody proceeding concerning the child in this or any other state of which he obtained information during this proceeding.

§ 9-13-210. Additional parties.

If the court learns from information furnished by the parties pursuant to § 9-13-209 or from other sources that a person not a party to the custody proceeding has physical custody of the child or claims to have custody or visitation rights with respect to the child, it shall order that person to be joined as a party and to be duly notified of the pendency of the proceeding and of his joinder as a party. If the person joined as a party is outside this state, he shall be served with process or otherwise notified in accordance with § 9-13-205.

§ 9-13-211. Appearance of parties and child.

(a) The court may order any party to the proceeding who is in this state to appear personally before the court. If that party has physical custody of the child, the court may order that he appear personally with the child.

(b) If a party to the proceeding whose presence is desired by the court is outside this state with or without the child, the court may order that the notice given under § 9-13-205 include a statement directing that party to appear personally with or without the child and declaring that failure to appear may result in a decision adverse to that party.

(c) If a party to the proceeding who is outside this state is directed to appear under subsection (b) or desires to appear personally before the court with or without the child, the court may require another party to pay to the clerk of the court travel and other necessary expenses of the party so appearing and of the child, if this is just and proper under the circumstances.

§ 9-13-212. Binding force and res judicata effect of custody decree.

A custody decree rendered by a court of this state which had jurisdiction under § 9-13-203 binds all parties who have been served in this state or notified in accordance with § 9-13-205, or who have submitted to the jurisdiction of the court, and who have been given an opportunity to be heard. As to these parties, the custody decree is conclusive as to all issues of law and fact decided and as to the custody determination made, unless and until that determination is modified pursuant to law, including the provisions of this subchapter.

§ 9-13-213. Recognition of out-of-state custody decrees.

The courts of this state shall recognize and enforce an initial or modification decree of a court of another state which had assumed jurisdiction under statutory provisions substantially in accordance with this subchapter, or which was made under factual circumstances meeting the jurisdictional standards of this subchapter, so long as this decree has not been modified in accordance with jurisdictional standards substantially similar to those of this subchapter.

§ 9-13-214. Modification of custody decree of another state.

(a) If a court of another state has made a custody decree, a court of this state shall not modify that decree unless (1) it appears to the court of this state that the court which rendered the decree does not now have jurisdiction under jurisdictional prerequisites substantially in accordance with this subchapter or has declined to assume jurisdiction to modify the decree and (2) the court of this state has jurisdiction.

(b) If a court of this state is authorized under subsection (a) and § 9-13-208 to modify a custody decree of another state, it shall give due consideration to the transcript of the record and other documents of all previous proceedings submitted to it in accordance with § 9-13-222.

§ 9-13-215. Filing and enforcement of custody decree of another state.

(a) A certified copy of a custody decree of another state may be filed in the office of the clerk of any chancery court of this state. The clerk shall treat the decree in the same manner as a custody decree of the chancery court of this state. A custody decree so filed has the same effect and shall be enforced in like manner as a custody decree rendered by a court of this state.

(b) A person violating a custody decree of another state which makes it necessary to enforce the decree in this state may be required to pay necessary travel and other expenses, including attorneys' fees, incurred by the party entitled to the custody or his witnesses.

§ 9-13-216. Registry of out-of-state custody decrees and proceedings.

The clerk of each chancery court shall maintain a registry in which he shall enter the following:

(1) Certified copies of custody decrees of other states received for filing;

(2) Communications as to the pendency of custody proceedings in other states;

(3) Communications concerning a finding of inconvenient forum by a court of another state; and

(4) Other communications or documents concerning custody proceedings in another state which may affect the jurisdiction of a court of this state or the disposition to be made by it in a custody proceeding.

§ 9-13-217. Certified copies of custody decree.

The clerks of the chancery courts of this state, at the request of the court of another state or at the request of any person who is affected by or has a legitimate interest in a custody decree, shall certify and forward a copy of the decree to that court or person.

§ 9-13-218. Taking testimony in another state.

In addition to other procedural devices available to a party, any party to the proceeding or a guardian ad litem or other representative of the child may adduce testimony of witnesses, including parties and the child, by deposition or otherwise, in another state. The court on its own motion may direct that the testimony of a person be taken in another state and may prescribe the manner in which and the terms upon which the testimony shall be taken.

§ 9-13-219. Hearings and studies in another state - Orders to appear.

(a) A court of this state may request the appropriate court of another state to hold a hearing to adduce evidence, to order a party to produce or give evidence under other procedures of that state, or to have social studies made with respect to the custody of a child involved in proceedings pending in the court of this state; and to forward to the court of this state certified copies of the transcript of the record of the hearing, the evidence otherwise adduced, or any social studies prepared in compliance with the request. The cost of the services may be assessed against the parties or, if necessary, ordered paid by the state.

(b) A court of this state may request the appropriate court of another state to order a party to custody proceedings pending in the court of this state to appear in the proceedings, and if that party has physical custody of the child, to appear with the child. The request may state that travel and other necessary expenses of the party and of the child whose appearance is desired will be assessed against another party or will otherwise be paid.

§ 9-13-220. Assistance to courts of other states.

(a) Upon request of the court of another state, the courts of this state which are competent to hear custody matters may order a person in this state to appear at a hearing to adduce evidence or to produce or give evidence under other procedures available in this state, or may order social studies to be made for use in a custody proceeding in another state. A certified copy of the transcript of the record of the hearing or the evidence otherwise adduced, and any social studies prepared, shall be forwarded by the clerk of the court to the requesting court.

(b) A person within this state may voluntarily give his testimony or statement in this state for use in a custody proceeding outside this state.

(c) Upon request of the court of another state, a competent court of this state may order a person in this state to appear alone or with the child in a custody proceeding in another state. The court may condition compliance with the request upon assurance by the other state that state travel and other necessary expenses will be advanced or reimbursed.

§ 9-13-221. Preservation of documents for use in other states.

In any custody proceeding in this state, the court shall preserve the pleadings, orders and decrees, any record that has been made of its hearings, social studies, and other pertinent documents until the child reaches eighteen (18) years of age. Upon appropriate request of the court of another state, the court shall forward to the other court certified copies of any or all of those documents.

§ 9-13-222. Request for court records of another state.

If a custody decree has been rendered in another state concerning a child involved in a custody proceeding pending in a court of this state, the court of this state, upon taking jurisdiction of the case, shall request of the court of the other state certified copy of the transcript of any court record and other documents mentioned in § 9-13-221.

§ 9-13-223. International application.

The general policies of this subchapter extend to the international area. The provisions of this subchapter relating to the recognition and enforcement of custody decrees of other states apply to custody decrees and decrees involving legal institutions similar in nature to custody institutions rendered by appropriate authorities of other nations if reasonable notice and opportunity to be heard were given to all affected persons.

§ 9-13-224. Priority.
Upon the request of a party to a custody proceeding which raises a question of existence or exercise of jurisdiction under this subchapter, the case shall be given calendar priority and handled expeditiously.

§ 9-13-225. Severability.
If any provision of this subchapter or the application thereof to any person or circumstance is held invalid, its invalidity does not affect other provisions or applications of the subchapter which can be given effect without the invalid provision or application, and to this end the provisions of this subchapter are severable.

§ 9-13-226. Short title.
This subchapter may be cited as the "Uniform Child Custody Jurisdiction Act."

§ 9-13-227. Repealer.
All laws and parts of laws in conflict with this subchapter are hereby repealed.

CALIFORNIA

UNIFORM CHILD CUSTODY JURISDICTION ACT

§ 5150. Purposes of act; construction of provisions.
(1) The general purposes of this title are to:

(a) Avoid jurisdiction competition and conflict with courts of other states in matters of child custody which have in the past resulted in the shifting of children from state to state with harmful effects on their well-being.

(b) Promote cooperation with the courts of other states to the end that a custody decree is rendered in that state which can best decide the case in the interest of the child.

(c) Assure that litigation concerning the custody of a child take place ordinarily in the state with which the child and his family have the closest connection and where significant evidence concerning his care, protection, training, and personal relationships is most readily available, and that courts of this state decline the exercise of jurisdiction when the child and family have a closer connection with another state.

(d) Discourage continuing controversies over child custody in the interest of greater stability of home environment and of secure family relationships for the child.

(e) Deter abductions and other unilateral removals of children undertaken to obtain custody awards.

(f) Avoid relitigation of custody decisions of other states in this state insofar as feasible.

(g) Facilitate the enforcement of custody decrees of other states.

(h) Promote and expand the exchange of information and other forms of mutual assistance between the courts of this state and those of other states concerned with the same child.

(i) To make uniform the law of those states which enact it.

(2) This title shall be construed to promote the general purposes stated in this section.

§ 5151. Definitions.
As used in this title:

(1) "Contestant" means a person, including a parent, who claims a right to custody or visitation rights with respect to a child;

(2) "Custody determination" means a court decision and court orders and instructions providing for the custody of a child, including visitation rights; it does not include a decision relating to child support or any other monetary obligation of any person.

(3) "Custody proceeding" includes proceedings in which a custody determination is one of several issues, such as an action for dissolution of marriage, or legal separation, and includes child neglect and dependency proceedings;

(4) "Decree" or "custody decree" means a custody determination contained in a judicial decree or order made in a custody proceeding, and includes an initial decree and a modification decree.

(5) "Home state" means the state in which the child immediately preceding the time involved lived with his parents, a parent,

or a person acting as parent, for at least six consecutive months, and in the case of a child less than six-months old the state in which the child lived from birth with any of the persons mentioned. Periods of temporary absence of any of the named persons are counted as part of the six-month or other period.

(6) "Initial decree" means the first custody decree concerning a particular child.

(7) "Modification decree" means a custody decree which modifies or replaces a prior decree, whether made by the court which rendered the prior decree or by another court.

(8) "Physical custody" means actual possession and control of a child.

(9) "Person acting as parent" means a person, other than a parent, who has physical custody of a child and who has either been awarded custody by the court or claims a right to custody.

(10) "State" means any state, territory, or possession of the United States, the Commonwealth of Puerto Rico, and the District of Columbia.

§ 5152. Jurisdiction; grounds.

(1) A court of this state which is competent to decide child custody matters has jurisdiction to make a child custody determination by initial or modification decree if the conditions as set forth in any of the following paragraphs are met:

(a) This state (i) is the home state of the child at the time of commencement of the proceeding, or (ii) had been the child's home state within six months before commencement of the proceeding and the child is absent from this state because of his removal or retention by a person claiming his custody or for other reasons, and a parent or person acting as parent continues to live in this state.

(b) It is in the best interest of the child that a court of this state assume jurisdiction because (i) the child and his parents, or the child and at least one contestant, have a significant connection with this state, and (ii) there is available in this state substantial evidence concerning the child's present or future care, protection, training, and personal relationships.

(c) The child is physically present in this state and (i) the child has been abandoned or (ii) it is necessary in an emergency to protect the child because he has been subjected to or threatened with mistreatment or abuse or is otherwise neglected or dependent.

(d) (i) It appears that no other state would have jurisdiction under prerequisites substantially in accordance with paragraphs (a), (b), (c), or another state has declined to exercise jurisdiction on the ground that this state is the more appropriate forum to determine the custody of the child, and (ii) it is in the best interest of the child that this court assume jurisdiction.

(2) Except under paragraphs (c) and (d) of subdivision (1), physical presence in this state of the child, or of the child and one of the contestants, is not alone sufficient to confer jurisdiction on a court of this state to make a child custody determination.

(3) Physical presence of the child, while desirable, is not a prerequisite for jurisdiction to determine his custody.

§ 5153. Notice and opportunity to be heard.

Before making a decree under this title, reasonable notice and opportunity to be heard shall be given to the contestants, any parent whose parental rights have not been previously terminated, and any person who has physical custody of the child. If any of these persons is outside this state, notice and opportunity to be heard shall be given pursuant to Section 5154.

§ 5154. Notice to persons outside this state; submission to jurisdiction.

(1) Notice required for the exercise of jurisdiction over a person outside this state shall be given in a manner reasonably calculated to give actual notice, and may be made in any of the following ways:

(a) By personal delivery outside this state in the manner prescribed for service of process within this state.

(b) In the manner prescribed by the law of the place in which the service is made for service of process in that place in an action in any of its courts of general jurisdiction.

(c) By any form of mail addressed to the person to be served and requesting a receipt.

(d) As directed by the court (including publication, if other means of notification are ineffective).

(2) Notice under this section shall be served, mailed, delivered, or last published at least 10 days before any hearing in this state.

(3) Proof of service outside this state may be made by affidavit of the individual who made the service, or in the manner prescribed by the law of this state, the order pursuant to which the service is made, or the law of the place in which the service is made. If service is made by mail, proof may be a receipt signed by the addressee or other evidence of delivery to the addressee.

(4) Notice is not required if a person submits to the jurisdiction of the court.

§ 5155. Simultaneous proceedings in other states.

(1) A court of this state shall not exercise its jurisdiction under this title if at the time of filing the petition a proceeding concerning the custody of the child was pending in a court of another state exercising jurisdiction substantially in conformity with this title, unless the proceeding is stayed by the court of the other state because this state is a more appropriate forum or for other reasons.

(2) Before hearing the petition in a custody proceeding the court shall examine the pleadings and other information supplied by the parties under Section 5159 and shall consult the child custody registry established under Section 5165 concerning the pendency of proceedings with respect to the child in other states. If the court has reason to believe that proceedings may be pending in another state it shall direct an inquiry to the state court administrator or other appropriate official of the other state.

(3) If the court is informed during the course of the proceeding that a proceeding concerning the custody of the child was pending in another state before the court assumed jurisdiction it shall stay the proceeding and communicate with the court in which the other proceeding is pending to the end that the issue may be litigated in the more appropriate forum and that information be exchanged in accordance with Sections 5168 through 5171. If a court of this state has made a custody decree before being informed of a pending proceeding in a court of another state it shall immediately inform that court of the fact. If the court is informed that a proceeding was commenced in another state after it assumed jurisdiction it shall likewise inform the other court to the end that the issues may be litigated in the more appropriate forum.

§ 5156. Inconvenient forum.

(1) A court which has jurisdiction under this title to make an initial or modification decree may decline to exercise its jurisdiction any time before making a decree if it finds that it is an inconvenient forum to make a custody determination under the circumstances of the case and that a court of another state is a more appropriate forum.

(2) A finding of inconvenient forum may be made upon the court's own motion or upon motion of a party or a guardian ad litem or other representative of the child.

(3) In determining if it is an inconvenient forum, the court shall consider if it is in the interest of the child that another state assume jurisdiction. For this purpose it may take into account the following factors, among others:

(a) If another state is or recently was the child's home state.

(b) If another state has a closer connection with the child and his family or with the child and one or more of the contestants.

(c) If substantial evidence concerning the child's present or future care, protection, training, and personal relationships is more readily available in another state.

(d) If the parties have agreed on another forum which is no less appropriate.

(e) If the exercise of jurisdiction by a court of this state would contravene any of the purposes stated in Section 5150.

(4) Before determining whether to decline or retain jurisdiction the court may communicate with a court of another state and exchange information pertinent to the assumption of jurisdiction by either court with a view to assuring that jurisdiction will be exercised by the more appropriate court and that a forum will be available to the parties.

(5) If the court finds that it is an inconvenient forum and that a court of another state is a more appropriate forum, it may dismiss the proceedings, or it may stay the proceedings upon condition that a custody proceeding be promptly commenced in another named state or upon any other conditions which may be just and proper, including the condition that a moving party stipulate his consent and submission to the jurisdiction of the other forum.

(6) The court may decline to exercise its jurisdiction under this title if a custody determination is incidental to an action for divorce or another proceeding while retaining jurisdiction over the divorce or other proceeding.

(7) If it appears to the court that it is clearly an inappropriate forum it may require the party who commenced the proceedings to pay, in addition to the costs of the proceedings in this state, necessary travel and other expenses, including attorney's fees, incurred by other parties or their witnesses. Payment is to be made to the clerk of the court for remittance to the proper party.

(8) Upon dismissal or stay of proceedings under this section the court shall inform the court found to be the more appropriate forum of this fact, or if the court which would have jurisdiction in the other state is not certainly known, shall transmit the information to the court administrator or other appropriate official for forwarding to the appropriate court.

(9) Any communication received from another state informing this state of a finding of inconvenient forum because a court of this state is the more appropriate forum shall be filed in the custody registry of the appropriate court. Upon assuming jurisdiction the court of this state shall inform the original court of this fact.

§ 5157. Jurisdiction declined by reason of conduct.

(1) If the petitioner for an initial decree has wrongfully taken the child from another state or has engaged in similar reprehensible conduct the court may decline to exercise jurisdiction for purposes of adjudication of custody if this is just and proper under the circumstances.

(2) Unless required in the interest of the child, the court shall not exercise its jurisdiction to modify a custody decree of another state if the petitioner, without consent of the person entitled to custody has improperly removed the child from the physical custody of the person entitled to custody or has improperly retained the child after a visit or other temporary relinquishment of physical custody. If the petitioner has violated any other provision of a custody decree of another state the court may decline to exercise its jurisdiction if this is just and proper under the circumstances.

(3) Where the court declines to exercise jurisdiction upon petition for an initial custody decree pursuant to subdivision (1), the court shall notify the parent or other appropriate person and the prosecuting attorney of the appropriate jurisdiction in the other state. If a request to that effect is received from the other state, the court shall order the petitioner to appear with the child in a custody proceeding instituted in the other state in accordance with Section 5169. If no such request is made within a reasonable time after such notification, the court may entertain a petition to determine custody by the petitioner if it has jurisdiction pursuant to Section 5152.

(4) Where the court refuses to assume jurisdiction to modify the custody decree of another state pursuant to subdivision (2) or pursuant to Section 5163, the court shall notify the person who has legal custody under the decree of the other state and the

prosecuting attorney of the appropriate jurisdiction in the other state and may order the petitioner to return the child to the person who has legal custody. If it appears that the order will be ineffective and the legal custodian is ready to receive the child within a period of a few days, the court may place the child in a foster care home for such period, pending return of the child to the legal custodian. At the same time, the court shall advise the petitioner that any petition for modification of custody must be directed to the appropriate court of the other state which has continuing jurisdiction, or, in the event that that court declines jurisdiction, to a court in a state which has jurisdiction pursuant to Section 5152.

(5) In appropriate cases a court dismissing a petition under this section may charge the petitioner with necessary travel and other expenses, including attorney's fees and the cost of returning the child to another state.

§ 5158. Information under oath to be submitted to court.

(1) Every party in a custody proceeding in his first pleading or in an affidavit attached to that pleading shall give information under oath as to the child's present address, the places where the child has lived within the last five years, and the names and present addresses of the persons with whom the child has lived during that period. In this pleading or affidavit every party shall further declare under oath as to each of the following whether:

(a) He has participated, as a party, witness, or in any other capacity, in any other litigation concerning the custody of the same child in this or any other state.

(b) He has information of any custody proceeding concerning the child pending in a court of this or any other state.

(c) He knows of any person not a party to the proceedings who has physical custody of the child or claims to have custody or visitation rights with respect to the child.

(2) If the declaration as to any of the above items is in the affirmative the declarant shall give additional information under oath as required by the court. The court may examine the parties under oath as to details of the information furnished and as to other matters pertinent to the court's jurisdiction and the disposition of the case.

(3) Each party has a continuing duty to inform the court of any custody proceeding concerning the child in this or any other state of which he obtained information during this proceeding.

§ 5159. Additional parties.

If the court learns from information furnished by the parties pursuant to Section 5158 or from other sources that a person not a party to the custody proceeding has physical custody of the child or claims to have custody or visitation rights with respect to the child, it shall order that person to be joined as a party and to be duly notified of the pendency of the proceeding and of his joinder as a party. If the person joined as a party is outside this state he shall be served with process or otherwise notified in accordance with Section 5154.

§ 5160. Appearance of parties and child.

(1) The court may order any party to the proceeding who is in this state to appear personally before the court. If that party has physical custody of the child the court may order that he appear personally with the child. If the party who is ordered to appear with the child cannot be served or fails to obey the order, or it appears the order will be ineffective, the court may issue a warrant of arrest against such party to secure his appearance with the child.

(2) If a party to the proceeding whose presence is desired by the court is outside this state with or without the child the court may order that the notice given under Section 5154 include a statement directing that party to appear personally with or without the child and declaring that failure to appear may result in a decision adverse to that party.

(3) If a party to the proceeding who is outside this state is directed to appear under subdivision (2) or desires to appear personally before the court with or without the child, the court may require another party to pay to the clerk of the court travel and other necessary expenses of the party so appearing and of the child if this is just and proper under the circumstances.

§ 5161. Binding force and res judicata effect of custody decree.

A custody decree rendered by a court of this state which had jurisdiction under Section 5152 binds all parties who have been served in this state or notified in accordance with Section 5154 or who have submitted to the jurisdiction of the court, and who have been given an opportunity to be heard. As to these parties the custody decree is conclusive as to all issues of law and fact decided and as to the custody determination made unless and until that determination is modified pursuant to law, including the provisions of this title.

§ 5162. Recognition of out-of-state custody decrees.

The courts of this state shall recognize and enforce an initial or modification decree of a court of another state which had assumed jurisdiction under statutory provisions substantially in accordance with this title or which was made under factual circumstances meeting the jurisdictional standards of the title, so long as this decree has not been modified in accordance with jurisdictional standards substantially similar to those of this title.

§ 5163. Modification of custody decree of another state.

(1) If a court of another state has made a custody decree, a court of this state shall not modify that decree unless (a) it appears to the court of this state that the court which rendered the decree does not now have jurisdiction under jurisdictional prerequisites substantially in accordance with this title or has declined to assume jurisdiction to modify the decree and (b) the court of this state has jurisdiction.

(2) If a court of this state is authorized under subdivision (1) and Section 5157 to modify a custody decree of another state it shall give due consideration to the transcript of the record and other documents of all previous proceedings submitted to it in accordance with Section 5171.

§ 5164. Filing and enforcement of custody decree of another state.

(1) A certified copy of a custody decree of another state may be filed in the office of the clerk of any superior court of this state. The clerk shall treat the decree in the same manner as a custody decree of the superior court of this state. A custody decree so filed has the same effect and shall be enforced in like manner as a custody decree rendered by a court of this state.

(2) A person violating a custody decree of another state which makes it necessary to enforce the decree in this state may be required to pay necessary travel and other expenses, including attorneys' fees, incurred by the party entitled to the custody or his witnesses.

§ 5165. Registry of out-of-state custody decrees and proceedings.

The clerk of each superior court shall maintain a registry in which he shall enter all of the following:

(1) Certified copies of custody decrees of other states received for filing.

(2) Communications as to the pendency of custody proceedings in other states.

(3) Communications concerning a finding of inconvenient forum by a court of another state.

(4) Other communications or documents concerning custody proceedings in another state which may affect the jurisdiction of a court of this state or the disposition to be made by it in a custody proceeding.

§ 5166. Certified copies of custody decree.

The clerk of a superior court of this state, at the request of the court of another state or at the request of any person who is affected by or has a legitimate interest in a custody decree, shall certify and forward a copy of the decree to that court or person.

§ 5167. Taking testimony in another state.

In addition to other procedural devices available to a party, any party to the proceeding or a guardian ad litem or other representative of the child may adduce testimony of witnesses, including parties and the child, by deposition or otherwise, in another state. The court on its own motion may direct that the testimony of a person be taken in another state and may prescribe the manner in which and the terms upon which the testimony shall be taken.

§ 5168. Hearings and studies in another state; orders to appear.

(1) A court of this state may request the appropriate court of another state to hold a hearing to adduce evidence, to order a party to produce or give evidence under other procedures of that state, or to have social studies made with respect to the custody of a child involved in proceedings pending in the court of this state; and to forward to the court of this state certified copies of the transcript of the record of the hearing, the evidence otherwise adduced, or any social studies prepared in compliance with the request. The cost of the services may be assessed against the parties or, if necessary, ordered paid by the state.

(2) A court of this state may request the appropriate court of another state to order a party to custody proceedings pending in the court of this state to appear in the proceedings, and if that party has physical custody of the child, to appear with the child. The request may state that travel and other necessary expenses of the party and of the child whose appearance is desired will be assessed against another party or will otherwise be paid.

§ 5169. Assistance to courts of other states.

(1) Upon request of the court of another state the courts of this state which are competent to hear custody matters may order a person in this state to appear at a hearing to adduce evidence or to produce or give evidence under other procedures available in this state. A certified copy of the transcript of the record of the hearing or the evidence otherwise adduced shall be forwarded by the clerk of the court to the requesting court.

(2) A person within this state may voluntarily give his testimony or statement in this state for use in a custody proceeding outside this state.

(3) Upon request of the court of another state a competent court of this state may order a person in this state to appear alone or with the child in a custody proceeding in another state. The court may condition compliance with the request upon assurance by the other state that travel and other necessary expenses will be advanced or reimbursed. If the person who has physical custody of the child cannot be served or fails to obey the order, or it appears the order will be ineffective, the court may issue a warrant of arrest against such person to secure his appearance with the child in the other state.

§ 5170. Preservation of records of custody proceedings; forwarding to another state.
In any custody proceeding in this state the court shall preserve the pleadings, orders and decrees, any record that has been made of its hearings, social studies, and other pertinent documents until the child reaches 18 years of age. Upon appropriate request of the court of another state the court shall forward to the other court certified copies of any or all of such documents.

§ 5171. Request for court records of another state.
If a custody decree has been rendered in another state concerning a child involved in a custody proceeding pending in a court of this state, the court of this state upon taking jurisdiction of the case shall request of the court of the other state a certified copy of the transcript of any court record and other documents mentioned in Section 5170.

§ 5172. International application.
The general policies of this title extend to the international area. The provisions of this title relating to the recognition and enforcement of custody decrees of other states apply to custody decrees and decrees involving legal institutions similar in nature to custody rendered by appropriate authorities of other nations if reasonable notice and opportunity to be heard were given to all affected persons.

§ 5173. Calendar priority.
Upon the request of a party to a custody proceeding which raises a question of existence or exercise of jurisdiction under this title the case shall be given calendar priority and handled expeditiously.

§ 5174. Short title.
This title may be cited as the Uniform Child Custody Jurisdiction Act.

COLORADO

UNIFORM CHILD CUSTODY JURISDICTION ACT

§ 14-13-101. Short title.
This article shall be known and may be cited as the "Uniform Child Custody Jurisdiction Act".

§ 14-13-102. Legislative declaration - construction of provisions.
(1) The general purposes of this article are to:

(a) Avoid jurisdictional competition and conflict with courts of other states in matters of child custody which have in the past resulted in the shifting of children from state to state with harmful effects on their well-being;

(b) Promote cooperation with the courts of other states to the end that a custody decree is rendered in that state which can best decide the case in the interest of the child;

(c) Assure that litigation concerning the custody of a child take place ordinarily in the state with which the child and his family have the closest connection and where significant evidence concerning his care, protection, training, and personal relationships is most readily available, and that courts of this state decline the exercise of jurisdiction when the child and his family have a closer connection with another state;

(d) Discourage continuing controversies over child custody in the interest of greater stability of home environment and of secure family relationships for the child;

(e) Deter abductions and other unilateral removals of children undertaken to obtain custody awards;

(f) Avoid relitigation of custody decisions of other states in this state insofar as feasible;

(g) Facilitate the enforcement of custody decrees of other states;

(h) Promote and expand the exchange of information and other forms of mutual assistance between the courts of this state and those of other states concerned with the same child; and

(i) Make uniform the law of those states which enact it.

(2) This article shall be construed to promote the general purposes stated in this section.

§ 14-13-103. Definitions.
As used in this article, unless the context otherwise requires:

(1) "Contestant" means a person, including a parent, who claims a right to custody or visitation rights with respect to a child.

(2) "Custody determination" means a court decision and court orders and instructions providing for the custody of a child, including visitation rights; it does not include a decision relating to child support or any other monetary obligation of any person.

(3) "Custody proceeding" includes proceedings in which a custody determination is one of several issues, such as an action for divorce, dissolution of marriage, or separation, and includes child neglect and dependency proceedings.

(4) "Decree" or "custody decree" means a custody determination contained in a judicial decree or order made in a custody proceeding and includes an initial decree and a modification decree.

(5) "Home state" means the state in which the child immediately preceding the time involved lived with his parents, a parent, or a person acting as parent, for at least six consecutive months, and in the case of a child less than six months old the state in which the child lived from birth with any of the persons mentioned. Periods of temporary absence of any of the named persons are counted as part of the six-month or other period.

(6) "Initial decree" means the first custody decree concerning a particular child.

(7) "Modification decree" means a custody decree which modifies or replaces a prior decree, whether made by the court which rendered the prior decree or by another court.

(8) "Person acting as parent" means a person, other than a parent, who has physical custody of a child and who has either been awarded custody by a court or claims a right to custody.

(9) "Physical custody" means actual possession and control of a child.

(10) "State" means any state, territory, or possession of the United States, the Commonwealth of Puerto Rico, and the District of Columbia.

§ 14-13-104. Jurisdiction.

(1) A court of this state which is competent to decide child custody matters has jurisdiction to make a child custody determination by initial or modification decree if:

(a) This state is the home state of the child at the time of commencement of the proceeding, or had been the child's home state within six months before commencement of the proceeding, and the child is absent from this state because of his removal or retention by a person claiming his custody or for other reasons, and a parent or person acting as parent continues to live in this state; or

(b) It is in the best interest of the child that a court of this state assume jurisdiction because the child and his parents, or the child and at least one contestant, have a significant connection with this state and there is available in this state substantial evidence concerning the child's present or future care, protection, training, and personal relationships; or

(c) The child is physically present in this state and the child has been abandoned or it is necessary in an emergency to protect the child because he has been subjected to or threatened with mistreatment or abuse or is otherwise neglected or dependent; or

(d) It appears that no other state would have jurisdiction under prerequisites substantially in accordance with paragraph (a), (b), or (c) of this subsection (1), or another state has declined to exercise jurisdiction on the ground that this state is the more appropriate forum to determine the custody of the child, and it is in the best interest of the child that this court assume jurisdiction.

(2) Except under paragraphs (c) and (d) of subsection (1) of this section, physical presence in this state of the child, or of the child and one of the contestants, is not alone sufficient to confer jurisdiction on a court of this state to make a child custody determination.

(3) Physical presence of the child, while desirable, is not a prerequisite for jurisdiction to determine his custody.

§ 14-13-105. Notice and opportunity to be heard.

Before making a decree under this article, reasonable notice and opportunity to be heard shall be given to the contestants, any parent whose parent-child legal relationship has not been previously terminated, and any person who has physical custody of the child. If any of these persons is outside this state, notice and opportunity to be heard shall be given pursuant to section 14-13-106.

§ 14-13-106. Notice to persons outside this state - submission to jurisdiction.

(1) Notice required for the exercise of jurisdiction over a person outside this state shall be given in a manner reasonably calculated to give actual notice, and such notice may be given:

(a) By personal delivery outside this state in the manner prescribed for service of process within this state;

(b) In the manner prescribed by the law of the place in which the service is made for service of process in that place in an action in any of its courts of general jurisdiction;

(c) By any form of mail addressed to the person to be served and requesting a receipt; or

(d) As directed by the court, including publication, if other means of notification are ineffective, upon an affirmative showing to that effect. If publication is directed, the court shall order one publication in a newspaper published or having general circulation in the county in which the proceeding is filed. The notice shall state the names of the parties, the action number, the nature of the action, that a copy of the petition may be obtained from the clerk of the court during regular business hours, and that default judgment may be entered against that party upon whom service is made by such notice if he fails to appear or file a response within thirty days after the date of publication. If a party is indigent or otherwise unable to pay such publication costs, the costs shall be paid by the court from funds appropriated for the purpose. Service of the notice shall be complete upon such publication, and a response or appearance by the party served by publication under this paragraph (d) shall be made within thirty days thereafter, or default judgment may be entered. No later than the day of publication, the clerk of the court shall also post for thirty consecutive days a copy of the process on a bulletin board in his office, and shall mail a copy of the process to the other party at his last-known address, and shall place in the file of the proceeding his certificate of posting and mailing. Proof of publication of the notice shall be by placing in the file a copy of the affidavit of publication, certified by the clerk of the court to be a true and correct copy of the original affidavit on file in the clerk's office.

(2) Notice under this section shall be served, mailed, delivered, or last published at least twenty days before any hearing in this state.

(3) Proof of service outside this state may be made by affidavit of the individual who made the service, or, in the manner prescribed by the law of this state, the order pursuant to which the service is made, or the law of the place in which the service is made. If service is made by mail, proof may be a receipt signed by the addressee or other evidence of delivery to the addressee.

(4) Notice is not required if a person submits to the jurisdiction of the court.

§ 14-13-107. Simultaneous proceedings in other states.

(1) A court of this state shall not exercise its jurisdiction under this article if at the time of filing the petition a proceeding concerning the custody of the child was pending in a court of another state exercising jurisdiction substantially in conformity with this article, unless the proceeding is stayed by the court of the other state because this state is a more appropriate forum or for other reasons.

(2) Before hearing the petition in a custody proceeding, the court shall examine the pleadings and other information supplied by the parties under section 14-13-110 and shall consult the child custody registry established under section 14-13-117 concerning the pendency of proceedings with respect to the child in other states. If the court has reason to believe that proceedings may be pending in another state, it shall direct an inquiry to the state court administrator or other appropriate official of the other state.

(3) If the court is informed during the course of the proceeding that a proceeding concerning the custody of the child was pending in another state before the court assumed jurisdiction, it shall stay the proceeding and communicate with the court in which the other proceeding is pending, to the end that the issue may be litigated in the more appropriate forum and that information may be exchanged in accordance with sections 14-13-120 to 14-13-123. If a court of this state has made a custody decree before being informed of a pending proceeding in a court of another state, it shall immediately inform that court of the fact. If the court is informed that a proceeding was commenced in another state after it assumed jurisdiction, it shall likewise inform the other court, to the end that the issues may be litigated in the more appropriate forum.

§ 14-13-108. Inconvenient forum.

(1) A court which has jurisdiction under this article to make an initial or modification decree may decline to exercise its jurisdiction any time before making a decree if it finds that it is an inconvenient forum to make a custody determination under the circumstances of the case and that a court of another state is a more appropriate forum.

(2) A finding of inconvenient forum may be made upon the court's own motion or upon motion of a party or a guardian ad litem or other representative of the child.

(3) In determining if it is an inconvenient forum, the court shall consider if it is in the interest of the child that another state assume jurisdiction. For this purpose it may take into account the following factors, among others:

(a) If another state is or recently was the child's home state;

(b) If another state has a closer connection with the child and his family or with the child and one or more of the contestants;

(c) If substantial evidence concerning the child's present or future care, protection, training, and personal relationships is more readily available in another state;

(d) If the parties have agreed on another forum which is no less appropriate; and

(e) If the exercise of jurisdiction by a court of this state would contravene any of the purposes stated in section 14-13-102.

(4) Before determining whether to decline or retain jurisdiction, the court may communicate with a court of another state and exchange information pertinent to the assumption of jurisdiction by either court with a view to assuring that jurisdiction will be exercised by the more appropriate court and that a forum will be available to the parties.

(5) If the court finds that it is an inconvenient forum and that a court of another state is a more appropriate forum, it may dismiss the proceedings, or it may stay the proceedings upon condition that a custody proceedings be promptly commenced in another named state or upon any other conditions which may be just and proper, including the condition that a moving party stipulate his consent and submission to the jurisdiction of the other forum.

(6) The court may decline to exercise its jurisdiction under this article if a custody determination is incidental to an action for divorce, dissolution of marriage, or another proceeding while retaining jurisdiction over the divorce, dissolution of marriage, or other proceeding.

(7) If it appears to the court that it is clearly an inappropriate forum, it may require the party who commenced the proceedings to pay, in addition to the costs of the proceedings in this state, necessary travel and other expenses, including attorneys' fees, incurred by other parties or their witnesses. Payment is to be made to the clerk of the court for remittance to the proper party.

(8) Upon dismissal or stay of proceedings under this section, the court shall inform the court found to be the more appropriate forum of this fact or, if the court which would have jurisdiction in the other state is not certainly known, shall transmit the information to the court administrator or other appropriate official for forwarding to the appropriate court.

(9) Any communication received from another state informing this state of a finding of inconvenient forum because a court of this state is the more appropriate forum shall be filed in the custody registry of the appropriate court. Upon assuming jurisdiction, the court of this state shall inform the original court of this fact.

§ 14-13-109. Jurisdiction declined by reason of conduct.

(1) If the petitioner for an initial decree has wrongfully taken the child from another state or has engaged in similar reprehensible conduct, the court may decline to exercise jurisdiction if this is just and proper under the circumstances.

(2) Unless required in the interest of the child, the court shall not exercise its jurisdiction to modify a custody decree of another state if the petitioner, without consent of the person entitled to custody, has improperly removed the child from the physical custody of the person entitled to custody or has improperly retained the child after a visit or other temporary relinquishment of physical custody. If the petitioner has violated any other provision of a custody decree of another state, the court may decline to exercise its jurisdiction if this is just and proper under the circumstances.

(3) In appropriate cases, a court dismissing a petition under this section may charge the petitioner with necessary travel and other expenses, including attorneys' fees, incurred by other parties or their witnesses.

§ 14-13-110. Information under oath to be submitted to the court.

(1) Every party in a custody proceeding under section 14-10-123 shall, in his first pleading or in an affidavit attached to that pleading, give information under oath as to the child's present address, the places where the child has lived within the last five years, and the names and present addresses of the persons with whom the child has lived during that period. In this pleading or affidavit, every party shall further declare under oath whether:

(a) He has participated, as a party or witness or in any other capacity, in any other litigation concerning the custody of the same child in this or any other state;

(b) He has information of any custody proceeding concerning the child pending in a court of this or any other state; and

(c) He knows of any person not a party to the proceedings who has physical custody of the child or claims to have custody or visitation rights with respect to the child.

(2) If the declaration as to any of the items in subsection (1) of this section is in the affirmative, the declarant shall give additional information under oath as required by the court. The court may examine the parties under oath as to details of the information furnished and as to other matters pertinent to the court's jurisdiction and the disposition of the case.

(3) Each party has a continuing duty to inform the court of any custody proceeding concerning the child in this or any other state of which he obtained information during this proceeding.

§ 14-13-111. Additional parties.

If the court learns from information furnished by the parties pursuant to section 14-13-110 or from other sources that a person not a party to the custody proceeding has physical custody of the child or claims to have custody or visitation rights with respect to the child, it shall order that person to be joined as a party and to be duly notified of the pendency of the proceeding and of his joinder as a party. If the person joined as a party is outside this state, he shall be served with process or otherwise notified in accordance with section 14-13-106.

§ 14-13-112. Appearance of parties and the child.

(1) The court may order any party to the proceeding who is in this state to appear personally before the court. If that party has physical custody of the child, the court may order that he appear personally with the child.

(2) If a party to the proceeding whose presence is desired by the court is outside this state with or without the child, the court may order that the notice given under section 14-13-106 include a statement directing that party to appear personally with or without the child and declaring that failure to appear may result in a decision adverse to that party.

(3) If a party to the proceeding who is outside this state is directed to appear under subsection (2) of this section or desires to appear personally before the court with or without the child, the court may require another party to pay to the clerk of the court travel and other necessary expenses of the party so appearing and of the child if this is just and proper under the circumstances.

§ 14-13-113. Binding force and res judicata effect of custody decree.

A custody decree rendered by a court of this state which had jurisdiction under section 14-13-104 binds all parties who have been served in this state or notified in accordance with section 14-13-106 or who have submitted to the jurisdiction of the court and who have been given an opportunity to be heard. As to these parties, the custody decree is conclusive as to all issues of law and fact decided and as to the custody determination made unless and until that determination is modified pursuant to law, including the provisions of this article.

§ 14-13-114. Recognition of out-of-state custody decrees.

The courts of this state shall recognize and enforce an initial or modification decree of a court of another state which had assumed jurisdiction under statutory provisions substantially in accordance with this article or which was made under factual circumstances meeting the jurisdictional standards of the article, so long as this decree has not been modified in accordance with jurisdictional standards substantially similar to those of this article.

§ 14-13-115. Modification of custody decree of another state.

(1) If a court of another state has made a custody decree, a court of this state shall not modify that decree unless it appears to the court of this state that the court which rendered the decree does not now have jurisdiction under jurisdictional prerequisites substantially in accordance with this article or has declined to assume jurisdiction to modify the decree and the court of this state has jurisdiction.

(2) If a court of this state is authorized under subsection (1) of this section and section 14-13-109 to modify a custody decree of another state, it shall give due consideration to the transcript of the record and other documents of all previous proceedings submitted to it in accordance with section 14-13-123.

§ 14-13-116. Filing and enforcement of custody decree of another state.

(1) A certified copy of a custody decree of another state may be filed in the office of the clerk of any distrtict court of this state pursuant to section 14-11-101. The clerk shall treat the decree in the same manner as a custody decree of the district court of this state. A custody decree so filed has the same effect and shall be enforced in like manner as a custody decree rendered by a court of this state.

(2) A person violating a custody decree of another state which makes it necessary to enforce the decree in this state may be required to pay necessary travel and other expenses, including attorneys' fees, incurred by the party entitled to the custody or his witnesses.

§ 14-13-117. Registry of out-of-state custody decrees and proceedings.

(1) The clerk of each district court shall maintain a registry in which he shall enter the following:

(a) Certified copies of custody decrees of other states received for filing;

(b) Communications as to the pendency of custody proceedings in other states;

(c) Communications concerning a finding of inconvenient forum by a court of another state; and

(d) Other communications or documents concerning custody proceedings in another state which may affect the jurisdiction of a court of this state or the disposition to be made by it in a custody proceeding.

§ 14-13-118. Certified copies of custody decree.

The clerk of the district court of this state, at the request of the court of another state or at the request of any person who is affected by or has a legitimate interest in a custody decree, shall certify and forward a copy of the decree to that court or person.

§ 14-13-119. Taking testimony in another state.

In addition to other procedural devices available to a party, any party to the proceeding or a guardian ad litem or other representative of the child may adduce testimony of witnesses, including parties and the child, by deposition or otherwise, in another state. The court on its own motion may direct that the testimony of a person be taken in another state and may prescribe the manner in which and the terms upon which the testimony shall be taken, and the court shall make payment for any costs related thereto.

§ 14-13-120. Hearings and studies in another state - orders to appear.

(1) A court of this state may request the appropriate court of another state to hold a hearing to adduce evidence, to order a party to produce or give evidence under other procedures of that state, or to have social studies made with respect to the custody of a child involved in proceedings pending in the court of this state and to forward to the court of this state certified copies of the transcript of the record of the hearing, the evidence otherwise adduced, or any social studies prepared in compliance with the request. The cost of the services may be assessed against the parties or, if a party against whom the costs are assessed is determined by the court to be indigent, paid by the state.

(2) A court of this state may request the appropriate court of another state to order a party to custody proceedings pending in the court of this state to appear in the proceedings and, if that party has physical custody of the child, to appear with the child. The request may state that travel and other necessary expenses of the party and of the child whose appearance is desired will be assessed against another party, or, if such party is determined by a court of this state to be indigent, the costs will be paid by this state.

§ 14-13-121. Assistance to courts of other states.

(1) Upon request of the court of another state, the courts of this state which are competent to hear custody matters may order a person in this state to appear at a hearing to adduce evidence or to produce or give evidence under other procedures available

in this state or may order social studies to be made for use in a custody proceeding in another state. A certified copy of the transcript of the record of the hearing or the evidence otherwise adduced and any social studies prepared shall be forwarded by the clerk of the court to the requesting court upon receipt of payment therefor from the requesting court.

(2) A person within this state may voluntarily give his testimony or statement in this state for use in a custody proceeding outside this state.

(3) Upon request of the court of another state, a competent court of this state may order a person in this state to appear alone or with the child in a custody proceeding in another state. The court may condition compliance with the request upon assurance by the other state that state travel and other necessary expenses will be advanced or reimbursed.

§ 14-13-122. Preservation of documents for use in other states.

In any custody proceeding in this state, the court shall preserve the pleadings, orders, and decrees, any record that has been made of its hearings, social studies, and other pertinent documents until the child reaches eighteen years of age. Upon appropriate request of and payment from the court of another state, the court shall forward to the other court certified copies of any or all of such documents.

§ 14-13-123. Request for court records of another state.

If a custody decree has been rendered in another state concerning a child involved in a custody proceeding pending in a court of this state, the court of this state upon taking jurisdiction of the case shall request of the court of the other state a certified copy of the transcript of any court record and other documents mentioned in section 14-13-122 and send payment therefor. If a party against whom the costs are assessed is determined by the court to be indigent, the costs shall be paid by the state.

§ 14-13-124. International application.

The general policies of this article extend to the international area. The provisions of this article relating to the recognition and enforcement of custody decrees of other states apply to custody decrees and decrees involving legal institutions similar in nature to custody institutions rendered by appropriate authorities of other nations if reasonable notice and opportunity to be heard were given to all affected persons.

§ 14-13-125. Priority.

Upon the request of a party to a custody proceeding which raises a question of existence or exercise of jurisdiction under this article, the case shall be given calendar priority and handled expeditiously.

§ 14-13-126. Severability.

If any provision of this article or the application thereof to any person or circumstance is held invalid, its invalidity does not affect other provisions or applications of the article which can be given effect without the invalid provision or application, and to this end the provisions of this article are severable.

CONNECTICUT

UNIFORM CHILD CUSTODY JURISDICTION ACT

Sec. 46b-90. Short title.

This chapter shall be known as and may be cited as the Uniform Child Custody Jurisdiction Act.

Sec. 46b-91. Purposes of act; construction of provisions.

(a) The general purposes of this chapter are to: (1) Avoid jurisdictional competition and conflict with courts of other states in matters of child custody which have in the past resulted in the shifting of children from state to state with harmful effects on their well-being; (2) promote cooperation with the courts of other states to the end that a custody decree is rendered in a state which can best decide the case in the interest of the child; (3) assure that litigation concerning the custody of a child take place ordinarily in the state with which the child and his family have the closest connection and where significant evidence concerning his care, protection, training and personal relationships is most readily available, and that courts of this state decline the exercise of jurisdiction when the child and his family have a closer connection with another state; (4) discourage continuing controversies over child custody in the interest of greater stability of home environment and of secure family relationships for the child; (5) deter abductions and other unilateral removals of children undertaken to obtain custody awards; (6) avoid relitigation of custody decisions of other states in this state insofar as feasible; (7) facilitate the enforcement of custody decrees of other states; (8) promote and expand the exchange of information and other forms of mutual assistance between the courts of this state and those of other states concerned with the same child; and (9) make uniform the laws of the states which enact the Uniform Child Custody Jurisdiction Act.

(b) This chapter shall be construed to promote the general purposes stated in this section.

Sec. 46b-92. Definitions.

As used in this chapter:

(1) "Contestant" means a person who claims a right to custody or visitation rights with respect to a child;

(2) "Custody determination" means a court decision and court orders and instructions providing for the custody of a child, including visitation rights; it does not include a decision relating to child support or any other monetary obligation of any person or any matter properly within the jurisdiction of any court of probate;

(3) "Custody proceeding" includes proceedings in which a custody determination is one of several issues, such as an action for dissolution of marriage, divorce or separation, and includes child neglect and dependency proceedings; it does not include any matter properly within the jurisdiction of any court of probate;

(4) "Decree" or "custody decree" means a custody determination contained in a judicial decree or order made in a custody proceeding, and includes an initial decree and a modification decree;

(5) "Home state" means the state in which the child immediately preceding the time involved lived with his parents, a parent, or a person acting as parent, for at least six consecutive months, and in the case of a child less than six months old, the state in which the child lived from birth with any of such persons. Periods of temporary absence of any of the named persons are counted as part of the six month or other period;

(6) "Initial decree" means the first custody decree concerning a particular child, including a temporary order of custody granted pendente lite;

(7) "Modification decree" means a custody decree which modifies or replaces a prior decree, whether made by the court which rendered the prior decree or by another court;

(8) "Physical custody" means actual possession and control of a child;

(9) "Person acting as parent" means a person, other than a parent, who has physical custody of a child and who has either been awarded custody by a court or claims a right to custody;

(10) "State" means any state, territory or possession of the United States, the Commonwealth of Puerto Rico, and the District of Columbia.

Sec. 46b-93. Jurisdiction.

(a) The superior court shall have jurisdiction to make a child custody determination by initial or modification decree if: (1) This state (A) is the home state of the child at the time of commencement of the proceeding, or (B) had been the child's home state within six months before the commencement of the proceeding and the child is absent from this state because of his removal or retention by a person claiming his custody or for other reasons, and a parent or person acting as parent continues to live in this state; or (2) it is in the best interest of the child that a court of this state assume jurisdiction because (A) the child and his parents, or the child and at least one contestant, have a significant connection with this state, and (B) there is available in this state substantial evidence concerning the child's present or future care, protection, training and personal relationships; or (3) the child is physically present in this state and (A) the child has been abandoned or (B) it is necessary in an emergency to protect the child because he has been subjected to or threatened with mistreatment or abuse or is otherwise neglected or dependent; or (4) (A) it appears that no other state would have jurisdiction under prerequisites substantially in accordance with subdivision (2) or (3) of this subsection, or another state has declined to exercise jurisdiction on the ground that this state is the more appropriate forum to determine the custody of the child, and (B) it is in the best interest of the child that this court assume jurisdiction.

(b) Except under subdivision (3) and (4) of subsection (a) of this section, physical presence in this state of the child, or of the child and one of the contestants, is not alone sufficient to confer jurisdiction on a court of this state to make a child custody determination.

(c) Physical presence of the child is not a prerequisite for jurisdiction to determine his custody.

Sec. 46b-94. Notice and opportunity to be heard.

Before making a decree under this chapter or section 46b-56 or 46b-57, reasonable notice and opportunity to be heard shall be given to the contestants, any parent whose parental rights have not been previously terminated and any person who has physical custody of the child. If any of these persons is outside this state, notice and opportunity to be heard shall be given pursuant to section 46b-95.

Sec. 46b-95. Notice to persons outside this state; submission to jurisdiction.

(a) Notice required for the exercise of jurisdiction over a person outside this state shall be given in a manner reasonably calculated to give actual notice, and may be; (2) in the manner prescribed by the law of the place in which the service is made for service of process in that place in an action in any of its courts of general jurisdiction; (3) any form of mail addressed to the person to be served and requesting a receipt; or (4) as directed by the court including publication, if other means of notification are ineffective.

(b) Notice under this section shall be served, mailed or delivered or last published at least twelve days before any hearing in this state.

(c) Proof of service outside this state may be made by affidavit of the individual who made the service, or in the manner prescribed by the law of this state, the other pursuant to which the service is made, or the law of the place in which the service is made. If service is made by mail, proof may be a receipt signed by the addressee or other evidence of delivery to the addressee.

(d) Notice is not required if a person submits to the jurisdiction of the court.

Sec. 46b-96. Simultaneous proceedings in other states.

(a) A court of this state shall not exercise its jurisdiction under this chapter if at the time of filing the petition a proceeding concerning the custody of the child is pending in a court of another state exercising jurisdiction substantially in conformity with this chapter, unless the proceeding is stayed by the court of the other state because this state is a more appropriate forum or for other reasons.

(b) Before hearing the petition in a custody proceeding, the court shall examine the pleadings and other information supplied by the parties under section 46b-99 and shall consult the child custody registry established under section 46b-106 concerning the pendency of proceedings with respect to the child in other states. If the court has reason to believe that proceedings may be pending in another state it shall direct an inquiry to the state court administrator or other appropriate official of the other state.

(c) If the court is informed during the course of the proceeding that a proceeding concerning the custody of the child was pending in another state before the court assumed jurisdiction, it shall stay the proceeding and communicate with the court in which the other proceeding is pending to the end that the issue may be litigated in the more appropriate forum and that information be exchanged in accordance with sections 46b-109 to 46b-112, inclusive. If a court of this state has made a custody decree before being informed of a pending proceeding in a court of another state, it shall immediately inform such court of the fact. If the court is informed that a proceeding was commenced in another state after it assumed jurisdiction, it shall likewise inform the other court to the end that the issues may be litigated in the more appropriate forum.

Sec. 46b-97. Inconvenient forum.

(a) A court which has jurisdiction under this chapter to make an initial or modification decree may decline to exercise its jurisdiction any time before making a decree if it finds that it is an inconvenient forum to make a custody determination under the circumstances of the case and that a court of another state is a more appropriate forum.

(b) A finding of inconvenient forum may be made upon the court's own motion or upon motion of a party or a guardian ad litem or other representative of the child.

(c) In determining if it is an inconvenient forum, the court shall consider if it is in the interest of the child that another state assume jurisdiction. For this purpose it may take into account the following factors, including but not limited to: (1) Another state is or recently was the child's home state; (2) another state has a closer connection with the child and his family or with the child and one or more of the contestants; (3) substantial evidence concerning the child's present or future care, protection, training and personal relationships is more readily available in another state; (4) the parties have agreed on another forum which is no less appropriate; and (5) the exercise of jurisdiction by a court of this state would contravene any of the purposes stated in section 46b-91.

(d) Before determining whether to decline or retain jurisdiction the court may communicate with a court of another state and exchange information pertinent to the assumption of jurisdiction by either court with a view to assuring that jurisdiction will be exercised by the more appropriate court and that a forum will be available to the parties.

(e) If the court finds that it is an inconvenient forum and that a court of another state is a more appropriate forum, it may dismiss the proceedings, or it may stay the proceedings upon condition that a custody proceeding be promptly commenced in another named state or upon any other conditions which may be just and proper, including the condition that a moving party stipulate his consent and submission to the jurisdiction of the other forum.

(f) The court may decline to exercise its jurisdiction under this chapter if a custody determination is incidental to an action for dissolution of marriage, divorce or another proceeding while retaining jurisdiction over the dissolution of marriage, divorce or other proceedings.

(g) If it appears to the court that it is clearly an inappropriate forum, it may require the party who commenced the proceedings to pay, in addition to the costs of the proceedings in this state, necessary travel and other expenses, including attorneys' fees, incurred by other parties or their witnesses. Payment is to be made to the clerk of the court for remittance to the proper party.

(h) Upon dismissal or stay of proceedings under this section, the court shall inform the court found to be the more appropriate forum of this fact, or if the court which would have jurisdiction in the other state is not certainly known, shall transmit the information to the court administrator or other appropriate official for forwarding to the appropriate court.

(i) Any communication received from another state informing this state of a finding of inconvenient forum because a court of this state is the more appropriate forum shall be filed in the custody registry of the appropriate court. Upon assuming jurisdiction the court of this state shall inform the original court of this fact.

Sec. 46b-98. Jurisdiction declined by reason of petitioner's reprehensible conduct.

(a) If the petitioner for an initial decree has wrongfully taken the child from another state or has engaged in similar reprehensible conduct, the court may decline to exercise jurisdiction if it is just and proper under the circumstances.

(b) Unless required in the interest of the child, the court shall not exercise its jurisdiction to modify a custody decree of another state if the petitioner, without consent of the person entitled to custody, has improperly removed the child from the physical custody of the person entitled to custody or has improperly retained the child after a visit or other temporary relinquishment of physical custody. If the petitioner has violated any other provision of a custody decree of another state, the court may decline to exercise its jurisdiction if it is just and proper under the circumstances.

(c) In appropriate cases, a court dismissing a petition under this section may charge the petitioner with necessary travel and other expenses, including attorneys' fees, incurred by other parties or their witnesses.

Sec. 46b-99. Information under oath to be submitted to the court.

(a) Every party in a custody proceeding in his first pleading or in an affidavit attached to that pleading shall give information under oath as to the child's present address, the places where the child has lived within the last five years, and the names and present addresses of the persons with whom the child has lived during that period. In this pleading or affidavit every party shall further declare under oath whether: (1) He has participated as a party, witness or in any other capacity in any other litigation concerning the custody of the same child in this or any other state; (2) he has information of any custody proceeding concerning the child pending in a court of this or any other state; and (3) he knows of any person not a party to the proceedings who has physical custody of the child or claims to have custody or visitation rights with respect to the child.

(b) If the declaration as to any of the above items is in the affirmative the declarant shall give additional information under oath as required by the court. The court may examine the parties under oath as to details of the information furnished and as to other matters pertinent to the court's jurisdiction and the disposition of the case.

(c) Each party has a continuing duty to inform the court of any custody proceeding concerning the child in this or any other state of which he obtained information during this proceeding.

Sec. 46b-100. Additional parties.

If the court learns from information furnished by the parties pursuant to section 46b-99 or from other sources that a person not a party to the custody proceeding has physical custody of the child or claims to have custody or visitation rights with respect to the child, it shall order that person to be joined as a party and to be duly notified of the pendency of the proceeding and of his joinder as a party. If the person joined as a party is outside this state, he shall be served with process or otherwise notified in accordance with section 46b-95.

Sec. 46b-101. Appearance of parties and the child.

(a) The court may order any party to the proceeding who is in this state to appear personally before the court. If that party has physical custody of the child the court may order that he appear personally with the child.

(b) If a party to the proceeding whose presence is desired by the court is outside this state with or without the child the court may order that the notice given under section 46b-95 include a statement directing that party to appear personally with or without the child and declaring that failure to appear may result in a decision adverse to that party.

(c) If a party to the proceeding who is outside this state is directed to appear under subsection (b) of this section or desires to appear personally before the court with or without the child, the court may require another party to pay to the clerk of the court travel and other necessary expenses of the party so appearing and of the child if it is just and proper under the circumstances.

Sec. 46b-102. Binding force and conclusive effect of custody decree.

A custody decree rendered by a court of this state which had jurisdiction under section 46b-93 binds all parties who have been served in this state or notified in accordance with section 46b-95 or who have submitted to the jurisdiction of the court, and who have been given an opportunity to be heard. As to these parties the custody determination made unless and until that determination is modified pursuant to law, including the provisions of this chapter and sections 46b-56 and 46b-57.

Sec. 46b-103. Recognition of out-of-state custody decrees.

The courts of this state shall recognize and enforce an initial or modification decree of a court of another state which had assumed jurisdiction under statutory provisions substantially in accordance with this chapter or which was made under factual circumstances meeting the jurisdictional standards of this chapter, so long as this decree has not been modified in accordance with jurisdictional standards substantially similar to those of this chapter.

Sec. 46b-104. Modification of custody decree of another state.

(a) If a court of another state has made a custody decree, a court of this state shall not modify that decree unless (1) it appears to the court of this state that the court which rendered the decree does not now have jurisdiction under jurisdictional prerequisites substantially in accordance with this chapter or has declined to assume jurisdiction to modify the decree and (2) the court of this state has jurisdiction.

(b) If a court of this state is authorized under subsection (a) of this section and section 46b-98 to modify a custody decree of another state it shall give due consideration to the transcript of the record and other documents of all previous proceedings submitted to it in accordance with section 46b-112.

Sec. 46b-105. Filing and enforcement of custody decree of another state.

(a) A certified copy of a custody decree of another state may be filed in the office of the clerk of the superior court. The clerk shall treat the decree in the same manner as a custody decree of the superior court. A custody decree so filed has the same effect and shall be enforced in like manner as a custody decree rendered by the superior court.

(b) A person violating a custody decree of another state which makes it necessary to enforce the decree in this state may be required to pay necessary travel and other expenses, including attorneys' fees, incurred by the party entitled to the custody or his witnesses.

Sec. 46b-106. Registry of out-of-state custody decrees and proceedings.

The clerk of the superior court for each judicial district shall maintain a registry in which he shall enter the following:

(1) Certified copies of custody decrees of other states received for filing;

(2) Communications as to the pendency of custody proceedings in other states;

(3) Communications concerning a finding of inconvenient forum by a court of another state; and

(4) Other communications or documents concerning custody proceedings in another state which may affect the jurisdiction of a court of this state or the disposition to be made by it in a custody proceeding.

Sec. 46b-107. Clerk to certify and forward copy of decree upon request.

The clerk of the superior court of each judicial district, at the request of the court of another state or at the request of any person who is affected by or has a legitimate interest in a custody decree, shall certify and forward a copy of the decree to that court or person.

Sec. 46b-108. Taking testimony in another state.

In addition to other procedural devices available to a party, any party to the proceeding or a guardian ad litem or other representative of the child may adduce testimony of witnesses, including parties and the child, by deposition or otherwise, in another state. The court on its own motion may direct that the testimony of a person be taken in another state and may prescribe the manner in which and the terms upon which the testimony shall be taken.

Sec. 46b-109. Hearings and studies in another state; orders to appear.

(a) A court of this state may request the appropriate court of another state to hold a hearing to adduce evidence, to order a party to produce or give evidence under other procedures of that state, or to have social studies made with respect to the custody of a child involved in proceedings pending in the court of this state; and to forward to the court of this state certified copies of the transcript of the record of the hearing, the evidence otherwise adduced, or any social studies prepared in compliance with the request. The cost of the services may be assessed against the parties or, if necessary, ordered paid by the state.

(b) A court of this state may request the appropriate court of another state to order a party to custody proceedings pending in the court of this state to appear in the proceedings, and if that party has physical custody of the child, to appear with the child. The request may state that travel and other necessary expenses of the party and of the child whose appearance is desired will be assessed against another party or will otherwise be paid.

Sec. 46b-110. Assistance to courts of other states.

(a) Upon request of the court of another state the courts of this state which are competent to hear custody matters may order a person in this state to appear at a hearing to adduce evidence or to produce or give evidence under other procedures available in this state or may order social studies to be made for use in a custody proceeding in another state. A certified copy of the transcript of the record of the hearing or the evidence otherwise adduced and any social studies prepared shall be forwarded by the clerk of the court to the requesting court.

(b) A person within this state may voluntarily give his testimony or statement in this state for use in a custody proceeding outside this state.

(c) Upon request of the court of another state, a competent court of this state may order a person in this state to appear alone or with the child in a custody proceeding in another state. The court may condition compliance with the request upon assurance by the other state that travel and other necessary expenses will be advanced or reimbursed.

Sec. 46b-111. Preservation of documents for use in other states.

In any custody proceeding in this state the court shall preserve the pleadings, orders and decrees, any record that has been made of its hearings, social studies and other pertinent documents until the child reaches eighteen years of age. Upon appropriate request of the court of another state, the court shall forward to the other court certified copies of any or all of such documents.

Sec. 46b-112. Request for court records of another state.

If a custody decree has been rendered in another state concerning a child involved in a custody proceeding pending in a court of this state, the court of this state upon taking jurisdiction of the case shall request of the court of the other state a certified copy of the transcript of any court record and other documents mentioned in section 46b-111.

Sec. 46b-113. International application.

The general policies of this chapter extend to the international area. The provisions of this chapter relating to the recognition and enforcement of custody decrees of other states apply to custody decrees and decrees involving legal institutions similar in nature to custody rendered by appropriate authorities of other nations if reasonable notice and opportunity to be heard were given to all affected persons.

Sec. 46b-114. Priority.

Upon the request of a party to a custody proceeding, which raises a question of existence or exercise of jurisdiction under this chapter, the case shall be given calendar priority and handled expeditiously.

Secs 46b-115 to 46b-119.

Reserved for future use.

DELAWARE

UNIFORM CHILD CUSTODY JURISDICTION ACT

§13-1901. Purposes of chapter; construction of provisions.

(a) The general purposes of this chapter are to:

(1) Avoid jurisdictional competition and conflict with courts of other states in matters of child custody which have in the past resulted in the shifting of children from state to state with harmful effects on the well-being of such children;

(2) Promote cooperation with the courts of other states to the end that a custody decree will be rendered in that state which can best decide the case in the interest of the child;

(3) Assure that litigation concerning the custody of the child takes place ordinarily in the state with which the child and his family have the closest connection and where significant evidence concerning his care, protection, training and personal relationships is most readily available, and that the courts of this State decline the exercise of jurisdiction when the child and his family have a closer connection with another state which has enacted the Uniform Child Custody Jurisdiction Act;

(4) Discourage continuing controversies over child custody in the interests of greater stability of home environment and of secure family relationships for the child;

(5) Deter abductions and other unilateral removals of children undertaken to obtain custody awards;

(6) Avoid the relitigation of custody decisions of other states in this State insofar as it is feasible;

(7) Facilitate the enforcement of custody decrees of other states;

(8) Promote and expand the exchange of information and other forms of mutual assistance between the courts of this State and those of other states concerned with the same child; and

(9) Make uniform the law of those states which enact child custody jurisdiction legislation.

(b) This chapter shall be construed to promote the general purposes stated in this section.

§13-1902. Definitions.

As used in this chapter:

(1) "Contestant" shall mean a person, including a parent, or an authorized social service agency, who claims a right to custody or visitation rights with respect to a child.

·(2) "Custody determination" shall mean a court decision and court orders and instructions providing for the custody of a child, including visitation rights; it does not include a decision relating to child support or any other monetary obligation of any person.

(3) "Custody proceeding" shall include proceedings in which a custody determination is one of several issues, such as an action for divorce or separation, and includes child neglect and dependency proceedings.

(4) "Decree" or "custody decree" shall mean a custody determination contained in a judicial decree or order made in a custody proceeding, and includes an initial decree and a modification decree.

(5) "Home state" shall means the state in which the child immediately preceding the time involved lived with his parents, a

parent or a person acting as parent, for at least 6 consecutive months, and in the case of a child less than 6 months old the state in which the child lived from birth with any of the persons mentioned. Periods of temporary absence of any of the named persons are counted as part of the 6 month or other period.

(6) "Initial decree" shall mean the first custody decree concerning a particular child.

(7) "Modification decree" shall mean a custody decree which modifies or replaces a prior decree, whether made by the court which rendered the prior decree or by another court.

(8) "Physical custody" shall mean actual possession and control of the child.

(9) "Person acting as parent" shall mean a person, other than a parent, who has physical custody of a child and who has either been awarded custody by a court or claims a right to custody.

(10) "State" shall mean any state, territory or possession of the United States, the Commonwealth of Puerto Rico and the District of Columbia.

§13-1903. Jurisdiction.

A court of this State which is competent to decide child custody matters has jurisdiction to make a child custody determination by initial or modification decree if:

(1) This State:

a. Is the home state of the child at the time of the commencement of the proceeding; or

b. Had been the child's home state within 6 months before commencement of the proceedings and the child is absent from this State because of his removal or retention by a person claiming his custody or for other reasons, and a parent or person acting as parent continues to live in this State; or

(2) It is in the best interests of the child that a court of this State assume jurisdiction because:

a. The child and his parents, or the child and at least 1 contestant, have a significant connection with this State; and

b. There is available in this State substantial evidence concerning the child's present or future care, protection, training and personal relationships; or

(3) The child is physically present in this State and:

a. The child has been abandoned; or

b. It is necessary in an emergency to protect the child because he has been subjected or threatened with mistreatment or abuse or is otherwise neglected or dependent; or

(4) It appears that no other state would have jurisdiction under prerequisites substantially in accordance with subdivisions (1), (2) and (3) of this section, or another state has declined to exercise jurisdiction on the ground that this State is the more appropriate forum to determine the custody of the child, and it is in the best interests of the child that this court assume jurisdiction.

Except as otherwise specifically stated in this section, the physical presence in this State of the child, or of the child and 1 of the contestants, is not alone sufficient to confer jurisdiction on a court of this State to make a child custody determination. Physical presence of the child, while desirable, is not a prerequisite for jurisdiction to determine his custody.

§13-1904. Notice and opportunity to be heard.

Before making a decree under this chapter, reasonable notice and opportunity to be heard shall be given to the contestants, any parent whose parental rights have not been previously terminated and any person who has physical custody of the child. If any of these persons are outside this State, notice and opportunity to be heard shall be given pursuant to § 1905 of this title.

§13-1905. Notice to persons outside this State.

(a) Notice required for the exercise of jurisdiction over a person outside this State shall be given in a manner reasonably calculated to give actual notice, and may be:

(1) By personal delivery outside this State in the manner prescribed for service of process within this State;

(2) In the manner prescribed by the law of the place at which the service is made for service of process in that place in an action in any of its courts of general jurisdiction;

(3) By any form of mail addressed to the person to be served and requesting a receipt; or

(4) As directed by the court, including publication if other means of notification are ineffective.

(b) Notice under this section shall be served, mailed, delivered or last published at least 20 days before any hearing in this State.

(c) Proof of service outside this State may be made by affidavit of the individual who made the service, or in the manner prescribed by the law of this State, the order pursuant to which the service is made, or the law of the place in which the service is made. If service is made by mail, proof may be a receipt signed by the addressee or other evidence of delivery to the addressee. Notice is not required if a person submits to the jurisdiction of the court.

§13-1906. Simultaneous proceedings in other states.

(a) A court of this State shall not exercise jurisdiction conferred by this chapter if at the time of filing the petition a proceeding concerning the custody of the child was pending in a court of another state exercising jurisdiction substantially in conformity with the Uniform Child Custody Jurisdiction Act, unless the proceeding is stayed by the court of the other state because this State is a more appropriate forum or for other reasons.

(b) Before hearing the petition in a custody proceeding, the court shall examine the pleadings and all other information supplied by the parties under § 1909 of this title, and shall consult the child custody registry established under § 1916 of this title concerning the pendency of proceedings with respect to the child in other states. If the court has reason to believe that proceedings may be pending in another state, it shall direct an inquiry to the State Court Administrator or other appropriate official of the other state.

(c) If the court is informed during the course of the proceeding that a proceeding concerning the custody of the child was pending in another state before the court assumed jurisdiction, it shall stay the proceeding and communicate with the court in which the other proceeding is pending to the end that the issue may be litigated in the more appropriate forum and that information be exchanged in accordance with § 1919 through § 1922 of this title. If a court of this State has made a custody decree before being informed of a pending proceeding in a court of another state, it shall immediately inform that court of the fact. If the court is informed that a proceeding was commenced in another state after it assumed jurisdiction, it shall likewise inform the other court to the end that the issues may be litigated in the more appropriate forum.

§13-1907. Forum non conveniens.

(a) A court which has jurisdiction under this chapter to make an initial or modification decree may decline to exercise its jurisdiction any time before making a decree, if it finds that it is an inconvenient forum to make a custody determination under the circumstances of the case and that a court of another state is a more appropriate forum.

(b) A finding of forum non conveniens may be made upon the court's own motion or upon motion of a party or guardian ad litem or other representative of the child.

(c) In determining if it is an inconvenient forum, the court shall consider whether or not it is in the best interests of the child that another state assume jurisdiction. For this purpose it may take into account the following factors, among others:

(1) If another state is or recently was the child's home state;

(2) If another state has a closer connection with the child and his family or with the child and 1 or more of the contestants;

(3) If substantial evidence concerning the child's present or future care, protection, training and personal relationships is more readily available in another state;

(4) If the parties have agreed on another forum which is no less appropriate; and

(5) If the exercise of jurisdiction by a court of this State would contravene any of the purposes stated in § 1901 of this title.

(d) Before determining whether to decline or retain jurisdiction, the court may communicate with a court of another state and exchange information pertinent to the assumption of jurisdiction by either court with a view to assuring that jurisdiction will be exercised by the more appropriate court and that a forum will be available to the parties.

(e) If the court finds that it is an inconvenient forum and that a court of another state is a more appropriate forum, it may dismiss the proceedings or it may stay the proceedings upon the condition that a custody proceeding be promptly commenced in another named state or upon any other conditions which may be just and proper, including the condition that a moving party stipulate his consent and submission to the jurisdiction of another forum.

(f) The court may decline to exercise its jurisdiction under this chapter if a custody determination is incidental to an action for divorce or other proceeding, and yet may retain jurisdiction over the divorce or other proceeding.

(g) If it appears to the court that it is clearly an inappropriate forum, it may require the party who commenced the proceedings to pay, in addition to the costs of the proceedings in this State, necessary travel and other expenses, including attorneys' fees, incurred by other parties or their witnesses. Payment is to be made to the clerk or other person designated by the court for remittance to the other party.

(h) Upon dismissal or a stay of proceedings under this section, the court shall inform the court found to be the more appropriate forum of this fact, or if the court which would have jurisdiction in the other state is not certainly known, shall transmit the information to the Court Administrator or other appropriate official for forwarding.

(i) Any communication received form another state informing this State of a finding of forum non conveniens because a court of this State is the more appropriate forum shall be filed in the custody registry of the appropriate court. Upon assuming jurisdiction the court of this State shall inform the original court of this fact.

§13-1908. Jurisdiction declined by reason of conduct.

(a) If the petitioner for an initial decree has wrongfully taken the child from another state or has engaged in similar reprehensible conduct, the court may decline to exercise jurisdiction if this is just and proper under the circumstances.

(b) Unless required in the interests of the child, the court shall not exercise its jurisdiction to modify a custody decree of another state if the petitioner, without consent of the person entitled to custody, has improperly removed the child from the physical custody of the person entitled to custody or has improperly retained the child after a visit or other temporary relinquishment of physical custody. If the petitioner has violated a custody decree of another state, the court may decline to exercise its jurisdiction if this is just and proper under the circumstances.

(c) In appropriate cases a court dismissing a petition under this section may charge the petitioner with necessary travel and other expenses, including attorneys' fees, incurred by other parties or their witnesses.

§13-1909. Information under oath to be submitted to the court.

(a) Every party in a custody proceeding, in his first pleading or in an affidavit attached to that pleading, shall give information under oath as to the child's present address, the places where the child has lived within the last 5 years and the names and present addresses of the persons with whom the child has lived during that period. In this pleading or affidavit every party shall further declare, under oath, whether:

(1) He has participated (as a party, witness or in any other capacity) in any other litigation concerning the custody of the same child in this or any other state;

(2) He has information of any custody proceeding concerning the child pending in a court of this or any other state; and

(3) He knows of any person not a party to the proceedings who has physical custody of the child or claims to have custody or visitation rights with respect to the child.

(b) If the declaration as to any of the above items is in the affirmative, the declarant shall give additional information under oath as required by the court. The court may examine the parties under oath as to details of the information furnished and as to other matters pertinent to the court's jurisdiction and the disposition of the case.

(c) Each party has a continuing duty to inform the court of any custody proceeding concerning the child in this or any other state of which he obtained information during this proceeding.

§13-1910. Additional parties.

If the court learns from the information furnished by the parties pursuant to § 1909 of this title or from other sources that a person not a party to the custody proceeding has physical custody of the child or claims to have custody or visitation rights with respect to the child, it shall order that person to be joined as a party and to be duly notified of the pendency of the proceeding and of his joinder as a party. If the person joined as a party is outside this State, he shall be served with process or otherwise notified in accordance with § 1905 of this title.

§13-1911. Appearance of parties and child.

(a) The court may order any party to the proceeding who is in the State to appear personally before the court. If that party has physical custody of the child, the court may order that such party appear personally with the child.

(b) If a party to the proceeding whose presence is desired by the court is outside this State, with or without the child, the court may order that the notice given under § 1905 of this title include a statement directing that party to appear personally, with or without the child, and declaring that failure to appear may result in a decision adverse to that party.

(c) If a party to the proceeding who is outside this State is directed to appear in accordance with this section, or desires to appear personally before the court, with or without the child, the court may require another party to pay travel and other necessary expenses of the party so appearing and of the child, if this is just and proper under the circumstances.

§13-1912. Binding force and res judicata effect of custody decree.

A custody decree rendered by a court of this State which had jurisdiction under § 1903 of this title binds all parties who have been served in this State or notified in accordance with § 1905 of this title, or who have submitted to the jurisdiction of the court, and who have been given an opportunity to be heard. As to these parties the custody decree is conclusive as to all issues of law and fact decided and as to the custody determination made, unless and until that determination is modified pursuant to the law, including this chapter.

§13-1913. Recognition of out-of-state custody decrees.

The courts of this State shall recognize and enforce an initial or modification decree of a court of another state which had assumed jurisdiction under statutory provisions substantially in accordance with the Uniform Child Custody Jurisdiction Act, or which was made under factual circumstances meeting the jurisdictional standards of the Uniform Act, so long as this decree has not been modified in accordance with jurisdictional standards substantially similar to those of this chapter.

§13-1914. Modification of custody decree of another state.

(a) If a court of another state has made a custody decree, a court of this State shall not modify that decree unless:

(1) It appears to the court of this State that the court which rendered the decree does not now have jurisdiction under jurisdictional prerequisites substantially in accordance with this chapter, or has declined to assume jurisdiction to modify the decree; and

(2) The court of this State has jurisdiction.

(b) If a court of this State is authorized under this section and § 1908 of this title to modify a custody decree of another state, it shall give due consideration to the transcript of the record and other documents of all previous proceedings submitted to it in accordance with § 1922 of this title.

§13-1915. Filing and enforcement of custody decree of another state.

(a) A certified copy of a custody decree of another state may be filed in the office of the Clerk of any Family Court of this State.

The Clerk shall treat the decree in the same manner as a custody decree of the Family Court of this State. A custody decree so filed has the same effect and shall be enforced in like manner as a custody decree rendered by a court of this State.

(b) A person violating a custody decree of another state which makes it necessary to enforce the decree in this State may be required to pay necessary travel and other expenses, including attorney's fees, incurred by the party entitled to the custody or his witnesses.

§13-1916. Registry of out-of-state custody decrees and proceedings.

The Clerk of each Family Court shall maintain a registry in which he shall enter the following:

(1) Certified copies of custody decrees of other states received for filing;

(2) Communications as to the pendency of custody proceedings in other states;

(3) Communications concerning a finding of forum non conveniens by a court of another state; and

(4) Other communications or documents concerning custody proceedings in another state which may affect the jurisdiction of a court of this State or the disposition to be made by it in a custody proceeding.

§13-1917. Certified copies of custody decree.

The Clerk of a Family Court of this State, at the request of the court of another state or at the request of any person who is affected by or who has a legitimate interest in a custody decree, shall certify and forward a copy of the decree to that court or person.

§13-1918. Taking testimony in another state.

In addition to other procedural devices available to a party, any party to the proceeding or a guardian ad litem or other representative of the child may adduce testimony of witnesses, including parties and the child, by deposition or otherwise, in another state. The court on its own motion may direct that the testimony of a person be taken in another state and may prescribe the manner in which and the terms upon which the testimony shall be taken.

§13-1919. Hearings and studies in another state.

(a) A court of this State may request the appropriate court of another state to hold a hearing to adduce evidence, to order a party to produce or give evidence under other procedures of that state or to have social studies made with respect to the custody of a child involved in proceedings pending in the court of this State, and to forward to the court of this State certified copies of the transcript of the record of the hearing, the evidence otherwise adduced or any social studies prepared in compliance with the request. The cost of the services may be assessed against the parties or, if necessary, ordered paid by the county or State.

(b) A court of this State may request the appropriate court of another state to order a party to custody proceedings pending in a court of this State to appear in the proceedings, and, if that party has physical custody of the child, to appear with the child. The request may state that travel and other necessary expenses of the party and of the child whose appearance is desired will be assessed against another party or will otherwise be paid.

§13-1920. Assistance to courts of other states.

(a) Upon request of the court of another state, the courts of this State which are competent to hear custody matters may order a person in this State to appear at a hearing to adduce evidence, or to produce or give evidence under other procedures available in this State or may order social studies to be made for use in a custody proceeding in another state. A certified copy of the transcript of the record of the hearing or the evidence otherwise adduced, and any social studies prepared, shall be forwarded by the clerk of the court to the requesting court.

(b) A person within this State may voluntarily give his testimony or statement in this State for use in a custody proceeding outside this State.

(c) Upon request of the court in another state, a competent court of this State may order a person in this State to appear alone or with the child in a custody proceeding in another state. The court may condition compliance with the request upon assurance by the other state that state travel and other necessary expenses will be advanced or reimbursed.

§13-1921. Preservation of documents for use in other states.

In any custody proceeding in this State, the court shall preserve the pleadings, orders and decrees, any records that have been made of its hearings, social studies and other pertinent documents until the child reaches 21 years of age. Upon appropriate request of the court of another state, the court shall forward to the other court certified copies of any or all of such documents.

§13-1922. Request for court records of another state.

If a custody decree has been rendered in another state concerning a child involved in a custody proceeding pending in a court of this State, the court of this State upon taking jurisdiction of the case shall request of the court of the other state a certified copy of the transcript of any court record and any other documents mentioned in § 1921 of this title.

§13-1923. International application.

The general policies of this chapter extend to the international area. The provisions of this chapter relating to the recognition and enforcement of custody decrees of other states apply to custody decrees and decrees involving legal institutions similar in nature to custody institutions rendered by appropriate authorities of other nations, if reasonable notice and opportunity to be heard were given to all affected persons.

§13-1924. Priority.

Upon the request of a party to a custody proceeding which raises a question of existence or exercise of jurisdiction under this chapter, the case shall be given calendar priority and handled expeditiously.

§13-1925. Short title.

This chapter may be cited as the Uniform Child Custody Jurisdiction Act.

DISTRICT OF COLUMBIA

UNIFORM CHILD CUSTODY JURISDICTION ACT

§ 16-4501. Purposes of chapter.

(a) The general purposes of this chapter are to:

(1) Avoid jurisdictional competition and conflict with courts of other states in matters of child custody which have in the past resulted in the shifting of children from state to state with harmful effects on their well-being;

(2) Promote cooperation with the courts of other states to the end that a custody decree is rendered in that state which can best decide the case in the interest of the child;

(3) Assure that litigation concerning the custody of a child takes place ordinarily in the state with which the child and his or her family have the closest connection and where significant evidence concerning the child's care, protection, training, and personal relationships is most readily available, and that courts of the District decline the exercise of jurisdiction when the child and his or her family have a closer connection with another state;

(4) Discourage continuing controversies over child custody in the interest of greater stability of home environment and of secure family relationships for the child;

(5) Deter abductions and other unilateral removals of children undertaken to obtain custody awards;

(6) Avoid relitigation of custody decisions of other states in the District insofar as feasible;

(7) Facilitate the enforcement of custody decision of other states;

(8) Promote and expand the exchange of information and other forms of mutual assistance between the courts of the District and those of other states concerned with the same child; and

(9) Make uniform the law of those states which enact it.

§ 16-4502. Definitions.

As used in this chapter, the term:

(1) "Custody determination" means a court decision and court orders and instructions providing for the custody of a child, including visitation rights. The term "custody determination" does not include a decision relating to child support or any other monetary obligation of any person.

(2) "Custody proceeding" means proceedings in which a custody determination is one of several issues, such as action for divorce, adoption, or separation, and includes child neglect and dependency proceedings.

(3) "Decree" or "custody decree" means a custody determination contained in a judicial decree or order made in a custody proceeding, and includes an initial decree and a modification decree.

(4) "District" means the District of Columbia.

(5) "Home state" means the state in which the child, immediately preceding the time involved, lived with his or her parents, a parent, or a person acting as parent, for at least 6 consecutive months, and in the case of a child less than 6 months old the state in which the child lived from birth with any of the persons mentioned. Periods of temporary absence of any of the named persons are counted as part of the 6-month or other period.

(6) "Initial decree" means the 1st custody decree concerning a particular child.

(7) "Modification decree" means a custody decree which modifies or replaces a prior decree, whether made by the court which rendered the prior decree or by another court.

(8) "Physical custody" means actual possession and control of a child.

(9) "Person acting as parent" means a person, other than a parent, who has physical custody of a child and who has either been awarded custody by a court or claims a right to custody.

(10) "Petitioner" means a person, including a parent, who claims a right to custody or visitation rights with respect to a child.

(11) "State" means any state, territory or possession of the United States, the Commonwealth of Puerto Rico, and the District of Columbia.

§ 16-4503. Exercise of jurisdiction.

(a) The Superior Court may exercise its jurisdiction to make a child custody determination by initial or modification decree if:

(1) The District (A) is the home state of the child at the time of commencement of the proceeding, or (B) had been the child's home state within 6 months before commencement of the proceeding and the child is absent from the District because of his or her removal or retention by a person claiming his or her custody or for other reasons, and a parent or person acting as parent continues to live in the District;

(2) It is in the best interest of the child that the Superior Court assume jurisdiction because (A) the child and his or her parents, or the child and at least 1 petitioner, have a significant connection with the District, and (B) there is available in the District substantial evidence concerning the child's present or future care, protection, training, and personal relationships;

(3) The child is physically present in the District and (A) the child has been abandoned, or (B) it is necessary in an emergency to protect the child because he or she has been subjected to or threatened with mistreatment or abuse or is otherwise neglected or dependent; or

(4) (A) It appears that no other state would have jurisdiction under prerequisites substantially in accordance with paragraphs (1), (2), or (3), or another state has declined to exercise jurisdiction on the ground that the District is the more appropriate forum to determine the custody of the child, and (B) it is in the best interest of the child that the Superior Court assume jurisdiction.

(b) Except as provided in subsection (a) (3) and (4), physical presence in the District of the child or of the child and 1 of the petitioners is not sufficient alone to permit the exercise of jurisdiction by the Superior Court to make a child custody determination.

(c) Physical presence of the child, while desirable, is not a prerequisite for jurisdiction to determine his or her custody.

§ 16-4504. Notice and opportunity to be heard.

Before making a decree under this chapter, reasonable notice and opportunity to be heard shall be given to the petitioners, any parent whose parental rights have not been previously terminated, and any person who has physical custody of the child. If any of these persons is outside the District, notice and opportunity to be heard shall be given pursuant to section 16-4505.

§ 16-4505. Notice to persons outside the District; submission to jurisdiction.

(a) Notice required for the exercise of jurisdiction over a person outside the District shall be given in a manner reasonably calculated to give actual notice, and may be:

(1) By personal delivery outside the District in the manner prescribed for service of process within the District;

(2) In the manner prescribed by the law of the place in which service of process be made;

(3) By any form of mail addressed to the person to be served and requesting a receipt; or

(4) As directed by the Superior Court, including publication if other means of notification are ineffective.

(b) Notice under this section shall be given at least 20 days before any hearing in the District.

(c) If service is made by mail pursuant to subsection (a) (3), proof may be a receipt signed by the addressee or other evidence of delivery to the addressee.

(d) Proof of service outside the District may be made by affidavit of the individual who made the service, or in the manner prescribed by the law of the District, the order pursuant to which the service is made, or the law of the place in which the service is made. If service is made by mail, proof may be a receipt signed by the addressee or other evidence of delivery to the addressee.

§ 16-4506. Simultaneous proceedings in other states.

(a) The Superior Court shall not exercise its jurisdiction under this chapter if at the time of filing the petition a proceeding concerning the custody of the child was pending in a court of another state exercising jurisdiction substantially in conformity with this chapter, unless the proceeding is stayed by the court of the other state because the District is a more appropriate forum or for other reasons.

(b) Before hearing the petition in a custody proceeding the Superior Court shall examine the pleadings and other informaiton supplied by the parties under section 16-4509 and shall consult the child custody registry established under section 16-4516 concerning the pendency of proceedings with respect to the child in other states.

(c) Where the Superior Court has reason to believe proceedings may be pending in another state, it shall direct an inquiry to the state court administrator or other appropriate official of the other state.

(d) If the Superior Court is informed during the course of the proceeding that a proceeding concerning the custody of the child was pending in another state before the court assumed jurisdiction, it shall stay the proceeding and communicate with the court in which the other proceeding is pending to the end that the issue may be litigated in the more appropriate forum and that information be exchanged in accordance with sections 16-4519 through 16-4522.

(e) If the Superior Court has made a custody decree before being informed of a pending proceeding in a court of another state, it shall immediately inform that court of the fact. If the Superior Court is informed that a proceeding was commenced in another state after it assumed jurisdiction it shall likewise inform the other court to the end that the issues may be litigated in the more appropriate forum.

§ 16-4507. Inconvenient forum.

(a) The Superior Court may decline to exercise its jurisdiction any time before making a decree if it finds that it is an inconvenient forum to make a custody determination under the circumstances of the case and that a court of another state is a more appropriate forum.

(b) A finding of inconvenient forum may be made upon the Superior Court's own motion or upon the motion of a party or a guardian ad litem or other representative of the child.

(c) In determining if it is an inconvenient forum, the court shall consider if it is in the interest of the child that another state assume jurisdiction. For this purpose it may take into account the following factors, among others:

(1) If another state is or recently was the child's home state;

(2) If another state has a closer connection with the child and his or her family or with the child and 1 or more of the petitioners;

(3) If substantial evidence concerning the child's present or future care, protection, training, and personal relationships is more available in another state;

(4) If the parties have agreed on another forum which is no less appropriate; and

(5) If the exercise of jurisdiction by the Superior Court would contravene any of the purposes stated in section 16-4501, or any of the provisions of the parental Kidnapping Prevention Act of 1980 (94 Stat. 3568).

(d) Before determining whether to decline or retain jurisdiction the Superior Court may communicate with a court of another state and exchange information pertinent to the assumption of jurisdiction by either court with a view to assuring that jurisdiction will be exercised by the more appropriate court and that a forum will be available to the parties.

(e) If the Superior Court finds that it is an inconvenient forum and that a court of another state is a more appropriate forum, it may dismiss the proceedings, or it may stay the proceedings upon condition that a custody proceeding be promptly commenced in another named state or upon any other conditions which may be just and proper, including the condition that a moving party stipulate his or her consent and submission to the jurisdiction of the other forum.

(f) The Superior Court may decline to exercise its jurisdiction under this chapter if a custody determination is incidental to an action for divorce or another proceeding while retaining jurisdiction over the divorce or other proceeding.

(g) If it appears to the Superior Court that it is clearly an inappropriate forum, it may require the party who commenced the proceedings to pay, in addition to the costs of the proceedings in the District, necessary travel and other expenses, including attorneys' fees, incurred by other parties or their witnesses. Payment is to be made to the Superior Court for remittance to the proper party.

(h) Upon dismissal or stay of proceedings under this section, the Superior Court shall inform the court found to be the more appropriate forum of this fact or, if the court which would have jurisdiction in the other state is not certainly known, shall transmit the information to the court administrator or other appropriate official for forwarding to the appropriate court.

(i) Any communication received form another state informing the District of a finding of inconvenient forum, because the Superior Court is a more appropriate forum, shall be filed in the Superior Court. Upon assuming jurisdiction the Superior Court shall inform the original court of this fact.

§ 16-4508. Jurisdiction declined by reason of conduct.

(a) If the petitioner seeking an initial decree from the Superior Court has wrongfully taken the child from another state or has engaged in similar reprehensible conduct, the Superior Court may decline to exercise jurisdiction if this is just and proper under the circumstances.

(b) Unless required in the interest of the child, the Superior Court shall not exercise its jurisdiction to modify a custody decree of another state if the petitioner, without consent of the person entitled to custody, has improperly removed the child from the physical custody of the person entitled to custody or has improperly retained the child after a visit or other temporary relinquishment of physical custody. If the petitioner has violated any other provision of a custody decree of another state the Superior Court may decline to exercise its jurisdiction if this is just and proper under the circumstances.

(c) In appropriate cases where the Superior Court dismisses a petition under this section, the Superior Court may charge the petitioner seeking the decree from the Superior Court with necessary travel and other expenses, including attorneys' fees, incurred by other parties or their witnesses.

§ 16-4509. Information under oath to be submitted to the Superior Court.

(a) Every party in a custody proceeding, in his or her 1st pleading or in an affidavit attached to that pleading, shall give information under oath as to the child's present address, the places where the child has lived within the last 5 years, and the names and present addresses of the persons with whom the child has lived during that period. In this pleading or affidavit every party shall further declare under oath whether:

(1) He or she has participated (as a party, witness, or in any other capacity) in any other litigation concerning the custody of the same child in the District or any other state;

(2) He or she has information of any custody proceeding concerning the child pending in the Superior Court or any other state; and

(3) He or she knows of any person not a party to the proceedings who has physical custody of the child or claims to have custody or visitation rights with respect to the child.

(b) If the declaration as to any of the above items is in the affirmative, the declarant shall give additional information under oath as required by the Superior Court.

(c) The Superior Court may examine the parties under oath as to details of the information furnished and as to other matters pertinent to the Superior Court's exercise of jurisdiction and the disposition of the case.

(d) Each party has a continuing duty to inform the Superior Court of any custody proceeding concerning the child in the District or any other state of which he or she obtained information during the proceeding in the Superior Court.

§ 16-4510. Additional parties.

(a) If the Superior Court learns from information furnished by the parties pursuant to section 16-4509 or from other sources that a person not a party to the custody proceeding has physical custody of the child or claims to have custody or visitation rights with respect to the child, it shall order that person to be joined as a party and to be duly notified of the pendency of the proceeding and of his or her joinder as a party.

(b) If the person joined as a party is outside the District, he or she shall be served with process or otherwise notified in accordance with section 16-4505.

§ 16-4511. Appearance of parties and the child.

(a) The Superior Court may order any party to the proceeding who is in the District to appear personally before the Superior Court. If that party has physical custody of the child, the Superior Court may order that he or she appear personally with the child.

(b) If a party to the proceeding whose presence is desired by the Superior Court is outside the District with or without the child, the Superior Court may order that the notice given under section 16-4505 include a statement directing that party to appear personally with or without the child and declaring that failure to appear may result in the decision adverse to that party.

(c) If a party to the proceeding who is outside the District is directed to appear under subsection (b) or desires to appear personally before the Superior Court with or without the child, the Superior Court may require another party to pay to the Superior Court travel and other necessary expenses of the party so appearing and of the child if this is just and proper under the circumstances.

§ 16-4512. Binding force and res judicata effect of custody decree.

A custody decree rendered by the Superior Court under section 16-4503 binds all parties who have been served in the District or notified in accordance with section 16-4505 or who have submitted to the jurisdiction of the Superior Court, and who have been given an opportunity to be heard. As to these parties the custody decree is prima facie evidence of the contents therein contained as to all issues of law and fact decided and as to the custody determination made unless and until that determination is modified pursuant to law, including the provisions of this chapter.

§ 16-4513. Recognition of out-of-state custody decrees.

The Superior Court shall recognize and enforce an initial or modification decree of a court of another state which had assumed jurisdiction under statutory provisions substantially in accordance with this chapter or which was made under factual circumstances meeting the jurisdictional standards substantially similar to those of this chapter, so long as this decree has not been modified in accordance with jurisdictional standards substantially similar to those in this chapter.

§ 16-4514. Modification of custody decree of another state.

(a) If a court of another state has made a custody decree, the Superior Court shall not modify that decree unless (1) it appears to the Superior Court that the court which rendered the decree presently does not have jurisdiction under jurisdictional prerequisites substantially in accordance with this chapter or has declined to assume jurisdiction to modify the decree, and (2) the Superior Court may exercise jurisdiction consistent with this chapter.

(b) If the Superior Court is authorized under subsection (a) and section 16-4508 to modify a custody decree of another state, it shall give due consideration to the transcript of the record and other documents of all previous proceedings submitted to it in accordance with section 16-4522.

§ 16-4515. Filing and enforcement of custody decree of another state.

(a) A certified copy of a custody decree of another state may be filed in the Superior Court.

(b) The certified decree shall be treated in the same manner as a custody decree of the Superior Court.

(c) A custody decree so filed has the same effect and shall be enforced in the same manner as a custody decree rendered by the Superior Court.

(d) A person violating a custody decree of another state which makes it necessary to enforce the decree in the District may be required to pay necessary travel and other expenses, including attorneys' fees, incurred by the party entitled to the custody or his or her witnesses.

§ 16-4516. Registry of out-of-state custody decrees and proceedings.

The Superior Court shall maintain a registry containing the following:

(a) Certified copies of custody decrees of other states received for filing;

(b) Communications as to the pendency of custody proceedings in other states;

(c) Communications concerning a finding of inconvenient forum by a court of another state; and

(d) Other communications or documents concerning custody proceedings in another state which may affect the exercise of jurisdiction by the Superior Court or the disposition to be made by it in a custody proceeding.

§ 16-4517. Certified copies of custody decree.

The Superior Court, at the request of the court of another state or at the request of any person who is affected by or has a legitimate interest in a custody decree, shall certify and forward a copy of the decree to that court or person.

§ 16-4518. Taking testimony in another state.

(a) In addition to other procedural devices available to a party, any party to the proceeding or a guardian ad litem or other representative of the child may adduce testimony of witnesses, including parties and the child, by deposition or otherwise, in another state.

(b) The Superior Court on its own motion may direct that the testimony of a person be taken in another state and may prescribe the manner in which and the terms upon which the testimony shall be taken.

§ 16-4519. Hearings and studies in another state; orders to appear.

(a) The Superior Court may request the appropriate court of another state to hold a hearing to adduce evidence, to order a party to produce or give evidence under other procedures of that state, or to have social studies made with respect to the custody of a child involved in proceedings pending in the Superior Court, and to forward to the Superior Court certified copies of the transcript of the record of the hearing, the evidence otherwise adduced, or any social studies prepared in compliance with the request. The costs of the services may be assessed against the parties.

(b) The Superior Court may request the appropriate court of another state to order a party to custody proceedings pending in the Superior Court to appear in the proceedings, and if the party has physical custody of the child, to appear with the child.

(c) The request pursuant to subsections (a) and (b) may state that travel and other necessary expenses of the party and of the child whose appearance is desired will be assessed against another party or will otherwise be paid.

§ 16-4520. Assistance to courts of other states.

(a) Upon request of the court of another state, the Superior Court may order a person in the District to appear at a hearing to adduce evidence or to produce or give evidence under other procedures available in the District, or may order social studies to be made for use in a custody proceeding in another state.

(b) A certified copy of the transcript of the record of the hearing of the evidence otherwise adduced and any social studies prepared pursuant to subsection (a) shall be forwarded by the Superior Court to the requesting court.

(c) A person within the District may voluntarily give his or her testimony or statement in the District for use in a custody proceeding outside the District.

(d) Upon request of the court of another state, the Superior Court may order a person in the District to appear alone or with the child in a custody proceeding in another state.

(e) The Superior Court may condition compliance with the request pursuant to subsection (d) upon assurance by the other state that travel and other necessary expenses will be advanced or reimbursed.

§ 16-4521. Preservation of documents for use in other states.

In any custody proceeding in the District, the Superior Court shall preserve the pleadings, orders, decrees, any record that has been made of its hearings, social studies, and other pertinent documents at least until the child reaches 21 years of age. Upon appropriate request of the court of another state, the Superior Court shall forward to the other court certified copies of any or all of these documents.

§ 16-4522. Request for court records of another state.

If a custody decree has been rendered in another state concerning a child involved in a custody proceeding pending in a court of the District, the Superior Court upon taking jurisdiction of the case shall request of the court of the other state a certified copy of the transcript of any court record and other documents mentioned in section 16-4521.

§ 16-4523. International application.

The provisions of this chapter relating to the recognition and enforcement of custody decrees of other states apply to custody decrees involving legal institutions similar in nature to custody institutions rendered by appropriate authorities of other nations if reasonable notice and opportunity to be heard were given to all affected persons.

§ 16-4524. Severability.

If any provision of this chapter's application thereof to any person or circumstance is held invalid, its invalidity does not affect other provisions or applications of the chapter which can be given effect without the invalid provision or applications, and to this end the provisions of this chapter are severable.

FLORIDA

UNIFORM CHILD CUSTODY JURISDICTION ACT

61.1302. Short title.

Sections 61.1302-61.1348 may be known and shall be cited as the "Uniform Child Custody Jurisdiction Act."

61.1304. Purposes of act; construction of provisions.

The general purposes of this act are to:

(1) Avoid jurisdictional competition and conflict with courts of other states in matters of child custody which have in the past resulted in the shifting of children from state to state with harmful effects on their well-being.

(2) Promote cooperation with the courts of other states to the end that a custody decree is rendered in the state which can best decide the case in the interest of the child.

(3) Assure that litigation concerning the custody of a child takes place ordinarily in the state with which the child and his family have the closest connection and where significant evidence concerning his care, protection, training, and personal relationships is most readily available, and that courts of this state decline the exercise of jurisdiction when the child and his family have a closer connection with another state.

(4) Discourage continuing controversies over child custody in the interest of greater stability of home environment and of secure family relationships for the child.

(5) Deter abductions and other unilateral removals of children undertaken to obtain custody awards.

(6) Avoid relitigation of custody decisions of other states in this state insofar as feasible.

(7) Facilitate the enforcement of custody decrees of other states.

(8) Promote and expand the exchange of information and other forms of mutual assistance between the courts of this state and those of other states concerned with the same child.

(9) Make uniform the law with respect to the subject of this act among states enacting it.

61.1306. Definitions.

As used in this act:

(1) "Contestant" means a person, including a parent, who claims a right to custody or visitation rights with respect to a child.

(2) "Custody determination" means a court decision and court orders and instruction providing for the custody of a child, including visitation rights; it does not include a decision relating to child support or any other monetary obligation of any person.

(3) "Custody proceeding" includes proceedings in which a custody determination is one of several issues, such as an action for dissolution of marriage or separation, and includes child neglect and dependency proceedings.

(4) "Decree" or "custody decree" means a custody determination contained in a judicial decree or order made in a custody proceeding, and includes an initial decree and a modification decree.

(5) "Home state" means the state in which the child, immediately preceding the time involved, lived with his parents, a parent, or a person acting as parent for at least 6 consecutive months or, in the case of a child less than 6 months old, the state in which the child lived form birth with any of the persons mentioned. Periods of temporary absence of any of the named persons are counted as part of the 6-months or other period.

(6) "Initial decree" means the first custody decree concerning a particular child.

(7) "Modification decree" means a custody decree which modifies or replaces a prior decree, whether made by the court which rendered the prior decree or by another court.

(8) "Physical custody" means actual possession and control of a child.

(9) "Person acting as parent" means a person, other than a parent, who has physical custody of a child and who has either been awarded custody by a court or claims a right to custody.

(10) "State" means any state, territory, or possession of the United States; the Commonwealth of Puerto Rico or the District of Columbia.

61.1308. Jurisdiction.

(1) A court of this state which is competent to decide child custody matters has jurisdiction to make a child custody determination by initial or modification decree if:

(a) This state:

1. Is the home state of the child at the time of commencement of the proceeding, or

2. Had been the child's home state within 6 months before commencement of the proceeding and the child is absent from this state because of his removal or retention by a person claiming his custody or for other reasons, and a parent or person acting as parent continues to live in this state;

(b) It is in the best interest of the child that a court of this state assume jurisdiction because:

1. The child and his parents, or the child and at least one contestant, have a significant connection with this state, and

2. There is available in this state substantial evidence concerning the child's present or future care, protection, training, and personal relationships;

(c) The child is physically present in this state and

1. The child has been abandoned, or

2. It is necessary in an emergency to protect the child because he has been subjected to or threatened with mistreatment or abuse or is otherwise neglected; or

(d) 1. It appears that no other state would have jurisdiction under prerequisites substantially in accordance with paragraph (a), paragraph (b), or paragraph (c), or another state has declined to exercise jurisdiction on the ground that this state is the more appropriate forum to determine the custody of the child, and

2. It is in the best interest of the child that a court of this state assume jurisdiction.

(2) Except under paragraph (c) or paragraph (d) of subsection (1), physical presence in this state of the child, or of the child and one of the contestants, is not alone sufficient to confer jurisdiction on a court of this state to make a child custody determination.

(3) Physical presence of the child, while desirable, is not a prerequisite for jurisdiction to determine his custody.

61.131. Notice and opportunity to be heard.

Before a decree is made under this act, reasonable notice and opportunity to be heard shall be given to the contestants, any parent whose parental rights have not been previously terminated, and any person who has physical custody of the child. If any of these persons is outside this state, notice and opportunity to be heard shall be given pursuant to s. 61.1312.

61.1312. Notice to persons outside this state; submission to jurisdiction.

(1) Notice required for the exercise of jurisdiction over a person outside this state shall be given in a manner reasonably calculated to give actual notice, and may be:

(a) By personal delivery outside this state in the manner prescribed for service of process within this state;

(b) In the manner prescribed by the law of the place in which the service is made for service of process in that place in an action in any of its courts of general jurisdiction;

(c) By any form of mail addressed to the person to be served and requesting a receipt; or

(d) As directed by the court, including publication, if other means of notification are ineffective.

(2) Notice under this section shall be served, mailed, delivered, or last published at least 20 days before any hearing in this state.

(3) Proof of service outside this state may be made by affidavit of the individual who made the service or in the manner prescribed by the law of this state, the order pursuant to which the service is made, or the law of the place in which the service is made. If service is made by mail, proof may be a receipt signed by the addressee or other evidence of delivery to the addressee.

(4) Notice is not required if a person submits to the jurisdiction of the court.

61.1314. Simultaneous proceedings in other states.

(1) A court of this state shall not exercise its jurisdiction under this act if, at the time the petition is filed, a proceeding concerning the custody of the child was pending in a court of another state exercising jurisdiction substantially in conformity with this act, unless the proceeding is stayed by the court of the other state because this state is a more appropriate forum or for other reasons.

(2) Before hearing the petition in a custody proceeding, the court shall examine the pleadings and other information supplied by the parties under s. 61.132 and shall consult the child custody registry established under s. 61.1334 concerning the pendency of proceedings with respect to the child in other states. If the court has reason to believe that proceedings may be pending in another

state, it shall direct an inquiry to the state court administrator or other appropriate official of the other state.

(3) If the court is informed during the course of the proceeding that a proceeding concerning the custody of the child was pending in another state before the court assumed jurisdiction, it shall stay the proceeding and communicate with the court in which the other proceeding is pending, to the end that the issue may be litigated in the more appropriate forum and that information be exchanged in accordance with ss. 61.134-61.1346. If a court of this state has made a custody decree before being informed of a pending proceeding in a court of another state, it shall immediately inform that court of the fact. If the court is informed that a proceeding was commenced in another state after it assumed jurisdiction, it shall likewise inform the other court to the end that the issues may be litigated in the more appropriate forum.

61.1316. Inconvenient forum.

(1) A court which has jurisdiction under this act to make an initial or modification decree may decline to exercise its jurisdiction any time before making a decree if it finds that it is an inconvenient forum to make a custody determination under the circumstances of the case and that a court of another state is a more appropriate forum.

(2) A finding of inconvenient forum may be made upon the court's own motion or upon motion of a party or a guardian ad litem or other representative of the child.

(3) In determining if it is an inconvenient forum, the court shall consider if it is in the interest of the child that another state assume jurisdiction. For this purpose it may take into account the following factors, among others:

(a) If another state is or recently was the child's home state;

(b) If another state has a closer connection with the child and his family or with the child and his family or with the child and one or more of the contestants;

(c) If substantial evidence concerning the child's present or future care, protection, training, and personal relationships is more readily available in another state;

(d) If the parties have agreed on another forum which is no less appropriate; and

(e) If the exercise of jurisdiction by a court of this state would contravene any of the purposes stated in s. 61.1304.

(4) Before determining whether to decline or retain jurisdiction, the court may communicate with a court of another state and exchange information pertinent to the assumption of jurisdiction by either court, with a view to assuring that jurisdiction will be exercised by the more appropriate court and that a forum will be available to the parties.

(5) If the court finds that it is an inconvenient forum and that a court of another state is a more appropriate forum, it may dismiss the proceedings, or it may stay the proceedings upon condition that a custody proceeding be promptly commenced in another named state or upon any other conditions which may be just and proper, including the condition that a moving party stipulate his consent and submission to the jurisdiction of the other forum.

(6) The court may decline to exercise its jurisdiction under this act if a custody determination is incidental to an action for dissolution of marriage or another proceeding while retaining jurisdiction over the dissolution of marriage or other proceeding.

(7) If it appears to the court that it is clearly an inappropriate forum, it may require the party who commenced the proceedings to pay, in addition to the costs of the proceedings in this state, necessary travel and other expenses, including attorneys' fees, incurred by other parties or their witnesses. Payment is to be made to the clerk of the court for remittance to the proper party.

(8) Upon dismissal or stay of proceedings under this section, the court shall inform the court found to be the more appropriate forum of this fact or, if the court which would have jurisdiction in the other state is not certainly known, shall transmit the information to the court administrator or other appropriate official for forwarding to the appropriate court.

(9) Any communication received from another state informing this state of a finding of inconvenient forum because a court of this state is the more appropriate forum shall be filed in the custody registry of the appropriate court. Upon assuming jurisdiction, the court of this state shall inform the original court of this fact.

61.1318. Jurisdiction declined by reason of conduct.

(1) If the petitioner for an initial decree has wrongfully taken the child from another state or has engaged in similar reprehensible conduct, the court may decline to exercise jurisdiction if this is just and proper under the circumstances.

(2) Unless required in the interest of the child, the court shall not exercise its jurisdiction to modify a custody decree of another state if the petitioner, without consent of the person entitled to custody, has improperly removed the child from the physical custody of the person entitled to custody or has improperly retained the child after a visit or other temporary relinquishment of physical custody. If the petitioner has violated any other provision of a custody decree of another state, the court may decline to exercise its jurisdiction if this is just and proper under the circumstances.

(3) In appropriate cases, a court dismissing a petition under this section may charge the petitioner with necessary travel and other expenses, including attorneys' fees, incurred by other parties or their witnesses.

61.132. Information under oath to be submitted to the court.

(1) Every party in a custody proceeding, in his first pleading or in an affidavit attached to that pleading, shall give information under oath as to the child's present address, the places where the child has lived within the last 5 years, and the names and present addresses of the persons with whom the child has lived during that period. In this pleading or affidavit every party shall further declare under oath whether:

(a) He has participated as a party or witness or in any other capacity in any other litigation concerning the custody of the same child in this or any other state;

(b) He has information of any custody proceeding concerning the child pending in a court of this or any other state; and

(c) He knows of any person not a party to the proceedings who has physical custody of the child or claims to have custody or visitation rights with respect to the child.

(2) If the declaration as to any of the above items is in the affirmative, the declarant shall give additional information under oath as required by the court. The court may examine the parties under oath as to details of the information furnished and as to other matters pertinent to the court's jurisdiction and the disposition of the case.

(3) Each party has a continuing duty to inform the court of any custody proceeding concerning the child in this or any other state of which he obtained information during this proceeding.

61.1322. Additional parties.

If the court learns from information furnished by the parties pursuant to s. 61.132 or from other sources that a person not a party to the custody proceeding has physical custody of the child or claims to have custody or visitation rights with respect to the child, it shall order that person to be joined as a party and to be duly notified of the pendency of the proceeding and of his joinder as a party. If the person joined as a party is outside this state, he shall be served with process or otherwise notified in accordance with s. 61.1312.

61.1324. Appearance of parties and the child.

(1) The court may order any party to the proceeding who is in this state to appear personally before the court. If that party has physical custody of the child, the court may order that he appear personally with the child.

(2) If a party to the proceeding whose presence is desired by the court is outside this state with or without the child, the court may order that the notice given under s. 61.1312 include a statement directing that party to appear personally with or without the child and declaring that failure to appear may result in a decision adverse to that party.

(3) If a party to the proceeding who is outside this state is directed to appear under subsection (2) or desires to appear personally before the court with or without the child, the court may require another party to pay to the clerk of the court travel and other necessary expenses of the party so appearing and of the child if this is just and proper under the circumstances.

61.1326. Binding force and res judicata effect of custody decree.

A custody decree rendered by a court of this state which has jurisdiction under s. 61.1308 binds all parties who have been served in this state or notified in accordance with s. 61.1312 or who have submitted to the jurisdiction of the court, and who have been given an opportunity to be heard. As to these parties, the custody decree is conclusive as to all issues of law and fact decided and as to the custody determination made unless and until that determination is modified pursuant to law, including the provisions of this act.

61.1328. Recognition of out-of-state custody decrees.

The courts of this state shall recognize and enforce an initial or modification decree of a court of another state which had assumed jurisdiction under statutory provisions substantially in accordance with this act, or which decree was made under factual circumstances meeting the jurisdictional standards of the act, so long as this decree has not been modified in accordance with jurisdictional standards substantially similar to those of this act.

61.133. Modification of custody decree of another state.

(1) If a court of another state has made a custody decree, a court of this state shall not modify that decree unless:

(a) It appears to the court of this state that the court which rendered the decree does not now have jurisdiction under jurisdictional prerequisites substantially in accordance with this act or has declined to assume jurisdiction to modify the decree; and

(b) The court of this state has jurisdiction.

(2) If a court of this state is authorized under subsection (1) and s. 61.1318 to modify a custody decree of another state, it shall give due consideration to the transcript of the record and other documents of all previous proceedings submitted to it in accordance with s. 61.1346.

61.1332. Filing and enforcement of custody decree of another state.

(1) A certified copy of a custody decree of another state may be filed in the office of the clerk of any circuit court of this state. The clerk shall treat the decree in the same manner as a custody decree of a circuit court of this state. A custody decree so filed has the same effect and shall be enforced in like manner.

(2) A person violating a custody decree of another state which makes it necessary to enforce the decree in this state may be required to pay necessary travel and other expenses, including attorney's fees, incurred by the party entitled to the custody or his witnesses.

61.1334. Registry of out-of-state custody decrees and proceedings.
The clerk of each circuit court shall maintain a registry in which he shall enter the following:

(1) Certified copies of custody decrees of other states received for filing.

(2) Communications as to the pendency of custody proceedings in other states.

(3) Communications concerning a finding of inconvenient forum by a court of another state.

(4) Other communications or documents concerning custody proceedings in another state which may affect the jurisdiction of a court of this state or the disposition to be made by it in a custody proceeding.

61.1336. Certified copies of custody decree.
The clerk of the circuit court, at the request of the court of another state or at the request of any person who is affected by, or has a legitimate interest in, a custody decree, shall certify and forward a copy of the decree to that court or person.

61.1338. Taking testimony in another state.
In addition to other procedural devices available to a party, any party to the proceeding or a guardian ad litem or other representative of the child may adduce testimony of witnesses, including parties and the child, by deposition or otherwise, in another state. The court on its own motion may direct that the testimony of a person be taken in another state and may prescribe the manner in which, and the terms upon which, the testimony shall be taken.

61.134. Hearings and studies in another state; orders to appear.
(1) A court of this state may request the appropriate court of another state to hold a hearing to adduce evidence, to order a party to produce or give evidence under other procedures of that state, or to have social studies made with respect to the custody of a child involved in proceedings pending in the court of this state; and to forward to the court of this state certified copies of the transcript of the record of the hearing, the evidence otherwise adduced, or any social studies prepared in compliance with the request. The cost of the services may be assessed against the parties or, if necessary, ordered paid by the state.

(2) A court of this state may request the appropriate court of another state to order a party to custody proceedings pending in the court of this state to appear in the proceedings and, if that party has physical custody of the child, to appear with the child. The request may state that travel and other necessary expenses of the party and of the child whose appearances are desired will be assessed against another party or will otherwise be paid.

61.1342. Assistance to courts of other states.
(1) Upon request of the court of another state, the courts of this state which are competent to hear custody matters may order a person in this state to appear at a hearing to adduce evidence or to produce or give evidence under other procedures available in this state or may order social studies to be made for use in a custody proceeding in another state. A certified copy of the transcript of the record of the hearing or the evidence otherwise adduced and any social studies prepared shall be forwarded by the clerk of the court to the requesting court.

(2) A person within this state may voluntarily give his testimony or statement in this state for use in a custody proceeding outside this state.

(3) Upon request of the court of another state, a competent court of this state may order a person in this state to appear alone or with the child in a custody proceeding in another state. The court may condition compliance with the request upon assurance by the other state that travel and other necessary expenses will be advanced or reimbursed.

61.1344. Preservation of documents for use in other states.
In any custody proceeding in this state, the court shall preserve the pleadings, orders, and decrees; any record that has been made of its hearings; social studies; and other pertinent documents until the child reaches 18 years of age. Upon appropriate request of the court of another state, the court shall forward to the other court certified copies of any or all of such documents.

61.1346. Request for court records of another state.
If a custody decree has been rendered in another state concerning a child involved in a custody proceeding pending in a court of this state, the court of this state, upon taking jurisdiction of the case, shall request of the court of the other state a certified copy of the transcript of any court record and other documents mentioned in s. 61.1344.

61.1348. International application.
The general policies of this act extend to the international area. The provisions of this act relating to the recognition and enforcement of custody decrees of other states apply to custody decrees, and decrees involving legal institutions similar in nature to custody institutions, rendered by appropriate authorities of other nations if reasonable notice and opportunity to be heard were given to all affected persons.

GEORGIA

UNIFORM CHILD CUSTODY JURISDICTION ACT

§ 19-9-40. Short title.

This article shall be known and may be cited as the "Uniform Child Custody Jurisdiction Act."

§ 19-9-41. Purposes of article; construction.

(a) The general purposes of this article are to:

(1) Avoid jurisdictional competition and conflict with courts of other states in matters of child custody, which competition and conflict have in the past resulted in the shifting of children from state to state with harmful effects on the children's well-being;

(2) Promote cooperation with the courts of other states, to the end that a custody decree is rendered in the state which can best decide the case in the interest of the child;

(3) Assure that litigation concerning the custody of a child takes place ordinarily in the state with which the child and his family have the closest connection and where significant evidence concerning his care, protection, training, and personal relationships is most readily available and also to assure that the courts of this state decline the exercise of jurisdiction when the child and his family have a closer connection with another state;

(4) Discourage continuing controversies over child custody, in the interest of greater stability of home environment and of secure family relationships for the child;

(5) Deter abductions and other unilateral removals of children undertaken to obtain custody awards;

(6) Avoid unnecessary relitigation in this state of custody decisions of other states;

(7) Facilitate the enforcement of custody decrees of other states;

(8) Promote and expand the exchange of information and other forms of mutual assistance between the courts of this state and those of other states concerned with the same child; and

(9) Make uniform the law of those states which enact the "Uniform Child Custody Jurisdiction Act."

(b) This article shall be construed to promote the general purposes stated in subsection (a) of this Code section.

§ 19-9-42. Definitions.

As used in this article, the term:

(1) "Contestant" means a person, including, but not limited to, a parent, who claims a right to custody or visitation rights with respect to a child.

(2) "Custody determination" means a court decision and court orders and instructions providing for the custody of a child, including, but not limited to, visitation rights. The term "custody determination" does not include a decision relating to child support or any other monetary obligation of any person.

(3) "Custody proceeding" includes proceedings in which a custody determination is one of several issues, such as an action for divorce or separation and includes child neglect and dependency proceedings and adoption proceedings.

(4) "Decree" or "custody decree" means a custody determination contained in a judicial decree or order made in a custody proceeding and includes, but is not limited to, an initial decree and a modification decree.

(5) "Home state" means the state in which the child, immediately preceding the time involved, lived with his parents, a parent, or a person acting as a parent for at least six consecutive months and, in the case of a child less than six months old, the state in which the child lived from birth with any of the persons mentioned. Periods of temporary absence of any of the named persons are counted as part of the six-month or other period.

(6) "Initial decree" means the first custody decree concerning a particular child.

(7) "Modification decree" means a custody decree which modifies or replaces a prior decree, whether made by the court which rendered the prior decree or by another court.

(8) "Person acting as parent" means a person, other than a parent, who has physical custody of a child and who either has been awarded custody by a court or claims a right to custody.

(9) "Physical custody" means actual possession and control of a child.

(10) "State" means any state, territory, or possession of the United States, the Commonwealth of Puerto Rico, and the District of Columbia and any foreign country.

§ 19-9-43. Jurisdiction to make child custody determination.

(a) A court of this state which is competent to decide child custody matters has jurisdiction to make a child custody determination by initial or modification decree if:

(1) This state:

(A) Is the home state of the child at the time of commencement of the proceeding; or

(B) Had been the child's home state within six months before commencement of the proceeding and the child is absent from this state because of his removal or retention by a person claiming his custody or for other reasons and a parent or person acting as parent continues to live in this state; or

(2) It is in the best interest of the child that a court of this state assume jurisdiction because:

(A) The child and his parents or the child and at least one contestant have a significant connection with this state; and

(B) There is available in this state substantial evidence concerning the child's present or future care, protection, training, and personal relationships; or

(3) The child is physically present in this state, and:

(A) The child has been abandoned; or

(B) It is necessary in an emergency to protect the child because he has been subjected to or threatened with mistreatment or abuse or is otherwise neglected or dependent; or

(4) (A) It appears that no other state would have jurisdiction under prerequisites substantially in accordance with paragraph (1), (2), or (3) of this subsection or that another state has declined to exercise jurisdiction on the ground that this state is the more appropriate forum to determine the custody of the child; and

(B) It is in the best interest of the child that this court assume jurisdiction.

(b) Except under paragraphs (3) and (4) of subsection (a) of this Code section, physical presence in this state of the child or of the child and one of the contestants is not alone sufficient to confer jurisdiction on a court of this state to make a child custody determination.

(c) Physical presence of the child, while desirable, is not a prerequisite for jurisdiction to determine his custody.

§ 19-9-44. To whom notice and opportunity to be heard to be given.

Before making a decree under this article, reasonable notice and opportunity to be heard shall be given to the contestants, to any parent whose parental rights have not been previously terminated, and to any person who has physical custody of the child. If any of these persons is outside this state, notice and opportunity to be heard shall be given pursuant to Code Section 19-9-45.

§ 19-9-45. How notice given to persons outside state; time of giving notice; proof of service; submission to court's jurisdiction.

(a) Notice required for the exercise of jurisdiction over a person outside this state shall be given in a manner reasonably calculated to give actual notice and may be made:

(1) By personal delivery outside this state in the manner prescribed for service of process within this state;

(2) In the manner prescribed by the law of the place in which the service is made for service of process in that place in an action in any of its courts of general jurisdiction;

(3) By any form of mail addressed to the person to be served and requesting a receipt; or

(4) As directed by the court. If other means of notification are ineffective, service under this paragraph may include, but need not be limited to, service by publication.

(b) Notice under this Code section shall be served, mailed, delivered, or last published at least 30 days before any hearing in this state.

(c) Proof of service outside this state may be made by affidavit of the individual who made the service or may be made in the manner prescribed by the law of this state, the order pursuant to which the service is made, or the law of the place in which the service is made. If service is made by mail, proof may be a receipt signed by the person to whom the service is addressed or other evidence of delivery to the person to whom the service is addressed.

(d) Notice is not required if a person submits to the jurisdiction of the court.

§ 19-9-46. Procedure where simultaneous proceedings pending in another state.

(a) A court of this state shall not exercise its jurisdiction under this article if at the time of filing the petition a proceeding concerning the custody of the child was pending in a court of another state exercising jurisdiction substantially in conformity with this article, unless the proceeding is stayed by the court of the other state because this state is a more appropriate forum or for other reasons.

(b) Before hearing the petition in a custody proceeding, the court shall examine the pleadings and other information supplied by the parties under Code Section 19-9-49 and shall consult the child custody registry established under Code Section 19-9-56 concerning the pendency of proceedings with respect to the child in other states. If the court has reason to believe that proceedings may be pending in another state, it shall direct an inquiry to the state court administrator or other appropriate official of the other state.

(c) If the court is informed during the course of the proceeding that a proceeding concerning the custody of the child was pending in another state before the court assumed jurisdiction, it shall stay the proceeding and communicate with the court in which the other proceeding is pending, to the end that the issue may be litigated in the more appropriate forum and that information may be exchanged in accordance with Code Sections 19-9-59 through 19-9-62. If a court of this state has made a custody decree before being informed of a pending proceeding in a court of another state, it shall immediately inform that court of the fact. If the court is informed that a proceeding was commenced in another state after it assumed jurisdiction, it shall likewise inform the other court, to the end that the issues may be litigated in the more appropriate forum.

§ 19-9-47. Finding of inconvenient forum; procedure thereupon; payment of expenses; communications between courts.

(a) A court which has jurisdiction under this article to make an initial or modification decree may decline to exercise its jurisdiction any time before making a decree, if it finds that it is an inconvenient forum to make a custody determination under the circumstances of the case and that a court of another state is a more appropriate forum.

(b) A finding of inconvenient forum may be made upon the court's own motion or upon motion of a party or a guardian ad litem or other representative of the child.

(c) In determining if it is an inconvenient forum, the court shall consider if it is in the interest of the child that another state assume jurisdiction. For this purpose it may take into account the following factors, among others:

(1) If another state is or recently was the child's home state;

(2) If another state has a closer connection with the child and his family or with the child and one or more of the contestants;

(3) If substantial evidence concerning the child's present or future care, protection, training, and personal relationships is more readily available in another state;

(4) If the parties have agreed on another forum which is no less appropriate; and

(5) If the exercise of jurisdiction by a court of this state would contravene any of the purposes stated in Code Section 19-9-41.

(d) Before determining whether to decline or retain jurisdiction, the court may communicate with a court of another state and exchange information pertinent to the assumption of jurisdiction by either court, with a view to assuring that jurisdiction will be exercised by the more appropriate court and that a forum will be available to the parties.

(e) If the court finds that it is an inconvenient forum and that a court of another state is a more appropriate forum, it may:

(1) Dismiss the proceedings; or

(2) Stay the proceedings upon condition that a custody proceeding be promptly commenced in another named state or upon any other conditions which may be just and proper, including, but not limited to, the condition that a moving party stipulate his consent and submission to the jurisdiction of the other forum.

(f) If a custody determination is incidental to an action for divorce or some other proceeding, the court may decline to exercise its jurisdiction under this article while retaining jurisdiction over the divorce or other proceeding.

(g) If it appears to the court that it is clearly an inappropriate forum, it may require the party who commenced the proceedings to pay, in addition to the costs of the proceedings in this state, necessary travel and other expenses, including, but not limited to, attorneys' fees, incurred by other parties or their witnesses. Payment is to be made to the clerk of the court, for remittance to the proper party.

(h) Upon dismissal or stay of proceedings under this Code section, the court shall inform the court found to be the more appropriate forum of this fact or, if the court which would have jurisdiction in the other state is not certainly known, shall transmit the information to the court administrator or other appropriate official for forwarding to the appropriate court.

(i) Any communication received from another state informing this state of a finding of inconvenient forum because a court of this state is the more appropriate forum shall be filed in the custody registry of the appropriate court. Upon assuming jurisdiction, the court of this state shall inform the original court of this fact.

§ 19-9-48. When court may decline to exercise jurisdiction; payment of expenses.

(a) If the petitioner seeking an initial decree has wrongfully taken the child from another state or has engaged in similar reprehensible conduct, the court may decline to exercise jurisdiction if this is just and proper under the circumstances.

(b) Unless required in the interest of the child, the court shall not exercise its jurisdiction to modify a custody decree of another state if the petitioner, without consent of the person entitled to custody, has improperly removed the child from the physical custody of the person entitled to custody or has improperly retained the child after a visit or other temporary relinquishment of physical custody. If the petitioner has violated any other provision of a custody decree of another state, the court may decline to exercise its jurisdiction if this is just and proper under the circumstances.

(c) In appropriate cases, a court dismissing a petition under this Code section may charge the petitioner with necessary travel and other expenses, including, but not limited to, attorneys' fees, incurred by the other parties or their witnesses.

§ 19-9-49. Information to be given under oath; examination; continuing duty to inform court.

(a) Every party in a custody proceeding, either in his first pleading or in an affidavit attached to that pleading, shall give the following information under oath:

(1) The child's present address;

(2) The places where the child has lived within the last five years; and

(3) The names and present addresses of the persons with whom the child has lived during the last five years.

(b) In his pleading or affidavit every party shall further declare under oath:

(1) Whether he has participated as a party or witness or in any other capacity in any other litigation concerning the custody of the same child in this or any other state;

(2) Whether he has information of any custody proceeding concerning the child pending in a court of this or any other state; and

(3) Whether he knows of any person not a party to the proceedings who has physical custody of the child or who claims to have custody or visitation rights with respect to the child.

(c) If the declaration required in paragraph (1), (2), or (3) of subsection (b) of this Code section is in the affirmative, the declarant shall give additional information under oath as required by the court. The court may examine the parties under oath as to details of the information furnished and as to other matters pertinent to the court's jurisdiction and the disposition of the case.

(d) Each party has a continuing duty to inform the court of any custody proceeding concerning the child, in this or any other state, of which he obtains information during this proceeding.

§ 19-9-50. Joinder of additional parties; service or notification.

If the court learns, from information furnished by the parties pursuant to Code Section 19-9-49 or from other sources, that a person not a party to the custody proceeding has physical custody of the child or claims to have custody or visitation rights with respect to the child, it shall order that person to be joined as a party and to be duly notified of the pendency of the proceeding and of his joinder as a party. If the person joined as a party is outside this state, he shall be served with process or otherwise notified in accordance with Code Section 19-9-45.

§ 19-9-51. Order for appearance of parties and child; notice to party outside state directing appearance; payment of expenses.

(a) The court may order any party to the proceeding who is in this state to appear personally before the court. If that party has physical custody of the child, the court may order that he appear personally with the child.

(b) If a party to the proceeding, whose presence is desired by the court, is outside this state with or without the child, the court may order that the notice given under Code Section 19-9-45 include a statement directing that party to appear personally with or without the child and declaring that failure to appear may result in a decision adverse to that party.

(c) If a party to the proceeding who is outside this state is directed to appear under subsection (b) of this Code section or desires to appear personally before the court with or without the child, the court may require another party to pay to the clerk of the court travel and other necessary expenses of the party so appearing and of the child, if this is just and proper under the circumstances.

§ 19-9-52. Who bound by custody decree; res judicata effect.

A custody decree rendered by a court of this state which has jurisdiction under Code Section 19-9-43 binds all parties who have been served in this state, have been notified in accordance with Code Section 19-9-45, or have submitted to the jurisdiction of the court and who have been given an opportunity to be heard. As to these parties, the custody decree is conclusive as to all issues of law and fact decided and as to the custody determination made, unless and until that determination is modified pursuant to law, including, but not limited to, this article.

§ 19-9-53. Recognition of foreign custody decrees.

The courts of this state shall recognize and enforce an initial or modification decree which was made by a court of another state which had assumed jurisdiction under statutory provisions substantially in accordance with this article or which was made under factual circumstances meeting the jurisdictional standards of this article, so long as the decree has not been modified in accordance with jurisdictional standards substantially similar to those of this article.

§ 19-9-54. When custody decree of another state may be modified; consideration of previous record.

(a) If a court of another state has made a custody decree, a court of this state shall not modify that decree unless:

(1) It appears to the court of this state that the court which rendered the decree does not now have jurisdiction under jurisdictional prerequisites substantially in accordance with this article or has declined to assume jurisdiction to modify the decree; and

(2) The court of this state has jurisdiction.

(b) If a court of this state is authorized under subsection (a) of this Code section and under Code Section 19-9-48 to modify a custody decree of another state, it may give due consideration to the transcript, the record, and other documents of all previous proceedings in the other court which are submitted to it in accordance with Code Section 19-9-62.

§ 19-9-55. Filing and enforcement of custody decree of another state; payment of expenses.

(a) A certified and exemplified copy of a custody decree of another state may be filed in the office of the clerk of any superior court of this state. The clerk shall treat the decree in the same manner as a custody decree of the superior court of this state. A custody decree so filed has the same effect and shall be enforced in like manner as a custody decree rendered by a court of this state.

(b) A person violating a custody decree of another state so as to make it necessary to enforce the decree in this state may be required to pay necessary travel and other expenses, including, but not limited to, attorneys' fees, incurred by the party entitled to the custody or by his witnesses.

§ 19-9-56. Registry of foreign custody decrees, proceedings, etc.

The clerk in each superior court shall maintain a registry in which he shall enter the following:

(1) Certified and exemplified copies of custody decrees of other states received for filing;

(2) Communications as to the pendency of custody proceedings in other states;

(3) Communications concerning a finding of inconvenient forum by a court of another state; and

(4) Other communications or documents concerning custody proceedings in another state which may affect the jurisdiction of a court of this state which may affect the jurisdiction of a court of this state or the disposition to be made by it in a custody proceeding.

§ 19-9-57. Certified copies of custody decrees to be supplied.

The clerk of each superior court in this state, at the request of the court of another state or at the request of any person who is affected by or has a legitimate interest in a custody decree, shall certify and forward a copy of the decree to that court or person.

§ 19-9-58. Taking testimony in another state.

In addition to other procedural devices available to a party, any party to the proceeding or a guardian ad litem or other representative of the child may adduce testimony of witnesses, including, but not limited to, the parties and the child, by deposition or otherwise, in another state. The court on its own motion may direct that the testimony of a person be taken in another state and may prescribe the manner in which and the terms upon which the testimony shall be taken.

§ 19-9-59. Hearings and studies in another state; costs; orders to appear.

(a) The court of this state may request the appropriate court of another state to hold a hearing to adduce evidence, to order a party to produce or give evidence under other procedures of that state, or to have social studies made, with respect to the custody of a child involved in proceedings pending in the court of this state, and to forward to the court of this state certified copies of the transcript and the record of the hearing, the evidence otherwise adduced, or any social studies prepared in compliance with the request. The cost of the services may be assessed against the parties or, if necessary, ordered paid by the state.

(b) A court of this state may request the appropriate court of another state to order a party to custody proceedings pending in the court of this state to appear in the proceedings and, if that party has physical custody of the child, to appear with the child. The request may state that travel and other necessary expenses of the party and of the child whose appearance is desired will be assessed against another party or will otherwise be paid.

§ 19-9-60. Assistance to courts of other states; voluntary testimony for use outside state.

(a) Upon request of the court of another state, the courts of this state which are competent to hear custody matters may order a person in this state to appear at a hearing to adduce evidence or to produce or give evidence under other procedures available in this state or may order social studies to be made for use in a custody proceeding in another state. A certified copy of the transcript and the record of the hearing or the evidence otherwise adduced and any social studies prepared shall be forwarded by the clerk of the court to the requesting court.

(b) A person within this state may voluntarily give his testimony or statement in this state for use in a custody proceeding outside this state.

(c) Upon request of the court of another state, a competent court of this state may order a person in this state to appear alone or with the child in a custody proceeding in another state. The court may condition compliance with the request upon assurance by the other state that state travel and other necessary expenses will be advanced or reimbursed.

§ 19-9-61. Preservation of custody documents during child's minority; furnishing copies to court of another state.

In a custody proceeding in this state, the court shall preserve the pleadings, the orders and decrees, any record that has been made of its hearings, any social studies, and other pertinent documents until the child reaches 18 years of age. Upon appropriate request of the court of another state, the court shall forward to the other court certified copies of any or all of such documents.

§ 19-9-62. Request for foreign court records.

If a custody decree has been rendered in another state, concerning a child involved in a custody proceeding pending in a court of this state, the court of this state, upon taking jurisdiction of the case, shall request of the court of the other state a certified and exemplified copy of the transcript of any court record and other documents mentioned in Code Section 19-9-61.

§ 19-9-63. International application of article.

The general policies of this article extend to the international area. The provisions of this article relating to the recognition and enforcement of custody decrees of other states apply to custody decrees and decrees involving legal institutions similar in nature to custody institutions rendered by appropriate authorities of other nations, if reasonable notice and opportunity to be heard were given to all affected persons.

§ 19-9-64. Calendar priority on jurisdictional questions.

Upon the request of a party to a custody proceeding which raises a question of the existence or exercise of jurisdiction under this article, the case shall be given calendar priority and handled expeditiously.

HAWAII

UNIFORM CHILD CUSTODY JURISDICTION ACT

[§ 583-1] Purposes of chapter; construction of provisions.

(a) The general purposes of this chapter are to:

(1) Avoid jurisdictional competition and conflict with courts of other states in matters of child custody which have in the past resulted in the shifting of children from state to state with harmful effects on their well-being;

(2) Promote cooperation with the courts of other states to the end that a custody decree is rendered in that state which can best decide the case in the interest of the child;

(3) Assure that litigation concerning the custody of a child take place ordinarily in the state with which the child and his family have the closest connection and where significant evidence concerning his care, protection, training, and personal relationships is most readily available, and that courts of this State decline the exercise of jurisdiction when the child and his family have a closer connection with another state;

(4) Discourage continuing controversies over child custody in the interest of greater stability of home environment and of secure family relationships for the child;

(5) Deter abductions and other unilateral removals of children undertaken to obtain custody awards;

(6) Avoid relitigation of custody decisions of other states in this State insofar as feasible;

(7) Facilitate the enforcement of custody decrees of other states;

(8) Promote and expand the exchange of information and other forms of mutual assistance between the courts of this State and those of other states concerned with the same child; and

(9) Make uniform the law of those states which enact it.

(b) This chapter shall be construed to promote the general purposes stated in this section, and shall apply only between those states which have enacted the same or similar legislation.

[§ 583-2]. Definitions.

As used in this chapter:

(1) "Contestant" means a person, including a parent, who claims a right to custody or visitation rights with respect to a child;

(2) "Custody determination" means a court decision and court orders and instructions providing for the custody of a child, including visitation rights; it does not include a decision relating to child support or any other monetary obligation of any person;

(3) "Custody proceeding" includes proceedings in which a custody determination is one of several issues, such as an action for divorce or separation, and includes child neglect and dependency proceedings;

(4) "Decree" or "custody decree" means a custody determination contained in a judicial decree or order made in a custody proceeding, and includes an initial decree and a modification decree;

(5) "Home state" means the state in which the child immediately preceding the time involved lived with his parents, a parent, or a person acting as parent, for at least six consecutive months, and in the case of a child less than six months old the state in which the child lived form birth with any of the persons mentioned. Periods of temporary absence of any of the named persons are counted as part of the six-month or other period;

(6) "Initial decree" means the first custody decree concerning a particular child;

(7) "Modification decree" means a custody decree which modifies or replaces a prior decree, whether made by the court which rendered the prior decree or by another court;

(8) "Physical custody" means actual possession and control of a child;

(9) "Person acting as parent" means a person, other than a parent, who has physical custody of a child and who has either been

awarded custody by a court or claims a right to custody; and

(10) "State" means any state, territory, or possession of the United States, the Commonwealth of Puerto Rico, and the District of Columbia.

[§ 583-3]. Jurisdiction.

(a) A court of this State which is competent to decide child custody matters has jurisdiction to make a child custody determination by initial or modification decree if:

(1) This State (A) is the home state of the child at the time of commencement of the proceeding, or (B) had been the child's home state within six months before commencement of the proceeding and the child is absent form this State because of his removal or retention by a person claiming his custody or for other reasons, and a parent or person acting as parent continues to live in this State; or

(2) It is in the best interest of the child that a court of this State assume jurisdiction because (A) the child and his parents, or the child and at least one contestant, have a significant connection with this State, and (B) there is available in this State substantial evidence concerning the child's present or future care, protection, training, and personal relationships; or

(3) The child is physically present in this State and (A) the child has been abandoned or (B) it is necessary in an emergency to protect the child because he has been subjected to or threatened with mistreatment or abuse or is otherwise neglected or dependent; or

(4) (A) It appears that no other state would have jurisdiction under prerequisites substantially in accordance with paragraphs (1), (2), or (3), or another state has declined to exercise jurisdiction on the ground that this State is the more appropriate forum to determine the custody of the child, and (B) it is in the best interest of the child, that this court assume jurisdiction.

(b) Except under paragraphs (3) and (4) of subsection (a), physical presence in this State of the child, or of the child and of the contestants, is not alone sufficient to confer jurisdiction on a court of this State to make a child custody determination.

(c) Physical presence of the child, while desirable, is not a prerequisite for jurisdiction to determine his custody.

[§ 583-4]. Notice and opportunity to be heard.

Before making a decree under this chapter, reasonable notice and opportunity to be heard shall be given to the contestants, any parent whose parental rights have not been previously terminated, and any person who has physical custody of the child. If any of these persons if outside this State, notice and opportunity to be heard shall be given pursuant to section 583-5.

[§ 583-5]. Notice to persons outside this State; submission to jurisdiction.

(a) Notice required for the exercise of jurisdiction over a person outside this State shall be given in a manner reasonably calculated to give actual notice, and may be:

(1) By personal delivery outside this State in the manner prescribed for service of process within this State;

(2) In the manner prescribed by the law of the place in which the service is made for service of process in that place in an action in any of its courts of general jurisdiction;

(3) By any form of mail addressed to the person to be served and requesting a receipt; or

(4) As directed by the court, including publication, if other means of notification are ineffective.

(b) Notice under this section shall be served, mailed, or delivered, or last published at least twenty days before any hearing in this State.

(c) Proof of service outside this State may be made by affidavit of the individual who made the service, or in the manner prescribed by the law of this State, the order pursuant to which the service is made, or the law of the place in which the service is made. If service is made by mail, proof may be a receipt signed by the addressee or other evidence of delivery to the addressee.

(d) Notice is not required if a person submits to the jurisdiction of the court.

[§ 583-6]. Simultaneous proceedings in other states.

(a) A court of this State shall not exercise its jurisdiction under this chapter if at the time of filing the petition a proceeding concerning the custody of the child was spending in a court of another state exercising jurisdiction substantially in conformity with this chapter, unless the proceeding is stayed by the court of the other state because this State is a more appropriate forum or for other reasons.

(b) Before hearing the petition in a custody proceeding the court shall examine the pleadings and other information supplied by the parties under section 583-9 and shall consult the child custody registry established under section 583-16 concerning the pendency of proceedings with respect to the child in other states. If the court has reason to believe that proceedings may be pending in another state it shall direct an inquiry to the state court administrator or other appropriate official of the other state.

(c) If the court is informed during the course of the proceeding that a proceeding concerning the custody of the child was pending in another state before the court assumed jurisdiction it shall stay the proceeding and communicate with the court in which the other proceeding is pending to the end that the issue may be litigated in the more appropriate forum and that information be exchanged in accordance with sections 583-19 through 583-22. If a court of this State has made a custody decree before being informed of a pending proceeding in a court of another state it shall immediately inform that court of the fact. If the court is informed that a proceeding was commenced in another state after it assumed jurisdiction it shall likewise inform the other court to the end that the issues may be litigated in the more appropriate forum.

[§ 583-7]. Inconvenient forum.

(a) A court which has jurisdiction under this chapter to make an initial or modification decree may decline to exercise its jurisdiction any time before making a decree if it finds that it is an inconvenient forum to make a custody determination under the circumstances of the case and that a court of another state is a more appropriate forum.

(b) A finding of inconvenient forum may be made upon the court's own motion or upon motion of a party or a guardian ad litem or other representative of the child.

(c) In determining if it is an inconvenient forum, the court shall consider if it is in the interest of the child that another state assume jurisdiction. For this purpose it may take into account the following factors, among others:

(1) If another state is or recently was the child's home state;

(2) If another state has a closer connection with the child and his family or with the child and one or more of the contestants;

(3) If substantial evidence concerning the child's present or future care, protection, training, and personal relationships is more readily available in another state;

(4) If the parties have agreed on another forum which is no less appropriate; and

(5) If the exercise of jurisdiction by a court of this State would contravene any of the purposes stated in section 583-1.

(d) Before determining whether to decline or retain jurisdiction the court may communicate with a court of another state and exchange information pertinent to the assumption of jurisdiction by either court with a view to assuring that jurisdiction will be exercised by the more appropriate court and that a forum will be available to the parties.

(e) If the court finds that it is an inconvenient forum and that a court of another state is a more appropriate forum, it may dismiss the proceedings, or it may stay the proceedings upon condition that a custody proceeding be promptly commenced in another named state or upon any other conditions which may be just and proper, including the condition that a moving party stipulate his consent and submission to the jurisdiction of the other forum.

(f) The court may decline to exercise its jurisdiction under this chapter if a custody determination is incidental to an action for divorce or another proceeding while retaining jurisdiction over the divorce or other proceeding.

(g) If it appears to the court that it is clearly an inappropriate forum it may require the party who commenced the proceedings to pay, in addition to the costs of the proceedings in this State, necessary travel and other expenses, including attorneys' fees, incurred by other parties or their witnesses. Such payment required by the court shall be made to the clerk of the court for remittance to the proper party.

(h) Upon dismissal or stay of proceedings under this section the court shall inform the court found to be the more appropriate forum of this fact, or if the court which would have jurisdiction in the other state is not certainly known, shall transmit the information to the court administrator or other appropriate official for forwarding to the appropriate court.

(i) Any communication received from another state informing this State of a finding of inconvenient forum because a court of this State is the more appropriate forum shall be filed in the custody registry of the appropriate court. Upon assuming jurisdiction the court of this State shall inform the original court of this fact.

[§ 583-8]. Jurisdiction declined by reason of conduct.

(a) If the petitioner for an initial decree has wrongfully taken the child from another state or has engaged in similar reprehensible conduct the court may decline to exercise jurisdiction if this is just and proper under the circumstances.

(b) Unless required in the interest of the child, the court shall not exercise its jurisdiction to modify a custody decree of another state if the petitioner, without consent of the person entitled to custody, has improperly removed the child from the physical custody of the person entitled to custody or has improperly retained the child after a visit or other temporary relinquishment of physical custody. If the petitioner has violated any other provision of a custody decree of another state the court may decline to exercise its jurisdiction if this is just and proper under the circumstances.

(c) In appropriate cases a court dismissing a petition under this section may charge the petitioner with necessary travel and other expenses, including attorneys' fees, incurred by other parties or their witnesses.

[§ 583-9]. Information under oath to be submitted to the court.

(a) Every party in a custody proceeding in his first pleading or in an affidavit attached to that pleading shall give information as to the child's present address, the places where the child has lived within the last five years, and the names and present addresses of the persons with whom the child has lived during that period. In this pleading or affidavit every party shall further declare whether:

(1) He has participated (as a party, witness, or in any other capacity) in any other litigation concerning the custody of the same child in this or any other state;

(2) He has information of any custody proceeding concerning the child pending in a court of this or any other state; and

(3) He knows of any person not a party to the proceedings who has physical custody of the child or claims to have custody or visitation rights with respect to the child.

(b) If the declaration as to any of the above items is in the affirmative the declarant shall give additional information as required by the court. The court may examine the parties under oath as to details of the information furnished and as to other matters pertinent to the court's jurisdiction and the disposition of the case.

(c) Each party has a continuing duty to inform the court of any custody proceeding concerning the child in this or any other state of which he obtained information during this proceeding.

[§ 583-10]. Additional parties.

If the court learns from information furnished by the parties pursuant to section 583-9 or from other sources that a person not a party to the custody proceeding has physical custody of the child or claims to have custody or visitation rights with respect to the child, it shall order that person to be joined as a party and to be duly notified of the dependency of the proceeding and of his joinder as a party. If the person joined as a party is outside this State he shall be served with process or otherwise notified in accordance with section 583-5.

[§ 583-11]. Appearance of parties and the child.

(a) The court may order any party to the proceeding who is in this State to appear personally before the court. If that party has physical custody of the child the court may order that he appear personally with the child.

(b) If a party to the proceeding whose presence is desired by the court is outside this State with or without the child the court may order that the notice given under section 583-5 include a statement directing that party to appear personally with or without the child and declaring that failure to appear may result in a decision adverse to that party.

(c) If a party to the proceeding who is outside this State is directed to appear under subsection (b) or desires to appear personally before the court with or without the child, the court may require another party to pay travel and other necessary expenses of the party so appearing and of the child if this is just and proper under the circumstances.

[§ 583-12]. Binding force and res judicata effect of custody decree.

A custody decree rendered by a court of this State which has jurisdiction under section 583-3 binds all parties who have been served in this State or notified in accordance with section 583-5 or who have submitted to the jurisdiction of the court, and who have been given an opportunity to be heard. As to these parties the custody decree is conclusive as to all issues of law and fact decided and as to the custody determination made unless and until that determination is modified pursuant to law, including the provisions of this chapter.

[§ 583-13]. Recognition of out-of-state custody decrees.

The courts of this State shall recognize and enforce an initial or modification decree of a court of another state which had assumed jurisdiction under statutory provisions substantially in accordance with this chapter or which was made under factual circumstances meeting the jurisdiction standards of the chapter, so long as this decree has not been modified in accordance with jurisdictional standards substantially similar to those of this chapter.

[§ 583-14]. Modification of custody decree of another state.

(a) If a court of another state has made a custody decree, a court of this State shall not modify that decree unless (1) it appears to the court of this State that the court which rendered the decree does not now have jurisdiction under jurisdictional prerequisites substantially in accordance with this chapter or has declined to assume jurisdiction to modify the decree and (2) the court of this State has jurisdiction.

(b) If a court of this State is authorized under subsection (a) and section 583-8 to modify a custody decree of another state it shall give due consideration to the transcript of the record and other documents of all previous proceedings submitted to it in accordance with section 583-22.

[§ 583-15]. Filing and enforcement of custody decree of another state.

(a) A certified copy of a custody decree of another state may be filed in the office of the clerk of any family court of this State. The clerk shall treat the decree in the same manner as a custody decree of the family court of this State. A custody decree so filed has the same effect and shall be enforced in like manner as a custody decree rendered by a court of this State.

(b) A person violating a custody decree of another state which makes it necessary to enforce the decree in this State may be required to pay necessary travel and other expenses, including attorneys' fees, incurred by the party entitled to the custody or his witnesses.

[§ 583-16]. Registry of out-of-state custody decrees and proceedings.

The clerk of each family court shall maintain a registry in which he shall enter the following:

(1) Certified copies of custody decrees of other states received for filing;

(2) Communications as to the pendency of custody proceedings in other states;

(3) Communications concerning a finding of inconvenient forum by a court of another state; and

(4) Other communications or documents concerning custody proceedings in another state which may affect the jurisdiction of a court of this State or the disposition to be made by it in a custody proceeding.

[§ 583-17]. Certified copies of custody decree.

The clerk of the family court of this State, at the request of the court of another state or at the request of any person who is affected by or has a legitimate interest in a custody decree, shall certify and forward a copy of the decree to that court or person.

[§ 583-18]. Taking testimony in another state.

In addition to other procedural devices available to a party, any party to the proceeding or a guardian ad litem or other representative of the child may adduce testimony of witnesses, including parties and the child, by deposition or otherwise, in another state. The court on its own motion may direct that the testimony of a person be taken in another state and may prescribe the manner in which and the terms upon which the testimony may be taken.

[§ 583-19]. Hearings and studies in another state; orders to appear.

(a) A court of this State may request the appropriate court of another state to hold a hearing to adduce evidence, to order a party to produce or give evidence under other procedures of that state, or to have social studies made with respect to the custody of a child involved in proceedings pending in the court of this State; and to forward to the court of this State certified copies of the transcript of the record of hearing, the evidence otherwise adduced, or any social studies prepared in compliance with the request. The cost of the services may be assessed against the parties.

(b) A court of this State may request the appropriate court of another state to order a party to custody proceedings pending in the court of this State to appear in the proceedings, and if that party has physical custody of the child, to appear with the child. The request may state that travel and other necessary expenses of the party and of the child whose appearance is desired will be assessed against another party or will otherwise be paid.

[§ 583-20]. Assistance to courts of other states.

(a) Upon request of the court of another state the courts of this State which are competent to hear custody matters may order a person in this State to appear at a hearing to adduce evidence or to produce or give evidence under other procedures available in this State or may order social studies to be made for use in a custody proceeding in another state. A certified copy of the transcript of the record of the hearing or the evidence otherwise adduced and any social studies prepared shall be forwarded by the clerk of the court to the requesting court.

(b) A person within this State may voluntarily give his testimony or statement in this State for use in a custody proceeding outside this State.

(c) Upon request of the court of another state a competent court of this State may order a person in this State to appear alone or with the child in a custody proceeding in another state. The court may condition compliance with the request upon assurance by the other state that travel and other necessary expenses will be advanced or reimbursed.

[§ 583-21]. Preservation of documents for use in other states.

In any custody proceeding in this State the court shall preserve the pleadings, orders and decrees, any record that has been made of its hearings, social studies, and other pertinent documents until the child reaches eighteen years of age. Upon appropriate request of the court of another state the court shall forward to the other court certified copies of any or all of such documents.

[§ 583-22]. Request for court records for another state.

If custody decree has been rendered in another state concerning a child involved in a custody proceeding pending in a court of this State, the court of this State upon taking jurisdiction of the case shall request of the court of the other state a certified copy of the transcript of any court record and other documents mentioned in section 583-21.

[§ 583-23]. International application.

The general policies of this chapter extend to the international area. The provisions of this chapter relating to the recognition and enforcement of custody decrees of other states apply to custody decrees and decrees involving legal institutions similar in nature to custody, rendered by appropriate authorities of other nations if reasonable notice and opportunity to be heard were given to all affected persons.

[§ 583-24]. Priority.

Upon the request of a party to a custody proceeding which raises a question of existence or exercise of jurisdiction under this chapter the case shall be given calendar priority and handled expeditiously.

[§ 583-25]. Short title.

This chapter may be cited as the Uniform Child Custody Jurisdiction Act.

[§ 583-26]. Severability.

If any provision of this chapter or the application thereof to any person or circumstance is held invalid, its invalidity does not affect other provisions or applications of the chapter which can be given effect without the valid provision or application, and to this end the provisions of this chapter are severable.

IDAHO

UNIFORM CHILD CUSTODY JURISDICTION ACT

§ 32-1101. Purposes of act - Construction of provisions.

(a) The general purposes of this chapter are to:

(1) Avoid jurisdictional competition and conflict with courts of other states in matters of child custody which have in the past resulted in the shifting of children from state to state with harmful effects on their well-being;

(2) Promote cooperation with the courts of other states to the end that a custody decree is rendered in that state which can best decide the case in the interest of the child;

(3) Assure that litigation concerning the custody of a child take place ordinarily in the state with which the child and his family have the closest connection and where significant evidence concerning his care, protection, training, and personal relationships is most readily available, and that courts of this state decline the exercise of jurisdiction when the child and his family have a closer connection with another state;

(4) Discourage continuing controversies over child custody in the interest of greater stability of home environment and of secure family relationships for the child;

(5) Deter abductions and other unilateral removals of children undertaken to obtain custody awards;

(6) Avoid relitigation of custody decisions of other states in this state insofar as feasible;

(7) Facilitate the enforcement of custody decrees of other states;

(8) Promote and expand the exchange of information and other forms of mutual assistance between the courts of this state and those of other states concerned with the same child; and

(9) Make uniform the law of those states which enact it.

(b) This shall be construed to promote the general purposes stated in this section.

§ 32-1102. Definitions.

As used in this chapter:

(1) "Contestant" means a person, including a parent, who claims a right to custody or visitation rights with respect to a child;

(2) "Custody determination" means a court decision and court orders and instructions providing for the custody of a child, including visitation rights; it does not include a decision relating to child support or any other monetary obligation of any person;

(3) "Custody proceeding" means proceedings in which a custody determination is one of several issues, and includes child neglect and dependency proceedings;

(4) "Decree" or "custody decree" means a custody determination contained in a judicial decree made in a custody proceeding, and includes an initial decree and a modification decree;

(5) "Home state" means the state in which the child immediately preceding the time involved lived with his parents, a parent, or a person acting as parent, for at least six (6) consecutive months, and in the case of a child less than six (6) months old the state in which the child lived from birth with any of the persons mentioned. Periods of temporary absence of any of the named persons are counted as part of the six (6) month or other period;

(6) "Initial decree" means the first custody decree concerning a particular child;

(7) "Modification decree" means a custody decree which modifies or replaces a prior decree, whether made by the court which rendered the prior decree or by another court;

(8) "Physical custody" means when a child resides with or is under the care and supervision of a parent or party;

(9) "Person acting as parent" means a person, other than a parent, who has physical custody of a child and who has either been awarded custody by a court or claims a right to custody; and

(10) "State" means any state, territory, or possession of the United States, the Commonwealth of Puerto Rico, and the District of Columbia.

§ 32-1103. Jurisdiction.

(a) A court of this state which is competent to decide child custody matters has jurisdiction to make a child custody determination by initial or modification decree if:

(1) This state (i) is the home state of the child at the time of commencement of the proceeding, or (ii) had been the child's home state within six (6) months before commencement of the proceeding and the child is absent from this state because of his removal or retention by a person claiming his custody or for other reasons, and a parent or person acting as parent continues to live in this state; or

(2) It is in the best interest of the child that a court of this state assume jurisdiction because (i) the child and his parents, or the child and at least one contestant, have a significant connection with this state, and (ii) there is available in this state substantial evidence concerning the child's present or future care, protection, training, and personal relationships; or

(3) The child is physically present in this state and (i) the child has been abandoned or (ii) it is necessary in an emergency to protect the child because he has been subjected to or threatened with mistreatment or abuse or is otherwise neglected or dependent; or

(4) (i) It appears that no other state would have jurisdiction under prerequisites substantially in accordance with paragraphs (1), (2), or (3) of this section, or another state has declined to exercise jurisdiction on the ground that this state is the more appropriate forum to determine the custody of the child, and (ii) it is in the best interest of the child that this court assume jurisdiction.

(b) Except under paragraphs (3) and (4) of subsection (a) of this section, physical presence in this state of the child, or of the child and one of the contestants, is not alone sufficient to confer jurisdiction on a court of this state to make a child custody determination.

(c) Physical presence of the child, while desirable, is not a prerequisite for jurisdiction to determine his custody.

§ 32-1104. Notice and opportunity to be heard.

Before making a decree under this chapter, reasonable notice and opportunity to be heard shall be given to the contestants, any parent whose parental rights have not been previously terminated, and any person who has physical custody of the child. If any of these persons is outside this state, notice and opportunity to be heard shall be given pursuant to section 32-1105, Idaho Code.

§ 32-1105. Notice to persons outside this state - Submission to jurisdiction.

(a) Notice required for the exercise of jurisdiction over a person outside this state shall be given in a manner reasonably calculated to give actual notice, and may be:

(1) By personal delivery outside this state in the manner prescribed for service of process within this state;

(2) In the manner prescribed by the law of the place in which the service is made for service of process in that place in an action in any of its courts of general jurisdiction;

(3) By any form of mail addressed to the person to be served and requesting a receipt; or

(4) As directed by the court, including publication, if other means of notification are ineffective.

(b) Notice under this section shall be served, mailed, delivered, or last published at least twenty (20) days before any hearing in this state.

(c) Proof of service outside this state may be made by affidavit of the individual who made the service, or in the manner prescribed by the law of this state, the order pursuant to which the service is made, or the law of the place in which the service is made. If service is made by mail, proof may be a receipt signed by the addressee or other evidence of delivery to the addressee.

(d) Notice is not required if a person submits to the jurisdiction of the court.

§ 32-1106. Simultaneous proceedings in other states.

(a) A court of this state shall not exercise its jurisdiction under this chapter if at the time of filing the petition a proceeding concerning the custody of the child was pending in a court of another state exercising jurisdiction substantially in conformity with this chapter, unless the proceeding is stayed by the court of the other state because this state is a more appropriate forum or for other reasons.

(b) Before hearing the petition in a custody proceeding the court shall examine the pleadings and other information supplied by the parties under section 32-1109, Idaho Code, and shall consult the child custody registry established under section 32-1117, Idaho Code, concerning the pendency of proceedings with respect to the child in other states. If the court has reason to believe that proceedings may be pending in another state it shall direct an inquiry to the state court administrator or other appropriate official of the other state.

(c) If the court is informed during the course of the proceeding that a proceeding concerning the custody of the child was pending in another state before the court assumed jurisdiction it shall stay the proceeding and communicate with the court in which the other proceeding is pending to the end that the issue may be litigated in the more appropriate forum and that information be exchanged in accordance with sections 32-1120 through 32-1123, Idaho Code. If a court of this state has made a custody decree before being informed of a pending proceeding in a court of another state it shall immediately inform that court of the fact. If the court is informed that a proceeding was commenced in another state after it assumed jurisdiction it shall likewise inform the other court to the end that the issues may be litigated in the most appropriate forum.

§ 32-1107. Inconvenient forum.

(a) A court which has jurisdiction under this chapter to make an initial or modification decree may decline to exercise its jurisdiction any time before making a decree if it finds that it is an inconvenient forum to make a custody determination under the circumstances of the case and that a court of another state is a more appropriate forum.

(b) A finding of inconvenient forum may be made upon the court's own motion or upon motion of a party or a guardian ad litem or other representative of the child.

(c) In determining if it is an inconvenient forum, the court shall consider if it is in the interest of the child that another state assume jurisdiction. For this purpose it may take into account the following factors, among others:

(1) If another state is or recently was the child's home state;

(2) If another state has a closer connection with the child and his family or with the child and one or more of the contestants;

(3) If substantial evidence concerning the child's present or future care, protection, training, and personal relationships is more readily available in another state;

(4) If the parties have agreed on another forum which is no less appropriate; and

(5) If the exercise of jurisdiction by a court of this state would contravene any of the purposes stated in section 32-1101, Idaho Code.

(d) Before determining whether to decline or retain jurisdiction the court may communicate with a court of another state and exchange information pertinent to the assumption of jurisdiction by either court with a view to assuring that jurisdiction will be exercised by the most appropriate court and that a forum will be available to the parties.

(e) If the court finds that it is an inconvenient forum and that a court of another state is a more appropriate forum, it may dismiss the proceedings, or it may stay the proceedings upon condition that a custody proceeding be promptly commenced in another named state or upon any other conditions which may be just and proper, including the condition that a moving party stipulate his consent and submission to the jurisdiction of the other forum.

(f) The court may decline to exercise its jurisdiction under this chapter if a custody determination is incidental to an action for divorce or another proceeding while retaining jurisdiction over the divorce or other proceeding.

(g) If it appears to the court that it is clearly an inappropriate forum it may require the party who commenced the proceedings to pay, in addition to the costs of the proceedings in this state, necessary travel and other expenses, including attorneys' fees, incurred by other parties or their witnesses. Payment is to be made to the clerk of the court for remittance to the proper party.

(h) Upon dismissal or stay of proceedings under this section the court shall inform the court found to be the more appropriate forum of this fact, or if the court which would have jurisdiction in the other state is not certainly known, shall transmit the information to the court administrator or other appropriate official for forwarding to the appropriate court.

(i) Any communication received from another state informing this state of a finding of inconvenient forum because a court of this state is the more appropriate forum shall be filed with the clerk of the appropriate court. Upon assuming jurisdiction the court of this state shall inform the original court of this fact.

§ 32-1108. Jurisdiction declined by reason of conduct.

(a) If the petitioner for an initial decree has wrongfully taken the child from another state or has engaged in similar reprehensible conduct the court may decline to exercise jurisdiction if this is just and proper under the circumstances.

(b) Unless required in the interest of the child and subject to subsection (a) of section 32-1114, Idaho Code, the court shall not exercise its jurisdiction to modify a custody decree of another state if the petitioner, without consent of the person entitled to custody, has improperly removed the child from the physical custody of the person entitled to custody or has improperly retained the child after a visit or other temporary relinquishment of physical custody. If the petitioner has violated any other provision of a custody decree of another state the court subject to subsection (a) of section 32-1114, Idaho Code, may decline to exercise jurisdiction if this is just and proper under the circumstances.

(c) In appropriate cases a court dismissing a petition under this section may charge the petitioner with necessary travel and other expenses, including attorneys' fees, incurred by other parties or their witnesses.

§ 32-1109. Information under oath to be submitted to the court.

(a) Every party in a custody proceeding in his first pleading or in an affidavit attached to that pleading shall give information under oath as to the child's present address, the places where the child has lived within the last five (5) years, and the names and present addresses of the persons with whom the child has lived during that period. In this pleading or affidavit every party shall further declare under oath if:

(1) He has participated (as a party, witness, or in any other capacity) in any other litigation concerning the custody of the same child in this or any other state;

(2) He has information of any custody proceeding concerning the child pending in a court of this or any other state; and

(3) He knows of any person not a party to the proceedings who has physical custody of the child or claims to have custody or visitation rights with respect to the child.

(b) If the declaration as to any of the above items is in the affirmative the declarant shall give additional information under oath as required by the court. The court may examine the parties under oath as to details of the information furnished and as to other matters pertinent to the court's jurisdiction and the disposition of the case.

(c) Each party has a continuing duty to inform the court of any custody proceeding concerning the child in this or any other state of which he obtained information during this proceeding.

§ 32-1110. Additional parties.

If the court learns from information furnished by the parties pursuant to section 32-1109, Idaho Code, or from other sources that a person not a party to the custody proceeding has physical custody of the child or claims to have custody or visitation rights with respect to the child, it shall order that person to be joined as a party. If the person joined as a party is outside this state he shall be served with process or otherwise notified in accordance with section 32-1105, Idaho Code.

§ 32-1111. Appearance of parties and the child.

(a) The court may order any party to the proceeding who is in this state to appear personally before the court. If that party has physical custody of the child the court may order that he appear personally with the child.

(b) If a party to the proceeding whose presence is desired by the court is outside this state with or without the child the court may order that the notice given under section 32-1105, Idaho Code, include a statement directing that party to appear personally with or without the child and declaring that failure to appear may result in a decision adverse to that party.

(c) If a party to the proceeding who is outside this state is directed to appear under subsection (b) of this section or desires to appear personally before the court with or without the child, the court may require another party to pay to the clerk of the court travel and other necessary expenses of the party so appearing and of the child if this is just and proper under the circumstances.

§ 32-1112. Binding force and res judicata effect of custody decree.

A custody decree rendered by a court of this state which had jurisdiction under section 32-1103, Idaho Code, binds all parties who have been served in this state or notified in accordance with section 32-1105, Idaho Code, or who have submitted to the jurisdiction of the court, and who have been given an opportunity to be heard. As to these parties the custody decree is conclusive as to all issues of law and fact decided and as to the custody determination made unless and until that determination is modified pursuant to law, including the provisions of this chapter.

§ 32-1113. Recognition of out-of-state custody decrees.

The courts of this state shall recognize and enforce an initial or modification decree of a court of another state which had assumed jurisdiction under statutory provisions substantially in accordance with this chapter or which was made under factual circumstances meeting the jurisdictional standards of the chapter, so long as this decree has not been modified in accordance with jurisdictional standards substantially similar to those of this chapter.

§ 32-1114. Modification of custody decree of another state.

(a) If a court of another state has made a custody decree, a court of this state shall not modify that decree unless (1) it appears that the court which rendered the decree does not have jurisdiction under jurisdictional prerequisites substantially in accordance with this chapter or has declined to assume jurisdiction to modify the decree and (2) the court of this state has jurisdiction.

(b) If a court of this state is authorized under subsection (a) of this section and section 32-1108, Idaho Code, to modify a custody decree of another state it shall give due consideration to the transcript of the record and other documents of all previous proceedings submitted to it in accordance with section 32-1123, Idaho Code.

§ 32-1115. Time and standard for modifying custody decree.

(a) No motion to modify a custody decree may be made earlier than two (2) years after its date, unless the court permits it to be made on the basis of affidavits that there is reason to believe the child's present environment may endanger seriously his physical, mental, moral or emotional health; except that nothing in this section shall be construed to prevent the court from reconsidering a custody decree entered upon legal separation in the event of application before the expiration of two (2) years by either party for a decree terminating the marriage.

(b) No modification decree shall be entered except upon a showing that a permanent material change has occurred since the prior decree and that it is in the best interests of the child that the decree be modified.

§ 32-1116. Filing and enforcement of custody decree of another state.

(a) A certified copy of a custody decree of another state may be filed in the office of the clerk of any district court of this state. The clerk shall treat the decree in the same manner as a custody decree of the district court of this state. A custody decree so filed has the same effect and shall be enforced in like manner as a custody decree rendered by a court of this state.

(b) A person violating a custody decree of another state which makes it necessary to enforce the decree in this state may be required to pay necessary travel and other expenses, including attorneys' fees, incurred by the party entitled to the custody or his witnesses.

§ 32-1117. Registry of out-of-state custody decrees and proceedings.

The clerk of each district court shall maintain a registry in which he shall enter the following:

(1) Certified copies of custody decrees of other states received for filing;

(2) Communications as to the pendency of custody proceedings in other states;

(3) Communications concerning a finding of inconvenient forum by a court of another state; and

(4) Other communications or documents concerning custody proceedings in another state which may affect the jurisdiction of a court of this state or the disposition to be made by it in a custody proceeding.

§ 32-1118. Certified copies of custody decree.

The clerk of a district court of this state, at the request of the court of another state or at the request of any person who is affected by or has a legitimate interest in a custody decree, shall certify and forward a copy of the decree to that court or person.

§ 32-1119. Testimony by deposition in another state.

In addition to other procedural devices available to a party, any party to the proceeding or a guardian ad litem or other representative of the child may adduce testimony of witnesses, including parties and the child, by deposition or otherwise, in another state. The court on its own motion may direct that the testimony of a person be taken in another state and may prescribe the manner in which and the terms upon which the testimony shall be taken.

§ 32-1120. Hearings and studies in another state.

(a) A court of this state may request the appropriate court of another state to hold a hearing to adduce evidence, to order a party to produce or give evidence under other procedures of that state, or to have social studies made with respect to the custody of a child involved in proceedings pending in the court of this state; and to forward to the court of this state certified copies of the transcript of the record of the hearing, the evidence otherwise adduced, or any social studies prepared in compliance with the request. The cost of the services may be assessed against the parties or, if necessary, ordered paid by the county.

(b) A court of this state may request the appropriate court of another state to order a party to custody proceedings pending in the court of this state to appear in the proceedings, and if that party has physical custody of the child, to appear with the child. The request may state that travel and other necessary expenses of the party and of the child whose appearance is desired will be assessed against another party or will otherwise be paid.

§ 32-1121. Assistance to courts of other states.

(a) Upon request of the court of another state the courts of this state which are competent to hear custody matters may order a person in this state to appear at a hearing to adduce evidence or to produce or give evidence under other procedures available in this state. A certified copy of the transcript of the record of the hearing or the evidence otherwise adduced shall be forwarded by the clerk of the court to the requesting court.

(b) A person within this state may voluntarily give his testimony or statement in this state for use in a custody proceeding outside this state.

(c) Upon request of the court of another state a competent court of this state may order a person in this state to appear alone or with the child in a custody proceeding in another state. The court may condition compliance with the request upon assurance by the other state that travel and other necessary expenses will be advanced or reimbursed.

§ 32-1122. Preservation of documents for use in other states.

In any custody proceeding in this state the court shall preserve the pleadings, orders and decrees, any record that has been made of its hearings, social studies, and other pertinent documents until the child reaches eighteen (18) years of age. Upon appropriate request of the court of another state the court shall forward to the other court certified copies of any or all of such documents.

§ 32-1123. Request for court records of another state.

If a custody decree has been rendered in another state concerning a child involved in a custody proceeding pending in a court of this state, the court of this state upon taking jurisdiction of the case shall request of the court of the other state a certified copy of the transcript of any court record and other documents mentioned in section 32-1122, Idaho Code.

§ 32-1124. International application.

The general policies of this chapter extend to the international area. The provisions of this chapter relating to the recognition and enforcement of custody decrees of other states apply to custody decrees and decrees involving legal institutions similar in nature to custody institutions rendered by appropriate authorities of other nations if reasonable notice and opportunity to be heard were given to all affected persons.

§ 32-1125. Priority.

Upon the request of a party to a custody proceeding which raises a question of existence or exercise of jurisdiction under this chapter the case shall be given calendar priority and handled expeditiously.

§ 32-1126. Short title.
This act may be cited as the "Uniform Child Custody Jurisdiction Act."

ILLINOIS

CHAPTER 40
UNIFORM CHILD CUSTODY JURISDICTION ACT

§ 2101. Short title.
This Act shall be known and may be cited as the "Uniform Child Custody Jurisdiction Act".

§ 2102. Purposes of Act - Construction of Provisions.
(a) The general purposes of this Act are to:

1. avoid jurisdictional competition and conflict with courts of other states in matters of child custody which have in the past resulted in the shifting of children from state to state with harmful effects on their well-being;

2. promote co-operation with the courts of other states to the end that a custody judgment is rendered in that state which can best decide the case in the interest of the child;

3. assure that litigation concerning the custody of a child take place ordinarily in the state with which the child and his family have the closest connection and where significant evidence concerning his care, protection, training, and personal relationships is most readily available, and that courts of this State decline the exercise of jurisdiction when the child and his family have a closer connection with another state;

4. discourage continuing controversies over child custody in the interest of greater stability of home environment and of secure family relationships for the child;

5. deter abductions and other unilateral removals of children undertaken to obtain custody awards;

6. avoid relitigation of custody decisions of other states in this State to the extent to which the avoidance of such relitigation is feasible;

7. facilitate the enforcement of custody judgments of other states;

8. promote and expand the exchange of information and other forms of mutual assistance between the courts of this State and those of other states concerned with the same child; and

9. make uniform the law of those states which enact it.

(b) This Act shall be construed to promote the general purposes stated in this Section.

§ 2103. Definitions.
As used in this Act unless the context otherwise requires, the terms specified in Sections 3.01 through 3.10 have the meanings ascribed to them in those Sections.

§ 2103.01. Contestant.
"Contestant" means a person, including a parent, who claims a right to custody or visitation rights with respect to a child.

§ 2103.02. Custody determination.
"Custody determination" means a court decision and court orders and instructions providing for the custody of a child, including visitation rights but such term does not include a decision relating to child support or any other monetary obligation of any person.

§ 2103.03. Custody proceeding.
"Custody proceeding" means proceedings in which a custody determination is one of several issues, and includes child neglect and dependency proceedings.

§ 2103.04. Home state.
"Home state" means the state in which the child immediately preceding the time involved lived with his parents, a parent, or a person acting as parent, for at least 6 consecutive months, and in the case of a child less than 6 months old the state in which the child lived from birth with any of the persons mentioned, however, periods of temporary absence of any of the named persons are counted as part of the 6-month or other period.

§ 2103.05. Initial judgment.

"Initial judgment" means the first custody judgment concerning a particular child.

§ 2103.06. Judgment or custody judgment.

"Judgment" or "custody judgment" means a custody determination made in a custody proceeding, and includes an initial judgment and a modification judgment.

§ 2103.07. Modification judgment.

"Modification judgment" means a custody judgment which modifies or replaces a prior judgment, whether made by the court which rendered the prior judgment or by another court.

§ 2103.08. Physical custody.

"Physical custody" means actual possession and control of a child.

§ 2103.09. Person acting as parent.

"Person acting as parent" means a person, other than a parent, who has physical custody of a child and who has either been awarded custody by a court or claims a right to custody.

§ 2103.10. State.

"State" means any state, territory, or possession of the United States, the Commonwealth of Puerto Rico, and the District of Columbia.

§ 2104. Jurisdiction.

(a) The circuit courts have jurisdiction to make a child custody determination by initial or modification judgment if:

    1. this State

        (i) is the home state of the child at the time of commencement of the proceeding, or

        (ii) had been the child's home state within 6 months before commencement of the proceeding and the child is absent from this State because of his removal or retention by a person claiming his custody or for other reasons, and a parent or person acting as a parent continues to live in this State; or

    2. it is in the best interest of the child that a court of this State assume jurisdiction because

        (i) the child and his parents, or the child and at least one contestant, have a significant connection with this State, and

        (ii) there is available in this State substantial evidence concerning the child's present or future care, protection, training, and personal relationships; or

    3. the child is physically present in this State and

        (i) the child has been abandoned or

        (ii) it is necessary in an emergency to protect the child because he has been subjected to or threatened with mistreatment or abuse or is otherwise neglected or dependent; or

    4. (i) it appears that no other state would have jurisdiction under prerequisites substantially in accordance with paragraphs 1., 2., or 3., or another state has declined to exercise jurisdiction on the ground that this State is the more appropriate forum to determine the custody of the child, and

        (ii) it is in the best interest of the child that this court assume jurisdiction.

(b) A court, once having obtained jurisdiction over a child, shall retain such jurisdiction unless it concedes jurisdiction to a foreign state or none of the parties to the action, including the child, remain in Illinois.

(c) Except under paragraphs 3. and 4. of subsection (a), physical presence in this State of the child, or of the child and one of the contestants, is not alone sufficient to confer jurisdiction on a court of this State to make a child custody determination.

(d) Physical presence of the child, while desirable, is not a prerequisite for jurisdiction to determine his custody.

§ 2105. Notice and opportunity to be heard.

Before making a judgment under this Act, reasonable notice and opportunity to be heard shall be given to the contestants, any parent whose parental rights have not been previously terminated, and any person who has physical custody of the child. If any of these persons is outside this State, notice and opportunity to be heard shall be given pursuant to Section 6.

§ 2106. Process and notice to persons outside this state.

(a) Process in initial custody proceedings shall be governed by the Civil Practice Law.

(b) Notice in all custody proceedings required for the exercise of jurisdiction over a person outside this State shall be given in a manner best calculated to give actual notice, and shall be either:

    1. by personal delivery outside this State in the manner prescribed for service of process within this State; or

2. in the manner prescribed by the law of the place in which the service is made for service of process in that place in an action in any of its courts of general jurisdiction; or

3. by any form of mail addressed to the person to be served and requesting a receipt; or

4. as directed by the court if other means of notification are ineffective.

(c) Notice under this Section shall be served, mailed or delivered at least 10 days before any hearing in this State.

(d) Proof of service outside this State may be made by affidavit of the individual who made the service, or in the manner prescribed by the law of this State, the order pursuant to which the service is made, or the law of the place in which the service is made. If service is made by mail, proof may be a receipt signed by the addressee or other evidence of delivery to the addressee.

§ 2107. Simultaneous proceedings in other states.

(a) A court of this State shall not exercise its jurisdiction under this Act if at the time of filing the petition a proceeding concerning the custody of the child was pending in a court of another state exercising jurisdiction substantially in conformity with this Act, unless the proceeding is stayed by the court of the other state because this State is a more appropriate forum or for other reasons.

(b) Before hearing the petition in a custody proceeding the court shall examine the pleadings and other information supplied by the parties under Section 10 and shall consult the child custody registry established under Section 17 concerning the pendency of proceedings with respect to the child in other states. If the court has reason to believe that proceedings may be pending in another state it shall direct an inquiry to the state court administrator or other appropriate official of the other state.

(c) If the court is informed during the course of the proceeding that a proceeding concerning the custody of the child was pending in another state before the court assumed jurisdiction it shall stay the proceeding and communicate with the court in which the other proceeding is pending to the end that the issue may be litigated in the more appropriate forum and that information be exchanged in accordance with Sections 20 through 23 of this Act. If a court of this State has made a custody judgment before being informed of a pending proceeding in a court of another state it shall immediately inform that court of the fact. If the court is informed that a proceeding was commenced in another state after it assumed jurisdiction it shall likewise inform the other court to the end that the issues may be litigated in the most appropriate forum.

§ 2108. Inconvenient forum.

(a) A court which has jurisdiction under this Act to make an initial or modification judgment may decline to exercise its jurisdiction any time before making a judgment if it finds that it is an inconvenient forum to make a custody determination under the circumstances of the case and that a court of another state is a more appropriate forum.

(b) A finding of inconvenient forum may be made upon the court's own motion or upon motion of a party or a guardian ad litem or other representative of the child.

(c) In determining if it is an inconvenient forum, the court shall consider if it is in the interest of the child that another state assume jurisdiction. For this purpose it may take into account the following factors, among others:

(d) Before determining whether to decline or retain jurisdiction the court may communicate with a court of another state and exchange information pertinent to the assumption of jurisdiction by either court with a view to assuring that jurisdiction will be exercised by the most appropriate court and that a forum will be available to the parties.

(e) If the court finds that it is an inconvenient forum and that a court of another state is a more appropriate forum, it may dismiss the proceedings upon condition that a custody proceeding be promptly commenced in another named state or upon any other conditions which may be just and proper, including the condition that a moving party stipulate his consent and submission to the jurisdiction of the other forum.

(f) The court may decline to exercise its jurisdiction under this Act if a custody determination is incidental to an action for dissolution of marriage or another proceeding while retaining jurisdiction over the action for dissolution of marriage or other proceeding.

(g) If it appears to the court that it is clearly an inappropriate forum it may require the party who commenced the proceedings to pay, in addition to the costs of the proceedings in this State, necessary travel and other expenses, including attorneys' fees, incurred by other parties or their witnesses. Payment is to be made to the clerk of the court for remittance to the proper party.

(h) Upon dismissal or stay of proceedings under this Section the court shall inform the court found to be the more appropriate forum of this fact, or if the court which would have jurisdiction in the other state is not certainly known, shall transmit the information to the court administrator or other appropriate official for forwarding to the appropriate court.

(i) Any communication received from another state informing this State of a finding of inconvenient forum because a court of this State is the more appropriate forum shall be filed in the custody registry of the appropriate court. Upon assuming jurisdiction the court of this State shall inform the original court of this fact.

§ 2109. Jurisdiction declined by reason of conduct.

(a) If the petitioner for an initial judgment has wrongfully taken the child from another state or has engaged in similar reprehensible conduct the court may decline to exercise jurisdiction if this is just and proper under the circumstances.

(b) Unless required in the interest of the child and subject to Section 15, paragraph (a), the court shall not exercise its jurisdiction to modify a custody judgment of another state if the petitioner, without consent of the person entitled to custody, has improperly removed the child from the physical custody of the person entitled to custody or has improperly retained the child after a visit or other temporary relinquishment of physical custody. If the petitioner has violated any other provision of a custody judgment of another state the court subject to Section 15, paragraph (a), may decline to exercise jurisdiction if this is just and proper under the circumstances.

(c) In appropriate cases a court dismissing a petition under this Section may charge the petitioner with necessary travel and other expenses, including attorneys' fees, incurred by other parties or their witnesses. Where the court finds that the petitioner has improperly removed the child from the physical custody of the person entitled to custody or has improperly retained the child after a visit or other temporary relinquishment of physical custody, the court shall notify the person entitled to custody as to the location of the child, as soon as is practicable.

§ 2110. Information under oath to be submitted to the court.

(a) Every party in a custody proceeding in his first pleading or in an affidavit attached to that pleading shall give information under oath as to the child's present address, the places where the child has lived within the last 5 years, and the names and present addresses of the persons with whom the child has lived during that period. In this pleading or affidavit every party shall further declare under oath if:

1. he has participated (as a party, witness, or in any other capacity) in any other litigation concerning the custody of the same child in this or any other state;

2. he has information of any custody proceeding concerning the child pending in a court of this or any other state; and

3. he knows of any person not a party to the proceedings who has physical custody of the child or claims to have custody or visitation rights with respect to the child.

(b) If the declaration as to any of the above items is in the affirmative the declarant shall give additional information under oath as required by the court. The court may examine the parties under oath as to details of the information furnished and as to other matters pertinent to the court's jurisdiction and the disposition of the case.

(c) Each party has a continuing duty to inform the court of any custody proceeding concerning the child in this or any other state of which he obtained information during this proceeding.

§ 2111. Additional parties.

If the court learns from information furnished by the parties pursuant to Section 10 or from other sources that a person not a party to the custody proceeding has physical custody of the child or claims to have custody or visitation rights with respect to the child, pursuant to an existing court order, it shall order that person to be joined as a party and to be duly notified of the pendency of the proceeding and of his joinder as a party. If the person joined as a party is outside this State he shall be served with process or otherwise notified in accordance with Section 6.

§ 2112. Appearance of parties and the child.

(a) The court may order any party to the proceeding who is in this State or over whom the court has personal jurisdiction to appear personally before the court. If that party has physical custody of the child the court may order that he appear personally with the child. For the protection of the child's best interests, the court may appoint counsel for the child. Reasonable attorney's fees shall be assessed in an equitable manner.

(b) If a party to the proceeding whose presence is desired by the court is outside this State with or without the child the court may order that the notice given under Section 5 include a statement directing that party to appear personally with or without the child and declaring that failure to appear may result in a decision adverse to that party.

(c) If a party to the proceeding who is outside this State is directed to appear under subsection (b) or desires to appear personally before the court with or without the child, the court may require another party to pay travel and other necessary expenses of the party so appearing and of the child if that is just and proper under the circumstances.

§ 2113. Binding force and res judicata effect of custody judgment.

A custody judgment rendered by a court of this State which had jurisdiction under Section 4 binds all parties who have been served in this State or notified in accordance with Section 6 or who have submitted to the jurisdiction of the court, and who have been given an opportunity to be heard. As to these parties the custody judgment is conclusive as to all issues of law and fact decided and as to the custody determination made unless and until that determination is modified pursuant to law, including the provisions of this Act.

§ 2114. Recognition of out-of-state custody judgments.

The courts of this State shall recognize and enforce an initial or modification judgment of a court of another state which had assumed jurisdiction under statutory provisions substantially in accordance with this Act or which was made under factual circumstances meeting the jurisdictional standards of the Act, so long as this judgment has not been modified in accordance with jurisdictional standards substantially similar to those of this Act.

§ 2115. Modification of custody judgment of another state.

(a) If a court of another state has made a custody judgment, a court of this State shall not modify that judgment unless:

1. it appears that the court which rendered the judgment does not have jurisdiction under jurisdictional prerequisites substantially in accordance with this Act or has declined to assume jurisdiction to modify the judgment or

2. the court of this State has jurisdiction.

(b) In a custody proceeding involving an out-of-state party, the court, prior to modifying a custody judgment, shall consult the registry of out-of-state judgments to determine whether there exists any communications or documents alleging that the child who is the subject of custody proceedings may have been improperly removed from the physical custody of the person entitled to custody or may have been improperly retained after a visit or other temporary relinquishment of physical custody. Where the court determines the existence of any such documents or communications, the court shall direct that notice of the pending custody proceedings be provided to the out-of-state party.

(c) If a court of this State is authorized under subsection (a) and Section 9 to modify a custody judgment of another state it shall give due consideration to the transcript of the record and other documents of all previous proceedings submitted to it in accordance with Section 23.

§ 2116. Filing and enforcement of custody judgment of another state.

(a) A certified copy of a custody judgment of another state may be filed in the office of the clerk of any circuit court of this State. The clerk shall treat the judgment in the same manner as a custody judgment of a circuit court of this State. A custody judgment so filed has the same effect and shall be enforced in like manner as a custody judgment rendered by a court of this State.

(b) A person violating a custody judgment of another state which makes it necessary to enforce the judgment in this State may be required to pay necessary travel and other expenses, including attorneys' fees, incurred by the party entitled to the custody or his witnesses.

§ 2117. Registry of out-of-state custody judgments and proceedings.

The clerk of each circuit court shall maintain a registry in which he shall enter the following:

(a) certified copies of custody judgments of other states received for filing;

(b) communications as to the pendency of custody proceedings in other states;

(c) communications concerning a finding of inconvenient forum by a court of another state;

(d) communications or documents concerning a child who may have been improperly removed from the physical custody of the person entitled to custody or may have been improperly retained after a visit or other temporary relinquishment of physical custody; and

(e) other communications or documents concerning custody proceedings in another state which may affect the jurisdiction of a court of this State or the disposition to be made by it in a custody proceeding.

The clerk of the court may provide for a schedule of fees for the registration of such judgments, communications or documents.

§ 2118. Certified copies of custody judgment.

The clerk of a circuit court of this State, at the request of the court of another state or at the request of any person who is affected by or has a legitimate interest in a custody judgment, shall certify and forward a copy of the judgment to that court or person.

The clerk of the court may charge a customary fee for such certification.

§ 2119. Testimony by deposition in another state.

In addition to other procedural devices available to a party any party to the proceeding or a guardian ad litem or other representative of the child may adduce testimony of witnesses, including parties and the child, by evidence or discovery deposition or otherwise, in another state. The court on its own motion may direct that the testimony of a person be taken in another state and may prescribe the manner in which and the terms upon which the testimony shall be taken.

§ 2120. Hearings and studies in another state.

(a) A court of this State may request the appropriate court of another state to hold a hearing to adduce evidence, to order a party to produce or give evidence under other procedures of that state, or to have social studies made with respect to the custody of a child involved in proceedings pending in the court of this State; and to forward to the court of this State certified copies of the transcript of the record of the hearing, the evidence otherwise adduced, or any social studies prepared in compliance with the request. The cost of the services may be assessed against the parties or, if necessary, ordered paid by the county.

(b) A court of this State may request the appropriate court of another state to order a party to custody proceedings pending in the court of this State to appear in the proceedings, and if that party has physical custody of the child, to appear with the child. The request may state that travel and other necessary expenses of the party and of the child whose appearance is desired will be assessed against another party or will otherwise be paid.

§ 2121. Assistance to courts of other states.

(a) Upon request of the court of another state the circuit courts of this State may order a person in this State to appear at a hearing to adduce evidence or to produce or give evidence under other procedures available in this State or may order social studies to be made for use in a custody proceeding in another state. A certified copy of the transcript of the record of the hearing or the evidence otherwise adduced and any social studies prepared shall be forwarded by the clerk of the court to the requesting court.

(b) A person within this State may voluntarily give his testimony or statement in this State for use in a custody proceeding outside this State.

(c) Upon request of the court of another state a circuit court of this State may order a person in this State to appear alone or with the child in a custody proceeding in another state. The court may condition compliance with the request upon assurance by the other state that travel and other necessary expenses will be advanced or reimbursed.

§ 2122. Preservation of documents for use in other states.

In any custody proceeding in this State the court shall preserve the pleadings, order and judgments, any record that has been made of its hearings, social studies, and other pertinent documents until the child reaches 21 years of age. Upon appropriate request of the court of another state the court shall forward to the other court certified copies of any or all of such documents.

§ 2123. Request for court records of another state.

If a custody judgment has been rendered in another state concerning a child involved in a custody proceeding pending in a court of this State, the court of this State upon taking jurisdiction of the case shall request of the court of the other state a certified copy of the transcript of any court record and other documents mentioned in Section 22.

§ 2124. International application.

The general policies of this Act extend to the international area. The provisions of this Act relating to the recognition and enforcement of custody judgments of other states apply to custody judgments and judgments involving legal institutions similar in nature to custody institutions rendered by appropriate authorities of other nations if reasonable notice and opportunity to be heard were given to all affected persons.

§ 2125. Priority.

Upon the request of a party to a custody proceeding which raises a question of existence or exercise of jurisdiction under this Act the case shall be given calendar priority and handled expeditiously.

§ 2126. Severability.

If any provision of this Act or the application thereof to any person or circumstance is held invalid, its invalidity does not affect other provisions or applications of the Act which can be given effect without the invalid provision or application, and to this end the provisions of this Act are severable.

INDIANA

UNIFORM CHILD CUSTODY JURISDICTION LAW

§ 31-1-11.6-1. Purposes and construction of law.

(a) The general purposes of this law are to:

(1) Avoid jurisdictional competition and conflict with courts of other states in matters of child custody which have in the past resulted in the shifting of children from state to state with harmful effects on their well-being;

(2) Promote cooperation with the courts of other states to the end that a custody decree is rendered in that state which can best decide the case in the interest of the child;

(3) Assure that litigation concerning the custody of a child take place ordinarily in the state with which the child and his family have the closest connection and where significant evidence concerning his care, protection, training, and personal relationships is most readily available, and that the courts of this state decline the exercise of jurisdiction when the child and his family have

a closer connection with another state;

(4) Discourage continuing controversies over child custody in the interest of greater stability of home environment and of secure family relationships for the child;

(5) Deter abductions and other unilateral removals of children undertaken to obtain custody awards;

(6) Avoid re-litigation of custody decisions of other states in this state insofar as feasible;

(7) Facilitate the enforcement of custody decrees of other states; and

(8) Promote and expand the exchange of information and other forms of mutual assistance between the courts of this state and those of other states concerned with the same child.

(b) This chapter shall be construed to promote the general purposes stated in this section.

§ 31-1-11.6-2. Definitions.

As used in this chapter:

(1) "Contestant" means a person, including a parent, who claims a right to custody or visitation rights with respect to a child;

(2) "Custody determination" means a court decision and court orders and instructions providing for the custody of a child, including visitation rights; it does not include a decision relating to child support or any other monetary obligation of any person;

(3) "Custody proceeding" includes proceedings in which a custody determination is one of several issues, such as an action for dissolution of marriage, and includes child neglect and dependency proceedings;

(4) "Decree" or "custody decree" means a custody determination contained in a judicial decree or order made in a custody proceeding, and includes an initial decree and a modification decree;

(5) "Home state" means the state in which the child, immediately preceding the time involved, lived with his parents, a parent, or a person acting as parent, for at least six [6] consecutive months, and in the case of a child less than six [6] months old the state in which the child lived from birth with any of the persons mentioned. Periods of temporary absence of any of the named persons are counted as part of the six-month or other period;

(6) "Initial decree" means the first custody decree concerning a particular child;

(7) "Modification decree" means a custody decree which modifies or replaces a prior decree, whether made by the court which rendered the prior decree or by another court;

(8) "Physical custody" means actual possession and control of a child;

(9) "Person acting as parent" means a person, other than a parent, who has physical custody of a child and who has either been awarded custody by a court or claims a right to custody; and

(10) "State" means any state, territory, or possession of the United States, the commonwealth of Puerto Rico, and the District of Columbia.

§ 31-1-11.6-3. Jurisdiction.

(a) A court of this state which is competent to decide child custody matters has jurisdiction to make a child custody determination by initial or modification decree if:

(1) This state (A) is the home state of the child at the time of commencement of the proceeding, or (B) had been the child's home state within six [6] months before commencement of the proceeding and the child is absent from this state because of his removal or retention by a person claiming his custody or for other reasons, and a parent or person acting as parent continues to live in this state; or

(2) It is in the best interest of the child that a court of this state assume jurisdiction because (A) the child and his parents, or the child and at least one contestant, have a significant connection with this state, and (B) there is available in this state substantial evidence concerning the child's present or future care, protection, training, and personal relationships; or

(3) The child is physically present in this state and (A) the child has been abandoned or (B) it is necessary in an emergency to protect the child because he has been subjected to or threatened with mistreatment or abuse or is otherwise neglected or dependent; or

(4) (A) It appears that no other state would have jurisdiction under prerequisites substantially in accordance with paragraphs (1), (2), or (3), or another state has declined to exercise jurisdiction on the grounds that this state is the more appropriate forum to determine the custody of the child, and (B) it is in the best interest of the child that this court assume jurisdiction.

(b) Except under paragraphs (3) and (4) of subsection (a), physical presence in this state of the child, or of the child and one [1] of the contestants, is not alone sufficient to confer jurisdiction on a court of this state to make a child custody determination.

(c) Physical presence of the child, while desirable, is not prerequisite for jurisdiction to determine his custody.

§ 31-1-11.6-4. Notice and opportunity to be heard.

Before making a decree under this chapter, reasonable notice and opportunity to be heard shall be given to the contestants, any parent whose parental rights have not been previously terminated, and any person who has physical custody of the child. If any of these persons is outside this state, notice and opportunity to be heard shall be given pursuant to section 5 [31-1-11.6-5] of this chapter.

§ 31-1-11.6-5. Notice to persons outside this state - Submission to jurisdiction.

(a) Notice required for the exercise of jurisdiction over a person outside this state shall be given in a manner reasonably calculated to give actual notice, and may be:

(1) By personal delivery outside this state in the manner prescribed for service of process within this state;

(2) In the manner prescribed by the law of the place in which the service is made for service of process in that place in an action in any of its courts of general jurisdiction;

(3) By and from of mail addressed to the person to be served and requesting a receipt; or

(4) As directed by the court.

(b) Notice under this section shall be served, mailed, or delivered, at least twenty [20] days before any hearing in this state.

(c) Proof of service outside this state may be made by affidavit of the individual who made the service, or in the manner prescribed by the law of this state, the order pursuant to which the service is made, or the law of the place in which the service is made. If service is made by mail, proof may be a receipt signed by the addressee or other evidence of delivery to the addressee.

(d) Notice is not required if a person submits to the jurisdiction of the court.

§ 31-1-11.6-6. Simultaneous proceedings in other states.

(a) A court of this state shall not exercise its jurisdiction under this chapter if at the time of filing the petition a proceeding concerning the custody of the child was pending in a court of another state exercising jurisdiction substantially in conformity with this chapter, unless the proceeding is stayed by the court of the other state because this state is a more appropriate forum or for other reasons.

(b) Before hearing the petition in a custody proceeding the court shall examine the pleadings and other information supplied by the parties under section 9 [31-1-11.6-9] of this chapter and shall consult the child custody registry established under section 16 [31-1-11.6-16] of this chapter concerning the pendency of proceedings with respect to the child in other states. If the court has reason to believe that proceedings may be pending in another state it shall direct an inquiry to the state court administrator or other appropriate official of the other state.

(c) If the court is informed during the course of the proceeding that a proceeding concerning the custody of the child was pending in another state before the court assumed jurisdiction it shall stay the proceeding and communicate with the court in which the other proceeding is pending to the end that the issue may be litigated in the more appropriate forum and that information be exchanged in accordance with sections 19 through 22 [31-1-11.6-19 - 31-1-11.6-22] of this chapter. If a court of this state has made a custody decree before being informed of a pending proceeding in a court of another state it shall immediately inform that court of the fact. If the court is informed that a proceeding was commenced in another state after it assumed jurisdiction it shall likewise inform the other court to the end that the issues may be litigated in the more appropriate forum.

§ 31-1-11.6-7. Inconvenient forum.

(a) A court which has jurisdiction under this chapter to make an initial or modification decree may decline to exercise its jurisdiction any time before making a decree if it finds that it is an inconvenient forum to make a custody determination under the circumstances of the case and that a court of another state is a more appropriate forum.

(b) A finding of inconvenient forum may be made upon the court's own motion or upon motion of a party or a guardian ad litem or other representative of the child.

(c) In determining if it is an inconvenient forum, the court shall consider if it is in the interest of the child that another state assume jurisdiction. For this purpose it may take into account the following factors, among others:

(1) If another state is or recently was the child's home state;

(2) If another state has a closer connection with the child and his family or with the child one or more of the contestants;

(3) If substantial evidence concerning the child's present or future care, protection, training, and personal relationships is more readily available in another state;

(4) If the parties have agreed on another forum which is no less appropriate; and

(5) If the exercise of jurisdiction by a court of this state would contravene any of the purposes stated in section 1 [31-1-11.6-1] of this chapter.

(d) Before determining whether to decline or retain jurisdiction the court may communicate with a court of another state and exchange information pertinent to the assumption of jurisdiction by either court with a view to assuring that jurisdiction will be exercised by the more appropriate court and that a forum will be available to the parties.

(e) If the court finds that it is an inconvenient forum and that a court of another state is a more appropriate forum, it may dismiss the proceedings, or it may stay the proceedings upon condition that a custody proceeding be promptly commenced in another named state or upon any other conditions which may be just and proper, including the condition that a moving party stipulate his consent and submission to the jurisdiction of the other forum.

(f) The court may decline to exercise its jurisdiction under this chapter if a custody determination is incidental to an action for dissolution of marriage or another proceeding while retaining jurisdiction over the dissolution of marriage or other proceeding.

(g) If it appears to the court that it is clearly an inappropriate forum it may require the party who commenced the proceedings to pay, in addition to the costs of the proceedings in this state, necessary travel and other expenses, including attorneys' fees,

incurred by other parties or their witnesses. Payment is to be made to the clerk of the court for remittance to the proper party.

(h) Upon dismissal or stay of proceedings under this section the court shall inform the court found to be the more appropriate forum of this fact, or if the court which would have jurisdiction in the other state is not certainly known, shall transmit the information to the court administrator or other appropriate official for forwarding to the appropriate court.

(i) Any communication received from another state informing this state of a finding of inconvenient forum because a court of this state is the more appropriate forum shall be filed in the custody registry of the appropriate court. Upon assuming jurisdiction the court of this state shall inform the original court of this fact.

§ 31-1-11.6-8. Denial of jurisdiction.

(a) If the petitioner for an initial decree has wrongfully taken the child from another state or has engaged in similar reprehensible conduct the court may decline to exercise jurisdiction if this is just and proper under the circumstances.

(b) Unless required in the interest of the child, the court shall not exercise its jurisdiction to modify a custody decree of another state if the petitioner, without consent of the person entitled to custody, has improperly removed the child from the physical custody of the person entitled to custody or has improperly retained the child after a visit or other temporary relinquishment of physical custody. If the petitioner has violated any other provision of a custody decree of another state the court may decline to exercise its jurisdiction if this is just and proper under the circumstances.

(c) In appropriate cases a court dismissing a petition under this section may charge the petitioner with necessary travel and other expenses, including attorneys' fees, incurred by other parties or their witnesses.

§ 31-1-11.6-9. Information to be submitted under oath.

(a) Every party in a custody proceeding, other than an action for dissolution of marriage, in his first pleading or in an affidavit attached to that pleading shall give information under oath as to the child's present address, the places where the child has lived within the last five [5] years, and the names and present addresses of the persons with whom the child has lived during that period. In this pleading or affidavit every party shall further declare under oath whether:

(1) He has participated (as a party, witness, or in any other capacity) in any other litigation concerning the custody of the same child in this or any other state;

(2) He has information of any custody proceeding concerning the child pending in a court of this or any other state; and

(3) He knows of any person not a party to the proceedings who has physical custody of the child or claims to have custody or visitation rights with respect to the child.

(b) If the declaration as to any of the above items is in the affirmative the declarant shall give additional information under oath as required by the court. The court may examine the parties under oath as to details of the information furnished and as to other matters pertinent to the court's jurisdiction and the disposition of the case.

(c) Each party has a continuing duty to inform the court of any custody proceeding concerning the child in this or any other state of which he obtained information during this proceeding.

§ 31-1-11.6-10. Additional parties.

If the court learns from information furnished by the parties pursuant to section 9 [31-1-11.6-9] of this chapter or from other sources that a person not a party to the custody proceeding has physical custody of the child or claims to have custody or visitation rights with respect to the child, it shall order that person to be joined as a party and to be duly notified of the pendency of the proceeding and of his joinder as a party. If the person joined as a party is outside this state he shall be served with process or otherwise notified in accordance with section 5 [31-1-11.6-5] of this chapter.

§ 31-1-11.6-11. Appearance of the parties and the child.

(a) The court may order any party to the proceeding who is in this state to appear personally before the court. If that party has physical custody of the child the court may order that he appear personally with the child.

(b) If a party to the proceeding whose presence is desired by the court is outside this state with or without the child the court may order that the notice given under section 5 [31-1-11.6-5] of this chapter include a statement directing that party to appear personally with or without the child and declaring that failure to appear may result in a decision adverse to that party.

(c) If a party to the proceeding who is outside this state is directed to appear under subsection (b) or desires to appear personally before the court with or without the child, the court may require another party to pay to the clerk of the court travel and other necessary expenses of the party so appearing and of the child if this is just and proper under the circumstances.

§ 31-1-11.6-12. Binding force and res judicata effect of custody decree.

A custody decree rendered by a court of this state which had jurisdiction under section 3 [31-1-11.6-3] of this chapter binds all parties who have been served in this state or notified in accordance with section 5 [31-1-11.6-5] of this chapter or who have submitted to the jurisdiction of the court, and who have been given an opportunity to be heard. As to these parties the custody decree is conclusive as to all issues of law and fact decided and as to the custody determination made unless and until that determination is modified pursuant to law, including the provisions of this chapter.

§ 31-1-11.6-13. Recognition of out-of-state custody decrees.

The courts of this state shall recognize and enforce an initial or modification decree of a court of another state which had assumed jurisdiction under statutory provisions substantially in accordance with this chapter or which was made under factual circumstances meeting the jurisdictional standards of this chapter, so long as this decree has not been modified in accordance with jurisdictional standards substantially similar to those of this chapter.

§ 31-1-11.6-14. Modification of custody decree of another state.

(a) If a court of another state has made a custody decree, a court of this state shall not modify that decree unless (1) it appears to the court of this state that the court which rendered the decree does not now have jurisdiction under jurisdictional prerequisites substantially in accordance with this chapter or has declined to assume jurisdiction to modify the decree and (2) the court of this state has jurisdiction.

(b) If a court of this state is authorized under section 8(a) [31-1-11.6-8(a)] of this chapter to modify a custody decree of another state it shall give due consideration to the transcript of the record and other documents of all previous proceedings submitted to it in accordance with section 22 [31-1-11.6-22] of this chapter.

§ 31-1-11.6-15. Filing and enforcement of custody decree of another state.

(a) A certified copy of a custody decree of another state may be filed in the office of the clerk of any circuit court of this state. The clerk shall treat the decree in the same manner as a custody decree of a circuit or superior court, or any court of this state which is competent to decide child custody matters. A custody decree so filed has the same effect and shall be enforced in like manner as a custody decree rendered by a court of this state.

(b) A person violating a custody decree of another state which makes it necessary to enforce the decree in this state may be required to pay necessary travel and other expenses, including attorneys' fees, incurred by the party entitled to the custody or his witnesses.

§ 31-1-11.6-16. Registry of out-of-state custody decrees and proceedings.

The clerk of each circuit court shall maintain a registry in which he shall enter the following:

(1) Certified copies of custody decrees of other states received for filing;

(2) Communications as to the pendency of custody proceedings in other states;

(3) Communications concerning a finding of inconvenient forum by a court of another state; and

(4) Other communications or documents concerning custody proceedings in another state which may affect the jurisdiction of a court of this state or the disposition to be made by it in a custody proceeding.

§ 31-1-11.6-17. Certified copies of custody decree.

The clerk of the circuit court of this state, at the request of the court of another state or at the request of any person who is affected by or has legitimate interest in a custody decree, shall certify and forward a copy of the decree to that court or person.

§ 31-1-11.6-18. Taking testimony in another state.

In addition to other procedural devices available to a party, any party to the proceeding or a guardian ad litem or other representatives of the child may adduce testimony of witnesses, including parties and the child, by deposition or otherwise, in another state. The court on its own motion may direct that the testimony of a person be taken in another state and may prescribe the manner in which and the terms upon which the testimony shall be taken.

§ 31-1-11.6-19. Hearings and studies in another state - Orders to appear.

(a) A court of this state may request the appropriate court of another state to hold a hearing to adduce evidence, to order a party to produce or give evidence under other procedures of that state, or to have social studies (an investigation and report pursuant to IC 31-1-11.5-22) made with respect to the custody of a child involved in proceedings pending in the court of this state; and to forward to the court of this state certified copies of the transcript of the record of the hearing, the evidence otherwise adduced, or any social studies prepared in compliance with the request. The cost of the services may be assessed against the parties, or, if necessary, ordered paid by the county.

(b) A court of this state may request the appropriate court of another state to order a party to custody proceedings pending in the court of this state to appear in the proceedings, and if that party has physical custody of the child, to appear with the child. The request may state that travel and other necessary expenses of the party and of the child whose appearance is desired will be assessed against another party or will otherwise be paid.

§ 31-1-11.6-20. Assistance to courts of other states.

(a) Upon request of the court of another state, the courts of this state which are competent to hear custody matters may order a person in this state to appear at a hearing to adduce evidence or to produce or give evidence under other procedures available in this state or may order social studies to be made for use in a custody proceeding in another state. A certified copy of the transcript of the record of the hearing or the evidence otherwise adduced and any social studies prepared shall be forwarded by the clerk of the court to the requesting court.

(b) A person within this state may voluntarily give his testimony or statement in this state for use in a custody proceeding outside this state.

(c) Upon request of the court of another state a competent court of this state may order a person in this state to appear alone or with the child in a custody proceeding in another state. The court may condition compliance with the request upon assurance by the other state that travel and other necessary expenses will be advanced or reimbursed.

§ 31-1-11.6-21. Preservation of documents for use in other states.

In any custody proceeding in this state the court shall preserve the pleadings, orders and decrees, any record that has been made of its hearings, social studies, and other pertinent documents until the child reaches twenty-one [21] years of age. Upon appropriate request of the court of another state the court shall forward to the other court certified copies of any or all of such documents.

§ 31-1-11.6-22. Request for court records of another state.

If a custody decree has been rendered in another state concerning a child involved in a custody proceeding pending in a court of this state, the court of this state upon taking jurisdiction of the case shall request of the court of the other state a certified copy of the transcript of any court record and other documents mentioned in section 21 [31-1-11.6-21] of this chapter.

§ 31-1-11.6-23. International application.

The general policies of this chapter extend to the international area. Except as provided in section 25 [31-1-11.6-25] of this chapter, the provisions of this chapter relating to the recognition and enforcement of custody decrees of other states apply to custody decrees and decrees involving legal institutions similar in nature to custody rendered by appropriate authorities of other nations if reasonable notice and opportunity to be heard were given to all affected persons.

§ 31-1-11.6-24. Priority.

Upon the request of a party to a custody proceeding which raises a question of existence or exercise of jurisdiction under this chapter the case shall be given calendar priority and handled expeditiously.

§ 31-1-11.6-25. Child custody and support determination by modification decree.

(a) Notwithstanding sections 3, 7, and 8 [31-1-11.6-3, 31-1-11.6-7, and 31-1-11.6-8] of this chapter, a court of this state has jurisdiction to make a child custody and support determination by modification decree if:

(1) The child is a citizen of the United States;

(2) A determination concerning the custody of the child has been made by a court in another nation;

(3) The child is physically present in this state; and

(4) There is a reasonable probability that the child will be moved outside of the United States if a determination concerning the custody of the child made by a court in another nation is given effect in the United States.

(b) If a court has jurisdiction to make a child custody and support determination under subsection (a), a parent or guardian of a child may file a petition seeking a modification decree concerning the custody and support of the child. The petition must be entitled "In re the modification of a determination concerning the custody and support of _____." The petition shall be verified and must set forth:

(1) The relationship of the parties;

(2) The present residence of each party;

(3) The name, age, and address of each child who will be affected by the modification decree sought under this subsection;

(4) A statement that the court has jurisdiction to make a child custody and support determination under subsection (a); and

(5) The relief sought.

A responsive pleading or a counter petition may be filed under this subsection. Proceedings provided for in this subsection must comply with the Indiana Rules of Trial Procedure.

(c) The court shall hold a hearing on the petition filed under subsection (b). At the hearing, the court shall hear evidence to determine whether the child custody and support determination should be modified. In making this determination, the court shall base its decision upon the best interests of the child, considering all relevant factors, including the factors set out in IC 31-1-11.5-12(a).

IOWA

UNIFORM CHILD CUSTODY JURISDICTION ACT

§ 598A.1. Legislative intent.

The general purposes of this chapter are to:

1. Avoid jurisdictional competition and conflict with courts of other states in matters of child custody, which have in the past resulted in the shifting of children from state to state with harmful effects on their well being.

2. Promote co-operation with the courts of other states to the end that a custody decree is rendered in the state which can best decide the case in the interest of the child.

3. Assure that litigation concerning the custody of a child takes place ordinarily in the state with which the child and the family have the closest connection and where significant evidence concerning the child's care, protection, training, and personal relationships is most readily available, and that courts of this state decline the exercise of jurisdiction when the child and the family have a closer connection with another state.

4. Discourage continuing controversies over child custody, in the interest of greater stability of home environment and of secure family relationships for the child.

5. Deter abductions and other unilateral removals of children undertaken to obtain custody awards.

6. Avoid relitigation of custody decisions of other states in this state insofar as feasible.

7. Facilitate the enforcement of custody decrees of other states.

8. Promote and expand the exchange of information and other forms of mutual assistance between the courts of this state and those of other states concerned with the same child.

9. Make uniform the law of those states which enact it.

This chapter shall be construed to promote the general purposes stated in this section.

§ 598A.2. Definitions.

As used in this chapter, unless the context otherwise requires:

1. "Contestant" means a person, including a parent, who claims a right to custody or visitation rights with respect to a child.

2. "Custody determination" means a court decision and court orders and instructions providing for the custody of a child, including visitation rights; it does not include a decision relating to child support or any other monetary obligation of any person.

3. "Custody proceeding" includes proceedings in which a custody determination is one of several issues, such as an action for divorce or separation, and includes child neglect and dependency proceedings.

4. "Decree" or "custody decree" means a custody determination contained in a judicial decree or order made in a custody proceeding, and includes an initial decree and a modification decree.

5. "Home state" means the state in which the child, immediately preceding the time involved, lived with the child's parents, a parent, or a person acting as parent, for at least six consecutive months, and in the case of a child less than six months old the state in which the child lived from birth with any of the persons mentioned. Periods of temporary absence of any of the named persons are counted as part of the six-month or other period.

6. "Initial decree" means the first custody decree concerning a particular child.

7. "Modification decree" means a custody decree which modifies or replaces a prior decree, whether made by the court which rendered the prior decree or by another court.

8. "Physical custody" means actual possession and control of a child.

9. "Person acting as parent" means a person, other than a parent, who has physical custody of a child and who has either been awarded custody by a court or claims a right to custody.

10. "State" means any state, territory, or possession of the United States, the Commonwealth of Puerto Rico, and the District of Columbia.

§ 598A.3. Jurisdiction.

1. A court of this state which is competent to decide child custody matters has jurisdiction to make a custody determination by initial or modification decree if:

a. This state is the home state of the child at the time of commencement of the proceeding, or had been the child's home state within six months before commencement of the proceeding and the child is absent from this state because of removal or retention by a person claiming custody or for other reasons, and a parent or person acting as parent continues to live in this state; or

b. It is in the best interest of the child that a court of this state assume jurisdiction because the child and the child's parents, or the child and at least one contestant, have a significant connection with this state, and there is available in this state substantial evidence concerning the child's present or future care, protection, training, and personal relationships; or

c. The child is physically present in this state, and the child has been abandoned or it is necessary in an emergency to protect the child because the child has been subjected to or threatened with mistreatment or abuse or is otherwise neglected or dependent; or

d. It appears that no other state would have jurisdiction under prerequisites substantially in accordance with paragraph "a", "b", or "c", or another state has declined to exercise jurisdiction on the ground that this state is the more appropriate forum to determine the custody of the child, and it is in the best interest of the child that this court assume jurisdiction.

2. Except under paragraphs "c" and "d" of subsection 1, physical presence in this state of the child, or of the child and one of the contestants, is not alone sufficient to confer jurisdiction on a court of this state to make a custody determination.

3. Physical presence of the child, while desirable, is not a prerequisite for jurisdiction to determine custody.

§ 598A.4. Notice - to whom.

Before making a decree under this chapter, reasonable notice and opportunity to be heard shall be given to the contestants, any parent whose parental rights have not been previously terminated, and any person who has physical custody of the child. If any of these persons is outside this state, notice and opportunity to be heard shall be given pursuant to section 598A.5.

§ 598A.5. Notice - methods.

Notice required for the exercise of jurisdiction over a person outside this state shall be given in a manner reasonably calculated to give actual notice, and may be:

1. By personal delivery outside this state in the manner prescribed for service of process within this state;

2. In the manner prescribed by the law of the place in which the service is made for service of process in that place in an action in any of its courts of general jurisdiction;

3. By publication and mailing in accordance with Iowa rules of civil procedure 60 to 63; or

4. As directed by the court.

Notice under this section shall be served, mailed, delivered, or last published at least twenty days before any hearing in this state.

Proof of service outside this state may be made by affidavit of the individual who made the service, or in the manner prescribed by the law of this state, the order pursuant to which the service is made, or the law of the place in which the service is made.

§ 598A.6. Jurisdiction withheld.

A court of this state shall not exercise its jurisdiction under this chapter if at the time of filing the petition a proceeding concerning the custody of the child was pending in a court of another state exercising jurisdiction substantially in conformity with this chapter, unless the proceeding is stayed by the court of the other state because this state is a more appropriate forum or for other reasons.

Before hearing the petition in a custody proceeding, the court shall examine the pleadings and other information supplied by the parties under section 598A.9 and shall consult the child-custody registry established under section 598A.16 concerning the pendency of proceedings with respect to the child in other states. If the court has reason to believe that proceedings may be pending in another state it shall direct an inquiry to the state court administrator or other appropriate official of the other state.

If the court is informed during the course of the proceeding that a proceeding concerning the custody of the child was pending in another state before the court assumed jurisdiction, it shall stay the proceeding and communicate with the court in which the other proceeding is pending, to the end that the issue may be litigated in the more appropriate forum and that information may be exchanged in accordance with sections 598A.19 to 598A.22. If a court of this state has made a custody decree before being informed of a pending proceeding in a court of another state, it shall immediately inform that court of the fact. If the court is informed that a proceeding was commenced in another state after it assumed jurisdiction, it shall likewise inform the other court, to the end that the issues may be litigated in the more appropriate forum.

§ 598A.7. Inconvenient forum.

1. A court which has jurisdiction under this chapter to make an initial or modification decree may decline to exercise its jurisdiction any time before making a decree if it finds that it is an inconvenient forum to make a custody determination under the circumstances of the case, and that a court of another state is a more appropriate forum.

2. A finding of inconvenient forum may be made upon the court's own motion or upon motion of a party or a guardian ad litem or other representative of the child.

3. In determining if it is an inconvenient forum, the court shall consider if it is in the interest of the child that another state assume jurisdiction. For this purpose it may take into account the following factors, among others:

a. Whether another state is or recently was the child's home state.

b. Whether another state has a closer connection with the child and the child's family or with the child and one or more of the contestants.

c. Whether substantial evidence concerning the child's present or future care, protection, training, and personal relationships is more readily available in another state.

d. Whether the parties have agreed on another forum which is no less appropriate.

e. Whether the exercise of jurisdiction by a court of this state would contravene any of the purposes stated in section 598A.1.

4. Before determining whether to decline or retain jurisdiction, the court may communicate with a court of another state and exchange information pertinent to the assumption of jurisdiction by either court, with a view to assuring that jurisdiction will be exercised by the more appropriate court and that a forum will be available to the parties.

5. If the court finds that is is an inconvenient forum and that a court of another state is a more appropriate forum, it may dismiss the proceedings, or it may stay the proceedings upon condition that a custody proceeding be promptly commenced in another named state, or upon any other conditions which may be just and proper, including the condition that a moving party give consent and submit to the jurisdiction of the other forum.

6. The court may decline to exercise its jurisdiction under this chapter if a custody determination is incidental to an action for divorce or another proceeding, while retaining jurisdiction over the divorce or other proceeding.

7. If it appears to the court that it is clearly an inappropriate forum, it may require the party who commenced the proceedings to pay, in addition to the costs of the proceedings in this state, necessary travel and other expenses, including attorneys' fees, incurred by other parties or their witnesses. Payment is to be made to the clerk of the court for remittance to the proper party.

8. Upon dismissal or stay of proceedings under this section, the court shall inform the court found to be the more appropriate forum of this fact, or if the court which would have jurisdiction in the other state is not known, shall transmit the information to the court administrator or other appropriate official for forwarding to the appropriate court.

9. Any communication received from another state informing this state of a finding of inconvenient forum because a court of this state is the more appropriate forum shall be filed in the custody registry of the appropriate court. Upon assuming jurisdiction, the court of this state shall inform the original court of this fact.

§ 598A.8. Jurisdiction declined by reason of conduct.

1. If the petitioner for an initial decree has wrongfully taken the child from another state or has engaged in similar reprehensible conduct, the court may decline to exercise jurisdiction if this is just and proper under the circumstances.

2. Unless required in the interest of the child, the court shall not exercise its jurisdiction to modify a custody decree of another state if the petitioner, without consent of the person entitled to custody, has improperly removed the child from the physical custody of the person entitled to custody or has improperly retained the child after a visit or other temporary relinquishment of physical custody. If the petitioner has violated any other provision of a custody decree of another state, the court may decline to exercise its jurisdiction if this is just and proper under the circumstances.

3. In appropriate cases a court dismissing a petition under this section may charge the petitioner with necessary travel and other expenses, including attorneys' fees, incurred by other parties or their witnesses.

§ 598A.9. Information submitted to court.

1. Every party in a custody proceeding, in that party's first pleading or in an affidavit attached to that pleading, shall give information under oath as to the child's present address, the places where the child has lived within the last five years, and the names and present addresses of the persons with whom the child has lived during that period. In this pleading or affidavit every party shall further declare under oath whether he or she:

a. Has participated as a party, witness or in any other capacity, in any other litigation concerning the custody of the same child in this or any other state.

b. Has information of any custody proceeding concerning the child pending in a court of this or any other state.

c. Knows of any person not a party to the proceedings who has physical custody of the child or claims to have custody or visitation rights with respect to the child.

2. If the declaration as to any of the above items is in the affirmative the declarant shall give additional information under oath as required by the court. The court may examine the parties under oath as to details of the information furnished and as to other matters pertinent to the court's jurisdiction and the disposition of the case.

3. Each party has a continuing duty to inform the court of any custody proceeding concerning the child in this or any other state, of which that party obtained information during this proceeding.

§ 598A.10. Additional parties.

If the court learns from information furnished by the parties pursuant to section 598A.9, or from other sources, that a person not a party to the custody proceeding has physical custody of the child or claims to have custody or visitation rights with respect to the child, it shall order that person to be joined as a party and to be duly notified of the pendency of the proceeding and of that person's joinder as a party. If the person joined as a party is outside this state, he or she shall be served with process or otherwise notified in accordance with section 598A.5.

§ 598A.11. Appearance.

1. The court may order any party to the proceeding who is in this state to appear personally before the court. If that party has physical custody of the child, the court may order that person to appear personally with the child.

2. If a party to the proceeding whose presence is desired by the court is outside this state with or without the child, the court may order that the notice given under section 598A.5 include a statement directing that party to appear personally with or without

the child, and declaring that failure to appear may result in a decision adverse to that party.

3. If a party to the proceeding who is outside this state is directed to appear or desires to appear personally before the court with or without the child, the court may require another party to pay to the clerk of the court travel and other necessary expenses of the party so appearing and of the child, if this is just and proper under the circumstances.

§ 598A.12. Effect of custody decree.

A custody decree rendered by a court of this state which had jurisdiction under section 598A.3 binds all parties who have been served in this state or notified in accordance with section 598A.5, or who have submitted to the jurisdiction of the court, and who have been given an opportunity to be heard. As to these parties the custody decree is conclusive as to all issues of law and fact decided and as to the custody determination made, unless and until that determination is modified pursuant to law.

§ 598A.13. Out-of-state custody decree.

The courts of this state shall recognize and enforce an initial or modification decree of a court of another state which had assumed jurisdiction under statutory provisions substantially in accordance with this chapter, or which was made under factual circumstances meeting the jurisdictional standards of this chapter, so long as this decree has not been modified in accordance with jurisdictional standards substantially similar to those of this chapter.

§ 598A.14. Modification of custody decree of another state.

If a court of another state has made a custody decree, a court of this state shall not modify that decree unless it appears to the court of this state that the court which rendered the decree does not now have jurisdiction under jurisdictional prerequisites substantially in accordance with this chapter, or has declined to assume jurisdiction to modify the decree, and the court of this state has jurisdiction.

If a court of this state is authorized under this section and section 598A.8 to modify a custody decree of another state, it shall give due consideration to the transcript of the record and other documents of all previous proceedings submitted to it in accordance with section 598A.22.

§ 598A.15. Filing and enforcement of out-of-state decrees.

A certified copy of a custody decree of another state may be filed in the office of the clerk of any district court of this state. The clerk shall treat the decree in the same manner as a custody decree of the district court of this state. A custody decree so filed has the same effect and shall be enforced in like manner as a custody decree rendered by a court of this state.

A person violating a custody decree of another state, which makes it necessary to enforce the decree in this state, may be required to pay necessary travel and other expenses, including attorney's fees, incurred by the party entitled to the custody or by that party's witnesses.

§ 598A.16. Registry of out-of-state decrees.

The clerk of each district court shall maintain a registry in which shall be entered the following:

1. Certified copies of custody decrees of other states received for filing.
2. Communications as to the pendency of custody proceedings in other states.
3. Communications concerning a finding of inconvenient forum by a court of another state.
4. Other communications or documents concerning custody proceedings in another state which may affect the jurisdiction of a court of this state or the disposition to be made by it in a custody proceeding.

§ 598A.17. Certified copies.

The clerk of the district court of this state, at the request of the court of another state or at the request of any person who is affected by or has a legitimate interest in a custody decree, shall certify and forward a copy of the decree to that court or person.

§ 598A.18. Taking testimony in another state.

In addition to other procedural devices available to a party, any party to the proceeding or a guardian ad litem or other representative of the child may adduce testimony of witnesses, including parties and the child, by deposition or otherwise, in another state. The court on its own motion may direct that the testimony of a person be taken in another state and may prescribe the manner in which and the terms upon which the testimony shall be taken.

§ 598A.19. Hearings in another state.

A court of this state may request the appropriate court of another state to hold a hearing to adduce evidence, to order a party to produce or give evidence under other procedures of that state, or to have social studies made with respect to the custody of a child involved in proceedings pending in the court of this state; and to forward to the court of this state certified copies of the transcript of the record of the hearing, the evidence otherwise adduced, or any social studies prepared in compliance with the request. The cost of the services may be assessed against the parties or, if necessary, ordered paid by the county.

A court of this state may request the appropriate court of another state to order a party to custody proceedings pending in the court of this state to appear in the proceedings, and if that party has physical custody of the child, to appear with the child. The request may state that travel and other necessary expenses of the party and of the child whose appearance is desired will be assessed against another party or will otherwise be paid.

§ 598A.20. Assistance to courts of other states.

Upon request of the court of another state, the courts of this state which are competent to hear custody matters may order a person in this state to appear at a hearing to adduce evidence or to produce or give evidence under other procedures available in this state, or may order social studies to be made for use in a custody proceeding in another state. A certified copy of the transcript of the record of the hearing or the evidence otherwise adduced, and any social studies prepared, shall be forwarded by the clerk of the court to the requesting court.

A person within this state may voluntarily give testimony or a statement in this state for use in a custody proceeding outside this state.

Upon request of the court of another state, a competent court of this state may order a person in this state to appear alone or with the child in a custody proceeding in another state. The court may condition compliance with the request upon assurance by the other state that state travel and other necessary expenses will be advanced or reimbursed.

§ 598A.21. Preservation of documents.

In any custody proceeding in this state, the court shall preserve the pleadings, orders and decrees, and any record that has been made of its hearings, social studies, and other pertinent documents until the child reaches eighteen years of age. Upon appropriate request of the court of another state, the court shall forward to the other court certified copies of any or all of such documents.

§ 598A.22. Request for records.

If a custody decree has been rendered in another state concerning a child involved in a custody proceeding pending in a court of this state, the court of this state upon taking jurisdiction of the case shall request of the court of the other state a certified copy of the transcript of any court record and other documents mentioned in section 598A.21.

§ 598A.23. International application.

The general policies of this chapter extend to the international area. The provisions of this chapter relating to the recognition and enforcement of custody decrees of other states apply to custody decrees and decrees involving legal institutions similar in nature to custody institutions rendered by appropriate authorities of other nations, if reasonable notice and opportunity to be heard were given to all affected persons.

§ 598A.24. Judicial priority.

Upon the request of a party to a custody proceeding which raises a question of existence or exercise of jurisdiction under this chapter, the case shall be given calendar priority and handled expeditiously.

§ 598A.25. Short title.

This chapter may be cited as the "Uniform Child Custody Jurisdiction Act".

KANSAS

UNIFORM CHILD CUSTODY JURISDICTION ACT

§ 38-1301. Purposes of act; construction of provisions.

(a) The general purposes of this act are to:

(1) Avoid jurisdictional competition and conflict with courts of other states in matters of child custody which have in the past resulted in the shifting of children from state to state with harmful effects on their well-being;

(2) promote cooperation with the courts of other states to the end that a custody decree is rendered in that state which can best decide the case in the interest of the child;

(3) assure that litigation concerning the custody of a child take place ordinarily in the state with which the child and the child's family have the closest connection and where significant evidence concerning the child's care, protection, training, and

personal relationships is most readily available, and that courts of this state decline the exercise of jurisdiction when the child and the child's family have a closer connection with another state;

(4) discourage continuing controversies over child custody in the interest of greater stability of home environment and of secure family relationships for the child;

(5) deter abductions and other unilateral removals of children undertaken to obtain custody awards;

(6) avoid re-litigation of custody decisions of other states in this state insofar as feasible;

(7) facilitate the enforcement of custody decrees of other states;

(8) promote and expand the exchange of information and other forms of mutual assistance between the courts of this state and those of other states concerned with the same child; and

(9) make uniform the law of those states which enact it.

(b) This act shall be construed to promote the general purposes stated in this section.

§ 38-1302. Definitions.

As used in the uniform child custody jurisdiction act:

(a) "Contestant" means a person, including a parent, who claims a right to custody or visitation rights with respect to a child.

(b) "Custody determination" means a court decision and court orders and instructions providing for the custody of a child, including visitation rights; it does not include a decision relating to child support or any other monetary obligation of any person.

(c) "Custody proceeding" includes proceedings in which a custody determination is one of several issues, such as an action for divorce or separation, and includes proceedings under the Kansas code for care of children.

(d) "Decree" or "custody decree" means a custody determination contained in a judicial decree or order made in a custody proceeding, and includes an initial decree and a modification decree.

(e) "Home state" means the state in which the child immediately preceding the time involved lived with the child's parents, a parent, or a person acting as parent, for at least six consecutive months, and in the case of a child less than six months old the state in which the child lived from birth with any of the persons mentioned. Periods of temporary absence of any of the named persons are counted as part of the six-month or other period.

(f) "Initial decree" means the first custody decree concerning a particular child.

(g) "Modification decree" means the first custody decree modifies or replaces a prior decree, whether made by the court which rendered the prior decree or by another court.

(h) "Physical custody" means actual possession and control of a child.

(i) "Person acting as parent" means a person, other than a parent, who has physical custody of a child and who has either been awarded custody by a court or claims a right to custody.

(j) "State" means any state, territory, or possession of the United States, the Commonwealth of Puerto Rico, and the District of Columbia.

§ 38-1303. Jurisdiction.

(a) A court of this state which is competent to decide child custody matters has jurisdiction to make a child custody determination by initial or modification decree if:

(1) This state (A) is the home state of the child at the time of commencement of the proceeding, or (B) had been the child's home state within six months before commencement of the proceeding and the child is absent from this state because of the child's removal or retention by a person claiming the child's custody or for other reasons, and a parent or person acting as parent continues to live in this state; or

(2) it is in the best interest of the child that a court of this state assume jurisdiction because (A) the child and the child's parents, or the child and at least one contestant, have a significant connection with this state, and (B) there is available in this state substantial evidence concerning the child's present or future care, protection, training, and personal relationships; or

(3) the child is physically present in this state and (A) the child has been abandoned or (B) it is necessary in an emergency to protect the child because the child has been subjected to or threatened with mistreatment or abuse or is otherwise a child in need of care; or

(4) (A) it appears that no other state would have jurisdiction under prerequisites substantially in accordance with paragraphs (1), (2), or (3), or another state has declined to exercise jurisdiction on the ground that this state is the more appropriate forum to determine the custody of the child, and (B) it is in the best interest of the child that this court assume jurisdiction.

(b) Except under paragraphs (3) and (4) of subsection (a), physical presence in this state of the child, or of the child and one of the contestants, is not alone sufficient to confer jurisdiction on a court of this state to make a child custody determination.

(c) Physical presence of the child, while desirable, is not a prerequisite for jurisdiction to determine the child's custody.

§ 38-1304. Notice and opportunity to be heard.

Before making a decree under this act, reasonable notice and opportunity to be heard shall be given to the contestants, any parent whose parental rights have not been previously terminated, and any person who has physical custody of the child. If any of these persons is outside this state, notice and opportunity to be heard shall be given pursuant to K.S.A. 38-1305.

§ 38-1305. Notice to persons outside this state; submission to jurisdiction.

(a) Notice required for the exercise of jurisdiction over a person outside this state shall be given in a manner reasonably calculated to give actual notice, and may be:

(1) By personal delivery outside this state in the manner prescribed for service of process within this state;

(2) in the manner prescribed by the law of the place in which the service is made for service of process in that place in an action in any of its courts of general jurisdiction;

(3) by any form of mail addressed to the person to be served and requesting a receipt; or

(4) as directed by the court, including publication, if other means of notification are ineffective.

(b) Notice under this section shall be served, mailed, or delivered, or last published at least thirty (30) days before any hearing in this state.

(c) Proof of service outside this state may be made by affidavit of the individual who made the service, or in the manner prescribed by the law of this state, the order pursuant to which the service is made, or the law of the place in which the service is made. If service is made by mail, proof may be a receipt signed by the addressee or other evidence of delivery to the addressee.

(d) Notice is not required if a person submits to the jurisdiction of the court.

§ 38-1306. Simultaneous proceedings in other states.

(a) A court of this state shall not exercise its jurisdiction under this act if at the time of filing the petition a proceeding concerning the custody of the child was pending in a court of another state exercising jurisdiction substantially in conformity with this act, unless the proceeding is stayed by the court of the other state because this state is a more appropriate forum or for other reasons.

(b) Before hearing the petition in a custody proceeding the court shall examine the pleadings and other information supplied by the parties under K.S.A. 38-1309 and shall consult the child custody registry established under K.S.A. 38-1316 concerning the pendency of proceedings with respect to the child in other states. If the court has reason to believe that proceedings may be pending in another state it shall direct an inquiry to the state court administrator or other appropriate official of the other state.

(c) If the court is informed during the course of the proceeding that a proceeding concerning the custody of the child was pending in another state before the court assumed jurisdiction it shall stay the proceeding and communicate with the court in which the other proceeding is pending to the end that the issue may be litigated in the more appropriate forum and that information be exchanged in accordance with K.S.A. 38-1319 to 38-1322, inclusive. If a court of this state has made a custody decree before being informed of a pending proceeding in a court of another state it shall immediately inform that court of the fact. If the court is informed that a proceeding was commenced in another state after it assumed jurisdiction it shall likewise inform the other court to the end that the issues may be litigated in the more appropriate forum.

§ 38-1307. Inconvenient forum.

(a) A court which has jurisdiction under this act to make an initial or modification decree may decline to exercise its jurisdiction any time before making a decree if it finds that it is an inconvenient forum to make a custody determination under the circumstances of the case and that a court of another state is a more appropriate forum.

(b) A finding of inconvenient forum may be made upon the court's own motion or upon motion of a party or a guardian ad litem or other representative of the child.

(c) In determining if it is an inconvenient forum, the court shall consider if it is in the interest of the child that another state assume jurisdiction. For this purpose it may take into account the following factors, among others:

(1) If another state is or recently was the child's home state;

(2) if another state has a closer connection with the child and the child's family or with the child and one or more of the contestants;

(3) if substantial evidence concerning the child's present or future care, protection, training, and personal relationships is more readily available in another state;

(4) if the parties have agreed on another forum which is no less appropriate; and

(5) if the exercise of jurisdiction by a court of this state would contravene any of the purposes stated in K.S.A. 38-1301.

(d) Before determining whether to decline or retain jurisdiction the court may communicate with a court of another state and exchange information pertinent to the assumption of jurisdiction by either court with a view to assuring that jurisdiction will be exercised by the more appropriate court and that a forum will be available to the parties.

(e) If the court finds that it is an inconvenient forum and that a court of another state is a more appropriate forum, it may dismiss the proceedings, or it may stay the proceedings upon condition that a custody proceeding be promptly commenced in another named state or upon any other conditions which may be just and proper, including the condition that a moving party stipulate such party's consent and submission to the jurisdiction of the other forum.

(f) The court may decline to exercise its jurisdiction under this act if a custody determination is incidental to an action for divorce or another proceeding while retaining jurisdiction over the divorce or other proceeding.

(g) If it appears to the court that it is clearly an inappropriate forum it may require the party who commenced the proceedings to pay, in addition to the costs of the proceedings in this state, necessary travel and other expenses, including attorneys' fees,

incurred by other parties or their witnesses. Payment is to be made to the clerk of the court for remittance to the proper party.

(h) Upon dismissal or stay of proceedings under this section the court shall inform the court found to be the more appropriate forum of this fact, or if the court which would have jurisdiction in the other state is not certainly known, shall transmit the information to the court administrator or other appropriate official for forwarding to the appropriate court.

(i) Any communication received from another state informing this state of a finding of inconvenient forum because a court of this state is the more appropriate forum shall be filed in the custody registry of the appropriate court. Upon assuming jurisdiction the court of this state shall inform the original court of this fact.

§ 38-1308. Jurisdiction declined by reason of conduct.

(a) If the petitioner for an initial decree has wrongfully taken the child from another state or has engaged in similar reprehensible conduct the court may decline to exercise jurisdiction if this is just and proper under the circumstances.

(b) Unless required in the interest of the child, the court shall not exercise its jurisdiction to modify a custody decree of another state if the petitioner, without consent of the person entitled to custody, has improperly removed the child from the physical custody of the person entitled to custody or has improperly retained the child after a visit or other temporary relinquishment of physical custody. If the petitioner has violated any other provision of a custody decree of another state the court may decline to exercise its jurisdiction if this is just and proper under the circumstances.

(c) In appropriate cases a court dismissing a petition under this section may charge the petitioner with necessary travel and other expenses, including attorneys' fees, incurred by other parties or their witnesses.

§ 38-1309. Information under oath to be submitted to the court.

(a) Every party in a custody proceeding in the party's first pleading or in an affidavit attached to that pleading shall give information under oath as to the child's present address, the places where the child has lived within the past five years, and the names and present addresses of the persons with whom the child has lived during that period. In this pleading or affidavit every party shall further declare under oath whether:

(1) The party has participated (as a party, witness, or in any other capacity) in any other litigation concerning the custody of the same child in this or any other state;

(2) the party has information of any custody proceeding concerning the child pending in a court of this or any other state; and

(3) the party knows of any person not a party to the proceedings who has physical custody of the child or claims to have custody of the child or claims to have custody or visitation rights with respect to the child.

(b) If the declaration as to any of the above items is in the affirmative the declarant shall give additional information under oath as required by the court. The court may examine the parties under oath as to details of the information furnished and as to other matters pertinent to the court's jurisdiction and the disposition of the case.

(c) Each party has a continuing duty to inform the court of any custody proceeding concerning the child in this or any other state of which the party obtained information during this proceeding.

(d) Any party who submits information pursuant to this section knowing the same to be false shall, upon conviction, be deemed guilty of a class C misdemeanor.

§ 38-1310. Additional parties.

If the court learns from information furnished by the parties pursuant to K.S.A. 38-1309 or from other sources that a person not a party to the custody proceeding has physical custody of the child or claims to have custody or visitation rights with respect to the child, it shall order that person to be joined as a party and to be duly notified of the pendency of the proceeding and of such person's joinder as a party. If the person joined as a party is outside this state the person shall be served with process or otherwise notified in accordance with K.S.A. 38-1305.

§ 38-1311. Appearance of parties and child.

(a) The court may order any party to the proceeding who is in this state to appear personally before the court. If that party has physical custody of the child the court may order that the party appear personally with the child.

(b) If a party to the proceeding whose presence is desired by the court is outside this state with or without the child, the court may order that the notice given under K.S.A. 38-1305 include a statement directing that party to appear personally with or without the child and declaring that failure to appear may result in a decision adverse to that party.

(c) If a party to the proceeding who is outside this state is directed to appear under subsection (b) or desires to appear personally before the court with or without the child, the court may require another party to pay to the clerk of the court travel and other necessary expenses of the party so appearing and of the child if this is just and proper under the circumstances.

§ 38-1312. Binding force and res judicata effect of custody decree.

A custody decree rendered by a court of this state which had jurisdiction under K.S.A. 38-1303 binds all parties who have been served in this state or notified in accordance with K.S.A. 38-1305 or who have submitted to the jurisdiction of the court, and who have been given an opportunity to be heard. As to these parties the custody decree is conclusive as to all issues of law and fact decided and as to the custody determination made unless and until that determination is modified pursuant to law, including the provisions of this act.

§ 38-1313. Recognition of out-of-state custody decrees.

The courts of this state shall recognize and enforce an initial or modification decree of a court of another state which had assumed jurisdiction under statutory provisions substantially in accordance with this act or which was made under factual circumstances meeting the jurisdictional standards of the act, so long as this decree has not been modified in accordance with jurisdictional standards substantially similar to those of this act.

§ 38-1314. Modification of custody decree of another state.

(a) If a court of another state has made a custody decree, a court of this state shall not modify that decree unless (1) it appears to the court of this state that the court which rendered the decree does not now have jurisdiction under jurisdictional prerequisites substantially in accordance with this act or has declined to assume jurisdiction to modify the decree and (2) the court of this state has jurisdiction.

(b) If a court of this state is authorized under subsection (a) and K.S.A. 38-1308 to modify a custody decree of another state it shall give due consideration to the transcript of the record and other documents of all previous proceedings submitted to it in accordance with K.S.A. 38-1322.

§ 38-1315. Filing and enforcement of custody decree of another state.

(a) A certified copy of a custody decree of another state may be filed in the office of the clerk of any district court of this state. The clerk shall treat the decree in the same manner as a custody decree of the district court of this state. A custody decree so filed has the same effect and shall be enforced in like manner as a custody decree rendered by a court of this state.

(b) A person violating a custody decree of another state which makes it necessary to enforce the decree in this state may be required to pay necessary travel and other expenses, including attorneys' fees, incurred by the party entitled to the custody or such party's witnesses.

§ 38-1316. Registry of out-of-state custody decrees and proceedings.

The clerk of each district court shall maintain a registry in which the clerk shall enter the following:

(a) Certified copies of custody decrees of other states received for filing;

(b) communications as to the pendency of custody proceedings in other states;

(c) communications concerning a finding of inconvenient forum by a court of another state; and

(d) other communications or documents concerning custody proceedings in another state which may affect the jurisdiction of a court of this state or the disposition to be made by it in a custody proceeding.

§ 38-1317. Certified copies of custody decree.

The clerk of the district court of this state, at the request of the court of another state or at the request of any person who is affected by or has a legitimate interest in a custody decree, shall certify and forward a copy of the decree to that court or person.

§ 38-1318. Taking testimony in another state.

In addition to other procedural devices available to a party, any party to the proceeding or a guardian ad litem or other representative of the child may adduce testimony of witnesses, including parties and the child, by deposition or otherwise, in another state. The court on its own motion may direct that the testimony of a person be taken in another state and may prescribe the manner in which and the terms upon which the testimony shall be taken.

§ 38-1319. Hearings and studies in another state; orders to appear.

(a) A court of this state may request the appropriate court of another state to hold a hearing to adduce evidence, to order a party to produce or give evidence under other procedures of that state, or to have social studies made with respect to the custody of a child involved in proceedings pending in the court of this state; and to forward to the court of this state certified copies of the transcript of the record of the hearing, the evidence otherwise adduced, or any social studies prepared in compliance with the request. The cost of the services may be assessed against the parties or, if necessary, ordered paid by the county.

(b) A court of this state may request the appropriate court of another state to order a party to custody proceedings pending in the court of this state to appear in the proceedings, and if that party has physical custody of the child, to appear with the child. The request may state that travel and other necessary expenses of the party and of the child whose appearance is desired will be assessed against another party or will otherwise be paid.

§ 38-1320. Assistance to courts of other states.

(a) Upon request of the court of another state the courts of this state which are competent to hear custody matters may order a person in this state to appear at a hearing to adduce evidence or to produce or give evidence under other procedures available in this state or may order social studies to be made for use in a custody proceeding in another state. A certified copy of the transcript of the record of the hearing or the evidence otherwise adduced and any social studies prepared shall be forwarded by the clerk of the court to the requesting court.

(b) A person within this state may voluntarily give testimony or statement in this state for use in a custody proceeding outside this state.

(c) Upon request of the court of another state a competent court of this state may order a person in this state to appear alone or with the child in a custody proceeding in another state. The court may condition compliance with the request upon assurance by the other state that travel and other necessary expenses will be advanced or reimbursed.

§ 38-1321. Preservation of documents for use in other states.

In any custody proceeding in this state the court shall preserve the pleadings, orders and decrees, any record that has been made of its hearings, social studies, and other pertinent documents until the child reaches eighteen (18) years of age. Upon appropriate request of the court of another state the court shall forward to the other court certified copies of any or all of such documents.

§ 38-1322. Requests for court records of other states.

If a custody decree has been rendered in another state concerning a child involved in a custody proceeding pending in a court of this state, the court of this state upon taking jurisdiction of the case shall request of the court of the other state a certified copy of the transcript of any court record and other documents mentioned in K.S.A. 38-1321.

§ 38-1323. International application.

The general policies of this act extend to the international area. The provisions of this act relating to the recognition and enforcement of custody decrees of other states apply to custody decrees and decrees involving legal institutions similar in nature to custody institutions similar in nature to custody institutions rendered by appropriate authorities of other nations if reasonable notice and opportunity to be heard were given to all affected persons.

§ 38-1324. Priority.

Upon the request of a party to a custody proceeding which raises a question of existence or exercise of jurisdiction under this act the case shall be given calendar priority and handled expeditiously.

§ 38-1325. Severability.

If any provision of this act or the application thereof to any person or circumstances is held invalid, its invalidity does not affect other provisions or applications of the act which can be given effect without the invalid provision or application, and to this end the provisions of this act are severable.

§ 38-1326. Short title.

K.S.A. 38-1301 to 38-1326, inclusive, may be cited as the uniform child custody jurisdiction act.

§§ 38-1327 to 38-1334. Reserved.

§ 38-1335. Continuation of jurisdiction until assumed by other state.

(a) The provisions of the uniform child custody jurisdiction act notwithstanding, the district court, having assumed jurisdiction to make a custody determination regarding a child, shall continue to have such jurisdiction until such time as a court of another state assumes jurisdiction to make a custody determination regarding such child.

(b) The definitions provided by K.S.A. 38-1302 shall apply to the terms used in this section.

KENTUCKY

UNIFORM CHILD CUSTODY JURISDICTION ACT

§ 403.400. Purposes - Construction.

(1) The general purposes of KRS 403.410 to 403.620 are to:

(a) Avoid jurisdictional competition and conflict with courts of other states in matters of child custody which have in the past resulted in the shifting of children from state to state with harmful effects on their well-being;

(b) Promote cooperation with the courts of other states to the end that a custody decree is rendered in that state which can best decide the case in the interest of the child;

(c) Assure that litigation concerning the custody of a child takes place ordinarily in the state with which the child and his family have the closest connection and where significant evidence concerning his care, protection, training, and personal relationships is most readily available, and that courts of this state decline the exercise of jurisdiction when the child and his family have closer connection with another state;

(d) Discourage continuing controversies over child custody in the interest of greater stability of home environment and of secure family relationships for the child;

(e) Deter abductions and other unilateral removals of children undertaken to obtain custody awards;

(f) Avoid re-litigation of custody decision of other states in this state insofar as feasible;

(g) Facilitate the enforcement of custody decrees of other states;

(h) Promote and expand the exchange of information and other forms of mutual assistance between the courts of this state and those of other states concerned with the same child; and

(i) Make uniform the law of those states which enact it.

(2) KRS 403.410 to 403.620 shall be construed to promote the general purposes stated in this section.

§ 403.410. Definitions.

(1) "Contestant" means a person, including a parent, who claims a right to custody or visitation rights with respect to a child;

(2) "Custody determination" means a court decision and court orders and instructions providing for the custody of a child, including visitation rights; it does not include a decision relating to child support or any other monetary obligation of any person;

(3) "Custody proceeding" includes proceedings in which a custody determination is one of several issues, such as an action for divorce or separation, and includes child neglect and dependency proceedings;

(4) "Decree" or "custody decree" means a custody determination contained in a judicial decree or order made in a custody proceeding, and includes an initial decree and a modification decree;

(5) "Home state" means the state in which the child immediately preceding the time involved lived with his parents, a parent, or a person acting as parent, for at least six (6) consecutive months, and in the case of a child less than six (6) months old the state in which the child lived from birth with any of the persons mentioned. Periods of temporary absence of any of the named persons are counted as part of the six (6)-month or other period;

(6) "Initial decree" means the first custody decree concerning a particular child;

(7) "Modification decree" means a custody decree which modifies or replaced a prior decree, whether made by the court which rendered the prior decree or by another court;

(8) "Physical custody" means actual possession and control of a child;

(9) "Person acting as parent" means a person, other than a parent, who has physical custody of a child and who has either been awarded custody by a court or claims a right to custody; and

(10) "State" means any state, territory, or possession of the United States, the Commonwealth of Puerto Rico, and the District of Columbia.

§ 403.420. Prerequisites to jurisdiction - Commencement of proceeding.

(1) A court of this state which is competent to decide child custody matters has jurisdiction to make a child custody determination by initial or modification decree if:

(a) This state is the home state of the child at the time of commencement of the proceeding, or had been the child's home state within six (6) months before commencement of the proceeding and the child is absent from this state because of his removal or retention by a person claiming his custody or for other reasons, and a parent or person acting as parent continues to live in this state; or

(b) It is in the best interest of the child that a court of this state assume jurisdiction because the child and his parents, or the child and at least one (1) contestant, have a significant connection with this state, and there is available in this state substantial evidence concerning the child's present or future care, protection, training, and personal relationships; or

(c) The child is physically present in this state and the child has been abandoned or it is necessary in an emergency to protect the child because he has been subjected to or threatened with mistreatment or abuse or is otherwise neglected or dependent; or

(d) It appears that no other state would have jurisdiction under prerequisites substantially in accordance with paragraphs (a), (b), or (c), or another state has declined to exercise jurisdiction on the ground that this state is the more appropriate forum to determine the custody of the child, and it is in the best interest of the child that this court assume jurisdiction.

(2) Except under paragraphs (c) and (d) of subsection (1) of this section, physical presence in this state of the child, or of the child and one (1) of the contestants, is not alone sufficient to confer jurisdiction on a court of this state to make a child custody determination.

(3) Physical presence of the child, while desirable, is not a prerequisite for jurisdiction to determine his custody.

(4) A child custody proceeding is commenced in the circuit court:
(a) By a parent, by filing a petition:
1. For dissolution or legal separation; or
2. For custody of the child in the county in which he is permanently resident or found; or
(b) By a person other than a parent, by filing a petition for custody of the child in the county in which he is permanently resident or found, but only if he is not in the physical custody of one (1) of his parents.

§ 403.430. Notice and opportunity to be heard.

Before making a decree under KRS 403.420 to 403.620, reasonable notice and opportunity to be heard shall be given to the contestants, any parent whose parental rights have not been previously terminated, and any person who has physical custody of the child. If any of these persons is outside this state, notice and opportunity to be heard shall be given pursuant to KRS 403.440.

§ 403.440. Notice to persons outside state - Exception.

(1) Notice required for the exercise of jurisdiction over a person outside this state shall be given in a manner reasonably calculated to give actual notice, and may be:
(a) By personal delivery outside this state in the manner prescribed for service of process within this state;
(b) In the manner prescribed by the law of the place in which the service is made for service of process in that place in an action in any of its courts of general jurisdiction;
(c) By any form of mail addressed to the person to be served and requesting a receipt; or
(d) As directed by the court.
(2) Notice under this section shall be served, mailed, or delivered at least twenty (20) days before any hearing in this state.
(3) Proof of service outside this state may be made by affidavit of the individual who made the service, or in the manner prescribed by the law of this state, the order pursuant to which the service is made, or the law of the place in which the service is made. If service is made by mail, proof may be a receipt signed by the addressee or other evidence of delivery to the addressee.
(4) Notice is not required if a person submits to the jurisdiction of the court.

§ 403.450. Simultaneous proceedings in other states.

(1) A court of this state shall not exercise its jurisdiction under KRS 403.420 to 403.620 if at the time of filing the petition a proceeding concerning the custody of the child was pending in a court of another state exercising jurisdiction substantially in conformity with KRS 403.420 to 403.620, unless the proceeding is stayed by the court of the other state because this state is a more appropriate forum or for other reasons.
(2) Before hearing the petition in a custody proceeding the court shall examine the pleadings and other information supplied by the parties under KRS 403.480 and shall consult the child custody registry established under KRS 403.550 concerning the pendency of proceedings with respect to the child in other states. If the court has reason to believe that proceedings may be pending in another state it shall direct an inquiry to the state court administrator or other appropriate official of the other state.
(3) If the court is informed during the course of the proceeding that a proceeding concerning the custody of the child was pending in another state before the court assumed jurisdiction it shall stay the proceeding and communicate with the court in which the other proceeding is pending to the end that the issue may be litigated in the more appropriate forum and that information be exchanged in accordance with KRS 403.580 to 403.610. If a court of this state has made a custody decree before being informed of a pending proceeding in a court of another state it shall immediately inform that court of the fact. If the court is informed that a proceeding was commenced in another state after it assumed jurisdiction it shall likewise inform the other court to the end that the issues may be litigated in the more appropriate forum.

§ 403.460. Inconvenient forum.

(1) A court which has jurisdiction under KRS 403.420 to 403.620 to make an initial or modification decree may decline to exercise its jurisdiction any time before making a decree if it finds that it is an inconvenient forum to make a custody determination under the circumstances of the case and that a court of another state is a more appropriate forum.
(2) A finding of inconvenient forum may be made upon the court's own motion or upon motion of a party or a guardian ad litem or other representative of the child.
(3) In determining if it is an inconvenient forum, the court shall consider if it is in the interest of the child that another state assume jurisdiction. For this purpose it may take into account the following factors, among others:
(a) If another state is or recently was the child's home state;
(b) If another state has a closer connection with the child and his family or with the child and one (1) or more of the contestants;
(c) If substantial evidence concerning the child's present or future care, protection, training, and personal relationships is more readily available in another state;
(d) If the parties have agreed on another forum which is no less appropriate; and
(e) If the exercise of jurisdiction by a court of this state would contravene any of the purposes stated in KRS 403.400.

(4) Before determining whether to decline or retain jurisdiction the court may communicate with a court of another state and exchange information pertinent to the assumption of jurisdiction by either court with a view to assuring that jurisdiction will be exercised by the more appropriate court and that a forum will be available to the parties.

(5) If the court finds that it is an inconvenient forum and that a court of another state is a more appropriate forum, it may dismiss the proceedings, or it may stay the proceedings upon condition that a custody proceeding be promptly commenced in another named state or upon any other conditions which may be just and proper, including the condition that a moving party stipulate his consent and submission to the jurisdiction of the other forum.

(6) The court may decline to exercise its jurisdiction under KRS 403.420 to 403.620 if a custody determination is incidental to an action for divorce or another proceeding while retaining jurisdiction over the divorce or other proceeding.

(7) If it appears to the court that it is clearly an inappropriate forum it may require the party who commenced the proceedings to pay, in addition to the costs of the proceedings in this state, necessary travel and other expenses, including attorneys' fees, incurred by other parties or their witnesses. Payment is to be made to the clerk of the court for remittance to the proper party.

(8) Upon dismissal or stay of proceedings under this section the court shall inform the court found to be the more appropriate forum of this fact or, if the court which would have jurisdiction in the other state is not certainly known, shall transmit the information to the court administrator or other appropriate official for forwarding to the appropriate court.

(9) Any communication received from another state informing this state of a finding of inconvenient forum because a court of this state is the more appropriate forum shall be filed in the custody registry of the appropriate court. Upon assuming jurisdiction the court of this state shall inform the original court of this fact.

§ 403.470. Jurisdiction declined by reason of conduct.

(1) If the petitioner for an initial decree has wrongfully taken the child from another state or has engaged in similar reprehensible conduct the court may decline to exercise jurisdiction if this is just and proper under the circumstances.

(2) Unless required in the interest of the child, the court shall not exercise its jurisdiction to modify a custody decree of another state if the petitioner, without consent of the person entitled to custody, has improperly removed the child from the physical custody of the person entitled to custody or has improperly removed the child from the physical custody of the person entitled to custody or has improperly retained the child after a visit or other temporary relinquishment of physical custody. If the petitioner has violated any other provision of a custody decree of another state the court may decline to exercise its jurisdiction if this is just and proper under the circumstances.

(3) In appropriate cases a court dismissing a petition under this section may charge the petitioner with necessary travel and other expenses, including attorneys' fees, incurred by other parties or their witnesses.

§ 403.480. Information under oath to be submitted to court - Continuing duty.

(1) Every party in a custody proceeding in his first pleading or in an affidavit attached to that pleading shall give information under oath as to the child's present address, the places where the child has lived within the last five (5) years, and the names and present addresses of the persons with whom the child has lived during that period. In this pleading or affidavit every party shall further declare under oath whether:

(a) He has participated (as a party, witness, or in any other capacity) in any other litigation concerning the custody of the same child in this or any other state;

(b) He has information of any custody proceeding concerning the child pending in a court of this or any other state; and

(c) He knows of any person not a party to the proceedings who has physical custody of the child or claims to have custody or visitation rights with respect to the child.

(2) If the declaration as to any of the above items is in the affirmative the declarant shall give additional information under oath as required by the court. The court may examine the parties under oath as to details of the information furnished and as to other matters pertinent to the court's jurisdiction and the disposition of the case.

(3) Each party has a continuing duty to inform the court of any custody proceeding concerning the child in this or any other state of which he obtained information during this proceeding.

§ 403.490. Joinder of parties.

If the court learns from information furnished by the parties pursuant to KRS 403.480 or from other sources that a person not a party to the custody proceeding has physical custody of the child or claims to have custody or visitation rights with respect to the child, it shall order that person to be joined as party and to be duly notified of the pendency of the proceeding and of his joinder as a party. If the person joined as a party is outside this state he shall be served with process or otherwise notified in accordance with KRS 403.440.

§ 403.500. Court appearance of parties and the child.

(1) The court may order any party to the proceeding who is in this state to appear personally before the court. If that party has physical custody of the child, the court may order that he appear personally with the child.

(2) If a party to the proceeding whose presence is desired by the court is outside this state with or without the child, the court

may order that the notice given under KRS 403.440 include a statement directing that party to appear personally with or without the child and declaring that failure to appear may result in a decision adverse to that party.

(3) If a party to the proceeding who is outside this state is directed to appear under subsection (2) of this section or desires to appear personally before the court with or without the child, the court may require another party to pay to the clerk of the court travel and other necessary expenses of the party so appearing and of the child if this is just and proper under the circumstances.

§ 403.510. Binding force and res judicata effect of custody decree.

A custody decree rendered by a court of this state which had jurisdiction under KRS 403.420 binds all parties who have been served in this state or notified in accordance with KRS 403.440 or who have submitted to the jurisdiction of the court, and who have been given an opportunity to be heard. As to these parties the custody decree is conclusive as to all issues of law and fact decided and as to the custody determination made unless and until that determination is modified pursuant to law, including the provisions of KRS 403.420 to 403.620.

§ 403.520. Recognition of out-of-state decree.

The courts of this state shall recognize and enforce an initial or modification decree of a court of another state which had assumed jurisdiction under statutory provisions substantially in accordance with KRS 403.420 to 403.620 or which was made under factual circumstances meeting the jurisdictional standards of KRS 403.420 to 403.620, so long as this decree has not been modified in accordance with jurisdictional standards substantially similar to those of KRS 403.420 to 403.620.

§ 403.530. Modification of decree of another state.

(1) If a court of another state has made a custody decree, a court of this state shall not modify that decree unless it appears to the court of this state that the court which rendered the decree does not now have jurisdiction under jurisdictional prerequisites substantially in accordance with KRS 403.420 to 403.620 or has declined to assume jurisdiction to modify the decree and the court of this state has jurisdiction.

(2) If a court of this state is authorized under subsection (1) of this section and KRS 403.470 to modify a custody decree of another state it shall give due consideration to the transcript of the record and other documents of all previous proceedings submitted to it in accordance with KRS 403.610.

§ 403.540. Filing and enforcement of custody decree of another state.

(1) A certified copy of a custody decree of another state may be filed in the office of the clerk of any circuit court of this state. The clerk shall treat the decree in the same manner as the custody decree of the state. A custody decree so filed has the same effect and shall be enforced in like manner as a custody decree rendered by a court of this state.

(2) A person violating a custody decree of another state which makes it necessary to enforce the decree in this state may be required to pay necessary travel and other expenses including attorneys' fees, incurred by the party entitled to the custody or his witnesses.

§ 403.550. Registry of out-of-state custody decrees and proceedings.

The clerk of each circuit court shall maintain a registry in which he shall enter the following:

(1) Certified copies of custody decrees of other states received for filing;

(2) Communications as to the pendency of custody proceedings in other states;

(3) Communications concerning a finding of inconvenient forum by a court of another state; and

(4) Other communications or documents concerning custody proceedings in another state which may affect the jurisdiction of a court of this state or the disposition to be made by it in a custody proceeding.

§ 403.560. Certified copies of custody decree.

The clerk of the circuit court of this state, at the request of the court of another state or at the request of any person who is affected by or has a legitimate interest in a custody decree, shall certify and forward a copy of the decree to that court or person.

§ 403.570. Taking testimony in another state.

In addition to other procedural devices available to a party, any party to the proceeding or a guardian ad litem or other representative of the child may adduce testimony of witnesses, including parties and the child, by deposition or otherwise, in another state. The court on its own motion may direct that the testimony of a person be taken in another state and may prescribe the manner in which and the terms upon which the testimony shall be taken.

§ 403.580. Hearings and studies in another state - Orders to appear.

(1) A court of this state may request the appropriate court of another state to hold a hearing to adduce evidence, to order a party to produce or give evidence under other procedures of that state, or to have social studies made with respect to the custody of a child involved in proceedings pending in the court of this state; and to forward to the court of this state certified copies of the

transcript of the record of the hearing, the evidence otherwise adduced, or any social studies prepared in compliance with the request. The cost of the services may be assessed against the parties or, if necessary, ordered paid by the state.

(2) A court of this state may request the appropriate court of another state to order a party to custody proceedings pending in the court of this state to appear in the proceedings, and if that party has physical custody of the child, to appear with the child. The request may state that travel and other necessary expenses of the party and of the child whose appearance is desired will be assessed against another party or will otherwise be paid.

§ 403.590. Assistance to courts of other states.

(1) Upon request of the court of another state the courts of this state which are competent to hear custody matters may order a person in this state to appear at a hearing to adduce evidence or to produce or give evidence under other procedures available in this state or may order social studies to be made for use in a custody proceeding in another state. A certified copy of the transcript of the record of the hearing or the evidence otherwise adduced and any social studies prepared shall be forwarded by the clerk of the court to the requesting court.

(2) A person within this state may voluntarily give his testimony or statement in this state for use in a custody proceeding outside this state.

(3) Upon request of the court of another state a competent court of this state may order a person in this state to appear alone or with the child in a custody proceeding in another state. The court may condition compliance with the request upon assurance by the other state that state travel and other necessary expenses will be advanced or reimbursed.

§ 403.600. Preservation of court records - Use in other states.

In any custody proceeding in this state the court shall preserve the pleadings, orders and decrees, any record that has been made of its hearings, social studies, and other pertinent documents until the child reaches eighteen (18) years of age. Upon appropriate request of the court of another state the court shall forward to the other court certified copies of any or all of such documents.

§ 403.610. Request for court records of another state.

If a custody decree has been rendered in another state concerning a child involved in a custody proceeding pending in a court of this state, the court of this state upon taking jurisdiction of the case shall request of the court of the other state a certified copy of the transcript of any court record and other documents mentioned in KRS 403.600.

§ 403.620. International application.

The general policies of KRS 403.420 to 403.620 extend to the international area. The provisions of KRS 403.420 to 403.620 relating to the recognition and enforcement of custody decrees of other states apply to custody decrees and decrees involving legal institutions similar in nature to custody institutions rendered by appropriate authorities of other nations if reasonable notice and opportunity to be heard were given to all affected persons.

§ 403.630. Short title.

KRS 403.400 to 403.620 may be cited as the "Uniform Child Custody Jurisdiction Act."

LOUISIANA

UNIFORM CHILD CUSTODY JURISDICTION LAW

§ 1700. Purposes of Part; construction of provisions.

A. The general purposes of this Part are to:

(1) Avoid jurisdictional competition and conflict with courts of other states in matters of child custody which have in the past resulted in the shifting of children from state to state with harmful effects on their well-being.

(2) Promote cooperation with the courts of other states to the end that a custody decree is rendered in that state which can best decide the case in the interests of the child.

(3) Assure that litigation concerning the custody of a child takes place ordinarily in the state with which the child and his family have the closest connection and where significant evidence concerning his care, protection, training, and personal relationships is most readily available, and to assure that the courts of this state decline the exercise of jurisdiction when the child and his family have closer connection with another state.

(4) Discourage continuing controversies over child custody in the interest of greater stability of home environment and of secure family relationships for the child.

(5) Deter abductions and other unilateral removals of children undertaken to obtain custody awards.

(6) Avoid relitigation of custody decisions of other states in this state insofar as feasible.

(7) Facilitate the enforcement of custody decrees of other states.

(8) Promote and expand the exchange of information and other forms of mutual assistance between the courts of this state and those of other states concerned with the same child, and

(9) Make uniform the law of those states which enact it.

B. This Part shall be construed to promote the general purposes stated in this Section.

§ 1701. Definitions.

(1) "Contestant" means a person, including a parent, who claims a right to custody or visitation rights with respect to a child.

(2) "Custody determination" means a court decision and court orders and instructions providing for the custody of a child, including visitation rights; it does not include a decision relating to child support or any other monetary obligation of any person.

(3) "Custody proceeding" includes proceedings in which a custody determination is one of several issues, such as an action for divorce or separation, and includes child neglect and dependency proceedings.

(4) "Decree" or "custody decree" means a custody determination contained in a judicial decree or order made in a custody proceeding, and includes an initial decree and a modification decree.

(5) "Home state" means the state in which the child immediately preceding the time involved lived with his parents, a parent, or a person acting as parent, for at least six consecutive months, and in the case of a child less than six months old the state in which the child lived from birth with any of the persons mentioned. Periods of temporary absence of any of the named persons are counted as part of the six-month or other period.

(6) "Initial decree" means the first custody decree concerning a particular child.

(7) "Modification decree" means a custody decree which modifies or replaces a prior decree, whether made by the court which rendered the prior decree or by another court.

(8) "Physical custody" means actual possession and control of a child.

(9) "Person acting as parent" means a person, other than a parent, who has physical custody of a child and who has either been awarded custody by a court or claims a right to custody, and

(10) "State" means any state, territory, or possession of the United States, the Commonwealth of Puerto Rico, and the District of Columbia.

§ 1702. Jurisdiction.

A. A court of this state which is competent to decide child custody matters has jurisdiction to make a child custody determination by initial or modification decree if:

(1) This state (i) is the home state of the child at the time of commencement of the proceeding, or (ii) had been the child's home state within six months before commencement of the proceeding and the child is absent from this state because of his removal or retention by a person claiming his custody or for other reasons, and a parent or person acting as parent continues to live in this state; or

(2) It is in the best interest of the child that a court of this state assume jurisdiction because (i) the child and his parents, or the child and at least one contestant, have a significant connection with this state, and (ii) there is available in this state substantial evidence concerning the child's present or future care, protection, training, and personal relationships; or

(3) The child is physically present in this state and (i) the child has been abandoned or (ii) it is necessary in an emergency to protect the child because he has been subjected to or threatened with mistreatment or abuse or is otherwise neglected or dependent; or

(4) (i) It appears that no other state would have jurisdiction under prerequisites substantially in accordance with Paragraphs (1), (2), or (3), or another state has declined to exercise jurisdiction on the ground that this state is the more appropriate forum to determine the custody of the child, and (ii) it is in the best interest of the child that this court assume jurisdiction.

B. Except under Paragraphs (3) and (4) of Subsection A, physical presence in this state of the child, or of the child and one of the contestants, is not alone sufficient to confer jurisdiction on a court of this state to make a child custody determination.

C. Physical presence of the child, while desirable, is not a prerequisite for jurisdiction to determine his custody.

§ 1703. Notice and opportunity to be heard.

Before making a decree under this Part, reasonable notice and opportunity to be heard shall be given to the contestants, any parent whose parental rights have not been previously terminated, and any person who has physical custody of the child. If any of these persons is outside this state, notice and opportunity to be heard shall be given pursuant to Section 1704.

§ 1704. Notice to persons outside this state; submission to jurisdiction.

A. Notice required for the exercise of jurisdiction over a person outside this state shall be given in a manner reasonably calculated to give actual notice, and may be:

(1) By personal delivery outside of this state in the manner prescribed for service of process within this state; or

(2) By registered or certified mail; or

(3) If the party is a nonresident or absentee who cannot be served by the methods provided in paragraphs (1) and (2) above, either personally or through an agent for service of process, and who has made no general appearance, the court shall appoint an attorney at law to represent him.

If the court appoints an attorney at law to represent the party, all proceedings against the party shall be conducted contradictorily against the attorney at law appointed by the court to represent him. The qualifications and duties of such attorney and his compensation shall be governed by the provisions of Articles 5092 through 5096 of the Code of Civil Procedure.

B. Notice under this Section shall be served, mailed and delivered, or last published at least ten days before any hearing in this state.

C. Proof of service outside this state may be made by affidavit of the individual who made the service, or in the manner prescribed by the law of this state, the order pursuant to which the service is made, or the law of the place in which the service is made. If service is made by mail, proof may be a receipt signed by the addressee or other evidence of delivery to the addressee.

§ 1705. Simultaneous proceedings in other states.

A. A court of this state shall not exercise its jurisdiction under this Part if at the time of filing the petition a proceeding concerning the custody of the child was pending in a court of another state exercising jurisdiction substantially in conformity with this Part, unless the proceeding is stayed by the court of the other state because this state is a more appropriate forum or for other reasons.

B. Before hearing the petition in a custody proceeding the court shall examine the pleadings and other information supplied by the parties under Section 1708 and shall consult the child custody registry established under Section 1715 concerning the pendency of proceedings with respect to the child in other states. If the court has reason to believe that proceedings may be pending in another state it shall direct an inquiry to the state court administrator or other appropriate official of the other state.

C. If the court is informed during the course of proceeding that a proceeding concerning the custody of the child was pending in another state before the court assumed jurisdiction it shall stay the proceeding and communicate with the court in which the other proceeding is pending to the end that the issue may be litigated in the more appropriate forum and that information be exchanged in accordance with Sections 1718 through 1721. If a court of this state has made a custody decree before being informed of a pending proceeding in a court of another state it shall immediately inform that court of the fact. If the court is informed that a proceeding was commenced in another state after it assumed jurisdiction it shall likewise inform the other court to the end that the issues may be litigated in the more appropriate forum.

§ 1706. Inconvenient forum.

A. A court which has jurisdiction under this Part to make an initial or modification decree may decline to exercise its jurisdiction any time before making a decree if it finds that it is an inconvenient forum to make a custody determination under the circumstances of the case and that a court of another state is a more appropriate forum.

B. A finding of inconvenient forum may be made upon the court's own motion or upon motion of a party or a curator ad hoc or other representative of the child.

C. In determining if it is an inconvenient forum, the court shall consider if it is in the interest of the child that another state assume jurisdiction. For this purpose it may take into account the following factors, amount others:

(1) If another state is or recently was the child's home state.

(2) If another state has a closer connection with the child and his family or with the child and one or more of the contestants.

(3) If substantial evidence concerning the child's present or future care, protection, training, and personal relationships is more readily available in another state.

(4) If the parties have agreed on another forum which is no less appropriate, and

(5) If the exercise of jurisdiction by a court of this state would contravene any of the purposes stated in Section 1700.

D. Before determining whether to decline or retain jurisdiction the court may communicate with a court of another state and exchange information pertinent to the assumption of jurisdiction by either court with a view to assuring that jurisdiction will be exercised by the more appropriate court and that a forum will be available to the parties.

E. If the court finds that it is an inconvenient forum and that a court of another state is a more appropriate forum, it may dismiss the proceedings, or it may stay the proceedings upon condition that a custody proceeding be promptly commenced in another named state or upon any other conditions which may be just and proper, including the condition that a moving party stipulate his consent and submission to the jurisdiction of the other forum.

F. The court may decline to exercise its jurisdiction under this Part if a custody determination is incidental to an action for divorce or another proceeding while retaining jurisdiction over the divorce or other proceeding.

G. If it appears to the court that it is clearly an inappropriate forum it may require the party who commenced the proceedings to pay, in addition to the costs of the proceedings, in this state, necessary travel and other expenses, including attorneys' fees, incurred by other parties or their witnesses. Payment is to be made to the clerk of the court for remittance to the proper party.

H. Upon dismissal or stay of proceedings under this Section the court shall inform the court found to be the more appropriate forum of this fact, or if the court which would have jurisdiction in the other state is not certainly known, shall transmit the information to the court administrator or other appropriate official for forwarding to the appropriate court.

I. Any communication received from another state informing this state of a finding of inconvenient forum because a court of this state is the more appropriate forum shall be filed in the custody registry of the appropriate court. Upon assuming jurisdiction the court of this state shall inform the original court of this fact.

§ 1707. Jurisdiction declined by reason of conduct.

A. If the petitioner for an initial decree has wrongfully taken the child from another state or has engaged in similar reprehensible conduct the court may decline to exercise jurisdiction if this is just and proper under the circumstances.

B. Unless required in the interest of the child, the court shall not exercise its jurisdiction to modify a custody decree of another state if the petitioner, without consent of the person entitled to custody, has improperly removed the child from the physical custody of the person entitled to custody or has improperly retained the child after a visit or other temporary relinquishment of physical custody. If the petitioner has violated any other provisions of a custody decree of another state the court may decline to exercise its jurisdiction if this is just and proper under the circumstances.

C. In appropriate cases a court dismissing a petition under this Section may charge the petitioner with necessary travel and other expenses, including attorneys' fees, incurred by other parties or their witnesses.

§ 1708. Information under oath to be submitted to the court only in actions commenced under this Part.

A. Every party in a custody proceeding in his first pleading or in an affidavit attached to that pleading shall give information under oath as to the child's present address, the places where the child has lived within the last five years, and the names and present addresses of the persons with whom the child has lived during that period. In this pleading or affidavit every party shall further declare under oath whether:

(1) He has participated (as a party, witness, or in any other capacity) in any other litigation concerning the custody of the same child in this or any other state.

(2) He has information of any custody proceeding concerning the child pending in a court of this or any other state, and

(3) He knows of any person not a party to the proceedings who has physical custody of the child or claims to have custody or visitation rights with respect to the child.

B. If the declaration as to any of the above items is in the affirmative the declarant shall give additional information under oath as required by the court. The court may examine the parties under oath as to details of the information furnished and as to other matters pertinent to the court's jurisdiction and the disposition of the case.

C. Each party has a continuing duty to inform the court of any custody proceeding concerning the child in this or any other state of which he obtained information during this proceeding.

§ 1709. Additional parties.

If the court learns from information furnished by the parties pursuant to Section 1708 or from other sources that a person not a party to the custody proceeding has physical custody of the child or claims to have custody or visitation rights with respect to the child, it shall order that person to be joined as a party and to be duly notified of the pendency of the proceeding and of his joinder as a party. If the person joined as a party outside this state he shall be served with process or otherwise notified in accordance with Section 1704.

§ 1710. Appearance of parties and the child.

A. The court may order any party to the proceeding who is in this state to appear personally before the court. If that party has physical custody of the child the court may order that he appear personally with the child.

B. If a party to the proceeding whose presence is desired by the court is outside this state with or without the child, the court may order that the notice given under Section 1704 include a statement directing that party to appear personally with or without the child and declaring that failure to appear may result in a decision adverse to that party.

C. If a party to the proceeding who is outside this state is directed to appear under Subsection B or desires to appear personally before the court with or without the child, the court may require another party to pay to the clerk of the court travel and other necessary expenses of the party so appearing and of the child if this is just and proper under the circumstances.

§ 1711. Binding force and res judicata effect of custody decree.

A custody decree rendered by a court of this state which had jurisdiction under Section 1702 binds all parties who have been served in this state or notified in accordance with Section 1704 or who have submitted to the jurisdiction of the court, and who have been given an opportunity to be heard. As to these parties, the custody decree is conclusive as to all issues of law and fact decided and as to the custody determination made unless and until that determination is modified pursuant to law, including the provisions of this Part.

§ 1712. Recognition of out-of-state custody decrees.

The courts of this state shall recognize and enforce an initial or modification decree of a court of another state which had assumed jurisdiction under statutory provisions substantially in accordance with this Part or which was made under factual circumstances meeting the jurisdictional standards of the Part, so long as this decree has not been modified in accordance with jurisdictional standards substantially similar to those of this Part.

§ 1713. Modification of custody decree of another state.

A. If a court of another state has made a custody decree, a court of this state shall not modify that decree unless it appears to the court of this state that the court which rendered the decree does not now have jurisdiction under jurisdictional prerequisites substantially in accordance with this Part or has declined to assume jurisdiction to modify the decree and the court of this state has jurisdiction.

B. If a court of this state is authorized under Subsection A of this Section and Section 1707 to modify a custody decree of another state it shall give due consideration to the transcript of the record and other documents of all previous proceedings submitted to it in accordance with Section 1721.

§ 1714. Filing and enforcement of custody decree of another state.

A. A certified copy of a custody decree of another state may be filed in the office of the clerk of any district court or family court of this state. The clerk shall treat the decree in the same manner as a custody decree of the district court or family court of this state. A custody decree so filed has the same effect and shall be enforced in like manner as a custody decree rendered by a court of this state.

B. A person violating a custody decree of another state which makes it necessary to enforce the decree in this state may be required to pay necessary travel and other expenses, including attorney's fees, incurred by the party entitled to the custody or his witnesses.

C. Upon filing of a certified copy of a custody decree of another state, valid on its face, and upon a showing of probable cause to believe that the person with physical custody of a child is likely to flee the jurisdiction of this state, the court may place the temporary custody of the child with the office of family services of the Department of Health and Human Resources pending a determination of the validity of the other state's custody decree. Temporary custody shall not exceed fifteen days unless the court extends the period upon a showing of good cause. In no case shall the custody period exceed sixty days.

§ 1715. Registry of out-of-state custody decrees and proceedings.

The clerk of each district court or family court shall maintain a registry in which he shall enter the following:

(1) Certified copies of custody decrees of other states received for filing.

(2) Communications as to the pendency of custody proceedings in other states.

(3) Communications concerning a finding of inconvenient forum by a court of another state, and

(4) Other communications or documents concerning custody proceedings in another state which may affect the jurisdiction of a court of this state or the disposition to be made by it in a custody proceeding.

§ 1716. Certified copies of custody decree.

The clerk of the district court or family court of this state, at the request of the court of another state or at the request of any person who is affected by or has a legitimate interest in a custody decree, shall certify and forward a copy of the decree to that court or person.

§ 1717. Taking testimony in another state.

In addition to other procedural devices available to a party, any party to the proceeding or a curator ad hoc or other representative of the child may adduce testimony of witnesses, including parties and the child, by deposition or otherwise, in another state. The court on its own motion may direct that the testimony of a person be taken in another state and may prescribe the manner in which and the terms upon which the testimony shall be taken.

§ 1718. Hearings and studies in another state; order to appear.

A. A court of this state may request the appropriate court of another state to hold a hearing to adduce evidence, to order a party to produce or give evidence under other procedures of that state, or to have social studies made with respect to the custody of a child involved in proceedings pending in the court of this state; and to forward to the court of this state certified copies of the transcript of the record of the hearing, the evidence otherwise adduced, or any social studies prepared in compliance with the request. The cost of the services may be assessed against the parties.

B. A court of this state may request the appropriate court of another state to order a party to custody proceedings pending in the court of this state to appear in the proceedings and if that party has physical custody of the child, to appear with the child. The request may state that travel and other necessary expenses of the party and of the child whose appearance is desired will be assessed against another party or will otherwise be paid.

§ 1719. Assistance to courts of other states.

A. Upon request of the court of another state the courts of this state which are competent to hear custody matters may order a person in this state to appear at a hearing to adduce evidence or to produce or give evidence under other procedures available in this state or may order social studies to be made for use in a custody proceeding in another state. A certified copy of the transcript of the record of the hearing or the evidence otherwise adduced and any social studies prepared shall be forwarded by the clerk of the court to the requesting court.

B. A person within this state may voluntarily give his testimony or statement in this state for use in a custody proceeding outside this state.

C. Upon request of the court of another state, a competent court of this state may order a person in this state to appear alone or with the child in a custody proceeding in another state. The court may condition compliance with the request upon assurance by the other state that travel and other necessary expenses will be advanced or reimbursed.

§ 1720. Preservation of documents for use in other states.

In any custody proceeding in this state the court shall preserve the pleadings, orders and decrees, any record that has been made of its hearings, social studies, and other pertinent documents until the child reaches eighteen (18) years of age. Upon appropriate request of the court of another state the court shall forward to the other court certified copies of any or all of such documents.

§ 1721. Request for court records of another state.

If a custody decree has been rendered in another state concerning a child involved in a custody proceeding pending in a court of this state, the court of this state upon taking jurisdiction of the case shall request of the court of the other state a certified copy of the transcript of any court record and other documents mentioned in Section 1720.

§ 1722. International application.

The general policies of this Part extend to the international area. The provisions of this Part relating to the recognition and enforcement of custody decrees of other states apply to custody decrees and decrees involving legal institutions similar in nature to custody institutions rendered by appropriate authorities of other nations if reasonable notice and opportunity to be heard were given to all affected persons.

§ 1723. Priority.

Upon the request of a party to a custody proceeding which raises a question of existence or exercise of jurisdiction under this Part, the case shall be given calendar priority and handled expeditiously.

§ 1724. Short title.

This Part may be cited as the Uniform Child Custody Jurisdiction Law.

MAINE

CHAPTER 16
UNIFORM CHILD CUSTODY JURISDICTION ACT

§ 801. Short title.

This chapter may be cited as the "Uniform Child Custody Jurisdiction Act."

§ 802. Purposes of Act; construction of provisions.

1. General purposes. The general purposes of this Act are to:

A. Avoid jurisdictional competition and conflict with courts of other states in matters of child custody which have in the past resulted in the shifting of children from state to state with harmful effects on their well-being;

B. Promote cooperation with the courts of other states to the end that a custody decree is rendered in that state which can best decide the case in the interest of the child;

C. Assure that litigation concerning the custody of a child take place ordinarily in the state with which the child and his family have the closest connection and where significant evidence concerning his care, protection, training and personal relationships is most readily available, and that courts of this State decline the exercise of jurisdiction when the child and his family have a closer connection with another state;

D. Discourage continuing controversies over child custody in the interest of greater stability of home environment and of secure family relationships for the child;

E. Deter abductions and other unilateral removals of children undertaken to obtain custody awards;

F. Avoid re-litigation of custody decisions of other states in this State insofar as feasible;

G. Facilitate the enforcement of custody decrees of other states;

H. Promote and expand the exchange of information and other forms of mutual assistance between the courts of this State and those of other states concerned with the same child; and

I. Make uniform the law of those states which enact it.

2. Construction. This Act shall be construed to promote the general purposes stated in this section.

§ 803. Definitions.

As used in this Act, unless the context indicates otherwise, the following terms shall have the following meanings.

1. Contestant. "Contestant" means a person, including a parent, who claims a right to custody or visitation rights with respect to a child.

2. Custody determination. "Custody determination" means a court decision and court orders and instructions providing for the custody of a child, including visitation rights; it does not include a decision relating to child support or any other monetary obligation of any person.

3. Custody proceeding. "Custody proceeding" includes proceedings in which custody determination is one of the several issues, such as an action for divorce or separation, and includes child neglect and dependency proceedings.

4. Decree or custody decree. "Decree" or "custody decree" means a custody determination contained in a judicial decree or order made in a custody proceeding, and includes an initial decree and a modification decree.

5. Home state. "Home state" means the state in which the child immediately preceding the time involved lived with his parents, a parent or a person acting as parent, for at least 6 consecutive months, and in the case of a child less than 6 months old the state in which the child lived from birth with any of the persons mentioned. Periods of temporary absence of any of the named persons are counted as part of the 6-month or other period.

6. Initial decree. "Initial decree" means the first custody decree concerning a particular child.

7. Modification decree. "Modification decree" means a custody decree which modifies or replaces a prior decree, whether made by the court which rendered the prior decree or by another court.

8. Physical custody. "Physical custody" means actual possession and control of a child.

9. Person acting as a parent. "Person acting as a parent" means a person, other than a parent, who has physical custody of a child and who has either been awarded custody by a court or claims a right to custody.

10. State. "State" means any state, territory or possession of the United States, the Commonwealth of Puerto Rico and the District of Columbia.

§ 804. Jurisdiction.

1. Grounds for jurisdiction. A court of this State which is competent to decide child custody matters has jurisdiction to make a child custody determination by initial or modification decree if:

A. This State is the home state of the child at the time of commencement of the proceeding, or has been the child's home state within 6 months before commencement of the proceeding and the child is absent from this State because of his removal or retention by a person claiming his custody or for other reasons, and a parent or person acting as parent continues to live in this State;

B. It is in the best interest of the child that a court of this State assume jurisdiction because the child and his parents, or the child and at least one contestant, have a significant connection with this State, and there is available in this State substantial evidence concerning the child's present or future care, protection, training and personal relationships;

C. The child is physically present in this State and the child has been abandoned or it is necessary in an emergency to protect the child because he has been subjected to or threatened with mistreatment or abuse or is otherwise neglected; or

D. It appears that no other state would have jurisdiction under prerequisites substantially in accordance with paragraphs A, B or C, or another state has declined to exercise jurisdiction on the ground that this State is the more appropriate forum to determine the custody of the child, and it is in the best interest of the child that this court assume jurisdiction.

2. Sufficiency of physical presence. Except under subsection 1, paragraphs C and D, physical presence in this State of the child, or of the child and one of the contestants, is not alone sufficient to confer jurisdiction on a court of this state to make a child custody determination.

3. Physical presence as prerequisite. Physical presence of the child, while desirable, is not a prerequisite for jurisdiction to determine his custody.

§ 805. Notice and opportunity to be heard.

Before making a decree under this Act, reasonable notice and opportunity to be heard shall be given to the contestants, any parent whose parental rights have not been previously terminated and any person who has physical custody of the child. If any of these persons is outside this State, notice and opportunity to be heard shall be given pursuant to section 806.

§ 806. Notice to persons outside the State; submission to jurisdiction.

1. Manner of notice. Notice required for the exercise of jurisdiction over a person outside this State shall be given in a manner reasonably calculated to give actual notice and may be:

A. By personal delivery outside this State in the manner prescribed for service of process within this State;

B. In the manner prescribed by the law of the place in which the service is made for service of process in that place in an action in any of its courts of general jurisdiction;

C. By any form of mail addressed to the person to be served and requesting a receipt; or

D. As directed by the court, including publication, if other means of notification are ineffective.

2. Time of notice. Notice under this section shall be served, mailed or delivered, or last published at least 20 days before any hearing in this State.

3. Proof of service. Proof of service outside this State may be made by affidavit of the individual who made the service, in the manner prescribed by the law of this State, the order pursuant to which the service is made, or the law of the place in which service is made. If service is made by mail, proof may be receipt signed by the addressee or other evidence of delivery to the addressee.

4. Notice not required. Notice is not required if a person submits to the jurisdiction of the court.

§ 807. Simultaneous proceedings in other states.

1. Prohibition on exercising jurisdiction. A court of this State shall not exercise its jurisdiction under this Act if at the time of filing the petition a proceeding concerning the custody of the child was pending in a court of another state exercising jurisdiction substantially in conformity with this Act, unless the proceeding is stayed by the court of the other state because this State is a more appropriate forum or for other reasons.

2. Investigating proceedings in other states. Before hearing the petition in a custody proceeding, the court shall examine the pleadings and other information supplied by the parties under section 810 and shall consult the child custody registry established under section 817 concerning the pendency of proceedings with respect to the child in other states. If the court has reason to believe that proceedings may be pending in another state, it shall direct an inquiry to the state court administrator or other appropriate official of the other state.

3. Resolution of multiple proceedings. If the court is informed during the course of the proceeding that a proceeding concerning the custody of the child was pending in another state before the court assumed jurisdiction, it shall stay the proceeding and communicate with the court in which the other proceeding is pending to the end that the issue may be litigated in the more appropriate forum and that information be exchanged in accordance with sections 820 through 823. If a court of this State has made a custody decree before being informed of a pending proceeding in a court of another state, it shall immediately inform that court of the fact. If the court is informed that a proceeding was commenced in another state after it assumed jurisdiction, it shall likewise inform the other court to the end that the issues may be litigated in the more appropriate forum.

§ 808. Inconvenient forum.

1. Decline to exercise jurisdiction. A court which has jurisdiction under this Act to make an initial or modification decree may decline to exercise its jurisdiction any time before making a decree if it finds that it is an inconvenient forum to make a custody determination under the circumstances of the case and that a court of another state is a more appropriate forum.

2. Motion for findings. A finding of inconvenient forum may be made upon the court's own motion or upon motion of a party or a guardian ad litem or other representative of the child.

3. Determination of inconvenient forum. In determining if it is an inconvenient forum, the court shall consider if it is in the interest of the child that another state assume jurisdiction. For this purpose it may take into account the following factors, among others:

A. If another state is or recently was the child's home state;

B. If another state has a closer connection with the child and his family or with the child and one or more of the contestants;

C. If substantial evidence concerning the child's present or future care, protection, training and personal relationships is more readily available in another state;

D. If the parties have agreed on another forum which is no less appropriate; and

E. If the exercise of jurisdiction by a court of this State would contravene any of the purposes stated in section 802.

4. Communicating with other states. Before determining whether to decline or retain jurisdiction, the court may communicate with a court of another state and exchange information pertinent to the assumption of jurisdiction by either court with a view to assuring that jurisdiction will be exercised by the more appropriate court and that a forum will be available to the parties.

5. Dismissal or stay. If the court finds that it is an inconvenient forum and that a court of another state is a more appropriate forum, it may dismiss the proceedings, or it may stay the proceedings upon condition that a custody proceeding be promptly commenced in another named state or upon any other conditions which may be just and proper, including the condition that a moving party stipulate his consent and submission to the jurisdiction of the other forum.

6. Separation of divorce and custody jurisdictions. The court may decline to exercise its jurisdiction under this Act if a custody determination is incidental to an action for divorce or another proceeding while retaining jurisdiction over the divorce or other proceeding.

7. Costs. If it appears to the court that it is clearly an inappropriate forum, it may require the party who commenced the proceedings to pay, in addition to the costs of the proceedings in this State, necessary travel and other expenses, including attorneys' fees, incurred by other parties or their witnesses. Payment is to be made to the clerk of the court for remittance to the proper party.

8. Informing another state. Upon dismissal or stay of proceedings under this section, the court shall inform the court found to be the more appropriate forum of this fact or, if the court which would have jurisdiction in the other state is not certainly known, shall transmit the information to the court administrator or other appropriate official for forwarding to the appropriate court.

9. Other state informing this State. Any communication received from another state informing this State of a finding of inconvenient forum because a court of this State is the more appropriate forum shall be filed in the custody registry of the appropriate court. Upon assuming jurisdiction, the court of this State shall inform the original court of this fact.

§ 809. Jurisdiction declined by reason of conduct.

1. Reprehensible conduct. If the petitioner for an initial decree has wrongfully taken the child from another state or has engaged in similar reprehensible conduct the court may decline to exercise jurisdiction if this is just and proper under the circumstances.

2. Improper removal of child. Unless required in the interest of the child, the court shall not exercise its jurisdiction to modify a custody decree of another state if the petitioner, without consent of the person entitled to custody, has improperly removed the child from the physical custody of the person entitled to custody or has improperly retained the child after a visit or other temporary relinquishment of physical custody. If the petitioner has violated any other provision of a custody decree of another state, the court may decline to exercise its jurisdiction if this is just and proper under the circumstances.

3. Costs. In appropriate cases, a court dismissing a petition under this section may charge the petitioner with necessary travel and other expenses, including attorneys' fees, incurred by other parties or their witnesses.

§ 810. Information under oath to be submitted to the court.

1. Information required in first pleading. Every party in a custody proceeding in his first pleading or in an affidavit attached to that pleading shall give information under oath or affirmation as to the child's present address, the places where the child has lived within the last 5 years and the names and present addresses of the persons with whom the child has lived during that period. In this pleading or affidavit, every party shall further declare under oath or affirmation whether:

A. He has participated as a party, witness or in any other capacity in any other litigation concerning the custody of the same child in this or any other state;

B. He has information of any custody proceeding concerning the child pending in a court of this or any other state; and

C. He knows of any person not a party to the proceedings who has physical custody of the child or claims to have custody or visitation rights with respect to the child.

2. Other information. If the declaration as to any item in subsection 1 is in the affirmative the declarant shall give additional information under oath or affirmation as required by the court. The court may examine the parties under oath or affirmation as to details of the information furnished and as to other matters pertinent to the court's jurisdiction and the disposition of the case.

3. Continuing duty of parties. Each party has a continuing duty to inform the court of any custody proceeding concerning the child in this or any other state of which he obtained information during this proceeding.

§ 811. Additional parties.

If the court learns from information furnished by the parties under section 810 or from other sources that a person not a party to the custody proceeding has physical custody of the child or claims to have custody or visitation rights with respect to the child, it shall order that person to be joined as a party and to be duly notified of the pendency of the proceeding and of his joinder as a party. If the person joined as a party is outside this State, he shall be served with process or otherwise notified in accordance with section 806.

§ 812. Appearance of parties and the child.

1. Personal appearance of in-state party. The court may order any party to the proceeding who is in this State to appear personally before the court. If that party has physical custody of the child, the court may order that he appear personally with the child.

2. Personal appearance of out-of-state party. If a party to the proceeding whose presence is desired by the court is outside this State with or without the child, the court may order that the notice given under section 806 include a statement directing that party to appear personally with or without the child and declaring that failure to appear may result in a decision adverse to that party.

3. Costs. If a party to the proceeding who is outside this State is directed to appear under subsection 2 or desires to appear personally before the court with or without the child, the court may require another party to pay the clerk of the court travel and other necessary expenses of the party so appearing and of the child if this is just and proper under the circumstances.

§ 813. Binding force and res judicata effect of custody decree.

A custody decree rendered by a court of this State which had jurisdiction under section 804 binds all parties who have been served in this State or notified in accordance with section 806 or who have submitted to the jurisdiction of the court and who have been given an opportunity to be heard. As to these parties, the custody decree is conclusive as to all issues of law and fact decided and as to the custody determination made unless and until that determination is modified pursuant to law, including the provisions of this Act.

§ 814. Recognition of out-of-state custody decrees.

The courts of this State shall recognize and enforce an initial or modification decree of a court of another state which had assumed jurisdiction under statutory provisions substantially in accordance with this Act or which was made under factual circumstances meeting the jurisdictional standards of the Act, so long as this decree has not been modified in accordance with jurisdictional standards substantially similar to those of this Act.

§ 815. Modification of custody decree of another state.

1. Limits on modification. If a court of another state has made a custody decree, a court of this State shall not modify that decree unless it appears to the court of this State that the court which rendered the decree does not now have jurisdiction under jurisdictional prerequisites substantially in accordance with this Act or has declined to assume jurisdiction to modify the decree and the court of this State has jurisdiction.

2. Consideration of proceedings in another state. If a court of this State is authorized under subsection 1 and section 809 to modify a custody decree of another state, it shall give due consideration to the transcript of the record and other documents of all previous proceedings submitted to it in accordance with section 823.

§ 816. Filing and enforcement of custody decree of another state.

1. Filing a decree of another state. A certified copy of a custody decree of another state may be filed in the office of the clerk of any court of this State having jurisdiction under section 804. The clerk shall treat the decree in the same manner as a custody decree of that court. A custody decree so filed has the same effect and shall be enforced in like manner as a custody decree rendered by a court of this State.

2. Costs. A person violating a custody decree of another state which makes it necessary to enforce the decree in this State may be required to pay necessary travel and other expenses, including attorneys' fees incurred by the party entitled to the custody or his witnesses.

3. Filing in registry. On receiving a custody decree of another state, the clerk shall send a certified copy of that decree for filing under section 817 to the State Court Administrator.

§ 817. Registry of out-of-state custody decrees and proceedings.

The State Court Administrator shall maintain a registry in which he shall enter the following:

1. Copies of decrees. Certified copies of custody decrees of other states received for filing;

2. Communications on pending decrees. Communications as to the pendency of custody proceedings in other states;

3. Communications on inconvenient forum findings. Communications concerning a finding of inconvenient forum by a court of another state; and

4. Other information. Other communications or documents concerning custody proceedings in another state which may affect the jurisdiction of a court of this State or the disposition to be made by it in a custody proceeding.

§ 818. Certified copies of custody decree.

The State Court Administrator at the request of the court of another state or at the request of any person who is affected by or has a legitimate interest in a custody decree, shall certify and forward a copy of the decree to that court or person. He shall provide copies at cost.

§ 819. Taking testimony in another state.

In addition to other procedural devices available to a party, any party to the proceeding or a guardian ad litem or other representative of the child may adduce testimony of witnesses, including parties and the child, by deposition or otherwise, in another state. The court on its own motion may direct that the testimony of a person be taken in another state and may prescribe the manner in which and the terms upon which the testimony shall be taken.

§ 820. Hearings and studies in another state; orders to appear.

1. Requesting another state to hold hearings. A court of this State may request the appropriate court of another state to hold a hearing to adduce evidence, to order a party to produce or give evidence under other procedures of that state or to have social studies made with respect to the custody of a child involved in proceedings pending in the court of this State; and to forward to the court of this State certified copies of the transcript of the record of the hearing, the evidence otherwise adduced or any social studies prepared in compliance with the request. The cost of the services may be assessed against the parties or, if necessary, ordered paid by the State.

2. Request another state to order personal appearance. A court of this State may request the appropriate court of another state

to order a party to custody proceedings pending in the court of this State to appear in the proceedings and if that party has physical custody of the child, to appear in the proceedings and if that party has physical custody of the child, to appear with the child. The request may state that travel and other necessary expenses of the party and of the child whose appearance is desired will be assessed against another party or will otherwise be paid.

§ 821. Assistance to courts of other states.

1. Responding to requests of other states. Upon request of the court of another state, the courts of this State which are competent to hear custody matters may order a person in this State to appear at a hearing to adduce evidence or to produce or give evidence under other procedures available in this State or may request social studies to be made for use in a custody proceeding in another state as provided under section 751 for proceedings in this State. A certified copy of the transcript of the record of the hearing or the evidence otherwise adduced and any social studies prepared shall be forwarded by the clerk of the court to the requesting court.

2. Voluntary testimony. A person within this State may voluntarily give his testimony or statement in this State for use in a custody proceeding outside this State.

3. Ordering personal appearance in another state. Upon request of the court of another state, a competent court of this State may order a person in this State to appear alone or with the child in a custody proceeding in another state. The court may condition compliance with the request upon assurance by the other state that state travel and other necessary expenses will be advanced or reimbursed.

§ 822. Preservation of documents for use in other states.

In any custody proceeding in this State, the court shall preserve the pleadings, orders and decrees, any record that has been made of its hearings, social studies and other pertinent documents until the child reaches 18 years of age. Upon appropriate request of the court of another state, the court shall forward to the other court certified copies of any or all of such documents.

§ 823. Request for court records of another state.

If a custody decree has been rendered in another state concerning a child involved in a custody proceeding pending in a court of this State, the court of this State upon taking jurisdiction of the case shall request of the court of the other state a certified copy of the transcript of any court record and other documents mentioned in section 822.

§ 824. International application.

The general policies of this Act extend to the international area. The provisions of this Act relating to the recognition and enforcement of custody decrees of other states apply to custody decrees and decrees involving legal institutions similar in nature to custody rendered by appropriate authorities of other nations if reasonable notice and opportunity to be heard were given to all affected persons.

§ 825. Priority.

Upon the request of a party to a custody proceeding which raises a question of existence or exercise of jurisdiction under this Act, the case shall be given calendar priority and handled expeditiously.

MARYLAND

MARYLAND UNIFORM CHILD CUSTODY JURISDICTION ACT

§ 9-201. Definitions.

(a) In general. In this subtitle the following words have the meanings indicated.

(b) Contestant. "Contestant" means a person, including a parent, who claims a right to custody or visitation rights with respect to a child.

(c) Custody determination.

(1) "Custody determination" means a judicial decision, order, or instruction that relates to the custody of a child or to visitation rights.

(2) "Custody determination" does not include a decision relating to child support or any other monetary obligation of any person.

(d) Custody proceeding.

(1) "Custody proceeding" includes any proceeding in which a custody determination is 1 of several issues, such as an action for divorce or separation.

(2) "Custody proceeding" includes a child neglect or dependency proceeding.

(e) Decree or custody decree.

(1) "Decree" or "custody decree" means a custody determination contained in a judicial decree or order made in a custody proceeding.

(2) "Decree" or "custody decree" includes an initial decree and a modification decree.

(f) Home state. "Home state" means the state in which the child, immediately preceding the time involved, lived with the child's parents, a parent, or a person acting as parent, for at least 6 consecutive months, and in the case of a child less than 6 months old, the state in which the child lived from birth with any of the persons mentioned. Periods of temporary absence of any of the named persons are counted as part of the 6-month or other period.

(g) Initial decree. "Initial decree" means the first custody decree concerning a particular child.

(h) Modification decree. "Modification decree" means a custody decree that modified or replaces a prior decree, whether made by the court that rendered the prior decree or by another court.

(i) Physical custody. "Physical custody" means actual possession and control of a child.

(j) Person acting as parent. "Person acting as parent" means a person, other than a parent, who has physical custody of a child and who has either been awarded custody by a court or claims a right to custody.

§ 9-202. Purpose and construction of subtitle.

(a) General purposes. The general purposes of this subtitle are to:

(1) avoid jurisdictional competition and conflict with courts of other states in matters of child custody which have in the past resulted in the shifting of children from state to state with harmful effects on their well-being;

(2) promote cooperation with the courts of other states to the end that a custody decree is rendered in that state which can best decide the case in the interest of the child;

(3) assure that litigation concerning the custody of a child takes place ordinarily in the state with which the child and the child's family have the closest connection and where significant evidence concerning the child's care, protection, training, and personal relationships is most readily available, and that courts of this State decline the exercise of jurisdiction when the child and the child's family have a closer connection with another state;

(4) discourage continuing controversies over child custody in the interest of greater stability of home environment and of secure family relationships for the child;

(5) deter abductions and other unilateral removals of children undertaken to obtain custody awards;

(6) avoid relitigation of custody decisions of other states in this State insofar as feasible;

(7) facilitate the enforcement of custody decrees of other states;

(8) promote and expand the exchange of information and other forms of mutual assistance between the courts of this State and those of other states concerned with the same child; and

(9) make uniform the law of those states which enact it.

(b) Construction. This subtitle shall be construed to promote the general purposes stated in this section.

§ 9-203. International scope of subtitle.

The general policies of this subtitle extend to the international area. The provisions of this subtitle relating to the recognition and enforcement of custody decrees of other states apply to custody decrees and decrees involving legal institutions similar in nature to custody institutions rendered by appropriate authorities of other nations if reasonable notice and opportunity to be heard were given to all affected persons.

§ 9-204. When court has jurisdiction.

(a) Grounds for jurisdiction. A court of this State which is competent to decide child custody matters has jurisdiction to make a child custody determination by initial decree or modification decree if:

(1) this State (i) is the home state of the child at the time of commencement of the proceeding, or (ii) had been the child's home state within 6 months before commencement of the proceedings and the child is absent from this State because of the child's removal or retention by a person claiming custody or for other reasons, and a parent or person acting as parent continues to live in this State;

(2) it is in the best interest of the child that a court of this State assume jurisdiction because (i) the child and the child's parents, or the child and at least 1 contestant, have a significant connection with this State, and (ii) there is available in this State substantial evidence concerning the child's present or future care, protection, training, and personal relationships;

(3) the child is physically present in this State and (i) the child has been abandoned or (ii) it is necessary in an emergency to protect the child because the child has been subjected to or threatened with mistreatment or abuse or is otherwise neglected or dependent; or

(4) (i) it appears that no other state would have jurisdiction under prerequisites substantially in accordance with items (1), (2), or (3) of this subsection or another state has declined to exercise jurisdiction on the ground that this State is the more appropriate forum to determine the custody of the child, and (ii) it is in the best interest of the child that this court assume jurisdiction.

(b) Effect of physical presence. Except under subsection (a) (3) and (4) of this section, physical presence in this State of the child, or of the child and 1 of the contestants, is not alone sufficient to confer jurisdiction on a court of this State to make a child custody determination.

(c) Physical presence not prerequisite. Physical presence of the child, while desirable, is not a prerequisite for jurisdiction to determine the child's custody.

§ 9-205. Notice and opportunity to be heard.

Before making a decree under this subtitle, reasonable notice and opportunity to be heard shall be given to the contestants, any parent whose parental rights have not been previously terminated, and any person who has physical custody of the child. If any of these persons is outside this State, notice and opportunity to be heard shall be given pursuant to the Maryland Rules of Procedure.

§ 9-206. Proceeding pending in another state.

(a) When other state more appropriate. Except where the child has been abandoned or it is necessary in an emergency to protect the child because the child has been subjected to or threatened with mistreatment or is otherwise neglected or dependent, a court of this State shall not exercise its jurisdiction under this subtitle if, at the time of filing the petition, a proceeding concerning the custody of the child was pending in a court of another state exercising jurisdiction substantially in conformity with this subtitle, unless the proceeding is stayed by the court of the other state because this State is a more appropriate forum or for other reasons.

(b) Inquiry before hearing as to proceeding in other state. Before hearing the petition in a custody proceeding, the court shall examine the pleadings and other information supplied by the parties under § 9-209 of this subtitle and shall consult the child custody registry established under § 9-216 of this subtitle concerning the pendency of proceedings with respect to the child in other states. If the court has reason to believe that proceedings may be pending in another state, it shall direct an inquiry to the state court administrator or other appropriate official of the other state.

(c) Stay during proceeding. If the court is informed during the course of the proceeding that a proceeding concerning the custody of the child was pending in another state before the court assumed jurisdiction, it shall stay the proceeding and communicate with the court in which the other proceeding is pending to the end that the issue may be litigated in the more appropriate forum and that information be exchanged in accordance with §§ 9-219 through 9-222 of this subtitle. If a court of this State has made a custody decree before being informed of a pending proceeding in a court of another state, it shall immediately inform that court of the fact. If the court is informed that a proceeding was commenced in another state after it assumed jurisdiction, it shall likewise inform the other court to the end that the issues may be litigated in a more appropriate forum.

§ 9-207. Finding that court is inconvenient forum.

(a) Action if this State is inconvenient forum. A court which has jurisdiction under this subtitle to make an initial decree or modification decree may decline to exercise its jurisdiction any time before making a decree if it finds that it is an inconvenient forum to make a custody determination under the circumstances of the case and that a court of another state is a more appropriate forum.

(b) Who may move for finding of inconvenient forum. A finding of inconvenient forum may be made on the court's own motion or on motion of a party or a guardian ad litem or other representative of the child.

(c) Factors in determination. In determining if it is an inconvenient forum, the court shall consider if it is in the interest of the child that another state assume jurisdiction. For this purpose, it may take into account the following factors, among others:

(1) if another state is or recently was the child's home state;

(2) if another state has a closer connection with the child and the child's family or with the child and 1 or more of the contestants;

(3) if substantial evidence concerning the child's present or future care, protection, training, and personal relationships is more readily available in another state;

(4) if the parties have agreed on another forum that is no less appropriate; and

(5) if the exercise of jurisdiction by a court of this State would contravene any of the purposes stated in § 9-202 of this subtitle.

(d) Communications with other courts. Before determining whether to decline or retain jurisdiction, the court may communicate with a court of another state and exchange information pertinent to the assumption of jurisdiction by either court with a view to assuring that jurisdiction will be exercised by the more appropriate court and that a forum will be available to the parties.

(e) Action on finding of inconvenient forum. If the court finds that it is an inconvenient forum and that a court of another state is a more appropriate forum, it may dismiss the proceedings, or it may stay the proceedings on condition that a custody proceeding be promptly commenced in another named state or on any other conditions which may be just and proper, including the condition that a moving party stipulate the party's consent and submission to the jurisdiction of the other forum.

(f) Effect of divorce or other proceeding. The court may decline to exercise its jurisdiction under this subtitle if a custody determination is incidental to an action for divorce or another proceeding while retaining jurisdiction over the divorce or other proceeding.

(g) Assessment of costs, expenses, and fees. If it appears to the court that it is clearly an inappropriate forum, it may require the party who commenced the proceedings to pay, in addition to the costs of the proceedings in this State, necessary travel and other expenses, including attorneys' fees, incurred by other parties or their witnesses. Payment is to be made to the clerk of the court for remittance to the proper party.

(h) Notice to other state. On dismissal or stay of proceedings under this section, the court shall inform the court found to be the more appropriate forum of this fact, or if the court which would have jurisdiction in the other state is not certainly known, shall transmit the information to the court administrator or other appropriate official for forwarding to the appropriate court.

(i) Action if other state defers to this State. Any communication received from another state informing this State of a finding of inconvenient forum because a court of this State is the more appropriate forum shall be filed in the custody registry of the appropriate court. On assuming jurisdiction, the court of this State shall inform the original court of this fact.

§ 9-208. When court may decline jurisdiction.

(a) No existing decree. If the petitioner for an initial decree has wrongfully taken the child from another state or has engaged in similar reprehensible conduct, the court may decline to exercise jurisdiction if this is just and proper under the circumstances.

(b) Existing decree. Unless required in the interest of the child, the court shall not exercise its jurisdiction to modify a custody decree of another state if the petitioner, without consent of the person entitled to custody, has improperly removed the child from the physical custody of the person entitled to custody or has improperly retained the child after a visit or other temporary relinquishment of physical custody. If the petitioner has violated any other provision of a custody decree of another state, the court may decline to exercise its jurisdiction if this is just and proper under the circumstances.

(c) Assessments of expenses and fees. In appropriate cases, a court dismissing a petition under this section may charge the petitioner with necessary travel and other expenses, including attorney's fees, incurred by other parties or their witnesses.

§ 9-209. Providing information as to child.

(a) In initial pleading. Every party in a custody proceeding in the party's first pleading or in an affidavit attached to that pleading shall give information under oath as to the child's present address, the places where the child has lived within the last 5 years, and the names and present addresses of the persons with whom the child has lived during that period. In this pleading or affidavit every party shall further declare under oath whether:

(1) the party has participated as a party, witness, or in any other capacity in any other litigation concerning the custody of the same child in this or any other state;

(2) the party has information of any custody proceeding concerning the child pending in a court of this or any other state; and

(3) the party knows of any person not a party to the proceedings who has physical custody of the child or claims to have custody or visitation rights with respect to the child.

(b) Court may require additional information. If the declaration as to any of the above items is in the affirmative, the declarant shall give additional information under oath as required by the court. The court may examine the parties under oath as to details of the information furnished and as to other matters pertinent to the court's jurisdiction and the disposition of the case.

(c) Continuing duty to inform court. Each party has a continuing duty to inform the court of any custody proceeding concerning the child in this or any other state of which the party obtained information during this proceeding.

§ 9-210. Joinder of person as a party.

If the court learns from information furnished by the parties pursuant to § 9-209 of this subtitle or from other sources that a person not a party to the custody proceeding has physical custody of the child or claims to have custody or visitation rights with respect to the child, it shall order that person to be joined as a party and to be notified of the pendency of the proceeding and of the person's joinder as a party. If the person joined as a party is outside this State, the person shall be served with process or otherwise notified in accordance with § 9-205 of this subtitle.

§ 9-211. Appearances before court.

(a) Order to appear. The court may order any party to the proceeding who is in this State to appear personally before the court. If that party has physical custody of the child, the court may order that party to appear personally with the child.

(b) Failure to appear. If a party to the proceeding whose presence is desired by the court is outside this State, with or without the child, the court may order that the notice include a statement directing that party to appear personally with or without the child and declaring that failure to appear may result in a decision adverse to that party.

(c) Travel and other expenses. If a party to the proceeding who is outside this State is directed to appear under subsection (b) of this section or desires to appear personally before the court with or without the child, the court may require another party to pay to the clerk of the court travel and other necessary expenses of the party so appearing and of the child if this is just and proper under the circumstances.

§ 9-212. Custody decree binding and conclusive.

A custody decree rendered by a court of this State which had jurisdiction under § 9-204 of this subtitle binds all parties who have been served in this State or notified in accordance with the Maryland Rules of Procedure, or who have submitted to the jurisdiction of the court, and who have been given an opportunity to be heard. As to these parties, the custody decree is conclusive as to all issues of law and fact decided and as to the custody determination made unless and until that determination is modified pursuant to law, including the provisions of this subtitle.

§ 9-213. Out-of-State decree - Recognition and enforcement.

The courts of this State shall recognize and enforce an initial decree or modification decree of a court of another state that had assumed jurisdiction under statutory provisions substantially in accordance with this subtitle, or that was made under factual circumstances meeting the jurisdictional standards of the subtitle, so long as this decree has not been modified in accordance with jurisdictional standards substantially similar to those of this subtitle.

§ 9-214. Same - Modification.

(a) Jurisdictional requirements. If a court of another state has made a custody decree, a court of this State shall not modify that decree unless (1) it appears to the court of this State that the court that rendered the decree does not now have jurisdiction under jurisdictional prerequisites substantially in accordance with this subtitle or has declined to assume jurisdiction to modify the decree and (2) the court of this State has jurisdiction.

(b) Documents to be considered. If a court of this State is authorized under subsection (a) of this section and § 9-204 of this subtitle to modify a custody decree of another state, the court shall give due consideration to the transcript of the record and other documents of all previous proceedings submitted to it in accordance with § 9-222 of this subtitle.

§ 9-215. Same - Filing; expenses of enforcement.

(a) Filing certified copy of decree; effect of filing. A certified copy of a custody decree of another state may be filed in the office of the clerk of any circuit court for any county. The clerk shall treat the decree in the same manner as a custody decree of that court. A custody decree so filed has the same effect and shall be enforced in like manner as a custody decree rendered by a court of this State.

(b) Liability for certain expenses of enforcement. A person violating a custody decree of another state which makes it necessary to enforce the decree in this State may be required to pay necessary travel and other expenses, including attorney's fees, incurred by the party entitled to the custody or the party's witnesses.

§ 9-216. Clerks to maintain registry; contents of registry.

The clerks of the circuit courts shall maintain a registry in which they shall enter the following:

(1) certified copies of custody decrees of other states received for filing;

(2) communications as to the pendency of custody proceedings in other states;

(3) communications concerning a finding of inconvenient forum by a court of another state; and

(4) other communications or documents concerning custody proceedings in another state which may affect the jurisdiction of a court of this State or the disposition to be made by it in a custody proceeding.

§ 9-217. Clerk to provide copy of decree.

The clerk of the court, at the request of the court of another state or at the request of any person who is affected by or has a legitimate interest in a custody decree, shall certify and forward a copy of the decree to that court or person.

§ 9-218. Obtaining testimony of witnesses in another state.

In addition to other procedural devices available to a party, any party to the proceeding or a guardian ad litem or other representative of the child may adduce testimony of witnesses, including parties and the child, by deposition or otherwise, in another state. The court on its own motion may direct that the testimony of a person be taken in another state and may prescribe the manner in which and the terms on which the testimony shall be taken.

§ 9-219. Requests to another state for evidence or for party to appear.

(a) Evidence that may be requested; assessment of costs. A court of this State may request the appropriate court of another state to hold a hearing to adduce evidence, to order a party to produce or give evidence under other procedures of that state, or to have social studies made with respect to the custody of a child involved in proceedings pending in the court of this State; and to forward to the court of this State certified copies of the transcript of the record of the hearing, the evidence otherwise adduced, or any social studies prepared in compliance with the request. The cost of the services may be assessed against the parties, or, if necessary, ordered paid by the State.

(b) Appearance of party; assessment of travel expenses. A court of this State may request the appropriate court of another state to order a party to custody proceedings pending in the court of this State to appear in the proceedings, and if that party has physical custody of the child, to appear with the child. The request may state that travel and other necessary expenses of the party and of the child whose appearance is desired will be assessed against another party or will otherwise be paid.

§ 9-220. Requests from another state.

(a) Evidence that may be requested. On request of the court of another state, the courts of this State which are competent to hear custody matters may order a person in this State to appear at a hearing to adduce evidence or to produce or give evidence under other procedures available in this State or may order social studies to be made for use in a custody proceeding in another state. A certified copy of the transcript of the record of the hearing or the evidence otherwise adduced and any social studies prepared shall be forwarded by the clerk of the court to the requesting court.

(b) Voluntary giving of evidence. A person within this State may voluntarily give testimony or a statement in this State for use in a custody proceeding outside this State.

(c) Appearance of party in another state; payment of expenses. On request of the court of another state, a competent court of this State may order a person in this State to appear alone or with the child in a custody proceeding in another state. The court may condition compliance with the request on assurance by the other state that travel and other necessary expenses will be advanced or reimbursed.

§ 9-221. Preservation of documents; certified copies to be provided.

In any custody proceeding in this State, the court shall preserve the pleadings, orders, and decrees, any record that has been made of its hearings, social studies, and other pertinent documents until the child reaches 18 years of age. On appropriate request of the court of another state, the court shall forward to the other court certified copies of any or all of the documents.

§ 9-222. Requesting court records and documents from another state.

If a custody decree has been rendered in another state concerning a child involved in a custody proceeding pending in a court of this State, the court of this State on taking jurisdiction of the case shall request of the court of the other state a certified copy of the transcript of any court record and other documents mentioned in § 9-216 of this subtitle.

§ 9-223. Cases given priority.

On the request of a party to a custody proceeding that raises a question of existence or exercise of jurisdiction under this subtitle, the case shall be given calendar priority and handled expeditiously.

§ 9-224. Short title.

This subtitle may be cited as the "Maryland Uniform Child Custody Jurisdiction Act".

MASSACHUSETTS

CHAPTER 209B
MASSACHUSETTS CHILD CUSTODY JURISDICTION ACT

§ 1. Definitions.

As used in this chapter the following words, unless the context requires otherwise, shall have the following meanings:

"Contestant", a person who claims a legal right to custody or visitation with respect to a child;

"Custody determination", any court order, instruction or judgment, whether temporary or final, providing for the custody of or visitation rights with a child; it shall not be deemed to include any order or judgment concerning other child-related matters except to the extent such order of judgment contains a custody determination as above-stated;

"Custody proceeding", includes proceedings in which a custody determination is one of several issues presented for resolution, such as an action for divorce or separation, guardianship, and care and protection;

"Judgment" or "Custody judgment", a custody determination made in a custody proceeding, and includes an initial judgment and a modification judgment;

"Home state", the state in which the child immediately preceding the date of commencement of the custody proceeding resided with his parents, a parent, or a person acting as parent, for at least 6 consecutive months, and in the case of a child less than 6 months old the state in which the child lived from birth with any of the persons mentioned. Periods of temporary absence of any of the named persons are counted as part of the 6-month or other period;

"Initial judgment", the first custody determination concerning a particular child;

"Modification judgment", a custody determination which modifies or replaces a prior custody determination, whether made by the court which rendered the prior custody determination, or by another court;

"Physical custody", actual possession and control of a child;

"Person acting as parent", a person other than a parent who has physical custody of a child and who has either been awarded custody of a child or claims a legal right to custody and includes an authorized social service agency exercising legal or physical custody of a child; and

"Parent", a biological, foster, or adoptive parent whose parental rights have not previously been terminated;

"State", any state, territory, or possession of the United States, the Commonwealth of Puerto Rico, and the District of Columbia.

§ 2. Jurisdiction.

(a) Any court which is competent to decide child custody matters has jurisdiction to make a custody determination by initial or modification judgment if:

(1) the commonwealth (i) is the home state of the child on the commencement of the custody proceeding, or (ii) had been the child's home state within six months before the date of the commencement of the proceeding and the child is absent from the commonwealth because of his or her removal or retention by a person claiming his or her custody or for other reasons, and a parent or person acting as parent continues to reside in the commonwealth; or

(2) it appears that no other state would have jurisdiction under paragraph (1) and it is in the best interest of the child that a court of the commonwealth assume jurisdiction because (i) the child and his or her parents, or the child and at least one contestant, have a significant connection with the commonwealth, and (ii) there is available in the commonwealth substantial evidence concerning the child's present or future care, protection, training, and personal relationships; or

(3) the child is physically present in the commonwealth and (i) the child has been abandoned or (ii) it is necessary in an emergency to protect the child from abuse or neglect or for other good cause shown, provided that in the event that jurisdictional prerequisites are not established pursuant to any other paragraph of this subsection and a court of another state shall be entitled to assert jurisdiction under any other subparagraph of this paragraph then a court exercising jurisdiction pursuant to this clause of paragraph (3) may do so only by entering such temporary order or orders as it deems necessary unless the court of the other state has declined to exercise jurisdiction, has stayed its proceedings or has otherwise deferred to the jurisdiction of a court of the commonwealth; or

(4) (i) it appears that no other state would have jurisdiction under prerequisites substantially in accordance with paragraph (1), (2) or (3), or another state has declined to exercise jurisdiction on the ground that the commonwealth is the more appropriate forum to determine the custody of the child, and (ii) it is in the best interest of the child that a court of the commonwealth assume jurisdiction.

(b) Except under subparagraphs (3) and (4) of paragraph (a), physical presence in the commonwealth of the child or of the child and one of the contestants, is not alone sufficient to confer jurisdiction on a court of the commonwealth to make a custody determination.

(c) Physical presence of the child, while desirable, is not a prerequisite for jurisdiction to make a custody determination.

(d) A court of the commonwealth shall not exercise jurisdiction in any custody proceeding commenced during the pendency of a proceeding in a court of another state where such court of that state is exercising jurisdiction consistently with the provisions of this section for the purpose of making a custody determination, except in accordance with paragraph (3) of subsection (a), unless the court of the other state shall decline jurisdiction pursuant to paragraph (4) of subsection (a) or shall stay its proceedings or otherwise defer to the jurisdiction of a court of the commonwealth.

(e) If a court of another state has made a custody determination in substantial conformity with this chapter, a court of the commonwealth shall not modify that determination unless (1) it appears to the court of the commonwealth that the court which made the custody determination does not now have jurisdiction under jurisdictional prerequisites substantially in accordance with this chapter or that such court has declined to assume jurisdiction to modify its determination and (2) a court of the commonwealth now has jurisdiction pursuant to this chapter.

§ 3. Matters to be Stated in Affidavit; Examination Under Oath; Amendments; Waiver of Disclosure of Address; Sanctions.

(a) Every party in any custody proceeding shall state in an affidavit which shall be filed together with his first pleading the following information:

(1) the child's present address of residence;

(2) each address at which the child has resided during the two years immediately prior to the filing of the instant custody proceeding;

(3) the names and, if known, the current residential addresses or, if unknown, the last and usual residential addresses, of all persons who have been parties to any custody proceedings involving the child during the said two-year period, other than any person whose rights have been terminated in any parental rights termination proceeding, and any other persons who, according to the knowledge and belief of the affiant, claim a legal right to the custody or physical possession of the child; and

(4) whether or not the party knows of or has participated in any prior custody proceeding involving the child in the commonwealth or in any other jurisdiction and the nature of his participation, as party, witness, or in any other capacity, in such prior proceeding.

(b) Unless the same have already been filed by another party, every party in any custody proceeding shall attach to the affidavit a certified copy of each pleading and of any determination entered in any custody proceeding he knows of or has participated in involving the child in the commonwealth or in any other jurisdiction.

(c) The court may examine any one or more of the parties under oath concerning the information required to be furnished under this section and concerning other matters pertinent to any jurisdictional or other issues before the court.

(d) Each party shall amend the affidavit at any time after filing to inform the court of any custody proceeding filed in any jurisdiction after the date of filing of the instant custody proceeding of which the affiant becomes aware after filing the affidavit and shall further amend the affidavit to include the names and addresses, in conformity with paragraph (3) of subsection (a), of any person of whom the affiant becomes aware after filing the affidavit who claims a legal right to the custody or physical possession of the child.

(e) Notwithstanding the provisions of this section, a court may waive disclosure of the present or prior address of the child or of a contestant when such waiver is necessary to protect the child or the contestant from physical or emotional abuse. Application for an order waiving disclosure under this paragraph shall be made upon such notice as the court shall prescribe. The court shall waive disclosure whenever the present or prior address of the child or of a contestant is a shelter for battered persons and their dependent children. The reasons for waiver of any disclosure requirement of this section shall be stated by the court in the record of the custody proceeding.

(f) The court may impose sanctions against any party who fails to act in conformity with this section without leave of court granted for good cause shown.

§ 4. Parties.

(a) After examination of the pleadings, affidavits, certified copies of the documentation relative to other custody proceedings and such oral testimony as it may require, the court shall determine the proper parties to the custody proceeding.

(b) During the pendency of the proceeding, the court may require the joinder of additional parties and in that event, the court shall specify that such additional parties be served with process in accordance with section five or six, as applicable, or that they be otherwise notified in such manner as the court shall determine.

§ 5. Notice; Waiver of Notice.

(a) Reasonable notice in conformity with section six and an opportunity to be heard shall be given to the contestants, to any parent whose parental rights have not been previously terminated, to any person acting as parent, and to any other persons designated proper parties by the court pursuant to section four, provided that in the event a court of the commonwealth assumes jurisdiction pursuant to clause (ii) of paragraph (3) of subsection (a) of section two, then the court may waive such notice requirement for such period as may be allowed under applicable court rules.

(b) Any notice shall include the nature of the action, copies of all pleadings filed with the court, and the statement that any person so notified may apply to the court concerning allocation of the costs of those reasonable and necessary expenses to be incurred in connection with the custody proceeding in accordance with applicable sections of this chapter.

§ 6. Notice; Manner of Serving; Voluntary Appearance.

(a) Notice to a person in the commonwealth shall be given in accordance with the applicable Massachusetts rules of court or in any such other manner as is prescribed by law.

(b) Notice required for the exercise of jurisdiction over a person outside the commonwealth shall be given in accordance with the applicable Massachusetts Rules of Court or statute or, in the discretion of the court, in the manner prescribed by the law of the place in which the service is made concerning service of process in an action of its court of general jurisdiction, provided, however, that in no event shall notice under this paragraph be served, mailed, delivered or last published less than twenty days before any custody determination is made in this state, other than a determination made pursuant to clause (ii) of paragraph (3) of subsection (a) of section two.

(c) Proof of service outside the commonwealth may be made by affidavit of the individual who made the service, in accordance with the applicable law or the Massachusetts rules of court, in accordance with the order pursuant to which the service is made, or, in the discretion of the court, otherwise in accordance with the law of the place in which the service is made.

(d) Notice is not required to be given to a contestant who submits to the jurisdiction of the court.

§ 7. Court May Decline Jurisdiction; Inconvenient Forum; Costs and Fees; Sanctions.

(a) A court which has jurisdiction pursuant to section two may decline to exercise its jurisdiction at any time prior to making a custody determination upon finding that its assumption of jurisdiction would be (i) violative of the purposes of this chapter; or (ii) would be based upon the illegal or otherwise wrongful conduct of a party; or (iii) would constitute an inconvenient forum and that a court of another state would constitute a more convenient forum.

(b) A court may decline jurisdiction for any of the reasons set forth in paragraph (a) upon motion of a party or of any representative of the child entitled to appear before the court or upon the court's own motion.

(c) In order to determine whether it is the appropriate forum, a court of the commonwealth may, in its discretion, at any time during the pendency of the custody proceeding, communicate and exchange information with a court or courts of any other relevant jurisdiction.

(d) For the purposes of this section, a court may consider the following factors:

(1) whether another state is or recently was the child's home state;

(2) whether another state has a closer connection with the child and his family or with the child and one or more of the contestants;

(3) whether more substantial evidence concerning the child's present or future care, protection, training, and personal relationships is available or whether such evidence is more readily available in another state;

(4) whether the parties have agreed on another forum which is not less appropriate; and

(5) whether the exercise of jurisdiction by a court of the commonwealth would contravene any of the purposes of this chapter.

(e) If a court shall find that a court of another jurisdiction is or may be a more appropriate forum under the terms of this chapter for the adjudication of the custody proceeding, it may do one or more of the following:

(1) dismiss the proceeding with or without prejudice;

(2) vacate any order or judgment already entered;

(3) stay the proceeding upon condition that a custody proceeding be initiated or prosecuted in another state in a timely manner or upon any other condition that the court might deem just;

(4) retain jurisdiction over any action to which the custody proceeding is incident, while declining to render a custody determination;

(5) enter such temporary order or orders as may be required, in the court's discretion, pursuant to clause (ii) of paragraph (3) of section two;

(6) assess any or all of the costs of the custody proceeding in this state, having due regard for the purposes of this chapter, including the reasonable travel and other expenses of any party and his or her witnesses, the reasonable attorneys' fees of any party, the costs of the court's communications and information exchanges with other courts and the fees and costs of any person entitled to appear before the court as the representative of a child;

(7) assess sanctions against any party whom the court finds has engaged in illegal or otherwise wrongful conduct;

(8) enter any other order or judgment which may be meet and just under the circumstances of the case.

(f) A court shall communicate to the court of any other relevant jurisdiction any determination or finding made pursuant to this section.

§ 8. Ordering Personal Appearance.

(a) The court may order any party to the proceeding who is in the commonwealth to appear personally before the court. If that party has physical custody of the child the court may order that he or she appear personally with the child.

(b) If a party to the proceeding whose presence is desired by the court is outside the commonwealth with or without the child, the court may order that the notice given under section five include a statement directing the party to appear personally with or without the child and declaring the failure to appear may result in a decision adverse to that party.

(c) If a party to the proceeding who is outside the commonwealth is directed to appear under paragraph (b) or desires to appear personally before the court with or without the child, the court may require another party to pay to the clerk or register of the court travel and other necessary expenses of the party so appearing and of the child if this is just and proper under the circumstances.

§ 9. Taking of Depositions.

In addition to other procedural devices available to a party, any party to the proceeding or a guardian ad litem or other representative of the child may adduce testimony of witnesses, including parties and the child, by deposition or otherwise, in another state. The court on its own motion may direct that the testimony of a person be taken in another state and may prescribe the manner in which and the terms upon which the testimony shall be taken.

§ 10. Requesting Assistance of Courts of Other States.

(a) A court of the commonwealth may request the appropriate court of another state to hold a hearing to adduce evidence, to order a party to produce or give evidence under other procedures of that state, or to have an investigation made with respect to the custody of a child involved in proceedings pending in the court of the commonwealth; and to forward to the court of the commonwealth certified copies of the transcript of the record of the hearing, the evidence otherwise adduced, or any investigation prepared in compliance with the request. The cost of these services may be assessed against the parties.

(b) A court of the commonwealth may request the appropriate court of another state to order a party to custody proceedings pending in the court of the commonwealth to appear in the proceeding, and if that party has physical custody of the child, to appear with the child. The request may state that travel and other reasonable and necessary expenses of the party and of the child whose appearance is desired may be assessed against another party or may otherwise be paid.

§ 11. Assisting Courts of Other States.

(a) Upon request of the court of another state the courts of the commonwealth which are competent to hear custody matters may order a person in the commonwealth to appear at a hearing to adduce evidence or to produce or give evidence under other procedures available in the commonwealth or may order investigations to be made for use in a custody proceeding in another state. A certified copy of the transcript of the record of the hearing or the evidence otherwise adduced and of any investigation shall be forwarded by the clerk or register of the court to the requesting court.

(b) Upon request of the court of another state a competent court of the commonwealth may order a person in the commonwealth to appear alone or with the child in a custody proceeding in another state. The court may condition compliance with the request upon assurance by the other state that travel and other necessary expenses will be advanced or reimbursed.

Notwithstanding any provision of this chapter to the contrary, no child shall be ordered or compelled to appear or attend such proceeding in another state when, after a hearing a judge makes a finding that there is probable cause to believe that such child may be placed in jeopardy or exposed to risk of mental or physical harm by such return to said other state.

§ 12. Enforcement of Judgments from Other States.

(a) A certified copy of a custody judgment of another state may be filed in the office of the clerk or register of any court of competent jurisdiction in the commonwealth. The clerk or register of any court of competent jurisdiction in the commonwealth. The clerk or register shall treat the judgment in the same manner as a custody judgment rendered by a court of the commonwealth.

(b) A person violating a custody judgment of another state the violation of which makes it necessary to enforce the judgment in the commonwealth may be required to pay the reasonable and necessary travel, witness and other expenses, including attorneys' fees, incurred by the party entitled to custody of the child.

§ 13. Preservation of Pleadings, Orders and Judgments; Transfer to Other Courts.

In any custody proceeding in the commonwealth the court shall preserve the pleadings, orders and judgments and any record that has been made of its hearings, investigations and other pertinent documents until the child reaches eighteen years of age. Upon appropriate request of the court of another state and receipt of payment therefor the court shall forward to the other court certified copies of any or all of such documents.

§ 14. Recognition of Foreign Judgments.

To the extent that the legal institutions of other nations have rendered custody determinations in substantial conformity with the provisions of this chapter, the courts of the commonwealth shall grant due recognition to such determinations.

MICHIGAN

UNIFORM CHILD CUSTODY JURISDICTION ACT

§ 600.651. Purposes; short title.

Sec. 651. (1) The general purposes of sections 651 to 673 are to:

(a) Avoid jurisdictional competition and conflict with courts of other states in matters of child custody which have in the past resulted in the shifting of children from state to state with harmful effects on their well-being.

(b) Promote cooperation with the courts of other states so that a custody decree or judgment is rendered in that state which can best decide the case in the interest of the child.

(c) Assure that litigation concerning the custody of a child take place ordinarily in the state with which the child and his family have the closest connection and where significant evidence concerning his care, protection, training, and personal relationships is most readily available, and that courts of this state decline the exercise of jurisdiction when the child and his family have a closer connection with another state.

(d) Discourage continuing controversies over child custody in the interest of greater stability of home environment and of secure family relationships for the child.

(e) Deter abductions and other unilateral removals of children undertaken to obtain custody awards.

(f) Avoid relitigation of custody decisions of other states in this state insofar as feasible.

(g) Facilitate the enforcement of custody decrees or judgments of other states.

(h) Promote and expand the exchange of information and other forms of mutual assistance between the courts of this state and those of other states concerned with the same child.

(i) Make uniform the law of those states which substantially conforms to sections 651 to 673.

(2) Sections 651 to 673 shall constitute the "uniform child custody jurisdiction act" and shall be construed to promote the general purposes stated in this section.

§ 600.652. Definitions.

Sec. 652. As used in sections 651 to 673:

(a) "Contestant" means a person, including a parent, who claims a right to custody or visitation rights with respect to a child.

(b) "Custody determination" means a court decision and court orders and instructions providing for the custody of a child, including visitation rights. Custody determination does not include a decision relating to child support or other monetary obligation of a person.

(c) "Custody proceeding" includes proceedings in which a custody determination is 1 of several issues, such as an action for divorce or separation, and includes child neglect and dependency proceedings.

(d) "Decree or judgment" or "custody decree or judgment" means a custody determination contained in a judicial decree or order made in a custody proceeding, and includes an initial decree or judgment and a modification decree or judgment.

(e) "Home state" means the state in which the child immediately preceding the time involved lived with his or her parents, a parent, or a person acting as parent, for at least 6 consecutive months, and in the case of a child less than 6 months old the state in which the child lived from birth with any of the persons mentioned. Periods of temporary absence of the named persons are counted as part of the 6-month or other period.

(f) "Initial decree or judgment" means the first custody decree or judgment concerning a particular child.

(g) "Modification decree or judgment" means a custody decree or judgment which modifies or replaces a prior decree or judgment, whether made by the court which rendered the prior decree or judgment or by another court.

(h) "Physical custody" means actual possession and control of a child.

(i) "Person acting as parent" means a person, other than a parent, who has physical custody of a child and who has either been awarded custody by a court or claims a right to custody.

(j) "State" means a state, territory, or possession of the United States, the Commonwealth of Puerto Rico, and the District of Columbia.

§ 600.653. Child custody determinations, jurisdiction.

Sec. 653. (1) A court of this state which is competent to decide child custody matters has jurisdiction to make a child custody determination by initial or modification decree or judgment if any of the following exist:

(a) This state is the home state of the child at the time of commencement of the proceeding or had been the child's home state within 6 months before commencement of the proceeding and the child is absent from this state because of his removal or retention by a person claiming his custody or for other reasons, and a parent or person acting as parent continues to live in this state.

(b) It is in the best interest of the child that a court of this state assume jurisdiction because the child and his parents, or the child and at least 1 contestant, have a significant connection with this state and there is available in this state substantial evidence concerning the child's present or future care, protection, training, and personal relationships.

(c) The child is physically present in this state and the child has been abandoned or it is necessary in an emergency to protect the child because the child has been subjected to or threatened with mistreatment or abuse or is otherwise neglected or dependent.

(d) It appears that no other state would have jurisdiction under prerequisites substantially in accordance with subdivisions (a), (b) or (c) or another state has declined to exercise jurisdiction on the ground that this state is the more appropriate forum to determine the custody of the child and it is in the best interest of the child that this court assume jurisdiction.

(2) Except under subsection (1)(c) and (d), the physical presence in this state of the child or of the child and 1 of the contestants is not alone sufficient to confer jurisdiction on a court of this state to make a child custody determination.

(3) Physical presence of the child, while desirable, is not a prerequisite for jurisdiction to determine his custody.

§ 600.654. Notice and hearing prior to determination.

Sec. 654. Before making a decree or judgment under sections 651 to 673, reasonable notice and opportunity to be heard shall be given to the contestants, a parent whose parental rights have not been previously terminated and a person who has physical custody of the child. If any of these persons is outside this state, notice and opportunity to be heard shall be given pursuant to section 655.

§ 600.655. Manner of giving notice and making proof of service.

Sec. 655. (1) Notice required for the exercise of jurisdiction over a person outside this state shall be given in a manner reasonably calculated to give actual notice, and may be:

(a) By personal delivery outside this state in the manner prescribed for service of process within this state.

(b) In the manner prescribed by the law of the place in which the service is made for service of process in that place in an action in any of its courts of general jurisdiction.

(c) By any form of mail addressed to the person to be served and requesting a receipt.

(d) As directed by the court including publication, if other means of notification are ineffective.

(2) Notice under this section shall be served, mailed, or delivered, or last published at least 20 days before a hearing in this state.

(3) Proof of service outside this state may be made by affidavit of the person who made the service or in the manner prescribed by the law of this state, the order pursuant to which the service is made or the law of the place in which the service is made. If service is made by mail, proof may be a receipt signed by the addressee or other evidence of delivery to the addressee.

(4) Notice is not required if a person submits to the jurisdiction of the court.

§ 600.656. Proceedings pending in another state.

Sec. 656. (1) A court of this state shall not exercise its jurisdiction under sections 651 to 673 if at the time of filing the petition a proceeding concerning the custody of the child is pending in a court of another state exercising jurisdiction substantially in conformity with sections 651 to 673, unless the proceeding is stayed by the court of the other state because this state is a more appropriate forum or for other reasons or unless temporary action by a court of this state is necessary in an emergency to protect the child because the child has been subjected to or threatened with mistreatment or abuse or is otherwise neglected or dependent.

(2) Before hearing the petition in a custody proceeding the court shall examine the pleadings and other information supplied by the parties under section 659 and shall consult the child custody registry established under section 666 concerning the pendency of proceedings with respect to the child in other states. If the court has reason to believe that proceedings may be pending in another state, it shall direct an inquiry to the state court administrator or other appropriate official of the other state.

(3) If the court is informed during the course of the proceeding that a proceeding concerning the custody of the child was pending in another state before the court assumed jurisdiction, it shall stay the proceeding and communicate with the court in which the other proceeding is pending to the end that the issue may be litigated in the more appropriate forum and that information be exchanged in accordance with section 669 to 672. If a court of this state has made a custody decree or judgment before being informed of a pending proceeding in a court of another state it shall immediately inform that court of the fact. If the court is informed that a proceeding was commenced in another state after it assumed jurisdiction, it shall likewise inform the other court to the end that the issues may be litigated in the more appropriate forum.

§ 600.657. Inconvenient or inappropriate forum.

Sec. 657. (1) A court which has jurisdiction under sections 651 to 673 to make an initial or modification decree or judgment may decline to exercise its jurisdiction before making a decree or judgment if it is an inconvenient forum to make a custody determination under the circumstances of the case and that a court of another state is a more appropriate forum.

(2) A finding of inconvenient forum may be made upon the court's own motion or upon motion of a party or a guardian ad litem or other representative of the child.

(3) In determining if it is an inconvenient forum, the court shall consider if it is in the best interest of the child that another state assume jurisdiction. For this purpose it may take into account the following factors, among others:

(a) If another state is or recently was the child's home state.

(b) If another state has a closer connection with the child and his family or with the child and 1 or more of the contestants.

(c) If substantial evidence concerning the child's present or future care, protection, training, and personal relationships is more readily available in another state.

(d) If the parties have agreed on another forum which is no less appropriate.

(e) If the exercise of jurisdiction by a court of this state would contravene any of the purposes stated in section 651.

(4) Before determining whether to decline or retain jurisdiction the court may communicate with a court of another state and exchange information pertinent to the assumption of jurisdiction by either court with a view to assuring that jurisdiction will be exercised by the more appropriate court and that a forum will be available to the parties.

(5) If the court finds that it is an inconvenient forum and that a court of another state is a more appropriate forum, it may dismiss the proceedings or it may stay the proceedings upon condition that a custody proceeding be commenced promptly in another named state or upon other conditions which may be just and proper, including the condition that a moving party stipulate his consent and submission to the jurisdiction of the other forum.

(6) The court may decline to exercise its jurisdiction under section 651 to 673 if a custody determination is incidental to an action for divorce or another proceeding while retaining jurisdiction over the divorce or other proceeding.

(7) If it appears to the court that it is clearly an inappropriate forum, it may require the party who commenced the proceedings to pay, in addition to the costs of the proceedings in this state, necessary travel and other expenses, including attorneys' fees, incurred by other parties or their witnesses. Payment is to be made to the clerk of the court for remittance to the proper party.

(8) Upon dismissal or stay of proceedings under this section the court shall inform the court found to be the more appropriate forum of this fact, or if the court which would have jurisdiction in the other state is not certainly known, shall transmit the information to the court administrator or other appropriate official for forwarding to the appropriate court.

(9) A communication received from another state informing this state of a finding of inconvenient forum because a court of this state is the more appropriate forum shall be filed in the custody registry of the appropriate court. Upon assuming jurisdiction the court of this state shall inform the original court of this fact.

§ 600.658. Reprehensible conduct by petitioner.

Sec. 658. (1) If the petitioner for an initial decree or judgment has wrongfully taken the child from another state or has engaged in similar reprehensible conduct, the court may decline to exercise jurisdiction if this is just and proper under the circumstances.

(2) Unless required in the interest of the child, the court shall not exercise its jurisdiction to modify a custody decree or judgment of another state if the petitioner, without consent of the person entitled to custody, has improperly removed the child from the physical custody of the person entitled to custody or has improperly retained the child after a visit or other temporary relinquishment of physical custody. If the petitioner has violated another provision of a custody decree or judgment of another state, the court may decline to exercise its jurisdiction if this is just and proper under the circumstances.

(3) In appropriate cases a court dismissing a petition under this section may charge the petitioner with necessary travel and other expenses, including attorneys' fees, incurred by other parties or their witnesses.

§ 600.659. Information required of parties; examination under oath.

Sec. 659. (1) Every party in a custody proceeding in his first pleading or in an affidavit attached to that pleading shall give information under oath as to the child's present address, the places where the child has lived within the last 5 years and the names and present addresses of the persons with whom the child has lived during that period. In this pleading or affidavit every party shall further declare under oath whether:

(a) He has participated as a party, witness, or in another capacity in other litigation concerning the custody of the same child in this state or any other state.

(b) He has information of a custody proceeding concerning the child pending in a court of this or another state.

(c) He knows of a person not a party to the proceedings who has physical custody of the child or claims to have custody or visitation rights with respect to the child.

(2) If the declaration as to any of the above items is in the affirmative the declarant shall give additional information under oath as required by the court. The court may examine the parties under oath as to details of the information furnished and as to other matters pertinent to the court's jurisdiction and the disposition of the case.

(3) A party has a continuing duty to inform the court of any custody proceeding concerning the child in this or another state of which he obtained information during this proceeding.

§ 600.660. Joinder of parties.

Sec. 660. If the court learns from information furnished by the parties pursuant to section 659 or from other sources that a person not a party to the custody proceeding has physical custody of the child or claims to have custody or visitation rights with respect to the child, it shall order that person to be joined as a party and to be duly notified of the pendency of the proceeding and of his joinder as a party. If the person joined as a party is outside this state he shall be served with process or otherwise notified in accordance with section 655.

§ 600.661. Ordering appearance of party and child.

Sec. 661. (1) The court may order a party to the proceeding who is in this state to appear personally before the court. If that party has physical custody of the child the court may order that the party appear personally with the child.

(2) If a party to the proceeding whose presence is desired by the court is outside this state with or without the child, the court may order that the notice given under section 655 include a statement directing that party to appear personally with or without the child and declaring that failure to appear may result in a decision adverse to that party.

(3) If a party to the proceeding who is outside this state is directed to appear under subsection (2) or desires to appear personally before the court with or without the child, the court may require another party to pay to the clerk of the court travel and other necessary expenses of the party so appearing and of the child if this is just and proper under the circumstances.

§ 600.662. Parties bound by custody decree or judgment; conclusiveness.

Sec. 662. A custody decree or judgment rendered by a court of this state which had jurisdiction under section 653 binds all parties who have been served in this state or notified in accordance with section 655 or who have submitted to the jurisdiction of the court and who were given an opportunity to be heard. As to these parties the custody decree or judgment is conclusive as to all issues of law and fact decided and as to the custody determination made unless that determination is modified pursuant to law, including the provisions of sections 651 to 673.

§ 600.663. Enforcement of foreign decrees or judgments.

Sec. 663. The courts of this state shall recognize and enforce an initial or modification decree or judgment of a court of another state which had assumed jurisdiction under statutory provisions substantially in accordance with sections 651 to 673 or which was made under factual circumstances meeting the jurisdictional standards of sections 651 to 673 as long as this decree or judgment has not been modified in accordance with jurisdictional standards substantially similar to those of sections 651 to 673.

§ 600.664. Modification of foreign custody decrees or judgments.

Sec. 664. (1) If a court of another state has made a custody decree or judgment, a court of this state shall not modify that decree or judgment unless it appears to the court of this state that the court which rendered the decree or judgment does not now have jurisdiction under jurisdictional prerequisites substantially in accordance with sections 651 to 673 or has declined to assume jurisdiction to modify the decree or judgment and the court of this state has jurisdiction.

(2) If a court of this state is authorized under subsection (1) and section 658 to modify a custody decree or judgment of another state, it shall give due consideration to the transcript of the records and other documents of all previous proceedings submitted to it in accordance with section 672.

§ 600.665. Filing, effect, and violations of foreign custody decrees or judgments.

Sec. 665. (1) A certified copy of a custody decree or judgment of another state may be filed in the office of the clerk of a court of this state. The clerk shall treat the decree or judgment in the same manner as a custody decree or judgment of a court of this state. A custody decree or judgment so filed has the same effect and shall be enforced in like manner as a custody decree or judgment rendered by a court of this state.

(2) A person violating a custody decree or judgment of another state which makes it necessary to enforce the decree in this state may be required to pay necessary travel and other expenses, including attorneys' fees, incurred by the party entitled to the custody or his witnesses.

§ 600.666. Court registries.

Sec. 666. The clerk of each circuit and probate court shall maintain a registry in which shall be entered the following:

(a) Certified copies of custody decrees or judgments of other states received for filing.

(b) Communications as to the pendency of custody proceedings in other states.

(c) Communications concerning a finding of inconvenient forum by a court of another state.

(d) Other communications or documents concerning custody proceedings in another state which may affect the jurisdiction of a court of this state or the disposition to be made by it in a custody proceeding.

§ 600.667. Forwarding copies of custody decrees or judgments.

Sec. 667. The clerk of the circuit or probate court of this state, at the request of the court of another state or at the request of a person who is affected by or has a legitimate interest in a custody decree or judgment shall certify and forward a copy of the decree or judgment to that court or person.

§ 600.668. Adducing testimony of witnesses.

Sec. 668. In addition to other procedural devices available to a party, a party to the proceeding or a guardian ad litem or other representative of the child may adduce testimony of witnesses, including parties and the child, by deposition or otherwise, in another state. The court on its own motion may direct that the testimony of a person be taken in another state and may prescribe the manner in which and the terms upon which the testimony shall be taken.

§ 600.669. Requests made to foreign courts by Michigan courts.

Sec. 669. (1) A court of this state may request the appropriate court of another state to hold a hearing to adduce evidence, to order a party to produce or give evidence under other procedures of that state or to have social studies made with respect to the custody of a child involved in proceedings pending in the court of this state; and to forward to the court of this state certified copies of the transcript of the record of the hearing, the evidence otherwise adduced or social studies prepared in compliance with the request. The cost of the services may be assessed against the parties or, if necessary, ordered paid by the county.

(2) A court of this state may request the appropriate court of another state to order a party to custody proceedings pending in the court of this state to appear in the proceedings and if that party has physical custody of the child, to appear with the child. The request may state that travel and other necessary expenses of the party and of the child whose appearance is desired will be assessed against another party or will otherwise be paid.

§ 600.670. Requests made to Michigan courts by foreign courts.

Sec. 670. (1) Upon request of the court of another state, the courts of this state which are competent to hear custody matters may order a person in this state to appear at a hearing to adduce evidence or to produce or give evidence under other procedures available in this state or may order social studies to be made for use in a custody proceeding in another state. A certified copy of the transcript of the record of the hearing or the evidence otherwise adduced and social studies prepared shall be forwarded by the clerk of the court to the requesting court.

(2) A person within this state voluntarily may give his testimony or statement in this state for use in a custody proceeding outside this state.

(3) Upon request of the court of another state, a competent court of this state may order a person in this state to appear alone or with the child in a custody proceeding in another state. The court may condition compliance with the request upon assurance by the other state that travel and other necessary expenses will be advanced or reimbursed.

§ 600.671. Records of Michigan custody proceedings.

Sec. 671. In a custody proceeding in this state the court shall preserve the pleadings, orders, and decrees or judgments, a record that has been made of its hearings, social studies, and other pertinent documents until the child reaches 18 years of age. Upon appropriate request of the court of another state, the court shall forward to the other court certified copies of any or all of those documents.

§ 600.672. Records and other documents in foreign custody proceeding.

Sec. 672. If a custody decree or judgment was rendered in another state concerning a child involved in a custody proceeding pending in a court of this state, the court of this state upon taking jurisdiction of the case shall request the court of the other state a certified copy of the transcript of the court record and other documents mentioned in section 671.

§ 600.673. International area, application.

Sec. 673. The general policies of sections 651 to 673 extend to the international area. The provisions of sections 651 to 673 relating to the recognition and enforcement of custody decrees or judgments of other states apply to custody decrees or judgments and decrees involving legal institutions similar in nature to custody rendered by appropriate authorities of other nations if reasonable notice and opportunity to be heard were given to all affected persons.

MINNESOTA

CHAPTER 518A
UNIFORM CHILD CUSTODY JURISDICTION ACT

518A.01. Purposes.

Subdivision 1. The general purposes of sections 518A.01 to 518A.25 are:

(a) To avoid jurisdictional competition and conflict with courts of other states in matters of child custody and to promote cooperation with the courts of other states so that a custody decree is rendered in the state which can best decide the case in the best interest of the child;

(b) To deter abductions and other unilateral removals of children undertaken to obtain custody awards;

(c) To avoid relitigation of custody decisions of other states in this state insofar as feasible, and to facilitate the enforcement of custody decrees of other states;

(d) To promote and expand the exchange of information and other forms of mutual assistance between the courts of this state and those of other states concerned with the same child; and

(e) To make uniform the law of those states which enact it.

Subd. 2. Sections 518A.01 to 518A.25 shall be construed to promote the general purposes stated in this section.

518A.02. Definitions.

As used in sections 518A.01 to 518A.25:

(a) "Contestant" means a person, including a parent, who claims a right to custody or visitation rights with respect to a child.

(b) "Custody determination" means a court decision and court orders and instructions providing for the custody of a child, including visitation rights, but does not include a decision relating to child support or any other monetary obligation of any person.

(c) "Custody proceeding" includes proceedings in which a custody determination is one of several issues, such as an action for dissolution, divorce or separation, and includes child neglect and dependency proceedings.

(d) "Decree" or "custody decree" means a custody determination contained in a judicial decree or order made in a custody proceeding, and includes an initial decree and a modification decree.

(e) "Home state" means the state in which the child immediately preceding the time involved lived with the child's parents, a parent, or a person acting as parent, for at least six consecutive months, and in the case of a child less than six months old the state in which the child lived from birth with any of the persons listed. Periods of temporary absence of any of the named persons are counted as part of the six month or other period.

(f) "Initial decree" means the first custody decree concerning a particular child.

(g) "Modification decree" means a custody decree which modifies or replaces a prior decree, whether made by the court which rendered the prior decree or by another court.

(h) "Physical custody" means actual possession and control of a child.

(i) "Person acting as parent" means a person, other than a parent, who has physical custody of a child and who has either been awarded custody by a court or claims a right to custody.

(j) "State" means any state, territory, or possession of the United States, the Commonwealth of Puerto Rico, and the District of Columbia.

518A.03. Jurisdiction.

Subdivision 1. A court of this state which is competent to decide child custody matters has jurisdiction to make a child custody determination by initial or modification decree if:

(a) this state (1) is the home state of the child at the time of commencement of the proceeding, or (2) had been the child's home state within six months before commencement of the proceeding and the child is absent from this state because of removal or retention by a person claiming custody or for other reasons, and a parent or person acting as parent continues to live in this state; or

(b) it is in the best interest of the child that a court of this state assume jurisdiction because (1) the child and the parents, or the child and at least one contestant, have a significant connection with this state, and (2) there is available in this state substantial evidence concerning the child's present or future care, protection, training, and personal relationships; or

(c) the child is physically present in this state and (1) the child has been abandoned or (2) it is necessary in an emergency to protect the child because the child has been subjected to or threatened with mistreatment or abuse or is otherwise neglected or dependent; or

(d) (1) it appears that no court in another state would have jurisdiction under prerequisites substantially in accordance with clause (a), (b), or (c), or a court of another state has declined to exercise jurisdiction on the ground that a court of this state is the more appropriate forum to determine the custody of the child, and (2) it is in the best interest of the child that a court of this state assume jurisdiction.

Subd. 2. Except under clauses (c) and (d) of subdivision 1, physical presence in this state of the child, or of the child and one of the contestants, is not alone sufficient to confer jurisdiction on a court of this state to make a child custody determination.

Subd. 3. Physical presence of the child, while desirable, is not a prerequisite for jurisdiction to determine custody.

518A.04. Notice And Opportunity To Be Heard.

Before making a decree under sections 518A.01 to 518A.25, reasonable notice and opportunity to be heard shall be given to the contestants, any parent whose parental rights have not been previously terminated, and any person who has physical custody of the child. If any of these persons is outside this state, notice and opportunity to be heard shall be given pursuant to section 518A.05.

518A.05. Notice To Persons Outside This State; Submission To Jurisdiction.

Subdivision 1. Notice required for the exercise of jurisdiction over a person outside this state shall be given in a manner reasonably calculated to give actual notice, and may be:

(a) by personal delivery outside this state in the manner prescribed for service of process within this state;

(b) in the manner prescribed by the law of the place in which the service is made for service of process in that place in an action in any of its courts of general jurisdiction;

(c) by any form of mail addressed to the person to be served and requesting a receipt; or

(d) as directed by the court, including publication, if other means of notification are ineffective.

Subd. 2. Notice under this section shall be served, mailed, or delivered, or last published at least 20 days before any hearing in this state.

Subd. 3. Proof of service outside this state may be made by affidavit of the individual who made the service, or in the manner prescribed by the law of this state, the order pursuant to which the service is made, or the law of the place in which the service is made. If service is made by mail, proof may be a receipt signed by the addressee or other evidence of delivery to the addressee.

Subd. 4. Notice is required if a person submits to the jurisdiction of the court.

518A.06. Simultaneous Proceedings In Other States.

Subdivision 1. A court of this state shall not exercise its jurisdiction under sections 518A.01 to 518A.25 if at the time of filing the petition a proceeding concerning the custody of the child was pending in a court of another state exercising jurisdiction substantially in conformity with the provisions of sections 518A.01 to 518A.25, unless the proceeding is stayed by the court of the other state because this state is a more appropriate forum or for other reasons.

Subd. 2. Before hearing the petition in a custody proceeding the court shall examine the pleadings and other information supplied by the parties under section 518A.09 and shall consult the child custody registry established under section 518A.16 concerning the pendency of proceedings with respect to the child in other states. If the court has reason to believe that proceedings may be pending in another state it shall direct an inquiry to the state court administrator or other appropriate official of the other state.

Subd. 3. If the court is informed during the course of the proceeding that a proceeding concerning the custody of the child was pending in another state before the court assumed jurisdiction, it shall stay the proceeding and communicate with the court in which the other proceeding is pending to ensure that the issue may be litigated in the more appropriate forum and that information be exchanged in accordance with sections 518A.19 to 518A.22. If a court of this state has made a custody decree before being informed of a pending proceeding in a court of another state, it shall immediately inform that court of the fact. If the court is informed that a proceeding was commenced in another state after it assumed jurisdiction, it shall likewise inform the other court to ensure that the issues may be litigated in the more appropriate forum.

518A.07. Inconvenient Forum.

Subdivision 1. A court which has jurisdiction under sections 518A.01 to 518A.25 to make an initial or modification decree may decline to exercise its jurisdiction any time before making a decree if it finds that it is an inconvenient forum to make a custody determination under the circumstances of the case and that a court of another state is a more appropriate forum.

Subd. 2. A finding of inconvenient forum may be made upon the court's own motion or upon motion of a party or a guardian ad litem or other representative of the child.

Subd. 3. In determining if it is an inconvenient forum, the court shall consider, if it is in the interest of the child that another state assume jurisdiction. For this purpose it shall consider all relevant factors, including but not limited to the following:

(a) if another state is or recently was the child's home state;

(b) if another state has a closer connection with the child and the child's family or with the child and one or more of the contestants;

(c) if substantial evidence concerning the child's present or future care, protection, training, and personal relationships is more readily available in another state;

(d) if the parties have agreed on another forum which is not less appropriate; and

(e) if the exercise of jurisdiction by a court of this state would contravene any of the purposes stated in section 518A.01.

Subd. 4. Before determining whether to decline or retain jurisdiction, the court may communicate with a court of another state and exchange information pertinent to the assumption of jurisdiction by either court with a view to assuring that jurisdiction will be exercised by the more appropriate court and that a forum will be available to the parties.

Subd. 5. If the court finds that it is an inconvenient forum and that a court of another state is a more appropriate forum, it may dismiss the proceedings, or it may stay the proceedings upon condition that a custody proceeding be promptly commenced in another named state or upon any other conditions which may be just and proper, including the condition that a moving party stipulate consent and submission to the jurisdiction of the other forum.

Subd. 6. The court may decline to exercise its jurisdiction under sections 518A.01 to 518A.25 if a custody determination is incidental to an action for dissolution or to another proceeding, while retaining jurisdiction over the dissolution or other proceeding.

Subd. 7. If it appears to the court that it is clearly an inappropriate forum, it may require the party who commenced the proceedings to pay, in addition to the costs of the proceedings in this state, necessary travel and other expenses, including attorneys' fees, incurred by other parties or their witnesses. Payment is to be made to the court administrator for remittance to the proper party.

Subd. 8. Upon dismissal or stay of proceedings under this section the court shall inform the court found to be the more appropriate forum of this fact, or if the court which would have jurisdiction in the other state is not yet determined, shall transmit the information to the court administrator or other appropriate official for forwarding to the appropriate court.

Subd. 9. Any communication received from another state informing this state of a finding of inconvenient forum because a court of this state is the more appropriate forum shall be filed in the custody registry of the appropriate court. Upon assuming jurisdiction the court of this state shall inform the original court of this fact.

518A.08. Jurisdiction Declined By Reason Of Conduct.

Subdivision 1. If the petitioner for an initial decree has wrongfully taken the child from another state or has engaged in similar reprehensible conduct the court may decline to exercise jurisdiction if this is just and proper under the circumstances.

Subd. 2. Unless required in the interest of the child, the court shall not exercise its jurisdiction to modify a custody decree of another state if the petitioner, without consent of the person entitled to custody, has improperly removed the child from the physical custody of the person entitled to custody or has improperly retained the child after a visit or other temporary relinquishment of physical custody. If the petitioner has violated any other provision of a custody decree of another state the court may decline to exercise its jurisdiction if this is just and proper under this circumstances.

Subd. 3. In appropriate cases a court dismissing a petition under this section may charge the petitioner with necessary travel and other expenses, including attorneys' fees, incurred by other parties or their witnesses.

518A.09. Information Under Oath To Be Submitted To The Court.

Subdivision 1. The court shall, upon motion or request of a party or upon its own initiative require a party to a custody proceeding to provide information under oath by affidavit or otherwise as to the child's present address, the places where the child has lived within the last five years, the names and present addresses of the persons with whom the child has lived during that period, and whether the party:

(a) has participated as a party, witness, or in any other capacity in any other litigation concerning the custody of the same child in this or any other state;

(b) has information of any custody proceeding concerning the child pending in a court of this or any other state; and

(c) knows of any person not a party to the proceedings who has physical custody of the child or claims to have custody or visitation rights with respect to the child.

Subd. 2. If the declaration as to any of the above items is in the affirmative the declarant shall give additional information under oath as required by the court. The court may examine the parties under oath as to details of the information furnished and as to other matters pertinent to the court's jurisdiction and the disposition of the case.

Subd. 3. Each party has a continuing duty to inform the court of any custody proceeding concerning the child in this or any other state of which the party obtained information during this proceeding.

518A.10. Additional Parties.

If the court learns from information furnished by the parties pursuant to section 518A.09 or from other sources that a person not a party to the custody proceeding has physical custody of the child or claims to have custody or visitation rights with respect to the child, it shall order that person to be joined as a party and to be duly notified of the pendency of the proceeding and of the joinder as party. If the person joined as a party is outside this state that person shall be served with process or otherwise notified in accordance with section 518A.05.

518A.11. Appearance Of Parties And The Child.

Subdivision 1. The court may order any party to the proceeding who is in this state to appear personally before the court. If that party has physical custody of the child the court may order that the party appear personally with the child.

Subd. 2. If a party to the proceeding whose presence is desired by the court is outside this state with or without the child the court may order that the notice given under section 518A.05 include a statement directing that party to appear personally with or without the child and declaring that failure to appear may result in a decision adverse to that party.

Subd. 3. If a party to the proceeding who is outside this state is directed to appear under subdivision 2 or desires to appear personally before the court with or without the child, the court may require another party to pay to the court administrator travel and other necessary expenses of the party so appearing and of the child if this is just and proper under the circumstances.

518A.12. Binding Force And Res judicata Effect Of Custody Decree.

A custody decree rendered by a court of this state which had jurisdiction under section 518A.03 binds all parties who have been served in this state or notified in accordance with section 518A.05 or who have submitted to the jurisdiction of the court, and who have been given an opportunity to be heard. As to these parties the custody decree is conclusive as to all issues of law and fact decided and as to the custody determination made unless and until that determination is modified pursuant to law, including the provisions of sections 518A.01 to 518A.25.

518A.13. Recognition Of Out Of State Custody Decrees.

The courts of this state shall recognize and enforce an initial or modification decree of a court of another state which had assumed jurisdiction under statutory provisions substantially in accordance with sections 518A.01 to 518A.25 or which was made under factual circumstances meeting the jurisdictional standards of the act, so long as this decree has not been modified in accordance with jurisdictional standards substantially similar to those of sections 518A.01 to 518A.25.

518A.14. Modification Of Custody Decree Of Another State.

Subdivision 1. If a court of another state has made a custody decree, a court of this state shall not modify that decree unless (1) it appears to the court of this state that the court which rendered the decree does not now have jurisdiction under jurisdictional prerequisites substantially in accordance with section 518A.01 to 518A.25 or has declined to assume jurisdiction to modify the decree and (2) the court of this state has jurisdiction.

Subd. 2. If a court of this state is authorized under subdivision 1 and section 518A.08 to modify a custody decree of another state, it shall give due consideration to the transcript of the record and other documents of all previous proceedings submitted to it in accordance with section 518A.22.

518A.15. Filing And Enforcement Of Custody Decree Of Another State.

Subdivision 1. A certified copy of a custody decree of another state may be filed in the office of the court administrator of any court of this state having jurisdiction of child custody matters. The court administrator shall treat the decree in the same manner as a custody decree of the court of this state. A custody decree so filed has the same effect and shall be enforced in like manner as a custody decree rendered by a court of this state.

Subd. 2. A person violating a custody decree of another state which makes it necessary to enforce the decree in this state may be required to pay necessary travel and other expenses, including attorney's fees, incurred by the party entitled to the custody or to the entitled party's witnesses.

518A.16. Registry Of Out Of State Custody Decrees And Proceedings.

The court administrator of each court having jurisdiction of child custody matters shall maintain a registry to enter the following:

(a) certified copies of custody decrees of other states received for filing;

(b) communications as to the pendency of custody proceedings in other states;

(c) communications concerning a finding of inconvenient forum by a court of another state; and

(d) other communications or documents concerning custody proceedings in another state which may affect the jurisdiction of a court of this state or the disposition to be made by it in a custody proceeding.

518A.17. Certified Copies Of Custody Decree.

The court administrator of the court of this state having jurisdiction of child custody matters, at the request of the court of another state or at the request of any person who is affected by or has a legitimate interest in a custody decree, shall certify and forward a copy of the decree to that court or person.

518A.18. Taking Testimony In Another State.

In addition to other procedural devices available to a party, any party to the proceeding or a guardian ad litem or other representative of the child may adduce testimony of witnesses, including parties and the child, by deposition or otherwise, in another state. The court on its own motion may direct that the testimony of a person be taken in another state and may prescribe the manner in which and the terms upon which the testimony shall be taken.

518A.19. Hearings And Studies In Another State; Orders To Appear.

Subdivision 1. A court of this state may request the appropriate court of another state to hold a hearing to adduce evidence, to order a party to produce or give evidence under other procedures of that state, or to have social studies made with respect to the custody of a child involved in proceedings pending in the court of this state; and to forward to the court of this state certified copies of the transcript of the record of the hearing, the evidence otherwise adduced, or any social studies prepared in compliance with the request. The cost of the services may be assessed against the parties or, if necessary, ordered paid by the county in which the proceedings are pending.

Subd. 2. A court of this state may request the appropriate court of another state to order a party to custody proceedings pending in the court of this state to appear in the proceedings, and if that party has physical custody of the child, to appear with the child. The request may state that travel and other necessary expenses of the party and of the child whose appearance is desired will be assessed against another party or will otherwise be paid.

518A.20. Assistance To Courts Of Other States.

Subdivision 1. Upon request of the court of another state the courts of this state which are competent to hear custody matters may order a person in this state to appear at a hearing to adduce evidence or to produce or give evidence under other procedures available in this state or may order social studies to be made under other procedures available in this state for use in a custody proceeding in another state. A certified copy of the transcript of the record of the hearing or the evidence otherwise adduced and any social studies prepared shall be forwarded by the court administrator of the court to the requesting court.

Subd. 2. A person within this state may voluntarily give testimony or statement in this state for use in a custody proceeding outside this state.

Subd. 3. Upon request of the court of another state a competent court of this state may order a person in this state to appear alone or with the child in a custody proceeding in another state. The court may condition compliance with the request upon assurance by the other state that state travel and other necessary expenses will be advanced or reimbursed.

518A.21. Preservation Of Documents For Use In Other States.

In any custody proceeding in this state the court shall preserve the pleadings, orders and decrees, any record that has been made of its hearings, social studies, and other pertinent documents until the child reaches 18 years of age. Upon appropriate request of the court of another state the court shall forward to the other court certified copies of any or all of those documents.

518A.22. Request For Court Records Of Another State.

If a custody decree has been rendered in another state concerning a child involved in a custody proceeding pending in a court of this state, the court of this state upon taking jurisdiction of the case shall request of the court of the other state a certified copy of the transcript of any court record and other pertinent documents which have been preserved by the court of the other state.

518A.23. International Application.

The general policies of sections 518A.01 to 518A.25 extend to international proceedings. The provisions of sections 518A.01 to 518A.25 relating to the recognition and enforcement of custody decrees of other states apply to custody decrees and decrees involving legal institutions similar in nature to custody institutions rendered by appropriate authorities of other nations if reasonable notice and opportunity to be heard were given to all affected persons.

518A.24. Priority.

Upon the request of a party to a custody proceeding which raises a question of existence or exercise of jurisdiction under sections 518A.01 to 518A.25 the case shall be given calendar priority and handled expeditiously.

518A.25. Citation.

Sections 518A.01 to 518A.25 may be cited as the uniform child custody jurisdiction act.

MISSISSIPPI

UNIFORM CHILD CUSTODY JURISDICTION ACT

§ 93-23-1. Short title.

This chapter may be cited as the Uniform Child Custody Jurisdiction Act.

§ 93-23-3. Definitions.

As used in this chapter:

(a) "Contestant" means a person, including a parent, who claims a right to custody or visitation rights with respect to a child;

(b) "Court" means any court of this state which is competent to hear and decide child custody matters under the laws of this state;

(c) "Custody determination" means a court decision and court orders and instructions providing for the custody of a child, including visitation rights; it does not include a decision relating to child support or any other monetary obligation of any person;

(d) "Custody proceeding" includes proceedings in which a custody determination is one of several issues, such as an action for divorce or separation, and includes child neglect and dependency proceedings;

(e) "Decree" or "custody decree" means a custody determination contained in a judicial decree or order made in a custody proceeding, and includes an initial decree and a modification decree;

(f) "Home state" means the state in which the child immediately preceding the time involved lived with his parents, a parent, or a person acting as parent, for at least six (6) consecutive months, and in the case of a child less than six (6) months old the state in which the child lived from birth with any of the persons mentioned. Periods of temporary absence of any of the named persons are counted as part of the six-month or other period;

(g) "Initial decree" means the first custody decree concerning a particular child;

(h) "Modification decree" means a custody decree which modifies or replaces a prior decree, whether made by the court which rendered the prior decree or by another court;

(i) "Physical custody" means actual possession and control of a child;

(j) "Person acting as parent" means a person, other than a parent, who has physical custody of a child and who has either been awarded custody by a court or claims a right to custody; and

(k) "State" means any state, territory or possession of the United States, the Commonwealth of Puerto Rico and the District of Columbia.

§ 93-23-5. Jurisdiction.

(1) A court of this state which is competent to decide child custody matters has jurisdiction to make a child custody determination by initial or modification decree if:

(a) This state (i) is the home state of the child at the time of commencement of the proceeding, or (ii) had been the child's home state within six (6) months before commencement of the proceeding and the child is absent from this state because of his removal or retention by a person claiming his custody or for other reasons, and a parent or person acting as parent continues to live in this state; or

(b) It is in the best interest of the child that a court of this state assume jurisdiction because (i) the child and his parents, or the child and at least one (1) contestant, have a significant connection with the state, and (ii) there is available in this state substantial evidence concerning the child's present or future care, protection, training and personal relationship; or

(c) The child is physically present in this state and (i) the child has been abandoned, or (ii) it is necessary in an emergency to protect the child because he has been subjected to or threatened with mistreatment or abuse or is otherwise neglected or dependent; or

(d) (i) It appears that no other state would have jurisdiction under prerequisites substantially in accordance with paragraphs (a), (b) or (c), or another state has declined to exercise jurisdiction on the ground that this state is the more appropriate forum to determine the custody of the child, and (ii) it is in the best interest of the child that this court assume jurisdiction.

(2) Except under paragraphs (c) and (d) of subsection (1) of this section, physical presence in this state of the child, or of the child and one of the contestants, is not alone sufficient to confer jurisdiction on a court of this state to make a child custody determination.

(3) Physical presence of the child, while desirable, is not a prerequisite for jurisdiction to determine his custody.

§ 93-23-7. Notice and opportunity to be heard.

Before making a decree under this chapter, reasonable notice and opportunity to be heard shall be given to the contestants, any parent whose parental rights have not been previously terminated, and any person who has physical custody of the child. If any of these persons is outside this state, notice and opportunity to be heard shall be given pursuant to section 93-23-9.

§ 93-23-9. Notice to person outside of state; submission to jurisdiction.

(1) Notice required for the exercise of jurisdiction over a person outside this state shall be given in the manner, time and form as provided by law for service of process.

(2) Notice is not required if a person submits to the jurisdiction of the court.

§ 93-23-11. Simultaneous proceeding in another state.

(1) A court of this state shall not exercise its jurisdiction under this chapter if at the time of filing the petition a proceeding concerning the custody of the child was pending in a court of another state exercising jurisdiction substantially in conformity with this chapter, unless the proceeding is stayed by the court of the other state because this state is a more appropriate forum or for other reasons.

(2) Before hearing the petition in a custody proceeding the court shall examine the pleadings and other information supplied by the parties under section 93-23-17 and shall consult the child custody registry established under section 93-23-31 concerning the pendency of proceedings with respect to the child in other states. If the court has reason to believe that proceedings may be pending in another state it shall direct an inquiry to the state court administrator or other appropriate official of the other state.

(3) If the court is informed during the course of the proceeding that a proceeding concerning the custody of the child was pending in another state before the court assumed jurisdiction, it shall stay the proceeding and communicate with the court in which the other proceeding is pending to the end that the issue may be litigated in the more appropriate forum and that information be exchanged in accordance with sections 93-23-37 through 93-23-43. If a court of this state has made a custody decree before being informed of a pending proceeding in a court of another state, it shall immediately inform that court of the fact. If the court is informed that a proceeding was commenced in another state after it assumed jurisdiction, it shall likewise inform the other court to the end that the issues may be litigated in the more appropriate forum.

§ 93-23-13. Inconvenient forum.

(1) A court which has jurisdiction under this chapter to make an initial or modification decree may decline to exercise its jurisdiction anytime before making a decree if it finds that it is an inconvenient forum to make a custody determination under the circumstances of the case and that a court of another state is a more appropriate forum.

(2) A finding of inconvenient forum may be made upon the court's own motion or upon motion of a party or a guardian ad litem or other representative of the child.

(3) In determining if it is an inconvenient forum, the court shall consider if it is in the interest of the child that another state assume jurisdiction. For this purpose it may take into account the following factors, among others:

(a) If another state is or recently was the child's home state;

(b) If another state has a closer connection with the child and his family or with the child and one or more of the contestants;

(c) If substantial evidence concerning the child's present or future care, protection, training and personal relationship is more readily available in another state;

(d) If the parties have agreed on another forum which is no less appropriate; and

(e) If the exercise of jurisdiction by a court of this state would contravene any of the provisions of this chapter.

(4) Before determining whether to decline or retain jurisdiction the court may communicate with a court of another state and exchange information pertinent to the assumption of jurisdiction by either court with a view to assuring that jurisdiction will be exercised by the more appropriate court and that a forum will be available to the parties.

(5) If the court finds that it is an inconvenient forum and that a court of another state is a more appropriate forum, it may dismiss the proceedings, or it may stay the proceedings upon condition that a custody proceeding be promptly commenced in another named state or upon any other conditions which may be just and proper, including the condition that a moving party stipulate his consent and submission to the jurisdiction of the other forum.

(6) The court may decline to exercise its jurisdiction under this chapter if a custody determination is incidental to an action for divorce or another proceeding which retaining jurisdiction over the divorce or other proceeding.

(7) If it appears to the court that it is clearly an inappropriate forum it may require the party who commenced the proceedings to pay, in addition to the costs of the proceedings in this state, necessary travel and other expenses, including attorneys' fees, incurred by other parties or their witnesses. Payment is to be made to the clerk of the court for remittance to the proper party.

(8) Upon dismissal or stay of proceeding under this section the court shall inform the court found to be the more appropriate forum of this fact or, if the court which would have jurisdiction in the other state is not certainly known, shall transmit the information to the court administrator or other appropriate official for forwarding to the appropriate court.

(9) Any communication received from another state informing this state of a finding of inconvenient forum because a court of this state is the more appropriate forum shall be filed in the custody registry of the appropriate court. Upon assuming jurisdiction the court of this state shall inform the original court of this fact.

§ 93-23-15. Jurisdiction declined by reason of petitioner's conduct.

(1) If the petitioner for an initial decree has wrongfully taken the child from another state or has engaged in similar reprehensible conduct the court may decline to exercise jurisdiction if this is just and proper under the circumstances.

(2) Unless required in the interest of the child, the court shall not exercise its jurisdiction to modify a custody decree of another state if the petitioner, without consent of the person entitled to custody, has improperly removed the child from the physical custody of the person entitled to custody or has improperly retained the child after a visit or other temporary relinquishment of physical custody. If the petitioner has violated any other provision of a custody decree of another state the court may decline to exercise its jurisdiction if this is just and proper under the circumstances.

(3) In appropriate cases a court dismissing a petition under this section may charge the petitioner with necessary travel and other expenses, including attorneys' fees, incurred by other parties or their witnesses.

§ 93-23-17. Information under oath to be submitted to court.

(1) Every party in a custody proceeding in his first pleading or in an affidavit attached to that pleading shall give information under oath as to the child's present address, the places where the child has lived within the last five (5) years, and the names and present addresses of the persons with whom the child has lived during that period. In this pleading or affidavit every party shall further declare under oath whether:

(a) He has participated (as a party, witness or in any other capacity), in any other litigation concerning the custody of the same child in this or any other state;

(b) He has information of any custody proceeding concerning the child pending in a court of this or any other state; and

(c) He knows of any person not a party to the proceedings who has physical custody of the child or claims to have custody or visitation rights with respect to the child.

(2) If the declaration as to any of the above items is in the affirmative the declarant shall give additional information under oath as required by the court. The court may examine the parties under oath as to details of the information furnished and as to other matter pertinent to the court's jurisdiction and the disposition of the case.

(3) Each party has a continuing duty to inform the court of any custody proceeding concerning the child in this or any other state of which he obtained information during this proceeding.

§ 93-23-19. Additional parties.

If the court learns from information furnished by the parties pursuant to section 93-23-17 or from other sources that a person not a party to the custody proceeding has physical custody of the child or claims to have custody or visitation rights with respect to the child, it shall order that person to be joined as a party and to be duly notified of the pendency of the proceeding and of his joinder as a party. If the person joined as a party is outside this state he shall be served with process or otherwise notified in accordance with section 93-23-9.

§ 93-23-21. Appearance of parties and child.

(1) The court may order any party to the proceeding who is in this state to appear personally before the court. If that party has physical custody of the child the court may order that he appear personally with the child.

(2) If a party to the proceeding whose presence is desired by the court is outside this state with or without the child the court may order that the notice given under section 93-23-9 include a statement directing that party to appear personally with or without the child and declaring that failure to appear may result in a decision adverse to that party.

(3) If a party to the proceeding who is outside this state is directed to appear under subsection (2) of this section or desires to appear personally before the court with or without the child, the court may require another party to pay to the clerk of the court travel and other necessary expenses of the party so appearing and of the child if this is just and proper under the circumstances.

§ 93-23-23. Binding force and res judicata effect of custody decree.

A custody decree rendered by a court of this state which had jurisdiction under section 93-23-5 binds all parties who have been served in this state or notified in accordance with section 93-23-9 or who have submitted to the jurisdiction of the court, and who have been given an opportunity to be heard. As to these parties the custody decree is conclusive as to all issues of law and fact decided and as to the custody determination made unless and until that determination is modified pursuant to law, including the provisions of this chapter.

§ 93-23-25. Recognition of custody decree from another state.

The courts of this state shall recognize and enforce an initial or modification decree of a court of another state which had assumed jurisdiction under statutory provisions substantially in accordance with this chapter or which was made under factual circumstances meeting the jurisdictional standards of the chapter, so long as this decree has not been modified in accordance with jurisdictional standards substantially similar to those of this chapter.

§ 93-23-27. Modification of custody decree of another state.

(1) If a court of another state has made a custody decree, a court of this state shall not modify that decree unless (a) it appears to the court of this state that the court which rendered the decree does not now have jurisdiction under jurisdictional prerequisites substantially in accordance with this chapter or has declined to assume jurisdiction to modify the decree, and (b) the court of this state has jurisdiction.

(2) If a court of this state is authorized under subsection (1) of this section and section 93-23-15 to modify a custody decree of another state it shall give due consideration to the transcript of the record and other documents of all previous proceedings submitted to it in accordance with section 93-23-43.

§ 93-23-29. Filing and enforcement of custody decree of another state.

(1) A certified copy of a custody decree of another state may be filed in the office of the clerk of the court of this state. The clerk shall treat the decree in the same manner as a custody decree of the court of this state. A custody decree so filed has the same effect and shall be enforced in like manner as a custody decree rendered by a court of this state.

(2) A person violating a custody decree of another state which makes it necessary to enforce the decree in this state may be required to pay necessary travel and other expenses, including attorneys' fees, incurred by the party entitled to the custody or his witness.

§ 93-23-31. Registry of custody decrees and communications from other states.

The clerk of each court shall maintain a registry in which he shall enter the following:

(a) Certified copies of custody decrees of other states received for filing;

(b) Communications as to the pendency of custody proceedings in other states;

(c) Communications concerning a finding of inconvenient forum by a court of another state; and

(d) Other communications or documents concerning custody proceedings in another state which may affect the jurisdiction of a court of this state or the disposition to be made by it in a custody proceeding.

§ 93-23-33. Certified copies of custody decrees.

The clerk of the court of this state, at the request of the court of another state or at the request of any person who is affected by or has a legitimate interest in a custody decree, shall certify and forward a copy of the decree to that court or person.

§ 93-23-35. Taking testimony in another state.

In addition to other procedural devices available to a party, any party to the proceeding or a guardian ad litem or other representative of the child may adduce testimony of witnesses, including parties and the child, by deposition or otherwise, in another state. The court on its own motion may direct that the testimony of a person be taken in another state and may prescribe the manner in which and the terms upon which the testimony shall be taken.

§ 93-23-37. Hearings and studies in another state; orders to appear.

(1) A court of this state may request the appropriate court of another state to hold a hearing to adduce evidence, to order a party to produce or give evidence under other procedures of that state, or to have social studies made with respect to the custody of a child involved in proceedings pending in the court of this state; and to forward to the court of this state certified copies of the transcript of the record of the hearing, the evidence otherwise adduced, or any social studies prepared in compliance with the request. The cost of the services may be assessed against the parties.

(2) A court of this state may request the appropriate court of another state to order a party to custody proceedings pending in the court of this state to appear in the proceeding, and if that party has physical custody of the child, to appear with the child. The request may state that travel and other necessary expenses of the party and of the child whose appearance is desired will be assessed against another party or will otherwise be paid.

§ 93-23-39. Assistance to courts of other states.

(1) Upon request of the court of another state the courts of this state which are competent to hear custody matters may order a person in this state to appear at a hearing to adduce evidence or to produce or give evidence under other procedures available in this state or may order social studies to be made for use in a custody proceeding in another state. A certified copy of the transcript of the record of the hearing or the evidence otherwise adduced and any social studies prepared shall be forwarded by the clerk of the court to the requesting court.

(2) A person within this state may voluntarily give his testimony or statement in this state for use in a custody proceeding outside this state.

(3) Upon request of the court of another state a competent court of this state may order a person in this state to appear alone or with the child in a custody proceeding in another state. The court may condition compliance with the request upon assurance by the other state travel and other necessary expenses will be advanced or reimbursed.

§ 93-23-41. Preservation of documents; certified copies to other states on request.

In any custody proceeding in this state the court shall preserve the pleadings, orders and decrees, any record that has been made of its hearings, social studies and other pertinent documents until the child reaches eighteen (18) years of age. Upon appropriate request of the court of another state the court shall forward to the other court certified copies of any or all of such documents.

§ 93-23-43. Request for copies of court records and related documents from another state.

If a custody decree has been rendered in another state concerning a child involved in a custody proceeding pending in a court of this state, the court of this state upon taking jurisdiction of the case shall request of the court of the other state a certified copy of the transcript of any court record and other documents mentioned in section 92-23-41.

§ 93-23-45. International application.

The general policies of this chapter extend to the international area. The provisions of this chapter relating to the recognition and enforcement of custody decrees of other states apply to custody decrees and decrees involving legal institutions similar in nature to custody institutions rendered by appropriate authorities of other nations if reasonable notice and opportunity to be heard were given to all affected persons.

§ 93-23-47. Calendar priority given cases involving jurisdictional issues.

Upon the request of a party to a custody proceeding which raises a question of existence or exercise of jurisdiction under this chapter the case shall be given calendar priority and handled expeditiously.

MISSOURI

UNIFORM CHILD CUSTODY JURISDICTION ACT

§ 452.440. Short title.

Sections 452.440 to 452.550 may be cited as the "Uniform Child Custody Jurisdiction Act".

§ 452.445. Definitions.

As used in sections 452.440 to 452.550:

(1) "Custody determination" means a court decision and court orders and instructions providing for the custody of a child, including visitation rights. This term does not include a decision relating to child support or any other monetary obligation of any person; but the court shall have the right in any custody determination where jurisdiction is had pursuant to section 452.460 and where it is in the best interest of the child to adjudicate the issue of child support;

(2) "Custody proceeding" includes proceedings in which a custody determination is one of several issues, such as an action for dissolution of marriage, legal separation, separate maintenance, appointment of a guardian of the person, child neglect or abandonment, but excluding actions for violation of a state law or municipal ordinance;

(3) "Decree" or "custody decree" means a custody determination contained in a judicial decree or order made in a custody proceeding, and includes an initial decree and a modification decree;

(4) "Home state" means the state in which, immediately preceding the filing of custody proceeding, the child lived with his parents, a parent, an institution; or a person acting as parent, for at least six consecutive months; or, in the case of a child less than six months old, the state in which the child lived from birth with any of the persons mentioned. Periods of temporary absence of any of the named persons are counted as part of the six-month or other period;

(5) "Initial decree" means the first custody decree concerning a particular child;

(6) "Litigant" means a person, including a parent, grandparent, or step-parent, who claims a right to custody or visitation with respect to a child.

§ 452.450. Jurisdiction.

1. A court of this state which is competent to decide child custody matters has jurisdiction to make a child custody determination by initial or modification decree if:

(1) This state:

(a) Is the home state of the child at the time of commencement of the proceeding; or

(b) Had been the child's home state within six months before commencement of the proceeding and the child is absent from this state for any reason, and a parent or person acting as parent continues to live in this state; or

(2) It is in the best interest of the child that a court of this state assume jurisdiction because:

(a) The child and his parents, or the child and at least one litigant, have a significant connection with this state; and

(b) There is available in this substantial evidence concerning the child's present or future care, protection, training, and personal relationships; or

(3) The child is physically present in this state and:

(a) The child has been abandoned; or

(b) It is necessary in an emergency to protect the child because he has been subjected to or threatened with mistreatment or abuse, or is otherwise being neglected; or

(4) It appears that no other state would have jurisdiction under prerequisites substantially in accordance with subdivision (1), (2), or (3), or another state has declined to exercise jurisdiction on the ground that this state is the more appropriate forum to determine the custody of the child, and it is in the best interest of the child that this court assume jurisdiction.

2. Except as provided in subdivisions (3) and (4) of subsection 1 of this section, physical presence of the child, or of the child and one of the litigants, in this state is not sufficient alone to confer jurisdiction on a court of this state to make a child custody determination.

3. Physical presence of the child, while desirable, is not a prerequisite for jurisdiction to determine his custody.

§ 452.455. Petition for modification—procedure.

1. Any petition for modification of child custody decrees filed under the provisions of section 452.410, or sections 452.440 to 452.450, shall be verified and, if the original proceeding originated in the state of Missouri, shall be filed in that original case, but service shall be obtained and responsive pleadings may be filed as in any original proceeding.

2. Before making a decree under the provisions of section 452.410, or sections 452.440 to 452.450, the litigants, any parent whose parental rights have not been previously terminated, and any person who has physical custody of the child must be served in the manner provided by the rules of civil procedure and applicable court rules and may within thirty days after the date of service (forty-five days if service by publication) file a verified answer. If any of these persons is outside this state, notice and opportunity to be heard shall be given pursuant to section 452.460.

§ 452.460. Notice to persons outside this state—submission to jurisdiction.

1. The notice required for the exercise of jurisdiction over a person outside this state shall be given in a manner reasonably calculated to give actual notice, and may be given in any of the following ways:

(1) By personal delivery outside this state in the manner prescribed for service of process within this state;

(2) In the manner prescribed by the law of the place in which the service is made for service of process in that place in an action in any of its courts of general jurisdiction;

(3) By certified or registered mail; or

(4) As directed by the court, including publication, if other means of notification are ineffective.

2. Proof of service outside this state may be made by affidavit of the individual who made the service, or in the manner prescribed by the law of this state, the order pursuant to which the service is made, or the law of the place in which the service is made. If service is made by mail, proof of service may be a receipt signed by the addressee or other evidence of delivery to the addressee.

3. The notice provided for in this section is not required for a person who submits to the jurisdiction of the court.

§ 452.465. Simultaneous proceedings in other states.

1. A court of this state shall not exercise its jurisdiction under sections 452.440 to 452.550 if, at the time of filing the petition, a proceeding concerning the custody of the child was pending in a court of another state exercising jurisdiction substantially in conformity with sections 452.440 to 452.550, unless the proceeding is stayed by the court of that other state for any reason.

2. Before hearing the petition in a custody proceeding, the court shall examine the pleadings and other information supplied by the parties under section 452.480 and shall consult the child custody registry established under section 452.515 concerning the pendency of proceedings with respect to the child in other states. If the court has reason to believe that proceedings may be pending in another state, it shall direct an inquiry to the state court administrator or other appropriate official of that state.

3. If the court is informed during the course of the proceeding that a proceeding concerning the custody of the child was pending in another state before the court assumed jurisdiction, it shall stay the proceeding and communicate with the court in which the other proceeding is pending in order that the issue may be litigated in the more appropriate forum and that information may be exchanged in accordance with sections 452.530 to 452.550. If a court of this state has made a custody decree before being informed of a pending proceeding in a court of another state, it shall immediately inform that court of the fact. If the court is informed that a proceeding was commenced in another state after it assumed jurisdiction, it shall likewise inform the other court in order that the issues may be litigated in the more appropriate forum.

§ 452.470. Inconvenient forum.

1. A court which has jurisdiction under this act to make an initial or modification decree may decline to exercise its jurisdiction any time before making a decree if it finds that it is an inconvenient forum to make a custody determination under the circumstances of the case and that a court of another state is a more appropriate forum.

2. A finding that a court is an inconvenient forum under subsection 1 above may be made upon the court's own motion or upon the motion of party or a guardian ad litem or other representative of the child. In determining if it is an inconvenient forum, the court shall consider if it is in the interest of the child that another state assume jurisdiction.

3. Before determining whether to decline or retain jurisdiction the court may communicate with a court of another state and exchange information pertinent to the assumption of jurisdiction by either court, with a view to assuring that jurisdiction will be exercised by the more appropriate court and that a forum will be available to the parties.

4. If the court finds that it is an inconvenient forum and that a court of another state is a more appropriate forum, it may dismiss the proceedings, or it may stay the proceedings upon condition that a custody proceeding be promptly commenced in another named state or upon any other conditions which may be just and proper, including the condition that a moving party stipulate his consent and submission to the jurisdiction of the other forum.

5. The court may decline to exercise its jurisdiction under this act if a custody determination is incidental to an action for dissolution of marriage or another proceeding while retaining jurisdiction over the dissolution of marriage or other proceeding.

6. If it appears to the court that it is clearly an inappropriate forum, it may require the party who commenced the proceedings to pay, in addition to the costs of the proceedings in this state, necessary travel and other expenses, including attorneys' fees, incurred by other parties or their witnesses. Payment is to be made to the clerk of the court for remittance to the proper party.

7. Upon dismissal or stay of proceedings under this section, the court shall inform the court found to be the more appropriate forum of this fact or, if the court which would have jurisdiction in the other state is not certainly known, shall transmit the information to the court administrator or other appropriate official for forwarding to the appropriate court.

8. Any communication received from another state informing this state of a finding that a court of this state is the more appropriate forum shall be filed in the custody registry of the appropriate court. Upon assuming jurisdiction the court of this state shall inform the original court of this fact.

§ 452.475. Jurisdiction declined because of conduct.

1. If the petitioner for an initial decree has wrongfully taken the child from another state or has engaged in similar reprehensible conduct, the court may decline to exercise jurisdiction if this is just and proper under the circumstances.

2. Unless required in the interest of the child, the court shall not exercise its jurisdiction to modify a custody decree of another state if the petitioner, without consent of the person entitled to custody, has improperly removed the child from the physical custody of the person entitled to custody or has improperly retained the child after a visit or other temporary relinquishment of physical custody. If the petitioner has violated any other provision of a custody decree of another state, the court may decline to exercise its jurisdiction if this is just and proper under the circumstances.

3. In appropriate cases a court dismissing a petition under this section may charge the petitioner with necessary travel and other expenses, including attorneys' fees, incurred by other parties or their witnesses.

§ 452.480. Information under oath to be submitted to the court.

1. In his first pleading, or in an affidavit attached to that pleading, every party in a custody proceeding shall give information under oath as to the child's present address, with whom the child is presently living and with whom and where the child lived, other than on a temporary basis, within the past six months. In this pleading or affidavit every party shall further declare under oath whether:

(1) He has participated in any capacity in any other litigation concerning the custody of the same child in this or any other state;

(2) He has information of any custody proceeding concerning the child pending in a court of this or any other state; and

(3) He knows of any person not a party to the proceedings who has physical custody of the child or claims to have custody or visitation rights with respect to the child.

2. If the declaration as to any of the items listed in subdivisions (1) through (3) of subsection 1 above is in the affirmative, the declaration shall give additional information under oath as required by the court. The court may examine the parties under oath as to details of the information furnished and as to other matters pertinent to the court's jurisdiction and the disposition of the case.

3. Each party has a continuing duty to inform the court of any change in information required by subsection 1 of this section.

§ 452.485. Additional parties.

If the court learns from information furnished by the parties pursuant to section 452.480 or from other sources that a person not a party to the custody proceeding has physical custody of the child or claims to have custody or visitation rights with respect to the child, it may order that person to be joined as a party and to be duly notified of the pendency of the proceeding and of his joinder as a party. If the person joined as a party is outside this state he shall be served with process or otherwise notified in accordance with section 452.460.

§ 452.490. Appearance of parties—child—guardian ad litem appointed, fee.

1. The court may order any party to the proceeding who is in this state to appear personally before the court. If the court finds the physical presence of the child in court to be in the best interests of the child, the court may order that the party who has physical custody of the child appear personally with the child.

2. If a party to the proceeding whose presence is desired by the court is outside this state, with or without the child, the court may order that the notice given under section 452.460 include a statement directing that party to appear personally with or without the child.

3. If a party to the proceeding who is outside this state is directed to appear under subsection 1 of this section or desires to appear personally before the court with or without the child, the court may require another party to pay to the clerk of the court travel and other necessary expenses of the party so appearing and of the child, if this is just and proper under the circumstances.

4. If the court finds it to be in the best interest of the child that a guardian ad litem be appointed, the court may appoint a guardian ad litem for the child. The guardian ad litem so appointed shall be an attorney licensed to practice law in the state of Missouri. The guardian ad litem may, for the purpose of determining custody of the child only, participate in the proceedings as if he were a party. The court shall allow a reasonable fee to the guardian ad litem to be taxed as costs in the proceeding.

§ 452.495. Binding force and res judicata effect of custody decree.

A custody decree rendered by a court of this state which had jurisdiction under section 452.450 binds all parties who have been served in this state or notified in accordance with section 452.460, or who have submitted to the jurisdiction of the court, and who have been given an opportunity to be heard. As to these parties the custody decree is conclusive as to all issues of law and fact decided and as to the custody determination made, unless and until that determination is modified pursuant to law, including the provisions of section 452.410 and sections 452.440 to 452.550.

§ 452.500. Recognition of out of state custody decrees.

The courts of this state shall recognize and enforce an initial or modification decree of a court of another state which had assumed jurisdiction under statutory provisions substantially in accordance with sections 452.440 to 452.550, or which was made under factual circumstances meeting the jurisdictional standards of sections 452.440 to 452.550, so long as this decree has not been modified in accordance with jurisdictional standards substantially similar to those of sections 452.440 to 452.550.

§ 452.505. Modification of custody decree of another state.

If a court of another state has made a custody decree, a court of this state shall not modify that decree unless it appears to the court of this state that the court which rendered the decree does not now have jurisdiction under jurisdictional prerequisites substantially in accordance with sections 452.440 to 452.550 or has declined to assume jurisdiction to modify the decree and the court of this state has jurisdiction.

§ 452.510. Filing and enforcement of custody decree of another state.

1. A certified copy of a custody decree of another state may be filed in the office of the clerk of any circuit court of this state. The clerk shall treat the decree in the same manner as a custody decree of the circuit court of this state. A custody decree so filed has the same effect and shall be enforced in like manner as a custody decree rendered by a court of this state.

2. A person violating a custody decree of another state which makes it necessary to enforce the decree in this state may be required to pay necessary travel and other expenses, including attorneys' fees, incurred by the party entitled to the custody or his witnesses.

§ 452.515. Registry of out of state custody decrees and proceedings.

The clerk of each circuit court shall maintain a registry in which he shall enter the following:

(1) Certified copies of custody decrees of other states received for filing;

(2) Communications as to the pendency of custody proceedings in other states;

(3) Communications concerning findings of inconvenient forum under section 452.470 by a court of another state; and

(4) Other communications or documents concerning custody proceedings in another state which in the opinion of the circuit judge may affect the jurisdiction of a court of this state or the disposition to be made by it in a custody proceeding.

§ 452.520. Certified copies of custody decrees.

The clerk of the circuit court of this state, at the request of the court of another state or at the request of the court of another state or at the request of any person who is affected by or has a legitimate interest in a custody decree, may, upon payment therefor, certify and forward a copy of the decree to that court or person.

§ 452.525. Taking testimony in another state.

In addition to other procedural devices available to a party, any party to the proceeding or a guardian ad litem or other representative of the child may obtain the testimony of witnesses, including parties and the child, by deposition or otherwise, in another state. The court on its own motion may direct that the testimony of a person be taken in another state and may prescribe the manner in which and the terms upon which the testimony shall be taken.

§ 452.530. Hearings and studies in another state—orders to appear.

1. A court of this state may request the appropriate court of another state to hold a hearing to obtain evidence, to order persons within that state to produce or give evidence under other procedures of that state, or to have social studies made with respect to the custody of a child involved in proceedings pending in the court of this state; and to forward to the court of this state certified copies of the transcript of the record of the hearing, the evidence otherwise obtained, or any social studies prepared in compliance with the request. The cost of the services may be assessed against the parties.

2. A court of this state may request the appropriate court of another state to order a party to custody proceedings pending in the court of this state to appear in the proceedings and, if that party has physical custody of the child, to appear with the child. The request may state that travel and other necessary expenses of the party and of the child whose appearance is desired will be assessed against the appropriate party.

452.535. Assistance to courts of other states.

1. Upon request of the court of another state, the courts of this state which are competent to hear custody matters may order a person in this state to appear at a hearing to obtain evidence or to produce or give evidence under other procedures available in this state for use in a custody proceeding in another state. A certified copy of the transcript of the record of the hearing or the evidence otherwise obtained may, in the discretion of the court and upon payment therefor, be forwarded to the requesting court.

2. A person within this state may voluntarily give his testimony or statement in this state for use in a custody proceeding outside this state.

3. Upon request of the court of another state, a competent court of this state may order a person in this state to appear alone or with the child in this state to appear alone or with the child in a custody proceeding in another state. The court may condition compliance with the request upon assurance by the other state that travel and other necessary expenses will be advanced or reimbursed.

§ 452.540. Preservation of documents for use in other states.

In any custody proceeding in this state the court shall preserve the pleadings, orders and decrees, any record that has been made of its hearings, social studies, and other pertinent documents until the child reaches eighteen years of age. When requested by the court of another state the court may, upon payment therefor, forward to the other court certified copies of any or all of such documents.

§ 452.545. Request for court records of another state.

If a custody decree has been rendered in another state concerning a child involved in a custody proceeding pending in a court of this state, the court of this state, upon taking jurisdiction of the case, shall request of the court of the other state a certified copy of the transcript of any court record and other documents mentioned in section 452.540.

§ 452.550. Priority.

Upon the request of a party to a custody proceeding which raises a question of existence or exercise of jurisdiction under section 452.440 to 452.550, determination of jurisdiction shall be given calendar priority and handled expeditiously.

MONTANA

UNIFORM CHILD CUSTODY JURISDICTION ACT

§ 40-7-101. Short title.

This chapter may be cited as the "Uniform Child Custody Jurisdiction Act".

§ 40-7-102. Purpose—construction.

(1) The general purposes of this chapter are to:

(a) avoid jurisdictional competition and conflict with courts of other states in matters of child custody which have in the past resulted in the shifting of children from state to state with harmful effects on their well-being;

(b) promote cooperation with the courts of other states to the end that a custody decree is rendered in that state which can best decide the case in the interest of the child;

(c) assure that litigation concerning the custody of a child takes place ordinarily in the state with which the child and his family have the closest connection and where significant evidence concerning his care, protection, training, and personal relationships is most readily available and that courts of this state decline the exercise of jurisdiction when the child and his family have a closer connection with another state;

(d) discourage continuing controversies over child custody in the interest of greater stability of home environment and of secure family relationships for the child;

(e) deter abductions and other unilateral removals of children undertaken to obtain custody awards;

(f) avoid relitigation of custody decisions of other states in this state insofar as feasible;

(g) facilitate the enforcement of custody decrees of other states;

(h) promote and expand the exchange of information and other forms of mutual assistance between the courts of this state and those of other states concerned with the same child; and

(i) make uniform the law of those states which enact it.

(2) This chapter shall be construed to promote the general purposes stated in this section.

§ 40-7-103. Definitions.

As used in this chapter, the following definitions apply:

(1) "Contestant" means a person, including a parent, who claims a right to custody or visitation rights with respect to a child.

(2) "Custody determination" means a court decision and court orders and instructions providing for the custody of a child, including visitation rights. It does not include a decision relating to child support or any other monetary obligation of any person.

(3) "Custody proceeding" includes proceedings in which a custody determination is one of several issues, such as an action for divorce or separation, and includes issues of custody in adoption proceedings. A "custody proceeding" is not a proceeding pursuant to title 41, chapter 3 or 5.

(4) "Decree" or "custody decree" means a custody determination contained in a judicial decree or order made in a custody proceeding and includes an initial decree and a modification decree.

(5) "Home state" means the state in which the child, immediately preceding the time involved, lived with his parents, a parent, or a person acting as parent, for at least 6 consecutive months and in the case of a child less than 6 months old the state in which the child lived from birth with any of the persons mentioned. Periods of temporary absence of any of the named persons are counted as part of the 6-month or other period.

(6) "Initial decree" means the first custody decree concerning a particular child.

(7) "Modification decree" means a custody decree which modifies or replaces a prior decree, whether made by the court which rendered the prior decree or by another court.

(8) "Physical custody" means actual possession and control of a child.

(9) "Person acting as parent" means a person other than a parent who has physical custody of a child and who has either been awarded custody by a court or claims a right to custody.

(10) "State" means any state, territory, or possession of the United States, the Commonwealth of Puerto Rico, and the District of Columbia.

§ 40-7-104. Jurisdiction.

The jurisdictional provisions of 40-4-211 apply to this chapter.

§ 40-7-105. Notice and opportunity to be heard.

Before making a decree under this chapter, reasonable notice and opportunity to be heard shall be given to the contestants, any parent whose parental rights have not been previously terminated, and any person who has physical custody of the child. If any of these persons are outside this state, notice and opportunity to be heard shall be given pursuant to 40-7-106.

§ 40-7-106. Notice to persons outside this state—submission to jurisdiction.

(1) Notice required for the exercise of jurisdiction over a person outside this state shall be given in a manner reasonably calculated to give actual notice and may be:

(a) by personal delivery outside this state in the manner prescribed for service of process within this state;

(b) in the manner prescribed by the law of the place in which the service is made for service of process in that place in an action in any of its courts of general jurisdiction;

(c) by any form of mail addressed to the person to be served and requesting a receipt; or

(d) as directed by the court, including publication, if other means of notification are ineffective.

(2) Notice under this section shall be served, mailed, or delivered or last published at least 10 days before any hearing in this state.

(3) Proof of service outside this state may be made by affidavit of the individual who made the service or in the manner prescribed by the law of this state, the order pursuant to which the service is made, or the law of the place in which the service is made. If service is made by mail, proof may be a receipt signed by the addressee or other evidence of delivery to the addressee.

(4) Notice is not required if a person submits to the jurisdiction of the court.

§ 40-7-107. Simultaneous proceedings in other states.

(1) A court of this state may not exercise its jurisdiction under this chapter if at the time of filing the petition a proceeding concerning the custody of the child was pending in a court of another state exercising jurisdiction substantially in conformity with this chapter unless the proceeding is stayed by the court of the other state because this state is a more appropriate forum or for other reasons.

(2) Before hearing the petition in a custody proceeding, the court shall examine the pleadings and other information supplied by the parties under 40-7-110 and shall consult the child custody registry established under 40-7-117 concerning the pendency of proceedings with respect to the child in other states. If the court has reason to believe that proceedings may be pending in another state, it shall direct an inquiry to the state court administrator or other appropriate official of the other state.

(3) If the court is informed during the course of the proceeding that a proceeding concerning the custody of the child was pending in another state before the court assumed jurisdiction, it shall stay the proceeding and communicate with the court in which the other proceeding is pending to the end that the issue may be litigated in the more appropriate forum and that information be exchanged in accordance with 40-7-120 through 40-7-123. If a court of this state has made a custody decree before being informed of a pending proceeding in a court of another state, it shall immediately inform that court of the fact. If the court is informed that a proceeding was commenced in another state after it assumed jurisdiction, it shall likewise inform the other court to the end that the issues may be litigated in the more appropriate forum.

§ 40-7-108. Inconvenient forum.

(1) A court which has jurisdiction under this chapter to make an initial or modification decree may decline to exercise its jurisdiction any time before making a decree if it finds that it is an inconvenient forum to make a custody determination under the circumstances of the case and that a court of another state is a more appropriate forum.

(2) A finding of inconvenient forum may be made upon the court's own motion or upon motion of a party or a guardian ad litem or other representative of the child.

(3) In determining if it is an inconvenient forum, the court shall consider if it is in the best interest of the child that another state assume jurisdiction. For this purpose it may take into account the following factors, among others:

(a) if another state is or recently was the child's home state;

(b) if another state has a closer connection with the child and his family or with the child and one or more of the contestants;

(c) if substantial evidence concerning the child's present or future care, protection, training, and personal relationships is more readily available in another state;

(d) if the parties have agreed on another forum which is no less appropriate; and

(e) if the exercise of jurisdiction by a court of this state would contravene any of the purposes stated in 40-7-102.

(4) Before determining whether to decline or retain jurisdiction, the court may communicate with a court of another state and exchange information pertinent to the assumption of jurisdiction by either court with a view to assuring that jurisdiction will be exercised by the more appropriate court and that a forum will be available to the parties.

(5) If the court finds that it is an inconvenient forum and that a court of another state is a more appropriate forum, it may dismiss the proceedings or it may stay the proceedings upon condition that a custody proceeding be promptly commenced in another named state or upon any other conditions which may be just and proper, including the condition that a moving party stipulate his consent and submission to the jurisdiction of the other forum.

(6) The court may decline to exercise its jurisdiction under this chapter if a custody determination is incidental to an action for divorce or another proceeding while retaining jurisdiction over the divorce or other proceeding.

(7) If it appears to the court that it is clearly an inappropriate forum, it may require the party who commenced the proceedings to pay, in addition to the costs of the proceedings in this state, necessary travel and other expenses, including attorneys' fees,

incurred by other parties or their witnesses. Payment is to be made to the clerk of the court for remittance to the proper party.

(8) Upon dismissal or stay of proceedings under this section the court shall inform the court found to be the more appropriate forum of this fact or, if the court which would have jurisdiction in the other state is not certainly known, transmit the information to the court administrator or other appropriate official for forwarding to the appropriate court.

(9) Any communication received from another state informing this state of a finding of inconvenient forum because a court of this state is the more appropriate forum shall be filed in the custody registry of the appropriate court. Upon assuming jurisdiction, the court of this state shall inform the original court of this fact.

§ 40-7-109. Jurisdiction declined by reason of conduct.

(1) If the petitioner for an initial decree has wrongfully taken the child from another petitioner for an initial decree has wrongfully taken the child from another state or has engaged in similar reprehensible conduct, the court may decline to exercise jurisdiction if this is just and proper under the circumstances.

(2) Unless required in the interest of the child, the court may not exercise its jurisdiction to modify a custody decree of another state if the petitioner, without consent of the person entitled to custody, has improperly removed the child from the physical custody of the person entitled to custody or has improperly retained the child after a visit or other temporary relinquishment of physical custody. If the petitioner has violated any other provision of a custody decree of another state, the court may decline to exercise its jurisdiction if this is just and proper under the circumstances.

(3) In appropriate cases a court dismissing a petition under this section may charge the petitioner with necessary travel and other expenses, including attorneys' fees, incurred by other parties or their witnesses.

§ 40-7-110. Information under oath to be submitted to the court.

(1) Each party in a custody proceeding in his first pleading or in an affidavit attached to that pleading shall give information under oath as to the child's present address, the places where the child has lived within the last 5 years, and the names and present addresses of the persons with whom the child has lived during that period. In this pleading or affidavit each party shall further declare under oath whether:

(a) he has participated (as a party, witness, or in any other capacity) in any other litigation concerning the custody of the same child in this or any other state;

(b) he has information of any custody proceeding concerning the child pending in a court of this or any other state; and

(c) he knows of any person not a party to the proceedings who has physical custody of the child or claims to have custody or visitation rights with respect to the child.

(2) If the declaration as to any of the above items is in the affirmative, the declarant shall give additional information under oath as required by the court. The court may examine the parties under oath as to details of the information furnished and as to other matters pertinent to the court's jurisdiction and the disposition of the case.

(3) Each party has a continuing duty to inform the court of any custody proceeding concerning the child in this or any other state of which he obtained information during this proceeding.

§ 40-7-111. Additional parties.

If the court learns from information furnished by the parties pursuant to 40-7-110 or from other sources that a person not a party to the custody proceeding has physical custody of the child or claims to have custody or visitation rights with respect to the child, it shall order that person to be joined as a party and to be duly notified of the pendency of the proceeding and of his joinder as a party. If the person joined as a party is outside this state, he shall be served with process or otherwise notified in accordance with 40-7-106.

§ 40-7-112. Appearance of parties and child.

(1) The court may order any party to the proceeding who is in this state to appear personally before the court. If that party has physical custody of the child, the court may order that he appear personally with the child.

(2) If a party to the proceeding whose presence is desired by the court is outside this state with or without the child, the court may order that the notice given under 40-7-106 include a statement directing that party to appear personally with or without the child and declaring that failure to appear may result in a decision adverse to that party.

(3) If a party to the proceeding who is outside this state is directed to appear under subsection (2) or desires to appear personally before the court with or without the child, the court may require another party to pay to the clerk of the court travel and other necessary expenses of the party so appearing and of the child, if this is just and proper under the circumstances.

§ 40-7-113. Legal effect of custody decree.

A custody decree rendered by a court of this state which had jurisdiction under 40-7-104 binds all parties who have been served in this state or notified in accordance with 40-7-106 or who have submitted to the jurisdiction of the court and who have been given an opportunity to be heard. As to these parties the custody decree is conclusive as to all issues of law and fact decided and as to the custody determination made unless and until that determination is modified pursuant to law, including the provisions of this chapter.

§ 40-7-114. Recognition of out-of-state custody decrees.

The courts of this state shall recognize and enforce an initial or modification decree of a court of another state which had assumed jurisdiction under statutory provisions substantially in accordance with this chapter or which was made under factual circumstances meeting the jurisdictional standards of the chapter, so long as this decree has not been modified in accordance with jurisdictional standards substantially similar to those of this chapter.

§ 40-7-115. Modification of custody decree of another state.

(1) If a court of another state has made a custody decree, a court of this state may not modify that decree unless it appears to the court of this state that the court which rendered the decree does not now have jurisdiction under jurisdictional prerequisites substantially in accordance with this chapter or has declined to assume jurisdiction to modify the decree and the court of this state has jurisdiction.

(2) If a court of this state is authorized under subsection (1) and 40-7-109 to modify a custody decree of another state, it shall give due consideration to the transcript of the record and other documents of all previous proceedings submitted to it in accordance with 40-7-123.

§ 40-7-116. Filing and enforcement of custody decree of another state.

(1) A certified copy of a custody decree of another state may be filed in the office of the clerk of any district court of this state. The clerk shall treat the decree in the same manner as a custody decree of the district court of this state. A custody decree so filed has the same effect and shall be enforced in like manner as a custody decree rendered by a court of this state.

(2) A person violating a custody decree of another state which makes it necessary to enforce the decree in this state may be required to pay necessary travel and other expenses, including attorneys' fees, incurred by the party entitled to the custody or his witnesses.

§ 40-7-117. Registry of out-of-state custody decrees and proceedings.

The clerk of each district court shall maintain a registry in which he shall enter the following:

(1) certified copies of custody decrees of other states received for filing;

(2) communications as to the pendency of custody proceedings in other states;

(3) communications concerning a finding of inconvenient forum by a court of another state; and

(4) other communications or documents concerning custody proceedings in another state which may affect the jurisdiction of a court of this state or the disposition to be made by it in a custody proceeding.

§ 40-7-118. Certified copies of custody decree.

The clerk of the district court of this state, at the request of the court of another state or at the request of any person who is affected by or has a legitimate interest in a custody decree, shall certify and forward a copy of the decree to that court or person.

§ 40-7-119. Taking testimony in another state.

In addition to other procedural devices available to a party, any party to the proceeding or a guardian ad litem or other representative of the child may adduce testimony of witnesses, including parties and the child, by deposition or otherwise, in another state. The court on its own motion may direct that the testimony of a person be taken in another state and may prescribe the manner in which and the terms upon which the testimony shall be taken.

§ 40-7-120. Hearings and studies in another state—orders to appear.

(1) A court of this state may request the appropriate court of another state to hold a hearing to adduce evidence, to order a party to produce or give evidence under other procedures of that state, or to have social studies made with respect to the custody of a child involved in proceedings pending in the court of this state; and to forward to the court of this state certified copies of the transcript of the record of the hearing, the evidence otherwise adduced, or any social studies prepared in compliance with the request. The cost of the services may be assessed against the parties or, if necessary, ordered paid by the state.

(2) A court of this state may require the appropriate court of another state to order a party to custody proceedings pending in the court of this state to appear in the proceedings and, if that party has physical custody of the child, to appear with the child. The request may state that travel and other necessary expenses of the party and of the child whose appearance is desired will be assessed against another party or will otherwise be paid.

§ 40-7-121. Assistance to courts of other states.

(1) Upon request of the court of another state the courts of this state which are competent to hear custody matters may order a person in this state to appear at a hearing to adduce evidence or to produce or give evidence under other procedures available in this state or may order social studies to be made for use in a custody proceeding in another state. A certified copy of the transcript of the record of the hearing or the evidence otherwise adduced and any social studies prepared shall be forwarded by the clerk of the court to the requesting court.

(2) A person within this state may voluntarily give his testimony or statement in this state for use in a custody proceeding outside this state.

(3) Upon request of the court of another state a competent court of this state may order a person in this state to appear alone or with the child in a custody proceeding in another state. The court may condition compliance with the request upon assurance by the other state that state travel and other necessary expenses will be advanced or reimbursed.

§ 40-7-122. Preservation of documents for use in other states.

In any custody proceeding in this state the court shall preserve the pleadings, orders and decrees, any record that has been made of its hearings, social studies, and other pertinent documents until the child reaches 18 years of age. Upon appropriate request of the court of another state, the court shall forward to the other court certified copies of any or all of such documents.

§ 40-7-123. Request for court records of another state.

If a custody decree has been rendered in another state concerning a child involved in a custody proceeding pending in a court of this state, the court of this state upon taking jurisdiction of the case shall request of the court of the other state a certified copy of the transcript of any court record and other documents mentioned in 40-7-122.

§ 40-7-124. International application.

The general policies of this chapter extend to the international area. The provisions of this chapter relating to the recognition and enforcement of custody decrees of other states apply to custody decrees and decrees involving legal institutions similar in nature to custody institutions rendered by appropriate authorities of other nations if reasonable notice and opportunity to be heard have been given to all affected persons.

§ 40-7-125. Priority.

A custody proceeding which raises a question of existence or exercise of jurisdiction under this chapter shall be given calendar priority and handled expeditiously.

NEBRASKA

NEBRASKA CHILD CUSTODY JURISDICTION ACT

43-1201. Purposes and construction.

(1) The general purposes of sections 43-1201 to 43-1225 are to:

(a) Avoid jurisdictional competition and conflict with courts of other states in matters of child custody which have in the past resulted in the shifting of children from state to state with harmful effects on their well-being;

(b) Promote cooperation with the courts of other states to the end that a custody decree is rendered in that state which can best decide the case in the interest of the child;

(c) Assure that litigation concerning the custody of a child take place ordinarily in the state with which the child and his family have the closest connection and where significant evidence concerning his care, protection, training, and personal relationships is most readily available, and that courts of this state decline the exercise of jurisdiction when the child and his family have a closer connection with another state;

(d) Discourage continuing controversies over child custody in the interest of greater stability of home environment and of secure family relationships for the child;

(e) Deter abductions and other unilateral removals of children undertaken to obtain custody awards;

(f) Avoid relitigation of custody decisions of other states in this state when feasible;

(g) Facilitate the enforcement of custody decrees of other states;

(h) Promote and expand the exchange of information and other forms of mutual assistance between the courts of this state and those of other states concerned with the same child; and

(i) Make uniform the law of those states which enact it.

(2) Sections 43-1201 to 43-1225 shall be construed to promote the general purposes stated in this section.

43-1202. Terms, defined.

As used in the Nebraska Child Custody Jurisdiction Act:

(1) Contestant shall mean a person, including a parent, who claims a right to custody or visitation rights with respect to a child;

(2) Custody determination shall mean a court decision and court orders and instructions providing for the custody of a child, including visitation rights, but shall not include a decision relating to child support or any other monetary obligation of any person;

(3) Custody proceeding shall mean:

(a) Proceeding in which a custody determination is one of several issues such as an action for dissolution, separation, or annulment of a marriage or an action involving a doubtful marriage;

(b) Proceedings in a juvenile court in which a person under the age of eighteen years is alleged to be a child as described in subdivision (3) of section 43-247;

(c) Proceedings to establish the rights of the father of a child born out of wedlock as such rights are allowed by section s 43-104.05 and 43-104.06; and

(d) Proceedings to determine custody as provided by section 43-111.01 after a court has denied a petition for adoption;

(4) Custody decree shall mean a custody determination contained in a judicial decree or order made in a custody proceeding and shall include an initial decree and a modification decree;

(5) Home state shall mean the state in which the child immediately preceding the time involved lived with his or her parents, a parent, or a person acting as parent, for at least six consecutive months, and in the case of a child less than six months old the state in which the child lived from birth with any of the persons mentioned. Periods of temporary absence of any of the named persons shall be counted as part of the six-month or other period;

(6) Initial decree shall mean the first custody decree concerning a particular child;

(7) Modification decree shall mean a custody decree which modifies or replaces a prior decree, whether made by the court which rendered the prior decree or by another court;

(8) Physical custody shall mean actual possession and control of a child;

(9) Person acting as parent shall mean a person, other than a parent, who has physical custody of a child and who has either been awarded custody by a court or claims a right to custody; and

(10) State shall mean any state, territory, or possession of the United States, the Commonwealth of Puerto Rico, and the District of Columbia.

43-1203. Court; jurisdiction; prerequisites.

(1) A court of this state which is competent to decide child custody matters has jurisdiction to make a child custody determination by initial or modification decree if:

(a) This state (i) is the home state of the child at the time of commencement of the proceeding, or (ii) had been the child's home state within six months before commencement of the proceeding and the child is absent from this state because of his or her removal or retention by a person claiming his or her custody or for other reasons, and a parent or person acting as parent continues to live in this state;

(b) It is in the best interest of the child that a court of this state assume jurisdiction because (i) the child and his or her parents, or the child and at least one contestant, have a significant connection with this state and (ii) there is available in this state substantial evidence concerning the child's present or future care, protection, training, and personal relationships;

(c) The child is physically present in this state and (i) the child has been abandoned or (ii) it is necessary in an emergency to protect the child because he or she has been subjected to or threatened with mistreatment or abuse or is otherwise neglected;

(d)(i) It appears that no other state would have jurisdiction under prerequisites substantially in accordance with subdivision (a), (b), or (c) of this section, or another state has declined to exercise jurisdiction on the ground that this state is the more appropriate forum to determine the custody of the child, and (ii) it is in the best interest of the child that this court assume jurisdiction; or

(e) The child is not an Indian child over which jurisdiction is otherwise provided under the Nebraska Indian Child Welfare Act.

(2) Except under subdivisions (c) and (d) of subsection (1) of this section, physical presence in this state of the child, or of the child and one of the contestants, is not alone sufficient to confer jurisdiction on a court of this state to make a child custody determination.

(3) Physical presence of the child, while desirable, is not a prerequisite for jurisdiction to determine his or her custody.

43-1204. Decree; notice and opportunity to be heard.

Except as otherwise provided in the Nebraska Indian Child Welfare Act, before making a decree under sections 43-1201 to 43-1225, reasonable notice and opportunity to be heard shall be given to the contestants, any parent whose parental rights have not been previously terminated, and any person who has physical custody of the child. If any of these persons is outside this state, notice and opportunity to be heard shall be given pursuant to section 43-1205.

43-1205. Notice; person outside state; manner given.

(1) Notice required for the exercise of jurisdiction over a person outside this state shall be given in the manner provided for service of a summons in a civil action.

(2) Notice under this section shall be served, delivered, or last published at least fourteen days before any hearing in this state.

(3) Proof of service outside this state may be made by affidavit of the individual who made the service or in the manner prescribed

by the law of this state, the order pursuant to which the service is made, or the law of the place in which the service is made.

(4) Notice is not required if a person submits to the jurisdiction of the court.

(5) The provisions of this section shall not apply to persons subject to the Nebraska Indian Child Welfare Act.

43-1206. Proceeding pending in another state; how treated.

(1) A court of this state shall not exercise its jurisdiction under sections 43-1201 to 43-1225 if at the time of filing the petition a proceeding concerning the custody of the child was pending in a court of another state exercising jurisdiction substantially in conformity with this act, unless the proceeding is stayed by the court of the other state because this state is a more appropriate forum or for other reasons.

(2) Before hearing the petition in a custody proceeding the court shall examine the pleadings and other information supplied by the parties under section 43-1209 and shall consult the child custody registry established under section 43-1216 concerning the pendency of proceedings with respect to the child in other states. If the court has reason to believe that proceedings may be pending in another state is shall direct an inquiry to the state court administrator or other appropriate official of the other state.

(3) If the court is informed during the course of the proceeding that a proceeding concerning the custody of the child was pending in another state before the court assumed jurisdiction it shall stay the proceeding and communicate with the court in which the other proceeding is pending to the end that the issue may be litigated in the more appropriate forum and that information be exchanged in accordance with sections 43-1219 to 43-1222. If a court of this state has made a custody decree before being informed of a pending proceeding in a court of another state it shall immediately inform that court of the fact. If the court is informed that a proceeding was commenced in another state after it assumed jurisdiction it shall likewise inform the other court to the end that the issues may be litigated in the more appropriate forum.

43-1207. Court; inconvenient forum; determination; communication with another court.

(1) A court which has jurisdiction under sections 43-1201 to 43-1225 to make an initial or modification decree may decline to exercise its jurisdiction any time before making a decree if it finds that it is an inconvenient forum to make a custody determination under the circumstances of the case and that a court of another state is a more appropriate forum.

(2) A finding of inconvenient forum may be made upon the court's own motion or upon motion of a party of a guardian ad litem or other representative of the child.

(3) In determining if it is an inconvenient forum, the court shall consider if it is in the interest of the child that another state assume jurisdiction. For this purpose it may take into account the following factors, among others:

(a) If another state is or recently was the child's home state;

(b) If another state has a closer connection with the child and his family or with the child and one or more of the contestants;

(c) If substantial evidence concerning the child's present or future care, protection, training, and personal relationships is more readily available in another state;

(d) If the parties have agreed on another forum which is no less appropriate; and

(e) If the exercise of jurisdiction by a court of this state would contravene any of the purposes stated in section 43-1201.

(4) Before determining whether to decline or retain jurisdiction the court may communicate with a court of another state and exchange information pertinent to the assumption of jurisdiction by either court with a view to assuring that jurisdiction will be exercised by the more appropriate court and that a forum will be available to the parties. The court shall give to the parties the substance of any communication or exchange of information under this subsection, and afford the parties reasonable opportunity to respond.

(5) If the court finds that it is an inconvenient forum and that a court of another state is a more appropriate forum, it may dismiss the proceedings, or it may stay the proceedings upon condition that a custody proceeding be promptly commenced in another named state or upon any other conditions which may be just and proper, including the condition that a moving party stipulate his consent and submission to the jurisdiction of the other forum.

(6) The court may decline to exercise its jurisdiction under sections 43-1201 to 43-1225 if a custody determination is incidental to an action for divorce or another proceeding while retaining jurisdiction over the divorce or other proceeding.

(7) If it appears to the court that it is clearly an inappropriate forum it may require the party who commenced the proceedings to pay, in addition to the costs of the proceedings in this state, necessary travel and other expenses, including attorneys' fees, incurred by other parties or their witnesses. Payment is to be made to the clerk of the court for remittance to the proper party.

(8) Upon dismissal or stay of proceeding under this section the court shall inform the court found to be the more appropriate forum of this fact or, if the court which would have jurisdiction in the other state is not certainly known, shall transmit the information to the court administrator or other appropriate official for forwarding to the appropriate court.

(9) Any communication received from another state informing this state of a finding of inconvenient forum because a court of this state is the more appropriate forum shall be filed in the custody registry of the appropriate court. Upon assuming jurisdiction the court of this state shall inform the original court of this fact.

43-1208. Petitioner; wrongful conduct; court; decline jurisdiction; when; expenses.

(1) If the petitioner for an initial decree has wrongfully taken the child from another state or has engaged in similar reprehensible

conduct the court may decline to exercise jurisdiction if this is just and proper under the circumstances.

(2) Unless required in the interest of the child, the court shall not exercise its jurisdiction to modify a custody decree of another state if the petitioner, without consent of the person entitled to custody, has improperly removed the child from the physical custody of the person entitled to custody or has improperly retained the child after a visit or other temporary relinquishment of physical custody. If the petitioner has violated any other provision of a custody decree of another state the court may decline to exercise its jurisdiction if this is just and proper under the circumstances.

(3) In appropriate cases a court dismissing a petition under this section may charge the petitioner with necessary travel and other expenses, including attorneys' fees, incurred by other parties or their witnesses.

43-1209. Pleading; contents; additional information.

(1) Every party in a custody proceeding in his first pleading or in an affidavit attached to that pleading shall give information under oath as to the child's present address, the places where the child has lived within the last five years, and the names and present addresses of the persons with whom the child has lived during that period. In this pleading or affidavit every party shall further declare under oath whether:

(a) He has participated as a party, witness, or in any other capacity in any other litigation concerning the custody of the same child in this or any other state;

(b) He has information of any custody proceeding concerning the child pending in a court of this or any other state; and

(c) He knows of any person not a party to the proceedings who has physical custody of the child or claims to have custody or visitation rights with respect to the child.

(2) If the declaration as to any of the above items is in the affirmative the declarant shall give additional information under oath as required by the court. The court may examine the parties under oath as to details of the information furnished and as to other matters pertinent to the court's jurisdiction and the disposition of the case.

(3) Each party has a continuing duty to inform the court of any custody proceeding concerning the child in this or any other state of which he obtained information during this proceeding.

43-1210. Joinder as a party; notice.

If the court learns from information furnished by the parties pursuant to section 43-1209 or from other sources that a person not a party to the custody proceeding has physical custody of the child or claims to have custody or visitation rights with respect to the child, it shall order that person to be joined as a party and to be duly notified of the pendency of the proceeding and of his joinder as a party. If the person joined as a parties outside this state he shall be served with process or otherwise notified in accordance with section 43-1205.

43-1211. Party; personal appearance; notice; expenses.

(1) The court may order any party to the proceeding who is in this state to appear personally before the court. If that party has physical custody of the child the court may order that he appear personally with the child.

(2) If a party to the proceeding whose presence is desired by the court is outside this state with or without the child the court may order that the notice given under section 43-1205 include a statement directing that party to appear personally with or without the child and declaring that failure to appear may result in a decision adverse to that party.

(3) If a party to the proceeding who is outside this state is directed to appear under subsection (2) of this section or desires to appear personally before the court with or without the child, the court may require another party to pay to the clerk of the court travel and other necessary expenses of the party so appearing and of the child if this is just and proper under the circumstances.

43-1212. Decree; effect.

A custody decree rendered by a court of this state which had jurisdiction under section 43-1203 binds all parties who have been served in this state or notified in accordance with section 43-1205 or who have submitted to the jurisdiction of the court, and who have been given an opportunity to be heard. As to these parties the custody decree is conclusive as to all issues of law and fact decided and as to the custody determination made unless and until that determination is modified pursuant to law, including the provisions of sections 43-1201 to 43-1225.

43-1213. Decree of a court of another state; recognized; when.

The courts of this state shall recognize and enforce an initial or modification decree of a court of another state which had assumed jurisdiction under statutory provisions substantially in accordance with sections 43-1201 to 43-1225 or which was made under factual circumstances meeting the jurisdictional standards of such sections, so long as this decree has not been modified in accordance with jurisdictional standards substantially similar to those of sections 43-1201 to 43-1225.

43-1214. Decree of another state; modification.

(1) If a court of another state has made a custody decree, a court of this state shall not modify that decree unless (a) it appears to the court of this state that the court which rendered the decree does not now have jurisdiction under jurisdictional prerequisites

substantially in accordance with sections 43-1201 to 43-1225 or has declined to assume jurisdiction to modify the decree and (b) the court of this state has jurisdiction.

(2) If a court of this state is authorized under subsection (1) of this section and section 42-1208 to modify a custody decree of another state it shall give due consideration to the transcript of the record and other documents of all previous proceedings submitted to it in accordance with section 43-1222.

43-1215. Decree of another state; certified copy; filing; effect; enforcement.

(1) A certified copy of a custody decree of another state may be filed in the office of the clerk of any district court of this state. The clerk shall treat the decree in the same manner as a custody decree of the district court of this state. A custody decree so filed has the same effect and shall be enforced in like manner as a custody decree rendered by a court of this state.

(2) A person violating a custody decree of another state which makes it necessary to enforce the decree in this state may be required to pay necessary travel and other expenses, including attorneys' fees, incurred by the party entitled to the custody of this witnesses.

(3) If a person seeks to enforce in this state a custody decree of another state with respect to child support or other monetary or property obligations contained in such decree as well as to enforce the custody determination of such decree, the person may commence any proceeding allowed by law for the enforcement in this state for such support or other obligation and may include in such proceeding a request for appropriate enforcement of the custody determination. In such proceeding, the court shall recognize and treat the custody determination in accordance with the provisions of sections 43-1201 to 43-1225.

43-1216. Registry; clerk of district court; maintain.

The clerk of each district court shall maintain a registry in which he shall enter the following:

(1) Certified copies of custody decrees of other states received for filing;

(2) Communications as to the pendency of custody proceedings in other states;

(3) Communications concerning a finding of inconvenient forum by a court of another state; and

(4) Other communications or documents concerning custody proceedings in another state which may affect the jurisdiction of a court of this state or the disposition to be made by it in a custody proceeding.

43-1217. Decree; clerk of district court; certify; provide copy.

The clerk of the district court of this state, at the request of the court of another state or at the request of any person who is affected by or has a legitimate interest in a custody decree, shall certify and forward a copy of the decree to that court or person.

43-1218. Testimony of witness.

In addition to other procedural devices available to a party, any party to the proceeding or a guardian ad litem or other representative of the child may adduce testimony of witnesses, including parties and the child, by deposition or otherwise, in another state. The court on its own motion may direct that the testimony of a person be taken in another state and may prescribe the manner in which and the terms upon which the testimony shall be taken.

43-1219. Court of this state; request assistance from court of another state; costs.

(1) A court of this state may request the appropriate court of another state to hold a hearing to adduce evidence, to order a party to produce or give evidence under other procedures of that state, or to have social studies made with respect to the custody of a child involved in proceedings pending in the court of this state; and to forward to the court of this state certified copies of the transcript of the record of the hearing, the evidence otherwise adduced, or any social studies prepared in compliance with the request. The cost of the services may be assessed against the parties or, if necessary, ordered paid by the county.

(2) A court of this state may request the appropriate court of this state to appear in the proceedings, and if that party has physical custody of the child, to appear with the child. The request may state that travel and other necessary expenses of the party and of the child whose appearance is desired will be assessed against another party or will otherwise be paid.

43-1220. Court of another state; request assistance from court of this state; expenses.

(1) Upon request of the court of another state the courts of this state which are competent to hear custody matters may order a person in this state to appear at a hearing to adduce evidence or to produce or give evidence under other procedures available in this state, or may order social studies to be made for use in a custody proceeding in another state. A certified copy of the transcript of the record of the hearing or the evidence otherwise adduced and any social studies prepared shall be forwarded by the clerk of the court to the requesting court.

(2) A person within this state may voluntarily give his testimony or statement in this state for use in a custody proceeding outside this state.

(3) Upon request of the court of another state a competent court of this state may order a person in this state to appear alone or with the child in a custody proceeding in another state. The court may condition compliance with the request upon assurance by the other state that travel and other necessary expenses will be advanced or reimbursed.

43-1221. Preservation of documents; duration; certified copies.

In any custody proceeding in this state the court shall preserve the pleadings, orders and decrees, any record that has been made of its hearings, social studies, and other pertinent documents until the child reaches nineteen years of age. Upon appropriate request of the court of another state the court shall forward to the other court certified copies of any or all of such documents.

43-1222. Court of this state; request transcript and documents of court of another state.

If a custody decree has been rendered in another state concerning a child involved in a custody proceeding pending in a court of this state, the court of this state upon taking jurisdiction of the case shall request of the court of the other state a certified copy of the transcript of any court record and other documents mentioned in section 43-1221.

43-1223. Recognition and enforcement of decrees of other nations; when.

The general policies of sections 43-1201 to 43-1225 extend to the international area. The provisions of sections 43-1201 to 43-1225 relating to the recognition and enforcement of custody decrees of other states apply to custody decrees and decrees involving legal institutions similar in nature to custody institutions rendered by appropriate authorities of other nations if reasonable notice and opportunity to be heard were given to all affected persons.

43-1224. Jurisdictional issue; calendar priority.

Upon the request of a party to a custody proceeding which raises a question of existence or exercise of jurisdiction under sections 43-1201 to 43-1225 the jurisdictional issue of the case shall be given calendar priority and handled expeditiously.

43-1225. Act, how cited.

Sections 43-1201 to 43-1225 shall be known and may be cited as the Nebraska Child Custody Jurisdiction Act.

NEVADA

UNIFORM CHILD CUSTODY JURISDICTION ACT

125A.010. Short title.

This chapter may be cited as the Uniform Child Custody Jurisdiction Act.

125A.020. Purposes of chapter.

The general purposes of this chapter are to:

1. Avoid jurisdictional competition and conflict with courts of other states in matters of child custody which have in the past resulted in the shifting of children from state to state with harmful effects on their well-being;

2. Promote cooperation with the courts of other states to the end that a custody decree is rendered in that state which can best decide the case in the interest of the child;

3. Assure that litigation concerning the custody of a child take place ordinarily in the state with which the child and his family have the closest connection and where significant evidence concerning his care, protection, training and personal relationships is most readily available, and that courts of this state decline the exercise of jurisdiction when the child and his family have a closer connection with another state;

4. Discourage continuing controversies over child custody in the interest of greater stability of home environment and of secure family relationship for the child;

5. Deter abductions and other unilateral removals of children undertaken to obtain custody awards;

6. Avoid relitigation of custody decisions of other states in this state insofar as feasible;

7. Facilitate the enforcement of custody decrees of other states;

8. Promote and expand the exchange of information and other forms of mutual assistance between the courts of this state and those of other states concerned with the same child; and

9. Make uniform the law of those states which enact it.

This chapter shall be construed to promote the general purposes stated in this section.

125A.030. Application of chapter to decrees of other nations.

The general policies of this chapter extend to other nations. The provisions of this chapter relating to the recognition and enforcement of custody decrees of other states apply to custody decrees and decrees involving legal institutions similar in nature to custody institutions rendered by appropriate authorities of other nations if reasonable notice and opportunity to be heard were given to all affected persons.

125A.040. Definitions.

As used in this chapter:

1. "Contestant" means a person, including a parent, or an Indian child's tribe as defined by the Indian Child Welfare Act of 1978 (25 U.S.C. §§ 1901 et seq.), who claims a right to custody or visitation rights with respect to a child.

2. "Custody determination" means a court decision and court orders and instructions providing for the custody of a child, including visitation rights. It does not include a decision relating to child support or any other monetary obligation of any person.

3. "Custody proceeding" includes proceedings in which a custody determination is one of several issues, such as an action for divorce or separation, and includes child neglect and dependency proceedings.

4. "Decree" or "custody decree" means a custody determination contained in a judicial decree or other made in a custody proceeding.

5. "Home state" means the state in which the child immediately preceding the time involved lived with his parents, a parent, or a person acting as parent, for at least 6 consecutive months, and in the case of a child less than 6 months old the state in which the child lived from birth with any of the persons mentioned. Periods of temporary absence of any of the named persons are counted as part of the 6-month or other period.

6. "Initial decree" means the first custody decree concerning a particular child.

7. "Modifying decree" means a custody decree which modifies or replaces a prior decree, whether made by the court which rendered the prior decree or by another court.

8. "Person acting as parent" means a person, other than a parent, who has physical custody of a child and who has either been awarded custody by a court or claims a right to custody.

9. "Physical custody" means actual possession and control of a child.

10. "State" means any state, territory or possession of the United States, the Commonwealth of Puerto Rico and the District of Columbia, or an Indian tribe in situations where the Indian Child Welfare Act of 1978 (25 U.S.C. §§ 1901 et seq.) applies.

125A.050. Jurisdiction.

1. A court of this state which is competent to decide child custody matters has jurisdiction to make a child custody determination by initial or modifying decree if:

(a) This state:

(1) Is the home state of the child at the time of commencement of the proceeding; or

(2) Had been the child's home state within 6 months before commencement of the proceeding and the child is absent from this state because of his removal or retention by a person claiming his custody or for other reasons, and a parent or person acting as parent continues to live in this state;

(b) It is in the best interest of the child that a court of this state assume jurisdiction because:

(1) The child and his parents, or the child and at least one contestant, have a significant connection with this state; and

(2) There is available in this state substantial evidence concerning the child's present or future care, protection, training and personal relationships;

(c) The child is physically present in this state and:

(1) The child has been abandoned; or

(2) It is necessary in an emergency to protect the child because he has been subjected to or threatened with mistreatment or abuse or is otherwise neglected;

(d) It appears that no other state would have jurisdiction under prerequisites substantially in accordance with paragraphs (a), (b) or (c), or another state has declined to exercise jurisdiction on the ground that this state is the more appropriate forum to determine the custody of the child, and it is in the best interest of the child that this court assume jurisdiction; or

(e) The child is not subject to the exclusive jurisdiction of an Indian tribe pursuant to the Indian Child Welfare Act of 1978 (25 U.S.C. §§ 1901 et seq.).

2. Except under paragraphs (c) and (d) of subsection 1, physical presence in this state of the child, or of the child and one of the contestants, is not alone sufficient to confer jurisdiction on a court of this state to make a child custody determination.

3. Physical presence of the child, while desirable, is not a prerequisite for jurisdiction to determine his custody.

125A.060. Exercise of jurisdiction: When custody proceedings pending in other states.

1. A court of this state shall not exercise its jurisdiction under this chapter if at the time of filing the petition a proceeding concerning the custody of the child was pending in a court of another state exercising jurisdiction substantially in conformity with the Uniform Child Custody Jurisdiction Act or the Indian Child Welfare Act of 1978 (25 U.S..C. §§ 1901 et seq.), unless the proceeding is stayed by the court of the other state because this state is a more appropriate forum or for other reasons.

2. Before hearing the petition in a custody proceeding the court shall examine the pleadings and other information supped by the parties under NRS 125A.120 and shall consult the child custody registry established under NRS 125A.200 concerning the

pendency of proceedings with respect to the child in other states. If the court has reason to believe that proceedings may be pending in another state it shall direct an inquiry to the state court administrator or other appropriate official of the other state.

3. If the court is informed during the course of the proceeding that a proceeding concerning the custody of the child was pending in another state before the court assumed jurisdiction it shall stay the proceeding and communicate with the court in which the other proceeding is pending to the end that the issue may be litigated in the more appropriate forum and that information be exchanged in accordance with NRS 125A.220 to 125A.250, inclusive. If a court of this state has made a custody decree before being informed of a pending proceeding in a court of another state it shall immediately inform that court of the fact. If the court is informed that a proceeding was commenced in another state after it assumed jurisdiction it shall likewise inform the other court to the end that the issues may be litigated in the more appropriate forum.

125A.070. Exercise of jurisdiction: when forum inappropriate.

1. A court which has jurisdiction under this chapter to make an initial or modifying decree may decline to exercise its jurisdiction any time before making a decree if it finds that it is an inappropriate forum to make a custody determination under the circumstances of the case and that a court of another state is a more appropriate forum.

2. A finding of inappropriate forum may be made upon the court's own motion or upon motion of a party or a guardian ad litem or other representative of the child.

3. In determining whether it is an inappropriate forum, the court shall consider if it is in the interest of the child that another state assume jurisdiction. For this purpose it may take into account the following factors, among others:

(a) Whether another state is or recently was the child's home state;

(b) Whether another state has a closer connection with the child and his family or with the child and one or more of the contestants;

(c) Whether substantial evidence concerning the child's present or future care, protection, training and personal relationships is more readily available in another state;

(d) Whether the parties have agreed on another forum which is no less appropriate; and

(e) Whether the exercise of jurisdiction by a court of this state would contravene any of the purposes stated in NRS 125A.020.

4. Before determining whether to decline or retain jurisdiction the court may communicate with a court of another state and exchange information pertinent to the assumption of jurisdiction by either court with a view to assuring that jurisdiction will be exercised by the more appropriate court and that a forum will be available to the parties.

5. If the court finds that it is an inappropriate forum and that a court of another state is a more appropriate forum, it may dismiss the proceedings, or it may stay the proceedings upon condition that a custody proceeding be promptly commenced in another named state or upon any other conditions which may be just and proper, including the condition that a moving party stipulate his consent and submission to the jurisdiction of the other forum.

6. The court may decline to exercise its jurisdiction under this chapter if a custody determination is incidental to an action for divorce or another proceeding while retaining jurisdiction over the divorce or other proceeding.

7. The court shall transfer the proceeding pursuant to the provisions of the Indian Child Welfare Act of 1978 (25 U.S.C. §§ 1901 et seq.) where those provisions so require.

8. If it appears to the court that it is clearly an inappropriate forum it may require the party who commenced the proceedings to pay, in addition to the costs of the proceedings in this state, necessary travel and other expenses, including attorney's fees, incurred by other parties or their witnesses. Payment is to be made to the clerk of the court for remittance to the proper party.

9. Upon dismissal or stay of proceedings under this section the court shall inform the court found to be the more appropriate forum of this fact or, if the court which would have jurisdiction in the other state is not certainly known, shall transmit the information to the court administrator or other appropriate official for forwarding to the appropriate court.

10. Any communication received from another state informing this state of a finding of inappropriate forum because a court of this state is the more appropriate forum shall be filed in the custody registry of the appropriate court. Upon assuming jurisdiction the court of this state shall inform the original court of this fact.

125A.080. Exercise of jurisdiction: When petitioner acts wrongfully.

1. If the petitioner for an initial decree has wrongfully taken the child from another state or has engaged in similar reprehensible conduct the court may decline to exercise jurisdiction if this is just and proper under the circumstances.

2. Unless required in the interest of the child, the court shall not exercise its jurisdiction to modify a custody decree of another state if the petitioner, without consent of the person entitled to custody, has improperly removed the child from the physical custody of the person entitled to custody or has improperly retained the child after a visit or other temporary relinquishment of physical custody. If the petitioner has violated any other provision of a custody decree of another state the court may decline to exercise its jurisdiction if this is just and proper under the circumstances.

3. Where the court declines to exercise jurisdiction pursuant to subsection 1, the court shall notify the parent or other appropriate person and the prosecuting attorney of the appropriate jurisdiction in the other state. Upon request of the court of the other state, the court of this state shall order the petitioner to appear with the child in a custody proceeding instituted in the other state in accordance with NRS 125A.230.

4. Where the court refused to assume jurisdiction to modify the custody decree of another state pursuant to subsection 2 or pursuant to NRS 125A.180, the court shall notify the person who has legal custody under the decree of the other state and the prosecuting attorney of the appropriate jurisdiction in the other state and may order the petitioner to return the child to the person who has legal custody. If it appears that the order will be ineffective and the legal custodian is ready to receive the child within 10 days, the court may place the child in a foster home approved by the welfare division of the department of human resources for that period, pending return of the child to the legal custodian. At the same time, the court shall advise the petitioner that any petition for modification of custody must be directed to the appropriate court of the other state which has continuing jurisdiction or, if that court declines jurisdiction, to a court in a state which has jurisdiction.

5. In appropriate cases a court dismissing a petition under this section may charge the petitioner with necessary travel and other expenses, including attorney's fees, incurred by other parties or their witnesses.

125A.090. Exercise of jurisdiction: Notice and opportunity to be heard.

Before making a decree under this chapter, reasonable notice and opportunity to be heard must be given to the contestants, any parent whose parental rights have not been previously terminated, and any person who has physical custody of the child. If any of these persons is outside this state, notice and opportunity to be heard must be given pursuant to NRS 125A.100.

125A.100. Notice to persons outside Nevada.

Unless the Indian Child Welfare Act of 1978 (25 U.S.C. §§ 1901 et seq.) applies and imposes a different requirement:

1. Notice required for the exercise of jurisdiction over a person outside this state must be given in a manner reasonably calculated to give actual notice, and may be:

(a) By personal delivery outside this state in the manner prescribed for service of process within this state;

(b) In the manner prescribed by the law of the place in which the service is made for service of process in that place in an action in any of its courts of general jurisdiction;

(c) By any form of mail addressed to the person to be served and requesting a receipt; or

(d) As directed by the court, including publication if other means of notification are ineffective.

2. Notice under this section must be served, mailed, delivered or last published at least 20 days before any hearing in this state.

3. Proof of service outside this state may be made by affidavit of the person who made the service, or in the manner prescribed by the law of this state, the order pursuant to which the service is made, or the law of the place in which the service is made. If service is made by mail, proof may be a receipt signed by the addressee or other evidence of delivery to the addressee.

4. Notice is not required if a person submits to the jurisdiction of the court.

125A.110. Priority of issues concerning jurisdiction.

Upon the request of a party to a custody proceeding which raises a question of existence or exercise of jurisdiction under this chapter, the issue of jurisdiction shall be given calendar priority and handled expeditiously.

125A.120. Information required with initial pleading.

1. Every party in a custody proceeding in his first pleading or in an affidavit attached to that pleading shall give information under oath as to the child's present address, the places where the child has lived within the last 5 years, and the names and present addresses of the persons with whom the child has lived during that period. In this pleading or affidavit every party shall further declare under oath whether:

(a) He has participated as a party, witness or in any other capacity in any other litigation concerning the custody of the same child in this or any other state;

(b) He has information of any custody proceeding concerning the child pending in a court of this or any other state; and

(c) He knows of any person not a party to the proceedings who has physical custody of the child or claims to have custody or visitation rights with respect to the child.

2. If the declaration as to any of the above items is in the affirmative the declarant shall give additional information under oath as required by the court. The court may examine the parties under oath as to details of the information furnished and as to other matters pertinent to the court's jurisdiction and the disposition of the case.

3. Each party has a continuing duty to inform the court of any custody proceeding concerning the child in this or any other state of which he obtained information during this proceeding.

125A.130. Joinder of additional parties.

Whenever the court learns that a person not a party to the custody proceeding has physical custody of the child or claims to have custody or visitation rights with respect to the child, it shall order that person to be joined as a party and to be duly notified of the pendency of the proceeding and of his joinder as a party. If the person joined as a party is outside this state he must be served with process or otherwise notified in accordance with NRS 125A.100.

125A.140. Appearance of parties.

1. The court may order any party to the proceeding who is in this state to appear personally before the court. If that party has physical custody of the child the court may order that he appear personally with the child.

2. If the party who is ordered to appear with the child cannot be served or fails to obey the order, or it appears the order will be ineffective, the court may issue a warrant of arrest against that party to secure his appearance with the child.

3. If a party to the proceeding whose presence is desired by the court is outside this state with or without the child the court may order that the notice given under NRS 125A.100 include a statement directing that party to appear personally with or without the child and declaring that failure to appear may result in a decision adverse to that party.

4. If a party to the proceeding who is outside this state is directed to appear under subsection 3, or desires to appear personally before the court with or without the child, the court may require another party to pay to the clerk of the court travel and other necessary expenses of the party so appearing and of the child if this is just and proper under the circumstances.

125A.150. Effect of decree upon parties.

A custody decree rendered by a court of this state which had jurisdiction under NRS 125A.050 binds all parties who have been served in this state or notified in a accordance with NRS 125A.100 or who have submitted to the jurisdiction of the court, and who have been given an opportunity to be heard. As to these parties the custody decree is conclusive as to all issues of law and fact decided and as to the custody determination made until that determination is modified pursuant to law, including the provisions of this chapter.

125A.160. Certification of copies of decree.

The clerk of the district court of this state, at the request of the court of another state or at the request of any person who is affected by or has a legitimate interest in a custody decree, shall certify and forward a copy of the decree to that court or person.

125A.170. Recognition of foreign decrees.

The courts of this state shall recognize and enforce an initial or modifying decree of a court of another state which had assumed jurisdiction under statutory provisions substantially in accordance with the Uniform Child Custody Jurisdiction Act, or the Indian Child Welfare Act of 1978 (25 U.S.C. §§ 1901 et seq.), or which was made under factual circumstances meeting the jurisdictional standards of those acts, so long as this decree has not been modified in accordance with jurisdictional standards substantially similar to those of those acts.

125A.180. Modification of foreign decrees.

1. If a court of another state has made a custody decree, a court of this state shall not modify that decree unless:

(a) It appears to the court of this state that the court which rendered the decree does not now have jurisdiction under jurisdictional prerequisites substantially in accordance with the Uniform Child Custody Jurisdiction Act, or the Indian Child Welfare Act of 1978 (25 U.S.C. §§ 1901 et seq.), or has declined to assume jurisdiction to modify the decree; and

(b) The court of this state has jurisdiction.

2. If a court of this state is authorized under subsection 1 and NRS 125A.080 to modify a custody decree of another state it shall give due consideration to the transcript of the record and other documents of all previous proceedings submitted to it in accordance with NRS 125A.250.

125A.190. Filing and enforcement of foreign decrees.

1. A certified copy of a custody decree of another state may be filed in the office of the clerk of any district court of this state. The clerk shall treat the decree in the same manner as a custody decree of the district court of this state. A custody decree so filed has the same effect and must be enforced in like manner as a custody decree rendered by a court of this state.

2. A person violating a custody decree of another state which makes it necessary to enforce the decree in this state may be required to pay necessary travel and other expenses, including attorney's fees, incurred by the party entitled to the custody of his witnesses.

125A.200. Registry of foreign decrees, communications and other documents.

The clerk of each district court shall maintain a registry in which he shall enter the following:

1. Certified copies of custody decrees of other states received for filing;

2. Communications as to the pendency of custody proceedings in other states;

3. Communications concerning a finding of inappropriate or inconvenient forum by a court of another state; and

4. Other communications or documents concerning custody proceedings in another state which may affect the jurisdiction of a court of this state or the disposition to be made by it in a custody proceeding.

125A.210. Examination of witnesses outside Nevada.

In addition to other procedural devices available to a party, any party to the proceeding or a guardian ad litem or other representative of the child may examine witnesses, including parties and the child, by deposition or otherwise, in another state. The court on its own motion may direct that the testimony of a person be taken in another state and may prescribe the terms upon which the testimony shall be taken.

125A.220. Assistance by courts of other states.

1. A court of this state may request the appropriate court of another state:

(a) To hold a hearing to adduce evidence, to order a party to produce or give evidence under other procedures of that state, or to have social studies made with respect to the custody of a child involved in a proceedings pending in the court of this state; and

(b) To forward to the court of this state certified copies of the transcript of the record of the hearing, the evidence otherwise adduced, or any social studies prepared in compliance with the request. The cost of the services may be assessed against the parties, or if necessary, ordered paid by the county.

2. A court of this state may request the appropriate court of another state to order a party to custody proceedings pending in the court of this state to appear in the proceedings, and if that party has physical custody of the child, to appear with the child. The request may state that travel and other necessary expenses of the party and of the child whose appearance is desired will be assessed against another party or will otherwise be paid.

125A.230. Assistance to courts of other states.

1. Upon request of the court of another state the courts of this state which are competent to hear custody matters may order a person in this state to appear at a hearing to adduce evidence or to produce or give evidence under other procedures available in this state. A certified copy of the transcript of the record of the hearing or the evidence otherwise adduced must be forwarded by the clerk of the court to the requesting court.

2. A person within this state may voluntarily give his testimony or statement in this state for use in a custody proceeding outside this state.

3. Upon request of the court of another state a competent court of this state may, except when required under NRS 125A.080, order a person in this state to appear alone or with the child in a custody proceeding in another state. The court may condition compliance with the request upon the condition that travel and other necessary expenses will be advanced or reimbursed.

125A.240. Preservation of documents for use in other states.

In any custody proceeding in this state the court shall preserve the pleadings, orders and decrees, any record that has been made of its hearings, social studies and other pertinent documents until the child reaches 18 years of age. Upon appropriate request of the court of another state the court shall forward to the other court certified copies of any or all of these documents.

125A.250. Request for court records and documents of another state.

If a custody decree has been rendered in another state concerning a child involved in a custody proceeding pending in a court of this state, the court of this state upon taking jurisdiction of the case shall request of the court of the other state a certified copy of the transcript of any court record and other documents mentioned in NRS 125A.240.

125A.350. Consent required from noncustodial parent or parent having joint custody to remove child from state; permission from court; change of custody.

If custody has been established and the custodial parent or a parent having joint custody intends to move his residence to a place outside of this state and to take the child with him, he must, as soon as possible and before the planned move, attempt to obtain the written consent of the other parent to move the child from the state. If the noncustodial parent or other parent having joint custody refuses to give that consent, the parent planning the move shall, before he leaves the state with the child, petition the court for permission to move the child. The failure of a parent to comply with the provisions of this section may be considered as a factor if a change of custody is requested by the noncustodial parent or other parent having joint custody.

NEW HAMPSHIRE

UNIFORM CHILD CUSTODY JURISDICTION ACT

458-A:1. Purposes of Chapter; construction of Provisions.

I. The general purposes of this chapter are to:

(a) Avoid jurisdictional competition and conflict with courts of other states in matters of child custody which have in the past resulted in the shifting of children from state to state with harmful effects on their well-being;

(b) Promote cooperation with the courts of other states to the end that a custody decree is rendered in that state which can best decide the case in the interest of the child;

(c) Assure that litigation concerning the custody of a child take place ordinarily in the state with which the child and his family have the closest connection and where significant evidence concerning his care, protection, training, and personal relationship is more readily available and that courts of this state decline the exercise of jurisdiction when the child and his family have a closer connection with another state;

(d) Discourage continuing controversies over child custody in the interest of greater stability of home environment and of secure family relationship for the child;

(e) Deter abductions and other unilateral removals of children undertaken to obtain custody awards;

(f) Avoid re-litigation of custody decisions of other states in this state insofar as feasible;

(g) Facilitate the enforcement of custody decrees of other states;

(h) Promote and expand the exchange of information and other forms of mutual assistance between the courts of this state and those of other states concerned with the same child;

(i) Make uniform the law of those states which enact it.

II. This chapter shall be construed to promote the general purposes stated in this section.

458-A:2. Definitions.

In this chapter:

I. "Contestant" means a person, including a parent, who claims a right to custody or visitation rights with respect to a child.

II. "Custody determination" means a court decision and court orders and instructions providing for the the temporary or permanent custody of a child, including visitation rights.

II. "Custody proceeding" includes proceedings in which a custody determination is at issue or is one of several issues including any action or proceeding brought to annul a marriage or to declare the nullity of a void marriage, or for a separation, or for a divorce, but not including proceedings for adoption, child protective proceedings or proceedings for permanent termination of parental custody, or proceedings involving the guardianship and custody of neglected or dependent children.

IV. "Decree" or "custody decree" means a custody determination contained in a judicial decree or other made in a custody proceeding, and includes an initial decree and a modification decree.

V. "Home state" means the state in which the child at the time of the commencement of the custody proceeding has resided with his parents, a parent, or a person acting as parent, for at least 6 consecutive months. In the case of a child less than 6 months old at the time of the commencement of the proceeding, "home state" means the state in which the child has resided with any of such persons for a majority of the time since birth.

VI. "Initial decree" means the first custody decree concerning a particular child.

VII. "Modification decree" means a custody decree which modifies or replaces a prior decree, whether made by the court which rendered the prior decree or by another court.

VIII. "Physical custody" means actual possession and control of a child.

IX. "Person acting as parent" means a person, other than a parent, who has physical custody of a child and who has either been awarded custody by a court or claims a right to custody.

X. "State" means any state, territory or possession of the United States, the Commonwealth of Puerto Rico and the District of Columbia.

458-A:3. Jurisdiction to Make Child Custody Determinations.

I. A court of this state which is competent to decide child custody matters has jurisdiction to make a child custody determination by initial or modification decree only when:

(a) This state (1) is the home state of the child at the time of commencement of the custody proceeding; or (2) has been the child's home state within 6 months before commencement of the proceeding and the child is absent from this state because of his removal or retention by a person claiming his custody or for other reasons, and a parent or person acting as parent continues to live in this state; or

(b) It is in the best interest of the child that a court of this state assume jurisdiction because (1) the child and his parents, or the child and at least one contestant, have a significant connection with this state, and (2) there is within the jurisdiction of the court substantial evidence concerning the child's present or future care, protection, training and personal relationships; or

(c) The child is physically present in this state and (1) the child has been abandoned or (2) it is necessary in an emergency to protect the child; or

(d)(1) It appears that no other state would have jurisdiction under prerequisites substantially in accordance with paragraphs (a), (b) or (c), or another state has declined to exercise jurisdiction on the ground that this state is the more appropriate forum to determine the custody of the child, and (2) it is in the best interest of the child that this court assume jurisdiction.

II. Except under subparagraphs I (c) and (d), physical presence in this state of the child, or of the child and one of the contestants, is not alone sufficient to confer jurisdiction on a court of this state to make a child custody determination.

III. Physical presence of the child, while desirable, is not a prerequisite for jurisdiction to determine his custody.

458-A:4. Notice and Opportunity to Be Heard.

Before making a decree under this chapter, reasonable notice and opportunity to be heard shall be given to the contestants, any parent whose parental rights have not been previously terminated, and any person who has physical custody of the child. If any of these persons is outside the state, notice and opportunity to be heard shall be given pursuant to RSA 458-A:5. Any person who is given notice and an opportunity to be heard pursuant to this section shall be deemed a party to the proceeding for all purposes under this chapter.

458-A:5. Notice to Persons Outside the State.

I. If a person cannot be personally served with notice within the state, the court shall require that such person be served in a manner reasonably calculated to give actual notice, as follows:

(a) By personal delivery outside the state in the manner prescribed in RSA 510;

(b) By any form of mail addressed to the person and requesting a receipt; or

(c) In such manner as the court, upon motion, directs, including publication, if service is impracticable under subparagraph I(a) or (b).

II. Notice under this section shall be served, mailed, delivered, or last published at least 20 days before any hearing in this state.

III. Proof of service outside the state shall be by affidavit of the individual who made the service, or in the manner prescribed by the order pursuant to which the service is made. If service is made by mail, proof may be a receipt signed by the addressee or other evidence of delivery to the addressee.

IV. Notice is not required if a person submits to the jurisdiction of the court.

458-A:6. Simultaneous Proceedings in Other States.

I. A court of this state shall not exercise its jurisdiction under this chapter if, at the time of filing the petition, a proceeding concerning the custody of the child was pending in a court of another state exercising jurisdiction substantially in conformity with this chapter, unless the proceeding is stayed by the court of the other state because this state is a more appropriate forum or for other reasons.

II. Before hearing the petition in a custody proceeding, the court shall examine the pleadings and other information supplied by the parties under RSA 458-A:9. If the court has reason to believe that proceedings may be pending in another state, it shall direct an inquiry to the state court administrator or other appropriate official of the other state.

III. If the court is informed during the course of the proceeding that a proceeding concerning the custody of the child was pending in another state before the court assumed jurisdiction, it shall stay the proceeding and communicate with the court in which the other proceeding is pending to the end that the issue may be litigated in the more appropriate forum and that information be exchanged in accordance with RSA 458-A:18-21. If a court of this state has made a custody decree before being informed of a pending proceeding in a court of another state, it shall immediately inform that court of the fact. If the court is informed that a proceeding was commenced in another state after it assumed jurisdiction, it shall likewise inform the other court to the end that the issues may be litigated in the more appropriate forum.

458-A:7. Inconvenient Forum.

I. A court which has jurisdiction under this chapter to make an initial or modification decree may decline to exercise its jurisdiction any time before making a decree if it finds that it is an inconvenient forum to make a custody determination under the circumstances of the case and that a court of another state is a more appropriate forum.

II. A finding of inconvenient forum may be made upon the court's own motion or upon motion of a party or a guardian ad litem or other representative of the child.

III. In determining if it is an inconvenient forum, the court shall consider if it is in the interest of the child that another state assume jurisdiction. For this purpose it may take into account the following factors, among others, whether:

(a) Another state is or recently was the child's home state;

(b) Another state has a closer connection with the child and his family or with the child and one or more of the contestants;

(c) Substantial evidence concerning the child's present or future care, protection, training, and personal relationships is more readily available in another state;

(d) The parties have agreed on another forum which is no less appropriate;

(e) The exercise of jurisdiction by a court of this state would contravene any of the purposes stated in RSA 458-A:1.

IV. Before determining whether to decline or retain jurisdiction, the court may communicate with a court of another state and exchange information pertinent to the assumption of jurisdiction by either court with a view to assuring that jurisdiction will be exercised by the more appropriate court and that a forum will be available to the parties.

V. If the court finds that it is an inconvenient forum, and that a court of another state is a more appropriate forum it may dismiss the proceedings or it may stay the proceeding upon condition that a custody proceeding be promptly commenced in another named state or upon any other conditions which may be just and proper, including the condition that a moving party stipulate his consent and submission to the jurisdiction of the other forum.

VI. Where the court has jurisdiction of an action or proceeding brought to annul a marriage or to declare the nullity of a void marriage or for a separation or for a divorce, the court may decline to exercise jurisdiction of an application for a custody determination made therein while retaining jurisdiction of the matrimonial action.

VII. If it appears to the court that it is clearly an inappropriate forum, it may require the party who commenced the proceedings to pay, in addition to the costs of the proceedings in this state, necessary travel and other expenses, including attorney's fees, incurred by other parties or their witnesses. Payment shall be made to the clerk of the court for remittance to the proper party.

VIII. Upon dismissal or stay of proceedings under this section, the court shall inform the court found to be the more appropriate forum of such dismissal or stay, or, if the court which would have jurisdiction in the other state is not certainly known, shall transmit the information to the court administrator or other appropriate official for forwarding to the appropriate court.

IX. Any communication received from another state to the effect that its courts have made a finding of inconvenient forum because a court of this state is the more appropriate forum shall be filed with the clerk of the appropriate court. Upon assuming jurisdiction the court of this state shall inform the original court of this fact.

458-A:8. Jurisdiction Declined Because of Conduct.

I. If the petitioner for an initial decree has wrongfully taken the child from another state or has engaged in similar reprehensible conduct, the court may decline to exercise jurisdiction if this is just and proper under the circumstances.

II. Unless required in the interest of the child, the court shall not exercise its jurisdiction to modify a custody decree of another state if the petitioner, without consent of the person entitled to custody, has improperly removed the child from the physical custody of the person entitled to custody or has improperly retained the child after a visit or other temporary relinquishment of physical custody. If the petitioner has violated any other provision of a custody decree of another state, the court may decline to exercise its jurisdiction if this is just and proper under the circumstances.

III. In appropriate cases, a court dismissing a petition under this section may charge the petitioner with necessary travel and other expenses, including attorney's fees, incurred by other parties or their witnesses.

458-A:9. Pleadings and Affidavits; Duty to Inform Court.

I. Except as provided in paragraph IV, every party to a custody proceeding shall, in his first pleading or in an affidavit attached to that pleading, give information under oath as to the child's present address, the places where the child has lived within the last 5 years, and the names and present addresses of the persons with whom the child has lived during that period. In this pleading or affidavit every party shall further declare under oath whether he:

(a) Has participated as a party, witness, or in any other capacity in any other litigation concerning the custody of the same child in this or any other state;

(b) Has information of any custody proceeding concerning the child pending in a court of this or any other state; and

(c) Knows of any person not a party to the proceedings who has physical custody of the child or claims to have custody or visitation rights with respect to the child.

II. If the declaration as to any of the above items is in the affirmative, the declarant shall give additional information under oath as required by the court. The court may examine the parties under oath as to details of the information furnished and as to other matters pertinent to the court's jurisdiction and the disposition of the case.

III. If, during the pendency of a custody proceeding, any party learns of another custody proceeding concerning the child in this or another state, he shall immediately inform the court of this fact.

IV. In an action for divorce or separation or to annul a marriage or to declare the nullity of void marriage, where neither party is in default in appearance or pleading and the issue of custody is uncontested, the affidavit required by this section need not be submitted. In any other such action, such affidavit shall be submitted by the parties within 20 days after joinder of issue on the question of custody, or at the time application for a default judgment is made.

458-A:10. Additional Parties.

If the court learns from information furnished by the parties pursuant to RSA 458-A:9, or from other sources, that a person not a party to the custody proceeding has physical custody of the child or claims to have custody or visitation rights with respect to the child, it shall order that person to be joined as a party and to be duly notified of the pendency of the proceeding and of his joinder as a party. If the person joined as a party is outside this state, he shall be served with process or otherwise notified in accordance with RSA 458-A:5.

458-A:11. Appearance of Parties and the Child.

I. The court may order any party to the proceeding who is in the state to appear personally before the court. If that party has physical custody of the child, the court may order that he appear personally with the child.

II. If a party to the proceeding whose presence is desired by the court is outside the state with or without the child, the court may order that the notice given under RSA 458-A:5 include a statement directing that party to appear personally with or without the child and declaring that failure to appear may result in a decision adverse to that party.

III. If a party to the proceeding who is outside the state is directed to appear under paragraph II, or desires to appear personally before the court with or without the child, the court may require another party to pay to the clerk of the court travel and other necessary expenses of the party so appearing and of the child if this is just and proper under the circumstances.

458-A:12. Force and Effect of Custody Decrees.

A custody decree rendered by a court of this state which had jurisdiction under RSA 458:3 shall be binding upon all parties who have been personally served in this state or notified pursuant to RSA 458-A:5 or who have submitted to the jurisdiction of the court, and who have been given an opportunity to be heard. As to these parties, the custody decree is conclusive as to all issues of law and fact decided and as to the custody determination made unless and until that determination is modified pursuant to law, including the provisions of this chapter.

458-A:13. Recognition of Out-of-State Custody Decrees.

The courts of this state shall recognize and enforce an initial or modification decree of a court of another state which had assumed jurisdiction under statutory provisions substantially in accordance with this chapter or which was made under factual circumstances meeting the jurisdictional standards of this chapter, so long as the decree has not been modified in accordance with jurisdictional standards substantially similar to those of this chapter.

458-A:14. Modification of Custody Decree of Another State.

I. If a court of another state has made a custody decree, a court of this state shall not modify that decree unless (a) it appears to the court of this state that the court which rendered the decree does not now have jurisdiction under jurisdictional prerequisites substantially in accordance with this chapter or has declined to assume jurisdiction to modify the decree and (b) the court of this state has jurisdiction.

II. If a court of this state is authorized under paragraph I and RSA 458-A:8 to modify a custody decree of another state, it shall give due consideration to the transcript of the record and other documents of all previous proceedings submitted to it in accordance with RSA 458-A:21.

458-A:15. Filing and Enforcement of Custody Decree of Another State.

I. A certified copy of a custody decree of another state may be filed in the office of the clerk of the superior court. The clerk shall treat the decree in the same manner as a custody decree of the superior court. A custody decree so filed has the same effect and shall be enforced in like manner as a custody decree rendered by a court of this state.

II. A person violating a custody decree of another state which makes it necessary to enforce the decree in this state may be required to pay necessary travel and other expenses, including attorney's fees, incurred by the party entitled to the custody or his witnesses.

458-A:16. Certified Copies of Custody Decrees.

The clerk of the superior court, at the request of the court of another state or, upon payment of the appropriate fees, if any, at the request of party to the custody proceeding, the attorney for a party or a representative of the child shall certify and forward a copy of the decree to that court or person.

458-A:17. Examination of Witnesses Outside the State.

In addition to other procedural devices available to a party, any party to the proceeding or a guardian ad litem or other representative of the child may examine witnesses, including parties and the child, in another state by deposition or otherwise in accordance with the applicable provisions of the RSA and rules of the superior court.

458-A:18. Hearings and Studies in Another State; Orders to Appear.

I. A court of this state may request the appropriate court of another state to hold a hearing to adduce evidence, to order a party to produce or give evidence under other procedures of that state, or to have social studies made with respect to the custody of a child involved in proceedings pending in the court of this state, and to forward to the court of this state certified copies of the transcript of the record of the hearing, the evidence otherwise adduced, or any social studies prepared in compliance with the request. The cost of the services may be assessed against the parties.

II. A court of this state may request the appropriate court of another state to order a party to custody proceedings pending in the court of this state to appear in the proceedings and, if that party has physical custody of the child, to appear with the child. The request may state that travel and other necessary expenses of the party and of the child whose appearance is desired will be assessed against another party or will otherwise be paid.

458-A:19. Assistance to Courts of Other States.
I. Upon request of the court of another state, the courts of this state which are competent to hear custody matters may order a party or witness in this state to appear at an examination to be conducted in the same manner as if such person were a party to or witness in an action pending in the superior court. A certified copy of the deposition or the evidence otherwise adduced shall be forwarded by the clerk of the court to the court which requested it.

II. A person within the state may voluntarily give his testimony or statement for use in a custody proceeding outside this state.

III. Upon request of the court of another state, a competent court of this state may order a person within the state to appear alone or with the child in a custody proceeding in another state. The court may condition compliance with the request upon assurance by the other state that travel and other necessary expenses will be advanced or reimbursed.

458-A:20. Preservation of Evidence for Use in Other States.
In any custody proceeding in this state, the court shall preserve the pleadings, orders and decrees, any record that has been made of its hearings, social studies, and other pertinent documents until the child reaches 21 years of age. Upon appropriate request of the court of another state, the court shall forward to the other court certified copies of any or all of such documents.

458-A:21. Request for Court Records from Another State.
If a custody decree has been rendered in another state concerning a child involved in a custody proceeding pending in a court of this state, the court of this state upon taking jurisdiction of the case shall request of the court of the other state a certified copy of the transcript of any court record and other documents mentioned in RSA 458-A:20.

458-A:22. International Application.
The general policies of this chapter extend to the international area. The provisions of this chapter relating to the recognition and enforcement of custody decrees of other states apply to custody decrees and decrees involving legal institutions similar in nature to custody institutions rendered by appropriate authorities of other nations if reasonable notice and opportunity to be heard were given to all affected persons.

458-A:23. Priority.
Upon the request of a party to a custody proceeding which raises a question of existence or exercise of jurisdiction under this chapter, the case shall be given calendar priority and handled expeditiously.

458-A:24. Separability.
If any part of this chapter or the application thereof to any person or circumstance is adjudged invalid by a court of competent jurisdiction, such judgment shall not affect or impair the validity of the remainder of such chapter or the application thereof to other persons and circumstances.

458-A:25. Inconsistent Provisions of Other Laws Superseded.
Insofar as the provisions of this chapter are inconsistent with the provisions of any other law, general, special or local, the provisions of this chapter shall be controlling.

NEW JERSEY

UNIFORM CHILD CUSTODY JURISDICTION ACT

§ 2A:34-28. Short title.
This act shall be known and may be cited as the "Uniform Child Custody Jurisdiction Act."

§ 2A:34-29. Legislative findings.
The Legislature finds that this act is necessary in order to;

a. Avoid jurisdictional competition and conflict with courts of other states in matters of child custody which have in the past resulted in the shifting of children from state to state with harmful effects on their well-being;

b. Promote cooperation with the courts of other states to the end that a custody decree is rendered in that state which can best decide the case in the interest of the child;

c. Assure that litigation concerning the custody of a child takes place ordinarily in the state with which the child and his family have the closest connection and where significant evidence concerning his care, protection, training, and personal relationships is most readily available, and that courts of this State decline the exercise of jurisdiction when the child and his family have a closer connection with another state;

d. Discourage continuing controversies over child custody in the interest of greater stability of home environment and of secure family relationships for the child;

e. Deter abductions and other unilateral removals of children undertaken to obtain custody awards;

f. Avoid relitigation of custody decisions of other states in this State insofar as feasible;

g. Facilitate the enforcement of custody decrees of other states; and

h. Promote and expand the exchange of information and other forms of mutual assistance between the courts of this State and those of other states concerned with the same child.

§ 2A:34-30. Definitions.
As used in this act:

a. "Contestant" means a person, including a parent, who claims a right to custody or visitation rights with respect to a child;

b. "Custody determination" means a court decision and court orders and instructions providing for the custody of a child, including visitation rights, and does not include a decision relating to child support or any other monetary obligation of any person;

c. "Custody proceeding" includes proceedings in which a custody determination is one of several issues, such as an action for divorce or separation, and includes child neglect and dependency proceedings;

d. "Decree" or "custody decree" means a custody determination contained in a judicial decree or order made in a custody proceeding, and includes an initial decree and a modification decree;

e. "Home state" means the state in which the child immediately preceding the time involved lived with his parents, a parent, or a person acting as parent, for a least 6 consecutive months, and in the case of a child less than 6 months old the state in which the child lived from birth with any of the persons mentioned. Periods of temporary absence of any of the named persons are counted as part of the 6-month or other period;

f. "Initial decree" means the first custody decree concerning a particular child;

g. "Modification decree" means a custody decree which modifies or replaces a prior decree, whether made by the court which rendered the prior decree or by another court;

h. "Physical custody" means actual possession and control of a child;

i. "Person acting as parent" means a person, other than a parent, who has physical custody of a child and who has either been awarded custody by a court or claims a right to custody; and

j. "State" means any state, territory, or possession of the United States, the Commonwealth of Puerto Rico, and the District of Columbia.

§ 2A:34-31. Jurisdiction of Superior Court.
a. The Superior Court of the State of New Jersey has jurisdiction to make a child custody determination by initial or modification decree if:

(1) This State (i) is the home state of the child at the time of commencement of the proceeding, or (ii) had been the child's home state within 6 months before commencement of the proceeding and the child is absent from this State because of his removal or retention by a person claiming his custody or for other reasons, and a parent or person acting as parent continues to live in this State; or

(2) It is in the best interest of the child that a court of this State assume jurisdiction because (i) the child and his parents, or the child and at least one contestant, have a significant connection with this State, and (ii) there is available in this State substantial evidence concerning the child's present or future care, protection, training, and personal relationships; or

(3) The child is physically present in this State and (i) the child has been abandoned or (ii) it is necessary in an emergency to protect the child because he has been subjected to or threatened with mistreatment or abuse or is otherwise neglected; or

(4) (i) It appears that no other state would have jurisdiction under prerequisites substantially in accordance with paragraphs (1), (2), or (3), or another state has declined to exercise jurisdiction on the ground that this State is the more appropriate forum to determine the custody of the child, and (ii) it is in the best interest of the child that this court assume jurisdiction.

b. Except under paragraphs (3) and (4) of subsection a., physical presence in this State of the child, or of the child and one of the contestants, is not alone sufficient to confer jurisdiction on a court of this State to make a child custody determination.

c. Physical presence of the child, while desirable, is not a prerequisite for jurisdiction to determine his custody.

§ 2A:34-32. Notice and opportunity to be heard.

Before a decree is made pursuant to this act, reasonable notice and opportunity to be heard shall be given in accordance with the Rules Governing the Courts of the State of New Jersey to the contestants, any parent whose parental rights have not been previously terminated, and any person who has physical custody of the child. If any of these persons is outside this State, notice and opportunity to be heard shall be given pursuant to section 6 of this act.

§ 2A:34-33. Notice to persons outside this state; submission to jurisdiction.

a. Notice required for the exercise of jurisdiction over a person outside this State shall be given in a manner reasonably calculated to give actual notice, and may be:

(1) By personal delivery outside this State in the manner prescribed for service of process within this State;

(2) In the manner prescribed by the law of the place in which the service is made for service of process in that place in an action in any of its courts of general jurisdiction;

(3) By any form of mail addressed to the person to be served; or

(4) As directed by the court.

b. Notice under this section shall be served, mailed, or delivered, at least 20 days before any hearing in this State, or such other time period as directed by the court if the matter is emergent.

c. Proof of service outside this State may be made by affidavit of the individual who made the service, or in the manner prescribed by the law of this State, the order pursuant to which the service is made, or the law of the place in which the service is made. If service is made by mail, proof may be a receipt signed by the addressee or other evidence of delivery to the addressee.

§ 2A:34-34. Simultaneous proceedings in other states.

a. A court of this State shall not exercise its jurisdiction under this act if at the time of filing the petition a proceeding concerning the custody of the child was pending in a court of another state exercising jurisdiction substantially in conformity with this act, unless the proceeding is stayed by the court of the other state because this State is a more appropriate forum or for other reasons.

b. Before hearing the petition in a custody proceeding the court shall examine the pleadings and other information supplied by the parties pursuant to section 10 of this act and shall consult the child custody registry established pursuant to section 17 of this act concerning the pendency of proceedings with respect to the child in other states. If the court has reason to believe that proceedings may be pending in another state it shall direct an inquiry to the state court administrator or other appropriate official of the other state.

c. If the court is informed during the course of the proceeding that a proceeding concerning the custody of the child was pending in another state before the court assumed jurisdiction it shall stay the proceeding and communicate with the court in which the other proceeding is pending to the end that the issue may be litigated in the more appropriate forum and that information be exchanged in accordance with sections 20 through 23. If a court of this State has made a custody decree before being informed of a pending proceeding in a court of another state it shall immediately inform that court of the fact. If the court is informed that a proceeding was commenced in another state after it assumed jurisdiction it shall likewise inform the other court to the end that the issues may be litigated in the more appropriate forum.

§ 2A:34-35. Finding of inconvenient forum; dismissal or stay; assessment of costs and expenses; communication from other state.

a. A court which has jurisdiction under this act to make an initial or modification decree may decline to exercise its jurisdiction any time before making a decree if it finds that is is an inconvenient forum to make a custody determination under the circumstances of the case and that a court of another state is a more appropriate forum.

b. A finding of inconvenient forum may be made upon the court's own motion or upon motion of a party or a guardian ad litem or other representative of the child.

c. In determining if it is an inconvenient forum, the court shall consider if it is in the interest of the child that another state assume jurisdiction. For this purpose it may take into account the following factors, among others:

(1) If another state is or recently was the child's home state;

(2) If another state has a closer connection with the child and his family or with the child and one or more of the contestants;

(3) If substantial evidence concerning the child's present or future care, protection, training, and personal relationships is more readily available in another state;

(4) If the parties have agreed on another forum which is no less appropriate; and

(5) If the exercise of jurisdiction by a court of this State would contravene any of the purposes stated in section one of this act.

d. Before determining whether to decline or retain jurisdiction the court may communicate with a court of another state and exchange information pertinent to the assumption of jurisdiction by either court with a view to assuring that jurisdiction will be exercised by the more appropriate court and that a forum will be available to the parties.

e. If the court finds that it is an inconvenient forum and that a court of another state is a more appropriate forum, it may dismiss the proceedings, or it may stay the proceedings upon condition that a custody proceeding be promptly commenced in another named state or upon any other conditions which may be just and proper, including the condition that a moving party stipulate his consent and submission to the jurisdiction of the other forum.

f. The court may decline to exercise its jurisdiction where a finding of inconvenient forum is made under this act whether or not a custody determination is incidental to an action for divorce or another proceeding while retaining jurisdiction over the divorce or other proceeding.

g. If it appears to the court that it is clearly an inappropriate forum it may assess, and if not paid enter a judgment against the party who commenced the proceedings for, in action to the costs of the proceedings in this State, necessary travel and other expenses, including attorneys' fees, incurred by other parties or their witnesses. Payment shall be made to the clerk of the court for remittance to the proper party or, in the event of a judgment, shall be collected in accordance with the normal procedures for the collection of judgments.

h. Upon dismissal or stay of proceedings under this section the court shall inform the court found to be the more appropriate forum of this fact, or if the court which would have jurisdiction in the other state is not certainly known, shall transmit the information to the court administrator or other appropriate official for forwarding to the appropriate court.

i. Any communication received from another state informing this State of a finding of inconvenient forum because a court of this State if the more appropriate forum shall be filed in the custody registry of the appropriate court. Upon assuming jurisdiction the court of this State shall inform the original court of this fact.

§ 2A:34-36. Jurisdiction declined by reason of conduct.

a. If the petitioner for an initial decree has wrongfully taken the child from another state or has engaged in similar reprehensible conduct the court may decline to exercise jurisdiction if this is just and proper under the circumstances.

b. Unless required in the interest of the child, the court shall not exercise its jurisdiction to modify a custody decree of another state if the petitioner, without consent of the person entitled to custody, has improperly removed the child from the physical custody of the person entitled to custody or has improperly retained the child after a visit or other temporary relinquishment of physical custody. If the petitioner has violated any other provision of a custody decree of another state the court may decline to exercise its jurisdiction if this is just and proper under the circumstances.

c. In appropriate cases a court dismissing a petition under this section may assess, and if not paid enter a judgment against the petitioner for necessary travel and other expenses, including attorneys' fees, incurred by other parties or their witnesses. Payment shall be made to the clerk of the court for remittance to the proper party, or in the event of a judgment shall be collected in accordance with the normal procedures for the collection of judgments.

§ 2A:34-37. Information under oath to be submitted to court.

a. Every party in a custody proceeding in his first pleading or in an affidavit attached to that pleading shall give information under oath as to the child's present address, the places where the child has lived within the last 5 years, and the names and present addresses of the persons with whom the child has lived during that period. In this pleading or affidavit every party shall further declare under oath whether:

(1) He has participated (as a party, witness, or in any other capacity) in any other litigation concerning the custody of the same child in this or any other state;

(2) He has information of any custody proceeding concerning the child pending in a court of this or any other state; and

(3) He knows of any person not a party to the proceedings who has physical custody of the child or claims to have custody or visitation rights with respect to the child.

b. If the declaration as to any of the above items is in the affirmative the declarant shall give additional information under oath as required by the court. The court may examine the parties under oath as to details of the information furnished and as to other matters pertinent to the court's jurisdiction and the disposition of the case.

c. Each party has a continuing duty to inform the court of any custody proceeding concerning the child in this or any other state of which he obtained information during this proceeding.

§ 2A:34-38. Additional parties.

If the court learns from information furnished by the parties pursuant to section 10 of this act, or from other sources that a person not a party to the custody proceeding has physical custody of the child or claims to have custody or visitation rights with respect to the child, it shall order that person to be joined as a party and to be duly notified of the pendency of the proceeding and of his joinder as a party. If the person joined as a party is outside that State he shall be served with process or otherwise notified in accordance with the provisions of section 6 of this act.

§ 2A:34-39. Appearance of parties and child.

a. The court may order any party to the proceeding who is in this State to appear personally before the court. If that party has physical custody of the child the court may order that he appear personally with the child.

b. If a party to the proceeding whose presence is desired by the court is outside this State, with or without the child the court may order that the notice given pursuant to section 6 of this act include a statement directing that party to appear personally with or without the child and declaring that failure to appear may result in a decision adverse to that party.

c. If a party to the proceeding who is outside this State is directed to appear under subsection b. or desires to appear personally before the court, with or without the child, the court may require another party to pay to the clerk of the court travel and other necessary expenses of the party so appearing and of the child, if this is just and proper under the circumstances.

§ 2A:34-40. Binding effect and res judicata effect of custody decree.

A custody decree rendered by a court of this State which had jurisdiction pursuant to section 4 of this act binds all parties who have been served in this State or notified in accordance with the provisions of section 6 of this act or who have submitted to the jurisdiction of the court, and who have been given an opportunity to be heard. As to these parties the custody decree is conclusive as to all issues of law and fact decided and as to the custody determination made unless and until that determination is modified pursuant to law, including the provisions of this act.

§ 2A:34-41. Recognition of out-of-state custody decrees.

The courts of this State shall recognize and enforce an initial or modification decree of a court of another state which had assumed jurisdiction under statutory provisions substantially in accordance with this act or which was made under factual circumstances meeting the jurisdictional standards of this act, so long as the decree has not been modified in accordance with jurisdictional standards substantially similar to those of this act.

§ 2A:34-42. Modification of custody decree of another state.

a. If a court of another state has made a custody decree, a court of this State shall not modify that decree unless (1) it appears to the court of this State that the court which rendered the decree does not now have jurisdiction under jurisdictional prerequisites substantially in accordance with this act or has declined to assume jurisdiction to modify the decree, and (2) the court of this State has jurisdiction.

b. If a court of this State is authorized pursuant to subsection a. and to section 9 of this act to modify a custody decree of another state it shall give due consideration to the transcript of the record and other documents of all previous proceedings submitted to it in accordance with section 23 of this act.

§ 2A:34-43. Filing and enforcement of custody decree of another state.

a. A certified copy of a custody decree of another state may be filed in the office of the clerk of the Superior Court of this State. The clerk shall treat the decree in the same manner as a custody decree of said court.

A custody decree so filed has the same effect and shall be enforced in like manner as a custody decree rendered by a court of this State.

b. A person violating a custody decree of another state, which makes it necessary to enforce the decree in this State, may be required to pay necessary travel and other expenses, including attorneys' fees, incurred by the party entitled to the custody or his witnesses.

§ 2A:34-44. Registry of out-of-state custody decrees and proceedings.

The office of the Clerk of the Superior Court shall maintain a registry which shall contain the following:

(1) Certified copies of custody decrees of other states received for filing;

(2) Communications as to the pendency of custody proceedings in other states;

(3) Communications concerning a finding of inconvenient forum by a court of another state; and

(4) Other communications or documents concerning custody proceedings in another state which may affect the jurisdiction of a court of this State or the disposition to be made by it in a custody proceeding.

§ 2A:34-45. Certified copies of custody decree.

The clerk of the Superior Court of this State, at the request of the court of another state or at the request of any person who is affected by or has a legitimate interest in a custody decree, shall certify and forward a copy of the decree to that court or person.

§ 2A:34-46. Taking testimony in another state.

In addition to other procedural devices available to a party, any party to the proceeding or a guardian ad litem or other representative of the child may adduce testimony of witnesses, including parties and the child, by deposition or other form of sworn statement, in another state. The court on its own motion may direct that the testimony of a person be taken in another state and may prescribe the manner in which and the terms upon which the testimony shall be taken.

§ 2A:34-47. Hearings and studies in other state; orders to appear; nonwaiver of right to contest jurisdiction.

a. A court of this State may request the appropriate court of another state to hold a hearing to adduce evidence, to order a party to produce or give evidence under other procedures of that state, or to have social studies made with respect to the custody of a child involved in proceedings pending in the court of this State; and to forward to the court of this State certified copies of the transcript of the record of the hearing, the evidence otherwise adduced, or any social studies prepared in compliance with the request. The cost of the services may be assessed against the parties or, if necessary, ordered paid by the county wherein the child resides.

b. A court of this State may request the appropriate court of another state to order a party to custody proceedings pending in the court of this State to appear in the proceedings, and if that party has physical custody of the child, to appear with the child. The request may state that travel and other necessary expenses of the party and of the child whose appearance is desired will be assessed against another party or will otherwise be paid to the clerk of the court for remittance to the proper party.

c. The appearance of a party residing outside the State pursuant to this section shall not constitute waiver of the party's right to contest the court's jurisdiction.

§ 2A:34-48. Assistance to courts of other states.

a. Upon request of the court of another state the courts of this State which are competent to hear custody matters may order a person in this State to appear at a hearing to adduce evidence or to produce or give evidence under other procedures available in this State or may order social studies to be made for use in a custody proceeding in another state. A certified copy of the transcript of the record of the hearing or the evidence otherwise adduced and any social studies prepared shall be forwarded by the clerk of the court to the requesting court.

b. A person within this State may voluntarily give his testimony or statement in this State for use in a custody proceeding outside this State.

c. Upon request of the court of another state a competent court of this State may, after a hearing, order a person in this State to appear alone or with the child in a custody proceeding in another state. The court may condition compliance with the request upon assurance by the other state that travel and other necessary expenses will be advanced or reimbursed.

§ 2A:34-49. Preservation of documents for use in other states.

In any custody proceeding in this State the court shall preserve the pleadings, orders and decrees, any record that has been made of its hearings, social studies, and other pertinent documents until the child reaches 21 years of age. Upon appropriate request of the court of another state the court shall forward to the other court certified copies of any or all of such documents.

§ 2A:34-50. Request for court records of another state.

If a custody decree has been rendered in another state concerning a child involved in a custody proceeding pending in a court of this State, the court of this State, upon taking jurisdiction of the case, shall request of the court of the other state a certified copy of the transcript of any court record and other documents mentioned in section 22 of this act.

§ 2A:34-51. International application.

The general policies of this act extend to the international area. The provisions of this act relating to the recognition and enforcement of custody decrees of other states apply to custody decrees and decrees involving legal institutions similar in nature and to custody rendered by appropriate authorities of other nations, if reasonable notice and opportunity to be heard were given to all affected persons.

§ 2A:34-52. Severability.

If any provision of this act or the application thereof to any person or circumstance is held invalid, its invalidity does not affect other provisions or applications of the act which can be given effect without the invalid provision or application, and to this end the provisions of this act are severable.

NEW MEXICO

CHILD CUSTODY JURISDICTION ACT

§ 40-10-1. Short title.
This act [40-10-1 to 40-10-24 NMSA 1978] may be cited as the "Child Custody Jurisdiction Act."

§ 40-10-2. Purpose.
It is the purpose of the Child Custody Jurisdiction Act [40-10-1 to 40-10-24 NMSA 1978] to:

A. avoid jurisdictional competition and conflict with courts of other states in matters of child custody which have in the past resulted in the shifting of children from state to state with harmful effects on their well-being;

B. promote cooperation with the courts of other states to the end that a custody decree is rendered in that state which can best decide the case in the interest of the child;

C. assure that litigation concerning the custody of a child take place ordinarily in the state with which the child and his family have the closest connection and where significant evidence concerning his care, protection, training and personal relationships is most readily available, and that courts of this state decline the exercise of jurisdiction when the child and his family have a closer connection with another state;

D. discourage continuing controversies over child custody in the interest of greater stability of home environment and of secure family relationships for the child;

E. deter abductions and other unilateral removals of children undertaken to obtain custody awards;

F. avoid relitigation of custody decisions of other states in this state, insofar as feasible;

G. facilitate the enforcement of custody decrees of other states;

H. promote and expand the exchange of information and other forms of mutual assistance between the courts of this state and those of other states concerned with the same child; and

I. make the laws of New Mexico uniform with the laws of other states which enact similar laws.

§ 40-10-3. Definitions.
As used in the Child Custody Jurisdiction Act [40-10-1 to 40-10-24 NMSA 1978]:

A. "contestant" means a person, including a parent, who claims a right to custody or visitation rights with respect to a child;

B. "custody determination" means a court decision and court orders and instructions providing for the custody of a child, including visitation rights, but it does not include a decision relating to child support or any other monetary obligation of any person;

C. "custody proceeding" includes proceedings in which a custody determination is one of several issues, such as an action for divorce or separation;

D. "decree" or "custody decree" means a custody determination contained in a judicial decree or order made in a custody proceeding, and includes an initial decree and a modification decree;

E. "home state" means the state in which the child, immediately preceding the time involved, lived with his parents, a parent or a person acting as a parent for at least six consecutive months, and in the case of a child less than six months old, the state in which the child lived from birth with any of the persons mentioned. Periods of temporary absence of any of the above-named persons are counted as part of the six-month period or any other period;

F. "initial decree" means the first custody decree concerning a particular child;

G. "modification decree" means a custody decree which modifies or replaces a prior custody decree, whether made by the court which rendered the prior decree or by another court;

H. "person acting as a parent" means a person, other than a parent, who has physical custody of a child and who has either been awarded custody by a court or claims a right to custody;

I. "physical custody" means actual possession and control of a child; and

J. "state" means any state, territory or possession of the United States, the commonwealth of Puerto Rico and the District of Columbia.

§ 40-10-4. Jurisdiction.
A. A district court of New Mexico which is competent to decide child custody matters has jurisdiction to make a child custody determination by initial decree or modification decree of a prior decree of another court under the following circumstances if:

(1) New Mexico:

(a) is the home state of the child at the time of commencement of the proceeding; or

(b) had been the child's home state within six months before commencement of the proceeding and the child is absent from New Mexico because of his removal or retention by a person claiming his custody or for other reasons, and a parent or person acting as parent continues to live in New Mexico;

(2) it is in the best interest of the child that a district court of New Mexico assume jurisdiction because:

(a) the child and his parents, or the child and at least one contestant, have a significant connection with New Mexico; and

(b) there is available in New Mexico substantial evidence concerning the child's present or future care, protection, training and personal relationships;

(3) the child is physically present in New Mexico and:

(a) the child has been abandoned; or

(b) it is necessary in an emergency to protect the child because he has been subjected to or threatened with mistreatment or abuse or is otherwise neglected; or

(4) it appears that:

(a) no other state would have jurisdiction under prerequisites substantially in accordance with Paragraph (1), (2) or (3) of this subsection, or another state has declined to exercise jurisdiction on the ground that New Mexico is the more appropriate forum to determine the custody of the child; and

(b) it is in the best interest of the child that the New Mexico district court assume jurisdiction.

B. A district court of New Mexico which is competent to decide child custody matters has jurisdiction to make a child custody determination by modification decree of a prior New Mexico decree if, since the prior New Mexico custody determination, New Mexico has remained the residence of the child or any contestant in the prior custody determination.

C. Except as provided under Paragraphs (3) and (4) of Subsection A of this section, physical presence in New Mexico of the child, or of the child and one of the contestants, is not alone sufficient to confer jurisdiction on a district court of New Mexico to make a child custody determination.

D. Physical presence of the child, while desirable, is not a prerequisite for jurisdiction to determine his custody.

§ 40-10-5. Notice and opportunity to be heard.

Before making a decree under the Child Custody Jurisdiction Act [40-10-1 to 40-10-24 NMSA 1978], reasonable notice and opportunity to be heard shall be given to the contestants, any parent whose parental rights have not been previously terminated and any person who has physical custody of the child. If any of these persons are outside New Mexico, notice and opportunity to be heard shall be given pursuant to Section 6 [40-10-6 NMSA 1978] of that act.

§ 40-10-6. Notice to persons outside New Mexico; submission to jurisdiction.

A. Notice required for the exercise of jurisdiction over a person outside New Mexico shall be given in a manner reasonably calculated to give actual notice, and may be:

(1) by personal delivery outside New Mexico in the manner prescribed for service of process within New Mexico;

(2) in the manner prescribed by the law of the place in which the service is made for service of process in that place in an action in any of its courts of general jurisdiction;

(3) by certified mail, return receipt requested, addressed to the person to be served and requesting a receipt; or

(4) as directed by the district court including publication, if other means of notification are ineffective.

B. Notice under this section shall be served, mailed or delivered or last published at least twenty days before any hearing in New Mexico.

C. Proof of service outside New Mexico may be made by affidavit of the individual who made the service or in the manner prescribed by the law of New Mexico, the order pursuant to which the service is made or the law of the place in which the service is made. If service is made by mail, proof may be a receipt signed by the addressee or other evidence of delivery to the addressee.

D. Notice is not required if a person submits to the jurisdiction of the district court.

§ 40-10-7. Simultaneous proceeding in other states.

A. A district court of New Mexico shall not exercise its jurisdiction under the Child Custody Jurisdiction Act [40-10-1 to 40-10-24 NMSA 1978] if at the time of filing the petition a proceeding concerning the custody of the same child was pending in a court of another state exercising jurisdiction substantially in conformity with the Child Custody Jurisdiction Act, unless the proceeding is stayed by the court of the other state because New Mexico is a more appropriate forum, or for other reasons.

B. Before hearing the petition in a custody proceeding, the district court shall examine the pleadings and other information supplied by the parties under Section 10 [40-10-10 NMSA 1978] of the Child Custody Jurisdiction Act and shall consult the child custody registry established under Section 17 [40-10-17 NMSA 1978] of that act, concerning the pendency of proceedings with respect to the child in other states. If the court has reason to believe that proceedings may be pending in another state, the court shall direct an inquiry to the state court administrator or other appropriate official of the other state.

C. If the district court is informed during the course of the proceeding that a proceeding concerning the custody of the child was pending in another state before the New Mexico district court assumed jurisdiction, the court shall stay the proceeding and communicate with the court in which the other proceeding is pending to the end that the issue may be litigated in the more appropriate forum and that information be exchanged in accordance with Sections 20 through 23 [40-10-20 to 40-10-23 NMSA 1978] of the Child Custody Jurisdiction Act. If a court of New Mexico has made a custody decree before being informed of a pending proceeding in a court of another state, it shall immediately inform that court of this fact. If the district court is informed that a proceeding was commenced in another state after the New Mexico court assumed jurisdiction, it shall likewise inform the other court, to the end that the issues may be litigated in the more appropriate forum.

§ 40-10-8. Inconvenient forum.

A. A district court which has jurisdiction under the Child Custody Jurisdiction Act [40-10-1 to 40-10-24 NMSA 1978] to make an initial decree or a modification decree may decline to exercise its jurisdiction any time before making a decree if it finds that it is an inconvenient forum to make a custody determination under the circumstances of the case and that a court of another state is a more appropriate forum.

B. A finding of inconvenient forum may be made upon a district court's own motion or upon motion of a party or of a guardian ad litem or other representative of the child.

C. In order to determine whether it is an inconvenient forum, the court shall consider whether it is in the interest of the child that another state assume jurisdiction, and for this purpose may take into account the following factors, among others; whether:

(1) another state is or recently was the child's home state;

(2) another state has a closer connection with the child and his family or with the child and one or more of the contestants;

(3) substantial evidence concerning the child's present or future care, protection, training and personal relationships is more readily available in another state;

(4) the parties have agreed on another forum which is no less appropriate;

(5) the parties have stipulated that New Mexico shall retain jurisdiction of custody matters;

(6) the out-of-state contestant has complied with any previous custody and visitation orders of the New Mexico court; and

(7) the exercise of jurisdiction by a court of New Mexico would contravene any of the purposes stated in Section 40-10-2 NMSA 1978.

D. Before determining whether to decline or retain jurisdiction, the district court may communicate with a court of another state and exchange information pertinent to the assumption of jurisdiction by either court, with a view to assuring that jurisdiction will be exercised by the more appropriate court and that a forum will be available to the parties.

E. If the court finds that it is an inconvenient forum and that a court of another state is a more appropriate forum, it may dismiss the proceedings or it may stay the proceedings upon condition that a custody proceeding be promptly commenced in another named state, or upon any other conditions which may be just and proper, including the condition that a moving party stipulate his consent and submission to the jurisdiction of the other forum.

F. The court may decline to exercise its jurisdiction under the Child Custody Jurisdiction Act if a custody determination is incidental to an action for dissolution of marriage or another proceeding, while retaining jurisdiction over the dissolution of marriage or other proceeding.

G. Whenever it appears to the court that it is clearly an inappropriate forum, it may require the party who commenced the proceedings to pay, in addition to the costs of the proceedings in New Mexico, necessary travel and other expenses, including attorneys' fees, incurred by other parties or their witnesses. Payment is to be made to the clerk of the court for remittance to the proper party.

H. Upon dismissal or stay of proceedings under this section, the district court shall inform the court found to be the more appropriate forum of this fact or, if the court which would have jurisdiction in the other state is not certainly known, shall transmit the information to the court administrator or other appropriate official for forwarding to the appropriate court.

I. Any communication received from another state informing New Mexico of a finding of inconvenient forum because a district court of New Mexico is the more appropriate forum shall be filed in the custody registry of the appropriate court. Upon assuming jurisdiction in the case, the court of New Mexico shall inform the original court of this fact.

§ 40-10-9. Jurisdiction declined by reason of conduct.

A. If the petitioner for an initial decree has wrongfully taken the child from another state, the district court in its discretion may decline to exercise jurisdiction.

B. Unless required in the interest of the child and subject to Subsection A of Section 15 [40-10-15 NMSA 1978] of the Child Custody Jurisdiction Act, the district court shall not exercise its jurisdiction to modify a custody decree of another state if the petitioner, without consent of the person entitled to custody, has improperly removed the child from the physical custody of the person entitled to custody or has improperly retained the child after a visit or other temporary relinquishment of physical custody. If the petitioner has violated any other provision of a custody decree of another state, the court in its discretion and subject to Subsection A of Section 15 of that act may decline to exercise jurisdiction.

C. In appropriate cases a district court dismissing a petition under this section may charge the petitioner with necessary travel expenses and other expenses, including attorneys' fees, incurred by other parties or their witnesses.

§ 40-10-10. Information under oath to be submitted to the court.

A. Every party in a custody proceeding in his first pleading or in an affidavit attached to that pleading shall give information under oath as to the child's present address, the places where the child has lived within the last three years, and the names and present addresses of the persons with whom the child has lived during that period. In this pleading or affidavit, every party shall further declare under oath whether he:

(1) has participated as a party, witness or in any other capacity in any other litigation concerning the custody of the same child in New Mexico or any other state;

(2) has information of any custody proceeding concerning the child pending in a court of this or any other state; and

(3) knows of any person not a party to the proceedings who has physical custody of the child or claims to have custody or visitation rights with respect to the child.

B. If the declaration pursuant to Subsection A of this section is in the affirmative, the declarant shall give additional information under oath as required by the court. The district court may examine the parties under oath as to details of the information furnished and as to other matters pertinent to the court's jurisdiction and the disposition of the case.

C. Each party has a continuing duty to inform the court of any custody proceeding concerning the child in New Mexico or any other state of which he has obtained information during this proceeding.

§ 40-10-11. Additional parties.

Whenever the district court learns from information furnished by the parties pursuant to Section 10 [40-10-10 NMSA 1978] of the Child Custody Jurisdiction Act or from other sources that a person not a party to the custody proceeding has physical custody of the child or claims to have custody or visitation rights with respect to the child, it shall order the person to be joined as a party and to be duly notified of the pendency of a proceeding and of his joinder as a party. If the person joined as a party is outside New Mexico, he shall be served with process or otherwise notified in accordance with Section 6 [40-10-6 NMSA 1978] of that act.

§ 40-10-12. Appearance of parties and the child.

A. The district court may order any party to the proceeding who is in New Mexico to appear personally before the district court, and, if that party has physical custody of the child, the court may order that he appear personally with the child.

B. If a party to the proceeding whose presence is desired by the district court is outside New Mexico with or without the child, the court may order that the notice given under Section 6 [40-10-6 NMSA 1978] of the Child Custody Jurisdiction Act include a statement directing that party to appear personally with or without the child and declaring that failure to appear may result in a decision adverse to that party.

C. If a party to the proceeding who is outside New Mexico is directed to appear pursuant to Subsection B of this section or desires to appear personally before the district court with or without the child, the court may require another party to pay to the clerk of the district court travel and other necessary expenses of the party so appearing and of the child, if this is just and proper under the circumstances.

§ 40-10-13. Binding force and res judicata effect of custody decree.

A custody decree rendered by a district court of New Mexico which had jurisdiction under Section 4 [40-10-4 NMSA 1978] of the Child Custody Jurisdiction Act binds all parties who have been served in New Mexico or notified in accordance with Section 6 [40-10-6 NMSA 1978] of that act or who have submitted to the jurisdiction of the court and who have been given an opportunity to be heard. As to these parties, the custody decree is conclusive as to all issues of law and fact decided and as to the custody determination made unless and until that determination is modified pursuant to law, including the provisions of the Child Custody Jurisdiction Act [40-10-1 to 40-10-24 NMSA 1978].

§ 40-10-14. Recognition of out-of-state custody decrees.

The district court of New Mexico shall recognize and enforce an initial or modification decree of a court of another state which had assumed jurisdiction under statutory provisions substantially in accordance with the Child Custody Jurisdiction Act [40-10-1 to 40-10-24 NMSA 1978] or which was made under factual circumstances meeting the jurisdictional standards of that act, so long as this decree has not been modified in accordance with jurisdictional standards substantially similar to those of the Child Custody Jurisdiction Act.

§ 40-10-15. Modification of custody decree of another state.

A. If a court of another state has made a custody decree, a district court of New Mexico shall not modify that decree unless:

(1) it appears that the court which rendered the decree does not now have jurisdiction under jurisdictional prerequisites substantially in accordance with the Child Custody Jurisdiction Act [40-10-1 to 40-10-24 NMSA 1978] or has declined to assume jurisdiction to modify the decree; and

(2) the district court of New Mexico has jurisdiction.

B. If a district court of New Mexico is authorized under Subsection A of this section and Section 9 [40-10-9 NMSA 1978] of the Child Custody Jurisdiction Act to modify a custody decree of another state, it shall give due consideration to the transcript of the record and other documents of all previous proceedings submitted to it in accordance with Section 23 [40-10-23 NMSA 1978] of that act.

§ 40-10-16. Filing and enforcement of custody decree of another state.

A. A certified copy of a custody decree of another state may be filed in the office of the clerk of any district court of New Mexico. The clerk shall treat the decree in the same manner as a custody decree of the district court of New Mexico. A custody decree so filed has the same effect and shall be enforced in like manner as a custody decree rendered by a court of New Mexico.

B. A person violating a custody decree of another state, making it necessary to enforce the decree in New Mexico, may be required to pay necessary travel and other expenses, including attorney's fees, incurred by the party entitled to the custody or his witnesses.

§ 40-10-17. Registry of out-of-state custody decrees and proceedings.

The clerk of each district court shall maintain a registry in which he shall enter the following:

A. certified copies of custody decrees of other states received for filing;

B. communications as to the pendency of custody proceedings in other states;

C. communications concerning a finding of inconvenient forum by a court of another state; and

D. other communications or documents concerning custody proceedings in another state which may affect the jurisdiction of a court of New Mexico or the disposition to be made by it in a custody proceeding.

§ 40-10-18. Certified copies of custody decree.

The clerk of a district court of New Mexico shall, at the request of the court of another state or at the request of any person who is affected by or has a legitimate interest in a custody decree, certify and forward a copy of the decree to that court or person.

§ 40-10-19. Testimony by deposition in another state.

In addition to other procedural devices available to a party, any party to the proceeding or a guardian ad litem or other representative of the child may adduce testimony of witnesses, including parties and the child, by deposition or otherwise, in another state. The district court on its own motion may direct that the testimony of a person be taken in another state and may prescribe the manner in which and the terms upon which the testimony shall be taken.

§ 40-10-20. Hearing and studies in another state.

A. A court of New Mexico may request the appropriate court of another state to hold a hearing to adduce evidence, to order a party to produce or give evidence under other procedures of that state or to have social studies made with respect to the custody of a child involved in proceedings pending in the district court of New Mexico, and to forward to the district court of New Mexico certified copies of the transcript of the record of the hearing, the evidence otherwise adduced or any social studies prepared in compliance with the request. The cost of the services may be assessed against the parties.

B. A district court of New Mexico may request the appropriate court of another state to order a party to custody proceedings pending in the court of New Mexico to appear in the proceedings and, if that party has physical custody of the child, to appear with the child. The request may state that travel and other necessary expenses of the party and of the child whose appearance is desired will be assessed against another party or will otherwise be paid.

§ 40-10-21. Assistance to courts of other states.

A. Upon request of the court of another state, the district courts of New Mexico which are competent to hear custody matters may order a person in New Mexico to appear at a hearing to adduce evidence or to produce or give evidence under other procedures available in New Mexico or may order social studies to be made for use in a custody proceeding in another state. A certified copy of the transcript of the record of the hearing or the evidence otherwise adduced and any social studies prepared shall be forwarded by the clerk of the district court to the requesting court.

B. A person within New Mexico may voluntarily give his testimony or statement in New Mexico for use in a custody proceeding outside New Mexico.

C. Upon request of the court of another state, a competent district court of New Mexico may order a person in New Mexico to appear alone or with the child in a custody proceeding in another state. The district court may condition compliance with the request upon assurance by the other state that travel and other necessary expenses will be advanced or reimbursed.

§ 40-10-22. Preservation of documents for use in other states.

In any custody proceeding in New Mexico, the district court shall preserve the pleadings, orders and decrees; any record that has been made of its hearings; social studies; and other pertinent documents until the child reaches the age of majority. Upon appropriate request of the court of another state, the district court of New Mexico shall forward to the other court certified copies of any or all of such documents.

§ 40-10-23. Request for court records of another state.

Whenever a custody decree has been rendered in another state concerning a child involved in a custody proceeding pending in a district court of New Mexico, the district court of New Mexico, upon taking jurisdiction of the case, shall request of the court of the other state a certified copy of the transcript of any court record and other documents mentioned in Section 22 [40-10-22 NMSA 1978] of the Child Custody Jurisdiction Act.

§ 40-10-24. Applicability.

The provisions of the Child Custody Jurisdiction Act [40-10-1 to 40-10-24 NMSA 1978] shall apply only between those states which have enacted the same or similar legislation.

NEW YORK

ARTICLE 5A
UNIFORM CHILD CUSTODY JURISDICTION ACT

§ 75-a. Short title.

This article shall be known as the "Uniform Child Custody Jurisdiction Act."

§ 75-b. Purposes of article; construction of provisions.

1. The general purposes of this article are to:

(a) avoid jurisdictional competition and conflict with courts of other states in matters of child custody which have in the past resulted in the shifting of children from state to state with harmful effects on their well-being;

(b) promote cooperation with the courts of other states to the end that a custody decree is rendered in that state which can best decide the case in the interest of the child;

(c) assure that litigation concerning the custody of a child take place ordinarily in the state with which the child and his family have the closest connection and where significant evidence concerning his care, protection, training, and personal relationships is most readily available, and that courts of this state decline the exercise of jurisdiction when the child and his family have a closer connection with another state;

(d) discourage continuing controversies over child custody in the interest of greater stability of home environment and of secure family relationships for the child;

(e) deter abductions and other unilateral removals of children undertaken to obtain custody awards;

(f) avoid re-litigation of custody decisions of other states in this state insofar as feasible;

(g) facilitate the enforcement of custody decrees of other states;

(h) promote and expand the exchange of information and other forms of mutual assistance between the courts of this state and those of other states concerned with the same child; and

(i) make uniform the law of those states which enact it.

2. This article shall be construed to promote the general purposes stated in this section.

§ 75-c. Definitions.

As used in this article, the following terms have the following meanings:

1. "Contestant" means a person, including a parent, who claims a right to custody or visitation rights with respect to a child.

2. "Custody determination" means a court decision and court orders and instructions providing for the temporary or permanent custody of a child, including visitation rights.

3 "Custody proceeding" includes proceedings in which a custody determination is at issue or is one of several issues including any action or proceeding brought to annul a marriage or to declare the nullity of a void marriage, or for a separation, or for a divorce, but not including proceedings for adoption, child protective proceedings or proceedings for permanent termination of parental custody, or proceedings involving the guardianship and custody of neglected or dependent children, or proceedings initiated pursuant to section three hundred fifty-eight-a of the social services law.

4. "Decree" or "custody decree" means a custody determination contained in a judicial decree or order made in a custody proceeding, and includes an initial decree and a modification decree.

5. "Home state" means the state in which the child at the time of the commencement of the custody proceeding, has resided with his parents, a parent, or a person acting as parent, for at least six consecutive months. In the case of a child less than six months old at the time of the commencement of the proceeding, home state means the state in which the child has resided with any of such persons for a majority of the time since birth.

6. "Initial decree" means the first custody decree concerning a particular child.

7. "Modification decree" means a custody decree which modifies or replaces a prior decree, whether made by the court which rendered the prior decree or by another court.

8. "Physical custody" means actual possession and control of a child.

9. "Person acting as parent" means a person, other than a parent, who has physical custody of a child and who has either been awarded custody by a court or claims a right to custody.

10. "State" means any state, territory, or possession of the United States, the Commonwealth of Puerto Rico, and the District of Columbia.

§ 75-d. Jurisdiction to make child custody determinations.

1. A court of this state which is competent to decide child custody matters has jurisdiction to make a child custody determination by initial or modification decree only when:

(a) this state (i) is the home state of the child at the time of commencement of the custody proceeding, or (ii) had been the child's home state within six months before a commencement of such proceeding and the child is absent from this state because of his removal or retention by a person claiming his custody or for other reasons, and a parent or person acting as parent continues to live in this state; or

(b) it is in the best interest of the child that a court of this state assume jurisdiction because (i) the child and his parents, or the child and at least one contestant, have a significant connection with this state, and (ii) there is within the jurisdiction of the court substantial evidence concerning the child's present or future care, protection, training, and personal relationships; or

(c) the child is physically present in this state and (i) the child has been abandoned or (ii) it is necessary in an emergency to protect the child; or

(d)(i) it appears that no other state would have jurisdiction under prerequisites substantially in accordance with paragraph (a), (b), or (c), or another state has declined to exercise jurisdiction on the ground that this state is the more appropriate forum to determine the custody of the child, and (ii) it is in the best interest of the child that this court assume jurisdiction.

2. Except under paragraphs (c) and (d) of subdivision one of this section, physical presence in this state of the child, or of the child and one of the contestants, is not alone sufficient to confer jurisdiction on a court of this state to make a child custody determination.

3. Physical presence of the child, while desirable, is not a prerequisite for jurisdiction to determine his custody.

§ 75-e. Notice and opportunity to be heard.

Before making a decree under this article, reasonable notice and opportunity to be heard shall be given to the contestants, any parent whose parental rights have not been previously terminated, and any person who has physical custody of the child. If any of these persons is outside the state, notice and opportunity to be heard shall be given pursuant to section seventy-five-f of this article. Any person who is given notice and an opportunity to be heard pursuant to this section shall be deemed a party to the proceeding for all purposes under this article.

§ 75-f. Notice to persons outside the state.

1. If a person cannot be personally served with notice within the state, the court shall require that such person be served in a manner reasonably calculated to give actual notice, as follows:

(a) by personal delivery outside the state in the manner prescribed in section three hundred thirteen of the civil practice law and rules;

(b) by any form of mail addressed to the person and requesting a receipt; or

(c) in such manner as the court, upon motion, directs, including publication, if service is impracticable under paragraph (a) or (b) of subdivision one of this section.

2. Notice under this section shall be served, mailed, delivered, or last published at least twenty days before any hearing in this state.

3. Proof of service outside the state shall be by affidavit of the individual who made the service, or in the manner prescribed by the order pursuant to which the service is made. If service is made by mail, proof may be a receipt signed by the addressee or other evidence of delivery to the addressee.

§ 75-g. Simultaneous proceedings in other states.

1. A court of this state shall not exercise its jurisdiction under this article if at any time of filing the petition a proceeding concerning the custody of the child was pending in a court of another state exercising jurisdiction substantially in conformity with this article, unless the proceeding is stayed by the court of the other state because this state is a more appropriate forum or for other reasons.

2. Before hearing the petition in a custody proceeding the court shall examine the pleadings and other information supplied by the parties under section seventy-five-j of this article. If the court has reason to believe that proceedings may be pending in another state it shall direct an inquiry to the state court administrator or other appropriate official of the other state.

3. If the court is informed during the course of the proceeding that a proceeding concerning the custody of the child was pending in another state before the court assumed jurisdiction it shall stay the proceeding and communicate with the court in which the other proceeding is pending to the end that the issue may be litigated in the more appropriate forum and that information be

exchanged in accordance with sections seventy-five-s through seventy-five-v of this article. If a court of this state has made a custody decree before being informed of a pending proceeding in a court of another state, it shall immediately inform that court of the fact. If the court is informed that a proceeding was commenced in another state after it assumed jurisdiction, it shall likewise inform the other court to the end that the issues may be litigated in the more appropriate forum.

§ 75-h. Inconvenient forum.

1. A court which has jurisdiction under this article to make an initial or modification decree may decline to exercise its jurisdiction any time before making a decree if it finds that it is an inconvenient forum to make a custody determination under the circumstances of the case and that a court of another state is a more appropriate forum.

2. A finding of inconvenient forum may be made upon the court's own motion or upon motion of a party or a guardian ad litem or other representative of the child.

3. In determining if it is an inconvenient forum, the court shall consider if it is in the interest of the child that another state assume jurisdiction. For this purpose it may take into account the following factors, among others, whether:

(a) another state is or recently was the child's home state;

(b) another state has a closer connection with the child and his family or with the child and one or more of the contestants;

(c) substantial evidence concerning the child's present or future care, protection, training, and personal relationships is more readily available in another state;

(d) the parties have agreed on another forum which is no less appropriate; and

(e) the exercise of jurisdiction by a court of this state would contravene any of the purposes stated in section seventy-five-b of this article.

4. Before determining whether to decline or retain jurisdiction the court may communicate with a court of another state and exchange information pertinent to the assumption of jurisdiction by either court with a view to assuring that jurisdiction will be exercised by the more appropriate court and that a forum will be available to the parties.

5. If the court finds that it is an inconvenient forum and that a court of another state is a more appropriate forum, it may dismiss the proceedings, or it may stay the proceedings upon condition that a custody proceeding be promptly commenced in another named state or upon any other conditions which may be just and proper, including the condition that a moving party stipulate his consent and submission to the jurisdiction of the other forum.

6. Where the court has jurisdiction of an action or proceeding brought to annul a marriage or to declare the nullity of a void marriage or for a separation or for a divorce, the court may decline to exercise jurisdiction of an application for a custody determination made therein while retaining jurisdiction of the matrimonial action.

7. If it appears to the court that it is clearly an inappropriate forum it may require the party who commenced the proceedings to pay, in addition to the costs of the proceedings in this state, necessary travel expenses, including attorneys' fees, incurred by other parties or their witnesses. Payment shall be made to the clerk of the court for remittance to the proper party.

8. Upon dismissal or stay of proceedings under this section the court shall inform the court found to be the more appropriate forum of such dismissal or stay, or if the court which would have jurisdiction in the other state is not certainly known, shall transmit the information to the court administrator or other appropriate official for forwarding to the appropriate court.

9. Any communication received from another state to the effect that its courts have made a finding of inconvenient forum because a court of this state is the more appropriate forum shall be filed with the clerk of the appropriate court. Upon assuming jurisdiction the court of this state shall inform the original court of this fact.

§ 75-i. Jurisdiction declined because of conduct.

1. If the petitioner for an initial decree has wrongfully taken the child from another state or has engaged in similar reprehensible conduct the court may decline to exercise jurisdiction if this is just and proper under the circumstances.

2. Unless required in the interest of the child, the court shall not exercise its jurisdiction to modify a custody decree of another state if the petitioner, without consent of the person entitled to custody, has improperly removed the child from the physical custody of the person entitled to custody or has improperly retained the child after a visit or other temporary relinquishment of physical custody. If the petitioner has violated any other provision of a custody decree of another state the court may decline to exercise its jurisdiction if this is just and proper under the circumstances.

3. In appropriate cases a court dismissing a petition under this section may charge the petitioner with necessary travel and other expenses, including attorneys' fees, incurred by other parties or their witnesses.

§ 75-j. Pleadings and affidavits; duty to inform court.

1. Except as provided in subdivisions four and five of this section, every party to a custody proceeding shall, in his or her first pleading or in an affidavit attached to that pleading, give information under oath as to the child's present address, the places where the child has lived within the last five years, and the names and present addresses of the persons with whom the child has lived during that period. In this pleading or affidavit every party shall further declare under oath whether he or she:

(a) has participated as a party, witness, or in any other capacity in any other litigation concerning the custody of the same child in this or any other state;

(b) has information of any custody proceeding concerning the child pending in a court of this or any other state; and

(c) knows of any person not a party to the proceedings who has physical custody of the child or claims to have custody or visitation rights with respect to the child.

2. If the declaration as to any of the above items is in the affirmative the declarant shall give additional information under oath as required by the court. The court may examine the parties under oath as to details of the information furnished and as to other matters pertinent to the court's jurisdiction and the disposition of the case.

3. If, during the pendency of a custody proceeding, any party learns of another custody proceeding concerning the child in this or another state, he shall immediately inform the court of this fact.

4. In an action for divorce or separation, or to annul a marriage or declare the nullity of a void marriage, (a) where neither party is in default in appearance or pleading and the issue of custody is uncontested, the affidavit required by this section need not be submitted. In any other such action, such affidavit shall be submitted by the parties within twenty days after joinder of issue on the question of custody, or at the time application for a default judgment is made.

(b) Notwithstanding any other provision of law, if the party seeking custody of the child has resided or resides in a special care home as defined in subdivision thirty-one of section two of the social services law, the present address of the child and the present address of the party seeking custody and the address of the special care home shall not be revealed.

(c) Notwithstanding any other provision of law, the court shall waive disclosure of the present and all prior addresses of the child or a party upon notice to the adverse party when such relief is necessary for the physical or emotional safety of a child or a party.

5. Notwithstanding any other provision of law, in any custody proceeding, the court shall waive disclosure of the present or a prior address of the child or a party when such relief is necessary for the physical or emotional safety of a child or a party. Application for an order waving disclosure of the present or a prior address of the child or a party shall be on notice to all other parties, who shall have an opportunity to be heard. Provided, however, that in no case shall the address of a special care home, as defined in subdivision thirty-one of section two of the social services law, be disclosed.

§ 75-k. Additional parties.

If the court learns from information furnished by the parties pursuant to section seventy-five-j of this article, or from other sources that a person not a party to the custody proceeding has physical custody of the child or claims to have custody or visitation rights with respect to the child, it shall order that person to be joined as a party and to be duly notified of the pendency of the proceeding and of his joinder as a party. If the person joined as a party is outside this state he shall be served with process or otherwise notified in accordance with section seventy-five-f of this article.

§ 75-l. Appearance of parties and the child.

1. The court may order any party to the proceeding who is in the state to appear personally before the court. If that party has physical custody of the child the court may order that he appear personally with the child.

2. If a party to the proceeding whose presence is desired by the court is outside the state with or without the child the court may order that the notice given under section seventy-five-f of this article include a statement directing that party to appear personally with or without the child and declaring that failure to appear may result in a decision adverse to that party.

3. If a party to the proceeding who is outside the state is directed to appear under subdivision two or desires to appear personally before the court with or without the child, the court may require another party to pay to the clerk of the court travel and other necessary expenses of the party so appearing and of the child if this is just and proper under the circumstances.

§ 75-m. Force and effect of custody decrees.

A custody decree rendered by a court of this state which had jurisdiction under section seventy-five-d of this article shall be binding upon all parties who have been personally served in this state or notified pursuant to section seventy-five-f of this article or who have submitted to the jurisdiction of the court, and who have been given an opportunity to be heard. As to these parties the custody decree is conclusive as to all issues of law and fact decided and as to the custody determination made unless and until that determination is modified pursuant to law, including the provisions of this article.

§ 75-n. Recognition of out-of-state custody decrees.

The courts of this state shall recognize and enforce an initial or modification decree of a court of another state which had assumed jurisdiction under statutory provisions substantially in accordance with this article or which was made under factual circumstances meeting the jurisdictional standards of this article, so long as the decree has not been modified in accordance with jurisdictional standards substantially similar to those of this article.

§ 75-o. Modification of custody decree of another state.

1. If a court of another state has made a custody decree, a court of this state shall not modify that decree unless (1) it appears to the court of this state that the court which rendered the decree does not now have jurisdiction under jurisdictional prerequisites substantially in accordance with this article or has declined to assume jurisdiction to modify the decree and (2) the court of this state has jurisdiction.

2. If a court of this state is authorized under subdivision one of this section and section seventy-five-i of this article to modify a custody decree of another state, it shall give due consideration to the transcript of the record and other documents of all previous proceedings submitted to it in accordance with section seventy-five-v of this article.

§ 75-p. Filing and enforcement of custody decree of another state.

1. A certified copy of a custody decree of another state may be filed in the office of the clerk of the supreme court or of the family court. The clerk shall treat the decree in the same manner as a custody decree of the supreme court or of the family court. A custody decree so filed has the same effect and shall be enforced in like manner as a custody decree rendered by a court of this state.

2. A person violating a custody decree of another state which makes it necessary to enforce the decree in this state may be required to pay necessary travel and other expenses, including attorneys' fees, incurred by the party entitled to the custody or his witnesses.

§ 75-q. Certified copies of custody decrees.

The clerk of the supreme court or the family court, at the request of the court of another state or, upon payment of the appropriate fees, if any, at the request of a party to the custody proceeding, the attorney for a party or a representative of the child shall certify and forward a copy of the decree to that court or person.

§ 75-r. Examination of witnesses outside the state.

In addition to other procedural devices available to a party, any party to the proceeding or a guardian ad litem or other representative of the child may examine witnesses, including parties and the child, in another state by deposition or otherwise in accordance with the applicable provisions of the civil practice law and rules.

§ 75-s. Hearings and studies in another state; orders to appear.

1. A court of this state may request the appropriate court of another state to hold a hearing to adduce evidence, to order a party within its jurisdiction, to produce or give evidence under other procedures of that state, or to have social studies made with respect to the custody of a child involved in proceedings pending in the court of this state; and to forward to the court of this state certified copies of the transcript of the record of the hearing, the evidence otherwise adduced, or any social studies prepared in compliance with the request. The cost of the services may be assessed against the parties.

2. A court of this state may request the appropriate court of another state to order a party to custody proceedings pending in the court of this state to appear in the proceedings, and if that party has physical custody of the child, to appear with the child The request may state that travel and other necessary expenses of the party and of the child whose appearance is desired will be assessed against another party or will otherwise be paid.

§ 75-t. Assistance to courts of other states.

1. Upon request of the court of another state the courts of this state which are competent to hear custody matters may order a party or witness in this state to appear at an examination to be conducted in the same manner as if such person were a party to or witness in an action pending in the supreme court. A certified copy of the deposition or the evidence otherwise adduced shall be forwarded by the clerk of the court to the court which requested it.

2. A person within the state may voluntarily give his testimony or statement for use in a custody proceeding outside this state.

3. Upon request of the court of another state a competent court of this state may order a person within the state to appear alone or with the child in a custody proceeding in another state. The court may condition compliance with the request upon assurance by the other state that travel and other necessary expenses will be advanced or reimbursed.

§ 75-u. Preservation of evidence for use in other states.

In any custody proceeding in this state the court shall preserve the pleadings, orders and decrees, any record that has been made of its hearings, social studies, and other pertinent documents until the child reaches twenty-one year of age. Upon appropriate request of the court of another state the court shall forward to the other court certified copies of any or all of such documents.

§ 75-v. Request for court records from another state.

If a custody decree has been rendered in another state concerning a child involved in a custody proceeding pending in a court of this state, the court of this state upon taking jurisdiction of the case shall request of the court of the other state a certified copy of the transcript of any court record and other documents mentioned in section seventy-five-u.

§ 75-w. International application.

The general policies of this article extend to the international area. The provisions of this article relating to the recognition and enforcement of custody decrees of other states apply to custody decrees and decrees involving legal institutions similar in nature to custody institutions rendered by appropriate authorities of other nations if reasonable notice and opportunity to be heard were given to all affected persons.

§ 75-x. Priority.

Upon the request of a party to a custody proceeding which raises a question of existence or exercise of jurisdiction under this article the case shall be given calendar priority and handled expeditiously.

§ 75-y. Separability.

In any part of this article or the application thereof to any person or circumstance is adjudged invalid by a court of competent jurisdiction, such judgment shall not affect or impair the validity of the remainder of such article or the application thereof to other persons and circumstances.

§ 75-z. Inconsistent provisions of other laws superseded.

Insofar as the provisions of this article are inconsistent with the provisions of any other law, general, special or local, the provisions of this article shall be controlling.

NORTH CAROLINA

UNIFORM CHILD CUSTODY JURISDICTION ACT

§ 50A-1. Purposes of Chapter; construction of provisions.

(a) The general purposes of this Chapter are to:

(1) Avoid jurisdictional competition and conflict with courts of other states in matters of child custody which have in the past resulted in the shifting of children from state to state with harmful effects on their well-being;

(2) Promote cooperation with the courts of other states to the end that a custody decree is rendered in that state which can best decide the case in the interest of the child;

(3) Assure that litigation concerning the custody of a child takes place ordinarily in the state with which the child and the child's family have the closest connection and where significant evidence concerning the child's care, protection, training, and personal relationships is most readily available, and that courts of this State decline the exercise of jurisdiction when the child and the child's family have a closer connection with another state;

(4) Discourage continuing controversies over child custody in the interest of greater stability of home environment and of secure family relationships for the child;

(5) Deter abductions and other unilateral removals of children undertaken to obtain custody awards;

(6) Avoid re-litigation of custody decisions of other states in this State insofar as feasible;

(7) Facilitate the enforcement of custody decrees of other states;

(8) Promote and expand the exchange of information and other forms of mutual assistance between the courts of this State and those of other states concerned with the same child; and

(9) Make uniform the law of those states which enact it.

(b) This Chapter shall be construed to promote the general purposes stated in this section.

§ 50A-2. Definitions.

As used in this Chapter:

(1) "Contestant" means a person, including a parent, who claims a right to custody or visitation rights with respect to a child;

(2) "Custody determination" means a court decision and court orders and instructions providing for the custody of a child, including visitation rights; it does not include a decision relating to child support or any other monetary obligation of any person;

(3) "Custody proceeding" includes proceedings in which a custody determination is one of several issues, such as an action for divorce or separation, and includes child neglect and dependency proceedings;

(4) "Decree" or "custody decree" means a custody determination contained in a judicial decree or order made in a custody proceeding, and includes an initial decree and a modification decree;

(5) "Home state" means the state in which the child immediately preceding the time involved lived with the child's parents, a parent, or a person acting as parent, for at least six consecutive months, and in the case of a child less than six months old, the state in which the child lived from birth with any of the persons mentioned. Period of temporary absence of any of the named persons are counted as part of the six-month or other period;

(6) "Initial decree" means the first custody decree concerning a particular child;

(7) "Modification decree" means a custody decree which modifies or replaces a prior decree, whether made by the court which rendered the prior decree or by another court;

(8) "Person acting as parent" means a person, other than a parent who has physical custody of a child and who has either been awarded custody by a court or claims a right to custody;

(9) "Physical custody" means actual possession and control of a child; and

(10) "State" means any state, territory, or possession of the United States, the Commonwealth of Puerto Rico, and the District of Columbia.

§ 50A-3. Jurisdiction.

(a) A court of this State authorized to decide child custody matters has jurisdiction to make a child custody determination by initial or modification decree if:

(1) This State (i) is the home state of the child at the time of commencement of the proceeding, or (ii) had been the child's home state within six months before commencement of the proceeding and the child is absent from this State because of the child's removal or retention by a person claiming the child's custody or for other reasons, and a parent or person acting as parent continues to live in this State; or

(2) It is in the best interest of the child that a court of this State assume jurisdiction because (i) the child and the child's parents, or the child and at least one contestant, have a significant connection with this State, and (ii) there is available in this State substantial evidence relevant to the child's present or future care, protection, training, and personal relationships; or

(3) The child is physically present in this State and (i) the child has been abandoned or (ii) it is necessary in an emergency to protect the child because the child has been subjected to or threatened with mistreatment or abuse or is otherwise neglected or dependent; or

(4) (i) It appears that no other state would have jurisdiction under prerequisites substantially in accordance with paragraphs (1), (2), or (3), or another state has declined to exercise jurisdiction on the ground that this State is the more appropriate forum to determine the custody of the child, and (ii) it is in the best interest of the child that this court assume jurisdiction.

(b) Except under paragraphs (3) and (4) of subsection (a), physical presence in this State of the child, or of the child and one of the contestants, is not alone sufficient to confer jurisdiction on a court of this State to make a child custody determination.

(c) Physical presence of the child, while desirable, is not a prerequisite for jurisdiction to determine his custody.

§ 50A-4. Notice and opportunity to be heard.

Before making a decree under this Chapter reasonable notice and opportunity to be heard shall be given to the contestants, any parent whose parental rights have not been previously terminated, and any person who has physical custody of the child.

§ 50A-5. Service of notice.

The notice required by G.S. 50A-4 shall be given in a manner reasonably calculated to give actual notice and shall be served in the same manner as the manner of service of process set out in G.S. 1A-1, Rule 4. Proof of the service of the notice required by G.S. 50A-4 shall be made in the same manner as the manner to prove the service of process set out in G.S. 1A-1, Rule 4.

§ 50A-6. Simultaneous proceedings in other states.

(a) If at the time of filing the petition a proceeding concerning the custody of the child was pending in a court of another state exercising jurisdiction substantially in conformity with this Chapter, a court of this State shall not exercise its jurisdiction under this Chapter, unless the proceeding is stayed by the court of the other state because this State is a more appropriate forum or for other reasons.

(b) Before hearing the petition in a custody proceeding the court shall examine the pleadings and other information supplied by the parties under G.S. 50A-9 and shall consult the child custody registry established under G.S. 50A-16 concerning the pendency of proceedings with respect to the child in other states. If the court has reason to believe that proceedings may be pending in another state it shall direct an inquiry to the state court administrator or other appropriate official of the other state.

(c) If the court is informed during the course of the proceeding that a proceeding concerning the custody of the child was pending in another state before the court assumed jurisdiction it shall stay the proceeding and communicate with the court in which the other proceeding is pending to the end that the issue may be litigated in the more appropriate forum and that information be exchanged in accordance with G.S. 50A-19 through G.S. 50A-22. If a court of this State has made a custody decree before being informed of a pending proceeding in a court of another state it shall immediately inform that court of the fact. If the court is informed that a proceeding was commenced in another state after it assumed jurisdiction it shall likewise inform the other court to the end that the issues may be litigated in the more appropriate forum.

§ 50A-7. Inconvenient forum.

(a) A court which has jurisdiction under this Chapter to make an initial or modification decree may decline to exercise its jurisdiction any time before making a decree if it finds that it is an inconvenient forum to make a custody determination under the circumstances of the case and that a court of another state is a more appropriate forum.

(b) A finding of inconvenient forum may be made upon the court's own motion or upon motion of a party or a guardian ad litem or other representative of the child.

(c) In determining if it is an inconvenient forum, the court shall consider if it is in the interest of the child that another state assume jurisdiction. For this purpose it may take into account the following factors, among others:

(1) If another state is or recently was the child's home state;

(2) If another state has a closer connection with the child and the child's family or with the child and one or more of the contestants;

(3) If substantial evidence relevant to the child's present or future care, protection, training, and personal relationships is more readily available in another state;

(4) If the parties have agreed on another forum which is no less appropriate; and

(5) If the exercise of jurisdiction by a court of this State would contravene any of the purposes stated in G.S. 50A-1.

(d) Before determining whether to decline or retain jurisdiction the court may communicate with a court of another state and exchange information pertinent to the assumption of jurisdiction by either court with a view to assuring that jurisdiction will be exercised by the more appropriate court and that a forum will be available to the parties.

(e) If the court finds that it is an inconvenient forum and that a court of another state is a more appropriate forum, it may dismiss the proceedings, or it may stay the proceedings upon condition that a custody proceeding be promptly commenced in another named state or upon any other conditions which may be just and proper, including the condition that a moving party stipulate such party's consent and submission to the jurisdiction of the other forum.

(f) The court may decline to exercise its jurisdiction under this Chapter if a custody determination is incidental to an action for divorce or another proceeding while retaining jurisdiction over the divorce or other proceeding.

(g) If it appears to the court that it is clearly an inappropriate forum it may require the party who commenced the proceedings to pay, in addition to the costs of the proceedings in this State, necessary travel and other expenses including attorneys' fees, incurred by other parties or their witnesses. Payment is to be made to the clerk of the court for remittance to the proper party.

(h) Upon dismissal or stay of proceedings under this section the court shall inform the court found to be the more appropriate forum of this fact, or if the court which would have jurisdiction in the other state is not certainly known, shall transmit the information to the court administrator or other appropriate official for forwarding to the appropriate court.

(i) Any communication received from another state informing this State of a finding of inconvenient forum because a court of this State is the more appropriate forum shall be filed in the custody registry of the appropriate court. Upon assuming jurisdiction the court of this State shall inform the original court of this fact.

§ 50A-8. Jurisdiction declined by reason of conduct.

(a) If the petitioner for an initial decree has wrongfully taken the child from another state or has engaged in similar reprehensible conduct the court may decline to exercise jurisdiction if this is just and proper under the circumstances.

(b) Unless required in the interest of the child, the court shall not exercise its jurisdiction to modify a custody decree of another state if the petitioner, without consent of the person entitled to custody, has improperly removed the child from the physical custody of the person entitled to custody or has improperly retained the child after a visit or other temporary relinquishment of physical custody. If the petitioner has violated any other provision of a custody decree of another state the court may decline to exercise its jurisdiction if this is just and proper under the circumstances.

(c) In appropriate cases a court dismissing a petition under this section may charge the petitioner with necessary travel and other expenses, including attorneys' fees, incurred by other parties or their witnesses.

§ 50A-9. Information under oath to be submitted to the court.

(a) Every party in a custody proceeding in such party's first pleading or in an affidavit attached to that pleading shall give information under oath as to the child's present address, the places where the child has lived within the last five years, and the names and present addresses of the persons with whom the child has lived during that period. In this pleading or affidavit every party shall further declare under oath whether:

(1) Such party has participated as party, witness, or in any other capacity in any other litigation concerning the custody of the same child in this or any other state;

(2) Such party has information of any custody proceeding concerning the child pending in a court of this or any other state; and

(3) Such party knows of any person not a party to the proceedings who has physical custody of the child or claims to have custody or visitation rights with respect to the child.

(b) If the declaration as to any of the above items is in the affirmative the declaration shall give additional information under oath as required by the court. The court may examine the parties under oath as required by the court. The court may examine the parties under oath as to details of the information furnished and as to other matters pertinent to the court's jurisdiction and the disposition of the case.

(c) Each party has a continuing duty to inform the court of any custody proceeding concerning the child in this or any other state of which such party obtained information during this proceeding.

§ 50A-10. Additional parties.

If the court learns from information furnished by the parties pursuant to G.S. 50A-9 or from other sources that a person not a party to the custody proceeding has physical custody of the child or claims to have custody or visitation rights with respect to the child, it shall order that person to be joined as a party and to be duly notified of the pendency of the proceeding and of such person's joinder as a party. Such person shall be served with process or otherwise notified in accordance with process or otherwise notified in accordance with G.S. 50A-5.

§ 50A-11. Appearance of parties and the child.

(a) The court may order any party to the proceeding to appear personally before the court. If that party has physical custody of the child, the court may order that such party appear personally with the child.

(b) The court may order that the notice given under G.S. 50A-5 include a statement directing that party to appear personally with or without the child and declaring that failure to appear may result in a decision adverse to that party.

(c) If a party to the proceeding who is outside this State is directed to appear under subsection (b) or desires to appear personally before the court with or without the child, the court may require another party to pay to the clerk of the court travel and other necessary expenses of the party so appearing and of the child if this is just and proper under the circumstances.

§ 50A-12. Binding force and res judicata effect of custody decree.

A custody decree rendered by a court of this State which has jurisdiction under G.S. 50A-3 binds all parties who have been served or notified in accordance with G.S. 50A-5 or who have submitted to the jurisdiction of the court, and who have been given an opportunity to be heard. As to those parties, the custody decree is conclusive as to all issues of law and fact decided and as to the custody determination made unless and until that determination is modified pursuant to law, including the provisions of this Chapter.

§ 50A-13. Recognition of out-of-state custody decrees.

The courts of this State shall recognize and enforce an initial or modification decree of a court of another state which had assumed jurisdiction under statutory provisions substantially in accordance with this Chapter or which was made under factual circumstances meeting the jurisdictional standards of this Chapter, so long as that decree has not been modified in accordance with jurisdictional standards substantially similar to those of this Chapter.

§ 50A-14. Modification of custody decree of another state.

(a) If a court of another state has made a custody decree, a court of this State shall not modify that decree unless (1) it appears to the court of this State that the court which rendered the decree does not now have jurisdiction under jurisdictional prerequisites substantially in accordance with this Chapter or has declined to assume jurisdiction to modify the decree and (2) the court of this State has jurisdiction.

(b) If a court of this State is authorized under subsection (a) and G.S. 50A-8 to modify a custody decree of another state it shall give due consideration to the transcript of the record and other documents of all previous proceedings submitted to it in accordance with G.S. 50A-22.

§ 50A-15. Filing and enforcement of custody decree of another state.

(a) An exemplified copy of a custody decree of another state may be filed in the office of the clerk of any superior court of this State. The clerk shall treat the decree in the same manner as a custody decree of a court of this State. A custody decree so filed has the same effect and shall be enforced in like manner as a custody decree rendered by a court of this State.

(b) A person violating a custody decree of another state which makes it necessary to enforce the decree in this State may be required to pay necessary travel and other expenses, including attorneys' fees, incurred by the party entitled to the custody or such party's witnesses.

§ 50A-16. Registry of out-of-state custody decrees and proceedings.

The clerk of each superior court shall maintain a registry in which he shall enter the following:

(1) Exemplified copies of custody decrees of other states received for filing;

(2) Communications as to the pendency of custody proceedings in other states;

(3) Communications concerning a finding of inconvenient forum by a court of another state; and

(4) Other communications or documents concerning custody proceedings in another state which may affect the jurisdiction of a court of this State or the disposition to be made by it in a custody proceeding.

§ 50A-17. Certified copies of custody decree.

The clerk of a superior court of this State, at the request of the court of another state or at the request of any person who is affected by or has a legitimate interest in a custody decree, shall certify and forward a copy of the decree to that court or person.

§ 50A-18. Taking testimony in another state.

In addition to other procedural devices available to a party, any party to the proceeding or a guardian ad litem or other representative of the child may adduce testimony of witnesses, including parties and the child, by deposition or otherwise, in another state. The court on its own motion may direct that the testimony of a person be taken in another state and may prescribe the manner in which and the terms upon which the testimony shall be taken.

§ 50A-19. Hearings and studies in another state; orders to appear.

(a) A court of this State may request the appropriate court of another state to hold a hearing to adduce evidence, to order a party to produce or give evidence under other procedures of that state; and to forward to the court of this State certified copies of the transcript of the record of the hearing, and the evidence otherwise adduced. The cost of the services may be assessed against the parties in the discretion of the court.

(b) A court of this State may request the appropriate court of another state to order a person notified under the provisions of G.S. 50A-4 in a custody proceeding pending in the court of this State to appear in the proceedings, and if that person has physical custody of the child, to appear with the child. The request may state that travel and other necessary expenses of the party and of the child whose appearance is desired will be assessed against another party or will otherwise be paid.

§ 50A-20. Assistance to courts of other states.

(a) Upon request of the court of another state the courts of this State which are authorized to hear custody matters may order a person in this State to appear at a hearing to adduce evidence or to produce or give evidence under other procedures available in this State or may order social studies to be made for use in a custody proceeding in another state. A certified copy of the transcript of the record of the hearing or other evidence otherwise adduced and any social studies prepared shall be forwarded by the clerk of the court to the requesting court.

(b) A person within this State may voluntarily give testimony or a statement in this State for use in a custody proceeding outside this State.

(c) Upon request of the court of another state a competent court of this State may order a person in this State to appear alone or with the child in a custody proceeding in another state. The court may condition compliance with the request upon assurance by the other state that state travel and other necessary expenses will be advanced or reimbursed.

§ 50A-21. Preservation of documents for use in other states.

In any custody proceeding in this State the court shall preserve the pleadings, orders and decrees, any record that has been made of its hearings, and other pertinent documents until the child reaches 18 years of age. Upon appropriate request of the court of another state the court shall forward to the other court certified copies of any or all of such documents.

§ 50A-22. Request for court records or another state.

If a custody decree has been rendered in another state concerning a child involved in a custody proceeding pending in a court of this State, the court of this State upon taking jurisdiction of the case may request of the court of the other state a certified copy of the transcript of any court record and other documents mentioned in G.S. 50A-21.

§ 50A-23. International application.

The general policies of this Chapter extend to the international area. The provisions of this Chapter relating to the recognition and enforcement of custody decrees of other states apply to custody decrees and decrees involving legal institutions similar in nature to custody institutions rendered by appropriate authorities of other nations if reasonable notice and opportunity to be heard were given to all affected persons.

§ 50A-24. Short title.

This Chapter may be cited as the "Uniform Child Custody Jurisdiction Act."

§ 50A-25. Emergency orders.

Nothing in this Chapter shall be interpreted to limit the authority of the court to issue an interlocutory order under the provisions of G.S. 50-13.5(d)(2); or an immediate custody order under the provisions of G.S. 7A-284.

NORTH DAKOTA

UNIFORM CHILD CUSTODY JURISDICTION ACT

§ 14-14-01. Purposes of chapter — Construction of provisions.

1. The general purposes of this chapter are to:

a. Avoid jurisdictional competition and conflict with courts of other states in matters of child custody which have in the past resulted in the shifting of children from state to state with harmful effects on their well-being;

b. Promote cooperation with the courts of other states to the end that a custody decree is rendered in that state which can best decide the case in the interest of the child;

c. Assure that litigation concerning the custody of a child takes place ordinarily in the state with which the child and his family have the closest connection and where significant evidence concerning his care, protection, training, and personal relationships is most readily available, and that courts of this state decline the exercise of jurisdiction when the child and his family have a closer connection with another state;

d. Discourage continuing controversies over child custody in the interest of greater stability of home environment and of secure family relationships for the child;

e. Deter abductions and other unilateral removals of children undertaken to obtain custody awards;

f. Avoid relitigation of custody decisions of other states in this state insofar as feasible;

g. Facilitate the enforcement of custody decrees of other states;

h. Promote and expand the exchange of information and other forms of mutual assistance between the courts of this state and those of other states concerned with the same child; and

i. Make uniform the law of those states which enact it.

2. This chapter shall be construed to promote the general purposes stated in this section.

§ 14-14-02. Definitions.

As used in this chapter:

1. "Contestant" means a person, including a parent, who claims a right to custody or visitation rights with respect to a child.

2. "Custody determination" means a court decision and court orders and instructions providing for the custody of a child, including visitation rights; it does not include a decision relating to child support or any other monetary obligation of any person.

3. "Custody proceeding" includes proceedings in which a custody determination is one of several issues, such as an action for divorce or separation, and includes child neglect, dependency, and deprivation proceedings.

4. "Decree" or "custody decree" means a custody determination contained in a judicial decree or order made in a custody proceeding, and includes an initial decree and modification decree.

5. "Home state" means the state in which the child immediately preceding the time involved lived with his parents, a parent, or a person acting as parent, for at least six consecutive months, and in the case of a child less than six months old the state in which the child lived from birth with any of the persons mentioned. Periods of temporary absence of any of the named persons are counted as part of the six-month or other period.

6. "Initial decree" means the first custody decree concerning a particular child.

7. "Modification decree" means a custody decree which modifies or replaces a prior decree, whether made by the court which rendered the prior decree or by another court.

8. "Physical custody" means actual possession and control of a child.

9. "Person acting as parent" means a person, other than a parent, who has physical custody of a child and who has either been awarded custody by a court or claims a right to custody.

10. "State" means any state, territory, or possession of the United States, the Commonwealth of Puerto Rico, and the District of Columbia.

§ 14-14-03. Jurisdiction.

1. A court of this state which is competent to decide child custody matters has jurisdiction to make a child custody determination by initial decree or modification decree if:

a. This state (1) is the home state of the child at the time of commencement of the proceeding, or (2) had been the child's home state within six months before commencement of the proceeding and the child is absent from this state because of his removal or retention by a person claiming his custody or for other reasons, and a parent or person acting as a parent continues to live in this state;

b. It is in the best interest of the child that a court of this state assume jurisdiction because (1) the child and his parents, or the child and at least one contestant, have a significant connection with this state, and (2) there is available in this state substantial evidence concerning the child's present or future care, protection, training, and personal relationships;

c. The child is physically present in this state and (1) the child has been abandoned or (2) it is necessary in an emergency to protect the child because he has been subjected to or threatened with mistreatment or abuse or is otherwise neglected, dependent, or

d. (1) It appears that no other state would have jurisdiction under prerequisites substantially in accordance with subdivision a, b, or c, or another state has declined to exercise jurisdiction on the ground that this state is the more appropriate forum to determine the custody of the child, and (2) it is in the best interest of the child that this court assume jurisdiction.

2. Except under subdivisions c and d of subsection 1, physical presence in this state of the child, or of the child and one of the contestants, is not alone sufficient to confer jurisdiction on a court of this state to make a child custody determination.

3. Physical presence of the child, while desirable, is not a prerequisite for jurisdiction to determine his custody.

§ 14-14-04. Notice and opportunity to be heard.

Before making a decree under this chapter, reasonable notice and opportunity to be heard shall be previously terminated, and any person who has physical custody of the child. If any of these persons are outside this state, notice and opportunity to be heard shall be given pursuant to section 14-14-05.

§ 14-14-05. Notice to persons outside the state — Submission to jurisdiction.

1. Notice required for the exercise of jurisdiction over a person outside this state shall be given in a manner reasonably calculated to give actual notice, and may be:

a. By personal delivery outside this state in the manner prescribed for service of process within this state;

b. In the manner prescribed by the law of the place in which the service is made for service of process in that place in an action in any of its courts of general jurisdiction;

c. By any form of mail addressed to the person to be served and requesting a receipt; or

d. As directed by the court, including publication, if other means of notification are ineffective.

2. Notice under this section shall be served, mailed, delivered, or last published at least twenty days before any hearing in this state.

3. Proof of service outside this state may be made by affidavit of the individual who made the service, or in the manner prescribed by the law of this state, the order pursuant to which the service is made, or the law of the place in which the service is made. If service is made by mail, proof may be a receipt signed by the addressee or other evidence of delivery to the addressee.

4. Notice is not required if a person submits to the jurisdiction of the court.

§ 14-14-06. Simultaneous proceedings in other states.

1. A court of this state shall not exercise its jurisdiction under this chapter if at the time of filing the petition a proceeding concerning the custody of the child was pending in a court of another state exercising jurisdiction substantially in conformity with this chapter, unless the proceeding is stayed by the court of the other state because this state is a more appropriate forum or for other reasons.

2. Before hearing the petition in a custody proceeding, the court shall examine the pleadings and other information supplied by the parties under section 14-14-09 and shall consult the child custody registry established under section 14-14-16 concerning the pendency of proceedings with respect to the child in other states. If the court has reason to believe that proceedings may be pending in another state, it shall direct an inquiry to the state court administrator or other appropriate official of the other state.

3. If the court is informed during the course of the proceeding that a proceeding concerning the custody of the child was pending in another state before the court assumed jurisdiction, it shall stay the proceeding and communicate with the court in which the other proceeding is pending to the end that the issues may be litigated in the more appropriate forum and that information be exchanged in accordance with sections 14-14-19 through 14-14-22. If a court of this state has made a decree before being informed of a pending proceeding in a court of another state, it shall immediately inform that court of the fact. If the court is informed that a proceeding was commenced in another state after it assumed jurisdiction, it shall likewise inform the other court to the end that the issues may be litigated in the most appropriate forum.

§ 14-14-07. Inconvenient forum.

1. A court which has jurisdiction under this chapter to make an initial decree or a modification decree may decline to exercise its jurisdiction any time before making a decree if it finds that it is an inconvenient forum to make a custody determination under the circumstances of the case and that a court of another state is a more appropriate forum.

2. A finding of inconvenient forum may be made upon the court's own motion or upon motion of a party or of a guardian ad litem or other representative of the child.

3. In determining whether it is an inconvenient forum, the court shall consider whether it is in the interest of the child that another state assume jurisdiction. For this purpose it may take into account the following factors, among others, whether:

a. Another state is or recently was the child's home state;

b. Another state has a closer connection with the child and his family or with the child and one or more of the contestants;

c. Substantial evidence concerning the child's present or future care, protection, training, and personal relationships is more readily available in another state;

    d. The parties have agreed on another forum which is no less appropriate; and

    e. The exercise of jurisdiction by a court of this state would contravene any of the purposes stated in section 14-14-01.

4. Before determining whether to decline or retain jurisdiction, the court may communicate with a court of another state and exchange information pertinent to the assumption of jurisdiction by either court with a view to assuring that jurisdiction will be exercised by the more appropriate court and that a forum will be available to the parties.

5. If the court finds that it is an inconvenient forum and that a court of another state is a more appropriate forum, it may (a) dismiss the proceedings, or (b) stay the proceedings upon condition that a custody proceeding be promptly commenced in another named state or upon any other conditions which may be just and proper, including the condition that a moving party stipulate his consent and submission to the jurisdiction of the other forum.

6. The court may decline to exercise its jurisdiction under this chapter if a custody determination is incidental to an action for divorce or another proceeding while retaining jurisdiction over the divorce or other proceeding.

7. If it appears to the court that it is clearly an inappropriate forum, it may require the party who commenced the proceedings to pay, in addition to the costs of the proceedings in this state, necessary travel and other expenses, including attorney's fees, incurred by other parties or their witnesses. Payment is to be made to the clerk of the court for remittance to the proper party.

8. Upon dismissal or stay of proceedings under this section, the court shall inform the court found to be the more appropriate forum of this fact or, if the court which would have jurisdiction in the other state is not certainly known, shall transmit the information to the court administrator or other appropriate official for forwarding to the appropriate court.

9. Any communication received from another state informing this state of a finding of inconvenient forum because a court of this state is the more appropriate forum shall be filed in the custody registry of the appropriate court. Upon assuming jurisdiction, the court of this state shall inform the original court of this fact.

§ 14-14-08. Jurisdiction declined by reason of conduct.

1. If the petitioner for an initial decree has wrongfully taken the child from another state or has engaged in similar reprehensible conduct, the court may decline to exercise jurisdiction if this is just and proper under the circumstances.

2. Unless required in the interest of the child, the court shall not exercise its jurisdiction to modify a custody decree of another state if the petitioner, without consent of the person entitled to custody, has improperly removed the child from the physical custody of the person entitled to custody or has improperly retained the child after a visit or other temporary relinquishment of physical custody. If the petitioner has violated any other provision of a custody decree of another state, the court may decline to exercise its jurisdiction if this is just and proper under the circumstances.

3. In appropriate cases a court dismissing a petition under this section may charge the petitioner with necessary travel and other expenses, including attorney's fees, incurred by other parties or their witnesses.

§ 14-14-09. Information under oath to be submitted to the court.

1. Every party in a custody proceeding in his first pleading or in an affidavit attached to that pleading shall give information under oath as to the child's present address, the places where the child has lived within the last five years, and the names and present addresses of the persons with whom the child has lived during that period. In this pleading or affidavit every party shall further declare under oath whether he:

    a. Has participated (as a party, witness, or in any other capacity) in any other litigation concerning the custody of the same child in this or any other state;

    b. Has information of any custody proceeding concerning the child pending in a court of this or any other state; and

    c. Knows of any person not a party to the proceedings who has physical custody of the child or claims to have custody or visitation rights with respect to the child.

2. If the declaration as to any of the above items is in the affirmative, the declarant shall give additional information under oath as required by the court. The court may examine the parties under oath as to details of the information furnished and as to other matters pertinent to the court's jurisdiction and the disposition of the case.

3. Each party has a continuing duty to inform the court of any custody proceeding concerning the child in this or any other state of which he obtained information during this proceeding.

§ 14-14-10. Additional parties.

If the court learns from information furnished by the parties pursuant to section 14-14-09 or from other sources that a person not a party to the custody proceeding has physical custody of the child or claims to have custody or visitation rights with respect to the child, it shall order that person to be joined as a party and to be duly notified of the pendency of the proceeding and of his joinder as a party. If the person joined as a party is outside this state, he shall be served with process or otherwise notified in accordance with section 14-14-05.

§ 14-14-11. Appearance of parties and the child.

1. The court may order any party to the proceeding who is in this state to appear personally before the court. If that party has

physical custody of the child, the court may order that he appear personally with the child.

2. If a party to the proceeding whose presence is desired by the court is outside this state with or without the child, the court may order that the notice given under section 14-14-05 include a statement directing that party to appear personally with or without the child and declaring that failure to appear may result in a decision adverse to that party.

3. If a party to the proceeding who is outside this state is directed to appear under subsection 2 or desires to appear personally before the court with or without the child, the court may require another party to pay to the clerk of the court travel and other necessary expenses of the party so appearing and of the child if this is just and proper under the circumstances.

§ 14-14-12. Binding force and res judicata effect of custody decree.

A custody decree rendered by a court of this state which had jurisdiction under section 14-14-03 bind all parties who have been served in this state or notified in accordance with section 14-14-05 or who have submitted to the jurisdiction of the court, and who have been given an opportunity to be heard. As to these parties the custody decree is conclusive as to all issues of law and fact decided and as to the custody determination made unless and until that determination is modified pursuant to law, including the provisions of this chapter.

§ 14-14-13. Recognition of out-of-state custody decrees.

The courts of this state shall recognize and enforce an initial decree or modification decree of a court of another state which had assumed jurisdiction under statutory provisions substantially in accordance with this chapter or which was made under factual circumstances meeting the jurisdictional standards of this chapter, so long as this decree has not been modified in accordance with jurisdictional standards substantially similar to those of this chapter.

§ 14-14-14. Modification of custody decree of another state.

1. If a court of another state has made a custody decree, a court of this state shall not modify that decree unless (a) it appears to the court of this state that the court which rendered the decree does not now have jurisdiction under jurisdictional prerequisites substantially in accordance with this chapter or has declined to assume jurisdiction to modify the decree and (b) the court of this state has jurisdiction.

2. If a court of this state is authorized under subsection 1 and section 14-14-08 to modify a custody decree of another state, it shall give due consideration to the transcript of the record and other documents of all previous proceedings submitted to it in accordance with section 14-14-22.

§ 14-14-15. Filing and enforcement of custody decree of another state.

1. A certified copy of a custody decree of another state may be filed in the office of the clerk of any district court or family court of this state. The clerk shall treat the decree in the same manner as a custody decree of the district court or family court of this state. A custody decree so filed has the same effect and shall be enforced in like manner as a custody decree rendered by a court of this state.

2. A person violating a custody decree of another state which makes it necessary to enforce the decree in this state may be required to pay necessary travel and other expenses, including attorney's fees, incurred by the party entitled to the custody or his witnesses.

§ 14-14-16. Registry of out-of-state decrees and proceedings.

The clerk of each district court or family court shall maintain a registry in which he shall enter the following:

1. Certified copies of custody decrees of other states received for filing.

2. Communications as to the pendency of custody proceedings in other states.

3. Communications concerning a finding of inconvenient forum by a court of another state.

4. Other communications or documents concerning custody proceedings in another state which may affect the jurisdiction of a court of this state or the disposition to be made by it in a custody proceeding.

§ 14-14-17. Certified copies of custody decrees.

The clerk of the district court or family court of this state, at the request of the court of another state or at the request of any person who is affected by or has a legitimate interest in a custody decree, shall certify and forward a copy of the decree to that court or person. ﹨

§ 14-14-18. Taking testimony in another state.

In addition to other procedural devices available to a party, any party to the proceeding or a guardian ad litem or other representative of the child may adduce testimony of witnesses, including parties and the child, by deposition or otherwise, in another state. The court on its own motion may direct that the testimony of a person be taken in another state and may prescribe the manner in which and the terms upon which the testimony shall be taken.

§ 14-14-19. Hearings and studies in another state — Orders to appear.

1. A court of this state may request the appropriate court of another state to hold a hearing to adduce evidence, to order a party to produce or give evidence under other procedures of that state, or to have social studies made with respect to the custody of a child involved in proceedings pending in the court of this state and to forward to the court of this state certified copies of the transcript of the record of the hearing, the evidence otherwise adduced, or any social studies prepared in compliance with the request. The cost of the services may be assessed against the parties or, if necessary, ordered paid by the county of the residence of the child for public assistance purposes.

2. A court of this state may request the appropriate court of another state to order a party to custody proceedings pending in the court of this state to appear in the proceedings and, if that party has physical custody of the child, to appear with the child. The request may state that travel and other necessary expenses of the party and of the child whose appearance is desired will be assessed against another party or will otherwise be paid.

§ 14-14-20. Assistance to courts of other states.

1. Upon request of the court of another state the courts of this state which are competent to hear custody matters may order a person in this state to appear at a hearing to adduce evidence or to produce or give evidence under other procedures available in this state or may order social studies to be made for use in a custody proceeding in another state. A certified copy of the transcript of the record of the hearing or the evidence otherwise adduced and any social studies prepared shall be forwarded by the clerk of the court to the requesting court.

2. A person within this state may voluntarily give his testimony or statement in this state for use in a custody proceeding outside this state.

3. Upon request of the court of another state, a competent court of this state may order a person in this state to appear alone or with the child in a custody proceeding in another state. The court may condition compliance with the request upon assurance by the other state that travel and other necessary expenses will be advanced or reimbursed.

§ 14-14-21. Preservation of documents for use in other states.

In any custody proceeding in this state the court shall preserve the pleadings, orders, and decrees, any record that has been made of its hearings, social studies, and other pertinent documents until the child becomes an adult. Upon appropriate request of the court of another state the court shall forward to the other court certified copies of any or all of such documents.

§ 14-14-22. Request for court records of another state.

If a custody decree has been rendered in another state concerning a child involved in a custody proceeding pending in a court of this state, the court of this state upon taking jurisdiction of the case shall request of the court of the other state a certified copy of the transcript of any court record and other documents mentioned in section 14-14-21.

§ 14-14-22.1. Removal of child from state in violation of custody decree — Penalty.

Any person who intentionally removes, causes the removal of, or detains his or her own child under the age of eighteen years outside North Dakota with the intent to deny another person's rights under an existing custody decree shall be guilty of a class C felony. Detaining the child outside North Dakota in violation of the custody decree for more than seventy-two hours shall be prima facie evidence that the person charged intended to violate the custody decree at the time of removal.

§ 14-14-23. International application.

The general policies of this chapter extend to the international area. The provisions of this chapter relating to the recognition and enforcement of custody decrees of other states apply to custody decrees and decrees involving legal institutions similar in nature to custody institutions rendered by appropriate authorities of other nations if reasonable notice and opportunity to be heard were given to all affected persons.

§ 14-14-24. Priority.

Upon the request of a party to a custody proceeding which raises a question of existence or exercise of jurisdiction under this chapter, the case shall be given calendar priority and handled expeditiously.

§ 14-14-25. Severability.

If any provision of this chapter or the application thereof to any person or circumstance is held invalid, its invalidity does not affect other provisions or applications of the chapter which can be given effect without the invalid provision or application, and to this end the provisions of this chapter are severable.

§ 14-14-26. Short title.

This chapter may be cited as the Uniform Child Custody Jurisdiction Act.

OHIO

UNIFORM CHILD CUSTODY JURISDICTION LAW

§ 3109.21. Definitions.

As used in sections 3109.21 to 3109.37 of the Revised Code:

(A) "Contestant" means a person, including a parent, who claims a right to custody or visitation rights with respect to a child.

(B) "Custody determination" means a court decision and court orders and instructions providing for the custody of a child, including visitation rights. It does not include a decision relating to child support or any other monetary obligation of any person.

(C) "Custody proceeding" includes proceedings in which a custody determination is one of several issues, such as an action for divorce or separation, and includes child neglect and dependency proceedings.

(D) "Decree" or "custody decree" means a custody determination contained in a judicial decree or order made in a custody proceeding, and includes an initial decree and a modification decree.

(E) "Home state" means the state in which the child, immediately preceding the time involved, lived with his parents, a parent, or a person acting as parent, for at least six consecutive months, and in the case of a child less than six months old the state in which the child lived from birth with any of the persons mentioned. Periods of temporary absence of any of the named persons are counted as part of the six-month or other period.

(F) "Initial decree" means the first custody decree concerning a particular child.

(G) "Modification decree" means a custody decree that modifies or replaces a prior decree, whether made by the court that rendered the prior decree or by another court.

(H) "Physical custody" means actual possession and control of a child.

(I) "Person acting as parent" means a person, other than a parent, who has physical custody of a child and who has either been awarded custody by a court or claims a right to custody.

§ 3109.22. Prerequisites to jurisdiction.

(A) No court of this state having jurisdiction to determine the custody of a child shall exercise that jurisdiction unless one of the following applies:

(1) This state is the home state of the child at the time of commencement of the proceeding, or this state had been the child's home state within six months before commencement of the proceeding and the child is absent from this state because of his removal or retention by a person claiming his custody or for other reasons, and a parent or person acting as parent continues to live in this state;

(2) It is in the best interest of the child that a court of this state assumes jurisdiction because the child and his parents, or the child and at least one contestant, have a significant connection with this state, and there is available in this state substantial evidence concerning the child's present or future care, protection, training, and personal relationships;

(3) The child is physically present in this state and either has been abandoned or it is necessary in an emergency to protect the child because he has been subjected to or threatened with mistreatment or abuse or is otherwise neglected or dependent;

(4) It appears that no other state would have jurisdiction under prerequisites substantially in accordance with division (A)(1), (2), or (3) of this section, or a court in another state has declined to exercise jurisdiction on the ground this state is the more appropriate forum to determine the custody of the child, and it is in the best interest of the child that his court assume jurisdiction.

(B) Except as provided in divisions (A)(3) and (4) of this section, physical presence in this state of the child, or of the child and one of the contestants, is not alone sufficient to confer jurisdiction on a court of this state to make a child custody determination.

(C) Physical presence of the child, while desirable, is not a prerequisite for jurisdiction to determine his custody.

§ 3109.23. Notice of custody proceeding; proof of service.

(A) Before making a custody decree, the court shall give reasonable notice of the custody proceeding and opportunity to be heard to the contestants, any parent whose parental rights have not been previously terminated, and any person or public agency who has physical custody of the child. If any of these persons or the public agency is outside this state, notice and opportunity to be heard shall be given in accordance with division (B) of this section.

(B) Notice required for the exercise of jurisdiction over a person or public agency outside this state shall be given either in accordance with the Rules of Civil Procedure governing service of process within this state or by one of the following methods:

(1) In the manner prescribed by the law of the place in which the service is made for service of process in that place in an action in any of its courts of general jurisdiction;

(2) As directed by the court, including publication, if other means of notification are ineffective.

(C) Notice under division (B) of this section shall be served, mailed, delivered, or last published at least twenty days before any hearing in this state.

(D) Proof of service outside this state may be made by affidavit of the individual who made the service, or in the manner prescribed by the Rules of Civil Procedure governing service of process within this state, the order pursuant to which the service is made, or the law of the place in which the service is made. If service is made by mail, proof may be a receipt signed by the addressee or other evidence of delivery to the addressee.

(E) Notice is not required if a person submits to the jurisdiction of the court.

§ 3109.24. Pendency of proceedings in another state.

(A) A court of this state shall not exercise its jurisdiction, if at the time of filing the petition a custody proceeding concerning the child was pending in a court of another state exercising jurisdiction substantially in conformity with sections 3109.21 to 3109.36 of the Revised Code, unless the proceeding is stayed by the court of the other state because this state is a more appropriate forum or for other reasons.

(B) Before hearing the petition in a custody proceeding, the court shall examine the pleadings and other information supplied by the parties under section 3109.27 of the Revised Code and shall consult the child custody registry established under division (A) of section 3109.33 of the Revised Code concerning the pendency of custody proceedings with respect to the child in other states. If the court has reason to believe that custody proceedings may be pending in another state, it shall direct an inquiry to the state court administrator or other appropriate official of the other state.

(C) If a court is informed during the court of a custody proceeding that a custody proceeding concerning the child was pending in a court of another state before the court assumed jurisdiction, it shall stay the proceeding and communicate with the court in which the other proceeding is pending for the purpose of litigating the issue in the more appropriate forum and to ensure that information is exchanged in accordance with sections 3109.34 to 3109.36 of the Revised Code. If a court of this state has made a custody decree before being informed of a pending proceeding in a court of another state, it shall immediately inform that court of the fact. If a court of this state is informed that a proceeding was commenced in another state after it assumed jurisdiction, it shall inform the other court for the purpose of litigating the issues in the more appropriate forum.

§ 3109.25. Inconvenient forum; more appropriate forum.

(A) A court that has jurisdiction to make an initial or modification decree may decline to exercise its jurisdiction any time before making a decree if it finds that it is an inconvenient forum to make a custody determination under the circumstances of the case and that a court of another state is a more appropriate forum.

(B) A finding of inconvenient forum may be made upon the court's own motion or upon motion of a party or a guardian ad litem or other representative of the child.

(C) In determining if it is an inconvenient forum, the court shall consider if it is in the interest of the child that another state assume jurisdiction. For this purpose it may take into account, but is not limited to, any of the following factors:

(1) If another state is or recently was the child's home state;

(2) If another state has a closer connection with the child and his family or with the child and one or more of the contestants;

(3) If substantial evidence concerning the child's present or future care, protection, training, and personal relationships is more readily available in another state;

(4) If the parties have agreed on another forum that is no less appropriate.

(D) Before determining whether to decline or retain jurisdiction, the court may communicate with a court of another state and exchange information pertinent to the assumption of jurisdiction by either court for the purpose of assuring that jurisdiction is exercised by the more appropriate court and that a forum is available to the parties.

(E) If the court finds that it is an inconvenient forum and that a court of another state is a more appropriate forum, it may dismiss the proceedings, or may stay the proceedings upon condition that a custody proceeding be promptly commenced in another named state or upon any other conditions that may be just and proper, including the condition that a moving party stipulate his consent and submission to the jurisdiction of the other forum.

(F) The court may decline to exercise its jurisdiction, if a custody determination is incidental to an action for divorce or another proceeding, while retaining jurisdiction over the divorce or other proceeding.

(G) If it appears to the court that it is clearly an inappropriate forum, it may require the party who commenced the proceedings to pay, in addition to the costs of the proceedings in this state, necessary travel and other expenses, including attorney's fees, incurred by other parties or their witnesses. Payment shall be made to the clerk of the court for remittance to the proper party.

(H) Upon dismissal or stay of proceedings under this section, the court shall inform the court found to be the more appropriate forum of this fact, or if the court which would have jurisdiction in the other state is not certainly known, shall transmit the information to the clerk of the court for forwarding to the appropriate court.

(I) Any communication received from another state informing this state of a finding of inconvenient forum because a court of this state is the more appropriate forum shall be filed in the custody registry of the appropriate court. Upon assuming jurisdiction, the court of this state shall inform the original court of this fact.

§ 3109.26. Improperly obtained custody.

(A) If the petitioner for an initial decree has wrongfully taken the child from another state or has engaged in similar conduct, the court may decline to exercise jurisdiction, if this is just and proper under the circumstances.

(B) Unless required in the interest of the child, the court shall not exercise its jurisdiction to modify a custody decree of another state if the petitioner, without consent of the person entitled to custody, has improperly removed the child from the physical custody of the person entitled to custody or has improperly retained the child after a visit or other temporary relinquishment of physical custody. If the petitioner has violated any other provision of a custody decree of another state, the court may decline to exercise its jurisdiction, if this is just and proper under the circumstances.

(C) In appropriate cases, a court dismissing a petition under this section may charge the petitioner with necessary travel and other expenses, including attorney's fees, incurred by other parties or their witnesses.

§ 3109.27. Facts to be pleaded.

(A) Every party in a custody proceeding, in his first pleading or in an affidavit attached to that pleading, shall give information under oath as to the child's present address, the places where the child has lived within the last five years, and the names and present addresses of the persons with whom the child has lived during that period. In this pleading or affidavit every party shall also include all of the following information:

(1) Whether the party has participated as a party, witness, or in any other capacity in any other litigation concerning the custody of the same child in this or any other state;

(2) Whether the party has information of any custody proceeding concerning the child pending in a court of this or any other state;

(3) Whether the party knows of any person not a party to the proceedings who has physical custody of the child or claims to have custody or visitation rights with respect to the child.

(B) If the declaration under division (A)(1), (2), or (3) of this section is in the affirmative, the court may require the declarant to give additional information under oath. The court may examine the parties under oath as to details of the information furnished and as to other matters pertinent to the court's jurisdiction and the disposition of the case.

(C) Each party has a continuing duty to inform the court of any custody proceeding concerning the child in this or any other state of which he obtained information during this proceeding.

§ 3109.28. Persons claiming rights to be made parties.

If the court learns from information furnished by the parties pursuant to section 3109.27 of the Revised Code or from other sources that a person not a party to the custody proceeding has physical custody of the child or claims to have custody or visitation rights with respect to the child, it shall order that person to be joined as a party and to be duly notified of the pendency of the proceeding and of his joinder as a party. If the person joined as a party is outside this state he shall be served with process or otherwise notified in accordance with division (B) of section 3109.23 of the Revised Code.

§ 3109.29. Personal appearance of parties may be required.

(A) The court may order any party to the proceeding who is in this state to appear personally before the court. If that party has physical custody of the child, the court may order that he appear personally with the child.

(B) If a party to the proceeding whose presence is desired by the court is outside this state with or without the child, the court may order that the notice given under division (B) of section 3109.23 of the Revised Code include a statement directing that party to appear personally with or without the child and declaring that failure to appear may result in a decision adverse to that party.

(C) If a party to the proceeding who is outside this state is directed to appear under division (B) of this section or desires to appear personally before the court with or without the child, the court may require another party to pay to the clerk of the court travel and other necessary expenses for the appearance of the party and the child who are outside this state, if this is just and proper under the circumstances.

§ 3109.30. Parties bound by decrees.

(A) A custody decree rendered by a court of this state that exercises its jurisdiction in conformity with sections 3109.21 to 3109.36 of the Revised Code binds all parties who have been served in this state or notified in accordance with division (B) of section 3109.23 of the Revised Code, or who have submitted to the jurisdiction of the court, and who have been given an opportunity to be heard. As to these parties, the custody decree is conclusive as to all issues of law and fact decided and as to the custody determination made, unless and until that determination is modified pursuant to law.

(B) The courts of this state shall recognize and enforce an initial or modification decree of a court of another state if that court assumed jurisdiction under statutory provisions substantially in accordance with sections 3109.21 to 3109.36 of the Revised Code or if the decree was made under factual circumstances meeting the jurisdictional standards of sections 3109.21 to 3109.36 of the Revised Code, so long as the decree has not been modified in accordance with jurisdictional standards substantially similar to those of these sections.

§ 3109.31. Modification of decree of another court.

(A) If a court of another state has made a custody decree, a court of this state shall not modify that decree, unless it appears to the court of this state that the court that rendered the decree does not now have jurisdiction under jurisdictional prerequisites substantially in accordance with sections 3109.21 to 3109.36 of the Revised Code, or has declined to assume jurisdiction to modify the decree, and the court of this state has jurisdiction.

(B) If a court of this state is authorized under division (A) of this section and section 3109.26 of the Revised Code to modify a custody decree of another state, it shall give due consideration to the transcript of the record and other documents of all previous proceedings submitted to it in accordance with division (B) of section 3109.36 of the Revised Code.

§ 3109.32. Filing decree from another state.

(A) A certified copy of a custody decree of another state may be filed in the office of the clerk of any court of this state that renders custody decrees. The clerk shall treat the decree in the same manner as a custody decree of an appropriate court of this state. Until modified, a custody decree so filed has the same effect and shall be enforced in like manner as a custody decree rendered by a court of this state.

(B) A person violating a custody decree of another state which makes it necessary to enforce the decree in this state may be required to pay necessary travel and other expenses, including attorney's fees, incurred by the party entitled to the custody or his witnesses.

§ 3109.34. Ancillary proceedings in other state.

(A) A court of this state may request the appropriate court of another state to hold a hearing to adduce evidence, to order a party to produce or give evidence under other procedures of that state, or to have social studies made with respect to the custody of a child involved in custody proceedings pending in the court of this state, and to forward to the court of this state certified copies of the transcript of the record of the hearing, the evidence otherwise adduced, or any social studies prepared in compliance with the request. The cost of the services may be assessed against the parties or, if necessary, paid from the county treasury and taxed as costs in the case.

(B) A court of this state may request the appropriate court of another state to order a party to custody proceedings pending in the court of this state to appear in the proceedings, and if that party has physical custody of the child, to appear with the child. The request may state that travel and other necessary expenses of the party and of the child whose appearance is desired will be assessed against another party or will otherwise be paid.

In addition to other procedural devices available to a party, any party to a custody proceeding or a guardian ad litem or other representative of the child may adduce testimony of witnesses, including parties and the child, by deposition or otherwise, in another state. The court on its own motion may direct that the testimony of a person be taken in another state and may prescribe the manner in which and the terms upon which the testimony shall be taken.

§ 3109.35. Ancillary proceedings in this state for courts of other state.

(A) Upon request of the court of another state, the courts of this state that render custody decrees may order a person in this state to appear at a hearing to adduce evidence or to produce or give evidence under other procedures available in this state or may order social studies to be made for use in a custody proceeding in another state. A certified copy of the transcript of the record of the hearing or the evidence otherwise adduced and any social studies prepared shall be forwarded by the clerk of the court to the requesting court.

(B) A person within this state may voluntarily give his testimony or statement in this state for use in a custody proceeding outside this state.

(C) Upon request of the court of another state, a court of this state may order a person in this state to appear alone or with the child in a custody proceeding in another state. The court may condition compliance with the request upon assurance by the other state that travel and other necessary expenses will be advanced or reimbursed.

§ 3109.36. Preservation and certification of records.

(A) In any custody proceeding in this state, the court shall preserve the pleadings, orders and decrees, any record that has been made of its hearings, social studies, and other pertinent documents until the child reaches eighteen years of age. Upon appropriate request of the court of another state, the court shall forward to the other court certified copies of any or all of such documents.

(B) If a custody decree has been rendered in another state concerning a child involved in a custody proceeding pending in a court of this state, the court of this state upon taking jurisdiction of the case shall request of the court of the other state a certified copy of the transcript of any court record and other documents mentioned in division (A) of this section.

§ 3109.37. Priority of handling of jurisdictional challenge.

Upon the request of a party to a custody proceeding which raises a question of existence or exercise of jurisdiction under sections 3109.21 to 3109.36 of the Revised Code, the case shall be given calendar priority and handled expeditiously.

OKLAHOMA

TITLE 10, CHAPTER 52
UNIFORM CHILD CUSTODY JURISDICTION ACT

§ 1601. Short title.
This act shall be known as the "Uniform Child Custody Jurisdiction Act".

§ 1602. Purpose of act.
The general purposes of this act are to:

1. Avoid jurisdictional competition and conflict with courts of other states in matters of child custody which have in the past resulted in the shifting of children from state to state with harmful effects on their well-being;

2. Promote cooperation with the courts of other states to the end that a custody decree is rendered in that state which can best decide the case in the interest of the child;

3. Assure that litigation concerning the custody of a child take place ordinarily in the state with which the child and his family have the closest connection and where significant evidence concerning his care, protection, training and personal relationships is most readily available, and that courts of this state decline the exercise of jurisdiction when the child and his family have a close connection with another state;

4. Discourage continuing controversies over child custody in the interest of greater stability of home environment and of secure family relationships for the child;

5. Deter abductions and other unilateral removals of children undertaken to obtain custody awards;

6. Avoid relitigation of custody decisions of other states in this state insofar as feasible;

7. Facilitate the enforcement of custody decrees of other states;

8. Promote and expand the exchange of information and other forms of mutual assistance between the courts of this state and those of other states concerned with the same child; and

9. Make uniform the law of those states which enact it.

§ 1603. Application of act.
The provisions of this act shall apply to all custody proceedings brought within this state, whether as an initial proceeding or modification, and regardless of the absence of jurisdictional dispute.

§ 1604. Definitions.
As used in this act:

1. "Contestant" means a person, including a parent, who claims a right to custody or visitation rights with respect to a child;

2. "Custody determination" means a court decision and court orders and instructions providing for the custody of a child, including visitation rights; it does not include a decision relating to child support or any other monetary obligation of any person;

3. "Custody proceeding" includes proceedings in which a custody determination is one of several issues, such as an action for divorce or separation, and includes child neglect or dependency proceedings;

4. "Decree" or "custody decree" means a custody determination contained in a judicial decree or order made in a custody proceeding, and includes an initial decree or modification decree;

5. "Home state" means the state in which the child immediately preceding the time involved lived with his parents, a parent, or a person acting as parent, for at least six (6) consecutive months, and in the case of a child less than six (6) months old the state in which the child lived from birth with any of the persons mentioned. Periods of temporary absence of any of the named persons are counted as part of the six-month or other period;

6. "Initial decree" means the first custody decree concerning a particular child;

7. "Modification decree" means a custody decree which modified or replaces a prior decree, whether made by the court which rendered the prior decree or by another court;

8. "Physical custody" means actual possession and control of a child;

9. "Person acting as parent" means a person, other than a parent, who has physical custody of a child and who has either been awarded custody by a court or claims a right to custody; and

10 "State" means any state, territory or possession of the United States, the Commonwealth of Puerto Rico, or the District of Columbia.

§ 1605. Prerequisites for jurisdiction.
A. A court of this state which is competent to decide child custody matters has jurisdiction to make a child custody determination by initial or modification decree if:

1. This state:

a. is the home state of the child at the time of commencement of the proceeding, or

b. had been the child's home state within six (6) months before commencement of the proceeding and the child is absent from this state because of his removal or retention by a person claiming his custody or for other reasons, and a parent or person acting as parent continues to live in this state; or

2. It is in the best interest of the child that a court of this state assume jurisdiction because:

a. the child and his parents, or the child and at least one contestant, have a significant connection with this state, and

b. there is available in this state substantial evidence concerning the child's present or future care, protection, training and personal relationships; or

3. The child is physically present in this state and:

a. the child has been abandoned, or

b. it is necessary in an emergency to protect the child because he has been subjected to or threatened with mistreatment abuse or is otherwise neglected or dependent; or

4. a. It appears that no other state would have jurisdiction under prerequisites substantially in accordance with paragraphs 1, 2 or 3 of this subsection, or another state has declined to exercise jurisdiction on the ground that this state is the more appropriate forum to determine the custody of the child, and

b. it is in the best interest of the child that this court assume jurisdiction

B. Except under paragraphs 3 and 4 of subsection A of this section, physical presence in this state of the child, or of the child and one of the contestants, is not alone sufficient to confer jurisdiction on a court of this state to make a child custody determination.

C. Physical presence of the child, while desirable, is not a prerequisite for jurisdiction to determine his custody.

D. The controlling criterion for awarding custody by a court of this state shall always be what is in the best interest of the child, other statutory provisions merely being factors which may be considered.

§ 1606. Right to notice and opportunity to be heard.

Before making a decree under this act, reasonable notice and opportunity to be heard shall be given to the contestants, any parent whose parental rights have not been previously terminated and any person who has physical custody of the child. If any of these persons is outside this state, notice and opportunity to be heard shall be given pursuant to Section 7 of this act.

§ 1607. Notice requirements for persons outside state—Proof of service—Exemption.

A. Notice required for the exercise of jurisdiction over a person outside this state shall be given in a manner reasonably calculated to give actual notice, and may be:

1. By personal delivery outside this state in the manner prescribed for service of process within this state;

2. In the manner prescribed by the law of the place in which the service is made for service of process in that place in an action in any of its courts of general jurisdiction;

3. By any form of mail addressed to the person to be served and requesting a receipt; or

4. As directed by the court, including publication, if other means of notification are ineffective.

B. Notice under this section shall be served, mailed, delivered or last published at least ten (10) days before any hearing in this state.

C. Proof of service outside this state may be made by affidavit of the individual who made the service, or in the manner prescribed by the law of this state, the order pursuant to which the service is made, or the law of the place in which the service is made. If service is made by mail, proof may be a receipt signed by the addressee or other evidence of delivery to the addressee.

D. Notice is not required if a person submits to the jurisdiction of the court.

§ 1608. Proceedings pending in other state—Stay of proceeding—Examination of pleadings and other information— Informing other court of decree.

A. A court of this state shall not exercise its jurisdiction under this act if at the time of filing the petition a proceeding concerning the custody of the child was pending in a court of another state exercising jurisdiction substantially in conformity with this act, unless the proceeding is stayed by the court of the other state because this state is a more appropriate forum or for other reasons.

B. Before hearing the petition in a custody proceeding the court shall examine the pleadings and other information supplied by the parties under Section 11 of this act and shall consult the child custody registry established under Section 18 of this act concerning the pendency of proceedings with respect to the child in other states, and shall also inquire to determine if juvenile proceedings alleging the child to be deprived, in need of supervision or delinquent are pending or have been adjudicated. If the court has reason to believe that proceedings may be pending in another state it shall direct an inquiry to the state court administrator or other appropriate official of the other state.

C. If the court is informed during the course of the proceeding that a proceeding concerning the custody of the child was pending in another state before the court assumed jurisdiction it shall stay the proceeding and communicate with the court in which the other proceeding is pending to the end that the issue may be litigated in the more appropriate forum and that information be exchanged in accordance with Sections 21 through 24 of this act. If a court of this state has made a custody decree before being informed of a pending proceeding in a court of another state it shall immediately inform that court of the fact. If the court is informed that a proceeding was commenced in another state after it assumed jurisdiction it shall likewise inform the other court to the end that the issues may be litigated in the more appropriate forum.

§ 1609. Inconvenient forum—Motion—Factors determining—Communication with court of other state—Findings and proceedings thereon.

A. A court which has jurisdiction under this act to make an initial or modification decree may decline to exercise its jurisdiction any time before making a decree if it finds that it is an inconvenient forum to make a custody determination under the circumstances of the case and that a court of another state is a more appropriate forum.

B. A finding of inconvenient forum may be made upon the court's own motion or upon motion of a party or a guardian ad litem or other representative of the child.

C. In determining if it is an inconvenient forum, the court shall consider if it is in the interest of the child that another state assume jurisdiction. For this purpose it may take into account the following factors, among others:

1. If another state is or recently was the child's home state;

2. If another state has a closer connection with the child and his family or with the child and one or more of the contestants;

3. If substantial evidence concerning the child's present or future care, protection, training and personal relationships is more readily available in another state;

4. If the parties have agreed on another forum which is no less appropriate; and

5. If the exercise of jurisdiction by a court of this state would contravene any of the purposes stated in Section 2 of this act.

D. Before determining whether to decline or retain jurisdiction the court may communicate with a court of another state and exchange information pertinent to the assumption of jurisdiction by either court with a view to assuring that jurisdiction will be exercised by the more appropriate court and that a forum will be available to the parties.

E. If the court finds that it is an inconvenient forum and that a court of another state is a more appropriate forum, it may dismiss the proceedings, or it may stay the proceedings upon condition that a custody proceeding be promptly commenced in another named state or upon any other conditions which may be just and proper, including the condition that a moving party stipulate his consent and submission to the jurisdiction of the other forum.

F. The court may decline to exercise its jurisdiction under this act if a custody determination is incidental to an action for divorce or another proceeding while retaining jurisdiction over the divorce or other proceeding.

G. If it appears to the court that it is clearly an inappropriate forum it may require the party who commenced the proceeding to pay, in addition to the costs of the proceedings in this state, necessary travel and other expenses, including attorneys' fees, incurred by other parties or their witnesses. Payment is to be made to the clerk of the court for remittance to the proper party.

H. Upon dismissal or stay of proceedings under this section the court shall inform the court found to be the more appropriate forum of this fact or, if the court which would have jurisdiction in the other state is not certainly known, shall transmit the information to the court administrator or other appropriate official for forwarding to the appropriate court.

I. Any communication received from another state informing this state of a finding of inconvenient forum because a court of this state is the more appropriate forum shall be filed in the custody registry of the appropriate court. Upon assuming jurisdiction, the court of this state shall inform the original court of this fact.

§ 1610. Improper removal of child from another state or physical custody of person entitled to custody.

A. If the petitioner for an initial decree has wrongfully taken the child from another state or has engaged in similar reprehensible conduct the court may decline to exercise jurisdiction if this is just and proper under the circumstances.

B. Unless required in the interest of the child, the court shall not exercise its jurisdiction to modify a custody decree of another state if the petitioner, without consent of the person entitled to custody, has improperly removed the child from the physical custody of the person entitled to custody or has improperly retained the child after a visit or other temporary relinquishment of physical custody. If the petitioner has violated any other provision of a custody decree of another state the court may decline to exercise it jurisdiction if this is just and proper under the circumstances.

C. In appropriate cases a court dismissing a petition under this section may charge the petitioner with necessary travel and other expenses, including attorneys' fees, incurred by other parties or their witnesses.

§ 1611. Pleading or affidavit—Oath—Information required.

A. Every party in a custody proceeding in his first pleading or in an affidavit attached to that pleading shall give information under oath as to the child's present address, the places where the child has lived within the last five (5) years, and the names and present addresses of the persons with whom the child has lived during that period. In this pleading or affidavit every party shall further declare under oath whether:

1. He has participated, as a party, witness, or in any other capacity, in any other litigation concerning the custody of the same child in this or any other state;

2. He has information of any custody proceeding concerning the child pending in a court of this or any other state; and

3. He knows of any person not a party to the proceedings who has physical custody of the child or claims to have custody or visitation rights with respect to the child.

B. If the declaration as to any of the above items is in the affirmative the declarant shall give additional information under oath as required by the court. The court may examine the parties under oath as to details of the information furnished and as to other matters pertinent to the court's jurisdiction and the disposition of the case.

C. Each party has a continuing duty to inform the court of any custody proceeding concerning the child in this or any other state of which he obtained information during this proceeding.

§ 1612. Joinder of party having physical custody or claim or custody or visitation rights to child.

If the court learns from information furnished by the parties pursuant to Section 11 of this act or from other sources that a person not a party to the custody proceeding has physical custody of the child or claims to have custody or visitation rights with respect to the child, it shall order that person to be joined as a party and to be duly notified of the pendency of the proceeding and of his joinder as a party. If the person joined as a party is outside this state he shall be served with process or otherwise notified in accordance with Section 6 of this act.

§ 1613. Order for party to appear—Parties outside state.

A. The court may order any party to the proceeding who is in this state to appear personally before the court. If that party has physical custody of the child the court may order that he appear personally with the child.

B. If a party to the proceeding whose presence is desired by the court is outside this state with or without the child the court may order that the notice given under Section 7 of this act include a statement directing that party to appear personally with or without the child and declaring that failure to appear may result in a decision adverse to that party.

C. If a party to the proceeding who is outside this state is directed to appear under subsection B of this section or desires to appear personally before the court with or without the child, the court may require another party to pay to the clerk of the court, travel and other necessary expenses of the party so appearing and of the child if this is just and proper under the circumstances.

§ 1614. Decrees—Operation and effect.

A custody decree rendered by a court of this state which had jurisdiction under Section 5 of this act binds all parties who have been served in this state or notified in accordance with Section 7 of this act or who have submitted to the jurisdiction of the court, and who have been given an opportunity to be heard. As to these parties the custody decree is conclusive as to all issues of law and fact decided and as to the custody determination made, unless and until that determination is modified pursuant to law, including the provisions of this act.

§ 1615. Enforcement of decree of another state.

The courts of this state shall recognize and enforce an initial or modification decree of a court of another state which had assumed jurisdiction under statutory provision substantially in accordance with this act or which was made under factual circumstances meeting the jurisdictional standards of the act, so long as this decree has not been modified in accordance with jurisdictional standards substantially similar to those of this act.

§ 1616. Modification of decree of another state.

A. If a court of another state has made a custody decree, a court of this state shall not modify that decree unless:

1. It appears to the court of this state that the court which rendered the decree does not now have jurisdiction under jurisdictional prerequisites substantially in accordance with this act or has declined to assume jurisdiction to modify the decree; and

2. The court of this state has jurisdiction.

B. If a court of this state is authorized under subsection A of this section and Section 10 of this act to modify a custody decree of another state it shall give due consideration to the transcript of the record and other documents of all previous proceedings submitted to it in accordance with Section 24 of this act.

§ 1617. Filing of decree from another state—Violation of decree.

A. A certified copy of a custody decree of another state may be filed in the office of the clerk of any district court of this state. The clerk shall treat the decree in the same manner as a custody decree of the district court of this state. A custody decree so filed has the same effect and shall be enforced in like manner as a custody decree rendered by a court of this state.

B. A person violating a custody decree of another state which makes it necessary to enforce the decree in this state may be required to pay necessary travel and other expenses, including attorneys' fees, incurred by the party entitled to the custody or his witnesses.

§ 1618. Registry—Contents.

The clerk of each district court shall maintain a registry in which he shall enter the following:

1. Certified copies of custody decrees of other states received for filing;

2. Communications as to the pendency of custody proceedings in other states;

3. Communications concerning a finding of inconvenient forum by a court of another state; and

4. Other communications or documents concerning custody proceedings in another state which may affect the jurisdiction of a court of this state or the disposition to be made by it in a custody proceeding.

§ 1619. Certification and forwarding copy of decree.

The clerk of the district court of this state, at the request of the court of another state or at the request of any person who is affected by or has a legitimate interest in a custody decree, shall certify and forward a copy of the decree to that court or person.

§ 1620. Witnesses in another state—Adducing testimony.

In addition to other procedural devices available to a party, any party to the proceeding or a guardian ad litem or other representative of the child may adduce testimony of witnesses, including parties and the child, by deposition or otherwise, in another state. The court on its own motion may direct that the testimony of a person be taken in another state and may prescribe the manner in which and the terms upon which the testimony shall be taken.

§ 1621. Request for another state to hold hearing—Costs—Parties—Travel and other expenses.

A. A court of this state may request the appropriate court of another state to hold a hearing to adduce evidence, to order a party to produce or give evidence under other procedures of that state, or to have social studies made with respect to the custody of a child involved in proceedings pending in the court of this state; and to forward to the court of this state certified copies of the transcript of the record of the hearing, the evidence otherwise adduced, or any social studies prepared in compliance with the request. The cost of the services may be assessed against the parties or, if necessary, ordered paid by the state.

B. A court of this state may request the appropriate court of another state to order a party to custody proceedings pending in the court of this state to appear in the proceedings, and if that party has physical custody of the child, to appear with the child. The request may state that travel and other necessary expenses of the party and of the child whose appearance is desired will be assessed against another party or will otherwise be paid.

§ 1622. Holding hearing at request of another state—Witnesses—Travel and other expenses.

A. Upon request of the court of another state the courts of this state which are competent to hear custody matters may order a person in this state to appear at a hearing to adduce evidence or to produce or give evidence under other procedures available in this state or may order social studies to be made for use in a custody proceeding in another state. A certified copy of the transcript of the record of the hearing or the evidence otherwise adduced and any social studies prepared shall be forwarded by the clerk of the court to the requesting court.

B. A person within this state may voluntarily give his testimony or statement in this state for use in a custody proceeding outside this state.

C. Upon request of the court of another state a competent court of this state may order a person in this state to appear alone or with the child in a custody proceeding in another state. The court may condition compliance with the request upon assurance by the other state that travel and other necessary expenses will be advanced or reimbursed.

§ 1623. Records—Preservation—Copies.

In any custody proceeding in this state the court shall preserve the pleadings, orders and decrees, any record that has been made of its hearings, social studies and other pertinent documents until the child reaches eighteen (18) years of age. Upon appropriate request of the court of another state the court shall forward to the other court certified copies of any or all such documents.

§ 1624. Transcripts of court record and other documents from another state.

If a custody decree has been rendered in another state concerning a child involved in a custody proceeding pending in a court of this state, the court of this state upon taking jurisdiction of the case shall request of the court of the other state a certified copy of the transcript of any court record and other documents mentioned in Section 23 of this act.

§ 1625. International application of act.

The general policies of this act extend to the international area. The provisions of this act relating to the recognition and enforcement of custody decrees of other states apply to custody decrees and decrees involving legal institutions similar in nature to custody institutions rendered by appropriate authorities of other nations if reasonable notice and opportunity to be heard were given to all affected persons.

§ 1626. Jurisdictional questions—Priority.

Upon the request of a party to a custody proceeding which raises a question of existence or exercise of jurisdiction under this act the case shall be given calendar priority and handled expeditiously.

§ 1627. Violations—Defenses.

A. Any parent or other person who violates an order of any court of this state, granting the custody of the child under the age of eighteen (18) years, to any person, agency or institution, with the intent to deprive the lawful custodian of the custody of a child under the age of eighteen (18) years, shall be guilty of a felony.

B. It shall be an affirmative defense either:

1. That the offender reasonably believes that the act was necessary to preserve the child from danger to his welfare; or

2. That the child, being at the time more than fourteen (14) years old, was taken away at his own instigation without enticement and without purpose to commit a criminal offense with or against the child.

Provided, however, that such defenses shall not apply if the offender committed said act within thirty (30) days of an order of the district court relating to custody of the minor.

§ 1628. Missing child 16 and under—Investigation of disappearance.

It is hereby made the duty of any sheriff, chief of police, city marshal, constable, or any other law enforcement officer, upon notification of a report of a missing child sixteen (16) years and under, to immediately initiate an investigation into the disappearance of said child.

OREGON

UNIFORM CHILD CUSTODY JURISDICTION ACT

§109.700. Citation of ORS 109.700 to 109.930.

ORS 109.700 to 109.930 may be cited as the Uniform Child Custody Jurisdiction Act.

§109.710. Definitions for ORS 109.700 to 109.930.

As used in ORS 109.700 to 109.930:

(1) "Contestant" means a person including a parent, who claims a right to custody or visitation rights with respect to a child.

(2) "Custody determination" means a court decision and court orders and instructions providing for the custody of a child, including visitation rights. "Custody determination" does not include a decision relating to child support or any other monetary obligation of any person.

(3) "Custody proceeding" includes proceedings in which a custody determination is one of several issues, such as an action for divorce or separation, and includes child neglect and dependency proceedings.

(4) "Decree" or "custody decree" means a custody determination contained in a judicial decree or order made in a custody proceeding, and includes an initial decree and a modification decree.

(5) "Home state" means the state in which the child, immediately preceding the time involved, lived with the parents of the child, a parent, or a person acting as parent, for at least six consecutive months, and, in the case of a child less than six months old, the state in which the child lived from birth with any of the persons mentioned. Periods of temporary absence of any of the named persons are counted as part of the six-month or other period.

(6) "Initial decree" means the first custody decree concerning a particular child.

(7) "Modification decree" means a custody decree which modifies or replaces a prior decree, whether made by the court which rendered the prior decree or by another court.

(8) "Physical custody" means actual possession and control of a child.

(9) "Person acting as parent" means a person, other than a parent, who has physical custody of a child and who has either been awarded custody by a court or claims a right to custody.

(10) "State" means any state, territory, or possession of the United States, the Commonwealth of Puerto Rico, and the District of Columbia.

§109.720. General purposes; application.

(1) The general purposes of ORS 109.700 to 109.930 are to:

(a) Avoid jurisdictional competition and conflict with courts of other states in matters of child custody which have in the past resulted in the shifting of children from state to state with harmful effects on their wellbeing;

(b) Promote cooperation with the courts of other states to the end that a custody decree is rendered in that state which can best decide the case in the interest of the child;

(c) Assure that litigation concerning the custody of a child takes place ordinarily in the state with which the child and the family of the child have the closest connection and where significant evidence concerning care, protection, training, and personal relationships of the child is most readily available, and that courts of this state decline the exercise of jurisdiction when the child and the family of the child have a closer connection with another state;

(d) Discourage continuing controversies over child custody in the interest of greater stability of home environment and of secure family relationships for the child;

(e) Deter abductions and other unilateral removals of children undertaken to obtain custody awards;

(f) Avoid relitigation of custody decisions of other states in this state in so far as feasible;

(g) Facilitate the enforcement of custody decrees of other states;

(h) Promote and expand the exchange of information and other forms of mutual assistance between the courts of this state and those of other states concerned with the same child; and

(j) Make uniform the law of those states which enact it.

(2) ORS 109.700 to 109.930 shall be construed to promote the general purposes stated in this section.

(3) The general policies of ORS 109.700 to 109.930 extend to the international area. The provisions of ORS 109.700 to 109.930 relating to the recognition and enforcement of custody decrees of other states apply to custody decrees and decrees involving legal institutions similar in nature to custody, rendered by appropriate authorities of other nations if reasonable notice and opportunity to be heard were given to all affected persons.

§109.730. Jurisdiction over child custody determination.

(1) A court of this state which is competent to decide child custody matters has jurisdiction to make a child custody determination by initial or modification decree if:

(a) This state is the home state of the child at the time of commencement of the proceeding, or had been the child's home state within six months before commencement of the proceeding and the child is absent from this state because of removal or retention by a person claiming custody or for other reasons, and a parent or person acting as parent continues to live in this state;

(b) It is in the best interest of the child that a court of this state assume jurisdiction because the child and the parents of the child, or the child and at least one contestant, have a significant connection with this state, and there is available in this state substantial evidence concerning the child's present or future care, protection, training, and personal relationships;

(c) The child is physically present in this state and the child has been abandoned or it is necessary in an emergency to protect the child because the child has been subjected to or threatened with mistreatment or abuse or is otherwise neglected or dependent; or

(d) It appears that no other state would have jurisdiction under prerequisites substantially in accordance with paragraph (a), (b) or (c) of this subsection, or another state has declined to exercise jurisdiction on the ground that this state is the more appropriate forum to determine the custody of the child, and it is in the best interest of the child that this court assume jurisdiction.

(2) Except under paragraphs (c) and (d) of subsection (1) of this section, physical presence in this state of the child, or of the child and one of the contestants, is not alone sufficient to confer jurisdiction on a court of this state to make a child custody determination.

(3) Physical presence of the child, while desirable, is not a prerequisite for jurisdiction to determine custody of the child.

§109.740. Notice and opportunity of hearing required.

Before making a decree under ORS 109.700 to 109.930, reasonable notice and opportunity to be heard shall be given to the contestants, any parent whose parental rights have not been previously terminated, and any person who has physical custody of the child. If any of these persons is outside this state, notice and opportunity to be heard shall be given pursuant to ORS 109.750.

§109.750. Method of notice.

(1) Notice required for the exercise of jurisdiction over a person outside this state shall be given in a manner reasonably calculated to give actual notice, and may be:

(a) By personal delivery outside this state in the manner prescribed for service of process within this state;

(b) In the manner prescribed by the law of the place in which the service is made for service of process in that place in an action in any of its courts of general jurisdiction;

(c) By any form of mail addressed to the person to be serviced and requesting a receipt; or

(d) As directed by the court, including publication, if other means of notification are ineffective.

(2) Notice under this section shall be serviced, mailed, delivered or last published at least 20 days before any hearing in this state.

(3) Proof of service outside this state may be made by affidavit of the individual who made the service, or in the manner prescribed by the law of this state, or the order pursuant to which the service is made or the law of the place in which the service is made. If service is made by mail, proof may be a receipt signed by the addressee or other evidence of delivery to the addressee.

(4) Notice is not required if a person submits to the jurisdiction of the court.

§109.760. Effect of proceedings pending elsewhere.

(1) A court of this state shall not exercise its jurisdiction under ORS 109.700 to 109.930 if at the time of filing the petition a proceeding concerning the custody of the child was pending in a court of another state exercising jurisdiction substantially in conformity with ORS 109.700 to 109.930, unless the proceeding is stayed by the court of the other state because this state is a more appropriate forum or for other reasons.

(2) Before hearing the petition in a custody proceeding, the court shall examine the pleadings and other information supplied

by the parties under ORS 109.790 and shall consult the child custody registry established under ORS 109.860 concerning the pendency of proceedings with respect to the child in other states. If the court has reason to believe that proceedings may be pending in another state it shall direct an inquiry to the state court administrator or other appropriate official of the other state.

(3) If the court is informed during the course of the proceeding that a proceeding concerning the custody of the child was pending in another state before the court assumed jurisdiction it shall stay the proceeding and communicate with the court in which the other proceeding is pending to the end that the issue may be litigated in the more appropriate forum and that information be exchanged in accordance with ORS 109.890 to 109.920. If a court of this state has made a custody decree before being informed of a pending proceeding in a court of another state it shall immediately inform that court of the fact. If the court is informed that a proceeding was commenced in another state after it assumed jurisdiction it shall likewise inform the other court to the end that the issues may be litigated in the more appropriate forum.

§109.770. Finding of court on inconvenient forum.

(1) A court which has jurisdiction under ORS 109.700 to 109.930 to make an initial or modification decree may decline to exercise its jurisdiction any time before making a decree if it finds that it is an inconvenient forum to make a custody determination under the circumstances of the case and that a court of another state is a more appropriate forum.

(2) A finding of inconvenient forum may be made upon the court's own motion or upon motion of a party or a guardian ad litem or other representative of the child.

(3) In determining if it is an inconvenient forum, the court shall consider if it is in the interest of the child that another state assume jurisdiction. For this purpose it may take into account the following factors, among others:

(a) If another state is or recently was the child's home state;

(b) If another state has a closer connection with the child and the family of the child or with the child and one or more of the contestants;

(c) If substantial evidence concerning the child's present or future care, protection, training, and personal relationships is more readily available in another state;

(d) If the parties have agreed on another forum which is no less appropriate; and

(e) If the exercise of jurisdiction by a court of this state would contravene any of the purposes stated in ORS 109.720 (1) and (2).

(4) Before determining whether to decline or retain jurisdiction the court may communicate with a court of another state and exchange information pertinent to the assumption of jurisdiction by either court with a view to assuring that jurisdiction will be exercised by the more appropriate court and that a forum will be available to the parties.

(5) If the court finds that it is an inconvenient forum and that a court of another state is a more appropriate forum, it may dismiss the proceedings, or it may stay the proceedings upon condition that a custody proceeding be promptly commenced in another named state or upon any other conditions which may be just and proper, including the condition that a moving party stipulate consent and submission to the jurisdiction of the other forum.

(6) The court may decline to exercise its jurisdiction under ORS 109.700 to 109.930 if a custody determination is incidental to an action for divorce or another proceeding while retaining jurisdiction over the divorce or other proceeding.

(7) If it appears to the court that it is clearly an inappropriate forum it may require the party who commenced the proceedings to pay, in addition to the costs of the proceedings in this state, necessary travel and other expenses, including attorney fees at trial and on appeal, incurred by other parties or their witnesses. Payment is to be made to the clerk of the court for remittance to the proper party.

(8) Upon dismissal or stay of proceedings under this section the court shall inform the court found to be the more appropriate forum of this fact, or if the court which would have jurisdiction in the other state is not certainly known, shall transmit the information to the court administrator or other appropriate official for forwarding to the appropriate court.

(9) Any communication received from another state informing this state of a finding of inconvenient forum because a court of this state is the more appropriate forum shall be filed in the custody registry of the appropriate court. Upon assuming jurisdiction the court of this state shall inform the original court of this fact.

§109.780. Effect of wrongful conduct of petitioner.

(1) If the petitioner for an initial decree has wrongfully taken the child from another state or has engaged in similar reprehensible conduct the court may decline to exercise jurisdiction if this is just and proper under the circumstances.

(2) Unless required in the interest of the child, the court shall not exercise its jurisdiction to modify a custody decree of another state if the petitioner, without consent of the person entitled to custody, has improperly removed the child from the physical custody of the person entitled to custody or has improperly retained the child after a visit or other temporary relinquishment of physical custody. If the petitioner has violated any other provision of a custody decree of another state the court may decline to exercise its jurisdiction if this is just and proper under the circumstances.

(3) In appropriate cases a court dismissing a petition under this section may charge the petitioner with necessary travel and other expenses, including attorney fees at trial and on appeal, incurred by other parties or their witnesses.

§109.790. Information required.

(1) Every party in a custody proceeding in the first pleading of the party or in an affidavit attached to that pleading shall give information under oath as to the child's present address, the places where the child has lived within the last five years, and the names and present addresses of the person with whom the child has lived during the period. In this pleading or affidavit every party shall further declare under oath whether:

(a) The party has participated, as a party, witness or in any other capacity, in any other litigation concerning the custody of the same child in this or any other state;

(b) The party has information of any custody proceeding concerning the child pending in a court of this or any other state; and

(c) The party knows of any person not a party to the proceedings who has physical custody of the child or claims to have custody or visitation rights with respect to the child.

(2) If the declaration as to any of the above items is in the affirmative, the declarant shall give additional information under oath as required by the court. The court may examine the parties under oath as to details of the information furnished and as to other matters pertinent to the court's jurisdiction and the disposition of the case.

(3) Each party has a continuing duty to inform the court of any custody proceedings concerning the child in this or any other state of which the party obtained information during this proceeding.

§109.800. Joinder of other persons as parties.

If the court learns from information furnished by the parties pursuant to ORS 109.790 or from other sources that a person not a party to the custody proceeding has physical custody of the child or claims to have custody or visitation rights with respect to the child, it shall order that person to be joined as a party and to be duly notified of the pendency of the proceeding and of joinder as a party. If the person joined as a party is outside this state the person shall be serviced with process or otherwise notified in accordance with ORS 109.750.

§109.810. Authority to order appearance of others; payment of expenses.

(1) The court may order any party to the proceeding who is in this state to appear personally before the court. If that party has physical custody of the child, the court may order that the party appear personally with the child.

(2) If a party to the proceeding whose presence is desired by the court is outside this state with or without the child, the court may order that the notice given under ORS 109.750 include a statement directing that party to appear personally with or without the child and declaring that failure to appear may result in a decision adverse to that party.

(3) If a party to the proceeding who is outside this state is directed to appear under subsection (2) of this section or desires to appear personally before the court with or without the child, the court may require another party to pay to the clerk of the court travel and other necessary expenses of the party so appearing and of the child if this is just and proper under the circumstances.

§109.820. Effect of decree.

A custody decree rendered by a court of this state which had jurisdiction under ORS 109.730 binds all parties who have been served in this state, or notified in accordance with ORS 109.750 or who have submitted to the jurisdiction of the court, and who have been given an opportunity to be heard. As to these parties the custody decree is conclusive as to the custody determination made unless and until that determination is modified pursuant to law, including the provisions of ORS 109.700 to 109.930.

§109.830. Enforcement of decree of another state.

The court of this state shall recognize and enforce an initial or modification decree by a court of another state which had assumed jurisdiction under statutory provisions substantially in accordance with ORS 109.700 to 109.930 or which was made under factual circumstances meeting the jurisdictional standards of ORS 109.700 to 109.930, so long as this decree has not been modified in accordance with jurisdictional standards substantially similar to those of ORS 109.700 to 109.930.

§109.840. Modification of decree of another state.

(1) If a court of another state has made a custody decree, a court of this state shall not modify that decree unless it appears to the court of this state that the court which rendered the decree does not now have jurisdiction under jurisdictional prerequisites substantially in accordance with ORS 109.700 to 109.930 or has declined to assume jurisdiction to modify the decree and the court of this state has jurisdiction.

(2) If a court of this state is authorized under subsection (1) of this section and ORS 109.780 to modify a custody decree of another state it shall give due consideration to the transcript of the record and other documents of all previous proceedings submitted to it in accordance with ORS 109.920.

§109.850. Filing of decree of another state; effect of violation.

(1) A certified copy of a custody decree of another state may be filed in the office of the clerk of any circuit court of this state. The clerk shall treat the decree in the same manner as a custody decree of the circuit court of this state. A custody decree so filed has the same effect and shall be enforced in like manner as a custody decree rendered by a court of this state.

(2) A person violating a custody decree of another state which makes it necessary to enforce the decree in this state may be required to pay necessary travel and other expenses, including attorney fees at trial and on appeal, incurred by the party entitled

to the custody or witnesses of the party.

§109.860. Clerk's registry.

The clerk of each circuit court shall maintain a registry in which the clerk shall enter the following:

(1) Certified copies of custody decrees of other states received for filing;

(2) Communications as to the pendencey of custody proceedings in other states;

(3) Communications concerning a finding of inconvenient forum by a court of another state; and

(4) Other communications or documents concerning custody proceedings in another state which may affect the jurisdiction of a court of this state or the disposition to be made by it in a custody proceeding.

§109.870. Certification of decree; copies.

The clerk of a circuit court of this state, at the request of the court of another state or at the request of any person who is affected by or has a legitimate interest in a custody decree, shall certify and forward a copy of the decree to that court or person.

§109.880. Depositions.

In addition to other procedural devices available to a party, any party to the proceeding or a guardian ad litem or other representative of the child may adduce testimony of witnesses, including parties and the child, by deposition or otherwise, in another state. The court on its own motion may direct that the testimony of a person be taken in another state and may prescribe the manner in which and the the terms upon which the testimony may be taken.

§109.890. Hearing in another state.

(1) A court of this state may request the appropriate court of another state to hold a hearing to adduce evidence, to order a party to produce or give evidence under other procedures of that state, or to have social studies made with respect to the custody of a child involved in proceedings pending in the court of this state and to forward to the court of this state certified copies of the transcript of the record of the hearing, the evidence otherwise adduced, or any social studies prepared in compliance with the request. the cost of the services may be assessed against the parties, or if necessary, ordered paid by the county or state.

(2) A court of this state may request the appropriate court of another state to order a party to custody proceedings pending in the court of this state to appear in the proceedings, and if that party has physical custody of the child, to appear with the child. The request may state that travel and other necessary expenses of the party and of the child whose appearance is desired will be assessed against another party or will otherwise be paid.

§109.900. Ordering appearance in another state; payment of expenses.

(1) Upon request of the court of another state, the courts of this state which are competent to hear custody matters may order a person in this state to appear at a hearing to adduce evidence or to produce or give evidence under other procedures available in this state or may order social studies to be made for use in a custody proceeding in another state. A certified copy of the transcript of the record of the hearing or the evidence otherwise adduced and any social studies prepared shall be forwarded by the clerk of the court to the requesting court.

(2) A person within this state may voluntarily give testimony or a statement in this state for use in a custody proceeding outside this state.

(3) Upon request of the court of another state, a competent court of this state may order a person in this state to appear alone or with the child in a custody proceeding in another state. The court may condition compliance with the request upon assurance by the other state that travel and other necessary expenses will be advanced or reimbursed.

§109.910. Preservation of record; copies to other courts.

In any custody proceeding in this state the court shall preserve the pleadings, orders and decrees, any record that has been made of its hearings; social studies, and other pertinent documents until the child reaches 21 years of age. Upon appropriate request of the court of another state, the court shall forward to the other court certified copies of any or all such documents.

§109.920. Obtaining transcript from another state.

If a custody decree has been rendered in another state concerning a child involved in a custody proceeding pending in a court of this state, the court of this state upon taking jurisdiction of the case shall request of the court of the other state a certified copy of the transcript of any court record and other documents mentioned in ORS 109.910.

§109.930. Calendar priority.

Upon the request of a party to a custody proceeding which raises a question of existence or exercise of jurisdiction under ORS 109.700 to 109.930, the case shall be given calendar priority and handled expeditiously.

§109.990. Penalty.

A person who violates ORS 109.311 (3) or who submits a false statement under ORS 109.311 (2) commits a Class C felony.

PENNSYLVANIA

Title 42
UNIFORM CHILD CUSTODY JURISDICTION ACT

§ 5341. Short title of subchapter.

This subchapter shall be known and may be cited as the "Uniform Child Custody Jurisdiction Act."

§ 5342. Purposes and construction of subchapter.

(a) Purposes.—The general purposes of this subchapter are to:

(1) Avoid jurisdictional competition and conflict with courts of other states in matters of child custody which have in the past resulted in the shifting of children from state to state with harmful effects on their well-being.

(2) Promote cooperation with the courts of other states to the end that a custody decree is rendered in that state which can best decide the case in the interest of the child.

(3) Assure that litigation concerning the custody of a child takes place ordinarily in the state with which the child and his family have the closest connection and where significant evidence concerning his care, protection, training, and personal relationships is most readily available, and that courts of this Commonwealth decline the exercise of jurisdiction when the child and his family have a closer connection with another state.

(4) Discourage continuing controversies over child custody in the interest of greater stability of home environment and of secure family relationships for the child.

(5) Deter abductions and other unilateral removals of children undertaken to obtain custody awards.

(6) Avoid relitigation of custody decisions of other states in this Commonwealth insofar as feasible.

(7) Facilitate the enforcement of custody decrees of other states.

(8) Promote and expand the exchange of information and other forms of mutual assistance between the court of this Commonwealth and those of other states concerned with the same child.

(b) Construction.—This subchapter shall be construed to promote the general purposes stated in this section.

§ 5343. Definitions.

The following words and phrases when used in this subchapter shall have, unless the context clearly indicates otherwise, the meanings given to them in this section:

"Contestant." An institution or an individual, including a parent, who claims a right to custody or visitation rights with respect to a child.

"Custody determination." A court decision and court orders and instructions providing for the custody of a child, including visitation rights; the term does not include a decision relating to child support or any other monetary obligation of any person.

"Custody proceeding." Includes proceedings in which a custody determination is one of several issues, such as an action for divorce or separation, and includes child neglect and dependency proceedings.

"Decree" or "custody decree." A custody determination contained in a judicial decree or order made in a custody proceeding, and includes an initial decree and a modification decree.

"Home state." The state in which the child immediately preceding the time involved lived with his parents, a parent, or a person acting as parent, or in an institution, for at least six consecutive months, and in the case of a child less than six months old the state in which the child lived from birth with any of the persons mentioned. Periods of temporary absence of any of the named persons are counted as part of the six-month or other period.

"Initial decree." The first custody decree concerning a particular child.

"Modification decree." A custody decree which modifies or replaces a prior decree, whether made by the court which rendered the prior decree or by another court.

"Person acting as parent." A person, including an institution other than a parent, who has physical custody of a child and who has either been awarded custody by a court or claims a right to custody.

"Physical custody." Actual possession and control of a child.

§ 5344. Jurisdiction.

(a) General rule.—A court of this Commonwealth which is competent to decide child custody matters has jurisdiction to make a child custody determination by initial or modification decree if:

(1) this Commonwealth:

(i) is the home state of the child at the time of commencement of the proceeding; or

(ii) had been the home state of the child within six months before commencement of the proceeding and the child is absent from this Commonwealth because of his removal or retention by a person claiming his custody or for other reasons, and a parent or person acting as parent continues to live in this Commonwealth;

(2) it is in the best interest of the child that a court of this Commonwealth assume jurisdiction because:

(i) the child and his parents, or the child and at least one contestant, have a significant connection with this Commonwealth; and

(ii) there is available in this Commonwealth substantial evidence concerning the present or future care, protection, training, and personal relationships of the child;

(3) the child is physically present in this Commonwealth, and:

(i) the child has been abandoned; or

(ii) it is necessary in an emergency to protect the child because he has been subjected to or threatened with mistreatment or abuse or is otherwise neglected or dependent;

(4)(i) it appears that no other state would have jurisdiction under prerequisites substantially in accordance with paragraph (1), (2) or (3), or another state has declined to exercise jurisdiction on the ground that this Commonwealth is the more appropriate forum to determine the custody of the child; and

(ii) it is in the best interest of the child that the court assume jurisdiction; or

(5) the child welfare agencies of the counties wherein the contestants for the child live, have made an investigation of the home of the person to whom custody is awarded and have found it to be satisfactory for the welfare of the child.

(b) Physical presence insufficient.—Except under subsection (a)(3) and (4), physical presence in this Commonwealth of the child, or of the child and one of the contestants, is not alone sufficient to confer jurisdiction on a court of this Commonwealth to make a child custody determination.

(c) Physical presence unnecessary.—Physical presence of the child, while desirable, is not a prerequisite for jurisdiction to determine his custody.

§ 5345. Notice and opportunity to be heard.

Before making a decree under this subchapter, reasonable notice and opportunity to be heard shall be given to the contestants, any parent whose parental rights have not been previously terminated, and any person who has physical custody of the child. If any of these persons is outside this Commonwealth, notice and opportunity to be heard shall be given pursuant to section 5346 (relating to notice to persons outside this Commonwealth; submission to jurisdiction).

§ 5346. Notice to persons outside this Commonwealth; submission to jurisdiction.

(a) General rule.—Notice required for the exercise of jurisdiction over a person outside this Commonwealth shall be given in a manner reasonably calculated to give actual notice, and may be:

(1) by personal delivery outside this Commonwealth in the manner prescribed for service of process within this Commonwealth;

(2) in the manner prescribed by the law of the place in which the service is made for service of process in that place in an action in any of its courts of general jurisdiction;

(3) by any form of mail addressed to the person to be served and requesting a receipt; or

(4) as directed by the court including publication, if other means of notification are ineffective.

(b) Duration.—Notice under this section shall be served, mailed, or delivered or last published at least 10 days before any hearing in this Commonwealth.

(c) Proof of service.—Proof of service outside this Commonwealth may be made by affidavit of the individual who made the service, or in the manner prescribed by the law of this Commonwealth, the order pursuant to which the service is made, or the law of the place in which the service is made. If service is made by mail, proof may be a receipt signed by the addressee or other evidence of delivery to the addressee.

(d) Submission to jurisdiction.—Notice is not required if a person submits to the jurisdiction of the court.

§ 5347. Simultaneous proceedings in other states.

(a) General rule.—A court of this Commonwealth shall not exercise its jurisdiction under this subchapter if at the time of filing the petition a proceeding concerning the custody of the child was pending in a court of another state exercising jurisdiction substantially in conformity with this subchapter, unless the proceeding is stayed by the court of the other state because this Commonwealth is a more appropriate forum or for other reasons.

(b) Procedure.—Before hearing the petition in a custody proceeding the court shall examine the pleadings and other information supplied by the parties under section 5350 (relating to information under oath to be submitted to the court) and shall consult the child custody registry established under section 5357 (relating to registry of out-of-state custody decrees and proceedings) concerning the pendency of proceedings with respect to the child in other states. If the court has reason to believe that proceedings may be pending in another state it shall direct an inquiry to the state court administrator or other appropriate official of the other state.

(c) Stay; communication with other court.—If the court is informed during the court of the proceeding that a proceeding concerning the custody of the child was pending in another state before the court assumed jurisdiction it shall stay the proceeding and communicate with the court in which the other proceeding is pending to the end that the issue may be litigated in the more appropriate forum and that information be exchanged in accordance with sections 5360 (relating to hearings and studies in another state; orders to appear) through 5363 (relating to request for court records of another state). If a court of this Commonwealth has made a custody decree before being informed of a pending proceeding in a court of another state it shall immediately inform that court of the fact. If the court is informed that a proceeding was commenced in another state after it assumed jurisdiction it shall likewise inform the other court to the end that the issues may be litigated in the more appropriate forum.

§ 5348. Inconvenient forum.

(a) General rule.—A court which has jurisdiction under this subchapter to make an initial or modification decree may decline to exercise its jurisdiction any time before making a decree if it finds that it is an inconvenient forum to make a custody determination under the circumstances of the case and that a court of another state is a more appropriate forum.

(b) Moving party.—A finding of inconvenient forum may be made upon the court's own motion or upon motion of a party or a guardian ad litem or other representative of the child.

(c) Factors to be considered.—In determining if it is an inconvenient forum, the court shall consider if it is in the interest of the child that another state assume jurisdiction. For this purpose it may take into account the following factors, among others:

(1) If another state is or recently was the home state of the child.

(2) If another state has a closer connection with the child and his family or with the child and one or more of the contestants.

(3) If substantial evidence concerning the present or future care, protection, training, and personal relationships of the child is more readily available in another state.

(4) If the parties have agreed on another forum which is no less appropriate.

(5) If the exercise of jurisdiction by a court of this Commonwealth would contravene any of the purposes stated in section 5342 (relating to purposes and construction of subchapter).

(d) Communication with other court.—Before determining whether to decline or retain jurisdiction the court may communicate with a court of another state and exchange information pertinent to the assumption of jurisdiction by either court with a view to assuring that jurisdiction will be exercised by the more appropriate court and that a forum will be available to the parties.

(e) Disposition.—If the court finds that it is an inconvenient forum and that a court of another state is a more appropriate forum on condition that a custody proceeding be promptly commenced in another named state or upon any other conditions which may be just and proper, including the condition that a moving party stipulate his consent and submission to the jurisdiction of the other forum.

(f) Effect on divorce or other proceeding.—The court may decline to exercise its jurisdiction under this subchapter if a custody determination is incidental to an action for divorce or another proceeding while retaining jurisdiction over the divorce or other proceeding.

(g) Costs and expenses.—Subject to general rules:

(1) If it appears to the court that it is clearly an inappropriate forum it may require the party who commenced the proceedings to pay, in addition to the costs of the proceedings in this Commonwealth, necessary travel and other expenses, including attorneys' fees, incurred by other parties or their witnesses.

(2) Payment is to be made to the office of the clerk of the court of common pleas for remittance to the proper party.

(h) Notice of disposition.—Upon dismissal or stay of proceedings under this section the court shall inform the court found to be the more appropriate forum of this fact, or if the court which would have jurisdiction in the other state is not certainly known, shall transmit the information to the court administrator or other appropriate official of the other state for forwarding to the appropriate court.

(i) Registry of out-of-state stay; notice of assumption of jurisdiction.—Any communication received from another state informing this Commonwealth of a finding of inconvenient forum because a court of this Commonwealth is the more appropriate forum shall be filed in the custody registry of the appropriate court. Upon assuming jurisdiction the court of this Commonwealth shall inform the original court of this fact.

§ 5349. Jurisdiction declined by reason of conduct.

(a) General rule.—If the petitioner for an initial decree has wrongfully taken the child from another state or has engaged in conduct intending to benefit his position in a custody hearing, the court may decline to exercise jurisdiction if this is just and proper under the circumstances.

(b) Restriction on modification of foreign decree.—Unless required in the interest of the child, the court shall not exercise its jurisdiction to modify a custody decree of another state if the petitioner, without consent of the person entitled to custody, has improperly removed the child from the physical custody of the person entitled to custody or has improperly retained the child after a visit or other temporary relinquishment of physical custody. If the petitioner has violated any other provision of a custody decree of another state the court may decline to exercise its jurisdiction unless the petitioner can show that conditions in the custodial household are physically or emotionally harmful to the child, the burden of proof being on the petitioner requesting the court to take jurisdiction.

(c) Costs and expenses.—Subject to general rules, in appropriate cases a court dismissing a petition under this section may charge the petitioner with necessary travel and other expenses, including attorney's fees, incurred by other parties or their witnesses.

§ 5350. Information under oath to be submitted to the court.

(a) General rule.—Every party in a custody proceeding in his first pleading or in an affidavit attached to that pleading shall give information under oath as to the present address of the child, the places where the child has lived within the last five years, and the names and present addresses of the persons with whom the child has lived during that period. In this pleading or affidavit every party shall further declare under oath whether:

(1) he has participated (as a party, witness, or in any other capacity) in any other litigation concerning the custody of the same child in this or any other state;

(2) he has information of any custody proceeding concerning the child pending in a court of this or any other state; and

(3) he knows of any person not a party to the proceedings who has physical custody of the child or claims to have custody or visitation rights with respect to the child.

(b) Additional information.—If the declaration as to any of the items set forth in subsection (a) is in the affirmative the declarant shall give additional information under oath as required by the court. The court may examine the parties under oath as to details of the information furnished and as to other matters pertinent to the jurisdiction of the court and the disposition of the case.

(c) Continuing duty.—Each party has a continuing duty to inform the court of any custody proceeding concerning the child in this Commonwealth or any other state of which he obtained information during proceedings under this subchapter.

§ 5351. Additional parties.

If the court learns from information furnished by the parties pursuant to section 5350 (relating to information under oath to be submitted to the court) or from other sources that a person not a party to the custody proceeding has physical custody of the child or claims to have custody or visitation rights with respect to the child, it shall order that person to be joined as a party and to be duly notified of the pendency of the proceeding and of his joinder as a party. If the person joined as a party is outside this Commonwealth he shall be served with process or otherwise notified in accordance with section 5346 (relating to notice to persons outside this Commonwealth; submission to jurisdiction).

§ 5352. Appearance of parties and the child.

(a) General rule.—The court may order any party to the proceeding who is in this Commonwealth to appear personally before the court. If that party has physical custody of the child the court may order that he appear personally with the child.

(b) Out-of-state persons.—If a party to the proceeding whose presence is desired by the court is outside this Commonwealth with or without the child the court may order that the notice given under section 5346 (relating to notice to persons outside this Commonwealth; submission to jurisdiction) include a statement directing that party to appear personally with or without the child and declaring that failure to appear may result in a decision adverse to that party.

(c) Costs and expenses.—If a party to the proceeding who is outside this Commonwealth is directed to appear under subsection (b) or desires to appear personally before the court with or without the child, the court may require another party to pay travel and other necessary expenses of the party so appearing and of the child if this is just and proper under the circumstances.

§ 5353. Binding force and res judicata effect of custody decree.

A custody decree rendered by a court of this Commonwealth which had jurisdiction under section 5344 (relating to jurisdiction) binds all parties who have been served in this Commonwealth or notified in accordance with section 5346 (relating to notice to persons outside this Commonwealth; submission to jurisdiction) or who have submitted to the jurisdiction of the court, and who have been given an opportunity to be heard. As to these parties the custody decree is conclusive as to all issues of law and fact decided and as to the custody determination made unless and until that determination is modified pursuant to law, including the provisions of this subchapter.

§ 5354. Recognition of out-of-state custody decrees.

The courts of this Commonwealth shall recognize and enforce an initial or modification decree of a court of another state which had assumed jurisdiction under statutory provisions substantially in accordance with this subchapter or which was made under factual circumstances meeting the jurisdictional standards of this subchapter, so long as the decree has not been modified in accordance with jurisdictional standards substantially similar to those of this subchapter.

§ 5355. Modification of custody decree of another state.

(a) General rule.—If a court of another state has made a custody decree, a court of this Commonwealth shall not modify that decree unless:

(1) it appears to the court of this Commonwealth that the court which rendered the decree does not now have jurisdiction under jurisdictional prerequisites substantially in accordance with this subchapter or has declined to assume jurisdiction to modify the decree; and

(2) the court of this Commonwealth has jurisdiction.

(b) Consideration of out-of-state record.—If a court of this Commonwealth is authorized under subsection (a) and section 5349 (relating to jurisdiction declined by reason of conduct) to modify a custody decree of another state it shall give due consideration to the transcript of the record and other documents of all previous proceedings submitted to it in accordance with section 5363 (relating to request for court records of another state).

§ 5356. Filing and enforcement of custody decree of another state.

(a) General rule.—A certified copy of a custody decree of another state whose decrees are recognized under section 5354 (relating to recognition of out-of-state custody decrees) may be filed in any office of the clerk of the court of common pleas of this Commonwealth. The clerk shall treat the decree in the same manner as a custody decree of a court of common pleas of this Commonwealth. A custody decree so filed has the same effect and shall be enforced in like manner as a custody decree rendered by a court of this Commonwealth.

(b) Costs and expenses.—A person violating a custody decree of another state which makes it necessary to enforce the decree in this Commonwealth may be required to pay necessary travel and other expenses, including attorneys' fees, incurred by the party entitled to the custody or his witnesses.

§ 5357. Registry of out-of-state custody decrees and proceedings.

Each office of the clerk of the court of common pleas shall maintain a registry in which it shall enter the following:

(1) Certified copies of custody decrees of other states received for filing.

(2) Communications as to the pendency of custody proceedings in other states.

(3) Communications concerning a finding of inconvenient forum by a court of another state.

(4) Other communications or documents concerning custody proceedings in another state which may affect the jurisdiction of a court of this Commonwealth or the disposition to be made by it in a custody proceeding.

§ 5358. Certified copies of custody decree.

The office of the clerk of the court of common pleas, at the request of the court of another state or at the request of any person who is affected by or has a legitimate interest in a custody decree, shall certify and forward a copy of the decree to that court or person.

§ 5359. Taking testimony in another state.

In addition to other procedural devices available to a party, any party to the proceeding or a guardian ad litem or other representative of the child may adduce testimony of witnesses, including parties and the child, by deposition or otherwise, in another state. The court on its own motion may direct that the testimony of a person be taken in another state and may prescribe the manner in which and the terms upon which the testimony shall be taken.

§ 5360. Hearings and studies in another state; orders to appear.

(a) Hearings and studies.—A court of this Commonwealth may request the appropriate court of another state to hold a hearing to adduce evidence, to order a party to produce or give evidence under other procedures of that state, or to have social studies made with respect to the custody of a child involved in proceedings pending in the court of this Commonwealth; and to forward to the court of this Commonwealth certified copies of the transcript of the record of the hearing, the evidence otherwise adduced, or any social studies prepared in compliance with the request. Subject to general rules, the cost of the services may be assessed against the parties or, if necessary, ordered paid by the county.

(b) Order to appear.—A court of this Commonwealth may request the appropriate court of another state to order a party to custody proceedings pending in the court of this Commonwealth to appear in the proceedings, and if that party has physical custody of the child, to appear with the child. The request may state that travel and other necessary expenses of the party and of the child whose appearance is desired will be assessed against another party or will otherwise be paid.

§ 5361. Assistance to courts of other states.

(a) General rule.—Upon request of the court of another state the courts of this Commonwealth which are competent to hear custody matters may order a person in this Commonwealth to appear at a hearing to adduce evidence or to produce or give evidence under other procedures available in this Commonwealth or may order social studies to be made for use in a custody proceeding in another state. A certified copy of the transcript of the record of the hearing or the evidence otherwise adduced, any psychological studies and any social studies prepared shall be forwarded to the requesting court.

(b) Voluntary testimony.—A person within this Commonwealth may voluntarily give his testimony or statement in this Commonwealth for use in a custody proceeding outside this Commonwealth.

(c) Appearance in other state.—Upon request of the court of another state a competent court of this Commonwealth may order a person in this Commonwealth to appear alone or with the child in a custody proceeding in another state. The court may condition compliance with the request upon assurance by the other state that travel and other necessary expenses will be advanced or reimbursed.

§ 5362. Preservation of documents for use in other states.

In any custody proceeding in this Commonwealth the court shall preserve the pleadings, orders and decrees, any record that has been made of its hearings, social studies, and other pertinent documents until the child reaches 18 years of age. Upon appropriate request of the court of another state the court shall forward to the other court certified copies of any or all of such documents.

§ 5363. Request for court records of another state.

If a custody decree has been rendered in another state concerning a child involved in a custody proceeding pending in a court of this Commonwealth, the court of this Commonwealth upon taking jurisdiction of the case shall request of the court of the other state a certified copy of the transcript of any court record and other documents mentioned in section 5362 (relating to preservation of documents for use in other states).

§ 5364. Intrastate application.

(a) General rule.—Except as otherwise provided in this section, the provisions of this subchapter allocating jurisdiction and functions between and among courts of different states shall also allocate jurisdiction and functions between and among the courts of common pleas of this Commonwealth.

(b) Home jurisdiction.—For the purposes of the definition of "home state" in section 5343 (relating to definitions) a period of temporary absence of the child from the physical custody of the parent, person acting as parent or institution shall not affect the six months or other period.

(c) Petitioner.—As used in this subchapter insofar as relates to the allocation of jurisdiction and functions between and among the courts of common pleas of this Commonwealth, the term "petitioner" means anyone seeking change in the status of custody of a child either by an affirmative action brought in a court or as a defense to a custody action brought by a person acting as parent who had previously been awarded custody of the child.

(d) Effect of agency investigation.—Section 5344(a)(5) (relating to jurisdiction) shall not be applicable for the purposes of this section.

(e) Period of notice.—Notice under section 5346 (relating to notice to persons outside this Commonwealth; submission to jurisdiction) shall be served, mailed, delivered or last published at least 20 days before any hearing.

(f) Jurisdiction declined by reason of conduct.—

(1) If it is just and proper under the circumstances, when the petitioner for an initial decree has wrongfully taken the child from another jurisdiction or has engaged in improper conduct intending to benefit his position in a custody proceeding, upon presentation of the petition, the court shall decline to exercise jurisdiction or shall exercise jurisdiction only to issue an order, pending a full hearing in the appropriate jurisdiction, returning the parties to the custodial status quo existing prior to the improper conduct or wrongful taking unless the petitioner can show that conditions in the former custodial household are physically or emotionally harmful to the child.

(2) Unless required in the interest of the child, the court shall not exercise its jurisdiction to modify a custody decree of another court if the petitioner, without consent of the person entitled to custody has:

(i) improperly removed the child from the physical custody of the person entitled to custody;

(ii) improperly retained the child after a visit or other temporary relinquishment of physical custody; or

(iii) removed the child from the jurisdiction of the court entering the decree without 20 days written notice to the court entering the decree and any party entitled to custody or visitation rights under the terms of the decree.

If the petitioner has violated any provision of a custody decree of another court, the court shall decline to exercise its jurisdiction unless the contestant can show that conditions in the custodial household are physically or emotionally harmful to the child. The burden of proof on this issue is on the contestant requesting the court to take jurisdiction.

(3) Subject to general rules, in appropriate cases a court dismissing a petition under this subsection may charge the petitioner with necessary travel and other expenses, including attorney's fees, incurred by other parties or their witnesses.

(g) Statewide orders.—A court may under section 5352(a) (relating to appearance of parties and the child) issue orders to any party to the proceeding who is in any judicial district of this Commonwealth.

(h) Modification of custody decrees.—

(1) If another court has made a custody decree, a court before which a petition for modification is pending shall not modify the decree of the other court unless it appears to the court before which the petition is pending that the other court which rendered the decree does not have jurisdiction under jurisdictional prerequisites substantially in accordance with this subchapter or has declined to assume jurisdiction to modify its decree and the provisions of subsection (f)(2) will not be violated by an exercise of jurisdiction by the court before which the petition is pending.

(2) If a court of this Commonwealth is authorized under paragraph (1) to modify a custody decree of another court it shall give due consideration to the transcript of the record and other documents of all previous proceedings submitted to it in accordance with section 5363 (relating to request for court records of another state).

RHODE ISLAND

UNIFORM CHILD CUSTODY JURISDICTION ACT

§15-14-1. Short title.—
This chapter may be cited as the "Uniform Child Custody Jurisdiction Act".

§15-14-2. Purpose—Liberal construction.—
(a) The general purposes of this chapter are to:

(1) Avoid jurisdictional competition and conflict with courts of other states in matters of child custody which have in the past resulted in the shifting of children from state to state with harmful effects on their well-being;

(2) Promote cooperation with the courts of other states to the end that a custody decree is rendered in that state which can decide the case in the best interest of the child;

(3) Assure that litigation concerning the custody of a child take place ordinarily in the state with which the child and his or her family have the closest connection and where significant evidence concerning his or her care, protection, training, and personal relationships is most readily available, and that courts of this state decline the exercise of jurisdiction when the child and his or her family have a closer connection with another state;

(4) Discourage continuing controversies over child custody in the interest of greater stability of home environment and of secure family relationships for the child;

(5) Deter abductions and other unilateral removals of children undertaken to obtain custody awards;

(6) Avoid relitigation of custody decisions of other states in this state insofar as feasible;

(7) Facilitate the enforcement of custody decrees of other states;

(8) Promote and expand the exchange of information and other forms of mutual assistance between the courts of this state and those of other states concerned with the same child; and

(9) Make uniform the law of those states which enact it.

(b) This chapter shall be construed to promote the general purposes stated in this section.

§15-14-3. Definitions.—
As used in this chapter:

(1) "Petitioner" means a person, including a parent, who claims a right to custody or visitation rights with respect to a child;

(2) "Respondent" means a person including a parent, or state agency, who disputes the actions of a petitioner claiming a right to custody or visitation rights with respect to a child;

(3) "Custody determination" means a court decision and court orders and instructions providing for the custody of a child, including visitation rights; it does not include a decision relating to child support or any other monetary obligation of any person;

(4) "Custody proceeding" includes proceedings in which a custody determination is one of several issues, such as an action for divorce or separation, and includes child neglect and dependency proceedings;

(5) "Decree" or "custody decree" means a custody determination contained in a judicial decree or order made in a custody proceeding, and includes an initial decree and modification decree;

(6) "Home state" means the state in which the child immediately preceding the time involved lived with his or her parents, a parent, or person acting as parent, for at least six (6) consecutive months, and in the case of a child less than six (6) months old the state in which the child lived from birth and any of the persons mentioned. Periods of temporary absence of any of the named persons are counted as part of the six (6) month or other period;

(7) "Initial decree" means the first custody decree concerning a particular child;

(8) "Modification decree" means a custody decree which modified or replaced a prior decree, whether made by the court which rendered the prior decree or by another court;

(9) "Physical custody" means actual possession and control of a child;

(10) "Person acting as parent" means a person, other than a parent, who has physical custody of a child and who has either been awarded custody by a court or claims a right to custody;

(11) "State" means any state, territory, or possession of the United States, the Commonwealth of Puerto Rico, and the District of Columbia; and

(12) "Court" shall mean the family court of the state of Rhode Island and Providence Plantations unless another meaning is so indicated.

§15-14-4. Jurisdiction.—
(a) The family court has jurisdiction to make a child custody determination by initial or modification decree if:

(1) The state of Rhode Island: (i) is the home state of the child at the time of commencement of the proceeding, or (ii) had

been the child's home state within six (6) months before commencement of the proceeding and the child is absent from Rhode Island because of his or her removal or retention by a person claiming his or her custody or for other reasons, and a parent or person acting as parent continues to live in Rhode Island; or

(2) It is in the best interest of the child that the family court assume jurisdiction because: (i) the child and his or her parents, or the child and at least one party, have significant connection with Rhode Island, and (ii) there is available in Rhode Island substantial evidence concerning the child's present or future care, protection, training, and personal relationships; or

(3) The child is physically present in Rhode Island and: (i) the child has been abandoned, or (ii) it is necessary in an emergency to protect the child because he or she has been subjected to or threatened with mistreatment or abuse or is otherwise neglected or dependent; or

(4)(i) It appears that no other state would have jurisdiction under prerequisites substantially in accordance with subsection (a)(1), (2), or (3), or another state has declined to exercise jurisdiction on the ground that Rhode Island is the more appropriate forum to determine the custody of the child, and (ii) it is in the best interest of the child that the family court assume jurisdiction.

(b) Except under subdivisions (3) and (4) of subsection (a), physical presence in Rhode Island of the child, or of the child and one of the parties, is not alone sufficient to confer jurisdiction on the family court to make a child custody determination.

(c) Physical presence of the child, while desirable, is not a prerequisite for jurisdiction to determine his or her custody.

§15-14-5. Notice and opportunity to be heard.—

Before making a decree under this chapter, reasonable notice and opportunity to be heard shall be given to the parties, any parent whose parental rights have not been previously terminated, and any person who has physical custody of the child. If any of these persons is outside Rhode Island, notice and opportunity to be heard shall be given pursuant to § 15-14-6.

§15-14-6. Notice to persons outside Rhode Island—Submission to jurisdiction.—

(a) Notice required for the exercise of jurisdiction over a person outside Rhode Island shall be given in a manner reasonably calculated to give actual notice, and may be:

(1) By personal delivery outside Rhode Island in the manner prescribed for service of process within this state;

(2) In the manner prescribed by law of the place in which the service is made for service of process in that place in an action in any of its courts of general jurisdiction;

(3) By any form of mail addressed to the person to be served and requesting a receipt; or

(4) As directed by the court (including publication, if other means of notification are ineffective).

(b) Notice under this section shall be served, mailed, or delivered, or last published, at least twenty (20) days before any hearing in Rhode Island.

(c) Proof of service outside Rhode Island may be made by affidavit of the individual who made the service, or in the manner prescribed by the law of Rhode Island, the order pursuant to which the service is made, or the law of the place in which the service is made. If service is made by mail, proof may be a receipt signed by the addressee or other evidence of delivery to the addressee.

(d) Notice is not required if a person submits to the jurisdiction of the court.

§15-14-7. Simultaneous proceedings in other states.—

(a) The family court shall not exercise its jurisdiction under this chapter if at the time of filing the petition a proceeding concerning the custody of the child was pending in a court of another state exercising jurisdiction substantially in conformity with this chapter, unless the proceeding is stayed by the court of the other state because Rhode Island is a more appropriate forum or for other reasons.

(b) Before hearing the petition in a custody proceeding the court shall examine the pleadings and other information supplied by the parties under § 15-14-10 and shall consult the child custody registry established under § 15-14-17 concerning the pendency of proceedings with respect to the child in other states. If the court has reason to believe that proceedings may be pending in another state it shall direct an inquiry to the state court administrator or other appropriate official of the other state.

(c) If the court is informed during the course of the proceeding that a proceeding concerning the custody of the child was pending in another state before the court assumed jurisdiction it shall stay the proceeding and communicate with the court in which the other proceeding is pending to the end that the issue may be litigated in the more appropriate forum and that information be exchanged in accordance with §§ 15-14-20 through 15-14-23. If the court has made a custody decree before being informed of a pending proceeding in a court of another state it shall immediately inform that court of the fact. If the court is informed that a proceeding was commenced in another state after it assumed jurisdiction it shall likewise inform the other court to the end that the issues may be litigated in the more appropriate forum.

§15-14-8. Inconvenient forum.—

(a) The family court may decline to exercise its jurisdiction any time before making a decree if it finds that it is an inconvenient forum to make a custody determination under the circumstances of the case and that a court of another state is a more appropriate forum.

(b) A finding of inconvenient forum may be made upon the court's own motion or upon motion of a party or guardian ad litem or other representative of the child.

(c) In determining if it is an inconvenient forum, the court shall consider if it is in the interest of the child that another state assume jurisdiction. For this purpose it may take into account the following factors, among others:

(1) If another state is or recently was the child's home state;

(2) If another state has a closer connection with the child and his or her family or with the child and one or more of the parties;

(3) If substantial evidence concerning the child's present or future care, protection, training, and personal relationships is more readily available in another state;

(4) If the parties have agreed on another forum which is no less appropriate; and

(5) If the exercise of jurisdiction by a court of this state would contravene any of the purposes stated in § 15-14-2.

(d) Before determining whether to decline or retain jurisdiction the court may communicate with a court of another state and exchange information pertinent to the assumption of jurisdiction by either court with a view to assuring that jurisdiction will be exercised by the more appropriate court and that a forum will be available to the parties.

(e) If the court finds that it is an inconvenient forum and that a court of another state is a more appropriate forum, it may dismiss the proceeding, or it may stay the proceedings upon condition that a custody proceeding be promptly commenced in another named state or upon any other conditions which may be just and proper, including the condition that a moving party stipulate his or her consent and submission to the jurisdiction of the other forum.

(f) The court may decline to exercise its jurisdiction under this chapter if a custody determination is incidental to an action for divorce or another proceeding while retaining jurisdiction over the divorce or other proceeding.

(g) If it appears to the court that it is clearly an inappropriate forum it may require the party who commenced the proceedings to pay, in addition to the costs of the proceedings in Rhode Island, necessary travel and related expenses, and any other reasonable fees which may be imposed by the court. Payment is to be made to the clerk of the family court for remittance to the proper party.

(h) Upon dismissal or stay of proceedings under this section the court shall inform the court found to be the more appropriate forum of this fact or, if the court which would have jurisdiction in the other state is not certainly known, shall transmit the information to the court clerk or other appropriate official for forwarding to the appropriate court.

(i) Any communication received from another state informing the family court of a finding of inconvenient forum because the family court is the more appropriate forum shall be filed in the custody registry of the appropriate court. Upon assuming jurisdiction the family court shall inform the original court of this fact.

§15-14-9. Jurisdiction declined by reason of conduct.—

(a) If the petitioner for an initial decree has wrongfully taken the child from another state or has engaged in similar reprehensible conduct the court may decline to exercise jurisdiction if this is just and proper under the circumstances.

(b) Unless required in the interest of the child, the court shall not exercise its jurisdiction to modify a custody decree of another state if the petitioner, without consent of the person entitled to custody, has improperly removed the child from the physical custody of the person entitled to custody or has improperly retained the child after a visit or other temporary relinquishment of physical custody. If the petitioner has violated any other provision of a custody decree of another state the court may decline to exercise its jurisdiction if this is just and proper under the circumstances.

(c) In appropriate cases a court dismissing a petition under this section may charge the petitioner with necessary travel and other expenses, including attorneys' fees, incurred by other parties or their witnesses.

§15-14-10. Information under oath to be submitted to the court.—

(a) Every party in a custody proceeding in his first pleading or in an affidavit attached to that pleading shall give information under oath as to the child's present address, the places where the child has lived within the last five (5) years, and the names and present addresses of the persons with whom the child has lived during that period. In this pleading or affidavit every party shall further declare under oath whether:

(1) He or she has participated as a party or witness, or in any other capacity, in any other litigation concerning the custody of the child in this or any other state;

(2) He or she has information of any custody proceeding concerning the child pending in a court of this or any other state; and

(3) He or she knows of any person not a party to the proceedings who has physical custody of the child or claims to have custody or visitation rights with respect to the child.

(b) If the declaration as to any of the above items is in the affirmative the declarant shall give additional information under oath as required by the court. The court may examine the parties under oath as to details of the information furnished and as to other matters pertinent to the court's jurisdiction and the disposition of the case.

(c) Each party has a continuing duty to inform the court of any custody proceeding concerning the child in this or any other state of which he or she obtained information during this proceeding.

§15-14-11. Additional parties.—

If the court learns from information furnished by the parties pursuant to § 15-14-10 or from other sources that a person not a party to the custody proceeding has physical custody of the child or claims to have custody or visitation rights with respect to the child, it shall order that person to be joined as a party and to be duly notified of the pendency of the proceeding and of his or her joinder as a party. If the person joined as a party is outside Rhode Island he or she shall be served with process or otherwise notified in accordance with § 15-14-6.

§15-14-12. Appearance of parties and the child.—

(a) The court may order any party to the proceeding who is in Rhode Island to appear personally before the court. If that party has physical custody of the child the court may order that he appear personally with the child.

(b) If a party to the proceeding whose presence is desired by the court is outside Rhode Island with or without the child the court may order that the notice given under § 15-14-6 include a statement directing that party to appear personally with or without the child and declaring that failure to appear may result in a decision adverse to that party.

(c) If a party to the proceeding who is outside Rhode Island is directed to appear under subsection (b) or desires to appear personally before the court with or without the child, the court may require another party to pay to the clerk of the family court travel and other necessary expenses of the party so appearing and of the child if this is just and proper under the circumstances.

§15-14-13. Binding force and res judicata effect of custody decree.—

A custody decree rendered by the family court which had jurisdiction under § 15-14-4 binds all parties who have been served in Rhode Island or notified in accordance with § 15-14-6 who have submitted to the jurisdiction of the court, and who have been given an opportunity to be heard. As to these parties the custody decree is conclusive as to all issues of law and fact decided and as to the custody determination made unless and until that determination is modified pursuant to law, including the provisions of this chapter.

§15-14-14. Recognition of out-of-state custody decrees.—

The courts of Rhode Island shall recognize and enforce an initial or modification decree of a court of another state which had assumed jurisdiction under statutory provisions substantially in accordance with this chapter or which was made under factual circumstances meeting the jurisdictional standards of the chapter, so long as this decree has been modified in accordance with jurisdictional standards substantially similar to those of this chapter.

§15-14-15. Modification of custody decree of another state.—

(a) If a court of another state has made a custody decree, the family court shall not modify that decree unless: (1) it appears to the court that the court which rendered the decree does not now have jurisdiction under jurisdictional prerequisites substantially in accordance with this chapter or has declined to assume jurisdiction to modify the decree, and (2) the family court has jurisdiction.

(b) If the court is authorized under subsection (a) and § 15-14-9 to modify a custody decree of another state it shall give due consideration to the transcript of the record and other documents of all previous proceedings submitted to it in accordance with § 15-14-23.

§15-14-16. Filing and enforcement of custody decree of another state.—

(a) A certified copy of a custody decree of another state may be filed in the office of the clerk of the family court. The clerk shall treat the decree in the same manner as a custody decree of the family court. A custody decree so filed has the same effect and shall be enforced in like manner as a custody decree by the family court.

(b) A person violating a custody decree of another state which makes it necessary to enforce the decree in Rhode Island may be required to pay necessary travel and related expenses and any other reasonable fees which may be imposed by the court.

§15-14-17. Registry of out-of-state custody decrees and proceedings.—

The clerk of the family court shall maintain a registry in which he or she shall enter the following:

(1) Certified copies of custody decrees of other states received for filing;

(2) Communications as to the pendency of custody proceedings in other states;

(3) Communications concerning a finding of inconvenient forum by a court of another state; and

(4) Other communications or documents concerning custody proceedings in another state which may affect the jurisdiction of the family court or the disposition to be made by it in a custody proceeding.

§15-14-18. Certified copies of custody decree.—

The clerk of the family court at the request of the court of another state or at the request of any person who is affected by or has legitimate interest in a custody decree shall, upon payment of the fee provided by law, certify and forward a copy of the decree to that court or person.

§15-14-19. Taking testimony in another state.—

In addition to other procedural devices available to a party, any party to the proceeding or a guardian ad litem or other representative of the child may adduce testimony of witnesses, including parties and the child, by deposition or otherwise in another state. The court on its own motion may direct that the testimony of a person be taken in another state and may prescribe the manner in which and the terms upon which the testimony shall be taken.

§15-14-20. Hearings and studies in another state—Orders to appear.—

(a) The family court may request the appropriate court of another state to hold a hearing to adduce evidence, to order a party to produce or give evidence under other procedures of that state, to have social studies made with respect to the custody of a child involved in proceedings pending in the family court, and to forward to the family court certified copies of the transcript of the record of the hearing, the evidence otherwise adduced, or any social studies prepared in compliance with the request. The cost of the services may be assessed against the parties or, if necessary, ordered paid by the state.

(b) The family court may request the appropriate court of another state to order a party to custody proceedings pending in the family court to appear in the proceedings and, if that party has physical custody of the child, to appear with the child. The request may state that travel and other necessary expenses of the party and of the child whose appearance is desired will be assessed against another party or will otherwise be paid.

§15-14-21. Assistance to courts of other states.—

(a) Upon request of the court of another state the family court may order a person in Rhode Island to appear at a hearing to adduce evidence or to produce or give evidence under other procedures available in Rhode Island or may order social studies to be made for use in a custody proceeding in another state. A certified copy of the transcript of the record of the hearing or the evidence otherwise adduced and any social studies prepared shall be forwarded by the clerk of the family court to the requesting court.

(b) A person within Rhode Island may voluntarily give his or her testimony or statement in Rhode Island for use in a custody proceeding outside Rhode Island.

(c) Upon request of the court of another state the family court may order a person in Rhode Island to appear alone or with the child in a custody proceeding in another state. The court may condition compliance with the request upon assurance by the other state that travel and other necessary expenses will be advanced or reimbursed.

§15-14-22. Preservation of documents for use in other states.—

In any custody proceeding in Rhode Island the court shall preserve the pleadings, order, decrees, any record that has been made of its hearings, social studies, and other pertinent documents until the child reaches eighteen (18) years of age. Upon appropriate request of the court of another state the family court shall forward to the other court certified copies of any or all such documents.

§15-14-23. Request for court records of another state.—

If a custody decree has been rendered in another state concerning a child involved in a custody proceeding pending in the family court, the family court upon taking jurisdiction of the case shall request of the court of the other state a certified copy of the transcript of any court record and other documents mentioned in § 15-14-22.

§15-14-24. International application.—

The general policies of this chapter extend to the international area. The provisions of this chapter relating to the recognition and enforcement of custody decrees of other states apply to custody decrees and decrees involving legal institutions similar in nature to custody institutions rendered by appropriate authorities of other nations if reasonable notice and opportunity to be heard were given to all affected persons.

§15-14-25. Priority.—

Upon the request of a party to a custody proceeding which raises a question of existence of exercise of jurisdiction under this chapter the case shall be given calendar priority and handled expeditiously.

§15-14-26. Severability.—

If any provision of this chapter or the application thereof to any person or circumstances is held invalid, its invalidity does not affect other provisions or applications of the chapter which can be given without the invalid provision or application, and to this end the provisions of this chapter are severable.

SOUTH CAROLINA

UNIFORM CHILD CUSTODY JURISDICTION ACT

§ 20-7-782. Short title.
This subarticle may be cited as the Uniform Child Custody Jurisdiction Act.

§ 20-7-784. Purposes; construction of provisions.
(a) The general purposes of this subarticle are to:

(1) avoid jurisdictional competition and conflict with courts of other states in matters of child custody which have in the past resulted in the shifting of children from state to state with harmful effects on their well-being;

(2) promote cooperation with the courts of other states to the end that a custody decree is rendered in that state which can best decide the case in the interest of the child;

(3) assure that litigation concerning the custody of a child take place ordinarily in the state with which the child and his family have the closest connection and where significant evidence concerning his care, protection, training and personal relationships is most readily available, and that courts of this State decline the exercise of jurisdiction when the child and his family have a closer connection with another state;

(4) discourage continuing controversies over child custody in the interest of greater stability of home environment and of secure family relationships for the child;

(5) deter abductions and other unilateral removals of children undertaken to obtain custody awards;

(6) avoid relitigation of custody decisions of other states in this State insofar as feasible;

(7) facilitate the enforcement of custody decrees of other states;

(8) promote and expand the exchange of information and other forms of mutual assistance between the courts of this State and those of other states concerned with the same child;

(9) make uniform the law of those states which enact it.

(b) This subarticle shall be construed to promote the general purposes stated in this section.

§ 20-7-786. Definitions.
As used in this subarticle, unless the context clearly indicates otherwise:

(1) "contestant" means a person, including a parent, who claims a right to custody or visitation rights with respect to a child;

(2) "custody determination" means a court decision and court orders and instructions providing for the custody of a child, including visitation rights; it does not include a decision relating to child support or any other monetary obligation of any person;

(3) "custody proceeding" includes proceedings in which a custody determination is one of several issues, such as an action for divorce or separation, and includes child neglect and dependency proceedings;

(4) "decree" or "custody decree" means a custody determination contained in a judicial decree or order made in a custody proceeding, and includes an initial decree and a modification decree;

(5) "home state" means the state in which the child immediately preceding the time involved lived with his parents, a parent, or a person acting as parent, for at least six consecutive months, and in the case of a child less than six months old the state in which the child lived from birth with any of the persons mentioned. Periods of temporary absence of any of the named persons are counted as part of the six-month or other period;

(6) "initial decree" means the first custody decree concerning a particular child;

(7) "modification decree" means a custody decree which modifies or replaces a prior decree, whether made by the court which rendered the prior decree or by another court;

(8) "physical custody" means actual possession and control of a child;

(9) "person acting as parent" means a person, other than a parent, who has physical custody of a child and who has either been awarded custody by a court or claims a right to custody;

(10) "state" means any state, territory or possession of the United States, the Commonwealth of Puerto Rico and the District of Columbia;

(11) "court" or "court of this State" means the statewide system of family courts established pursuant to §§ 14-21-410 et seq.

(12) "clerk of the court" or "clerk of the family court" means the clerk of a respective family court or the person in charge of administration of a family court if not designated as clerk of that court.

§ 20-7-788. Jurisdiction.
(a) A court of this State which is competent to decide child custody matters has jurisdiction to make a child custody determination by initial or modification decree if:

(1) this State (i) is the home state of the child at the time of commencement of the proceeding, or (ii) had been the child's home

state within six months before commencement of the proceeding and the child is absent from this State because of his removal or retention by a person claiming his custody or for other reasons, and a parent or person acting as parent continues to live in this State; or

(2) it is in the best interest of the child that a court of this State assume jurisdiction because (i) the child and his parents, or the child and at least one contestant, have a significant connection with this State and (ii) there is available in this State substantial evidence concerning the child's present or future care, protection, training and personal relationships; or

(3) the child is physically present in this State and (i) the child has been abandoned or (ii) it is necessary in an emergency to protect the child because he has been subjected to or threatened with mistreatment or abuse or is otherwise neglected or dependent; or

(4) (i) it appears that no other state would have jurisdiction under prerequisites substantially in accordance with paragraphs (1), (2) or (3) of subsection (a), or another state has declined to exercise jurisdiction on the ground that this State is the more appropriate forum to determine the custody of the child and (ii) it is in the best interest of the child that this court assume jurisdiction.

(b) Except under paragraphs (3) and (4) of subsection (a), physical presence in this State of the child, or of the child and one of the contestants, is not alone sufficient to confer jurisdiction on a court of this State to make a child custody determination.

(c) Physical presence of the child, while desirable, is not a prerequisite for jurisdiction to determine his custody.

§ 20-7-790. Notice and opportunity to be heard.

Before making a decree under this subarticle, reasonable notice and opportunity to be heard shall be given to the contestants, any parent whose parental rights have not been previously terminated, and any person who has physical custody of the child. If any of these persons is outside this State, notice and opportunity to be heard shall be given pursuant to § 20-7-792.

§ 20-7-792. Notice to persons outside this state; submission to jurisdiction.

(a) Notice required for the exercise of jurisdiction over a person outside this State shall be given in a manner reasonably calculated to give actual notice, and may be:

(1) by personal delivery outside this State in the manner prescribed for service of process within this State;

(2) in the manner prescribed by the law of the place in which the service is made for service of process in that place in an action in any of its courts of general jurisdiction;

(3) by any form of mail addressed to the person to be served and requesting a receipt;

(4) as directed by the court, including publication, if other means of notification are ineffective.

(b) Notice under this section shall be served, mailed or delivered, or last published, at least twenty days before any hearing in this State. *Provided*, however, that in proceedings pursuant to § 20-7-788 (a) (3) above, upon a showing by the moving party that an emergency or abandonment situation exists within the meaning of § 20-7-788 (a) (3) so as to place the child in jeopardy, the court may shorten the notice period to such period as it may deem to be in the best interests of the child.

(c) Proof of service outside this State may be made by affidavit of the individual who made the service, or in the manner prescribed by the law of this State, the order pursuant to which the service is made, or the law of the place in which the service is made. If service is made by mail, proof may be a receipt signed by the addressee of other evidence of delivery to the addressee.

(d) Notice is not required if a person submits to the jurisdiction of the court.

§ 20-7-794. Simultaneous proceedings in other states.

(a) A court of this State shall not exercise its jurisdiction under this subarticle if at the time of filing the petition a proceeding concerning the custody of the child was pending in a court of another state exercising jurisdiction substantially in conformity with this subarticle, unless the proceeding is stayed by the court of the other state because this State is a more appropriate forum or for other reasons.

(b) Before hearing the petition in a custody proceeding the court shall examine the pleadings and other information supplied by the parties under § 20-7-800 and shall consult the child custody registry established under § 20-7-814 concerning the pendency of proceedings with respect to the child in other states. If the court has reason to believe that proceedings may be pending in another state it shall direct an inquiry to the state court administrator or other appropriate official of the other state.

(c) If the court is informed during the course of the proceeding that a proceeding concerning the custody of the child was pending in another state before the court assumed jurisdiction it shall stay the proceeding and communicate with the court in which the other proceeding is pending to the end that the issue may be litigated in the more appropriate forum and that information be exchanged in accordance with §§ 20-7-820 through 20-7-826. If a court of this State has made a custody decree before being informed of a pending proceeding in a court of another state it shall immediately inform that court of the fact. If the court is informed that a proceeding was commenced in another state after it assumed jurisdiction it shall likewise inform the other court to the end that the issues may be litigated in the more appropriate forum.

§ 20-7-796. Inconvenient forum.

(a) A court which has jurisdiction under this subarticle to make an initial or modification decree may decline to exercise its jurisdiction anytime before making a decree if it finds that it is an inconvenient forum to make a custody determination under the circumstances of the case and that a court of another state is a more appropriate forum.

(b) A finding of inconvenient forum may be made upon the court's own motion or upon motion of a party or a guardian ad litem or other representative of the child.

(c) In determining if it is an inconvenient forum, the court shall consider if it is in the interest of the child that another state assume jurisdiction. For this purpose it may take into account the following factors, among others:

(1) if another state is or recently was the child's home state;

(2) if another state has a closer connection with the child and his family or with the child and one or more of the contestants;

(3) if substantial evidence concerning the child's present or future care, protection, training and personal relationships are more readily available in another state;

(4) if the parties have agreed on another forum which is no less appropriate;

(5) if the exercise of jurisdiction by a court of this State would contravene any of the purposes stated in § 20-7-784.

(d) Before determining whether to decline or retain jurisdiction the court may communicate with a court of another state and exchange information pertinent to the assumption of jurisdiction by either court with a view to assuring that jurisdiction will be exercised by the more appropriate court and that a forum will be available to the parties.

(e) If the court finds that it is an inconvenient forum and that a court of another state is a more appropriate forum, it may dismiss the proceedings, or it may stay the proceedings upon condition that a custody proceeding be promptly commenced in another named state or upon any other conditions which may be just and proper, including the condition that a custody proceeding be promptly commenced in another named state or upon any other conditions which may be just and proper, including the condition that a moving party stipulate his consent and submission to the jurisdiction of the other forum.

(f) The court may decline to exercise its jurisdiction under this subarticle if a custody determination is incidental to an action for divorce or another proceeding while retaining jurisdiction over the divorce or other proceeding.

(g) If it appears to the court that it is clearly an inappropriate forum it may require the party who commenced the proceedings to pay necessary travel and other expenses, including attorneys' fees, incurred by other parties or their witnesses. Payment is to be made to the clerk of the court for remittance to the proper party.

(h) Upon dismissal or stay of proceedings under this section the court shall inform the court found to be the more appropriate forum of this fact, or if the court which would have jurisdiction in the other state is not certainly known, shall transmit the information to the court administrator or other appropriate official for forwarding to the appropriate court.

(i) Any communication received from another state informing this State of a finding of inconvenient forum because a court of this State is the more appropriate forum shall be filed in the custody registry of the appropriate court. Upon assuming jurisdiction the court of this State shall inform the original court of this fact.

§ 20-7-798. Jurisdiction declined by reason of conduct.

(a) If the petitioner for an initial decree has wrongfully taken the child from another state or has engaged in similar reprehensible conduct the court may decline to exercise jurisdiction if this is just and proper under the circumstances.

(b) Unless required in the interest of the child, the court shall not exercise its jurisdiction to modify a custody decree of another state if the petitioner, without consent of the person entitled to custody, has improperly removed the child from the physical custody of the person entitled to custody or has improperly retained the child after a visit or other temporary relinquishment of physical custody. If the petitioner has violated any other provision of a custody decree of another state the court may decline to exercise its jurisdiction if this is just and proper under the circumstances.

(c) In appropriate cases a court dismissing a petition under this section may charge the petitioner with necessary travel and other expenses, including attorneys' fees, incurred by other parties or their witnesses.

§ 20-7-800. Information under oath to be submitted to the court.

(a) Every party in a custody proceeding in his first pleading or in an affidavit attached to that pleading shall give information under oath as to the child's present address, the places where the child has lived within the last five years and the names and present addresses of the persons with whom the child has lived during that period. In this pleading or affidavit every party shall further declare under oath whether:

(1) he has participated (as a party, witness or in any other capacity) in any other litigation concerning the custody of the same child in this or any other state;

(2) he has information of any custody proceeding concerning the child pending in a court of this or any other state;

(3) he knows of any person not a party to the proceeding who has physical custody of the child or claims to have custody or visitation rights with respect to the child.

(b) If the declaration as to any of the above items is in the affirmative the declarant shall give additional information under oath as required by the court. The court may examine the parties under oath as to details of the information furnished and as to other matters pertinent to the court's jurisdiction and the disposition of the case.

(c) Each party shall have a continuing duty to inform the court of any custody proceeding concerning the child in this or any other state of which he obtained information during this proceeding.

§ 20-7-802. Additional parties.

If the court learns from information furnished by the parties pursuant to § 20-7-800 or from other sources that a person not a party to the custody proceeding has physical custody of the child or claims to have custody or visitation rights with respect to the child, it shall order that person to be joined as a party and to be duly notified of the pendency of the proceeding and of his joinder as a party. If the person joined as a party is outside this State he shall be served with process or otherwise notified in accordance with § 20-7-792.

§ 20-7-804. Appearance of parties and the child.

(a) The court may order any party to the proceeding who is in this State to appear personally before the court. If that party has physical custody of the child the court may order that he appear personally with the child.

(b) If a party to the proceeding whose presence is desired by the court is outside this State with or without the child the court may order that the notice given under § 20-7-792 include a statement directing that party to appear personally with or without the child and declaring that failure to appear may result in a decision adverse to that party.

(c) If a party to the proceeding who is outside this State is directed to appear under subsection (b) or desires to appear personally before the court with or without the child, the court may require another party to pay to the clerk of the court travel and other necessary expenses of the party so appearing and of the child if this is just and proper under the circumstances.

§ 20-7-806. Binding force and res judicata effect of custody decree.

A custody decree rendered by a court of this State which had jurisdiction under § 20-7-788 binds all parties who have been served in this State or notified in accordance with § 20-7-792 or who have submitted to the jurisdiction of the court, who have been given an opportunity to be heard. As to these parties the custody decree is conclusive as to all issues of law and fact decided and as to the custody determination made unless and until that determination is modified pursuant to law, including the provisions of this subarticle.

§ 20-7-808. Recognition of out-of-state custody decrees.

The courts of this State shall recognize and enforce an initial or modification decree of a court of another state which had assumed jurisdiction under statutory provisions substantially in accordance with this subarticle or which was made under factual circumstances meeting the jurisdictional standards of the subarticle, so long as this decree has not been modified in accordance with jurisdictional standards substantially similar to those of this subarticle.

§ 20-7-810. Modification of custody decree of another state.

(a) If a court of another state has made a custody decree, a court of this State shall not modify that decree unless (1) it appears to the court of this State that the court which rendered the decree does not now have jurisdiction under jurisdictional prerequisites substantially in accordance with this subarticle or has declined to assume jurisdiction to modify the decree and (2) the court of this State has jurisdiction.

(b) If a court of this State is authorized under subsection (a) and § 20-7-798 to modify a custody decree of another state it shall give due consideration to the transcript of the record and other documents of all previous proceedings submitted to it in accordance with § 20-7-826.

§ 20-7-812. Filing and enforcement of custody decree of another state.

(a) A certified copy of a custody decree of another state may be filed in the office of the clerk of any family court of this State. The clerk shall treat the decree in the same manner as a custody decree of the family court of this State. A custody decree so filed has the same effect and shall be enforced in like manner as a custody decree rendered by a court of this State.

(b) A person violating a custody decree of another state which makes it necessary to enforce the decree in this State may be required to pay necessary travel and other expenses, including attorneys' fees, incurred by the party entitled to the custody or his witnesses.

§ 20-7-814. Registry of out-of-state custody decrees and proceedings.

The clerk of each family court of this State shall maintain a registry in which he shall enter the following:

(1) certified copies of custody decrees of other states received for filing;

(2) communications as to the pendency of custody proceedings in other states;

(3) communications concerning a finding of inconvenient forum by a court of another state.

(4) other communications or documents concerning custody proceedings in another state which may affect the jurisdiction of a court of this State or the disposition to be made by it in a custody proceeding.

§ 20-7-816. Certified copies of custody decree.

The clerk of a family court of this State, at the request of the court of another state or at the request of any person who is affected by or has a legitimate interest in a custody decree, shall certify and forward a copy of the decree to that court or person.

§ 20-7-818. Taking testimony in another state.

In addition to other procedural devices available to a party, any party to the proceeding or a guardian ad litem or other representative of the child may adduce testimony of witnesses, including parties and the child, by deposition or otherwise, in another state. The court on its own motion may direct that the testimony of a person be taken in another state and may prescribe the manner in which and the terms upon which the testimony shall be taken.

§ 20-7-820. Hearings and studies in another state; orders to appear.

(a) A court of this State may request the appropriate court of another state to hold a hearing to adduce evidence, to order a party to produce or give evidence under other procedures of that state, or to have social studies made with respect to the custody of a child involved in proceedings pending in the court of this State; and to forward to the court of this State certified copies of the transcript of the record of the hearing, the evidence otherwise adduced, or any social studies prepared in compliance with the request. The court in its discretion may order that the cost of these services be assessed against particular parties to the action.

(b) A court of this State may request the appropriate court of another state to order a party to custody proceedings pending in the court of this State to appear in the proceedings, and if that party has physical custody of the child, to appear with the child. The request may state that travel and other necessary expenses of the party and of the child whose appearance is desired will be assessed against another party to the action.

§ 20-7-822. Assistance to courts of other states.

(a) Upon request of the court of another state the courts of this State which are competent to hear custody matters may order a person in this State to appear at a hearing to adduce evidence or to produce or give evidence under other procedures available in this State or may order social studies to be made for use in a custody proceeding in another state. A certified copy of the transcript of the record of the hearing or the evidence otherwise adduced and any social studies prepared shall be forwarded by the clerk of the court to the requesting court.

(b) A person within this State may voluntarily give his testimony or statement in this State for use in a custody proceeding outside this State.

(c) Upon request of the court of another state a competent court of this State may order a person in this State to appear alone or with the child in a custody proceeding in another state. The court may condition compliance with the request upon assurance by the other state that travel and other necessary expenses will be advanced or reimbursed.

§ 20-7-824. Preservation of documents for use in other state.

In any custody proceeding in this State the court shall preserve the pleadings, orders and decrees, any record that has been made of its hearings, social studies and other pertinent documents until the child reaches eighteen years of age. Upon appropriate request of the court of another state the court shall forward to the other court certified copies of any or all of such documents.

§ 20-7-826. Request for court records of another state.

If a custody decree has been rendered in another state concerning a child involved in a custody proceeding pending in a court of this State, the court of this State upon taking jurisdiction of the case shall request of the court of the other state a certified copy of the transcript of any court record and other documents mentioned in § 20-7-824

§ 20-7-828. Jurisdiction in family courts.

The statewide system of family courts established pursuant to §§ 14-21-410 et seq. is hereby declared to be the courts of this State where the provisions of this subarticle shall be enforced or litigated; *provided*, however, that where the provisions of this subarticle require any action which is not within the jurisdiction of the family courts, the circuit courts of this State shall have jurisdiction to perform or order such action.

§ 20-7-830. International application.

The general policies of this subarticle extend to the international area. The provisions of this subarticle relating to the recognition and enforcement of custody decrees of other states apply to custody decrees and decrees involving legal institutions similar in nature to custody, rendered by appropriate authorities of other nations if reasonable notice and opportunity to be heard were given to all affected persons.

SOUTH DAKOTA

UNIFORM CHILD CUSTODY JURISDICTION ACT

§ 26-5A-2. Definition of terms.

Terms used in this chapter, unless the context otherwise requires, mean:

(1) "Contestant," a person, including a parent, who claims a right to custody or visitation rights with respect to a child;

(2) "Custody determination," a court decision and court orders and instructions providing for the custody of a child, including visitation rights; it does not include a decision relating to child support or any other monetary obligation of any person;

(3) "Custody proceeding" includes proceedings in which a custody determination is one of several issues, such as an action for divorce or separation, and includes child neglect and dependency proceedings;

(4) "Decree" or "custody decree," a custody determination contained in a judicial decree or order made in a custody proceeding, and includes an initial decree and a modification decree;

(5) "Home state," the state in which the child immediately preceding the time involved lived with his parents, a parent, or a person acting as parent, for at least six consecutive months, and in the case of a child less than six months old the state in which the child lived from birth with any of the persons mentioned. Periods of temporary absence of any of the named persons are counted as part of the six-month or other period;

(6) "Initial decree," the first custody decree concerning a particular child;

(7) "Modification decree," a custody decree which modified or replaces a prior decree, whether made by the court which gave the prior decree or by another court;

(8) "Physical custody," actual possession and control of a child;

(9) "Person acting as parent," a person, other than a parent, who has physical custody of a child and who has either been awarded custody by a court or claims a right to custody;

(10) "State," any state, territory, or possession of the United States, the commonwealth of Puerto Rico, and the District of Columbia.

§ 26-5A-3. Jurisdiction.

A court of this state which is competent to decide child custody matters has jurisdiction to make a child custody determination by initial or modification decree if:

(1) This state is the home state of the child at the time of commencement of the proceeding, or had been the child's home state within six months before commencement of the proceeding and the child is absent from this state because of his removal or retention by a person claiming his custody or for other reasons, and a parent or person acting as parent continues to live in this state; or

(2) It is in the best interest of the child that a court of this state assume jurisdiction because the child and his parents, or the child and at least one contestant, have a significant connection with this state, and there is available in this state substantial evidence concerning the child's present or future care, protection, training, and personal relationships; or

(3) The child is physically present in this state and the child has been abandoned or it is necessary in an emergency to protect the child because he has been subjected to or threatened with mistreatment or abuse or is otherwise neglected or dependent; or

(4) It appears that no other state would have jurisdiction under prerequisites substantially in accordance with subdivisions (1), (2), or (3) of this section, or another state has declined to exercise jurisdiction on the ground that this state is the more appropriate forum to determine the custody of the child, and it is in the best interest of the child that this court assume jurisdiction.

Except under subdivisions (3) and (4) of this section physical presence in this state of the child, or of the child and one of the contestants, is not alone sufficient to confer jurisdiction on a court of this state to make a child custody determination.

Physical presence of the child, while desirable, is not a prerequisite for jurisdiction to determine his custody.

§ 26-5A-3.1. Court authorized to order mediation or investigation — Allocation of costs.

In any custody dispute between parents, the court may order mediation to assist the parties in formulating or modifying a plan, or in implementing a plan, for custody and may allocate the cost of the mediation between the parties. The court may also direct that an investigation be conducted to assist the court in making a custody determination and may allocate the costs of such investigation between the parties.

§ 26-5A-4. Notice and opportunity to be heard.

Before making a decree under this chapter, reasonable notice and opportunity to be heard shall be given to the contestants, any parent whose parental rights have not been previously terminated, and any person who has physical custody of the child. If any of these persons is outside this state, notice and opportunity to be heard shall be given pursuant to § 26-5A-5.

§ 26-5A-5. Notice to persons outside this state — Submission to jurisdiction.

Notice required for the exercise of jurisdiction over a person outside this state shall be given in a manner reasonably calculated to give actual notice, and may be:

(1) By personal delivery outside this state in the manner prescribed for service of process within this state;

(2) In the manner prescribed by the law of the place in which the service is made for service of process in that place in an action in any of its courts of general jurisdiction;

(3) By any form of mail addressed to the person to be served and requesting a receipt; or

(4) As directed by the court.

Notice under this section shall be served, mailed, or delivered, at least twenty days before any hearing in this state.

Proof of service outside this state may be made by affidavit of the individual who made the service, or in the manner prescribed by the law of this state, the order pursuant to which the service is made, or the law of the place in which the service is made. If service is made by mail, proof may be a receipt signed by the addressee or other evidence of delivery to the addressee.

Notice is not required if a person submits to the jurisdiction of the court.

§ 26-5A-6. Simultaneous proceedings in other states.

A court of this state may not exercise its jurisdiction under this chapter if at the time of filing the petition a proceeding concerning the custody of the child was pending in a court of another state exercising jurisdiction substantially in conformity with this chapter, unless the proceeding is stayed by the court of the other state because this state is a more appropriate forum or for other reasons.

Before hearing the petition in a custody proceeding the court shall examine the pleadings and other information supplied by the parties under § 26-5A-9 and shall consult the child custody registry established under § 26-5A-16 concerning the pendency of proceedings with respect to the child in other states. If the court has reason to believe that proceedings may be pending in another state it shall direct an inquiry to the state court administrator or other appropriate official of the other state.

If the court is informed during the course of the proceeding that a proceeding concerning the custody of the child was pending in another state before the court assumed jurisdiction it shall stay the proceeding. It shall communicate with the court in which the other proceeding is pending in order that the issue may be litigated in the more appropriate forum and that information be exchanged in accordance with §§ 26-5A-19 and 26-5A-22. If a court of this state has made a custody decree before being informed of a pending proceeding in a court of another state, it shall immediately inform that court of the fact. If the court is informed that a proceeding was commenced in another state after it assumed jurisdiction, it shall likewise inform the other court in order that the issues may be litigated in the more appropriate forum.

§ 26-5A-7. Inconvenient forum.

A court which has jurisdiction under this chapter to make an initial or modification decree may decline to exercise its jurisdiction any time before making a decree if it finds that it is an inconvenient forum to make a custody determination under the circumstances of the case and that a court of another state is a more appropriate forum.

A finding of inconvenient forum may be made upon the court's own motion or upon motion of a party or a guardian ad litem or other representative of the child.

In determining if it is an inconvenient forum, the court shall consider if it is in the interest of the child that another state assume jurisdiction. For this purpose it may take into account the following factors, including:

(1) If another state is or recently was the child's home state;

(2) If another state has a closer connection with the child and his family or with the child and one or more of the contestants;

(3) If substantial evidence concerning the child's present or future care, protection, training, and personal relationships is more readily available in another state;

(4) If the parties have agreed on another forum which is no less appropriate.

Before determining whether to decline or retain jurisdiction the court may communicate with a court of another state and exchange information pertinent to the assumption of jurisdiction by either court assuring that jurisdiction will be exercised by the more appropriate court and that a forum will be available to the parties.

If the court finds that it is an inconvenient forum and that a court of another state is a more appropriate forum, it may dismiss the proceedings, or it may stay the proceedings upon condition that a custody proceeding be promptly commenced in another named state or upon any other conditions which may be just and proper, including the condition that a moving party stipulate his consent and submission to the jurisdiction of the other forum.

The court may decline to exercise its jurisdiction under this chapter if a custody determination is incidental to an action for divorce or another proceeding while retaining jurisdiction over the divorce or other proceeding.

If it appears to the court that it is clearly an inappropriate forum it may require the party who commenced the proceedings to pay, in addition to the costs of the proceedings, in this state, necessary travel and other expenses, including attorneys' fees, incurred by other parties or their witnesses. Payment is to be made to the clerk of the court for remittance to the proper party.

Upon dismissal or stay of proceedings under this section, the court shall inform the court found to be the more appropriate forum of this fact. If the court which would have jurisdiction in the other state is not certainly known, the court shall transmit the information to the court administrator or other appropriate official for forwarding to the appropriate court.

Any communications received from another state informing this state of a finding of inconvenient forum because a court of this state is the more appropriate forum shall be filed in the custody registry of the appropriate court. Upon assuming jurisdiction the court of this state shall inform the original court of this fact.

§ 26-5A-8. Jurisdiction declined by reason of conduct.

If the petitioner for an initial decree was wrongfully taken the child from another state or has engaged in similar reprehensible conduct, the court may decline to exercise jurisdiction if this is just and proper under the circumstances.

Unless required in the interest of the child, the court may not exercise its jurisdiction to modify a custody decree of another state if the petitioner, without consent of the person entitled to custody, has improperly removed the child from the physical custody of the person entitled to custody, or has improperly retained the child after a visit or other temporary relinquishment of physical custody. If the petitioner has violated any other provision of a custody decree of another state the court may decline to exercise its jurisdiction if this is just and proper under the circumstances.

In appropriate cases a court dismissing a petition under this section may charge the petitioner with necessary travel and other expenses, including attorneys' fees, incurred by other parties or their witnesses.

§ 26-5A-9. Information under oath to be submitted to the court.

The court shall, upon motion or request of a party or upon its own initiative require any party to a custody proceeding to provide information under oath by affidavit or otherwise as to the child's present address, the places where the child has lived within the last five years, and the names and present addresses of the persons with whom the child has lived during that period and whether:

(1) He has participated (as a party, witness, or in any other capacity) in any other litigation concerning the custody of the same child in this or any other state;

(2) He has information of a custody proceeding concerning the child pending in a court of this or any other state; and

(3) He knows of any person not a party to the proceedings who has physical custody of the child or claims to have custody or visitation rights with respect to the child.

If the declaration as to any of the above items is in the affirmative the declarant shall give additional information under oath as required by the court. The court may examine the parties under oath as to details of the information furnished and as to other matters pertinent to the court's jurisdiction and the disposition of the case.

Each party has a continuing duty to inform the court of any custody proceeding concerning the child in this or any other state of which he obtained information during this proceeding.

§ 26-5A-10. Additional parties.

If the court learns from information furnished by the parties pursuant to § 26-5A-9 or from other sources that a person not a party to the custody proceeding has physical custody of the child or claims to have custody or visitation rights with respect to the child, it shall order that person to be joined as a party and to be duly notified of the pendency of the proceeding and of his joinder as a party. If the person joined as a party is outside this state he shall be served with process or otherwise notified in accordance with § 26-5A-5.

§ 26-5A-11. Appearance of parties and the child.

The court may order any party to the proceeding who is in this state to appear personally before the court. If that party has physical custody of the child the court may order that he appear personally with the child.

If a party to the proceeding whose presence is desired by the court is outside this state with or without the child, the court may order that the notice given under § 26-5A-5 include a statement directing that party to appear personally with or without the child and declaring that failure to appear may result in a decision adverse to that party.

If a party to the proceeding who is outside this state is directed to appear or desires to appear personally before the court with or without the child, the court may require another party to pay to the clerk of the court travel and other necessary expenses of the party so appearing and of the child if this is just and proper under the circumstances.

§ 26-5A-12. Binding force and res judicata effect of custody decree.

A custody decree given by a court of this state which had jurisdiction under § 26-5A-3 binds all parties who have been served in this state or notified in accordance with § 26-5A-3 binds all parties who have been served in this state or notified in accordance with § 26-5A-5 or who have submitted to the jurisdiction of the court, and who have been given an opportunity to be heard. As to these parties the custody decree is conclusive as to all issues of law and fact decided and as to the custody determination made unless and until that determination is modified pursuant to law, including the provisions of this chapter.

§ 26-5A-13. Recognition of out-of-state custody decrees.

The courts of this state shall recognize and enforce an initial or modification decree of a court of another state which had assumed jurisdiction under statutory provisions substantially in accordance with this chapter or which was made under factual circumstances meeting the jurisdictional standards of the chapter, so long as this decree has not been modified in accordance with jurisdictional standards substantially similar to those of this chapter.

§ 26-5A-14. Modification of custody decree of another state.

If a court of another state has made a custody decree, a court of this state shall not modify that decree unless it appears to the court of this state that the court which gave the decree does not now have jurisdiction under jurisdictional prerequisites substantially in accordance with this chapter or has declined to assume jurisdiction to modify the decree and the court of this state has jurisdiction.

If a court of this state is authorized to modify a custody decree of another state it shall give due consideration to the transcript of the record and other documents of all previous proceedings submitted to it in accordance with § 26-5A-22.

§ 26-5A-15. Filing and enforcement of custody decree of another state.

A certified copy of a custody decree of another state may be filed in the office of the clerk of any circuit court of this state. The clerk shall treat the decree in the same manner as a custody decree of the circuit court of this state. A custody decree so filed has the same effect and shall be enforced in like manner as a custody decree given by a court of this state.

A person violating a custody decree of another state which makes it necessary to enforce the decree in this state may be required to pay necessary travel and other expenses, including attorneys' fees, incurred by the party entitled to the custody or his witnesses.

§ 26-5A-16. Registry of out-of-state custody decrees and proceedings.

The clerk of each circuit court shall maintain a registry in which he shall enter the following:

(1) Certified copies of custody decrees of other states received for filing;

(2) Communications as to the pendency of custody proceedings in other states;

(3) Communications concerning a finding of inconvenient forum by a court of another state; and

(4) Other communications or documents concerning custody proceedings in another state which may affect the jurisdiction of a court of this state or the disposition to be made by it in a custody proceeding.

§ 26-5A-17. Certified copies of custody decree.

The clerk of the circuit court of this state, at the request of the court of another state or at the request of any person who is affected by or has a legitimate interest in a custody decree, shall certify and forward a copy of the decree to that court or person.

§ 26-5A-18. Taking testimony in another state.

In addition to other procedural devices available to a party, any party to the proceeding or a guardian ad litem or other representative of the child may adduce testimony of witnesses, including parties and the child, by deposition or otherwise, in another state. The court on its own motion may direct that the testimony of a person be taken in another state and may prescribe the manner in which and the terms upon which the testimony shall be taken.

§ 26-5A-19. Hearings and studies in another state — Orders to appear.

A court of this state may request the appropriate court of another state to hold a hearing to adduce evidence, to order a party to produce or give evidence under other procedures of that state, or to have social studies made with respect to the custody of a child involved in proceedings pending in the court of this state. In addition, the court may request the court of another state to forward to the court of this state certified copies of the transcript of the record of the hearing, the evidence otherwise adduced, or any social studies prepared in compliance with the request. The cost of the services may be assessed against the parties or, if necessary, ordered paid by the state.

A court of this state may request the appropriate court of another state to order a party to custody proceedings pending in the court of this state to appear in the proceedings, and if that party has physical custody of the child, to appear with the child. The request may state that travel and other necessary expenses of the party and of the child whose appearance is desired will be assessed against another party or will otherwise be paid.

§ 26-5A-20. Assistance to courts of other states.

Upon request of the court of another state the courts of this state which are competent to hear custody matters may order a person in this state to appear at a hearing to adduce evidence or to produce or give evidence under other procedures available in this state. A certified copy of the transcript of the record of the hearing or the evidence otherwise adduced shall be forwarded by the clerk of the court to the requesting court.

A person within this state may voluntarily give his testimony or statement in this state for use in a custody proceeding outside this state.

Upon request of the court of another state a competent court of this state may order a person in this state to appear alone or with the child in a custody proceeding in another state. The court may condition compliance with the request upon assurance by the other state that travel and other necessary expenses will be advanced or reimbursed.

§ 26-5A-21. Preservation of documents for use in other states.

In any custody proceeding in this state the court shall preserve the pleadings, orders and decrees, any record that has been made of its hearings, social studies, and other pertinent documents until the child reaches eighteen years of age. Upon appropriate request of the court of another state the court shall forward to the other court certified copies of any or all of such documents.

§ 26-5A-22. Request for court records of another state.
If a custody decree has been given in another state concerning a child involved in a custody proceeding pending in a court of this state, the court of this state upon taking jurisdiction of the case shall request of the court of the other state a certified copy of the transcript of any court record and other documents mentioned in § 26-5A-21.

§ 26-5A-23. Reserved.

§ 26-5A-24. Priority.
Upon the request of a party to a custody proceeding which raises a question of existence or exercise of jurisdiction under this chapter the case shall be given calendar priority and handled expeditiously.

§ 26-5A-25. Reserved.

§ 26-5A-26. Citation of chapter.
This chapter may be cited as the Uniform Child Custody Jurisdiction Act.

TENNESSEE

UNIFORM CHILD CUSTODY JURISDICTION ACT

§ 36-6-201. Purposes and construction of part.
(a) The general purposes of this part are to:

(1) Avoid jurisdictional competition and conflict with courts of other states in matters of child custody which have in the past resulted in the shifting of children from state to state with harmful effects on their well-being;

(2) Promote cooperation with the courts of other states to the end that a custody decree is rendered in that state which can best decide the case in the interest of the child;

(3) Assure that litigation concerning the custody of a child take place ordinarily in the state with which the child and his family have the closest connection and where significant evidence concerning the child's care, protection, training, and personal relationships is most readily available, and that courts of this state decline the exercise of jurisdiction when the child and his family have a closer connection with another state;

(4) Discourage continuing controversies over child custody in the interest of greater stability of home environment and of secure family relationships for the child;

(5) Deter abductions and other unilateral removals of children undertaken to obtain custody awards;

(6) Avoid re-litigation of custody decisions of other states in this state insofar as feasible;

(7) Facilitate the enforcement of custody decrees of other states;

(8) Promote and expand the exchange of information and other forms of mutual assistance between the courts of this state and those of other states concerned with the same child; and

(9) Make uniform the law of those states which enact it.

(b) This part shall be construed to promote the general purposes stated in this section.

§ 36-6-202. Definitions.
As used in this part:

(1) "Contestant" means a person, including a parent, who claims a right to custody or visitation rights with respect to a child;

(2) "Custody determination" means a court decision and court orders and instructions providing for the custody of a child, including visitation rights; it does not include a decision relating to child support or any other monetary obligation of any person;

(3) "Custody proceeding" includes proceedings in which a custody determination is one of several issues, such as an action for divorce or separation, and includes habeas corpus proceedings, but specifically excludes Interstate Juvenile Compact matters and other proceedings pursuant to title 37, except proceedings to determine custody pursuant to § 37-1-104 and pursuant to § 37-1-103 as to dependent and neglected children when an original party or person acting as a parent files the petition or when the petition involves facts arising from another state;

(4) "Decree" or "custody decree" means a custody determination contained in a judicial decree or order made in a custody

proceeding, and includes an initial decree and a modification decree;

(5) "Home state" means the state in which the child immediately preceding the time involved lived with his or her parents, a parent, or a person acting as parent, for at least six (6) consecutive months, and in the case of a child less than six (6) months old the state in which the child lived from birth with any of the persons mentioned. Periods of temporary absence of any of the named persons are counted as part of the six (6) months or other period;

(6) "Initial decree" means a custody decree concerning a particular child;

(7) "Modification decree" means a custody decree which modifies or replaces a prior decree, whether made by the court which rendered the prior decree or by another court;

(8) "Person acting as parent" means a person, other than a parent, who has physical custody of a child and who has either been awarded custody by a court or claims a right to custody;

(9) "Physical custody" means actual possession and control of a child; and

(10) "State" means any state, territory, or possession of the United States, the Commonwealth of Puerto Rico, and the District of Columbia.

§ 36-6-203. Jurisdiction to make custody determination.

(a) A court of this state which is competent to decide child custody matters has jurisdiction to make a child custody determination by initial or modification decree if:

(1) This state:

(A) Is the home state of the child at the time of commencement of the proceeding; or

(B) Had been the child's home state within six (6) months before commencement of the proceeding and the child is absent from this state because of the child's removal or retention by a person claiming custody or for other reasons, and a parent or person acting as parent continues to live in this state; or

(2) (A) It appears that no state has jurisdiction under subdivision (a)(1), or each state with jurisdiction under subdivision (a)(1) has declined to exercise jurisdiction on the ground that this state is the more appropriate forum to determine the custody of the child; and

(B) The child and at least one contestant have a significant connection with this state; and

(C) There is available in this state substantial evidence concerning the child's present or future care, protection, training and personal relationship; and

(D) It is in the best interest of the child that a court of this state assume jurisdiction; or

(3) It appears that no state has jurisdiction under subdivision (a)(1) or (a)(2) or each state has refused jurisdiction on the ground that this is the more appropriate forum to determine child custody, and it is in the best interest of the child that a court of this state assume jurisdiction.

(b) Except under subdivision (a)(3) of this section, physical presence in this state of the child, or of the child and one (1) of the contestants, is not alone sufficient to confer jurisdiction on a court of this state to make a child custody determination.

(c) Physical presence of the child, while desirable, is not a prerequisite for jurisdiction to determine his or her custody.

(d) Jurisdiction shall not be exercised to modify an existing custody decree except in accordance with § 36-6-215.

§ 36-6-204. Temporary decrees — Obtaining permanent custody decree.

(a) A court of this state which is competent to decide child custody matters has limited jurisdiction to suspend temporarily enforcement of an existing decree and to make a temporary decree for a period not longer than sixty (60) days if the child is physically present in this state and:

(1) The child has been abandoned; or

(2) It is necessary in an emergency to protect the child because the child has been subjected to or is immediately threatened with serious harm to life or with serious bodily injury.

(b) In order to obtain a permanent custody decree, the petitioning party shall file in a state which has jurisdiction as set out in § 36-6-203.

§ 36-6-205. Notice and opportunity to be heard.

Before making a decree under this part, reasonable notice and opportunity to be heard shall be given to the contestants, any parent whose parental rights have not been previously terminated, and any person who has physical custody of the child. If any of these persons is outside this state, notice and opportunity to be heard shall be given pursuant to § 36-6-206.

§ 36-6-206. Requirements for notice.

(a) Notice required for the exercise of jurisdiction over a person outside this state shall be given in a manner reasonably calculated to give actual notice, and may be:

(1) By personal delivery outside this state in the manner prescribed for service of process within this state;

(2) In the manner prescribed by the law of the place in which the service is made for service of process in that place in an action in any of its courts of general jurisdiction;

(3) By any form of mail addressed to the person to be served and requesting a receipt; or

(4) As directed by the court including publication, if other means of notification are ineffective.

(b) Notice under this section shall be served, mailed, or delivered, or last published at least twenty (20) days before any hearing in this state.

(c) Proof of service outside this state may be made by affidavit of the individual who made the service, or in the manner prescribed by the law of this state, the order pursuant to which the service is made, or the law of the place in which the service is made. If service is made by mail, proof may be a receipt signed by the addressee or other evidence of delivery to the addressee.

(d) Notice is not required if a person submits to the jurisdiction of the court.

§ 36-6-207. Proceedings pending in another state.

(a) A court of this state shall not exercise its jurisdiction under this part if at the time of filing the petition a proceeding concerning the custody of the child was pending in a court of another state exercising jurisdiction substantially in conformity with this part, unless the proceeding is stayed by the court of the other state because this state is a more appropriate forum or for other reasons.

(b) Before hearing the petition in a custody proceeding the court shall examine the pleadings and other information supplied by the parties under § 36-6-210 and shall consult the child custody registry established under § 36-6-217 concerning the pendency of proceedings with respect to the child in other states. If the court has reason to believe that proceedings may be pending in another state it shall direct an inquiry to the state court administrator or other appropriate official of the other state.

(c) If the court is informed during the course of the proceeding that a proceeding concerning the custody of the child was pending in another state before the court assumed jurisdiction, it shall stay the proceeding and communicate with the court in which the other proceeding is pending to the end that the issue may be litigated in the more appropriate forum and that information be exchanged in accordance with §§ 36-6-220 — 36-6-223. If a court of this state has made a custody decree before being informed of a pending proceeding in a court of another state, it shall immediately inform that court of the fact. If the court is informed that a proceeding was commenced in another state after it assumed jurisdiction, it shall likewise inform the other court to the end that the issues may be litigated in the more appropriate forum.

§ 36-6-208. Proceedings under finding of inconvenient forum.

(a) A court which has jurisdiction under this part to make an initial or modification decree may decline to exercise its jurisdiction any time before making a decree if it finds that it is an inconvenient forum to make a custody determination under the circumstances of the case and that a court of another state is a more appropriate forum. The court may appoint a guardian ad litem to represent the child if the court finds such appointment to be in the best interest of the child. The court may, in its discretion, order that the guardian ad litem's fee be paid by one (1), or in part by both, of the contesting parties.

(b) A finding of inconvenient forum may be made upon the court's own motion or upon motion of a party or a guardian ad litem or other representative of the child.

(c) In determining if it is an inconvenient forum, the court shall consider if it is in the interest of the child that another state assume jurisdiction. For this purpose it may take into account the following factors, among others:

(1) If another state is or recently was the child's home state;

(2) If another state has a closer connection with the child and family or with the child and one or more of the contestants;

(3) If substantial evidence concerning the child's present or future care, protection, training, and personal relationships is more readily available in another state;

(4) If the parties have agreed on another forum which is no less appropriate; and

(5) If the exercise of jurisdiction by a court of this state would contravene any of the purposes stated in § 36-6-201.

(d) Before determining whether to decline or retain jurisdiction the court may communicate with a court of another state and exchange information pertinent to the assumption of jurisdiction by either court with a view to assuring that jurisdiction will be exercised by the more appropriate court and that a forum will be available to the parties.

(e) If the court finds that it is an inconvenient forum and that a court of another state is a more appropriate forum, it may dismiss the proceedings, or it may stay the proceedings upon condition that a custody proceeding be promptly commenced in another named state or upon any other conditions which may be just and proper, including the condition that a moving party stipulate consent and submission to the jurisdiction of the other forum.

(f) The court may decline to exercise its jurisdiction under this part if a custody determination is incidental to an action for divorce or another proceeding while retaining jurisdiction over the divorce or other proceeding.

(g) If it appears to the court that it is clearly an inappropriate forum it may require the party who commenced the proceedings to pay, in addition to the costs of the proceedings in this state, necessary travel and other expenses, including attorneys' fees, incurred by other parties or their witnesses. Payment is to be made to the clerk of the court for remittance to the proper party.

(h) Upon dismissal or stay of proceedings under this section the court shall inform the court found to be the more appropriate forum of this fact or, if the court which would have jurisdiction in the other state is not certainly known, shall transmit the information to the court administrator or other appropriate official for forwarding to the appropriate court.

(i) Any communication received from another state informing this state of a finding of inconvenient forum because a court of this state is the more appropriate forum shall be filed in the custody registry of the appropriate court. Upon assuming jurisdiction the court of this state shall inform the original court of this fact.

§ 36-6-209. Declining jurisdiction.

(a) If the petitioner for an initial decree has wrongfully taken the child from another state or has engaged in similar reprehensible conduct the court may decline to exercise jurisdiction if this is just and proper under the circumstances.

(b) Unless required in the interest of the child and subject to § 36-6-215(a), the court shall not exercise its jurisdiction to modify a custody decree of another state if the petitioner, without consent of the person entitled to custody, has improperly removed the child from the physical custody of the person entitled to custody or has improperly retained the child after a visit or other temporary relinquishment of physical custody. If the petitioner has violated any other provision of a custody decree of another state the court, subject to § 36-6-215(a), may decline to exercise its jurisdiction if this is just and proper under the circumstances.

(c) In appropriate cases a court dismissing a petition under this section may charge the petitioner with necessary travel and other expenses, including attorney's fees, incurred by other parties or their witnesses.

§ 36-6-210. Information in first pleading or affidavit — Continuing duty to inform court.

(a) Every party in a custody proceeding in his first pleading or in an affidavit attached to that pleading shall give information under oath as to the child's present address, the places where the child has lived within the last five (5) years, and the names and present addresses of the persons with whom the child has lived during that period. In this pleading or affidavit every party shall further declare under oath whether:

(1) The party has participated (as a party, witness, or in any other capacity) in any other litigation concerning the custody of the same child in this or any other state;

(2) The party has information of any custody proceeding concerning the child pending in a court of this or any other state; and

(3) The party knows of any person not a party to the proceedings who has physical custody of the child or claims to have custody or visitation rights with respect to the child.

(b) If the declaration as to any of the above items is in the affirmative the declarant shall give additional information under oath as required by the court. The court may examine the parties under oath as to details of the information furnished and as to other matters pertinent to the court's jurisdiction and the disposition of the case.

(c) Each party has a continuing duty to inform the court of any custody proceeding concerning the child in this or any other state of which he obtained information during this proceeding.

§ 36-6-211. Joinder of party having physical custody of child or visitation rights.

If the court learns from information furnished by the parties pursuant to § 36-6-210 or from other sources that a person not a party to the custody proceeding has physical custody of the child or claims to have custody or visitation rights with respect to the child, it shall order that person to be joined as a party and to be duly notified of the pendency of the proceeding and of his joinder as a party. If the person joined as a party is outside this state the person shall be served with process or otherwise notified in accordance with § 36-6-206.

§ 36-6-212. Order to appear before court — Payment of expenses.

(a) The court may order any party to the proceeding who is in this state to appear personally before the court. If that party has physical custody of the child the court may order that the party appear personally with the child.

(b) If a party to the proceeding whose presence is desired by the court is outside this state with or without the child the court may order that the notice given under § 36-6-206 include a statement directing that party to appear personally with or without the child and declaring that failure to appear may result in a decision adverse to that party.

(c) If a party to the proceeding who is outside this state is directed to appear under subsection (b) or desires to appear personally before the court with or without the child, the court may require another party to pay to the clerk of the court travel and other necessary expenses of the party so appearing and of the child if this is just and proper under the circumstances.

§ 36-6-213. Binding and conclusive nature of court decree.

A custody decree rendered by a court of this state which had jurisdiction under § 36-6-203 binds all parties who have been served in this state or notified in accordance with § 36-6-206 or who have submitted to the jurisdiction of the court, and who have been given an opportunity to be heard. As to these parties the custody decree is conclusive as to all issues of law and fact decided and as to the custody determination made unless and until that determination is modified pursuant to law, including the provisions of this part.

§ 36-6-214. Recognition and enforcement of foreign decree.

(a) If a court of another state has made a custody decree recognizable and enforceable under § 36-6-213, a court of this state shall not modify that decree unless (1) it appears to the court of this state that the court which rendered the decree does not now have jurisdiction under jurisdictional prerequisites substantially in accordance with this part or has declined to assume jurisdiction to modify the decree and (2) the court of this state has jurisdiction.

(b) If a court of this state is authorized under subsection (a) and § 36-6-209 to modify a custody decree of another state it shall give due consideration to the transcript of the record and other documents of all previous proceedings submitted to it in accordance with § 36-6-223.

§ 36-6-216. Filing of foreign decree — Payment of expenses upon enforcement of foreign decree.

(a) A certified copy of a custody decree of another state may be filed in the office of the clerk of any court of this state which is competent to decide child custody matters. The clerk shall treat the decree in the same manner as a custody decree of the court of this state. A custody decree so filed has the same effect and shall be enforced in like manner as a custody decree rendered by a court of this state.

(b) A person violating a custody decree of another state which makes it necessary to enforce the decree in this state may be required to pay necessary travel and other expenses, including attorneys' fees, incurred by the party entitled to the custody or his witness.

§ 36-6-217. Registry maintained by clerk.

The clerk of each court of this state which is competent to decide child custody matters shall maintain a registry in which he or she shall enter the following:

(1) Certified copies of custody decrees of other states received for filing;

(2) Communications as to the pendency of custody proceedings in other states;

(3) Communications concerning a finding of inconvenient forum by a court of another state; and

(4) Other communications or documents concerning custody proceedings in another state which may affect the jurisdiction of a court of this state or the disposition to be made by it in a custody proceeding.

§ 36-6-218. Furnishing copies of decree.

The clerk of any court of this state which is competent to decide child custody matters, at the request of the court of another state or at the request of any person who is affected by or has a legitimate interest in a custody decree, shall certify and forward a copy of the decree to that court or person.

§ 36-6-219. Testimony of persons in another state.

In addition to other procedural devices available to a party, any party to the proceeding or a guardian ad litem or other representative of the child may adduce testimony of witnesses, including parties and the child, by deposition or otherwise, in another state. The court on its own motion may direct that the testimony of a person be taken in another state and may prescribe the manner in which and the terms upon which the testimony shall be taken.

§ 36-6-220. Request for hearing in another state — Ordering party to appear in this state.

(a) A court of this state may request the appropriate court of another state to hold a hearing to adduce evidence, to order a party to produce or give evidence under other procedures of that state, or to have social studies made with respect to the custody of a child involved in proceedings pending in the court of this state; and to forward to the court of this state certified copies of the transcript of the record of the hearing, the evidence otherwise adduced, or any social studies prepared in compliance with the request. The cost of the services may be assessed against the parties or, if necessary, ordered paid by the state.

(b) A court of this state may request the appropriate court of another state to order a party to custody proceedings pending in the court of this state to appear in the proceedings, and if that party has physical custody of the child, to appear with the child. The request may state that travel and other necessary expenses of the party and of the child whose appearance is desired will be assessed against another party or will otherwise be paid.

§ 36-6-221. Foreign requests for hearing in this state — Requests for person to appear in another state.

(a) Upon request of the court of another state the courts of this state which are competent to hear custody matters may order a person in this state to appear at a hearing to adduce evidence or to produce or give evidence under other procedures available in this state or may order social studies to be made for use in a custody proceeding in another state. A certified copy of the transcript of the record of the hearing or the evidence otherwise adduced (and any social studies prepared) shall be forwarded by the clerk of the court to the requesting court.

(b) A person within this state may voluntarily give his testimony or statement in this state for use in a custody proceeding outside this state.

(c) Upon request of the court to appear alone or with the child with the request upon assurance by the other state that state travel and other necessary expenses will be advanced or reimbursed.

§ 36-6-222. Preservation of documents — Furnishing copies of documents.

In any custody proceeding in this state the court shall preserve the pleadings, orders and decrees, any record that has been made of its hearings, social studies, and other pertinent documents until the child reaches eighteen (18) years of age. Upon appropriate request of the court of another state the court shall forward to the other court certified copies of any or all of such documents.

§ 36-6-223. Requesting transcript and documents from foreign state.

If a custody decree has been rendered in another state concerning a child involved in a custody proceeding pending in a court of this state, the court of this state upon taking jurisdiction of the case shall request of the court of the other state a certified copy of the transcript of any court record and other documents mentioned in § 36-6-222.

§ 36-6-224. International application of part.

The general policies of this part extend to the international area. The provisions of this part relating to the recognition and enforcement of custody decrees of other states apply to custody decrees and decrees involving legal institutions similar in nature to custody institutions rendered by appropriate authorities of other nations if reasonable notice and opportunity to be heard were given to all affected persons.

§ 36-6-225. Priority of jurisdictional questions.

Upon the request of the party to a custody proceeding which raises a question of existence or exercise of jurisdiction under this part the case shall be given calendar priority and handled expeditiously.

TEXAS

UNIFORM CHILD CUSTODY JURISDICTION ACT

§ 11.51. Purposes; Construction of Provisions.

(a) The general purposes of this subchapter are to:

(1) avoid jurisdictional competition and conflict with courts of other states in matters of child custody that have in the past resulted in the shifting of children from state to state with harmful effects on their well-being;

(2) promote cooperation with the courts of other states to the end that a custody decree is rendered in the state that can best decide the case in the interest of the child;

(3) assure that litigation concerning the custody of a child takes place ordinarily in the state with which the child and his family have the closest connection and where significant evidence concerning his care, protection, training, and personal relationships is most readily available, and that courts of this state decline the exercise of jurisdiction when the child and his family have a closer connection with another state;

(4) discourage continuing controversies over child custody in the interest of greater stability of home environment and of secure family relationships for the child;

(5) deter abductions and other unilateral removals of children undertaken to obtain custody awards;

(6) avoid relitigation of custody decisions of other states in this state insofar as feasible;

(7) facilitate the enforcement of custody decrees of other states;

(8) promote and expand the exchange of information and other forms of mutual assistance between the courts of this state and those of other states concerned with the same child; and

(9) make uniform the law of those states that enact it.

(b) This subchapter shall be construed to promote the general purposes stated in this section.

§ 11.52. Definitions.

In this subchapter:

(1) "Contestant" means a person, including a parent, who claims a right to custody or visitation rights, with respect to a child.

(2) "Custody determination" means a court decision and court orders and instructions providing for the custody of a child, including visitation rights, but does not include a decision relating to child support or any other monetary obligation of any person.

(3) "Custody proceeding" includes a proceeding in which a custody determination is one of several issues, such as an action for divorce or separation, and includes child neglect and dependency proceedings.

(4) "Decree" or "custody decree" means a custody determination contained in a judicial decree or order made in a custody proceeding and includes an initial decree and a modification decree.

(5) "Home state" means the state in which the child immediately preceding the time involved lived with his parents, a parent, or a person acting as parent, for at least six consecutive months, and in the case of a child less than six months old, the state in which the child lived from birth with any of the persons mentioned. Periods of temporary absence of any of the named persons are counted as part of the six-month or other period.

(6) "Initial decree" means the first custody decree concerning a particular child.

(7) "Modification decree" means a custody decree that modifies or replaces a prior decree, whether made by the court that rendered the prior decree or by another court.

(8) "Physical custody" means actual possession and control of a child.

(9) "Person acting as parent" means a person, other than a parent, who has physical custody of a child and who has either been awarded custody by a court or claims a right to custody.

(10) "Custody" means managing conservatorship of a child.

(11) "Visitation" means possession of or access to a child.

§ 11.53. Jurisdiction.

(a) A court of this state that is competent to decide child custody matters has jurisdiction to make a child custody determination by initial decree or modification decree or order if:

(1) this state:

(A) is the home state of the child on the date of the commencement of the proceeding; or

(B) had been the child's home state within six months before the date of the commencement of the proceeding and the child is absent from this state because of his removal or retention by a person claiming his custody or for other reasons, and a parent or person acting as parent continues to live in this state;

(2) it appears that no other state would have jurisdiction under Subdivision (1) of Subsection (a) of this section and it is in the best interest of the child that a court of this state assume jurisdiction because:

(A) the child and his parents or the child and at least one contestant have a significant connection with this state other than mere physical presence in this state; and

(B) there is available in this state substantial evidence concerning the child's present or future care, protection, training, and personal relationships;

(3) the child is physically present in this state and:

(A) the child has been abandoned; or

(B) it is necessary in an emergency to protect the child because he has been subjected to or threatened with mistreatment or abuse or is otherwise neglected or there is a serious and immediate question concerning the welfare of the child; or

(4) it is in the best interest of the child that this court assume jurisdiction and:

(A) it appears that no other state would have jurisdiction under prerequisites substantially in accordance with Subdivision (1), (2), or (3) of this subsection; or

(B) another state has declined to exercise jurisdiction on the ground that this state is the more appropriate forum to determine the custody of the child.

(b) Except under Subdivisions (3) and (4) of Subsection (a) of this section, physical presence in this state of the child or of the child and one of the contestants is not alone sufficient to confer jurisdiction on a court of this state to make a child custody determination.

(c) Physical presence of the child, while desirable, is not a prerequisite for jurisdiction to determine his custody.

(d) Except on written agreement of all the parties, a court may not exercise its continuing jurisdiction to modify custody if the child and the party with custody have established another home state unless the action to modify was filed before the new home state was acquired.

§ 11.54. Notice and Opportunity to be Heard.

Before making a custody decree based on jurisdiction established under this subchapter, reasonable notice and opportunity to be heard must be given to the contestants, to any parent whose parental rights have not been previously terminated, and to any person who has physical custody of the child. If any of these persons is outside this state, notice and opportunity to be heard must be given under Section 11.55 of this code.

§ 11.55. Notice to Persons Outside This State; Submission to Jurisdiction.

(a) Notice required for the exercise of jurisdiction over a person outside this state must be given in a manner reasonably calculated to give actual notice and may be:

(1) by personal delivery outside this state in the manner prescribed for service of process within this state;

(2) in the manner prescribed by the law of the place in which the service is made for service of process in that place in an action in any of its courts of general jurisdiction;

(3) by any form of mail addressed to the person to be served and requesting a receipt, subject to the requirements of the Texas Rules of Civil Procedure; or

(4) as directed by the court, including publication, if other means of notification are ineffective, subject to the requirements of the Texas Rules of Civil Procedure.

(b) Notice under this section must be delivered, mailed, or published with sufficient time to allow for filing of an answer before any hearing in this state, in accordance with the Texas Rules of Civil Procedure applicable to the filing of an original lawsuit. Each party whose rights, privileges, duties, or powers may be affected by the action is entitled to receive notice by citation and shall be commanded to appear by filing a written answer. Thereafter, the proceedings shall be as in civil cases generally.

(c) Proof of service outside this state may be made by the affidavit of the individual who made the service, or in the manner prescribed by the law of this state, by the order under which the service is made. If service is made by mail, proof may be a receipt signed by the addressee or other evidence of delivery to the addressee.

(d) Notice is not required if a person submits to the jurisdiction of the court.

§ 11.56. Simultaneous Proceedings in Other State.

(a) A court of this state may not exercise its jurisdiction under this subchapter if, at the time of filing the petition, a proceeding concerning the custody of the child was pending in a court of another state exercising jurisdiction substantially in conformity with this subchapter, unless the proceeding is stayed by the court of the other state because this state is a more appropriate forum or for other reasons.

(b) Before hearing the petition in a custody proceeding, the court shall examine the pleadings and other information supplied by the parties under Section 11.59 of this code and shall consult the child custody registry established under Section 11.66 of this code concerning the pendency of proceedings with respect to the child in other states. If the court has reason to believe that proceedings may be pending in another state, it shall direct an inquiry to the state court administrator or other appropriate official of the other state.

(c) If the court is informed during the course of the proceeding that a proceeding concerning the custody of the child was pending in another state before the court assumed jurisdiction, it shall stay the proceeding and communicate with the court in which the other proceeding is pending to the end that the issue may be litigated in the more appropriate forum and that information be exchanged in accordance with Sections 11.69 through 11.72 of this code. If a court of this state has made a custody decree before being informed of a pending proceeding in a court of another state, it shall immediately inform that court of the fact. If the court is informed that a proceeding was commenced in another state after it assumed jurisdiction, it shall likewise inform the other court to the end that the issues may be litigated in the more appropriate forum.

§ 11.57. Inconvenient Forum.

(a) A court that has jurisdiction under this chapter to make an initial or modification decree may decline to exercise its jurisdiction any time before making a decree if it finds that it is an inconvenient forum to make a custody determination under the circumstances of the case and that a court of another state is a more appropriate forum.

(b) A finding of inconvenient forum may be made on the court's own motion or on the motion of a party or a guardian ad litem or other representative of the child.

(c) In determining if it is an inconvenient forum, the court shall consider if it is in the best interest of the child that another state assume jurisdiction. For this purpose it may take into account the following factors, among others:

(1) if another state is or recently was the child's home state;

(2) if another state has a closer connection with the child and his family or with the child and one or more of the contestants;

(3) if substantial evidence concerning the child's present or future care, protection, training, and personal relationships is more readily available in another state;

(4) if the parties have agreed on another forum that is no less appropriate; and

(5) if the exercise of jurisdiction by a court of this state would contravene any of the purposes stated in Section 11.51 of this code.

(d) Before determining whether to decline or retain jurisdiction, the court may communicate with a court of another state and exchange information pertinent to the assumption of jurisdiction by either court with a view to assuring that jurisdiction will be exercised by the more appropriate court and that a forum will be available to the parties.

(e) If the court finds that it is an inconvenient forum and that a court of another state is a more appropriate forum, it may dismiss the proceedings, or it may stay the proceedings on condition that a custody proceeding be promptly commenced in another named state or on any other conditions that may be just and proper, including the condition that a moving party stipulate his consent and submission to the jurisdiction of the other forum.

(f) The court may decline to exercise its jurisdiction under this subchapter if a custody determination is incidental to an action for divorce or another proceeding while retaining jurisdiction over the divorce or other proceeding.

(g) If it appears to the court that it is clearly an inappropriate forum, it may require the party who commenced the proceedings to pay, in addition to the costs of the proceedings in this state, necessary travel and other expenses, including attorney's fees, incurred by other parties or their witnesses. Payment is to be made to the clerk of the court for remittance to the proper party.

(h) On dismissal or stay of proceedings under this section, the court shall inform the court found to be the more appropriate forum of this factor, if the court that would have jurisdiction in the other state is not certainly known, shall transmit the information to the court administrator or other appropriate official for forwarding to the appropriate court.

(i) Any communication received from another state informing this state of a finding of inconvenient forum because a court of this state is the more appropriate forum shall be filed in the custody registry of the appropriate court. On assuming jurisdiction, the court of this state shall inform the original court of this fact.

§ 11.58. Jurisdiction Declined by Reason of Conduct.

(a) If the petitioner for an initial decree has wrongfully taken the child from another state or has engaged in similar reprehensible conduct, the court may decline to exercise jurisdiction if this is just and proper under the circumstances.

(b) Unless required in the interest of the child, the court may not exercise its jurisdiction to modify a custody decree of another state if the petitioner, without consent of the person entitled to custody, has improperly removed the child from the physical custody of the person entitled to custody or has improperly retained the child after a visit or other temporary relinquishment of physical custody. If the petitioner has violated any other provision of a custody decree of another state, the court may decline to exercise its jurisdiction if this is just and proper under the circumstances.

(c) In an appropriate case, a court dismissing a petition under this section may charge the petitioner with necessary travel and other expenses, including attorney's fees, incurred by other parties or their witnesses.

§ 11.59. Information Under Oath to be Submitted to the Court.

(a) Unless all the contestants are residing in this state, every party in a custody proceeding in his first pleading or in an affidavit attached to that pleading shall give information under oath as to the child's present address, the places where the child has lived within the last five years, and the names and present addresses of the persons with whom the child has lived during that period. In this pleading or affidavit every party shall further declare under oath whether:

(1) he has participated (as a party, witness, or in any other capacity) in any other litigation concerning the custody of the same child in this or any other state;

(2) he has information of any proceeding concerning the child pending in a court of this or any other state; and

(3) he knows of any person not a party to the proceedings who has physical custody of the child or claims to have custody or visitation rights with respect to the child.

(b) If the declaration as to any of the items in Subsection (a) of this section is in the affirmative, the declarant shall give additional information under oath as required by the court. The court may examine the parties under oath as to details of the information furnished and as to other matters pertinent to the court's jurisdiction and the disposition of the case.

(c) Each party has a continuing duty to inform the court of any custody proceeding concerning the child in this or any other state of which he obtained information during this proceeding.

§ 11.60. Additional Parties.

(a) If the court learns from information furnished by the parties under Section 11.59 of this code or from other sources that a person not a party to the custody proceeding has physical custody of the child or claims to have custody or visitation rights with respect to the child, it shall order that the person:

(1) be joined as a party; and

(2) be notified of the pendency of the proceeding and of his joinder as a party.

(b) If the person joined as a party is outside this state, he must be served with process or otherwise notified in accordance with Section 11.55 of this code.

§ 11.61. Appearance of Parties and the Child.

(a) The court may order any party to the proceeding who is in this state to appear personally before the court. If that party has physical custody of the child, the court may order that he appear personally with the child.

(b) If a party to the proceeding whose presence is desired by the court is outside this state, with or without the child, the court may order that the notice given under Section 11.55 of this code include a statement directing that party to appear personally, with or without the child, and declaring that failure to appear may result in a decision adverse to that party.

(c) If a party to the proceeding who is outside this state is directed to appear under Subsection (b) of this section or desires to appear personally before the court, with or without the child, the court may require another party to pay to the clerk of the court travel and other necessary expenses of the party appearing and of the child if this is just and proper under the circumstances.

§ 11.62. Binding Force and Res Judicata Effect of Custody Decree.

A custody decree of a court of this state that has jurisdiction under Section 11.53 of this code binds all parties who have been served in this state or notified in accordance with Section 11.55 of this code or who have submitted to the jurisdiction of the court and who have been given an opportunity to be heard. As to these parties, the custody decree is conclusive as to all issues of law and fact decided and as to the custody determination made, unless and until that determination is modified.

§ 11.63. Recognition of Out-of-State Custody Decrees.

The courts of this state shall recognize and enforce an initial or modification decree of a court of another state that had assumed jurisdiction under statutory provisions substantially in accordance with this subchapter or that was made under factual circumstances meeting the jurisdictional standards of this subchapter, so long as this decree has not been modified in accordance with jurisdictional standards substantially similar to those of this subchapter.

§ 11.64. Modification of Custody Decree of Another State.

(a) If a court of another state has made a custody decree, a court of this state may not modify the decree unless:

(1) it appears to the court of this state that the court that rendered the decree does not have jurisdiction under jurisdictional prerequisites substantially in accordance with this subchapter or has declined to assume jurisdiction to modify the decree; and

(2) the court of this state has jurisdiction.

(b) If a court of this state is authorized under Subsection (a) of this section and Section 11.58 of this code to modify a custody decree of another state, it shall give due consideration to the transcript of the record and other documents of all previous proceedings submitted to it in accordance with Section 11.72 of this code.

§ 11.65. Filing and Enforcement of Custody Decree of Another State.

(a) On payment of proper fees, a certified copy of a custody decree of another state may be filed in the office of the clerk of any district court or other appropriate court of this state. The clerk shall treat the decree in the same manner as a custody decree of a district court or other appropriate court of this state. A custody decree so filed has the same effect and shall be enforced in like manner as a custody decree rendered by a court of this state.

(b) A person whose violation of a custody decree of another state makes it necessary to enforce the decree in this state may be required to pay necessary travel and other expenses, including attorney's fees, incurred by the party entitled to the custody or his witnesses.

§ 11.66. Registry of Out-of-State Custody Decrees and Proceedings.

The clerk of each district court or other appropriate court shall maintain a registry in which he shall enter:

(1) certified copies of custody decrees of other states received for filing;

(2) communications as to the pendency of custody proceedings in other states;

(3) communications concerning a finding of inconvenient forum by a court of another state; and

(4) other communications or documents concerning custody proceedings in another state that may affect the jurisdiction of a court of this state or the disposition to be made by it in a custody proceeding.

§ 11.67. Certified Copies of Custody Decree.

The clerk of the district court or other appropriate court of this state at the request of the court of another state or at the request of any person who is affected by or has a legitimate interest in a custody decree, shall, on payment of proper fees, certify and forward a copy of the decree to that court or person.

§ 11.68. Taking Testimony in Another State.

In addition to other procedural devices available to a party, any party to the proceeding or a guardian ad litem or other representative of the child may adduce testimony of witnesses, including parties and the child, by deposition or otherwise, in another state. The court on its own motion may direct that the testimony of a person be taken in another state and may prescribe the manner in which and the terms on which the testimony shall be taken.

§ 11.69. Hearings and Studies in Another State; Orders to Appear.

(a) A court of this state may request the appropriate court of another state to hold a hearing to adduce evidence, to order a party to produce or give evidence under other procedures of that state, to have social studies made with respect to the custody of a child involved in proceedings pending in the court of this state, and to forward to the court of this state certified copies of the transcript of the record of the hearing, the evidence otherwise adduced, or any social studies prepared in compliance with the request. The cost of the services may be assessed against the parties or, if necessary, ordered paid by the state as costs of court.

(b) A court of this state may request the appropriate court of another state to order a party to custody proceedings pending in the court of this state to appear in the proceedings, and if that party has physical custody of the child, to appear with the child. The request may state that travel and other necessary expenses of the party and of the child whose appearance is desired will be assessed against another party or will otherwise be paid.

§ 11.70. Assistance to Courts of Other States.

(a) On request of the court of another state, the courts of this state that are competent to hear custody matters may order a person in this state to appear at a hearing to adduce evidence or to produce or give evidence under other procedures available in this state or may order social studies to be made for use in a custody proceeding in another state. A certified copy of the transcript of the record of the hearing or the evidence otherwise adduced and any social studies prepared shall be forwarded by the clerk of the court to the requesting court.

(b) A person in this state may voluntarily give his testimony or statement in this state for use in a custody proceeding outside this state.

(c) On request of the court of another state, a competent court of this state may order a person in this state to appear alone or with the child in a custody proceeding in another state. The court may condition compliance with the request on assurance by the other state that state travel and other necessary expenses will be advanced or reimbursed.

§ 11.71. Preservation of Documents for Use in Other States.

In any custody proceeding in this state, the court shall preserve the pleadings, orders, and decrees, any record that has been made of its hearings, social studies, and other pertinent documents until the child reaches 18 years of age or in accordance with the law of this state. On appropriate request of the court of another state and payment of proper fees, the court shall forward to the other court certified copies of the documents.

§ 11.72. Request for Court Records of Another State.

If a custody decree has been rendered in another state concerning a child involved in a custody proceeding pending in a court of this state, the court of this state on taking jurisdiction of the case may request of the court of the other state a certified copy of the transcript of any court record and other documents mentioned in Section 11.71 of this code.

§ 11.73. International Application.

The general policies of this subchapter extend to the international area. The provisions of this subchapter relating to the recognition and enforcement of custody decrees of other states apply to custody decrees and decrees involving legal institutions similar in nature to custody institutions rendered by appropriate authorities of other nations if reasonable notice and opportunity to be heard were given to all affected persons.

§ 11.74. Priority.

On the request of a party to a custody proceeding that raises a question of existence or exercise of jurisdiction under this subchapter, the case shall be given calendar priority and handled expeditiously.

UTAH

UNIFORM CHILD CUSTODY JURISDICTION

§ 78-45c-1. Purposes — Construction.

(1) The general purposes of this act are to:

(a) avoid jurisdiction competition and conflict with courts of other states in matters of child custody which have in the past resulted in the shifting of children from state to state with harmful effects on their well-being;

(b) promote cooperation with the courts of other states to the end that a custody decree is rendered in that state which can best decide the case in the interest of the child;

(c) assure that litigation concerning the custody of a child take place ordinarily in the state with which the child and his family have the closest connection and where significant evidence concerning his care, protection, training, and personal relationships is most readily available, and that courts of this state decline the exercise of jurisdiction when the child and his family have a closer connection with another state;

(d) discourage continuing controversies over child custody in the interest of greater stability of home environment and of secure family relationships for the child;

(e) deter abductions and other unilateral removals of children undertaken to obtain custody awards;

(f) avoid relitigation of custody decisions of other states in this state insofar as feasible;

(g) facilitate the enforcement of custody decrees of other states;

(h) promote and expand the exchange of information and other forms of mutual assistance between the courts of this state and those of other states concerned with the same child; and

(i) to make uniform the law of those states which enact it.

(2) This title shall be construed to promote the general purposes stated in this section.

§ 78-45c-2. Definitions.

As used in this act:

(1) "Contestant" means a person, including a parent, who claims a right to custody or visitation rights with respect to a child;

(2) "Custody determination" means a court decision and court orders and instructions providing for the custody of a child, including visitation rights; it does not include a decision relating to child support or any other monetary obligation of any person;

(3) "Custody proceeding" includes proceedings in which a custody determination is one of several issues, such as an action for dissolution of marriage, or legal separation, and includes child neglect and dependency proceedings;

(4) "Decree" or "custody decree" means a custody determination contained in a judicial decree or order made in a custody

proceeding, and includes an initial decree and a modification decree;

(5) "Home state" means the state in which the child immediately preceding the time involved lived with his parents, a parent, or a person acting as parent, for at least six consecutive months, and in the case of a child less than six months old the state in which the child lived from birth with any of the persons mentioned. Periods of temporary absence of any of the named persons are counted as part of the six-month or other period;

(6) "Initial decree" means a custody decree concerning a particular child;

(7) "Modification decree" means a custody decree which modifies or replaces a prior decree, whether made by the court which rendered the prior decree or by another court;

(8) "Physical custody" means actual possession and control of a child;

(9) "Person acting as parent" means a person, other than a parent, who has physical custody of a child and who has either been awarded custody by the court or claims a right to custody; and

(10) "State" means any state, territory or possession of the United States, the Commonwealth of Puerto Rico, and the District of Columbia.

§ 78-45c-3. Bases of jurisdiction in this state.

(1) A court of this state which is competent to decide child custody matters has jurisdiction to make a child custody determination by initial or modification decree if the conditions as set forth in any of the following paragraphs are met:

(a) This state (i) is the home state of the child at the time of commencement of the proceeding, or (ii) had been the child's home state within six months before commencement of the proceeding and the child is absent from this state because of his removal or retention by a person claiming his custody or for other reasons, and a parent or person acting as parent continues to live in this state;

(b) It is in the best interest of the child that a court of this state assume jurisdiction because (i) the child and his parents, or the child and at least one contestant, have a significant connection with this state, and (ii) there is available in this state substantial evidence concerning the child's present or future care, protection, training, and personal relationships;

(c) The child is physically present in this state and (i) the child has been abandoned or (ii) it is necessary in an emergency to protect the child because he has been subjected to or threatened with mistreatment or abuse or is otherwise neglected or dependent; or

(d)(i) It appears that no other state would have jurisdiction under prerequisites substantially in accordance with Paragraphs (a), (b), or (c), or another state has declined to exercise jurisdiction on the ground that this state is the more appropriate forum to determine the custody of the child, and (ii) it is in the best interest of the child that this court assume jurisdiction.

(2) Except under Paragraphs (c) and (d) of Subsection (1), physical presence in this state of the child, or of the child and one of the contestants, is not alone sufficient to confer jurisdiction on a court of this state to make a child custody determination.

(3) Physical presence of the child, while desirable, is not a prerequisite for jurisdiction to determine his custody.

§ 78-45c-4. Persons to be notified and heard.

Before making a decree under this act, reasonable notice and opportunity to be heard shall be given to the contestants, any parent whose parental rights have not been previously terminated, and any person who has physical custody of the child. If any of these persons is outside this state, notice and opportunity to be heard shall be given pursuant to § 78-45c-5.

§ 78-45c-5. Service of notice outside state — Proof of service — Submission to jurisdiction.

(1) Notice required for the exercise of jurisdiction over a person outside this state shall be given in a manner reasonably calculated to give actual notice, and may be made in any of the following ways:

(a) by personal delivery outside this state in the manner prescribed for service of process within this state;

(b) in the manner prescribed by the law of the place in which the service is made for service of process in that place in an action in any of its courts of general jurisdiction;

(c) by any form of mail addressed to the person to be served and requesting a receipt; or

(d) as directed by the court (including publication, if other means of notification are ineffective).

(2) Notice under this section shall be served, mailed, delivered, or last published at least 10 days before any hearing in this state.

(3) Proof of service outside this state may be made by affidavit of the individual who made the service, or in the manner prescribed by the law of this state, the order pursuant to which the service is made, or the law of the place in which the service is made. If service is made by mail, proof may be a receipt signed by the addressee or other evidence of delivery to the addressee.

(4) Notice is not required if a person submits to the jurisdiction of the court.

§ 78-45c-6. Proceedings pending elsewhere — Jurisdiction not exercised — Inquiry to other state — Information exchange — Stay of proceeding on notice of another proceeding.

(1) A court of this state shall not exercise its jurisdiction under this act if at the time of filing the petition a proceeding concerning the custody of the child was pending in a court of another state exercising jurisdiction substantially in conformity with this act, unless the proceeding is stayed by the court of the other state because this state is a more appropriate forum or for other reasons.

(2) Before hearing the petition in a custody proceeding the court shall examine the pleadings and other information supplied by the parties under § 78-45c-10 and shall consult the child custody registry established under § 78-45c-16 concerning the pendency of proceedings with respect to the child in other states. If the court has reason to believe that proceedings may be pending in another state it shall direct an inquiry to the state court administrator or other appropriate official of the other state.

(3) If the court is informed during the course of the proceeding that a proceeding concerning the custody of the child was pending in another state before the court assumed jurisdiction it shall stay the proceeding and communicate with the court in which the other proceeding is pending to the end that the issue may be litigated in the more appropriate forum and that information be exchanged in accordance with §§ 78-45c-19 through 78-45c-22. If a court of this state has made a custody decree before being informed of a pending proceeding in a court of another state it shall immediately inform that court of the fact. If the court is informed that a proceeding was commenced in another state after it assumed jurisdiction it shall likewise inform the other court to the end that the issues may be litigated in the more appropriate forum.

§ 78-45c-7. Declining jurisdiction on finding of inconvenient forum — Factors in determination — Communication with other court — Awarding costs.

(1) A court which has jurisdiction under this act to make an initial or modification decree may decline to exercise its jurisdiction any time before making a decree if it finds that it is an inconvenient forum to make a custody determination under the circumstances of the case and that a court of another state is a more appropriate forum.

(2) A finding of inconvenient forum may be made upon the court's own motion or upon motion of a party or a guardian ad litem or other representative of the child.

(3) In determining if it is an inconvenient forum, the court shall consider if it is in the interest of the child that another state assume jurisdiction. For this purpose it may take into account the following factors, among others:

    (a) if another state is or recently was the child's home state;

    (b) if another state has a closer connection with the child and his family or with the child and one or more of the contestants;

    (c) if substantial evidence concerning the child's present or future care, protection, training, and personal relationships is more readily available in another state;

    (d) if the parties have agreed on another forum which is no less appropriate; and

    (e) if the exercise of jurisdiction by a court of this state would contravene any of the purposes stated in § 78-45c-1.

(4) Before determining whether to decline or retain jurisdiction the court may communicate with a court of another state and exchange information pertinent to the assumption of jurisdiction by either court with a view to assuring that jurisdiction will be exercised by the more appropriate court and that a forum will be available to the parties.

(5) If the court finds that it is an inconvenient forum and that a court of another state is a more appropriate forum, it may dismiss the proceedings, or it may stay the proceedings upon condition that a custody proceeding be promptly commenced in another named state or upon any other conditions which may be just and proper, including the condition that a moving party stipulate his consent and submission to the jurisdiction of the other forum.

(6) The court may decline to exercise its jurisdiction under this act if a custody determination is incidental to an action for divorce or another proceeding while retaining jurisdiction over the divorce or other proceeding.

(7) If it appears to the court that it is clearly an inappropriate forum it may require the party who commenced the proceedings to pay, in addition to the costs of the proceedings in this state, necessary travel and other expenses, including attorney's fees, incurred by other parties or their witnesses. Payment is to be made to the clerk of the court for remittance to the proper party.

(8) Upon dismissal or stay of proceedings under this section the court shall inform the court found to be the more appropriate forum of this fact, or if the court which would have jurisdiction in the other state is not certainly known, shall transmit the information to the court administrator or other appropriate official for forwarding to the appropriate court.

(9) Any communication received from another state informing this state of a finding of inconvenient forum because a court of this state is the more appropriate forum shall be filed in the custody registry of the appropriate court. Upon assuming jurisdiction the court of this state shall inform the original court of this fact.

§ 78-45c-8. Misconduct of petitioner as basis for refusing jurisdiction — Notice to another jurisdiction — Ordering petitioner to appear in other court or to return child — Awarding costs.

(1) If the petitioner for an initial decree has wrongfully taken the child from another state or has engaged in similar reprehensible conduct the court may decline to exercise jurisdiction for purposes of adjudication of custody if this is just and proper under the circumstances.

(2) Unless required in the interest of the child, the court shall not exercise its jurisdiction to modify a custody decree of another state if the petitioner, without consent of the person entitled to custody has improperly removed the child from the physical custody of the person entitled to custody or has improperly retained the child after a visit or other temporary relinquishment of physical custody. If the petitioner has violated any other provision of a custody decree of another state the court may decline to exercise its jurisdiction if this is just and proper under the circumstances.

(3) Where the court declines to exercise jurisdiction upon petition for an initial custody decree pursuant to Subsection (1), the court shall notify the parent or other appropriate person and the prosecuting attorney of the appropriate jurisdiction in the other

state. If a request to that effect is received from the other state, the court shall order the petitioner to appear with the child in a custody proceeding instituted in the other state in accordance with § 78-45c-20. If no such request is made within a reasonable time after such notification, the court may entertain a petition to determine custody by the petitioner if it has jurisdiction pursuant to § 78-45c-2.

(4) Where the court refuses to assume jurisdiction to modify the custody decree of another state pursuant to Subsection (2) or pursuant to § 78-45c-14, the court shall notify the person who has legal custody under the decree of the other state and the prosecuting attorney of the appropriate jurisdiction in the other state and may order the petitioner to return the child to the person who has legal custody. If it appears that the order will be ineffective and the legal custodian is ready to receive the child within a period of a few days, the court may place the child in a foster care home for such period, pending return of the child to the legal custodian. At the same time, the court shall advise the petitioner that any petition for modification of custody must be directed to the appropriate court of the other state which has continuing jurisdiction, or, in the event that that court declines jurisdiction, to a court in a state which has jurisdiction pursuant to § 78-45c-3.

(5) In appropriate cases a court dismissing a petition under this section may charge the petitioner with necessary travel and other expenses, including attorney's fees and the cost of returning the child to another state.

§ 78-45c-9. Information as to custody of child and litigation concerning required in pleadings — Verification — Continuing duty to inform court.

(1) Every party in a custody proceeding in his first pleading or in an affidavit attached to that pleading shall give information under oath as to the child's present address, the places where the child has lived within the last five years, and the names and present addresses of the persons with whom the child has lived during that period. In this pleading or affidavit every party shall further declare under oath as to each of the following whether:

(a) he has participated, as a party, witness, or in any other capacity, in any other litigation concerning the custody of the same child in this or any other state;

(b) he has information of any custody proceeding concerning the child pending in a court of this or any other state; and

(c) he knows of any person not a party to the proceedings who has physical custody of the child or claims to have custody or visitation rights with respect to the child.

(2) If the declaration as to any of the above items is in the affirmative the declarant shall give additional information under oath as required by the court. The court may examine the parties under oath as to details of the information furnished and as to other matters pertinent to the court's jurisdiction and the disposition of the case.

(3) Each party has a continuing duty to inform the court of any custody proceeding concerning the child in this or any other state of which he obtained information during this proceeding.

§ 78-45c-10. Joinder of persons having custody or claiming custody or visitation rights.

If the court learns from information furnished by the parties pursuant to § 78-45c-9 or from other sources that a person not a party to the custody proceeding has physical custody of the child or claims to have custody or visitation rights with respect to the child, it shall order that person to be joined as a party and to be duly notified of the pendency of the proceeding and of his joinder as a party. If the person joined as a party is outside this state he shall be served with process or otherwise notified in accordance with § 78-45c-5.

§ 78-45c-11. Ordering party to appear — Enforcement — Out-of-state party — Travel and other expenses.

(1) The court may order any party to the proceeding who is in this state to appear personally before the court. If that party has physical custody of the child the court may order that he appear personally with the child. If the party who is ordered to appear with the child cannot be served or fails to obey the order, or it appears the order will be ineffective, the court may issue a warrant of arrest against such party to secure his appearance with the child.

(2) If a party to the proceeding whose presence is desired by the court is outside this state with or without the child the court may order that the notice given under § 78-45c-5 include a statement directing that party to appear personally with or without the child and declaring that failure to appear may result in a decision adverse to that party.

(3) If a party to the proceeding who is outside this state is directed to appear under Subsection (2) or desires to appear personally before the court with or without the child, the court may require another party to pay to the clerk of the court travel and other necessary expenses of the party so appearing and of the child if this is just and proper under the circumstances.

§ 78-45c-12. Parties bound by custody decree — Conclusive unless modified.

A custody decree rendered by a court of this state which had jurisdiction under § 78-45c-3, binds all parties who have been served in this state or notified in accordance with § 78-45c-5 or who have submitted to the jurisdiction of the court, and who have been given an opportunity to be heard. As to these parties the custody decree is conclusive as to all issues of law and fact decided and as to the custody determination made unless and until that determination is modified pursuant to law, including the provisions of this act.

§ 78-45c-13. Recognition and enforcement of foreign decrees.

The courts of this state shall recognize and enforce an initial or modification decree of a court of another state which had assumed jurisdiction under statutory provisions substantially in accordance with this act or which was made under factual circumstances meeting the jurisdictional standards of the act, so long as this decree has not been modified in accordance with jurisdictional standards substantially similar to those of this act.

§ 78-45c-14. Modification of foreign decree — Prerequisites — Factors considered.

(1) If a court of another state has made a custody decree, a court of this state shall not modify that decree unless (a) it appears to the court of this state that the court which rendered the decree does not now have jurisdiction under jurisdictional prerequisites substantially in accordance with this act or has declined to assume jurisdiction to modify the decree and (b) the court of this state has jurisdiction.

(2) If a court of this state is authorized under Subsection (1) and § 78-45c-8 to modify a custody decree of another state it shall give due consideration to the transcript of the record and other documents of all previous proceedings submitted to it in accordance with § 78-45c-22.

§ 78-45c-15. Filing foreign decree — Effect — Enforcement — Award of expenses.

(1) A certified copy of a custody decree of another state may be filed in the office of the clerk of any district court of this state. The clerk shall treat the decree in the same manner as a custody decree of the district court of this state. A custody decree so filed has the same effect and shall be enforced in like manner as a custody decree rendered by a court of this state.

(2) A person violating a custody decree of another state which makes it necessary to enforce the decree in this state may be required to pay necessary travel and other expenses, including attorney's fees, incurred by the party entitled to the custody or his witnesses.

§ 78-45c-16. Registry maintained by clerk of court — Documents entered.

The clerk of each court shall maintain a registry in which he shall enter all of the following:

(1) certified copies of custody decrees of other states received for filing;

(2) communications as to the pendency of custody proceedings in other states;

(3) communications concerning a finding of inconveneint forum by a court of another state; and

(4) other communications or documents concerning custody proceedings in another state which may affect the jurisdiction of a court of this state or the disposition to be made by it in a custody proceeding.

§ 78-45c-17. Certified copies of decrees furnished by clerk of court.

The clerk of a district court of this state, at the request of the court of another state or at the request of any person who is affected by or has a legitimate interest in a custody decree, shall certify and forward a copy of the decree to that court or person.

§ 78-45c-18. Taking testimony of persons in other states.

In addition to other procedural devices available to a party, any party to the proceeding or a guardian ad litem or other representative of the child may adduce tesitmony of witnesses, including parties and the child, by deposition or otherwise, in another state. The court on its own motion may direct that the tesitmony of a person be taken in another state and may prescribe the manner in which and the terms upon which the testimony shall be taken.

§ 78-45c-19. Request to court of another state to take evidence, to make studies or to order appearance of party — Payment of costs.

(1) A court of this state may request the appropriate court of another state to hold a hearing to adduce evidence, to order a party to produce or give evidence under other procedures of that state, or to have social studies made with respect to the custody of a child involved in proceedings pending in the court of this state; and to forward to the court of this state certified copies of the transcript of the record of the hearing, the evidence otherwise adduced, or any social studies prepared in compliance with the request. The cost of the services may be assessed against the parties.

(2) A court of this state may request the appropriate court of another state to order a party to custody proceedings pending in the court of this state to appear in the proceedings, and if that party has physical custody of the child, to appear with the child. The request may state that travel and other necessary expenses of the party and of the child whose appearance is desired will be assessed against another party or will otherwise be paid.

§ 78-45c-20. Taking evidence for use in court of another state — Ordering appearance in another state — Costs — Enforcement.

(1) Upon request of the court of another state the courts of this state which are competent to hear custody matters may order a person in this state to appear at a hearing to adduce evidence or to produce or give evidence under other procedures available in this state. A certified copy of the transcript of the record of the hearing or the evidence otherwise adduced shall be forwarded by the clerk of the court to the requesting court.

(2) A person within this state may voluntarily give his testimony or statement in this state for use in a custody proceeding outside this state.

(3) Upon request of the court of another state a competent court of this state may order a person in this state to appear alone or with the child in a custody proceeding in another state. The court may condition compliance with the request upon assurance by the other state that travel and other necessary expenses will be advanced or reimbursed. If the person who has physical custody of the child cannot be served or fails to obey the order, or it appears the order will be ineffective, the court may issue a warrant of arrest against such person to secure his appearance with the child in the other state.

§ 78-45c-21. Preservation of records of proceedings — Furnishing copies to other state courts.

In any custody proceeding in this state the court shall preserve the pleadings, orders and decrees, any record that has been made of its hearings, social studies, and other pertinent documents until the child reaches 18 years of age. Upon appropriate request of the court of another state the court shall forward to the other court certified copies of any or all of such documents.

§ 78-45c-22. Requesting court records from another state.

If a custody decree has been rendered in another state concerning a child involved in a custody proceeding pending in a court of this state, the court of this state upon taking jurisdiction of the case shall request of the court of the other state a certified copy of the transcript of any court record and other documents mentioned in § 78-45c-21.

§ 78-45c-23. Foreign counties — Application of general policies.

The general policies of this act extend to the international area. The provisions of this act relating to the recognition and enforcement of custody decrees of other states apply to custody decrees and decrees involving legal institutions similar in nature to custody rendered by appropriate authorities of other nations if reasonable notice and opportunity to be heard were given to all affected persons.

§ 78-45c-24. Priority on court calendar.

Upon the request of a party to a custody proceeding which raises a question of existence or exercise of jurisdiction under this act the case shall be given calendar priority and handled expeditiously.

§ 78-45c-25. Notices — Orders to appear — Manner of service.

(1) Whenever the terms of this act impose a duty upon the court to notify a party or court of a particular fact or action, such notification may be accomplished by the clerk of the court or a party to the action upon order of the court.

(2) Orders of the court for parties or persons to appear before the court in accordance with the terms of this act shall include legal and sufficient service of process in accordance with the Utah Rules of Civil Procedure unless otherwise ordered for good cause shown.

§ 78-45c-26. Short title.

This act may be cited as the "Utah Uniform Child Custody Jurisdiction Act."

VERMONT

UNIFORM CHILD CUSTODY JURISDICTION ACT
TITLE 15

§ 1031. Definitions.

For the purposes of this chapter unless the context otherwise clearly requires:

(1) "contestant" means a person, including a parent, who claims a right to custody or visitation rights with respect to a child;

(2) "custody determination" means a court decision and court orders and instructions providing for the custody of a child, including visitation rights; it does not include a decision relating to child support or any other monetary obligation of any person;

(3) "custody proceeding" includes proceedings in which a custody determination is one of several issues, such as an action for divorce or separation, and includes child neglect and dependency proceedings;

(4) "decree" or "custody decree" means a custody determination contained in a judicial decree or order made in a custody proceeding, and includes an initial decree and a modification decree;

(5) "home state" means the state in which the child immediately preceding the time involved lived with his parents, a parent,

or a person acting as parent, for at least six consecutive months, and in the case of a child less than six months old the state in which the child lived from birth with any of the persons mentioned. Periods of temporary absence of any of the named persons are counted as part of the six-month or other period;

(6) "initial decree" means the first custody decree concerning a particular child;

(7) "modification decree" means a custody decree which modifies or replaces a prior decree, whether made by the court which rendered the prior decree or by another court;

(8) "physical custody" means actual possession and control of a child;

(9) "persons acting as parent" means a person, other than a parent, who has physical custody of a child and who has either been awarded custody by a court or claims a right to custody; and

(10) "state" means any state, territory, or possession of the United States; the Commonwealth of Puerto Rico, and the District of Columbia.

§ 1032. Jurisdiction.

(a) A court of this state which is competent to decide child custody matters has jurisdiction to make a child custody determination by initial or modification decree if:

(1) this state

(A) is the home state of the child at the time of commencement of the proceeding, or

(B) had been the child's home state within six months before commencement of the proceeding and the child is absent from this state because of his removal or retention by a person claiming his custody or for other reasons, and a parent or person acting as parent continues to live in this state; or

(2) it is in the best interest of the child that a court of this state assume jurisdiction because

(A) the child and his parents, or the child and at least one contestant, have a significant connection with this state, and

(B) there is available in this state substantial evidence concerning the child's present or future care, protection, training, and personal relationships; or

(3) the child is physically present in this state and

(A) the child has been abandoned or

(B) it is necessary in an emergency to protect the child because he has been subjected to or threatened with mistreatment or abuse or is otherwise neglected, or

(4) it appears that no other state would have jurisdiction under prerequisites substantially in accordance with divisions (1), (2), or (3) of this subsection, or another state has declined to exercise jurisdiction on the ground that this state is the more appropriate forum to determine the custody of the child, and it is in the best interest of the child that this court assume jurisdiction.

(b) Physical presence in this state of the child, or of the child and one of the contestants, is not alone sufficient to confer jurisdiction on a court of this state to make a child custody determination, except under divisions (3) and (4) of subsection (a) of this section (and then only when the conditions in the division are met).

(c) Physical presence of the child, while desirable, is not a prerequisite for jurisdiction to determine his custody.

§ 1033. Notice and opportunity to be heard.

Before making a decree under this chapter, reasonable notice and opportunity to be heard shall be given to the contestants, any parent whose parental rights have not been previously terminated, and any person who has physical custody of the child. If any of these persons is outside this state, notice and opportunity to be heard shall be given pursuant to section 1034 of this title.

§ 1034. Notice to persons outside this state; submission to jurisdiction.

(a) Notice required for the exercise of jurisdiction over a person outside this state shall be given pursuant to the Vermont Rules of Civil Procedure.

(b) Notice under this section shall be served, mailed, delivered, or published at least 20 days before any hearing in this state.

§ 1035. Simultaneous proceedings in other states.

(a) A court of this state shall not exercise its jurisdiction under this chapter if at the time of filing the petition a proceeding concerning the custody of the child was pending in a court of another state exercising jurisdiction substantially in conformity with this chapter, unless the proceeding is stayed by the court of the other state because this state is a more appropriate forum or for other reasons.

(b) Before hearing the petition in a custody proceeding the court shall examine the pleadings and other information supplied by the parties under section 1038 of this title and shall consult the child custody registry established under section 1045 of this title concerning the pendency of proceedings with respect to the child in other states. If the court has reason to believe that proceedings may be pending in another state, it shall direct an inquiry to the state court administrator or other appropriate official of the other state.

(c) If the court is informed during the court of the proceeding that a proceeding concerning the custody of the child was pending in another state before the court assumed jurisdiction it shall stay the proceeding and communicate with the court in which the other proceeding is pending to the end that the issue may be litigated in the more appropriate forum and that information be exchanged in accordance with sections 1047-1050 of this title. If a court of this state has made a custody decree before being informed of a pending proceeding in a court of another state it shall immediately inform that court of the fact. If the court is informed that a proceeding was commenced in another state after it assumed jurisdiction, it shall likewise inform the other court to the end that the issues may be litigated in the more appropriate forum.

§ 1036. Inconvenient or inappropriate forum.

(a) A court which has jurisdiction under this chapter to make an initial or modification decree may decline to exercise its jurisdiction any time before making a decree if it finds that it is an inconvenient forum to make a custody determination under the circumstances of the case and that a court of another state is a more appropriate forum.

(b) A finding of inconvenient forum may be made upon the court's own motion or upon motion of a party or a guardian ad litem or other representative of the child.

(c) In determining if it is an inconvenient forum, the court shall consider if it is in the interest of the child that another state assume jurisdiction. For this purpose it may take into account the following factors, among others:

(1) if another state is or recently was the child's home state;

(2) if another state has a closer connection with the child and his family or with the child and one or more of the contestants;

(3) if substantial evidence concerning the child's present or future care, protection, training, and personal relationships is more readily available in another state;

(4) if the parties have agreed on another forum which is no less appropriate; and

(5) if the exercise of jurisdiction by a court of this state would contravene any of the purposes of this chapter.

(d) Before determining whether to decline or retain jurisdiction, the court may communicate with a court of another state and exchange information pertinent to the assumption of jurisdiction by either court with a view to assuring that jurisdiction will be exercised by the more appropriate court and that a forum will be available to the parties.

(e) If the court finds that it is an inconvenient forum and that a court of another state is a more appropriate forum, it may dismiss the proceedings, or it may stay the proceedings upon condition that a custody proceeding be promptly commenced in another named state or upon any other conditions which may be just and proper, including the condition that a moving party stipulate his consent and submission to the jurisdiction of the other forum.

(f) The court may decline to exercise its jurisdiction under this chapter if a custody determination is incidental to an action for divorce or another proceeding while retaining jurisdiction over the divorce or other proceeding.

(g) If it appears to the court that it is clearly an inappropriate forum, it may require the party who commenced the proceedings to pay, in addition to the costs of the proceedings in this state, necessary travel and other expenses, including attorneys' fees, incurred by other parties or their witnesses. Payment is to be made to the clerk of the court for remittance to the proper party.

(h) Upon dismissal or stay or proceedings under this section, the court shall inform the court found to be the more appropriate forum of this fact, or if the court which would have jurisdiction in the other state is not certainly known, shall transmit the information to the court administrator or other appropriate official for forwarding to the appropriate court.

(j) Any communication received from another state informing this state of a finding of inconvenient forum because a court of this state is the more appropriate forum shall be filed in the custody registry. Upon assuming jurisdiction the court of this state shall inform the original court of this fact.

§ 1037. Information under oath.

(a) Every party in a custody proceeding in his first pleading or in an affidavit attached to that pleading shall give information under oath as to the child's present address, the places where the child has lived within the last five years, and the names and present addresses of the persons with whom the child has lived during that period. In this pleading or affidavit every party shall further declare under oath whether:

(1) he has participated as a party, witness, or in any other capacity in any other litigation concerning the custody of the same child in this or any other state;

(2) he has information of any custody proceeding concerning the child pending in a court of this or any other state; and

(3) he knows of any person not a party to the proceedings who has physical custody of the child or claims to have custody or visitation rights with respect to the child.

(b) If the declaration as to any of the above items is in the affirmative, the declarant shall give additional information under oath as required by the court. The court may examine the parties under oath as to details of the information furnished and as to other matters pertinent to the court's jurisdiction and the disposition of the case.

(c) Each party has a continuing duty to inform the court of any custody proceeding concerning the child in this or any other state of which he obtained information during this proceeding.

§ 1038. Additional parties.

If the court learns from information furnished by the parties pursuant to section 1037 of this title or from other sources that a person not a party to the custody proceeding has physical custody of the child or claims to have custody or visitation rights with respect to the child, it shall order that person to be joined as a party and to be duly notified of the pendency of the proceeding and of his joinder as a party. If the person joined as a party is outside this state, he shall be served with process or otherwise notified in accordance with section 1034 of this title.

§ 1039. Appearance of parties and the child.

(a) The court may order any party to the proceeding who is in this state to appear personally before the court. If that party has physical custody of the child the court may order that he appear personally with the child.

(b) If a party to the proceeding whose presence is desired by the court is outside this state with or without the child, the court may order that the notice given under section 1034 of this title include a statement directing that party to appear personally with or without the child and declaring that failure to appear may result in a decision adverse to that party.

(c) If a party to the proceeding who is outside this state is directed to appear under subsection (b) of this section or desires to appear personally before the court with or without the child, the court may require another party to pay to the clerk of the court travel and other necessary expenses of the party so appearing and of the child if this is just and proper under the circumstances.

§ 1040. Binding force; res judicata effect of custody decree.

A custody decree rendered by a court of this state which had jurisdiction under section 1032 of this title binds all parties who have been served in this state or notified in accordance with section 1034 of this title or who have submitted to the jurisdiction of the court, and who have been given an opportunity to be heard. As to these parties the custody decree is conclusive as to all issues of law and fact decided and as to the custody determination made unless and until that determination is modified pursuant to law, including the provision of this chapter.

§ 1041. Recognition of out-of-state custody decrees.

The courts of this state shall recognize and enforce an initial or modification decree of a court of another state which had assumed jurisdiction under statutory provisions substantially in accordance with this chapter or which was made under factual circumstances meeting the jurisdictional standards of the chapter so long as this decree has not been modified in accordance with jurisdictional standards substantially similar to those of this chapter.

§ 1042. Modification of custody decree of another place.

(a) If a court of another state has made a custody decree, a court of this state shall not modify that decree unless

(1) it appears to the court of this state that the court which rendered the decree does not now have jurisdiction under jurisdictional prerequisites substantially in accordance with this chapter or has declined to assume jurisdiction to modify the decree and or has declined to assume jurisdiction to modify the decree and

(2) the court of this state has jurisdiction.

(b) Unless required in the interest of the child, the court shall not modify a custody decree of another state if the petitioner, without consent of the person entitled to custody, has improperly removed the child from the physical custody of the person entitled to custody or has improperly retained the child after a visit or other temporary relinquishment of physical custody.

(c) If a court of this state is authorized under subsections (a) or (b) of this section to modify a custody decree of another state, it shall give due consideration to the transcript of the record and other documents of all previous proceedings submitted to it in accordance with section 1049 of this title.

§ 1043. Filing and enforcement of custody decree of another state.

(a) A certified copy of a custody decree of another state may be filed in the office of the court administrator of this state. A custody decree so filed has the same effect and shall be enforced in like manner as a custody decree rendered by a court of this state.

(b) A person violating a custody decree of another state which makes it necessary to enforce the decree in this state may be required to pay necessary travel and other expenses, including attorneys' fees, incurred by the party entitled to the custody or his witnesses.

§ 1044. Registry of out-of-state custody decrees and proceedings.

The court administrator shall maintain a registry in which he shall enter the following:

(1) certified copies of custody decrees of other states received for filing;

(2) court documents as to the pendency of custody proceedings in other states;

(3) court documents concerning a finding of inconvenient forum by a court of another state; and

(4) court documents concerning custody proceedings in another state which may affect the jurisdiction of a court of this state or the disposition to be made by it in a custody proceeding.

§ 1045. Certified copies of custody decree.

The court administrator or the clerk of the court of competent jurisdiction of this state at the request of the court of another state or at the request of any person who is affected by or has a legitimate interest in a custody decree, shall certify and forward a copy of the decree to that court or person.

§ 1046. Taking testimony in another state.

In addition to other procedural devices available to a party, any party to the proceeding or a guardian ad litem or other representative of the child may adduce testimony of witnesses, including parties and the child, by deposition or otherwise, in another state.

§ 1047. Hearings and studies in another state; orders to appear.

(a) A court of this state may request the appropriate court of another state to hold a hearing to adduce evidence and to forward to the court of this state certified copies of the transcript of the record of the hearing and the evidence otherwise adduced. The cost of the services may be assessed against the parties, or if necessary, ordered paid by the state.

(b) A court of this state may request the appropriate court of another state to order a party to custody proceedings pending in the court of this state to appear in the proceedings, and if that party has physical custody of the child, to appear with the child. The request may state that travel and other necessary expenses of the party and of the child whose appearance is desired will be assessed against another party or will otherwise be paid.

§ 1048. Assistance to courts of other states.

(a) Upon request of the court of another state the courts of this state which are competent to hear custody matters may order a person in this state to appear at a hearing to adduce evidence or to produce or give evidence under other procedures available in this state. A certified copy of the transcript of the record of the hearing or the evidence otherwise adduced shall be forwarded by the clerk of the court to the requesting court.

(b) A person within this state may voluntarily give his testimony or statement in this state for use in a custody proceeding outside this state.

§ 1049. Preservation of documents for use in other states.

In any custody proceeding in this state the court shall preserve the pleadings, orders and decrees, any record that has been made of its hearings, social studies, and other pertinent documents until the child reaches 18 years of age. Upon appropriate request of the court of another state the court shall forward to the other court certified copies of any or all such documents.

§ 1050. Request for court records of another state.

If a custody decree has been rendered in another state concerning a child involved in a custody proceeding pending in a court of this state, the court of this state upon taking jurisdiction of the case shall request of the court of the other state a certified copy of the transcript of any court record and other documents mentioned in section 1049 of this title.

§ 1051. International application.

The general policies of this chapter extend to the international area. The provisions of this chapter relating to the recognition and enforcement of custody decrees of other states apply to custody decrees and decrees involving legal institutions similar in nature to custody rendered by appropriate authorities of other nations if reasonable notice and opportunity to be heard were given to all affected persons.

VIRGINIA

CHAPTER 7
UNIFORM CHILD CUSTODY JURISDICTION ACT

§20-125. Definitions.—

As used in this chapter:

1. *"Contestant"* means a person, including a parent, who claims a right to custody or visitation rights with respect to a child;

2. *"Custody determination"* means a court decision and court orders and decrees providing for the custody of a child, including visitation rights; it does not include a decision relating to child support or any other monetary obligation of any person;

3. *"Custody proceeding"* includes proceedings in which a custody determination is an issue, such as an action for divorce or separation, and includes child neglect and dependency proceedings;

4. *"Decree"* or *"custody decree"* means a custody determination contained in a judicial decree or order made in a custody proceeding, and includes an initial decree and a modification decree;

5. *"Home state"* means the state in which the child immediately preceding the time involved lived with his parents, a parent, a person acting as parent, for at least six consecutive months, and in the case of a child less than six months old the state in which

the child lived from birth with any of the persons mentioned. Periods of temporary absence of any of the named persons are counted as part of the six-month or other period;

6. "*Initial decree*" means the first custody decree concerning a particular child;

7. "*Modification decree*" means a custody decree which modifies or replaces a prior decree, whether made by the court which rendered the prior decree or by another court;

8. "*Physical custody*" means actual possession and control of a child;

9. "*Person acting as parent*"means a person, other than a parent, who has physical custody of a child and who has either been awarded custody by a court or claims a right to custody; and

10."*State*" means any state, territory, or possession of the United States, the Commonwealth of Puerto Rico, and the District of Columbia.

§20-126. Grounds for jurisdiction.—

A. A court of this State which is competent to decide child custody matters has jurisdiction to make a child custody determination by initial or modification decree if:

1. This State (i) is the home state of the child at the time of commencement of the proceeding, or (ii) had been the child's home state within six months before commencement of the proceeding and the child is absent from this State because of his removal or retention by a person claiming his custody or for other reasons, and a parent or person acting as parent continues to live in this State; or

2. It is in the best interest of the child that a court of this State assume jurisdiction because (i) the child and his parents, or the child and at least one contestant, have a significant connection with this State, and (ii) there is available in this State substantial evidence concerning the child's present or future care, protection, training, and personal relationships; or

3. The child is physically present in this State and (i) the child has been abandoned, or (ii) it is necessary in an emergency to protect the child because he has been subjected to or threatened with mistreatment or abuse or is otherwise neglected or dependent; or

4. (i) It appears no other state would have jurisdiction under prerequisites substantially in accordance with paragraphs 1, 2, or 3, or another state has declined to exercise jurisdiction on the ground that this State is the more appropriate forum to determine the custody of the child, and (ii) it is in the best interest of the child that this court assume jurisdiction.

B. Except under paragraphs 3 and 4 of subsection A physical presence in this State of the child, or of the child and one of the contestants, is not alone sufficient to confer jurisdiction on a court of this State to make a child custody determination.

C. Physical presence of the child, while desirable, is not a prerequisite for jurisdiction to determine his custody.

§20-127. Notice and opportunity to be heard required.—

Before making a decree under this chapter, reasonable notice and opportunity to be heard shall be given to the contestants, any parent whose parental rights have not been previously terminated, and any person who has physical custody of the child. If any of these persons is outside this State, notice and opportunity shall be given pursuant to § 20-128.

§20-128. Notice to persons outside this Commonwealth; submission to jurisdiction.—

A. Notice required for the exercise of jurisdiction over a person outside this Commonwealth shall be given in a manner reasonably calculated to give actual notice, and may be:

1. By personal delivery outside this Commonwealth in the manner prescribed for services of process within this Commonwealth;

2. In the manner prescribed by the law of the place in which the service is made for service of process in that place in an action in any of its courts of record;

2a. By certified or registered mail, return receipt requested, addressed to the person to be served;

3. As directed by the court including an order of publication, if the other means of notification are ineffective.

B. Notice under this section shall be served, mailed, or delivered, or last published at least twenty-one days before any hearing in this Commonwealth.

C. Proof of service outside this Commonwealth may be made by affidavit of the individual who made the service, or in the manner prescribed by the law of this Commonwealth, the order pursuant to which the service is made, or the law of the place in which the service is made. If service is made by mail, proof shall also include a receipt signed by the addressee.

D. Notice is not required if a person submits to the jurisdiction of the court.

§20-129. Simultaneous proceedings in other states.—

A. A court of this State shall not exercise its jurisdiction under this chapter if at the time of filing the petition to a proceeding concerning the custody of the child was pending in a court of another state exercising jurisdiction substantially in conformity with this chapter, unless the proceeding is stayed by the court of the other state because this State is a more appropriate forum or for other reasons.

B. Before hearing the petition in a custody proceeding the court shall examine the pleadings and other information supplied by the parties under § 20-132 and shall consult the child custody registry established under § 20-139 concerning the pendency of proceedings with respect to the child in other states. If the court has reason to believe that proceedings may be pending in another state it shall direct an inquiry to the clerk of the court or other appropriate official of the other state.

C. If the court is informed during the course of the proceeding that a proceeding concerning the custody of the child was pending in another state before the court assumed jurisdiction it shall stay the proceeding and communicate with the court in which the other proceeding is pending to the end that the issue may be litigated in the more appropriate forum and that information be exchanged in accordance with §§ 20-142 through 20-145. If a court of this State has made a custody decree before being informed of a pending proceeding in a court of another state it shall immediately inform that court of the fact. If the court is informed that a proceeding was commenced in another state after it assumed jurisdiction it shall likewise inform the other court to the end that the issues may be litigated in the more appropriate forum.

§20-130. Jurisdiction declined upon finding of inconvenient forum.—

A. A court which has jurisdiction under this chapter to make an initial or modification decree may decline to exercise its jurisdiction any time before making a decree if it finds that it is an inconvenient forum to make a custody determination under the circumstances of the case and that a court of another state is a more appropriate forum.

B. A finding of inconvenient forum may be made upon the court's own motion or upon motion of a party of a guardian ad litem or other representative of the child.

C. In determining if it is an inconvenient forum, the court shall consider if it is in the interest of the child that another state assume jurisdiction. For this purpose it may take into account the following factors, among others:

1. If another state is or recently was the child's home state;

2. If another state has a close connection with the child and his family or with the child and one or more of the contestants;

3. If substantial evidence concerning the child's present or future care, protection, training, and personal relationships is more readily available in another state; and

4. If the parties have agreed on another forum which is no less appropriate.

D. Before determining whether to decline or retain jurisdiction the court may communicate with a court of another state and exchange information pertinent to the assumption of jurisdiction by either court with a view to assuring that jurisdiction will be exercised by the more appropriate court and that a forum will be available to the parties.

E. If the court finds that it is an inconvenient forum and that a court of another state is a more appropriate forum, it may dismiss the proceedings, or it may stay the proceedings upon condition that a custody proceeding be promptly commenced in another named state or upon any other conditions which may be just and proper, including the condition that a moving party stipulate his consent and submission to the jurisdiction of the other forum.

F. The court may decline to exercise its jurisdiction under this chapter if a custody determination is incidental to an action for divorce or another proceeding while retaining jurisdiction over the divorce or other proceeding.

G. If it appears to the court that it is clearly an inappropriate forum it may require the party who commenced the proceedings to pay, in addition to the costs of the proceedings in this State, necessary travel and other expenses, including attorneys' fees, incurred by other parties or their witnesses.

H. Upon dismissal or stay of the proceedings under this section the court shall inform that court found to be the more appropriate forum of this fact, or if the court which would have jurisdiction in the other state is not certainly known, shall transmit the information to the court administrator or other appropriate official for forwarding to the appropriate court.

I. Any communication received from another state informing this State of a finding of inconvenient forum because a court of this State is the more appropriate forum shall be filed in the appropriate court. Upon assuming jurisdiction the court of this State shall inform the original court of this fact.

§20-131. Jurisdiction declined by reason of conduct.—

A. If the petitioner for an initial decree has wrongfully taken the child from another state or has engaged in similar reprehensible conduct the court may decline to exercise jurisdiction if this is just and proper under the circumstances.

B. Unless required in the interest of the child, the court shall not exercise its jurisdiction to modify a custody decree of another state if the petitioner, without consent of the person entitled to custody, has improperly removed the child from the physical custody of the person entitled to custody or has improperly retained the child after a visit or other temporary relinquishment of physical custody. If the petitioner has violated any other provision of a custody decree of another state the court may decline to exercise its jurisdiction if this is just and proper under the circumstances.

C. In appropriate cases a court dismissing a petition under this section may charge the petitioner with necessary travel and other expenses, including attorneys' fees, incurred by other parties or their witnesses.

§20-132. Information under oath to be submitted to court.—

A. Every party in a custody proceeding in his first pleading or in an affidavit attached to that pleading shall give information under oath as to the child's present address, the places where the child has lived within the last five years, and the names and present addresses of the persons with whom the child has lived during that period. In this pleading or affidavit every party shall further declare under oath whether:

1. He has participated as a party, witness, or in any other capacity, in any other litigation concerning the custody of the same child in this or any other state;

2. He has information of any custody proceeding concerning the child pending in a court of this or any other state; and

3. He knows of any person not a party to the proceeding who has physical custody of the child or claims to have custody or visitation rights with respect to the child.

B.If the declaration as to any of the above items is in the affirmative the declarant shall give additional information under oath as required by the court. The court may examine the parties under oath as to details of the information furnished and as to other matters pertinent to the court's jurisdiction and disposition of the case.

C. Each party has a continuing duty to inform the court of any custody proceeding concerning the child in this or any other state of which he obtained information during this proceeding.

D. Any decree of divorce granted pursuant to §§ 20-116 and 20-117 of this Code shall be deemed valid notwithstanding failure to comply with the provisions of this section.

E. The provisions of this section shall not be applicable to a divorce proceeding under § 20-91 or § 20-95 or an annulment proceeding under § 20-89.1, unless child custody is a contested issue in the proceedings.

§20-133. Joinder of additional parties.—

If the court learns from information furnished by the parties pursuant to § 20-132 or from other sources that a person not a party to the custody proceeding has physical custody of the child or claims to have custody or visitation rights with respect to the child, it shall order that person to be joined as a party and to be duly notified of the pendency of the proceeding and of his joinder as a party. If the person joined as a party is outside this State he shall be served with process or otherwise notified in accordance with § 20-128.

§20-134. Appearance of parties and child.—

A. The court may order any party to the proceeding who is in this State to appear personally before the court. If that party has physical custody of the child the court may order that he appear personally with the child.

B. If a party to the proceedings whose presence is desired by the court is outside this State with or without the child the court may order that the notice given under § 20-128 include a statement directing that party to appear personally with or without the child and declaring that failure to appear may result in a decision adverse to that party.

C. If a party to the proceeding who is outside this State is directed to appear under Subsection B or desires to appear personally before the court with or without the child, the court may require another party to pay the clerk of the court travel and other expenses of the party so appearing and of the child if this is just and proper under the circumstances.

§20-135. Res judicata effect of custody decree.—

A custody decree rendered by a court of this State which had jurisdiction under § 20-126 binds all parties who have been served in this State or notified in accordance with § 20-128 or who have submitted to the jurisdiction of the court, and who have been given an opportunity to be heard. As to these parties the custody decree is conclusive as to all issues of law and fact decided and as to the custody determination made unless and until that determination is modified pursuant to law, including the provisions of this chapter.

§20-136. Recognition of out-of-state custody decrees.—

The courts of this State shall recognize and enforce an initial or modification decree of a court of another state which has assumed jurisdiction under statutory provisions substantially in accordance with this chapter or which was made under factual circumstances meeting the jurisdictional standards of the chapter, so long as this decree has not been modified in accordance with jurisdictional standards substantially similar to those of this chapter.

§20-137. Modification of custody decree of another state.—

A. If a court of another state has made a custody decree, a court of this State shall not modify that decree unless (1) it appears to the court of this State that the court which rendered the decree does not now have jurisdiction under jurisdictional prerequisites substantially in accordance with this chapter or has declined to assume jurisdiction to modify the decree and (2) the court of this State has jurisdiction.

B. If a court of this State is authorized under subsection A and § 20-131 to modify a custody decree of another state it shall give due consideration to the transcript of the record and other documents of all previous proceedings submitted to it in accordance with § 20-145.

§20-138. Filing and enforcement of custody decree of another state.—

A. A certified copy of a custody decree of another state may be filed in the office of the clerk of any juvenile and domestic relations district court of this State. The clerk shall treat the decree in the same manner as a custody decree of the juvenile and domestic relations court of this State. A custody decree so filed has the same effect and shall be enforced in like manner as a custody decree rendered by a court of this State.

B. A person violating a custody decree of another state which makes it necessary to enforce the decree in this State may be required to pay necessary travel and other expenses, including attorney's fees, incurred by the party entitled to the custody or his witnesses.

§20-139. Registry of out-of-state custody decrees and proceedings.—
The clerk of each juvenile and domestic relations district court of this State shall maintain a registry in which he shall enter the following:
1. Certified copies of custody decrees of other states received for filing;
2. Communications as to the pendency of custody proceedings in other states;
3. Communications concerning a finding of inconvenient forum by a court of another state; and
4. Other communications or documents concerning custody proceedings in another state which may affect the jurisdiction of a court of this State or the disposition to be made by it in a custody proceeding.

§20-140. Certified copies of custody decrees.—
The clerk of the juvenile and domestic relations district court of this State, at the request of the court of another state or at the request of any person who is affected by or has a legitimate interest in a custody decree, shall certify and forward a copy of the decree to that court or person.

§20-141. Taking testimony in another state.—
In addition to other procedural devices available to a party, any party to the proceeding or a guardian ad litem or other representative of the child may adduce testimony of witnesses, including parties and the child, by deposition or otherwise, in another state. The court on its own motion may direct that the testimony of a person be taken in another state and may prescribe the manner in which and the terms upon which the testimony shall be taken.

§20-142. Requests for hearings and studies in another state; orders to appear.—
A. A court of this State may request the appropriate court of another state to hold a hearing to adduce evidence, to order a party to produce or give evidence under other procedures of that state, or to have social studies made with respect to the custody of a child involved in proceedings pending in the court of this State; and to forward to the court of this State certified copies of the transcript of the record of the hearing, the evidence otherwise adduced, or any social studies prepared in compliance with request. The cost of the services may be assessed against the parties or, if necessary, ordered paid by the State.

B. A court of this State may request the appropriate court of another state to order a party to custody proceedings pending in the court of this State to appear in the proceedings and if that party has physical custody of the child to appear with the child. The request may state that travel and other necessary expenses of the party and of the child whose appearance is ordered will be assessed against another party or otherwise paid.

§20-143. Assistance to courts of other states.—
A. Upon request of the court of another state the courts of this State which are competent to hear custody matters may order a person in the State to appear at a hearing to adduce evidence or produce or give evidence under other procedures available in this State or may order social studies to be made for use in a custody proceeding in another state. A certified copy of the transcript of the record of the hearing or the evidence otherwise adduced and any social studies prepared shall be forwarded by the clerk of the court to the requesting court.

B. A person within this State may voluntarily give his testimony or statement in this State for use in a custody proceeding outside this State.

C. Upon request of the court of another state a competent court of this State may order a person in this State to appear alone or with the child in a custody proceeding in another state. The court may condition compliance with the request upon assurance by the other state that State travel and other necessary expenses will be advanced or reimbursed.

§20-144. Preservation of documents for use in other states.—
In any custody proceeding in this State the court shall preserve the pleadings, orders and decrees, any record that has been made of its hearings, social studies, and other pertinent documents until the child reaches eighteen years of age. Upon appropriate request of the court of another state the courts shall forward to the other court certified copies of any or all of such documents.

§20-145. Request for court records of another state.—
If a custody decree has been rendered in another state concerning a child involved in a custody proceeding pending in a court of this State, the court of this State upon taking jurisdiction of the case shall request of the court of the other state a certified copy of the transcript of any court record and other documents mentioned in § 20-144.

§20-146. International application.—
The general policies of this chapter extend to the international area. The provisions of this chapter relating to the recognition and enforcement of custody decrees of other states apply to custody decrees and decrees involving legal institutions similar in

nature to custody institutions rendered by appropriate authorities of other nations if reasonable notice and opportunity to be heard were given to all affected persons.

WASHINGTON

UNIFORM CHILD CUSTODY JURISDICTION ACT

§ 26.27.010. Purposes of chapter — Construction of provisions.

(1) The general purposes of this chapter are to:

(a) Avoid jurisdiction competition and conflict with courts of other states in matters of child custody which have in the past resulted in the shifting of children from state to state with harmful effects on their well-being;

(b) Promote cooperation with the courts of other states to the end that a custody decree is rendered in that state which can best decide the case in the interest of the child;

(c) Assure that litigation concerning the custody of a child take place ordinarily in the state with which the child and his family have the closest connection and where significant evidence concerning his care, protection, training, and personal relationships is most readily available, and that courts of this state decline the exercise of jurisdiction when the child and his family have a closer connection with another state;

(d) Discourage continuing controversies over child custody in the interest of greater stability of home environment and of secure family relationships for the child;

(e) Deter abductions and other unilateral removals of children undertaken to obtain custody awards;

(f) Avoid relitigation of custody decisions of other states in this state insofar as feasible;

(g) Facilitate the enforcement of custody decrees of other states;

(h) Promote and expand the exchange of information and other forms of mutual assistance between the courts of this state and those of other states concerned with the same child; and

(i) Make uniform the law of those states which enact it.

(2) This chapter shall be construed to promote the general purposes stated in this section.

§ 26.27.020. Definitions.

As used in this chapter:

(1) "Contestant" means a person, including a parent, who claims a right to custody or visitation rights with respect to a child;

(2) "Custody determination" means a court decision and court orders and instructions providing for the custody of a child, including visitation rights; it does not include a decision relating to child support or any other monetary obligation of any person;

(3) "Custody proceeding" includes proceedings in which a custody determination is one of several issues, such as an action for dissolution of marriage, or legal separation, and includes child neglect and dependency proceedings;

(4) "Decree" or "custody decree" means a custody determination contained in a judicial decree or order made in a custody proceeding, and includes an initial decree and a modification decree;

(5) "Home state" means the state in which the child immediately preceding the time involved lived with his parents, a parent, or a person acting as parent, for at least six consecutive months, and in the case of a child less than six months old the state in which the child lived from birth with any of the persons mentioned. Periods of temporary absence of any of the named persons are counted as part of the six-month or other period;

(6) "Initial decree" means the first custody decree concerning a particular child;

(7) "Modification decree" means a custody decree which modifies or replaces a prior decree, whether made by the court which rendered the prior decree or by another court;

(8) "Physical custody" means actual possession and control of a child;

(9) "Person acting as parent" means a person, other than a parent, who has physical custody of a child and who has either been awarded custody by the court or claims a right to custody; and

(10) "State" means any state, territory, or possession of the United States, the Commonwealth of Puerto Rico, and the District of Columbia.

§ 26.27.030. Jurisdiction.

(1) A court of this state which is competent to decide child custody matters has jurisdiction to make a child custody determination by initial or modification decree if the conditions as set forth in any of the following paragraphs are met:

(a) This state (i) is the home state of the child at the time of commencement of the proceeding, or (ii) had been the child's home state within six months before commencement of the proceeding and the child is absent from this state because of his removal or retention by a person claiming his custody or for other reasons, and a parent or person acting as parent continues to live in this state; or

(b) It is in the best interest of the child that a court of this state assume jurisdiction because (i) the child and his parents, or the child and at least one contestant, have a significant connection with this state, and (ii) there is available in this state substantial evidence concerning the child's present or future care, protection, training, and personal relationships; or

(c) The child is physically present in this state and (i) the child has been abandoned or (ii) it is necessary in an emergency to protect the child because he has been subjected to or threatened with mistreatment or abuse or is otherwise neglected or dependent; or

(d)(i) It appears that no other state would have jurisdiction under prerequisites substantially in accordance with paragraphs (a), (b), or (c) of this subsection, or another state has declined to exercise jurisdiction on the ground that this state is the more appropriate forum to determine the custody of the child, and (ii) it is in the best interest of the child that this court assume jurisdiction.

(2) Except under subsection (1)(c) and (d) of this section, physical presence in this state of the child, or of the child and one of the contestants, is not alone sufficient to confer jurisdiction on a court of this state to make a child custody determination.

(3) Physical presence of the child, while desirable, is not a prerequisite for jurisdiction to determine his custody.

§ 26.27.040. Notice and opportunity to be heard.

Before making a decree under this chapter, reasonable notice and opportunity to be heard shall be given to the contestants, any parent whose parental rights have not been previously terminated, and any person who has physical custody of the child. If any of these persons is outside this state, notice and opportunity to be heard shall be given under RCW 26.27.050.

§ 26.27.050. Notice to persons outside this state — Submission to jurisdiction.

(1) Notice required for the exercise of jurisdiction over a person outside this state shall be given in a manner reasonably calculated to give actual notice, and may be made in any of the following ways:

(a) By personal delivery outside this state in the manner prescribed for service of process within this state;

(b) In the manner prescribed by the law of the place in which the service is made for service of process in that place in an action in any of its courts of general jurisdiction;

(c) By any form of mail addressed to the person to be served and requesting a receipt; or

(d) As directed by the court (including publication, if other means of notification are ineffective).

(2) Notice under this section shall be served, mailed, delivered, or last published at least ten days before any hearing in this state.

(3) Proof of service outside this state may be made by affidavit of the individual who made the service, or in the manner prescribed by the law of this state, the order pursuant to which the service is made, or the law of the place in which the service is made. If service is made by mail, proof may be a receipt signed by the addressee or other evidence of delivery to the addressee.

(4) Notice is not required if a person submits to the jurisdiction of the court.

§ 26.27.060. Simultaneous proceedings in other states.

(1) A court of this state shall not exercise its jurisdiction under this chapter if at the time of filing the petition a proceeding concerning the custody of the child was pending in a court of another state exercising jurisdiction substantially in conformity with this chapter, unless the proceeding is stayed by the court of the other state because this state is a more appropriate forum or for other reasons.

(2) Before hearing the petition in a custody proceeding the court shall examine the pleadings and other information supplied by the parties under RCW 26.27.090 and shall consult the child custody registry established under RCW 26.27.160 concerning the pendency of proceedings with respect to the child in other states. If the court has reason to believe that proceedings may be pending in another state it shall direct an inquiry to the state court administrator or other appropriate official of the other state.

(3) If the court is informed during the course of the proceeding that a proceeding concerning the custody of the child was pending in another state before the court assumed jurisdiction it shall stay the proceeding and communicate with the court in which the other proceeding is pending to the end that the issue may be litigated in the more appropriate forum and that information be exchanged in accordance with RCW 26.27.190 through 26.27.220. If a court of this state has made a custody decree before being informed of a pending proceeding in a court of another state it shall immediately inform that court of the fact. If the court is informed that a proceeding was commenced in another state after it assumed jurisdiction it shall likewise inform the other court to the end that the issues may be litigated in the more appropriate forum.

§ 26.27.070. Inconvenient forum.

(1) A court which has jurisdiction under this chapter to make an initial or modification decree may decline to exercise its jurisdiction any time before making a decree if it finds that it is an inconvenient forum to make a custody determination under the circumstances of the case and that a court of another state is a more appropriate forum.

(2) A finding of inconvenient forum may be made upon the court's own motion or upon motion of a party or a guardian ad litem or other representative of the child.

(3) In determining if it is an inconvenient forum, the court shall consider if it is in the interest of the child that another state assume jurisdiction. For this purpose it may take into account the following factors, among others:

(a) If another state is or recently was the child's home state;

(b) If another state has a closer connection with the child and his family or with the child and one or more of the contestants;

(c) If substantial evidence concerning the child's present or future care, protection, training, and personal relationships is more readily available in another state;

(d) If the parties have agreed on another forum which is no less appropriate; and

(e) If the exercise of jurisdiction by a court of this state would contravene any of the purposes stated in RCW 26.27.010.

(4) Before determining whether to decline or retain jurisdiction the court may communicate with a court of another state and exchange information pertinent to the assumption of jurisdiction by either court with a view to assuring that jurisdiction will be exercised by the more appropriate court and that a forum will be available to the parties.

(5) If the court finds that it is an inconvenient forum and that a court of another state is a more appropriate forum, it may dismiss the proceedings, or it may stay the proceedings upon condition that a custody proceeding be promptly commenced in another named state or upon any other conditions which may be just and proper, including the condition that a moving party stipulate his consent and submission to the jurisdiction of the other forum.

(6) The court may decline to exercise its jurisdiction under this chapter if a custody determination is incidental to an action for dissolution of marriage or another proceeding while retaining jurisdiction over the dissolution of marriage or other proceeding.

(7) If it appears to the court that it is clearly an inappropriate forum it may require the party who commenced the proceedings to pay, in addition to the costs of the proceedings in this state, necessary travel and other expenses, including attorney's fees, incurred by other parties or their witnesses. Payment is to be made to the clerk of the court of remittance to the proper party.

(8) Upon dismissal or stay of proceedings under this section the court shall inform the court found to be the more appropriate forum of this fact, or if the court which would have jurisdiction in the other state is not certainly known, shall transmit the information to the court administrator or other appropriate official for forwarding to the appropriate court.

(9) Any communication received from another state informing this state of a finding of inconvenient forum because a court of this state is the more appropriate forum shall be filed in the custody registry of the appropriate court. Upon assuming jurisdiction the court of this state shall inform the original court of this fact.

§ 26.27.080. Jurisdiction declined by reason of conduct.

(1) If the petitioner for an initial decree has wrongfully taken the child from another state or has engaged in similar reprehensible conduct the court may decline to exercise jurisdiction for purposes of adjudication of custody if this is just and proper under the circumstances.

(2) Unless required in the interest of the child, the court shall not exercise its jurisdiction to modify a custody decree of another state if the petitioner, without consent of the person entitled to custody has improperly removed the child from the physical custody of the person entitled to custody or has improperly retained the child after a visit or other temporary relinquishment of physical custody. If the petitioner has violated any other provision of a custody decree of another state the court may decline to exercise its jurisdiction if this is just and proper under the circumstances.

(3) Where the court declines to exercise jurisdiction upon petition for an initial custody decree under subsection (1) of this section, the court shall notify the parent or other appropriate person and the prosecuting attorney of the appropriate jurisdiction in the other state. If a request to that effect is received from the other state, the court shall order the petitioner to appear with the child in a custody proceeding instituted in the other state in accordance with RCW 26.27.200. If no such request is made within a reasonable time after the notification, the court may entertain a petition to determine custody by the petitioner if it has jurisdiction under RCW 26.27.030.

(4) Where the court refuses to assume jurisdiction to modify the custody decree of another state under subsection (2) of this section or under RCW 26.27.140, the court shall notify the person who has legal custody under the decree of the other state and the prosecuting attorney of the appropriate jurisdiction in the other state and may order the petitioner to return the child to the person who has legal custody. If it appears that the order will be ineffective and the legal custodian is ready to receive the child within a period of a few days, the court may place the child in a foster care home for the period, pending return of the child to the legal custodian. At the same time, the court shall advise the petitioner that any petition for modification of custody must be directed to the appropriate court of the other state which has continuing jurisdiction, or, in the event that that court declines jurisdiction, to a court in a state which has jurisdiction under RCW 26.27.030.

(5) In appropriate cases a court dismissing a petition under this section may charge the petitioner with necessary travel and other expenses, including attorney's fees and the cost of returning the child to another state.

§ 26.27.090. Information under oath to be submitted to court.

(1) Every party in a custody proceeding in his first pleading or in an affidavit attached to that pleading shall give information under oath as to the child's present address, the places where the child has lived within the last five years, and the names and present addresses of the persons with whom the child has lived during that period. In this pleading or affidavit every party shall further declare under oath as to each of the following whether:

(a) He has participated, as a party, witness, or in any other capacity, in any other litigation concerning the custody of the same child in this or any other state;

(b) He has information of any custody proceeding concerning the child pending in a court of this or any other state; and

(c) He knows of any person not a party to the proceedings who has physical custody of the child or claims to have custody or visitation rights with respect to the child.

(2) If the declaration as to any of the above items is in the affirmative the declarant shall give additional information under oath as required by the court. The court may examine the parties under oath as to details of the information furnished and as to other matters pertinent to the court's jurisdiction and the disposition of the case.

(3) Each party has a continuing duty to inform the court of any custody proceeding concerning the child in this or any other state of which he obtained information during this proceeding.

§ 26.27.100. Additional parties.

If the court learns from information furnished by the parties under RCW 26.27.090 or from other sources that a person not a party to the custody proceeding has physical custody of the child or claims to have custody or visitation rights with respect to the child, it shall order that person to be joined as a party and to be duly notified of the pendency of the proceeding and of his joinder as a party. If the person joined as a party is outside this state he shall be served with process or otherwise notified in accordance with RCW 26.27.050.

§ 26.27.110. Appearance of parties and child.

(1) The court may order any party to the proceeding who is in this state to appear personally before the court. If that party has physical custody of the child the court may order that he appear personally with the child. If the party who is ordered to appear with the child cannot be served or fails to obey the order, or it appears the order will be ineffective, the court may issue a warrant of arrest against the party to secure his appearance with the child.

(2) If a party to the proceeding whose presence is desired by the court is outside this state with or without the child the court may order that the notice given under RCW 26.27.050 include a statement directing that party to appear personally with or without the child and declaring that failure to appear may result in a decision adverse to that party.

(3) If a party to the proceeding who is outside this state is directed to appear under subsection (2) of this section or desires to appear personally before the court with or without the child, the court may require another party to pay to the clerk of the court travel and other necessary expenses of the party so appearing and of the child if this is just and proper under the circumstances.

§ 26.27.120. Binding force and res judicata effect of custody decree.

A custody decree rendered by a court of this state which had jurisdiction under RCW 26.27.030 binds all parties who have been served in this state or notified in accordance with RCW 26.27.050 or who have submitted to the jurisdiction of the court, and who have been given an opportunity to be heard. As to these parties the custody decree is conclusive as to all issues of law and fact decided and as to the custody determination made unless and until that determination is modified pursuant to law, including the provisions of this chapter.

§ 26.27.130. Recognition of out-of-state custody decrees.

The courts of this state shall recognize and enforce an initial or modification decree of a court of another state which had assumed jurisdiction under statutory provisions substantially in accordance with this chapter or which was made under factual circumstances meeting the jurisdictional standards of this chapter, so long as this decree has not been modified in accordance with jurisdictional standards substantially similar to those of this chapter.

§ 26.27.140. Modification of custody decree of another state.

(1) If a court of another state has made a custody decree, a court of this state shall not modify that decree unless (a) it appears to the court of this state that the court which rendered the decree does not now have jurisdiction under jurisdictional prerequisites substantially in accordance with this chapter or has declined to assume jurisdiction to modify the decree and (b) the court of this state has jurisdiction.

(2) If a court of this state is authorized under subsection (1) of this section and RCW 26.27.080 to modify a custody decree of another state it shall give due consideration to the transcript of the record and other documents of all previous proceedings submitted to it in accordance with RCW 26.27.220.

§ 26.27.150. Filing and enforcement of custody decree of another state.

(1) A certified copy of a custody decree of another state may be filed in the office of the clerk of any superior court of this state. The clerk shall treat the decree in the same manner as a custody decree of the superior court of this state. A custody decree so filed has the same effect and shall be enforced in like manner as a custody decree rendered by a court of this state.

(2) A person violating a custody decree of another state which makes it necessary to enforce the decree in this state may be required to pay necessary travel and other expenses, including attorneys' fees, incurred by the party entitled to the custody or his witnesses.

§ 26.27.160. Registry of out-of-state custody decrees and proceedings.

(1) The clerk of each superior court shall maintain a registry in which he or she shall enter certified copies of custody decrees of other states received for filing to which the clerk shall assign an individual cause number.

(2) The clerk shall maintain the following at no charge as miscellaneous filing:

(a) Communications as to the pendency of custody proceedings in other states;

(b) Communications concerning a finding of inconvenient forum by a court of another state; and

(c) Other communications or documents concerning custody proceedings in another state which may affect the jurisdiction of a court of this state or the disposition to be made by it in a custody proceeding.

§ 26.27.170. Certified copies of custody decree.

The clerk of a superior court of this state, at the request of the court of another state or at the request of any person who is affected by or has a legitimate interest in a custody decree, shall certify and forward a copy of the decree to that court or person.

§ 26.27.180. Taking testimony in another state.

In addition to other procedural devices available to a party, any party to the proceeding or a guardian ad litem or other representative of the child may adduce testimony of witnesses, including parties and the child, by deposition or otherwise, in another state. The court on its own motion may direct that the testimony of a person be taken in another state and may prescribe the manner in which and the terms upon which the testimony shall be taken.

§ 26.27.190. Hearings and studies in another state — Orders to appear.

(1) A court of this state may request the appropriate court of another state to hold a hearing to adduce evidence, to order a party to produce or give evidence under other procedures of that state, or to have social studies made with respect to the custody of a child involved in proceedings pending in the court of this state; and to forward to the court of this state certified copies of the transcript of the record of the hearing, the evidence otherwise adduced, or any social studies prepared in compliance with the request. The cost of the services may be assessed against the parties or, if necessary, ordered paid by the state.

(2) A court of this state may request the appropriate court of another state to order a party to custody proceedings pending in the court of this state to appear in the proceedings, and if that party has physical custody of the child, to appear with the child. The request may state that travel and other necessary expenses of the party and of the child whose appearance is desired will be assessed against another party or will otherwise be paid.

§ 26.27.200. Assistance to courts of other states.

(1) Upon request of the court of another state the courts of this state which are competent to hear custody matters may order a person in this state to appear at a hearing to adduce evidence or to produce or give evidence under other procedures available in this state or may order social studies under RCW 26.09.220 to be made for use in a custody proceeding in another state. A certified copy of the transcript of the record of the hearing or the evidence otherwise adduced and any social studies made shall be forwarded by the clerk of the court to the requesting court.

(2) A person within this state may voluntarily give his testimony or statement in this state for use in a custody proceeding outside this state.

(3) Upon request of the court of another state a competent court of this state may order a person in this state to appear alone or with the child in a custody proceeding in another state. The court may condition compliance with the request upon assurance by the other state that travel and other necessary expenses will be advanced or reimbursed. If the person who has physical custody of the child cannot be served or fails to obey the order, or it appears the order will be ineffective, the court may issue a warrant of arrest against such person to secure his appearance with the child in the other state.

§ 26.27.210. Preservation of records of custody proceedings — Forwarding to another state.

In any custody proceeding in this state the court shall preserve the pleadings, orders and decrees, any record that has been made of its hearings, social studies, and other pertinent documents until the child reaches eighteen years of age. Upon appropriate request of the court of another state the court shall forward to the other court certified copies of any or all of such documents.

§ 26.27.220. Request for court records of another state.

If a custody decree has been rendered in another state concerning a child involved in a custody proceeding pending in a court of this state, the court of this state upon taking jurisdiction of the case shall request of the court of the other state a certified copy of the transcript of any court record and other documents mentioned in RCW 26.27.210.

§ 26.27.230. International application.

The general policies of this chapter extend to the international area. The provisions of this chapter relating to the recognition and enforcement of custody decrees of other states apply to custody decrees and decrees involving legal institutions similar in nature to custody rendered by appropriate authorities of other nations if reasonable notice and opportunity to be heard were given to all affected persons.

§ 26.27.900. Construction with chapter 26.09 RCW.

This chapter is in addition to and shall be construed in conjunction with chapter 26.09 RCW. In the event of an irreconcilable conflict between this chapter and chapter 26.09 RCW, chapter 26.09 RCW shall control.

§ 26.27.910. Short title.

This chapter may be cited as the Uniform Child Custody Jurisdiction Act.

§ 26.27.920. Severability — 1979 c 98.

If any provision of this act, or its application to any person or circumstance is held invalid, the remainder of the act, or the application of the provision to other persons or circumstances is not affected.

§ 26.27.930. Section captions.

Section captions used in this act shall constitute no part of the law.

WEST VIRGINIA

UNIFORM CHILD CUSTODY JURISDICTION ACT

§ 48-10-1. Purposes; construction.

(a) The general purposes of this article are to:

(1) Avoid jurisdictional competition and conflict with courts of other states in matters of child custody which have in the past resulted in the shifting of children from state to state with harmful effects on their well-being;

(2) Promote cooperation with the courts of other states to the end that a custody decree is rendered in that state which can best decide the case in the interest of the child;

(3) Assure that litigation concerning the custody of a child takes place ordinarily in the state with which the child and his family have the closest connection and where significant evidence concerning his care, protection, training, and personal relationships is most readily available, and that courts of this State decline the exercise of jurisdiction when the child and his family have a closer connection with another state;

(4) Discourage continuing controversies over child custody in the interest of greater stability of home environment and of secure family relationships for the child;

(5) Deter abductions and other unilateral removals of children undertaken to obtain custody awards;

(6) Avoid relitigation of custody decisions of other states in this State insofar as feasible;

(7) Facilitate the enforcement of custody decrees of other states;

(8) Promote and expand the exchange of information and other forms of mutual assistance between the courts of this State and those of other states concerning the same child; and

(9) Make uniform the law of those states which enact it.

(b) This article shall be construed to promote the general purposes stated in this section.

§ 48-10-2. Definitions.

As used in this article:

(1) "Contestant" means a person, including a parent, who claims a right to custody or visitation rights with respect to a child;

(2) "Custody determination" means a court decision and court orders and instructions providing for the custody of a child, including visitation rights; it does not include a decision relating to child support or any other monetary obligation of any person;

(3) "Custody proceeding" includes proceedings in which a custody determination is one of several issues, such as an action for divorce or separation, and includes child neglect and dependency proceedings;

(4) "Decree" or "custody decree" means a custody determination contained in a judicial decree or order made in a custody proceeding and includes an initial decree and a modification decree;

(5) "Home state" means the state in which the child immediately preceding the time involved lived with his parents, a parent or a person acting as parent for at least six consecutive months and, in the case of a child less than six months old, the state in which the child lived from birth with any of the persons named. Periods of temporary absence of any of the named persons are counted as part of the six-month or other period;

(6) "Initial decree" means the first custody decree concerning a particular child;

(7) "Modification decree" means a custody decree which modifies or replaces a prior decree, whether made by the court which rendered the prior decree or by another court;

(8) "Physical custody" means actual possession and control of a child;

(9) "Person acting as parent" means a person, other than a parent, who has physical custody of a child and who has either been awarded custody by a court or claims a right to custody; and

(10) "State" means any state, territory or possession of the United States, the Commonwealth of Puerto Rico and the District of Columbia.

§ 48-10-3. Jurisdiction.

(a) A court of this State which is competent to decide child custody matters has jurisdiction to make a child custody determination by initial or modification decree if:

(1) This State (i) is the home state of the child at the time of commencement of the proceeding or (ii) has been the child's home state within six months before commencement of the proceeding, the child is absent from this State because of his removal or retention by a person claiming his custody or for other reasons and a parent or person acting as parent continues to live in this State; or

(2) It is in the best interest of the child that a court of this State assume jurisdiction because (i) the child and his parents, or the child and at least one contestant, have a significant connection with this State, and (ii) there is available in this State substantial evidence concerning the child's present or future care, protection, training and personal relationships; or

(3) The child is physically present in this state, and (i) the child has been abandoned, or (ii) it is necessary in an emergency to protect the child because he has been subjected to or threatened with mistreatment or abuse or is otherwise neglected or dependent; or

(4) (i) It appears that no other state would have jurisdiction under prerequisites substantially in accordance with subdivision (1), (2) or (3) of this subsection, or another state has declined to exercise jurisdiction on the ground that this State is the more appropriate forum to determine the custody of the child, and (ii) it is in the best interest of the child that this court assume jurisdiction.

(b) Except under subdivisions (3) and (4) of subsection (a), physical presence in this State of the child, or of the child and one of the contestants, is not alone sufficient to confer jurisdiction on a court of this State to make a child custody determination.

(c) Physical presence of the child, while desirable, is not a prerequisite for jurisdiction to determine his custody.

§ 48-10-4. Notice and opportunity to be heard.

Before making a decree under this article, reasonable notice and opportunity to be heard shall be given to the contestants, any parent whose parental rights have not been previously terminated and any person who has physical custody of the child. If any of these persons is outside this State, notice and opportunity to be heard shall be given pursuant to section five [§ 48-10-5] of this article.

§ 48-10-5. Notice to persons outside State; submission to jurisdiction.

(a) Notice required for the exercise of jurisdiction over a person outside this State shall be given in a manner reasonably calculated to give actual notice and may be:

(1) By personal delivery outside this State in the manner prescribed for service of process within this State;

(2) In the manner prescribed by the law of the place in which the service is made for service of process in that place in an action in any of its courts of general jurisdiction;

(3) By any form of mail addressed to the person to be served and requesting a receipt; or

(4) As directed by the court, including publication, if other means of notification are ineffective.

(b) Notice under this section shall be served, mailed, or delivered, or last published at least twenty days before any hearing in this State.

(c) Proof of service outside this State may be made by affidavit of the individual who made the service, or in the manner prescribed by the law of this State, by the order pursuant to which the service is made or by the law of the place in which the service is made. If service is made by mail, proof may be a receipt signed by the addressee or other evidence of delivery to the addressee.

(d) Notice is not required if a person submits to the jurisdiction of the court.

§ 48-10-6. Simultaneous proceedings in other states.

(a) A court of this State shall not exercise its jurisdiction under this article if at the time of filing the petition a proceeding concerning the custody of the child was pending in a court of another state exercising jurisdiction substantially in conformity with this article, unless the proceeding is stayed by the court of the other state because this State is a more appropriate forum or for other reasons.

(b) Before hearing the petition in a custody proceeding, the court shall examine the pleadings and other information supplied by the parties under section nine [§ 48-10-9] of this article and shall consult the child custody registry established under section sixteen [§ 48-10-16] of this article concerning the pendency of proceedings with respect to the child in other states. If the court has reason to believe that proceedings may be pending in another state, it shall direct an inquiry to the state court administrator or other appropriate official of the other state.

(c) If the court is informed during the course of the proceeding that a proceeding concerning the custody of the child was pending in another state before the court assumed jurisdiction, it shall stay the proceeding and communicate with the court in which the other proceeding is pending to the end that the issue may be litigated in the more appropriate forum and that information be exchanged in accordance with sections nineteen, twenty, twenty-one and twenty-two [§§ 48-10-19, 48-10-20, 48-10-21 and 48-10-22] of this article. If a court of this State has made a custody decree before being informed of a pending proceeding in a court of another state, it shall immediately inform that court of the fact. If the court is informed that proceeding was commenced in another state after it assumed jurisdiction, it shall likewise inform the other court to the end that the issues may be litigated in the more appropriate forum.

§ 48-10-7. Inconvenient forum.

(a) A court which has jurisdiction under this article to make an initial or modification decree may decline to exercise its jurisdiction any time before making a decree if it finds that it is an inconvenient forum to make a custody determination under the circumstances of the case and that a court of another state is a more appropriate forum.

(b) A finding of inconvenient forum may be made upon the court's own motion or upon motion of a party or a guardian ad litem or other representative of the child.

(c) In determining if it is an inconvenient forum, the court shall consider if it is in the interest of the child that another state assume jurisdiction. For this purpose it may take into account the following factors, among others:

(1) If another state is or recently was the child's home state.

(2) If another state has a closer connection with the child and his family or with the child and one or more of the contestants;

(3) If substantial evidence concerning the child's present or future care, protection, training and personal relationships is more readily available in another state;

(4) If parties have agreed on another forum which is no less appropriate; and

(5) If the exercise of jurisdiction by a court of this State would contravene any of the purposes stated in section one [§ 48-10-1] of this article.

(d) Before determining whether to decline or retain jurisdiction, the court may communicate with a court of another state and exchange information pertinent to the assumption of jurisdiction by either court with a view to assuring that jurisdiction will be exercised by the more appropriate court and that a forum will be available to the parties.

(e) If the court finds that it is an inconvenient forum and that a court of another state is a more appropriate forum, it may dismiss the proceedings, or it may stay proceedings upon condition that a custody proceeding be promptly commenced in another named state or upon any other conditions which may be just and proper, including the condition that a moving party stipulate his consent and submission to the jurisdiction of the other forum.

(f) The court may decline to exercise its jurisdiction under this article if a custody determination is incidental to an action for divorce or another proceeding while retaining jurisdiction over the divorce or other proceeding.

(g) If it appears to the court that it is clearly an inappropriate forum, it may require the party who commenced the proceedings to pay, in addition to the costs of the proceedings in this State, necessary travel and other expenses, including attorneys' fees, incurred by other parties or their witnesses. Payment is to be made to the clerk of the court for remittance to the proper party.

(h) Upon dismissal or stay of proceedings under this section the court shall inform the court found to be the more appropriate forum of this fact or, if the court which would have jurisdiction in the other state is not certainly known, shall transmit the information to the court administrator or other appropriate official for forwarding to the appropriate court.

(i) Any communication received from another state informing this State of a finding of inconvenient forum because a court of this State is the more appropriate forum shall be filed in the custody registry of the appropriate court. Upon assuming jurisdiction the court of this State shall inform the original court of this fact.

§ 48-10-8. Jurisdiction declined by reason of conduct.

(a) If the petitioner for an initial decree has wrongfully taken the child from another state or has engaged in similar reprehensible conduct, the court may decline to exercise jurisdiction if this is just and proper under the circumstances.

(b) Unless required in the interest of the child, the court shall not exercise its jurisdiction to modify a custody decree of another state if the petitioner, without consent of the person entitled to custody, has improperly removed the child from the physical custody of the person entitled to custody or has improperly retained the child after a visit or other temporary relinquishment of physical custody. If the petitioner has violated any other provision of a custody decree of another state, the court may decline to exercise its jurisdiction if this is just and proper under the circumstances.

(c) In appropriate cases a court dismissing a petition under this section may charge the petitioner with necessary travel and other expenses, including attorneys' fees, incurred by other parties or their witnesses.

§ 48-10-9. Information under oath to be submitted to the court.

(a) Every party in a custody proceeding in his first pleading or in an affidavit attached to that pleading shall give information under oath as to the child's present address, the places where the child has lived within the last five years, and the names and present addresses of the persons with whom the child has lived during that period. In this pleading or affidavit every party shall further declare under oath whether:

(1) He has participated (as a party, witness or in any other capacity) in any other litigation concerning the custody of the same child in this or any other state;

(2) He has information of any custody proceeding concerning the child pending in a court of this or any other state; and

(3) He knows of any person not a party to the proceedings who has physical custody of the child or claims to have custody or visitation rights with respect to the child.

(b) If the declaration as to any of the above items is in the affirmative, the declarant shall give additional information under oath as required by the court. The court may examine the parties under oath as to details of the information furnished and as to other matters pertinent to the court's jurisdiction and the disposition of the case.

(c) Each party has a continuing duty to inform the court of any custody proceeding concerning the child in this or any other state of which he obtained information during this proceeding.

§ 48-10-10. Additional parties.

If the court learns from information furnished by the parties pursuant to section nine [§ 48-10-9] of this article or from other sources that a person not a party to the custody proceeding has physical custody of the child or claims to have custody or visitation rights with respect to the child, it shall order that person to be joined as a party and to be duly notified of the pendency of the proceeding and of his joinder as a party. If the person joined as a party is outside this State, he shall be served with process or otherwise notified in accordance with section five [§ 48-10-5] of this article.

§ 48-10-11. Appearance of parties and the child.

(a) The court may order any party to the proceeding who is in this State to appear personally before the court. If that party has physical custody of the child, the court may order that he appear personally with the child.

(b) If a party to the proceeding whose presence is desired by the court is outside this State with or without the child, the court may order that the notice given under section five [§ 48-10-5] of this article include a statement directing that party to appear personally with or without the child and declaring that failure to appear may result in a decision adverse to that party.

(c) If a party to the proceeding who is outside this State is directed to appear under subsection (b) of this section or desires to appear personally before the court with or without the child, the court may require another party to pay to the clerk of the court travel and other necessary expenses of the party so appearing and of the child if this is just and proper under the circumstances.

§ 48-10-12. Psychological evidence.

In a proceeding under this article in which a circuit court in this State must determine or advise upon the issue of custody, testimony by a licensed psychologist relevant to a child's (a) academic skills and progress, (b) socialization, (c) physical well-being, and (d) emotional and mental status shall be admissible, subject however to all the rules of evidence ordinarily applicable to such testimony: Provided, That for the sole purpose of evidence relevant to the child's academic skills and progress, the testimony of a school psychologist shall be admissible. Any party may move for a psychological evaluation of the child at such reasonable time and place as the court shall, for good cause, order, for the purpose of preparing such testimony. Unless it appears that all the parties litigating the issue of custody desire to adduce evidence resulting from such an evaluation, the court may, on its own motion, order an independent evaluation by a licensed psychologist selected by agreement of the parties or, in the absence of such agreement, by the court. The court may assess as a cost of the proceeding the reasonable costs of transportation to the place of such evaluation, the evaluation, and the attendance in court by the psychologist for the giving of evidence, including expert witness fees. Costs shall be allocated among the parties as equity may, in the discretion of the court, require.

§ 48-10-13. Binding force and res judicata effect of custody decree.

A custody decree rendered by a court of this State which had jurisdiction under section three [§ 48-10-3] of this article binds all parties who have been served in this State or notified in accordance with section five [§ 48-10-5] of this article or who have submitted to the jurisdiction of the court, and who have been given an opportunity to be heard. As to these parties the custody decree is conclusive as to all issues of law and fact decided and as to the custody determination made unless and until that determination is modified pursuant to law, including the provisions of this article.

§ 48-10-14. Recognition of out-of-state custody decrees.

The courts of this State shall recognize and enforce an initial or modification decree of a court of another state which had assumed jurisdiction under statutory decree of a court of another state which had assumed jurisdiction under statutory provisions substantially in accordance with this article or which was made under factual circumstances meeting the jurisdictional standards of this article, so long as this decree has not been modified in accordance with jurisdictional standards substantially similar to those of this article.

§ 48-10-15. Modification of custody decree of another state.

(a) If a court of another state has made a custody decree, a court of this State shall not modify that decree unless (1) it appears to the court of this State that the court which rendered the decree does not now have jurisdiction under jurisdictional prerequisites substantially in accordance with this article or has declined to assume jurisdiction to modify the decree and (2) the court of this

State has jurisdiction.

(b) If a court of this State is authorized under subsection (a) of this section and section eight [§ 48-10-8] of this article to modify a custody decree of another state, it shall give due consideration to the transcript of the record and other documents of all previous proceedings submitted to it in accordance with section twenty-two [§ 48-10-22] of this article.

§ 48-10-16. Filing and enforcement of custody decree of another state.

(a) A certified copy of a custody decree of another state may be filed in the office of the clerk of any circuit court of this State. The clerk shall treat the decree in the same manner as a custody decree of a circuit court, or of any court of this State of competent jurisdiction. A custody decree so filed has the same effect and shall be enforced in like manner as a custody decree rendered by a court of this State.

(b) A person violating a custody decree of another state which makes it necessary to enforce the decree in this State may be required to pay necessary travel and other expenses, including attorneys' fees, incurred by the party entitled to the custody or his witnesses.

§ 48-10-17. Registry of out-of-state custody decrees and proceedings.

The clerk of each circuit court shall maintain a registry in which he shall enter the following:

(1) Certified copies of custody decrees of other states, received for filing;

(2) Communications as to the pendency of custody proceedings of other states;

(3) Communications concerning a finding of inconvenient forum by a court of another state; and

(4) Other communications or documents concerning custody proceedings in another state which may affect the jurisdiction of a court of this State or the disposition to be made by it in a custody proceeding.

§ 48-10-18. Certified copies of custody decree.

The clerk of the circuit court of this State, at the request of the court of another state or at the request of any person who is affected by or has a legitimate interest in a custody decree, shall certify and forward a copy of the decree to that court or person.

§ 48-10-19. Taking testimony in another state.

In addition to other procedural devices available to a party, any party to the proceeding or a guardian ad litem or other representative of the child may adduce testimony of witnesses, including parties and the child, by deposition or otherwise, in another state. The court on its own motion may direct that the testimony of a person be taken in another state and may prescribe the manner in which and the terms upon which the testimony shall be taken.

§ 48-10-20. Hearings and studies in another state; orders to appear.

(a) A court of this State may request the appropriate court of another state to hold a hearing to adduce evidence, to order a party to produce or give evidence under other procedures of that state, or to have social studies made with respect to the custody of a child involved in proceedings pending in the court of this State; and to forward to the court of this State certified copies of the transcript of the record of the hearing, the evidence otherwise adduced or any social studies prepared in compliance with the request. The cost of the services may be assessed against the parties or, if necessary, ordered paid out of the treasury of the state upon certificate of the court wherein the case is pending.

(b) A court of this State may request the appropriate court of another state to order a party to custody proceedings pending in the court of this State to appear in the proceedings, and, if that party has physical custody of the child, to appear with the child. The request may state that travel and other necessary expenses of the party and of the child whose appearance is desired will be assessed against another party or will otherwise be paid.

§ 48-10-21. Assistance to courts of other states.

(a) Upon request of the court of another state, the courts of this State which are competent to hear custody matters may order a person in this State to appear at a hearing to adduce evidence or to produce or give evidence under other procedures available in this State or may order social studies to be made for use in a custody proceeding in another state. A certified copy of the transcript of the record of the hearing or the evidence otherwise adduced and any social studies prepared shall be forwarded by the clerk of the court to the requesting court.

(b) A person within this State may voluntarily give his testimony or statement in this State for use in a custody proceeding outside this State.

(c) Upon request of the court of another state a competent court of this State may order a person in this State to appear alone or with the child in a custody proceeding in another state. The court may condition compliance with the request upon assurance by the other state that state travel and other necessary expenses will be advanced or reimbursed.

§ 48-10-22. Preservation of documents for use in other states.

In any custody proceeding in this State the court shall preserve the pleadings, orders and decrees, any record that has been made of its hearings, social studies and other pertinent documents until the child reaches eighteen years of age. Upon appropriate request of the court of another state the court shall forward to the other court certified copies of any or all of such documents.

§ 48-10-23. Request for court records of another state.
If a custody decree has been rendered in another state concerning a child involved in a custody proceeding pending in a court of this State, the court of this State upon taking jurisdiction of the case shall request of the court of the other state a certified copy of the transcript of any court record and other documents mentioned in section twenty-one [§ 48-10-21] of this article.

§ 48-10-24. International application.
The general policies of this article extend to the international area. The provisions of this article relating to the recognition and enforcement of custody decrees of other states apply to custody decrees and decrees involving legal institutions similar in nature to custody institutions rendered by appropriate authorities of other nations if reasonable notice and opportunity to be heard were given to all affected persons.

§ 48-10-25. Priority.
Upon request of a party to a custody proceeding which raises a question of existence or exercise of jurisdiction under this article, the case shall be given calendar priority and handled expeditiously.

§ 48-10-26. Short title.
This article may be cited as the "Uniform Child Custody Jurisdiction Act."

WISCONSIN

UNIFORM CHILD CUSTODY JURISDICTION ACT

§ 822.01. Purposes; construction of provisions.
(1) The general purposes of this chapter are to:

(a) Avoid jurisdictional competition and conflict with courts of other states in matters of child custody which have in the past resulted in the shifting of children from state to state with harmful effects on their well-being;

(b) Promote cooperation with the courts of other states to the end that a custody decree is rendered in that state which can best decide the case in the interest of the child;

(c) Assure that litigation concerning the custody of a child takes place ordinarily in the state with which the child and family have the closest connection and where significant evidence concerning the child's care, protection, training, and personal relationships is most readily available, and that courts of this state decline the exercise of jurisdiction when the child and family have a closer connection with another state;

(d) Discourage continuing controversies over child custody in the interest of greater stability of home environment and of secure family relationships for the child;

(e) Deter abductions and other unilateral removals of children undertaken to obtain custody awards;

(f) Avoid relitigation of custody decisions of other states in this state insofar as feasible;

(g) Facilitate the enforcement of custody decrees of other states;

(h) Promote and expand the exchange of information and other forms of mutual assistance between the courts of this state and those of other states concerned with the same child; and

(i) Make uniform the law of those states which enact it.

(2) This chapter shall be construed to promote the general purposes stated in this section.

§ 822.015. Custody of Indian children.
The Indian child welfare act, 25 USC 1911 to 1963, supersedes the provisons of this chapter in any child custody proceeding governed by that act.

§ 822.02. Definitions.
As used in this chapter:

(1) "Contestant" means a person, including a parent, who claims a right to legal custody, physical placement or visitation with respect to a child.

(2) "Custody determination" means a court decision and court orders and instructions providing for legal custody, physical

placement or visitation rights. It does not include a decision relating to child support or any other monetary obligation of any person.

(3) "Custody proceeding" includes proceedings in which a custody determination is one of several issues, such as an action for divorce or separation, and includes child neglect and dependency proceedings.

(4) "Decree" or "custody decree" means a custody determination contained in a judicial decree or order made in a custody proceeding, and includes an initial decree and a modification decree.

(5) "Home state" means the state in which the child immediately preceding the time involved lived with the child's parents, a parent, or a person acting as parent, for at least 6 consecutive months, and in the case of a child less than 6 months old the state in which the child lived from birth with any of the persons mentioned. Periods of temporary absence of any of the named persons are counted as part of the 6-month or other period.

(6m) "Legal custody" has the meaning given in s. 767.001(2).

(7) "Modification decree" means a custody decree which modifies or replaces a prior decree, whether made by the court which rendered the prior decree or by another court.

(8) "Person acting as parent" means a person, other than a parent, who has physical custody of a child and who has either been awarded custody by a court or claims a right to custody.

(9m) "Physical placement" has the meaning given in s. 767.001(5).

(10) "State" means any state, territory, or possession of the United States, the commonwealth of Puerto Rico, and the District of Columbia.

§ 822.03. Jurisdiction.

(1) A court of this state which is competent to decide child custody matters has jurisdiction to make a child custody determination by initial or modification decree if:

(a) This state is the home state of the child at the time of commencement of the proceeding, or had been the child's home state within 6 months before commencement of the proceeding and the child is absent from this state because of the child's removal or retention by a person claiming custody or for other reasons, and a parent or person acting as parent continues to live in this state; or

(b) It is in the best interest of the child that a court of this state assume jurisdiction because the child and the child's parents, or the child and at least one contestant, have a significant connection with this state, and there is available in this state substantial evidence concerning the child's present or future care, protection, training, and personal relationships; or

(c) It appears that no other state would have jurisdiction under prerequisites substantially in accordance with par. (a), (b) or (c), or another state has declined to exercise jurisdiction on the ground that this state is the more appropriate forum to determine the custody of the child, and it is in the best interest of the child that this court assume jurisdiction.

(2) Except under sub. (1)(c) and (d), physical presence in this state of the child, or of the child and one of the contestants, is not alone sufficient to confer jurisdiction on a court of this state to make a child custody determination.

(3) Physical presence of the child, while desirable, is not a prerequisite for jurisdiction to determine custody.

§ 822.04. Notice and opportunity to be heard.

Before making a decree under this chapter, reasonable notice and opportunity to be heard shall be given to the contestants, any parent whose parental rights have not been previously terminated, and any person who has physical custody of the child. If any of these persons is outside this state, notice and opportunity to be heard shall be given under s. 822.05.

§ 822.05. Notice to persons outside this state; submission to jurisdiction.

(1) Notice required for the exercise of jurisdiction over a person outside this state shall be given in a manner reasonably calculated to give actual notice, and may be:

(a) By personal delivery outside this state in the manner prescribed for service of process within this state;

(b) In the manner prescribed by the law of the place in which the service is made for service of process in that place in an action in any of its courts of general jurisdiction.

(c) By any form of mail addressed to the person to be served and requesting a receipt; or

(d) As directed by the court, including publication, if other means of notification are ineffective.

(2) Notice under this section shall be served, mailed, delivered or last published at least 10 days before any hearing in this state.

(3) Proof of service outside this state may be made by affidavit of the individual who made the service, or in the manner prescribed by the law of this state, the order pursuant to which the service is made, or the law of the place in which the service is made. If service is made by mail, proof may be a receipt signed by the addressee or other evidence of delivery to the addressee.

(4) Notice is not required if a person submits to the jurisdiction of the court.

§ 822.06. Simultaneous proceedings in other states.

(1) A court of this state shall not exercise its jurisdiction under this chapter if at the time of filing the petition a proceeding concerning the custody of the child was pending in a court of another state exercising jurisdiction substantially in conformity with

this chapter, unless the proceeding is stayed by the court of the other state because this state is a more appropriate forum or for other reasons.

(2) Before hearing the petition in a custody proceeding the court shall examine the pleadings and other information supplied by the parties under s. 822.09 and shall consult the child custody registry established under s. 822.16 concerning the pendency of proceedings with respect to the child in other states. If the court has reason to believe that proceedings may be pending in another state it shall direct an inquiry to the state court administrator or other appropriate official of the other state.

(3) If the court is informed during the course of the proceeding that a proceeding concerning the custody of the child was pending in another state before the court assumed jurisdiction it shall stay the proceeding and communicate with the court in which the other proceeding is pending to the end that the issue may be litigated in the more appropriate forum and that information be exchanged in accordance with ss. 822.19 to 822.22. If a court of this state has made a custody decree before being informed of a pending proceeding in a court of another state it shall immediately inform that court of the fact. If the court is informed that a proceeding was commenced in another state after it assumed jurisdiction it shall likewise inform the other court to the end that the issues may be litigated in the more appropriate forum.

(4) The communication between courts called for by sub. (3) or s. 822.07(4) may be conducted on the record by telephone conference to which the courts and all counsel are parties.

§ 822.07. Inconvenient forum.

(1) A court which has jurisdiction under this chapter to make an initial or modification decree may decline to exercise its jurisdiction any time before making a decree if it finds that it is an inconvenient forum to make a custody determination under the circumstances of the case and that a court of another state is a more appropriate forum.

(2) A finding of inconvenient forum may be made upon the court's own motion or upon motion of a party or a guardian ad litem or other representative of the child. Motions under this subsection may be heard on the record as prescribed in s. 807.13.

(3) In determining if it is an inconvenient forum, the court shall consider if it is in the interest of the child that another state assume jurisdiction. For this purpose it may take into account the following factors, among others:

(a) If another state is or recently was the child's home state;

(b) If another state has a closer connection with the child and family or with the child and one or more of the contestants;

(c) If substantial evidence concerning the child's present or future care, protection, training, and personal relationships is more readily available in another state;

(d) If the parties have agreed on another forum which is no less appropriate; and

(e) If the exercise of jurisdiction by a court of this state would contravene any of the purposes stated in s. 822.01.

(4) Before determining whether to decline or retain jurisdiction the court may communicate with a court of another state and exchange information pertinent to the assumption of jurisdiction by either court with a view to assuring that jurisdiction will be exercised by the more appropriate court and that a forum will be available to the parties.

(5) If the court finds that it is an inconvenient forum and that a court of another state is a more appropriate forum, it may dismiss the proceedings, or it may stay the proceedings upon condition that a custody proceedings be promptly commenced in another named state or upon any other conditions which may be just and proper, including the condition that a moving party stipulate consent and submission to the jurisdiction of the other forum.

(6) The court may decline to exercise its jurisdiction under this chapter if a custody determination is incidental to an action for divorce or another proceeding while retaining jurisdiction over the divorce or other proceeding.

(7) If it appears to the court that it is clearly an inappropriate forum it may require the party who commenced the proceedings to pay, in addition to the costs of the proceedings in this state, necessary travel and other expenses, including attorneys' fees, incurred by other parties or their witnesses. Payment is to be made to the clerk of the court for remittance to the proper party.

(8) Upon dismissal or stay of proceedings under this section the court shall inform the court found to be the more appropriate forum of this fact, or if the court which would have jurisdiction in the other state is not certainly known, shall transmit the information to the court administrator or other appropriate official for forwarding to the appropriate court.

(9) Any communication received from another state informing this state of a finding of inconvenient forum because a court of this state is the more appropriate forum shall be filed in the custody registry of the appropriate court. Upon assuming jurisdiction the court of this state shall inform the original court of this fact.

§ 822.08. Jurisdiction declined by reason of conduct.

(1) If the petitioner for an initial decree has wrongfully taken the child from another state or has engaged in similar reprehensible conduct the court may decline to exercise jurisdiction if this is just and proper under the circumstances.

(2) Unless required in the interest of the child, the court shall not exercise its jurisdiction to modify a custody decree of another state if the petitioner, without consent of the person entitled to custody, has improperly removed the child from the physical custody of the person entitled to custody or has improperly retained the child after a visit or other temporary relinquishment of physical custody. If the petitioner has violated any other provision of a custody decree of another state the court may decline to exercise its jurisdiction if this is just and proper under the circumstances.

(3) In appropriate cases a court dismissing a petition under this section may charge the petitioner with necessary travel and other

expenses, including attorneys' fees, incurred by other parties or their witnesses.

§ 822.09. Information under oath to be submitted to the court.

(1) Every party in a custody proceeding in the first pleading or in an affidavit attached to that pleading shall give information under oath as to the child's present address, the places where the child has lived within the last 5 years, and the names and present addresses of the persons with whom the child has lived during that period. In this pleading or affidavit every party shall further declare under oath whether:

(a) The party has participated as a party, witness, or in any other capacity in any other litigation concerning the custody of the same child in this or any other state;

(b) The party has information of any custody proceeding concerning the child pending in a court of this or any other state; and

(c) The party knows of any person not a party to the proceedings who has physical custody of the child or claims to have legal custody, physical placement or visitation rights with respect to the child.

(2) If the declaration as to any of the above items is in the affirmative the declarant shall give additional information under oath as required by the court. The court may examine the parties under oath as to details of the information furnished and as to other matters pertinent to the court's jurisdiction and the disposition of the case.

(3) Each party has a continuing duty to inform the court of any custody proceeding concerning the child in this or any other state of which the party obtained information during this proceeding.

§ 822.10. Additional parties.

If the court learns from information furnished by the parties pursuant to s. 822.09 or from other sources that a person not a party to the custody proceeding has physical custody of the child or claims to have legal custody, physical placement or visitation rights with respect to the child, it shall order that person to be joined as a party and to be duly notified of the pendency of the proceeding and of the person's joinder as a party. If the person joined as a party is outside this state the person shall be served with process or otherwise notified in accordance with s. 822.05.

§ 822.11. Appearance of parties and the child.

(1) The court may order any party to the proceeding who is in this state to appear personally before the court. If that party has physical custody of the child the court may order that the party appear personally with the child.

(2) If a party to the proceeding whose presence is desired by the court is outside this state with or without the child the court may order that the notice given under s. 822.05 include a statement directing that party to appear personally with or without the child and declaring that failure to appear may result in a decision adverse to that party.

(3) If a party to the proceeding who is outside this state is directed to appear under sub. (2) or desires to appear personally before the court with or without the child, the court may require another party to pay to the clerk of the court travel and other necessary expenses of the party so appearing and of the child if this is just and proper under the circumstances.

§ 822.12. Binding force and res judicata effect of custody decree.

A custody decree rendered by a court of this state which had jurisdiction under s. 822.03 binds all parties who have been served in this state or notified in accordance with s. 822.05 or who have submitted to the jurisdiction of the court, and who have been given an opportunity to be heard. As to these parties the custody decree is conclusive as to all issues of law and fact decided and as to the custody determination made unless and until that determination is modified pursuant to law, including the provisions of this chapter.

§ 822.13. Recognition of out-of-state custody decrees.

The courts of this state shall recognize and enforce an initial or modification decree of a court of another state which had assumed jurisdiction under statutory provisions substantially in accordance with this chapter or which was made under factual circumstances meeting the jurisdictional standards of this chapter, so long as this decree has not been modified in accordance with jurisdictional standards substantially similar to those of this chapter.

§ 822.14. Modification of custody decree of another state.

(1) If a court of another state has made a custody decree, a court of this state shall not modify that decree unless it appears to the court of this state that the court which rendered the decree does not now have jurisdiction under jurisdictional prerequisites substantially in accordance with this chapter or has declined to assume jurisdiction to modify the decree and the court of this state has jurisdiction.

(2) If a court of this state is authorized under sub. (1) and s. 822.08 to modify a custody decree of another state it shall give due consideration to the transcript of the record and other documents of all previous proceedings submitted to it in accordance with s. 822.22.

§ 822.15. Filing and enforcement of custody decree of another state.

(1) A certified copy of a custody decree of another state may be filed in the office of the clerk of any circuit court of this state. The clerk shall treat the decree in the same manner as a custody decree of a circuit court of this state. A custody decree so filed has the same effect and shall be enforced in like manner as a custody decree rendered by a circuit court of this state.

(2) A person violating a custody decree of another state which makes it necessary to enforce the decree in this state may be required to pay necessary travel and other expenses, including attorneys' fees, incurred by the party entitled to the custody or his or her witnesses.

§ 822.16. Registry of out-of-state custody decrees and proceedings.

The clerk of each circuit court shall maintain a registry in which he or she shall enter the following:

(1) Certified copies of custody decrees of other states received for filing;

(2) Communications as to the pendency of custody proceedings in other states;

(3) Communications concerning a finding of inconvenient forum by a court of another state; and

(4) Other communications or documents concerning custody proceedings in another state which may affect the jurisdiction of a court of this state or the disposition to be made by it in a custody proceeding.

§ 822.17. Certified copies of custody decree.

The clerk of a circuit court of this state, at the request of the court of another state or at the request of any person who is affected by or has a legitimate interest in a custody decree, shall certify and forward a copy of the decree to that court or person.

§ 822.18. Taking testimony in another state.

In addition to other procedural devices available to a party, any party to the proceeding or a guardian ad litem or other representative of the child may adduce testimony of witnesses, including parties and the child, by deposition or otherwise, in another state. The court on its own motion may direct that the testimony of a person be taken in another state and may prescribe the manner in which and the terms upon which the testimony shall be taken.

§ 822.19. Hearings and studies in another state; orders to appear.

(1) A court of this state may request the appropriate court of another state to hold a hearing to adduce evidence, to order a party to produce or give evidence under other procedures of that state, or to have social studies made with respect to the custody of a child involved in proceedings pending in the court of this state; and to forward to the court of this state certified copies of the transcript of the record of the hearing, the evidence otherwise adduced, or any social studies prepared in compliance with the request. The cost of the services may be assessed against the parties or, if necessary, ordered paid by the state.

(2) A court of this state may request the appropriate court of another state to order a party to custody proceedings pending in the court of this state to appear in the proceedings, and if that party has physical custody of the child, to appear with the child. The request may state that travel and other necessary expenses of the party and of the child whose appearance is desired will be assessed against another party or will otherwise be paid.

§ 822.20. Assistance to courts of other states.

(1) Upon request of the court of another state the courts of this state which are competent to hear custody matters may order a person in this state to appear at a hearing to adduce evidence or to produce or give evidence under other procedures available in this state or may order social studies to be made for use in a custody proceeding in another state. A certified copy of the transcript of the record of the hearing or the evidence otherwise adduced and any social studies prepared shall be forwarded by the clerk of the court to the requesting court.

(2) A person within this state may voluntarily give testimony or a statement in this state for use in a custody proceeding outside this state.

(3) Upon request of the court of another state a competent court of this state may order a person in this state to appear alone or with the child in a custody proceeding in another state. The court may condition compliance with the request upon assurance by the other state that state travel and other necessary expenses will be advanced or reimbursed.

§ 822.21. Preservation of documents for use in other states.

In any custody proceeding in this state the court shall preserve the pleadings, orders and decrees, any record that has been made of its hearings, social studies, and other pertinent documents until the child reaches 18 years of age. Upon appropriate request of the court of another state the court shall forward to the other court certified copies of any or all of such documents.

§ 822.22. Request for court records of another state.

If a custody decree has been rendered in another state concerning a child involved in a custody proceeding pending in a court of this state, the court of this state upon taking jurisdiction of the case shall request of the court of the other state a certified copy of the transcript of any court record and other documents mentioned in s. 822.21.

§ 822.23. International application.
The general policies of this chapter extend to the international area. The provisions of this chapter relating to the recognition and enforcement of custody decrees of other states apply to custody decrees and decrees involving legal institutions similar in nature to custody institutions rendered by appropriate authorities of other nations if reasonable notice and opportunity to be heard were given to all affected persons.

§ 822.24. Priority.
Upon the request of a party to a custody proceeding which raises a question of existence or exercise of jurisdiction under this chapter the case shall be given calendar priority and handled expeditiously.

§ 822.25. Short title.
This act may be cited as the "Uniform Child Custody Jurisdiction Act".

WYOMING

UNIFORM CHILD CUSTODY JURISDICTION ACT

§ 20-5-101. Title.
This act may be cited as the Uniform Child Custody Jurisdiction Act.

§ 20-5-102. Purpose.
(a) The general purposes of this act are:

(i) To avoid jurisdictional competition and conflict with courts of other states in matters of child custody which have in the past resulted in the shifting of children from state to state with harmful effects on their well-being;

(ii) To promote cooperation with the courts of other states to the end that a custody decree is rendered in that state which can best decide the case in the interest of the child;

(iii) To assure that litigation concerning the custody of a child take place ordinarily in the state with which the child and his family have the closest connection and where significant evidence concerning his care, protection, training and personal relationships is most readily available, and that courts of this state decline the exercise of jurisdiction when the child and his family have a closer connection with another state;

(iv) To discourage continuing controversies over child custody in the interest of greater stability of home environment and of secure family relationships for the child;

(v) To deter abductions and other unilateral removals of children undertaken to obtain custody awards;

(vi) To avoid relitigation of custody decisions of other states in this state insofar as feasible;

(vii) To facilitate the enforcement of custody decrees of other states;

(viii) To promote and expand the exchange of information and other forms of mutual assistance between the courts of this state and those of other states concerned with the same child; and

(ix) To make uniform the law of those states which enact it.

(b) The provisions of this act shall be construed to promote the general purposes stated in this section.

§ 20-5-103. Definitions.
(a) As used in this act:

(i) "Contestant" means a person who claims a right to custody or visitation rights with respect to a child;

(ii) "Custody determination" means a court order and instructions providing for the custody of a child including visitation rights, but does not include a decision relating to child support or any other monetary obligation of any person;

(iii) "Custody proceeding" includes proceedings in which a custody determination is one of several issues, such as an action for divorce or separation, and includes child neglect and dependency proceedings;

(iv) "Decree" or "custody decree" means a custody determination contained in a judicial decree made in a custody proceeding, and includes an initial decree and a modification decree;

(v) "Home state" means the state in which the child immediately preceding the time involved has lived with his parents, a parent or a person acting as parent, for at least six (6) consecutive months, and in the case of a child less than six (6) months old the state in which the child has lived since birth with any of the persons mentioned. Periods of temporary absence of any of the named persons are counted as part of the six (6) month or other period;

(vi) "Initial decree" means the first custody decree concerning a particular child;

(vii) "Modification decree" means a custody decree which modifies or replaces a prior decree, whether made by the court which rendered the prior decree or by another court;

(viii) "Physical custody" means actual possession and control of a child;

(ix) "Person acting as parent" means a person other than a parent who has physical custody of a child and who has either been awarded custody by a court or claims a right to custody;

(x) "State" means any state, territory or possession of the United States, the commonwealth of Puerto Rico or the District of Columbia;

(xi) "This act" means W.S. 20-5-101 through 20-5-125.

§ 20-5-104. Jurisdiction to make child custody determination.

(a) A court of this state competent to decide child custody matters has jurisdiction to make a child custody determination by initial decree or modification decree if:

(i) This state is the home state of the child at the time of commencement of the proceeding, or was the child's home state within six (6) months before commencement of the proceeding and the child is absent from the state because of his removal or retention by a person claiming his custody or for other reasons, and a parent or person acting as parent continues to live in this state;

(ii) It is in the best interest of the child that a court of this state assume jurisdiction because the child and his parents, or the child and at least one (1) contestant, have a significant connection with the state and there is available in this state substantial evidence concerning the child's present or future care, protection, training and personal relationships;

(iii) The child is physically present in this state and has been abandoned or if it is necessary in an emergency to protect the child because he has been subjected to or threatened with mistreatment or abuse or is otherwise neglected or dependent; or

(iv) It appears that no other state would have jurisdiction under prerequisites substantially in accordance with paragraphs (i), (ii) or (iii) of this subsection, or another state has declined to exercise jurisdiction on the ground that this state is the more appropriate forum to determine the custody of the child and it is in the best interest of the child that this court assume jurisdiction.

(b) Except under paragraphs (a)(iii) and (iv) of this section, physical presence in this state of the child or of the child and one (1) of the contestants is not alone sufficient to confer jurisdiction on a court of this state to make a child custody determination.

(c) Physical presence of the child, while desirable, is not a prerequisite for jurisdiction to determine his custody.

§ 20-5-105. Notice before decree.

Before making a decree under this act reasonable notice and opportunity to be heard shall be given to the contestants, any parent whose parental rights have not been previously terminated and any person who has physical custody of the child. If any of these persons are outside this state notice and opportunity to be heard shall be given pursuant to W.S. 20-5-106.

§ 20-5-106. Notice for exercise of jurisdiction over person outside this state; time; service; exception.

(a) Notice required for the exercise of jurisdiction over a person outside this state shall be given in a manner reasonably calculated to give actual notice, and may be:

(i) By personal delivery outside this state in the manner prescribed for service of process within this state;

(ii) In the manner prescribed by the law of the place in which the service is made for service of process in that place in an action in any of its courts of general jurisdiction;

(iii) By any form of mail addressed to the person to be served and requesting a receipt; or

(iv) As directed by the court including publication if other means of notification are ineffective.

(b) Notice under this section shall be served, mailed, delivered or last published at least twenty (20) days before any hearing in this state.

(c) Proof of service outside this state may be made by affidavit of the individual who made the service, or in the manner prescribed by the law of this state, the order pursuant to which the service is made or the law of the place in which the service is made. If service is made by mail, proof may be a receipt signed by the addressee or other evidence of delivery to the addressee.

(d) Notice is not required if a person submits to the jurisdiction of the court.

§ 20-5-107. Exercise of jurisdiction by court in this state; proceedings in other states.

(a) A court of this state shall not exercise its jurisdiction under this act if at the time of filing the petition a proceeding concerning the custody of the same child was pending in a court of another state exercising jurisdiction substantially in conformity with this act, unless the proceeding is stayed by the court of the other state because this state is a more appropriate forum or for other reasons.

(b) Before hearing the petition in a custody proceeding, the court shall examine the pleadings and other information supplied by the parties under W.S. 20-5-110 and shall consult the child custody registry established under W.S. 20-5-117 concerning the pendency of proceedings with respect to the child in other states. If the court has reason to believe that proceedings may be pending in another state the court shall direct an inquiry to the state court administrator or other appropriate official of the other state.

(c) If the court is informed during the course of the proceeding that a proceeding concerning the custody of the child was pending in another state before this court assumed jurisdiction, the court shall stay the proceeding and communicate with the court in which the other proceeding is pending to the end that the issue may be litigated in the more appropriate forum and that information be exchanged in accordance with W.S. 20-5-120 through 20-5-123. If a court of this state has made a custody decree before being informed of a pending proceeding in a court of another state it shall immediately inform that court of this fact. If the court is informed that a proceeding was commenced in another state after this court assumed jurisdiction it shall likewise inform the other court to the end that the issues may be litigated in the most appropriate forum.

§ 20-5-108. Court may decline to exercise jurisdiction.

(a) A court which has jurisdiction under this act to make an initial decree or a modification decree may decline to exercise its jurisdiction any time before making a decree if it finds that it is an inconvenient forum to make a custody determination under the circumstances of the case and that a court of another state is a more appropriate forum.

(b) A finding of inconvenient forum may be made upon a court's own motion or upon motion of a party or a guardian ad litem or other representative of a child.

(c) In order to determine whether it is an inconvenient forum, the court shall consider whether it is in the interest of the child that another state assume jurisdiction and for this purpose may take into account the following factors, among others:

(i) Whether another state is or recently was the child's home state;

(ii) Whether another state has a closer connection with the child and his family or with the child and one (1) or more of the contestants;

(iii) Whether substantial evidence concerning the child's present or future care, protection, training and personal relationships is more readily available in another state;

(iv) Whether the parties have agreed on another forum which is no less appropriate; and

(v) Whether the exercise of jurisdiction by a court of this state would contravene any of the purposes stated in W.S. 20-5-102.

(d) Before determining whether to decline or retain jurisdiction the court may communicate with a court of another state and exchange information pertinent to the assumption of jurisdiction by either court with a view to assuring that jurisdiction will be exercised by the most appropriate court and that a forum will be available to the parties.

(e) If the court finds that it is an inconvenient forum and that a court of another state is a more appropriate forum, it may dismiss the proceedings, or it may stay the proceedings upon the condition that a custody proceeding be promptly commenced in another named state or upon any other conditions which may be just and proper including the condition that a moving party stipulate his consent and submission to the jurisdiction of the other forum.

(f) The court may decline to exercise its jurisdiction under this act if a custody determination is incidental to an action for divorce or other proceeding, while retaining jurisdiction over the divorce or other parties or their witnesses. Payment is to be made to the clerk of the court for remittance to the proper party.

(g) Whenever it appears to the court that it is clearly an inappropriate forum it may require the party who commenced the proceedings to pay, in addition to the costs of the proceedings in this state, necessary travel and other expenses including attorneys' fees incurred by other parties or their witnesses. Payment is to be made to the clerk of the court for remittance to the proper party.

(h) Upon dismissal or stay of proceedings under this section, the court shall inform the court found to be the more appropriate forum of this fact, or if the court which would have jurisdiction in the other state is not certainly known, shall transmit the information to the court administrator or other appropriate official for forwarding to the appropriate court.

(j) Any communication received from another state informing this state of a finding of inconvenient forum because a court of this state is the more appropriate forum shall be filed in the custody registry of the appropriate court. Upon assuming jurisdiction in the case the court of this state shall inform the original court of this fact.

§ 20-5-109. Wrongful or improper removal of a child from another state.

(a) If the petitioner for an initial decree has wrongfully taken the child from another state or has engaged in similar reprehensible conduct, the court in its discretion may decline to exercise jurisdiction.

(b) Unless required in the interest of the child and subject to W.S. 20-5-115(a), the court shall not exercise its jurisdiction to modify a custody decree of another state if the petitioner without consent of the person entitled to custody has improperly removed the child from the physical custody of the person entitled to custody or has improperly retained the child after a visit or other temporary relinquishment of physical custody. If the petitioner has violated any other provision of a custody decree of another state the court in its discretion and subject to W. S. 20-5-115(a) may decline to exercise jurisdiction.

(c) In appropriate cases a court dismissing a petition under this section may charge the petitioner with necessary travel expenses and other expenses, including attorneys' fees, incurred by other parties or their witnesses.

§ 20-5-110. Custody proceeding; required information.

(a) Every party in a custody proceeding in his first pleading or in an affidavit attached to that pleading shall give information under oath as to the child's present address, the places where the child has lived within the last five (5) years and the names and present addresses of the persons with whom the child has lived during that period. In this pleading or affidavit every party shall further declare under oath:

(i) Whether he has participated in any capacity in any other litigation concerning the custody of the same child in this or any other state;

(ii) Whether he has information of any custody proceeding concerning the child pending in a court of this or any other state; and

(iii) Whether he knows of any person not a party to the proceedings who has physical custody of the child or claims to have custody or visitation rights with respect to the child.

(b) If the declaration as to any of the above items is in the affirmative, the declarant shall give additional information under oath as required by the court. The court may examine the parties under oath as to details of the information furnished and as to other matters pertinent to the court's jurisdiction and the disposition of the case.

(c) Each party has a continuing duty to inform the court of any custody proceeding concerning the child in this or any other state of which he obtained information during this proceeding.

§ 20-5-111. Person having custody to be joined as a party.

Whenever the court learns that a person not a party to the custody proceeding has physical custody of the child or claims to have custody or visitation rights with respect to the child it shall order that person to be joined as a party and to be duly notified of the pendency of the proceeding and of his joinder as a party. If the person joined as a party is outside this state he shall be served with process or otherwise notified in accordance with W.S. 20-5-106.

§ 20-5-112. Court may order party to proceeding to appear.

(a) The court may order any party to the proceeding who is in the state to appear personally before the court. If that party has physical custody of the child the court may order that he appear personally with the child.

(b) If a party to the proceeding whose presence is desired by the court is outside the state with or without the child, the court may order that the notice given under W.S. 20-5-106 include a statement directing that party to appear personally with or without the child and declaring that failure to appear may result in a decision adverse to that party.

(c) If a party to the proceeding who is outside the state is directed to appear under subsection (b) of this section or desires to appear personally before the court with or without the child, the court may require another party to pay to the clerk of the court travel and other necessary expenses of the party so appearing and of the child

§ 20-5-113. Custody decree binding on all parties.

A custody decree rendered by a court of this state which had jurisdiction under W.S. 20-5-104 binds all parties who have been served in this state or notified in accordance with W.S. 20-5-106 or who have submitted to the jurisdiction of the court, and who have been given an opportunity to be heard. As to these parties the custody decree is conclusive as to all issues of law and fact decided and as to the custody determination made until that determination is modified pursuant to law.

§ 20-5-114. Recognition and enforcement of initial or modification decree made by court of another state.

The courts of this state shall recognize and enforce an initial or modification decree of a court of another state which has assumed jurisdiction under statutory provisions substantially in accordance with this act, or which was made under factual circumstances meeting the jurisdictional standards of the act, so long as this decree has not been modified in accordance with jurisdictional standards substantially similar to those of this act.

§ 20-5-115. Modifying custody decree made by court of another state.

(a) If a court of another state has made a custody decree a court of this state shall not modify that decree unless it appears that the court which rendered the decree does not now have jurisdiction under jurisdictional prerequisites substantially in accordance with this act or has declined to assume jurisdiction to modify the decree, and the court of this state has jurisdiction.

(b) If a court of this state is authorized under subsection (a) of this section and W.S. 20-5-109 to modify a custody decree of another state, it shall give due consideration to the transcript of the record and other documents of all previous proceedings submitted to it in accordance with W.S. 20-5-123.

§ 20-5-116. Effect of custody decree made by court of another state.

(a) A certified copy of a custody decree of another state may be filed in the office of the clerk of any district court of this state. The clerk shall treat the decree in the same manner as a custody decree of the district court of this state. A custody decree so filed has the same effect and shall be enforced in like manner as a custody decree rendered by a court of this state.

(b) A person violating a custody decree of another state making it necessary to enforce the decree in this state may be required to pay necessary travel and other expenses including attorneys' fees incurred by the party entitled to the custody or his witnesses.

§ 20-5-117. Clerk of district court to maintain registry; contents.

(a) The clerk of each district court shall maintain a registry in which he shall enter:

(i) Certified copies of custody decrees of other states received for filing;

(ii) Communications as to the pendency of custody proceedings in other states;

(iii) Communications concerning a finding of inconvenient forum by a court of another state; and

(iv) Other communications or documents concerning custody proceedings in another state which may affect the jurisdiction of a court of this state or the disposition to be made by it in a custody proceeding.

§ 20-5-118. Forwarding copy of decree.

At the request of the court of another state or at the request of any person who is affected by or has a legitimate interest in a custody decree, the clerk of the district court of this state shall certify and forward a copy of the decree to that court or person.

§ 20-5-119. Testimony of witnesses; method of obtaining.

In addition to other procedural devices available to a party, any party to the proceeding or a guardian ad litem or other representative of the child may adduce testimony of witnesses including parties and the child by deposition or otherwise in another state. The court on its own motion may direct that the testimony of a person be taken in another state and may prescribe the manner in which and the terms upon which the testimony shall be taken.

§ 20-5-120. Requesting court of another state to adduce evidence; order party to appear.

(a) A court of this state may request the appropriate court of another state to hold a hearing to adduce evidence, to order a party to produce or give evidence under other procedures of that state or to have social studies made with respect to the custody of a child involved in proceedings pending in the court of this state, and to forward to the court of this state certified copies of the transcript of the record of the hearing, the evidence otherwise adduced or any social studies prepared in compliance with the request. The cost of the services may be assessed against the parties or if necessary ordered paid by the county.

(b) A court of this state may request the appropriate court of another state to order a party to custody proceeding pending in the court of this state to appear in the proceedings, and if that party has physical custody of the child to appear with the child. The request may state that travel and other necessary expenses of the party and of the child whose appearance is desired will be assessed against another party or will otherwise be paid.

§ 20-5-121. Request from courts of another state.

(a) Upon request of the court of another state the courts of this state which are competent to hear custody matters may order a person in this state to appear at a hearing to adduce evidence or to produce or give evidence under other procedures available in this state or may order social studies to be made for use in a custody proceeding in another state. A certified copy of the transcript of the record of the hearing or the evidence otherwise adduced and any social studies prepared shall be forwarded by the clerk of the court to the requesting court.

(b) A person within this state may voluntarily give his testimony or statement in this state for use in custody proceeding outside this state.

(c) Upon request of the court of another state a competent court of this state may order a person in this state to appear alone or with the child in a custody proceeding in another state. The court may condition compliance with the request upon assurance by the other state that travel and other necessary expenses will be advanced or reimbursed.

§ 20-5-122. Preserving records of custody proceeding.

In any custody proceeding in this state the court shall preserve the pleadings, orders and decrees, any record that has been made of its hearings, social studies and other pertinent documents until the child reaches twenty-one (21) years of age. Upon appropriate request of the court of another state, the court shall forward to the other court certified copies of any or all of such documents.

§ 20-5-123. Custody proceeding; record from another state.

Whenever a custody decree has been rendered in another state concerning a child involved in a custody proceeding pending in a court of this state, the court of this state, upon taking jurisdiction of the case, shall request of the court of the other state a certified copy of the transcript of any court record and other documents mentioned in W.S 20-5-122.

§ 20-5-124. Policies of act applicable to international area.

The general policies of this act extend to the international area. The provisions of this act relating to the recognition and enforcement of custody decrees of other states apply to custody decrees and decrees involving legal institutions similar in nature to custody rendered by appropriate authorities of other nations if reasonable notice and opportunity to be heard was given to all affected persons.

§ 20-5-125. Priority of custody proceeding raising question of jurisdiction.

Upon request of a party to a custody proceeding which raises a question of existence or exercise of jurisdiction under this act, the case shall be given calendar priority and handled expeditiously.

GLOSSARY

Ab initio—From the beginning, first and foremost, initially, primarily, originally.

Abandonment—The surrender, relinquishment, disclaimer, desertion of property or rights, foregoing of parental duties.

Abeyance—In deadlock, dormancy, interim, stalemate, suspension, while awaiting action.

Abrogate—To abolish, annul, void, invalidate, overrule, revoke.

Abscond—To avoid process by hiding, concealing, evading, departing.

Abuse—The breach of trust, exploitation, injury by physical or emotional, mishandle.

Acquiesce—To give an implied consent to any act by silence, without express assent or acknowledgment.

Acquittance—A written discharge where one is freed from an obligation to pay money or perform a duty.

Action in rem—A proceeding that takes no cognizance of owner but determines right in specific property against all of the world, equally binding on everyone.

Actuary—A statistician who computes insurance and pension rates and premiums on the basis of experience tables.

Ad hoc—A special purpose, for this use only.

Ad litem—For the purposes of the suit; pending the suit.

Adjudication—The formal giving or pronouncing a judgment or decree, also the judgment given.

Adverse—In resistance or opposition to a claim or proceeding.

Advocacy—The act of pleading for, supporting, aiding, assisting.

Affiant—The person who makes and subscribes an affidavit.

Affidavit—A statement under oath, written declaration of facts given voluntarily.

Affinity—A close relation or agreement held to exist between certain persons.

Affirmation—The solemn testimony that an affidavit is true.

Alienation—The aversion, separation, disfavor, withdrawal of affections or property.

Alimony—The allowances which husband or wife by court order pays other spouse for maintenance.

Alimony pendente lite—An allowance made pending a suit for divorce.

Ameliorate—To correct or change for the better.

Amicable—Friendly, agreement to by parties having conflicting interests.

Ancillary—Aiding; attendant upon; describing a proceeding attendant upon or which aids another proceeding considered as principal..

Annulment—The cancellation or undoing of a marriage as if it never existed.

Antenuptial—Made or done before a marriage.

Appeal—To request for review or seek reexamination.

Appellate—Pertaining to or having knowledge of other appeals.

Apprised—To advise, communicate or counsel.

Arbitrate—To arrive at a conclusion, bring to terms.

Arraignment—The procedure by which the accused is brought before the court to plead to the charges.

Aver—To declare or allege.

Bastardizes issue—To give evidence of illegitimacy of an issue or topic.

Bifurcate—To separate, branch out or halve.

Bigamy—The criminal offense of willfully and knowingly contracting a second marriage while the first marriage is still legal.

Bona fide—In good faith, honestly, openly, without fraud.

Capias—A document that requires the officer to take the body of the defendant into custody.

Capricious—Unreliable, apt to change ones mind impulsively.

Certiorari—To be informed of.

Chancery—Equity; equitable jurisdiction; a court of equity.

Charge D'Affaires—The title of a diplomatic representative of inferior rank.

Chattels—The personal assets, belongings or interests of a person.

Child Custody—The care, control and maintenance of children awarded by court.

Child Support—The legal obligation of parents to contribute to economic maintenance of their children.

Circumvent—To avoid doing, bypass, defraud, as to circumvent the law.

Codicil—A supplement or addendum to a will.

Collusion—The working together or agreement to defraud or for the accomplishment of unlawful purpose.

Comity—The courtesy to grant a privilege out of good will.

Commencement of actions—To initiate or begin by performing the first act.

Commingled Property—The combination of property together.

Common Law—Principles and rules of action deriving their authority solely from usages and customs rather than law created from legislation.

Complaint—The pleading or charge by which an action is commenced

Condonation—The pardon of a matrimonial offense by one of the married parties on the condition being that the offense shall not be repeated.

Confidentiality—Private, not for publication.

Connivance—The conspiracy or permission to allow an unlawful act by another.

Consanguinity—Kinship, of the same blood or common ancestry.

Construe—To ascertain the meaning of.

Contemnor—One who has committed contempt of court.

Contestant—The challenger of or adverse party.

Corpus—The collection or total of, the main body or principal of a trust.

Corroboration—The assurance or endorsement of.

Counsel—To advise or assist someone in legal matters.

Coverture—The legal status of a married woman.

Curtesy—The common-law right of a husband in his wife's property which arises from the marriage.

Custodial interference—To intervene or prevent custodial parent from duties on behalf of children.

Custody—The care or control of a thing or a person.

De novo—A second time, a fresh or new trial.

Decree—A final determination of rights of the parties in an action.

Decretal—The granting or denying of remedy sought.

Default—The omission or failure to perform.

Defendant—The accused; the party against whom relief or recovery is sought.

Denominating—Calling by name, giving title to.

Derogation—The partial repeal of a law which limits its force.

Desertion—The abandonment of responsibility or support of family.

Determinate—That which is ascertained.

Detinue—A common-law remedy for the recovery of property wrongfully withheld from the plaintiff.

Devolution—The assignment or transfer of property.

Diminution—The signifying that a record sent up from an inferior court to a superior court is incomplete.

Disparate—Conflicting, different, ill-matched.

Displaced Homemakers—Persons who were primary homemakers become homeless.

Disposition—The parting with or giving up of property or giving testimony.

Disseminate—To announce or communicate, the publication of a libel.

Dissolution—To terminate; end a marriage.

Distraint—The process of seizure.

Divorce—Legal separation of man and wife by decree of court.

Divorce a vinculo matrimonii—To release parties of a marriage wholly from their matrimonial obligations.

Docket—The calendar or list of cases.

Domestic Violence—The unlawful exercise of physical force, outrage or fury on persons relating to or belonging in a home or domicile.

Domicile—That place where a person has a true, fixed and permanent home.

Dower—The provision which the law makes for a widow out of the lands or tenements of her husband, for her support and the nurture of her children.

Duces tecum—The name of certain species of writs, of which the *subpoena duces tecum* is the most usual, requiring a party who is summoned to appear in court to bring with him some document, piece of evidence, or other thing to be used or inspected by the court.

Effectuate—To accomplish or bring to maturity.

Elicit—To arouse or bring forth or initiate.

Erroneous—Involving error, deviating from the law.

Et seq.—An abbreviation for *et sequentes*, a reference to more than one following page.

Evidentiary—Having the quality of evidence.

Ex parte temporary protection order—A temporary protection order made on behalf of one party only.

Exigencies—Something arising suddenly out of the current of events calling for immediate action or remedy.

Expeditiously—An act performed with fast, efficient action.

Expend—To lay out , consume or use up.

Extradition—The surrender by one state or country to another of an individual accused or convicted of an offense outside its own territory and within the territorial jurisdiction of the other.

Extrinsic—Foreign, from outside sources.

Facilitate—To aid or assist or simplify.

Felony—A crime of a graver or more serious nature than those designated as misdemeanors.

Forma pauperis—In the character of manner of a pauper; permission given to a poor person to proceed without liability for court fees or costs.

Furloughed—Leave of absence.

Garnishment—A statutory proceeding whereby person's property, money, or credits in possession or under control of, or owing by, another are applied to payment of former's debt to third person by proper statutory process against debtor and garnishee.

Guardian ad litem—A special guardian appointed by the court to prosecute or defend, in behalf of an infant or incompetent.

Imminent—Near at hand, impending.

Impetus—Encouragement, stimulus.

Incest—The crime of sexual intercourse or cohabitation between a man and woman who are related to each other with the degrees wherein marriage is prohibited by law.

Inchoate—Imperfect; partial; unfinished.

Indeterminate—That which is uncertain or not particularly designated.

Indicia—Indications or circumstances which point to the existence of a given fact as probable, but not certain.

Indict—An accusation in writing found and presented by a grand jury, charging that a person has done some act that is punishable.

Infamous—Shameful or disgraceful.

Inference—In the law of evidence, a truth drawn from another which is supposed or admitted to be true.

Interdict—A prohibitory decree.

Interlocutory—Temporary, tentative.

Intestate—Without making a will.

Intrastate—Within a state.

Intrinsic—Internal; inherent, the essential nature of a thing.

Inure—To take effect; to result, to fix ones' interest within.

Irretrievable breakdown—As a no-fault ground for divorce means one in which either or both parties are unable to cohabitate.

Joinder of parties—Bringing together or union of parties.

Joint tenants—The combined, united sharing of a premise.

Judgment by default—Determines right of plaintiff to recover at least nominal damages and costs.

Judgments—The final decision of a court of justice resolving the dispute and determining the rights and obligations of the parties.

Judicature—The state or profession of those officers who are employed in administering justice.

Judicial Attaches—The authority of a judge to seize property.

Jurat—The statement which confirms information on an affidavit.

Jurisdiction—The authority to hear and decide a case.

Jurisdiction in rem or quasi in rem—Power of a court over a thing so that its judgment is valid as against the rights of every person in the thing.

Jurisprudence—Knowledge of law, doctrines of lawmaking.

Jury trials—Trial of matter or cause before a jury as opposed to trial before a judge.

Legitimacy—Justifiability; genuine;a child proven to be born by parent.

Libels—False accusations.

Licentious—Disorderly, unrestrained will without regard to rights of others.

Lis pendens—A pending suit.

Litigant—The petitioner or plaintiff.

Mandamus—A writ issued from a court to direct the restoration of the complainant to rights or privileges of which he has been illegally deprived.

Mediation—The settlement of disputes through negotiations.

Mensa et thoro—From bed and board.

Movant Party—The applicant for a rule or order.

Municipality—A legally incorporated area of inhabitants for local governmental or other public purposes.

Nihil—Nothing.

Nisi—Unless.

Non-support—The failure or neglect to support those to whom an obligation of support is due.

Nonage—A minor.

Nonresident—One who does not live within the jurisdiction in question.

Nullity—The decision to overrule a prior decision, invalidity.

Nunc pro tunc—A phrase applied to acts allowed to be done after the time when they should be done.

Obligee—The party to whom someone else is obligated under a contract or court order.

Obligor—The person who is obligated to perform some under a contract or court order.

Obviate—Arrest, prevent, turn aside.

Onerous—When obligations to a contract are unreasonably exceed the advantage to be derived from it.

Ore tenus—By word of mouth.

Palpable—Unquestionable, unscreened, evident.

Parentage—Ancestors, bloodline, family.

Pari delecto—Equal in guilt or legal fault.

Particeps criminis—One who shares in a criminal offense.

Partition—Any division of real or personal property between co-owners, resulting in individual ownership of the interests of each.

Paternity—Ancestry, fatherhood.

Pecuniary—Monetary or that which can be valued as money.

Perjury—Act of oathbreaking, distortion of the truth.

Plaintiff—A person who sues in a civil action and seeks relief for an injury to rights.

Pleadings—Written statements of accusation or allegation of facts and defenses.

Polygamy—The act of having multiple spouses.

Praecipe—A writ commanding the defendant to do the thing required or prove why it has not been done.

Prima facie evidence—Evidence which, if unexplained or uncontradicted, is sufficient to sustain a judgment in favor of the issue which it supports, but which may be contradicted by other evidence.

Pro Rata—According to a certain rate, percentage or proportion.

Pro Se—Appearing for oneself, as one who does not retain a lawyer.

Probate—To confirm the validity of a will.

Probation—A conditional suspension of sentence, period of testing.

Proceedings—Course of action at law, trial.

Procure—To initiate a proceeding; persuade or cause someone to do something.

Prohibition—Act or law prohibiting something; banishment; block.

Propound—To advance; allege; offer; present.

Proviso—A condition, stipulation or provision which is inserted in a contract, and on the performance or nonperformance of which the validity of the contract frequently depends.

Putative Spouse—One thought to be the spouse of another in a marriage in opposition to which there are impediments.

Rebuttable—An argument against; to countercharge; take a stand against.

Receivership—The state or condition of a corporation, partnership or individual over whom a receiver has been appointed for protection of its assets and for ultimate sale and distribution to creditors.

Recision—The right to cancel a contract upon the occurrence of certain kinds of default by the other contracting party.

Reconciliation—In law of domestic relations, a voluntary resumption of marital relations in the fullest sense.

Recrimination—A charge made by an accused person against the accuser, in particular a counter-charge of adultery or cruelty made by one charged with the same offense in a suit for divorce against the person who has charged him or her.

Registry—A book authorized or recognized by law, kept for the recording or registration of facts or documents.

Replevin—A action whereby the owner entitled to repossession of property may recover that property from one who wrongfully detains that property.

Res judicata—A matter adjudged; a thing judicially acted upon or decided.

Rescript—A written order from the court to the clerk, giving directions concerning the further disposition of a case.

Restitution—Act of restoring anything to its rightful owner.

Restraining order—An order forbiding the defendant to do the threatened act until a hearing on the application can be had.

Revoke—To withdraw; suspend; annul; cancel.

Scire facias—A process to revive a judgment, after the lapse of a certain time.

Separation—A cessation of cohabitation of husband and wife by mutual agreement.

Sequester—To confine; separate; quarantine.

Sequestration—In general, the process by which property or funds are attached pending the outcome of litigation.

Severability—Capable of carrying on an independent existence; a statute that can still be valid even in one part of it is struck down as invalid by a court.

Stipulation—A material condition, requirement, or article in an agreement.

Subpoenas—A command to appear at a certain time and place to give testimony upon a certain matter.

Subrogation—The exchange of one person in the place of another with reference to a lawful claim.

Subsidiary—Under anothers control; subordinate.

Sui juris—Of his own right; not under any legal disability, or power of another.

Sundry—Separate, divers, or various.

Surety—A vow or contract to pay money or to do any other act in event that his principal falls therein.

Susceptible—Yielding, nonresistant, impressionable, easily affected.

Temporary protection order—An order of a court whose purpose is to protect a person from further harassment as an emergency remedy until the trial court can hear arguments.

Testimony—Evidence given by a competent witness under oath or affirmation.

Tort—A breach of legal duty, civil wrong.

Unambiguous—Certain, clear-cut, well defined.

Unconscionable—Conniving, conscienceless, unscrupulous.

Venue—The particular county, or geographical area, in which a court with jurisdiction may hear and determine a case.

Vilifying—Abusing, verbal attacking.

Vinculo matrimonii—A divorce from the bond of marriage.

Visitation—In a custody suit, permission granted to a parent to visit children.

Viva voce—By word of mouth.

Viz—Namely, that is to say, to wit.

Void or Voidable—Having no legal force or binding effect.

INDEX